In Memory of
    Robert Earl Kennedy and
Arnold Remington Pilling

Irregular connexions between the sexes have on the whole established a tendency to increase along with the progress of civilization.

Edward Westermarck, *The History of Human Marriage*

Contents

ILLUSTRATIONS

Acknowledgments

Because this book is the culmination of research projects we undertook over many summers and two sabbaticals over a 22-year period, we owe thanks to many individuals and institutions.

We would like to acknowledge the help of three research assistants who helped us in the early stages of the project: Dr. Mary Fair Deschene, Dr. Fabian Dapila, and our former colleague, the late Dr. Judith Abwunza. In the latter stages of the project, Mr. Stephan Dobson acted as an editorial assistant.

Our research was supported by a Short Term Research Grant from Wilfrid Laurier University and a Research Grant (no. 410-91-1361) from the Social Sciences and Humanities Research Council of Canada (1991–96). Harriet Lyons also received a Grace Anderson Research Fellowship from Wilfrid Laurier University.

We would like to thank librarians at the following institutions: Wilfrid Laurier University, Waterloo, Ontario; the University of Waterloo; McMaster University (Bertrand Russell Archive); the Sterling Library at Yale University (Bronislaw Malinowski Papers and Havelock Ellis Papers); the London School of Economics and Political Science and Dr. Angela Raspin, archivist (Bronislaw Malinowski Correspondence); the Library of the Wellcome Institute for the History of Medicine; the old British Library, including the Western Manuscripts Room (Marie C. Stopes–Havelock Ellis Correspondence); the Huntington Library, San Marino, California (Sir Richard Burton Archive); the Library of Congress (Margaret Mead Papers); the Bodleian Library, Oxford University, including the Bodleian Library of Commonwealth and African Studies at Rhodes House; the Institute of Social and Cultural Anthropology, Oxford University; and the Robarts Library of the University of Toronto.

The late Edwards Huntington Metcalf gave us access to some of his personal collection of Richard Burton's books and papers, which are stored at the Huntington Library.

There are a number of scholars and friends with whom we have shared ideas during the time we have worked on this project. They include Dorothy and David Counts, Ann Chowning, Bill and Marla Powers, the late Arnold Pilling, the late Ashley Montagu, the late Bob Kennedy, and Robert Gordon.

We would like to thank the editors of this series, Regna Darnell and Stephen Murray, for a stimulating exchange of ideas that helped us greatly in the preparation of our final manuscript. Naturally, any errors of scholarship and interpretation that remain are our own.

Finally, for those who are curious, we should mention that this is a totally cooperative endeavor. The order in which our names are listed is strictly alphabetical.

Some portions of chapters 4 and 6, which discuss Malinowski, Ellis, and Russell, first appeared in the *Canadian Journal of Anthropology*. We would like once again to thank Ms. Helena Wayne (Malinowska) for permission to quote materials from the Malinowski collections at Yale and at the London School of Economics.

Permission to quote from the diary of Mrs. E. M. Falk (MSS. Afr. S. 1000) has been granted by the Bodleian Library of Commonwealth and African Studies at Rhodes House. Permission to publish an illustration from *The Muria and Their Ghotul* by Verrier Elwin has been granted by Oxford University Press, New Delhi, India.

Series Editors' Introduction

Although the variety of human sexuality has been a rich topic in Anglo-American public culture, it has received surprisingly little anthropological attention. This lacuna may be attributable to the aura of the exotic or scandalous that clings to the topic within a discipline that has long aspired to the status of "science." Andrew Lyons and Harriet Lyons attempt to redress the omissions, emphasizing the ethnocentrism of cross-cultural sexuality studies.

Where we might expect alternative approaches to sexuality to engender a critique of post-Enlightenment cultural biases, we find instead a "conscription" or co-optation of ethnographically attested alternatives to preexisting agendas arising from a cultural context beyond the discipline of anthropology. Race and culture have been inextricably joined, with oversexed Africans, undersexed Native Americans, and promiscuous Polynesians feeding the mainstream's view of itself.

Americanists will be fascinated by a narrative that moves comfortably back and forth across the Atlantic. Although there are certainly distinctive features of the British and American national traditions, in matters of sexuality studies crossovers are legion (with the collaboration of Margaret Mead and Gregory Bateson as a paramount example). At each chronological juncture, American and British voices intersect, for example, Lewis Henry Morgan and the High Victorian evolutionism of John McLennan, Sir John Lubbock, and Johann Jakob Bachofen, a legacy interjected into American anthropology by the cosmopolitan European theoretical scope of Franz Boas and his early students. Margaret Mead tested the claims of psychologist G. Stanley Hall about the universality of adolescence, while Bronislaw Malinowski applied Freudian metanarratives to the cultural assumptions of Trobriand Islanders. National traditions are mediated by what Richard

Fardon called "localizing strategies," the ways of thinking anthropologically that emerge in particular areas of the globe.

Commonalities of Pacific sexualities abound in contrast to Native North American practices. Ethnography in turn invites reflexivity. Much is reported that strikes unhappy resonances to modern ears. The Lyonses frame their narrative as an exercise in disciplinary reflexivity.

Both the introduction and conclusion invite anthropologists and other students of sexuality in cross-cultural contexts to observe themselves observing through often unrecognized biases. Despite an uncompromising exposure of previous limitations of standpoint, Lyons and Lyons do not apologize for the past sins of anthropologists or despair of the grounds on which they and their readers now stand. To have raised the questions at all is the challenge accepted by the anthropology of sexuality. The historicism and *longue durée* of the irregular connections they catalog invite continuing revisionism as ethnographic studies of sexuality become better integrated with feminist, gay–lesbian, queer, and other theories and documentations of sexual practices in our own society. This volume strikes a balance between power–knowledge in its approach to the particulars of a topic–theme through a critical disciplinary history.

Regna Darnell and Stephen O. Murray

IRREGULAR CONNECTIONS

Introduction

If conjectures and opinions formed at a distance, have not sufficient authority in the history of mankind, the domestic antiquities of every nation must, for this very reason, be received with caution. They are, for most part, the mere conjectures or the fictions of subsequent ages; and even where at first they contained some resemblance of truth, they still vary with the imagination of those by whom they are transmitted, and in every generation receive a different form. They are made to bear the stamp of the times through which they have passed in the form of tradition, not of the ages to which their pretended descriptions relate. The information they bring, is not like the light reflected from a mirror, which delineates the object from which it originally came; but, like rays that come broken and dispersed from an opaque or unpolished surface, only give the colours and features of the body from which they were last reflected.

Adam Ferguson, An Essay on the History of Civil Society

Jenny sat down in a folding chair by the window and pretended to read a copy of the National Geographic *for July 1946 that someone had left about. It had native girls with bare busts. (Why did native busts not count?)*

Kingsley Amis, Take a Girl Like You

Many people still believe that anthropology is largely about sex. There is a persistent image of the anthropologist as a voyeur. Moreover, information about "primitives" is often used to justify or deplore Western sexual desire and practice. This is a recurring theme in writings of various kinds. It can be found, to name but a few famous sources, in the work of Charles Darwin, Sigmund Freud, Havelock Ellis, Margaret Mead, Bronislaw Malinowski, and Bertrand Russell. The sexual liberation movements of the 1970s, 1980s, and 1990s continued to use the sexuality of others as model or contrast.

It is a curious fact that sexuality has rarely been a dominant theme in ethnographic research, despite strong interest in the topic on the part of some of anthropology's founding practitioners and a few of their descendants. There are obvious and not-so-obvious reasons for this reticence. One of them is the quite obvious fact that many people and peoples are discreet about the subject, that the information they may provide may be unreliable, unrepresentative, or unverifiable. In recent articles, Donald Tuzin and Ernestine Friedl have drawn our attention to the important but surprisingly seldom-noted fact that with occasional ceremonial exceptions sexual acts are almost universally performed in private (Tuzin 1991:270–274, 1995:265, 266; Friedl 1994), a point Mead (1961:1434–1435) had noted some time earlier. Furthermore, there are both ethical and practical constraints on the activities of anthropological fieldworkers. Despite this reserve the mass media retain their hunger for anthropological statements about the sexuality of non-Western peoples.

During the mid-1980s the *New York Times* (e.g., January 31, 1983) and other leading media devoted much attention to claims that Margaret Mead's fieldwork in Samoa was sloppy and that her famous book was based on unreliable data. Specifically, there was much interest in Derek Freeman's allegations (1983, 1999) that Mead had been misled by her adolescent informants and had falsely portrayed Samoa as a society free of sexual repression and its social and psychological accompaniments.

Debate over female genital mutilation continues to surface in the media, inside and outside of the countries where it is practiced. The first work (by Harriet Lyons in 1981) that either of the authors of this book undertook with regard to anthropologists' treatment of sexuality was concerned with discourses surrounding clitoridectomy and male circumcision. Controversy about female circumcision pits concern about women's health against cultural relativism. The presumption that the traditional practices of all cultures deserve respect is a moral stance that has spread beyond anthropology to influence a broad spectrum of contemporary opinion. On issues like clitoridectomy anthropological knowledge may have direct implications for public policy.

The early spread of HIV/AIDS among Africans and homosexuals has unfortunately served as a vehicle for stigmatization and stereotyping. We shall examine some roots of these stereotypes in our account of anthropological writings in the 18th and 19th centuries.

A decade or so ago, the psychologist J. Philippe Rushton received considerable public attention, including television appearances in Canada and the United States, for his assertions about an alleged inverse relationship between intelligence and penis size in men and breast size in women (see Rushton and Bogaert 1987; Rushton 1988, 1992, 1994, 1997). Rushton adheres to the belief that the size of the male genitals is an index of fertility and the size of the cranium is an index of intelligence. On Rushton's scale, blacks are scored lowest in head size and intelligence and highest in genital size, production of spermatozoa, ovulatory rate, frequency of twinning, and susceptibility to HIV/AIDS (see, e.g., 1997:113–146, 165–183, 261, 262). Rushton places whites in the middle and rates Asians most intelligent but least genitally endowed. The social implications of these alleged correlations, along with the links Rushton finds between large genitals, low intelligence, and antisocial behavior (1997:214–216), have caused him to be taken seriously by a number of authors and politicians during a conservative era, although his ideas have had a hostile reception among anthropologists (see, e.g., Lieberman 2001). Knowledge of anthropological history would reveal just how old and how inappropriate many of the sources of such ideas about sex and intelligence are and how easily negative judgments about the sexuality of resented populations can be accepted as "science." Accordingly, the following paragraphs introduce some of the historical themes with which we will be concerned.

Most anthropologists and many nonanthropologists have heard of the speculations of 19th-century evolutionist thinkers concerning primitive sexual communism, mother right, and marriage by capture. Nineteenth-century interest in primitive sexuality was not merely sociological in nature. A literature of primitive exotica, which occupied the borderline between anthropology and pornography, as these genres were then perceived, was produced by Sir Richard Burton and some of his friends. Some publications of this type abandoned all but a ritual pretense at science. It was, rather surprisingly, one of these writings (*Untrodden Fields of Anthropology* [1898], attributed to "Jacobus X" or a "French army surgeon") that Rushton used in his more controversial publications (1992, 1994, 1997:150, 166). In more reputable areas of scholarship, published speculation about the adaptive significance of the incest taboo and supposed archaic forms of the family was an important part of the discourse of biological and social evolution. Several other types of 19th-century writing included sections on primitive sexual customs; medical writers, journalists, missionaries, and urban evangelists are among those who made use of such data.

A large popular audience in the late 1920s and 1930s was introduced to anthropological texts by the writings of Margaret Mead. Some of these readers perceived sexual behavior to be the main concern of those texts and others like them. After achieving fame, Mead took pains to set the record straight, pointing out that the topic *sex* appeared on only 68 pages of *Coming of Age in Samoa* (1928). However, this was at least 60 more pages on the topic than might be found in most other anthropological works of the 20th century, and Mead's work did comprise the most well known example of the use of ethnology by 20th-century advocates of sexual reform. Some of Malinowski's writings between 1918 and 1930, particularly *Sex and Repression in Savage Society* (1927) and *The Sexual Life of Savages in Northwestern Melanesia* (1929), though their audience was more restricted, were written with contemporary debates about sexual mores very much in mind.

In the 1950s and 1960s it was usual for anthropology students to be warned about the dangers of romantic ethnographies that described "love among the palm trees." The theoretical direction of anthropology in Britain had for some time ruled out any consideration of individual motivation and bodily processes, including not only sex but even hunger. American anthropology was more open to such considerations, though it is notable that even the neo-Freudian culture and personality movement produced few ethnographic descriptions of adult sexual behavior.

The 1980s saw a renewal of interest in the anthropology of sex. The publication of a number of books dealing with homoerotic practices in New Guinea Highlands society and elsewhere, for example, Gilbert Herdt's *Guardians of the Flutes* (1981), the emergence of feminist anthropology, and the controversies surrounding Mead's portrayal of adolescent promiscuity in Samoa brought sexuality back into the mainstream of anthropological debate. Michel Foucault's ideas on the relationship between sex and power (1980:5) have been a continuing influence throughout this period.

It is a truism of contemporary intellectual colloquy that the discourses of race, sex, class, and gender are closely interconnected. We shall discuss just a few of the many ways in which they figure in the history of anthropology.

Between 1860 and 1950 both academic anthropology and sociology as well as multiple forms of social work, counseling, and public administration underwent a gradual process of professionalization, somewhat intensified during and after the two world wars. The boundaries between anthropology and other emerging ventures were not impenetrable. Observations and speculations concerning the sexuality of primitives were sometimes used as implicit or explicit justifications for Victorian and Edwardian sexual mores, gender hierarchies, and colonial ventures. Conversely, such ventures and hierarchies undoubtedly helped to condition the kinds of questions anthropologists asked and the conclusions to which they were drawn. "Backward races," women, children, and members of the lower orders of Victorian society were all assumed to have certain characteristics in common that could be represented in art or studied by science. Such shared characteristics served to demarcate either fundamental innocence or inherent corruption, with corresponding requirements for control or protection.

The era in which anthropology has flourished as a discipline, roughly the last 130 years, has seen many watersheds in the history of sexuality in Western culture. The high Victorian era and its sexual double standard were followed by a fin de siècle reaction in which the status quo was challenged both by those who argued for greater sexual permissiveness and by those who favored stricter controls. The rejection of Victorian prudery by some segments of society during the flapper era of the 1920s was followed by the constraints of the Great Depression and the stresses (and, for some, greater sexual freedom) of World War II. The "mini-Victorian" era of the 1950s was followed by the sexual revolution, the conservative reaction to it, and the HIV/AIDS epidemic of the current period. During each of these periods there were writers who turned to "primitive" societies for evidence of what Westerners should or should not be doing in their sexual lives. The primitive has served ideologies of sexual restraint and of sexual freedom. Primitive sexuality has been cited in connection with the celebration of variance and with the insistence upon normative heterosexuality. Male dominance, female dominance, and gender equality have all been seen to have primitive reflections. There is little if any justification in cultural "facts" themselves for such sweeping pronouncements. Sometimes discourse was loud; sometimes it was relatively muted. Even "silences," however, must be interpreted in terms of social contexts.

This book is an endeavor to interrogate the employment of these extraordinary data in order to explore the motivation behind their persistent appearance. The main part of this book concerns the period between 1860 and 1970 in British and American anthropology. These two national traditions have always been closely interconnected, at times more than their proponents would like to acknowledge. This book explores the embeddedness of an important aspect of anthropological writings in the cultural and sexual politics of their locales. We are predominantly concerned with individuals who described themselves or were described as being anthropologists, but we shall occasionally stray beyond disciplinary bounds, particularly during our discussion of the formative phase of anthropological knowledge between 1800 and 1910.

Necessarily, our prologue begins before the Victorian era itself and therefore before the emergence of professional anthropology. Herodotus, who traveled widely, wrote about the many peoples he encountered and related stories, some true and others fantastic, about populations who lived beyond the fringes of the classical world. Medieval encyclopedists wrote about monsters and mythical beings. Sixteenth-century theologians argued about the humanity of American Indians. Political philosophers speculated about the origins of society. There could, therefore, be a case for beginning our narrative half a millennium or two millennia ago. However, the late 18th century, the latter part of the Enlightenment, is a good place to begin because it marks the advent of modern scientific and political discourse.

Traditionally, or at the very least since Saint Augustine, Christendom has held sex in low esteem. Those who existed outside Christendom's umbrella were generally regarded as tainted with sin. The Enlightenment's stress on reason and science pitted itself against both religious antipathy to sex and aristocratic decadence. A "natural" indulgence was permissible to those who accepted Enlightenment ideas, but many areas were problematic (masturbation, homosexuality, female adultery), and the advocates of chastity were never silent. (See Porter and Hall 1995:14–121 for an excellent summary of the 18th-century sexual environment.) Much of the sexually "permissive" art and literature of the Enlightenment employed various techniques for separating sex from the serious business of life – irony, parody, and an exaggeration that bordered on the grotesque. Distancing oneself from disquieting tendencies is a familiar psychological strategy for maintaining self-esteem.

The Victorian era in many ways began more than three decades before the queen's accession. The period of bowdlerism preceded her by a few years. The 19th century began and ended with significant manifestations of public prudery, the so-called social purity movements. The third quarter of the century is usually thought of as the high-water mark of sexual Victorianism, marked by the apogee of the double standard of sexual morality and sentimentalized images of domesticity. This period was also marked by various attempts to document, regulate, and otherwise combat prostitution, which loomed as a threat to Christian marriage. Orthodoxy was challenged from viewpoints that were diverse and in some cases radically opposed.

Male libertarians opposed excessive restraints on their freedom. Evangelical Christians and some feminists bemoaned the failure of legislation to protect women from sexual exploitation. On the other side, alliances between sexual radicals and "scientific" defenders of racial hierarchies were sometimes rooted in a common anticlericalism. This was because opposition to slavery and the worst colonial abuses, advocacy of purity, and suspicion of the rising natural sciences had tended to be linked positions. In the last years of the century these divisions and alliances were intensified. Feminism became more visible as a social and political movement and influenced some legislative changes. Homosexuality was labeled as a social issue, and homosexuals talked about "the love that dare not speak its name." Some became martyrs in doing so. These were the years of jingoism in both Britain and America, an imperialistic frenzy that served barely to conceal worries about economic and moral decline. These anxieties were reflected in a growing body of post-Darwinian literature on degeneration and decline. Such was the turbulent social context in which the intellectual foundations of the new discipline of anthropology were established.

Like Claude Lévi-Strauss's *bricoleurs*, Victorian theorists assembled and manipulated images and symbols from a plethora of sources devised for a multitude of uses. These images and symbols are encountered in a variety of discourses, encompassing the debates between the Darwinians and their opponents, speculations about primitive promiscuity and the origins of marriage, examination of erotic elements in Oriental religions, racial theorizing, as well as texts where anthropology provided an excuse for the frankly pornographic. The creators of anthropology and their reading public also had access to several other textual traditions: the travelogues of explorers, the reports of missionaries, apologies for slavery and attacks on it, preDarwinian science, and natural theology.

In both the late 18th and the 19th centuries, discourses that were otherwise at odds, like science and theology or conservatism and social reform, often intertwined in their encounter with unfamiliar sexualities. Primitives were usually portrayed as lacking in emotional control and rationality and were seen to be sexually more excitable (and more physical generally) than Europeans. Males were seen as sexually aggressive and promiscuous. Africans in particular were seen as sexually rapacious and domineering. Their genital endowments were exaggerated, their cranial capacity was underestimated. The women in such societies were more ambiguously portrayed. They were depicted either as rapacious Amazons or as brutalized and exploited by their menfolk. Africa is central to racialized discourses about sex and sexualized discourses about race, and one subject we shall consider in this book is how such images were created and have endured.

In a few cases the portrayal of the American Indian differs from that described for Africans and other allegedly oversexed populations. The prudery of some North American societies with respect to heterosexual relations, the toleration of institutionalized homosexuality (the institution of the berdache), the males' relative lack of body hair and beard, and a decline in population suggested an alternative model: the undersexed rather than the oversexed savage. Although some authors attributed to other groups of primitive males a greater interest in the employment of women for drudgery than for venery, this characterization was particularly common in the case of some North American groups.

It has become almost a cliché of the postmodern movement in anthropology to state that primitive Others represent a projection of the anxieties and aspirations of those who have written about them. We need to go beyond such sweeping characterizations, however, and examine the specific preoccupations, both political and "psychological," that have shaped each generation's reading of particular bodies of data. With regard to sex, such an examination reveals an interesting paradox caused by the juxtaposition of ambivalence about sex and ambivalence about primitives. It has been extremely rare for anthropologists to maintain relativism concerning both at the same time. Sometimes both primitives and sex are looked upon with disdain or at least nervousness; on other occasions appreciation for one is accompanied by disdain for the other. A full-bodied primitivism has constituted a third position, in which primitives have been represented as enjoying a level of sexual health and happiness that eludes humans spoiled by modernity. Inevitably, as the evolutionary paradigm declined and better empirical data became available, a realization grew that not all primitive societies were alike, that, in fact, they greatly differed in their attitudes toward sex. However, evolutionism's decline and the birth of fieldwork based on participant observation did not fully prevent the promulgation of statements about "the sexuality" of "the primitive." The construction of the ethnographic account is always to some degree preformed by received wisdom, and there is always a tendency to generalize from those "Others" with whom the ethnographer is most familiar. Malinowski is notorious for so doing, but he is not the only sinner.

At the end of the 19th century official disdain for sexual expression was challenged by a revised definition of sexual "health." Foucault and others have written about the construction of "healthy" sexuality during this period in the writings of sexologists, psychiatrists, and reformers. Anxieties about excessive sexuality did not disappear, but there were now insistent voices worrying about sexual insufficiency. As this atmosphere set in, a new stereotype of primitive sexuality fought for space with the old ones, although its antecedents might be seen in some of the early views of Native North Americans. Primitive sexuality was now seen to be fraught with anxieties, repressions, and taboos born of physical or mental underdevelopment and nurtured by religions based in superstition and ignorance. Primitive sexuality as a signifier shifted from denotations of superfluity to implications of lack. The signified, the essence of the Other, was, in one crucial way, unchanged: the primitive was still viewed as animal-like in behavior. The image of animality, albeit sometimes healthy and natural animality, was reinforced by statements that primitives, like animals, go into heat. It is no coincidence that this period saw the efflorescence of theories of the incest taboo, a supposed cultural universal at once reassuringly primal, arguably adaptive, and overtly restrictive. At the time that these views were pronounced, most particularly by Ernest Crawley and Havelock Ellis, some weaker versions of the older view persisted in the writings of W. H. R. Rivers, James G. Frazer, and, a generation later, Robert Briffault.

It is not, we argue, a coincidence that Havelock Ellis was involved in a movement for sexual liberation. His particular focus was, of course, on the liberation of male sexuality, but he also supported the sexual emancipation of women, albeit not in terms all feminists of his period and ours would accept. Ellis endorsed various forms of premarital sex and trial marriage. Both he and Edward Westermarck believed that homosexuality should be tolerated, although they did not engage in political advocacy on this issue.

Unlike their predecessors, who wrote before the era of systematic anthropological fieldwork, Mead and Malinowski were aware that the sexual mores of "primitive" societies were quite variable, a fact that Westermarck had stressed and fieldwork had elucidated. Mead's study of Manus demonstrated that free love was not ubiquitous in the South Seas. In Mead's Samoa and Malinowski's Trobriands, however, there was much sexual experimentation before marriage, whereas married life was stable but relatively dull. Curiously, the experimentation led to few pregnancies. The discovery of such "social facts" may not be unconnected with Malinowski's advocacy of a moderate form of "trial" and "companionate" marriage and his interest both in birth control and in those who advocated it.

It is generally understood (see Suggs and Marshall 1971a:220–221; Vance 1991; Herdt 1999:224) that during the Great Depression and the two decades following World War II there was a relative silence among anthropologists concerning sex. Like all such generalizations, this requires much qualification. Books and articles describing sexual mores continued to be written by anthropologists, but in a number of ways the topic was decentralized. This silencing involved the professional marginalization of certain anthropologists who studied sex and the redefinition of some traditional subjects in nonsexual terms. Perhaps the most important way in which this occurred was by reconceptualizing discussions of sex (and gender) under the more disembodied terms *marriage, family,* and *social structure.* Sir E. E. Evans-Pritchard collected material on Zande homosexual and heterosexual eroticism in the 1920s but did not publish it in venues normally read by anthropologists until the 1970s. In his late monograph *Man and Woman among the Azande,* Evans-Pritchard suggested that his generation of anthropologists may have "lost the flesh and blood" in their writings about African societies (1974:9). In 1932 Malinowski had apologized for writing so many books with "sex" in the title (1932b:x). Mead was criticized by some of her contemporaries for her interest in the topic (see Lutkehaus 1995). Social structure rather than sex was stressed when talking about traditional problems such as cross-dressing and ritual operations on the sexual organs. In the postwar years the influence of Lévi-Strauss and ensuing theoretical developments in Britain and the United States focused attention on ritual and cosmology, including sexual symbolism. One of the key tenets of structuralism, however, one that its practitioners specifically cited as differentiating it from psychoanalytic theory, was that symbols of sex and the body were not primary but equal links on chains of symbols that might include referents to plants, colors, geographical features, jural groups, and other culturally defined categories.

Although public interest in the right way to "do" sex did not disappear during this period, it had to compete with pressing matters such as the Great Depression, World War II, and the cold war. Many anthropologists who discussed sex in this period (e.g., Sir Raymond Firth on the Tikopia, Isaac Schapera on the Kgatla, George Devereux on the Mohave) did not link their anthropology to overt political agendas. Those very few anthropologists who were unafraid to advocate radical sexual politics such as Verrier Elwin were academically and geographically peripheral. Anxiety concerning gender roles in a period of economic and political uncertainty resulted in a flurry of writing about supposed maternal neglect and neurotic sexuality in other cultures (Cora Du Bois, Ralph Linton, Abram Kardiner). Some information about sexuality was submerged in strategic reports and monographs on the "modal personality" of allies and enemies by writers such as Mead (Britain), Ruth Benedict (Japan), and Geoffrey Gorer (Japan and Russia) who engaged in "the study of culture at a distance." Racial inequality in the United States came under increasing attack during these decades, and anthropologists were more closely involved with this project than with sexual reform. British anthropologists, though they rarely opposed the colonial project directly, were concerned with improving colonial governance. The elevation of public opinion concerning the people anthropologists studied may have come at the price of discretion about certain aspects of other cultures.

This was also a period during which anthropology was concerned to establish itself as a legitimate discipline and a genuine science. Gentlemen (and lady) anthropologists with private incomes all but disappeared. One price of legitimation was greater concern with the politics of universities, themselves expanding to provide an avenue to middle-class status to a wider sector of the population. It was vital that anthropology appear "serious." For many anthropologists it may also have been important to avoid becoming targets of the periodic episodes of political panic, during which there was intense scrutiny of traces of deviant sexuality, strongly believed to be connected to unorthodox opinion and suspicious affiliations. In all these matters anthropology was as sensitive to its social context as it had been during earlier periods. Some consequences of that sensitivity will be explored in the latter part of this book when we discuss the anthropological response to the Kinsey Report as well as the subsequent McCarthyite efforts to deny funding to Alfred C. Kinsey's Institute for Sex Research.

Recently, anthropology has purportedly, in Carole Vance's words, "rediscovered sex" (1991). The anthropology that accompanied the sexual and political "thaw" of the decades after the 1960s has been more introspective than any that preceded it. In many ways it has been engaged in producing its own history. While we certainly will examine current developments in the anthropology of sexuality alluded to earlier, our discussion will be *relatively* brief, given the huge volume of material that has been published. We are inclined to refer the reader to its many practitioners, most of them alive and active and busy writing their own stories. However, we do highlight and comment upon key trends such as the new anthropology of homosexualities and gender identity and the related problem of constructionism versus essentialism.

Having provided a synopsis of the subject matter of our book, we need to acquaint the reader with the theoretical perspectives that have guided us.

The field we are to explore is mined with contestations and obscured by queries. Lest the reader be misled as to our purpose, we must examine what we mean by *sexuality* and what we designate as anthropological discourse, and we must describe the trajectory of our historical inquiry.

Sexuality is not merely a loaded term, it is preeminently ambiguous. It might be said, like the word *game*, to be a Wittgensteinian odd-job word, a signifier with numerous, sometimes contradictory referents. It can be used to mean a biological given, whether a propensity or a drive; it may refer to individuals or groups; it may refer to "unconscious" or conscious impulses; it may describe behavior, whether indulged in, observed, desired, or related in narrative; it may be a concept in discourse that refers to some or all of the preceding.

The broadness of such a discursive concept may reflect the view that there is no verifiable reality beyond talk – that sexuality is best viewed as a social construct. "Sex" itself is similarly ambiguous. It can be seen as the biological "counterpoint" to socially constructed "gender," in which event either category could be and has been viewed as dependent on the other. Our viewpoint is clearly constructionist, and our focus is on sexuality as a discursive category. By this we do not mean to deny the obvious biological component in sexuality, as some extreme constructionists may appear to do, but to state that our focus is on the "constructs" or "fictions" that anthropologists and other writers have created about people in their own and other societies. Such "fictions" have necessarily informed, illuminated, reflected, refracted, and distorted studies of human sexual behavior. We suggest that the study of variations in human sexual behavior is a very legitimate part of anthropology, but we note that few scholars have succeeded in asking or answering apparently simple questions such as "What do the X people do in bed?" and "Is homosexual behavior present in all human groups?" without revealing a social and political agenda. When anthropologists analyze sexual behavior, they are usually examining what is said about such actions rather than eyewitness accounts. So one examines (perhaps) acts, the rules to which acts do or do not conform, the ways in which rules are enforced, the rules prescribing and proscribing talk about sex among the group studied, and the rules of academic discourse that prescribe guidelines or rules for the inquiring anthropologist.

We accordingly accept Foucault's insight that *sexuality* is a peculiarly dense transfer point for relations of power. It is one of the major means by which experts, the possessors of knowledge, exercise control over patients and clients; it is deployed in securing a regime of bodily control, categorizing and disciplining behavior and identity. Foucault's attention was devoted to the alienists, psychiatrists, social reformers, legal authorities, sexologists, and educators who extended the power of civil authority and interviewed, surveyed, regulated, and named their chosen subjects. The latter were prisoners, students, patients, and sexual "deviants." The "state" that controlled their lives was understood to be more extensive than the political and legal authorities as conventionally defined. The surveillance to which they were subjected took place in the interview room or on the alienist's couch, our modern "confessionals." The "gaze" to which they were subjected was often quite literal, the observation tower or panopticon in the prison and, doubtless, the statistical research instrument as well as the video camera. The ultimate realization of power is the self-regulated and self-scrutinizing subject. It should be stressed that in Foucault's formulation the watchers do not create sexual behaviors or insane ideation. They label them, diagnose them, and give them social reality.

There are omissions, whole or partial, deliberate or involuntary, in Foucault's accounts in volume 1 of *The History of Sexuality*. Inasmuch as he wished to refute what he called "the repressive hypothesis," arguing that restrictive regulation could constitute an incitement to discourse, and because he asserted that each "liberation" (e.g., permission for heterosexual pleasure within companionate marriage) inevitably meant the creation of new categories for social surveillance (e.g., "homosexuals"), he chose not to discuss the very real limits that social rules and actions placed on individual behavior and quotidian talk. The prosecutions of Bradlaugh in the 1870s (disseminating a book about contraceptive practices), Oscar Wilde, George Bedborough (distributing Havelock Ellis's book *Sexual Inversion* in 1898), Malinowski's fear of being labeled a "sexologist," the legal action concerning Eustace Chesser's *Love and Fear* in 1942, the 30-year struggle to publish the unexpurgated version of D. H. Lawrence's *Lady Chatterley's Lover*, and countless other laws, rules, limitations, and cautions reveal that discourse was often angry and that "freedoms" were hard to win.[1] (See Porter and Hall 1995 for a similar argument.)

Furthermore, there was also misrecognition of the salience of social class in modern society, although it was a central concern of Foucault's analysis of sexual penetration in ancient Greece and Rome. Foucault depicts the four main subjects of sexual discourse in the late 19th century (the Malthusian couple, the hysterical female, the masturbating child, the sexual pervert) as quasi-racial categories, but he has little to say in the main body of his works about "race," a hierarchical social category that so often intersects and intertwines with class, sex, and gender. Stoler (1995) has written about Foucault's lectures on race in the mid-1970s. It must be noted that Foucault's attention was primarily confined to racial categorization in France at the turn of the 20th century and its background in European history. He had little to say about race outside the metropolis and the central places. He was not concerned with the peripheral theaters of action, where slavery had flourished and was succeeded by imperialism and, more recently, by neocolonialism (see Stoler 1995:19–54). In these theaters there were many players: the slave owners and their opponents, colonial administrators, explorers, traders, missionaries, settlers, wives and mistresses, raciologists, armchair anthropologists, and fieldworkers. The voices of colonialism spoke through relatively few channels, and there were many, of course, about whom we hear only through the narratives of those who controlled the discourses of the colonial encounter. We could, if we liked, distinguish between activity in the colonies and discourses at the center of power. What we wish to stress is that much of 18th-, 19th-, and 20th-century physical and social anthropology may be viewed as a product of social relations not merely in the metropolis but also in the colonial periphery.

Anthropology has always been concerned with the affirmation or negation of categories such as race, sexuality, gender, and class as well as with their complex intersections and interweavings. It has affirmed or challenged their place or placing in Nature and discussed their role in Culture. Arguably, it has never attained the power and influence of Foucault's preferred metropolitan fields of discourse – criminology, psychiatry, and educational psychology. There is no precise equivalent to the panopticon, but that may not be for any lack of trying.

Another matter that must be addressed in considering the history of anthropologists' depictions of sexuality is that European culture, at home and in its colonial manifestation, is not the only locale in which sex has been a transfer point for power. Sex also serves such purposes in societies that anthropologists have studied. This may partially explain the perceived plethora of sex in anthropological writings.

Insofar as the plethora of ethnographic prurience is illusory, the apparent prominence of sex in ethnological texts may be an artifact of the invisibility of the Foucauldian panopticon when it is working smoothly in familiar surroundings. To understand alien sexuality we need to make it explicit and, therefore, memorable. On the other hand, a well-scrubbed family celebrating Mother's Day at a suburban restaurant is one of many domestic scenarios in which neither the sexual nor the political overtones would have been particularly visible to a North American observer before certain radical feminists foregrounded them by giving them the name "compulsory heterosexuality." Anthropologists wrote about "sex." A sociologist of the 1950s, describing the Mother's Day lunch, would have been writing about the importance of the nuclear family in the American social structure.

Of course, when anthropologists did write about the sexuality of others, they were not always alert for indigenous displays and transfers of power. More often, exotic sexuality was, as we have indicated, employed as a foil in arguments about sexuality at home. If it was not, the dictates of relativism were likely to preclude an investigation of the "winners" and "losers" created by foreign sexual systems. Some anthropologists, particularly those currently writing under the influence of Foucault, feminism, or "queer theory," have tried to examine the connections between sex and power in the cultures they describe, but they are often conscious of writing against the grain. Anthropologists' reactions to others' sexual politics is a theme that we will explore further in this book.

If the definition of "sex" is not obvious, neither is the demarcation of "anthropology" or "history." Anthropology is conventionally understood to involve the comparison of different peoples in different spaces and "times" with a view to comprehending both their similarities and their differences.

In practice, many anthropologists have concentrated their attention on a few societies at most. While it is possible to date the beginnings of anthropology to Herodotus or, arguably, to Ibn Khaldun or Ibn Battuta, the discipline is normally considered to have its real roots in the Enlightenment (e.g., see Harris 1969). It is hardly a coincidence that modern and secular rather than religious conceptions of the body, "sex," and "race" date to this period, the late 18th century. Anthropology was a response to two concerns of Enlightenment thinkers, namely, political controversies concerning emancipation and individualism and the scientific developments that were to lead to Darwin and Mendel. These projects were, as we shall see, closely intertwined, though science could be used to challenge as well as support egalitarianism and was itself not immune to external attack and internal controversy.

Supposed biological difference was used as a reason for excluding blacks and women from political and economic emancipation and was also employed by some such as the diplomat, historian, and raciologist Arthur, comte de Gobineau in the mid–19th century as the rationale for questioning the entire Enlightenment movement from hierarchy to equality.[2]

Early anthropology was not clearly demarcated from neighboring disciplines such as biology and sociology. (Indeed, the latter term was not invented by Auguste Comte until the second quarter of the 19th century.) There was as yet no clear separation between race and culture; rather, it was assumed that there was a connection between physical type and cultural achievement. The one was an index of the other. In a brilliant recent book, Robert Young (1995) has clearly demonstrated how intertwined "race" and "culture" were not only in the writings of raciologists such as Robert Knox and Josiah Clark Nott but also in the work of Ernest Renan and Matthew Arnold. The period between 1770 and 1870 witnessed a revolution in both geology and history that profoundly altered our conception of human origins and biological and social evolution. By 1870 biological anthropology and the new evolutionary social anthropology had begun to diverge, although their ultimate separation and divorce was a long, slow process. Since the time of Émile Durkheim and Franz Boas (1890–1920), social anthropologists have been decreasingly inclined to employ race as an explanation of difference between cultures. It has taken a little longer for them to question the "naturalness" of gender differentiation as a principle of social order, however much it might vary across cultures in its specific manifestations.

Early anthropologists did not do fieldwork but, rather, engaged in what we call "armchair anthropology," assessing data collected by explorers, traders, missionaries, and administrators. Some of the missionaries, explorers, and armchair anthropologists, however, such as Sir Richard Burton and Lewis Henry Morgan, did experience firsthand contact with indigenous, supposedly "primitive" peoples. Obviously, observations of sexuality in other cultures that are based on limited and usually secondhand data are by their very nature superficial and questionable.

The institutionalization of anthropology and the placement of anthropologists within universities was a slow process. The period between 1860 and 1890 witnessed the foundation of anthropological societies in London, Paris, and Washington DC. The Bureau of American Ethnology was founded in 1879. The development of anthropology as a university discipline was a tardier process. The reign of the amateur anthropologist did not end until after World War I (see Kuklick 1991; Darnell 1998).

We are justified in beginning our narrative with the era of the Enlightenment for the very simple reason that modern social anthropology is still intimately related to Enlightenment ideas, some of which it affirms and others it most assuredly denies. The very fervor with which some of us proclaim Culture's independence of Nature ("Omnis cultura ex cultura" [All culture springs from culture], as Alfred Kroeber once put it) is a reaction to our proximity to other, secular notions that affirmed that racial and gender hierarchies were determined by physical type.

This book examines an important aspect of anthropology's history, but it differs radically from many writings by historians of anthropology. In *After Tylor* George Stocking remarks: "Although such issues are only touched on here and there in the present volume, the history of British social anthropology might be written in terms of its relationship to changing views of sexual prudery and pornography. (For hints or gestures toward such a general interpretation, see Leach 1984:35, 218; Lyons and Lyons 1986; Tuzin 1994.)" (Stocking 1995:28). Although there is an element of exaggeration in Stocking's remark (we don't think that the history of anthropology is *only* the history of sexuality), the point is taken. Its implications are critical. Most historical writing on the development of anthropology tends to explain theoretical and institutional developments purely in terms of their significance within anthropology itself. An example might be an examination of the relationship between the functionalism of Malinowski and the structuralism of A. R. Radcliffe-Brown that considered differences in theoretical modeling, personal interactions, and institutional histories, with perhaps the odd references to metropolitan and colonial funding agencies. Our approach to anthropologists' attitudes toward the sexuality of other peoples, which sees such attitudes as very much the product of conflicts, dialogues, and social movements in Britain, the United States, and their dependencies, thus marks a departure from customary procedure. We believe such connections are worth pursuing, though they may be difficult to prove.

Some of the individuals we discuss (e.g., Ernest Crawley) were reticent about their opinions on political, social, and sexual issues; others such as Bronislaw Malinowski were extremely forthright. Our role is to raise very important questions, even if we cannot always answer them with an emphatic "quod erat demonstrandum." Better that than to leave unexplained why so many anthropologists felt it necessary to express such firm opinions on an area of human conduct about which so remarkably little was known.

We shall devote particular attention to a number of books and monographs that had an influence not only among anthropologists but also among the intelligentsia in general and, more recently, among that larger class of the population that is exposed to anthropology in the classroom or through the mass media. These "publics" have included politicians and policy makers as well as the implementers of policy in institutions such as schools, hospitals, and social service agencies. Thus, their sources of anthropological information are a significant interface between anthropology and history. We should note that anthropologists differ from sociologists and psychologists in the importance they assign to book-length field reports, although we do not privilege these exclusively.

We give the name "conscription" to the concept that has informed most of our writing in this book. By conscription we mean the deployment of data about sexual discourses and practices among "Others" within discourses of power, morality, pleasure, and therapy in the metropolitan cultures where anthropological texts have predominantly been read and produced. Conscription may imply the reaffirmation of existing social hierarchies, or it may involve what Marcus and Fischer (1986) call "cultural critique." The two positions, of course, need not be mutually exclusive – critiques of some social practices may reinforce others. Conscription is a live metaphor. It implies force and inequality and, more often than not, the absence of true dialogue. Conscription may be "positive," inasmuch as the heterosexual practices of "primitives" are viewed as a "natural," uncorrupted form of behavior from which "we" have wrongfully departed and toward which we should now return. Another mode of conscription consists in the demonstration that erotic actions and sentiments that we prohibit or discourage are permitted or even in some cases prescribed elsewhere for certain individuals (e.g., "homosexual" berdaches or "two-spirit people" among North American First Nations) or at certain stages in the life cycle (e.g., homoerotic features of male initiation in Melanesia). It may be "negative" inasmuch as primitive sexual behavior shows us how biologically different "they" are from "us," how lucky or righteous we are that we have evolved morally and they haven't, or, indeed, how their "degeneracy" is clear evidence of what will happen if we allow our own social misfits to survive or take control of our destinies. Negative conscription is particularly associated with the racialism of the 19th century, but we shall see that it is also more subtly present in 20th-century accounts of dystopia in Alor (Indonesia) and the Marquesas (Polynesia). Our discussion of the portrayal of Samoa by Mead and the Trobriand Islands by Malinowski will show that conscription can indeed be ambiguous. Both authors respected the freedom supposedly present in premarital sexuality, which showed that there was an alternative to the alleged miseries of Western adolescence, but also regretted the absence of passion in heterosexual courtship and marriage. We must note that the relationship between conscription and ethnographic "fact" is tangential inasmuch as the same selective data may support both a negative and a positive conscription.

We prefer the word "conscription" to more common notions in contemporary anthropology such as "co-option" and "appropriation." All three words imply an inequality in anthropological (or artistic and literary) encounters with "Others." However, co-option and appropriation have become synonymous with modes of conscription in which the author enlists the ideas or experience of others into some present argument (what we call positive conscription). We don't wish nihilistically to imply that the continuance of a scintilla (at the very least) of conscription in contemporary anthropology condemns our discipline to moral danger or scientific obloquy. We believe that a century of ethnographic writing has produced a record of uniformities and variance in human sexual morality that is, admittedly, spotty but does have much value. We are also aware that fieldworkers today are more inclined than ever before to consider ethical questions concerning subject consent and that university ethics committees reinforce such determination. These concerns are reflected, for the most part, in the recent anthropology of sexuality. Because anthropologists bring their ethical values and their particular sexual morality to the field with them, because they are political animals, and because, however "dialogic" and participatory their fieldwork methods may be, ethnographic authority still rests in their hands, conscription is inevitably an ethnographic and theoretical strategy. Self-awareness and self-knowledge may enable us to review absences as well as presences in our fieldwork notes so that we do not wholly fictionalize others in our own interests. Inasmuch as most ethnographic subjects today are all too aware of the possible repercussions of sensitive records, contemporary anthropologists have to balance the varied interests of "their" people and the urgency of anthropological knowledge. In other words, there is nothing wrong with using the astonishing record of human variability as well as human uniformity to critique our own institutions, provided we do not harm the peoples we study and provided that our awareness of who we are and what we are doing stops us from misrepresenting what we see and hear. This is a difficult task, but it is by no means impossible. The story we are about to tell has a simple point. If as anthropologists we do not become aware of the moral snares and scientific pitfalls that repeatedly mark the social history of our discipline, we can still make some very bad mistakes.

CHAPTER 1

Three Images of Primitive Sexuality and the Definition of Species

T hree persistent images of primitive sexuality emerged in the 18th century. Each of them had political as well as scientific resonances. Each of them was linked to the fact of miscegenation through processes of affirmation or denial. The politics of miscegenation (and/or interracial copulation) appear to be linked to controversies concerning the definition of the biological concept of species.

It was at this time that an image of Polynesia emerged that has endured and is still resonant. Tahitians were said to occupy a paradise of natural luxury and sexual liberty. This positive image was not uncontested, particularly by Evangelical Christians. Nonetheless, it distinguished the Tahitians from other non-Western groups. Africans of both sexes were portrayed as lascivious and bestial. The Hottentot, often racially distinguished from the Negro, was viewed as the symbol of the worst form of sexual excess. The appearance and size of the genitals in sub-Saharan Africans and African Americans was the visible index of moral degeneration. The sexuality of South American Indians, Lapps, and Inuit was also depicted in negative fashion. It too was excessive. In contrast, some North American groups such as the Iroquois supposedly lacked sexual ardor. Given that this too was a departure from the European norm, such continence was also seen as unnatural. Underlying all three images was a notion of a natural, biological sexuality. Where and among whom it existed was another matter. If savagery might diminish or exaggerate it, civilization was said to repress it, for better or worse. The happy mean, according to some Enlightenment thinkers, was to be found in the newly discovered South Seas.

Roy Porter (1990) has drawn our attention to the significance of early writings about Tahiti. He discusses the eyewitness accounts of Samuel Wallis, Phillibert Commerson, Louis Antoine de Bougainville, James Cook, Sir Joseph Banks, and Georg Forster as well as Denis Diderot's philosophical commentary *Le Supplément au voyage de Bougainville*. Our examination of Diderot's *Supplément* reveals that there is continuity between some of the earliest portrayals of South Seas societies and the scientific monographs of 20th-century anthropology.

After Wallis's vessel arrived there in 1767, Tahiti was visited three more times in the next five years (by Bougainville and subsequently two voyages of Captain Cook). The various crews were entertained by scantily clad Tahitian ladies who exceeded contemporary European standards of beauty. The cost of this entertainment was cheap. Because there was no iron in Tahiti, nails were a welcome item of exchange. Tahitian males were not loath to share their daughters and even their wives with the European newcomers. Bougainville observed that in Tahiti there was an abundance of natural resources and that commonality in both property and sexual partners was part of the idyll. Banks indicated that both he and other members of Cook's 1769 crew amply enjoyed the sexual opportunities they were offered (Porter 1990).

There were dissenting opinions. Cook noted that Tahitian marriages were stable, stating that the women who presented themselves to the crew were from the lower orders of Tahitian society and were in every way comparable to the prostitutes who abounded in English port cities (Porter 1990). The equation of primitive women and prostitutes is one we shall discuss later. However, Cook's aim was to avoid exoticism by remarking that not all Tahitian women were comparable to prostitutes. For the same reason, he expressed his doubts that there could be common ownership of property in any society that relied on individual labor in horticulture. The Evangelical Forster, who was also an officer on Cook's ship, was distressed by the morality both of the Tahitians and of the European visitors who had taken advantage of them.

Diderot's *Supplément* relies on Bougainville's account rather than Cook's. It also relies a little on Plutarch and Plato, who may be presumed not to have visited Tahiti. It contains a dialogic commentary by two individuals, A and B, into which are inserted two set pieces. One consists of a speech supposedly made by a Tahitian elder bidding an angry adieu to the *chef des brigands* (Bougainville) and his crew (Diderot 1989:589–595), who have corrupted Tahitian innocence and communalism with Western notions of property and colonial territory:

> We follow the pure instinct of Nature, and you have tried to erase its mark from our souls. Here everything belongs to all, and you have

preached to us some unspeakable distinction between thine and mine. Our daughters and our wives are shared in common; you have partaken in this privilege with us and have begun to kindle unknown passions among them. We are free, and behold! you have buried the deed of our future slavery beneath our own land. . . . Were a Tahitian someday to disembark on your shores and were he to carve on one of your stones or on the bark of one of your trees, "This country belongs to the inhabitants of Tahiti," what would you think? (Diderot 1989:591, our translation) [1]

The second set piece is an imagined dialogue between a Tahitian sage, Orou, and the ship's chaplain (*aumônier*) that concerns what we may call the cultural relativity of morals (Diderot 1989:599–613, 617–627). The chaplain is appalled by the offer of Orou's daughters and wife, although he is quickly drawn into a sexual relationship with the youngest daughter. His defense of Christian morals is undermined by Orou's defense of Tahitian alternatives. The incident ends with the semiconversion of the chaplain, whose sexual encounters with the sage's wife and remaining two daughters are punctuated with cries of "Mais ma religion! Mais mon état!" [But my religion! But my state!] (Diderot 1989:626). At one point, Orou expresses his moral indignation at the European custom of monogamous marriage for life. The chaplain has portrayed it as following the law of God, but the sage views it as contrary to nature to suppose that a free, thinking, sentient human could be made the property of his or her fellow being (Diderot 1989:604). Tahitian marriage is a terminable, consensual relationship:

> *The Chaplain:* What is marriage like among you?
> *Orou:* An agreement to live in the same hut and to lie in the same bed, so long as we are satisfied with the arrangement.
> *The Chaplain:* And when you're dissatisfied?
> *Orou:* We split. (Diderot 1989:609, our translation) [2]

Subsequently, Orou challenges the necessity of an incest taboo, including not merely parent-child but also sibling incest, a stance that would have been as alien to the real Polynesians as it was to the imaginary chaplain (Diderot 1989:619–620).

Michèle Duchet (1971) has appropriately remarked that Diderot's *Supplément* is a critique of French institutions, particularly the marriage laws and the role of the Catholic clergy, and that the Tahitians were merely a foil. While Diderot may thus be absolved of any genuine ethnographic intent, his and Bougainville's Tahitians were surely the adumbrations of Mead's Samoans, Malinowski's Trobrianders, the subjects of Gauguin's portraits, and countless other representations and fictions. Opposed to the paradisiacal image of Oceania is a counterimage of a verdant, subtropical Hell, the world of Somerset Maugham's *Rain*. The counterpart of these fictions is a Polynesia that has become the haunt of sometimes exploitative European males, who visit as voyagers, penetrators, or voyeurs.

Cornélius Jaenen (1982) has remarked that representations of North American Indian society in the 18th century often replicated "concepts and constructs" of the pre-Columbian as well as post-Columbian era. These included "the Terrestrial Paradise, the Golden Age, the Millennial Kingdom, the Monstrous Satanic World, the Utopian New World, the Chain of Being, etc." (Jaenen 1982:45). In *Deconstructing America* (1990) Peter Mason observes that 16th-century Europeans accommodated the strangeness and apparent incommensurability of the New World by means of preexistent representations concerning internal strangers and distant aliens. Commonly, these representations involved symbolic inversion, monstrosities, and liminal phenomena. They included elements of the medieval image of the witch, the wild man or woman, the madman, and the fool. The teratological tradition of Hesiod, Herodotus, Pliny the Elder, Solinus, and John Mandeville was extended to the Americas, which found a new home for depleted humans with one eye, leg, or testicle or with no breasts and for phantasmagoric confusions such as the Blemmyae (who had no heads but had eyes on their shoulders), the Cynocephalae (dog-headed people), and others who mixed animal and human features. Ideas of inverted behavior (cannibalism, extravagant sexuality, or sexual depletion) are the correlates of bodily deformation. The existence of similar "ethnoanthropologies" among Amerindian peoples (e.g., accounts of the headless Ewaipanoma given to Sir Walter Raleigh by inhabitants of Guiana) added another layer to the creative invention of the New World. Mason argues persuasively that accounts of effeminate males, Amazons, and sexually voracious females and transgressive sexuality (incestuous copulation in the writings of Amerigo Vespucci, homosexuality in the writings of Oviedo, lesbianism in the illustrations to Theodor de Bry's *America*), which are common during this period, are fictions that interweave renewed mythologies and ethnoanthropologies. To Mason the "factuality" of these accounts is beyond, or almost beyond, the point. For us, what is significant is that over 300 years of culture contact these images may have softened but were hardly obliterated. By the 17th and 18th centuries, groups who had converted to Christianity were less likely to be viewed as devil worshipers and perverts. On the other hand, 18th-century images of degeneration were utilized to contradict paradisiacal and Utopian images. One specific image that persisted through this time was that of the effeminate, sexless Amerindian male.

Georges Louis Leclerc, comte de Buffon, the prominent French savant and naturalist, was dismayed to find that his portrayal of North American Indians as weak, ignoble, and sexless savages was utilized to support anti-Utopian ideas of moral decline (rather than a more neutral notion of "degeneration" or alteration in type). His remarks about them in his *Histoire naturelle* (which appeared in several volumes between 1749 and 1788) were intended merely to demonstrate that "human nature was everywhere the same but there were racial or national differences because of such factors as climate, region, degrees of civility, government, or other accidental causes" (Jaenen 1982:49). The following is Jaenen's translation of the relevant text by Buffon:

> For though the American savage be nearly of the same stature with men in polished societies, yet this is not sufficient exception to the general contraction of animated Nature throughout the whole Continent. In the savage, the organs of generation are feeble. He has no hair, no beard, no ardour for the female. Though nimbler than the European, because more accustomed to running, his strength is not so great. His sensations are less acute: and yet he is more cowardly and timid. He has no vivacity, no activity of mind. . . . Destroy his appetite for victuals and drink, and you will at once annihilate the active principle of all his movements; he remains, in stupid repose, on his limbs or couch for whole days. (Jaenen 1982:49)

The abbé Guillaume Thomas François Raynal believed that the supposed sexual inadequacy of Amerindians was a sign of their immaturity, indeed, of the infancy of the continent (Jaenen 1982:51). Perhaps immaturity as a condition is preferable to degeneracy. William Byrd of Virginia spoke of their "Constitutions untainted by Lewdness" (Jordan 1969:162). Cornelius de Pauw announced that the Amerindian penis was smaller than that of Europeans (Jordan 1969:163).

One wonders if such a belief has any other basis than superstition and prejudice. One obvious explanation is the relative lack of facial hair among Amerindian males, to which Buffon indeed refers. Another is the strong sexual honor code that was manifest in many traditional North American cultures along with rules prescribing sexual abstinence for warriors in time of battle or for participants in some rituals. This resulted in a significant cultural difference: "Indians in eastern North America did not rape female captives; Europeans did" (Abler 1992:13). As William Smith noted in 1765, "No woman . . . need fear violation of her honour" (quoted in Abler 1992:14). Ironically, it would appear that their failure to make sexual prey out of female war captives may have led European commentators to cast aspersions on the virility of Amerindian males!

Significantly, Winthrop Jordan remarks that, although white–Indian miscegenation in the American South may not have been as frequent as miscegenation between whites and blacks, "the entire interracial sexual complex did not pertain to the Indian" (Jordan 1969:163). Indeed, "of the various laws which penalized illicit miscegenation, none applied to Indians, and only North Carolina's (and Virginia's for a very brief period) prohibited intermarriage. On the contrary, several colonists were willing to allow, even advocate, intermarriage with the Indian – an unheard of proposition concerning Negroes" (Jordan 1969:163). The gist of Jordan's argument is that there is a correlation between the image of the Other's sexuality and attitudes and practices concerning miscegenation with that Other. Inasmuch as Tahiti was and still is a sexual Utopia for some Europeans and Tahitian standards of beauty appealed to them, the European attitude to miscegenation was positive. Because Native North Americans were viewed as sexually nonthreatening, there was no bar to miscegenation. We shall discuss attitudes toward Africans and African Americans shortly.

We move from supposed deficiencies in male, heterosexual ardor to a related question, the presence (or absence) of what we might now call a "third gender" or "transgender phenomenon." Early reports of transvestism and/or homosexuality among Aztecs, Incas, and Cueva (Panama) and in various parts of South America are, quite simply, unreliable. Gonzalo Fernández de Oviedo y Valdés, the early-16th-century chronicler of the Spanish conquest, reported that the "lords and chieftains" of the Cueva kept young men who were transvestites, household servants, and passive homosexuals. Such individuals were the object of derision (Trexler 1995:90, 91). Oviedo also reported that same-sex relations between males were common throughout the new Spanish territories (Trexler 1995:1, 2). The existence of male temple prostitutes in the Valley of Mexico was reported by Bernal Díaz del Castillo (Trexler 1995:104; Keen 1971:61). In 1516 Peter Martyr reported that in Panama Vasco Núñez de Balboa had supposedly thrown 40 transvestites to the dogs (Trexler 1995:82). In the middle of the 16th century, when Juan Ginés de Sepúlveda and Bartolomé de Las Casas conducted their famous debate concerning the possibility of saving Indian souls, the credibility of such reports was at stake. Sepúlveda was inclined to believe most of them, whereas Las Casas was skeptical about claims that deviant sexuality was common and openly tolerated. No one suggested that some of the reported behaviors might indeed exist and that there might be nothing intrinsically wrong with them. This limitation of argument was to persist for 400 years.

From the 16th to the 18th century Spanish and French observers, including René Goulaine de Laudonnière, Jacques Le Moyne, and François Coréal, described "hermaphrodites" and "effeminate youths" they encountered among the Timacuans of Florida. These "hermaphrodites" cared for and fed the sick, carried provisions to the battlefield, and acted as messengers. They wore a distinctive headdress but otherwise tended to wear female attire. Some of them married men and may have practiced sodomy (Roscoe 1988:48–50). Europeans were later to encounter similar institutions when they explored the western part of the continent, both in the Great Plains and the southwestern pueblos. For example, the Cheyenne *hemaneh* (half-man, half-woman) wore feminine attire, did not engage in battle, and assumed the role of master of ceremonies at certain rites of passage. The French applied the term *berdache* (from a Persian word meaning "kept boy") to "passive partners in homosexual relationships between Native American males" (Midnight Sun 1988:34; Angelino and Shedd 1955:121). It should be emphasized that the berdache role was not, in fact, synonymous with homosexuality; it also implied transvestism, ceremonial roles, and occupational specialization.

Needless to say, such an institution did not meet with the approval of most European observers. The Catholic fathers sought and received confessions from the Timacuans. The most secular of authorities also disapproved. In his *Essai sur les moeurs* Voltaire remarked that homosexuality, "the Socratic vice," was not contrary to human nature, although it was contrary to Nature's purpose. Revolting customs were to be found in both savage and civilized societies. Among Amerindians, the Socratic vice had the same ill effect as among the ancient Greeks (Duchet 1971:304).

Representations of the sexuality of South American Indians and circumpolar groups were sometimes very different from those attributed to many Native North American groups. Voltaire's opinion of Brazilian Indians reflects the beliefs of both his contemporaries and his predecessors. Amazonian peoples were devoid of government, law, and religion. They were slaves to their senses. The men coupled indiscriminately with their mothers, sisters, and daughters. Worst of all, they were cannibals (Duchet 1971:303).

Buffon was not particularly fond of the circumpolar populations, all of whom he regarded as degenerated Tartars. This was hardly a compliment, given that the Tartars were without "decency in their manners" (Buffon 1791, vol. 3:67). He assumed that these physical and moral changes had been caused by the harsh climate and poor diet. The Samoyeds, Lapps, and Eskimo were all similar in culture. The Lapps were typical in one notable respect: "They offer their wives and daughters to strangers, and esteem it the highest affront if the offer is rejected" (Buffon 1791, vol. 3:62). Such unfortunate individuals bore the stigmata of their degeneration on their bodies, which showed an excess of some secondary sexual characteristics and a deficit of others: "Among all these people, the women are fully as ugly as the men, whom they resemble so much that the distinction is not easily perceived. . . . Their breasts are so long and pliable, that they can suckle their children over their shoulders. Their nipples are as black as jet, and their skin is of a very deep olive colour. Some travellers alledge that these women have no hair on their heads, and are not subject to the menstrual evacuation" (Buffon 1791, vol. 3:59, 60).

We must remark that there were a few who were skeptical of all these tall tales. One such person was Johann Friedrich Blumenbach of Göttingen (1752–1840), who is regarded by many as the founder of physical anthropology. He is, unfortunately, remembered as the inventor of the term *Caucasian*, by which he designated a population he believed to be particularly beautiful, although he was a believer in the potential equality of all races. In the third edition of *De Generis Humani Varietate Nativa*, which appeared in 1795, Blumenbach commented on stories about the beardlessness of American Indians. He granted that the quantity of facial hair varied from one population to another and that American Indian beards were "thin and scanty." However, a scanty beard did not mean no beard at all. Some Amerindian groups, in fact, encouraged the men to grow beards; among others the beard was systematically plucked out. He regretted that he had taken such "unnecessary trouble" to obtain a "heap of testimony" about this matter (Blumenbach 1969:272). Furthermore, he had investigated another story and found it too wanting in evidence:

The fabulous report that the American Indian women have no menstruation, seems to have its origin in this, that the Europeans when they discovered the new world, although they saw numbers of the female inhabitants entirely naked, never seem to have observed in them the stains of that excretion. For this it seems likely that there were two reasons; first, that amongst those nations of America, the women during menstruation are, by a fortunate prejudice, considered as poisonous, and are prohibited from social intercourse, and for so long enjoy a beneficial repose in the more secluded huts far from the view of men; secondly, because, as has been noticed, they are so commendably clean in their bodies, and the commissure of their legs so conduces to modesty, that no vestiges of the catamenia ever strike the eye. (Blumenbach 1969:272–273)

Images of African sexuality exhibit another kind of pathology that is intimately connected with the pathology exhibited by European colonialism since its inception. Africans of both sexes were regarded as supple, agile, dexterous, and possessed of "an extreme disposition toward sensations and excitations" (Virey 1824, vol. 2: 39–40; see also 42–43). Julien Virey, the author of Histoire naturelle du genre humain, also remarked that black females had large sexual organs and that black males had "very voluminous" genitals, all of which were the counterpart of their superstition, low intelligence, and poor linguistic facility (1824, vol. 2:46, 47–53). Virey's accomplishment was to lend the support of the fledgling science of physical anthropology to a folk tradition that was already 350 years old.

Jordan remarks that the idea that blacks had huge penises was current before the discovery of the Americas and possibly before the Portuguese exploration of the West African coast: "Several fifteenth century cartographers decorated parts of Africa with little naked figures which gave the idea graphic expression, and in due course, in the seventeenth century, English accounts of West Africa [Jordan mentions Richard Jobson and John Ogilby] were carefully noting the 'extraordinary greatness' of the Negroes' 'members'" (1969:158).

Jordan cites, as shall we, evidence that such beliefs were common in scientific circles. It is surely more difficult to surmise popular attitudes, but he suggests that they were probably similar. Recently, it was rumored that one racial scientist was attempting to prove this hypothesis by obtaining a statistical sample of verifiable measurements. Whether or not there is a small difference in the average size of the penis between different populations is unclear; what is palpably clear is that the extensive attention to the matter by certain people at certain times is, as Jordan suggests (1969:159), an index of European sexual insecurity. In the late 18th century, before the dismal science of statistics was born, a sample size of one was considered significant! Otherwise, one might refer to observations of "several" individuals.

Our sources are the English anatomist and racial determinist Charles White and the normally cautious Johann Friedrich Blumenbach: "It is generally said that the penis in the Negro is very large. And this assertion is so far borne out by the remarkable genital apparatus of an Aethiopian which I have in my anatomical collection. Whether this prerogative be constant and peculiar to the nation I do not know. It is said that women when eager for venery prefer the embraces of Negroes to those of other men" (Blumenbach 1969:249).

Apparently, there were some who said that "this prerogative" was shared by the Scottish highlanders, "who do not wear trowsers." However, with a possibly feigned gravity, Blumenbach remarks, "I have shown however on the weightiest testimony that this assertion is incorrect" (1969:249).[3] There is no irony in any of Charles White's statements about penis size:

> That the penis of an African is larger than that of an European, has, I believe, been shown in every anatomical school in London. Preparations of them are preserved in most anatomical museums; and I have one in mine. I have examined several living negroes, and found it invariably to be the case. A surgeon of reputation informs me that . . . he assisted at the dissection of a negro whose PENIS WAS AD LONGITUDINEM POLLICUM DUODECIM [12 inches long]. . . . Haller, in his PRIMAE LINIAE, speaking of the Africans, says, "IN HOMINIBUS ETIAM PENIS EST LONGIOR ET MULTO LAXIOR" [among humans, moreover, the penis is longer and much looser]; but I say, MULTO FIRMIOR ET DURIOR [firmer by far and harder]. In SIMIAE the penis is still longer in proportion to the size of their bodies. (1799:61)

Although the two anatomists agreed about the alleged peculiarity of black males, White's last remark indicates their substantial difference in philosophy. Blumenbach was convinced that a considerable gap separated humans from apes and monkeys and that bipedal locomotion, the use of the hands, menstruation, and the brain's structure and power were distinguishing features. White believed in a medieval notion that enjoyed renewed popularity in the 18th century, the Great Chain (otherwise Scale or Ladder) of Being. God, it was said, had constructed a continuous hierarchy in creation, ranging from stones and metallic objects at the bottom to the angels on high. In between were invertebrates, reptiles, fish, birds, and mammals. Monkeys and apes occupied the rung below humanity. It was believed that the Chain or Ladder of Being was a perfect creation. There were no gaps, no missing links or rungs. Accordingly, unlike Buffon and Blumenbach,

White believed that the "lower races" of humankind bridged the gap between the apes (the "orang-outang," which he and others could not yet distinguish from the chimpanzee) and the higher races such as the European. Sexuality was just one of the criteria of difference. Besides noting the size of the Negro penis, White also stated that apes and baboons menstruated less than black females, who in turn menstruated less than white females (1799:58–61), thereby exhibiting that "regular gradation" that was evident in so many other respects. White's own original research had consisted in some painstaking measurements of the ulna and radius among Negroes and Europeans. One particularly long forearm belonged to a Negro "in the lunatic asylum in Liverpool." He had measured the forearms of many Englishmen. None of them could surpass or even approximate that of the black lunatic (White 1799:53–54). The apes, however, had relatively larger forearms than even black humans.

Regular gradation was also present with respect to the skull's size and capacity, the placement of the foramen magnum, the capacity of the orbital cavities, and the width of the external auditory meatus. At the end of his remarks on the skeleton, White offered his readers a comprehensive list of other anatomical and physiological features that were proof of the principle of hierarchical ranking:

> We will now proceed to show that a similar gradation takes place in the cartilages, muscles, tendons, skin, hair, sweat, catamenia, rank smell, and heat of the body, duration of life, testes and scrotum, and fraenum preputii, clitoris, nymphae and mammae, size of the brain, reason, speech and language, sense of feeling, parturition, diseases and manner of walking; and likewise that a gradation takes place in the senses of hearing, seeing and smelling; in memory and the powers of mastication: but in these last particulars the order is changed, the European being the lowest, the African higher, and the brute creation still higher in the scale. (1799:56, 57)

It will be noted that White referred to a gradation in the "nymphae," by which he meant female external genitalia. By the time he wrote in 1799, a number of reports had been received from residents of and visitors to the Dutch colony in the Cape, which had been established in the late 17th century, about the peculiarities of the indigenous Khoi (Hottentot) and San (Bushman) peoples. Sometimes, the Khoi and San were identified with the black or Bantu populations; on other occasions they were deemed to be racially or even specifically distinct, rivaling the Australian Aborigines for a position at the bottom of the scale of humanity. Technologically, these people appeared unsophisticated: the San were hunter-gatherers, and the Khoi mixed hunting and gathering with pastoralism and other pursuits. They exhibited a degree of egalitarianism with respect to gender roles, a cultural feature that may have caused disquiet among their patriarchal Afrikaner conquerors, a disquiet that was perhaps expressed in dubious statements about the sexual forwardness of Khoi women (Gordon 1992a:189–193). Both groups spoke languages in which a variety of "clicks" or clucking sounds were used as phonemes. To some European listeners, Khoisan languages sounded like the utterances of birds or other animals. Individuals of both groups were quite small.

The supposed presence and absence of certain sexual features were felt by some to be the decisive evidence of the liminal physical status of the Khoisan peoples. Some early-16th- and 17th-century accounts of the Khoi said that the men were monorchids, but by 1800 attention was diverted from this dubious stigmatum to female sexual characteristics (Gordon 1992a:188,189). Steatopygia, the presence of large amounts of fat in the female buttocks, is a genuinely distinctive feature of both groups. It may represent a form of adaptation to harsh climes; in other words, it is a way of storing food. Otherwise, it could exemplify a process of Darwinian sexual selection. However, it was the structure of the external genitalia in the female that attracted the most attention.[4]

In successive editions of his *Essai sur les moeurs* that appeared in 1761, 1769, and 1775 Voltaire referred to the Hottentot apron as the specific character, the distinguishing characteristic, of these people. It was, he said, "skin [epidermis, from the French *surpeau*] hanging from the navel, which covers the organs of generation, in the form of an apron which can be raised or lowered" (Duchet 1971:292, our translation). It was a sign, for him, of their lowly status.

In the late 17th and early 18th centuries a number of reports on the subject had been received such as those by Olfert Dapper, Wilhelm ten Rhyne, and François Leguat. Leguat was a Huguenot refugee; his account and an accompanying picture may have been the source of the legend of the Hottentot apron (Baker 1974:313, 314).

It would appear that the "apron" was an exaggeration of a misunderstood cultural phenomenon. In any event, no apron of skin hung from the navel. It is, however, a fact that the labia minora in many Hottentot and San women were elongated to a length of half an inch to three inches. In some groups the labia were widened as well. During the 20th century anthropologists reported that many South African Bantu groups see elongated labia as a sign of beauty, and the labia are accordingly enlarged during female initiation rites (see Turner 1968:248).

In 1773 the traveler Jacques Henri Bernardin de Saint-Pierre, in his *Voyage à l'île de France*, portrayed the Hottentots as honest, egalitarian pastoralists who loved their children. He denounced reports of the Hottentot apron as a "fable" (Duchet 1971:51). Anders Sparrman, a Swedish member of Captain Cook's expedition, agreed with Bernardin de Saint-Pierre's opinion (Duchet 1971:52). Cook himself investigated the so-called *Sinus pudoris* (Linnaeus's term for the apron) and relayed a description of Hottentot labia supplied to him by a local physician (Baker 1974:314). About the same time, Lord Gordon, a Scots soldier, explored the interior of South Africa. Meeting with Diderot, he answered the Encyclopedist's questions about Hottentot anatomy with some accuracy. It would appear that he had learnt some Khoi. His information was included in the *Additions* to Buffon's *Histoire naturelle* (Duchet 1971:52). In 1798 the French naturalist François Le Vaillant had surmised that the apron was produced by artificial means. His illustration of a woman with such a *tablier* was based on firsthand observation. He had pleaded with a Hottentot woman to show her the apron, and she had, despite much shame and confusion, agreed to the request. Sadly, Le Vaillant's acknowledgment that the woman had normal human sensibilities and that some sort of consent was necessary was a precedent that others did not follow (Schiebinger 1993:165–168).

The leading naturalists and anatomists of the late 18th and early 19th centuries partook in the debate about the nature and significance of Hottentot female genitalia. Buffon, who also wrote about the "debauched" females of Guinea and Sierra Leone, gave a somewhat lurid description of the alleged apron (Buffon 1791:145, 156). On the other hand, Samuel Thomas von Soemmering, a distinguished German anatomist, in the course of a discussion of African racial characteristics, remarked that "the parts of generation, contrary to a vulgar notion, are of no uncommon size." However, he noted that "the female breasts, according to various writers, are flaccid and pendulous" and also remarked that the Negro skull was the reverse of the Grecian ideal (Soemmering 1799: clvii, cliv, cxlv). Blumenbach was also skeptical about the stories of Hottentot pudenda, suggesting that Hottentot aprons were artificially elongated labia and not some racially specific structure (1969:250). Most skeptical of all were the comments of John Hunter, an army physician from Edinburgh whose *Disputatio Inauguralis quaedam de hominum varietatibus, et harum causis exponens* appeared in 1795. Modern stories about beardless men, pendulous mammae that could be thrown over the shoulders (Buffon), and Hottentot pudenda were the equivalent of Pliny's tall stories about the one-eyed Arimaspi, the Androgyni, and the dog-headed Cynocephali. Men of supposedly beardless races plucked out their beards. The shape of the breasts was affected by the way women fed their infants. The Hottentot apron, he argued, represented nothing more than a somewhat greater frequency of labial characteristics that were not unknown among women in Europe (Hunter in Blumenbach 1969:384).

Unfortunately, a living specimen, a human object, was to appear in London and Paris some 35 to 40 years later (Gould 1982; Gilman 1985:83–89, 1989:291–296). Saat-Jee, a young San woman, did not possess an apron, or tablier, but her elongated labia and steatopygia rendered her the victim of the ogling gaze of scientists and paying spectators. After five years of notoriety, Saat-Jee died at the age of 25. She is remembered as the "Hottentot Venus." While abolitionists had protested her exhibition in London in 1810 "in a manner offensive to decency" (quoted in Gilman 1985:88), the final indecency still awaited her. Reports of her postmortem dissection were written by Henri de Blainville and Baron Georges Cuvier, the doyen of anatomy in France. They were particularly interested in her steatopygia. As for the genitals, Cuvier prepared them in such a way that members of the academy could clearly view her labia (Gilman 1989:293). Cuvier's report was reprinted at the beginning of his *Histoire naturelle des mammifères,* which he coauthored with his distinguished colleague Geoffroy St. Hilaire. Cuvier's dissection was utilized by Virey in his work on race (Gilman 1989:293). In April 2002 Saat-Jee's remains were finally returned to South Africa for burial.

Sander Gilman has remarked that "it is indeed in the physical appearance of the Hottentot that the central icon for sexual difference between the European and the black was found" (1985:83); further, that "Sarah Bartmann's [Saat-Jee's] sexual parts, her genitalia and her buttocks, serve as the central image of the black female throughout the nineteenth century" (1989:293); and, significantly, that "the genitalia and the buttocks of the black female attracted much greater interest in part because they were seen as evidence of an anomalous sexuality not only in black women but in all women" (1985:89). This is an unusual synecdoche. Gilman is brilliantly right except insofar as he seems to discount the importance of parallel images of Negro *male* sexuality. The last remark we quote from him points to a problem we discuss later, the transfer of a powerful imagery of primitivity from the colonial periphery to the metropolis and the equation of the lumpen proletariat and prostitutes in particular with those peoples who were supposedly least advanced or most degraded.

To label the Other's sexuality anomalous is to render him or her inappropriate as a partner, not merely because emotions of repulsion or at very least indifference are evoked but also because the Other by virtue of his or her genitalia is situated or, rather, moved to or beyond the boundary of the category "human." There is some relationship between scientists' comments about the Hottentot apron and the degree of racial prejudice exhibited toward the Hottentot and Negro as well as their opinions on the biological status of the latter group.

Voltaire, White, and Virey were all *polygenists* who believed that blacks and whites were members of separate biological species (see our later discussion). Blumenbach and Hunter, who were skeptical about the apron, were *monogenists*. Adherence to monogenesis did not always imply freedom from prejudice. Buffon was credulous concerning the apron. He believed that Africans had "little genius" but did grant them some good qualities, albeit in a tone that appears patronizing to our ears. They were "naturally affectionate" and, furthermore, "were endowed with excellent hearts and possess the seeds of every human virtue." The slave owners and slave traders were "hardened monsters" (Buffon 1791:201–203).

We must conclude our remarks on the "discovery" of Hottentot sexuality with a wry observation. Some of the early Dutch settlers in the Cape did not find anything in Hottentot females so peculiarly repulsive that they were biologically restrained from mating with them and producing offspring. Contemporary populations such as the Rehebother Bastaards are largely the product of such unions. When it was deemed safe to export an adequate number of Dutch women to the Cape, the barriers to interracial mating were raised higher and higher. We need to examine the relationship between the images of sexuality we have discussed, the realities of miscegenation, and the debate concerning the definition of species and the unity and plurality of the human race. We shall suggest that this relationship was quite intimate.

THE DEBATE OVER SPECIES

The debate between the monogenists, who believed in the unity of the human species, and their polygenist opponents occupied approximately 120 years (1750–1870). Readers, particularly those versed in the history of anthropology, may be very familiar with its details, which can be gleaned from several secondary sources (e.g., Stocking 1968, 1987; Banton 1967; Barzun

1965; Harris 1969; Stanton 1960; Young 1995) as well as from a doctoral dissertation written by one of us (Lyons 1974). We hope we shall be indulged as brief a recital as is necessary for our argument.

The modern concept of "species" may be dated to John Ray's work *The Wisdom of God Manifest in the Works of Creation*, which appeared in the late 17th century. It is conceivable that Buffon may have been the first to use the word "race" to describe a biological population rather than a lineage. (On changes in the word's meaning, see Guillaumin 1995:37–52.) The speculations and theories we shall discuss need to be placed in their historical context before the advent and triumph of Darwinian evolutionary theory and before the posthumous triumph of Mendel. It was believed by many in the 18th century that the world was no more than 6,000 years old and that events such as the Flood really happened. These views eventually lost credibility in the light of scientific evidence. The discovery of mammoth skeletons in Siberia, mastodon skeletons in New York State, the remains of dinosaurs in various locales, as well as other extinct fauna gave birth to the new science of paleontology. Geologists such as Cuvier and Charles Lyell unearthed the proof of extensive changes in the mineral, floral, and faunal content of rock strata over a much-extended period of time. Slowly but surely, many came to appreciate the words of the geologist James Hutton, who stated in 1795 that the world's history was infinitely long, with "no vestige of a beginning, no prospect of an end" (Greene 1959:78). Newly discovered living animal populations presented the scientific community with fascinating and perplexing problems. Because of the shyness of orangs and gorillas and because of the limits of European exploration, it was not until the end of the 18th century that the anatomical difference between the species of great apes was fully appreciated. Not surprisingly, Linnaeus's illustrator, Hoppius (Christian Emanuel Hoppe), portrayed the apes with surprisingly human features (see Greene 1959).

The birth of secular geology and biology did not occur without pain and tribulation. The century of warfare between science and religion, as it has sometimes been called, had ramifications in the debate over the nature of species. This is an area where religion, politics, and science intermingle in a complex fashion that, for reasons of space, we can only partially deconstruct.

The monogenists adhered, whether by religious faith, scientific conviction, or a mixture of both, to the dogma expressed in the well-known verse "And [God] hath made of one blood all nations of men for to dwell on all the face of the earth" (Acts 17:26, King James version). The so-called races of man were not separate species but rather *varieties* of a single species. Such variation was produced by environmental factors, for example, climate, diet, and mode of life. This variation followed human migration to new corners of the earth, which occurred either for reasons stated in the Bible (e.g., events following the Flood, the fall of the Tower of Babel, the expulsion of the Lost Tribes of Israel, etc.) or for more secular purposes. A warm climate might create a progressive tanning of the skin, inherited and enhanced each generation. This process of the creation of varieties by means of the inheritance of acquired characteristics was known as *degeneration*, a term that sometimes implied merely physical but on other occasions also implied moral change. Depending on their degree of faith in received Old Testament chronology, monogenists had more or less difficulty in explaining how such variation could have occurred over thousands rather than millions of years.

Polygenists believed that human races were separate species. Some of them dismissed the Old Testament as myth, others utilized such ideas as a preadamite creation to explain the existence of several species. Polygenists believed that the races, like other species, were fixed in form. To use a modern term, each human species was adapted to its *ecosystem*. There was no way that racial variations in skin color, stature, head shape, and size could have developed over 6,000 or even (if one did not literally interpret the Bible) 30,000 or 40,000 years. Some 18th-century polygenists such as the Jamaican planter and historian Edward Long and the anatomist Charles White believed in versions of the Great Chain of Being. All polygenists ranked races in a rigid hierarchy. Monogenists also ranked races, but with a few exceptions they did so less rigidly. In some cases, polygenists were motivated by a strong political belief in innate inequality (some endorsed slavery); in other cases such as Voltaire and the mid-19th-century American polygenist Josiah Clark Nott, an antireligious prejudice was also influential. Most monogenists, for example, Buffon, Blumenbach, and the American Samuel Stanhope Smith, believed that variation caused by unfavorable environmental circumstances was at least partially reversible. A few monogenists such as the proslavery writer John Bachman were motivated primarily by strong religious beliefs.

In order to demonstrate the existence of different human types, which might, depending on one's opinion, be either varieties or species, monogenists and polygenists discussed hair color, shape, and texture; skin color; skull size, shape, and capacity; the degree of prognathism of the jaw; the position of the foramen magnum, which determines the carriage of the skull, brain capacity, and convolutions; stature; size of limbs; sensory abilities; size of genitals and sexuality; and intelligence. They also sometimes appended such information as they had about the great apes. Some of these phenotypical characteristics still interest modern physical anthropologists, albeit they ask different questions from different premises. Finally, we must note that monogenists and polygenists disagreed about the concept that was at the core of their discussion, namely, species.

The account of creation in Genesis was viewed as scientifically and historically accurate by some monogenists. Not only were there many who denied the possibility of fresh creation or even the extinction of species in the face of growing evidence of the latter, but there were some who insisted that monogenesis implied the common descent of all humans from Adam and Eve. Unity of species implied unity of descent. Conversely, plurality of species implied descent from many ancestors.

Both species and varieties were conceived as ideal types. There was an insistence that all members of a species conformed to type and that they resembled each other more than they resembled members of other species. Polygenists and monogenists disagreed on the degree of resemblance between human races. Both camps agreed on the principle of fixity or permanence of type, but monogenists allowed for a degree of plasticity resulting from environmental influence and/or the effects of domestication.

The most critical disagreement was over another criterion of species that is now known as reproductive isolation, a criterion that is still accepted today. It was originally advocated by Buffon and Immanuel Kant. Members of the same species interbreed with each other and produce fertile offspring. They do not habitually interbreed with other populations. Matings between members of different species very seldom result in the birth of offspring. Should this happen, the offspring would normally be sterile.

Sexuality and sexual imagery have long been intrinsic to biological classification. Linnaeus's taxonomy of plant species was based on their sexual characteristics (number of and placement of stamens, pistils, etc.), and he even wrote of the marriages of plants (Schiebinger 1993:11–39). One prominent British critic, William Smellie, regarded such language as indecent (Schiebinger 1993:29). Schiebinger also noted Linnaeus's significant choice of the breasts as the distinguishing feature of the class Mammalia (1993:40–74). Furthermore, the readers of Linnaeus, both male and female, presumably included literate gardeners, animal breeders, and some slave owners. We stress that discussions of species in the 18th and 19th centuries and, in particular, discussions of the unity or plurality of the human species may simultaneously concern the scientific concept of species and both popular and scientific notions of sexuality. The debate about species concerns the possibility, desirability, and outcomes of miscegenation. Robert Young voices this notion succinctly: "Theories of race were thus also covert theories of desire" (1995:9).

Polygenists disputed the validity of the criterion of reproductive isolation. There was a thread of consistency in their arguments, although sometimes the thread was lost or stretched. They maintained the following positions:

1. There were reports that animals of separate species, for example, sheep and goats, wolves and dogs, interbreed. It was possible that the offspring of some sexual unions between different species might be interfertile if not with each other then with one or both parent stocks.

2. Domesticated varieties of dogs were, in fact, separate species. They had remained fixed for thousands of years. If indeed they did interbreed, it was proof that different, allied species could do so.

3. While there was evident proof of matings between members of certain human races, matings between members of far-flung groups (e.g., Australian Aborigines and Eskimo) might well not have occurred, and the outcome was clearly uncertain.

4. It was not clear that racial hybrids were as reproductively viable as their parent stocks. Indeed, miscegenation might adversely affect the potential of a group to reproduce its own kind. As late as the 1860s, the French polygenist Paul Broca reported an account by Count Strzlecki that maintained that Australian Aborigine women who had mated with Europeans were subsequently infertile with members of their own group (1864:55–59).

5. Mulattoes were higher in intelligence than their black parents but stupider than their white parents. In the long term, mulatto stocks were not viable. They tended to die out. There were no advantages inherent in hybridity.

6. If sheep and goats, wolves and dogs occasionally mated, no one should be surprised at accounts of unions between apes and black females, although these might not be voluntary on the latter's part.

The presence of the last argument in polygenist discourse more than anything else reveals the nature of the fantasies that underpinned that mode of science. Edward Long saw Negroes and orangutans as occupying adjacent rungs on the Great Chain of Being:

> For my own part, I conceive that probability favours the opinion, that human organs were not given him ["the orang," i.e., the great ape] for nothing: that this race have some language by which their meaning is communicated; whether it resembles the gobbling of turkies

like that of the Hottentots, or the hissing of serpents, is of very little consequence, so long as it is intelligible among themselves: nor, for what hitherto appears, do they seem at all inferior in the intellectual faculties to many of the Negro race, with some of whom they have the most intimate connexion and consanguinity. The amorous intercourse between them may be frequent; the Negroes themselves bear testimony that such intercourses actually happen; and it is certain that both races agree perfectly in lasciviousness and disposition. (1774, vol. 2:370)

The "orangs" who are granted some sort of language are beneficiaries of Long's account. The reader should note the equations made by Long between apes, Negroes, Hottentots, turkeys, and serpents. A new vision of temptation in Eden without the gift of knowledge!

It could be argued that Long was a historian, a proslavery apologist who strayed into the realms of science. Charles White was a doctor and scientist who described slavery as "pernicious" and who claimed that he only wished "to investigate the truth" (1799:v). This quest led him in interesting directions:

All those who have had opportunities of making observations on the orang-outangs, agree in ascribing to them, not only a remarkable docility of disposition, but also actions and affections similar to those observable in the human kind. They make themselves huts for their accommodation; they defend themselves with stones and clubs; and they bury their dead by covering the body with leaves, etc. They discover signs of modesty; and instances are related of the strongest attachment of the male to the female. When sick, these animals have been known to suffer themselves to be blooded, and even to invite the operation; and to submit to other necessary treatment like rational creatures. They groan like the human kind, when under circumstances of anxiety or oppression: and their sagacity in avoiding danger, in certain instances, is not exceeded by that of man. They have been taught to play upon musical instruments, as the pipe and the harp. *They have been known to carry off negro boys, girls and even women, with a view of making them subservient to their wants and slaves, or as objects of brutal passion: and it has been asserted by some, that women have had offspring from such connections. This last circumstance is not, however, certain. Supposing it to be true, it would be an object of inquiry, whether such offspring would propagate, or prove to be mules.* (White 1799:33–34, emphasis added)

White's paean of praise to the orang's intellectual and musical abilities, not to mention its moral virtues, terminates at the point where he refers to their brutal passions, which bring them into connection with blacks. Finally, the language becomes more sober as White expresses an element of doubt and appeals to the spirit of scientific inquiry.

The fiction of sexual intercourse between blacks and orangs is not confined to polygenist discourse. Gustav Jahoda has noted its occurrence in some 17th-century travelers' narratives and folklore (1999:24, 36). Buffon was aware of it (Hays 1972:163). Thomas Jefferson, who was, inter alia, a monogenist, also mentions stories involving male apes and Negresses. He also stated that blacks would be incapable of comprehending Euclid (Jefferson 1944:256, 257). To balance our account, we should note that the late-17th-century anatomist Edward Tyson believed that male apes preferred blondes (Schiebinger 1993:95).

As Jordan has noted, females, whether black or white, are usually the passive partners in such irregular liaisons. Males thrust upward, rising from one rung in the Chain of Being to penetrate into the higher zones. In such a way were fantasy and fear opposed to everyday evidence, which detailed liaisons between white slave owners and overseers and their female slaves. If we combine representations concerning intercourse between members of different species with images of genital anomaly, we can understand something of the climate that the "peculiar institution," slavery, created.

Scientific polygenism, as opposed to the folk myths that sustained it, had little appeal in the antebellum South until the last decade before the Civil War, when it finally attained popularity. The reason was the antireligious rhetoric of some of its advocates. In Europe the popularity of polygenism reached its peak in the 1850s. Even so, monogenism remained the dominant position. It is left to us to stress that polygenism was merely one end of the spectrum of intolerance, the most consistent expression of hierarchical views, which either affirmed a "natural" oligarchy or sought exclusions from Enlightenment or post-Enlightenment "fraternity." The reader of many monogenist writers such as Buffon, Soemmering, and Samuel Stanhope Smith finds their work replete with deprecations of non-European morality or intelligence. However, there were some such as Blumenbach and the English physician James Cowles Prichard who believed in "the natural equality of the African Negro and the European" (Prichard 1826, vol. 1:176–

178). Whether monogenist or polygenist, the new raciology tended to assume that most of culture – performances as well as ideas – had a "natural," physical root that could be explained by the new secular biology.

It is true that the victory of Darwinism spelled the end of the debate between the monogenists and polygenists, inasmuch as the common descent of humanity from an apelike creature gained scientific and popular credence. However, racialist views of the intelligence, morality, and sexuality of nonwhites flourished. Darwinian chronology allowed an ample time span for substantial differentiation. This allowed ideas of radical difference to persist in the new evolutionary social anthropology, although social evolutionists were much less obsessed with correlations between culture, morality, intelligence, and physical type.

THREE IMAGES REVISITED

There is a palpable correspondence between the three images of "primitive sexuality" we outlined at the beginning of this chapter and the historical facts related to miscegenation. These images are linked to stereotypical representations that we conventionally describe as noble or ignoble savagery. In turn, all of these factors have an explanation in comparative political economy.

In South and Central America and Polynesia representations of noble savagery predominate at times of first contact, when little attempt has been made to integrate the newly discovered Other into the Western economic system. This was true of Hispaniola, when Columbus met the Caribs, and of Tahiti in the time of Cook and Bougainville. If the Tahitians were oversexed, their indulgence was "natural," their social world a Utopia for the delight of European eyes and bodies. We have noted that Cook himself was less naive and that Forster was positively puritanical.

Different Amerindian groups have represented noble or ignoble savagery for different peoples at different times. Elements of both representations are to be found in depictions of northeastern groups such as the Iroquois – undersexed, brave, somewhat sadistic, but honorable.[5] The romantic image of northeastern Amerindians (e.g., James Fenimore Cooper's Chingachgook) was revived after any military threat disappeared. We have noted that attitudes toward miscegenation were not entirely negative. Despite trading contacts, wars, and military alliances, Amerindians tended to remain at the periphery of the North American economic system (which does not mean that some, e.g., those who traded furs, were not part of it). Perhaps a critical development was the failure of Europeans forcefully to integrate Amerindian groups in North America into a caste or class system of the type found in the southern plantations. South America is a more complicated case, but postcontact developments do not play a significant role in the literature we are considering.

While it may well be true, as Jordan (1969) suggested, that negative images of Africa preceded the slave trade, the elaboration of the whole complex of ideas about sexuality and miscegenation owes everything to the transatlantic traffic and the plantation economy. African culture and African peoples were usually portrayed harshly. The Africans were deemed the most ignoble of savages. [6] It was precisely the integration of Africans as slaves to European households, their intimate propinquity, and the frequency of sexual relations between masters and slave mistresses that made the drawing of social or sexual boundaries a necessary operation. It did not suffice to place Africans at the lowest rung of the human hierarchy; rather, they were placed one rung beneath it so that undesired sexual contact (i.e., between black males and white females) became bestiality. The viability of the "mixed breeds" created by sexual contact was not acknowledged lest they threaten the hierarchical principle. Surely there were, as Genovese has observed, cases where the white male and his black mistress loved each other and cared for their family (1974:198). This could not be acknowledged by the defenders of racial separation. Surely there were countless black families who successfully resisted white sexual aggression; this too would not have accorded with racialist stereotypes.

It is rather surprising that the reverse stereotype, the noble savage, was rarely developed with respect to Africans. There was a tradition of romantic, antislavery fiction, beginning with Aphra Behn's *Oroonoko* in the mid–17th century, in which some Africans are portrayed as noble. Dykes (1962) traced this tradition from Behn's time until the end of the 18th century. The chivalrous hero of Behn's fiction is particularly solicitous of the needs of his beloved. However, Behn contrasts his noble features (his nose, mouth, and lips) with those of other Africans. As Gallagher remarks, Behn portrays Oroonoko as a wonder because "blackness and heroism are normally thought to be mutually exclusive qualities" (1994:70). Unlike the Amerindians of Surinam, where Oroonoko and his beloved, Imoinda, are exiled as slaves, normal Africans are presumably savage but not noble. "The reader is frequently invited to marvel that Oroonoko, *although black*, behaves like a conventional European tragic hero" (Gallagher 1994:70).

Now that we have outlined our contrasting images of sexual alterity, we must consider how they were employed implicitly or explicitly to demarcate and rationalize gender and class images at home. Then we can see how disputed terrains of gender and class in Victorian and post-Victorian society may have been projected in anthropologists' representations of the sexuality of others and how such representations, in their turn, were instilled into Victorian debates about sexuality, gender, and class.

A strong linkage between 19th-century ideas concerning sexuality at the colonial periphery and gender relations in the metropolis has been asserted by some prominent recent writers (Gilman 1985:76–108; Levy 1991). The stagnant, fetid, plague-ridden tropics were equated by hygienists such as Southwood Smith with the crowded, filthy tenements of the London poor: "The room of a fever patient, in a small and heated apartment of London, with no perflation of fresh air, is perfectly analogous to a stagnant pool in Ethiopia full of the bodies of dead locusts" (Southwood Smith 1830 in Mort 1987:29). According to Frank Mort, many saw a link between incest and other perversions and the tropical-like miasmas they associated with slum dwellings: "'Ethiopia,' like the culture of the urban poor and especially the Irish, signified the animalism and lack of civilization which was in danger of pulling the whole of civilized society back into the abyss" (1987:29). Perceptions such as these were utilized by advocates of public sanitation and state regulation in the United Kingdom. The coincidence of humoral pathology as manifested in "noxious miasmas," tropical disease, and supposedly low morality provided a rationale for the work of missionaries such as Robert Moffat, David Livingstone, and their successors who wished to regulate and clothe African bodies and "save" African souls (Comaroff and Comaroff 1992:224–226).

Sexual excess had long been associated with tropical environments. This was a mainstay of Enlightenment environmentalism. In terms of the discourses we have already examined such excess might result either from the action of environmental stimuli on uniform human nature or, alternatively, from predetermined and primordial racial difference. The equation between the oversexed, tropical primitive and the underclass of industrial Europe was diffuse and unsystematic. It consisted of a parallelism in social hierarchy, the use of metaphor and allusion, implicit understandings, pictorial representations; perhaps all of this is not enough to justify postmodern critics' assertions. However, Anita Levy in *Other Women* has drawn our attention to a cross-cultural analysis of marriage and sexual customs contained in volume 4 of Henry Mayhew's *London Labour and the London Poor*, which, she argues, transferred "a notion of female sexual deviance to the urban working classes as a whole" and, furthermore, provided "a model for all anthropological procedures, which . . . universalized a class- and culture-specific notion of the family on the basis of deviant sexuality" (1991:48). The picture is a little more complex than Levy suggests, because Mayhew and his coauthors are somewhat kinder to the poor women of London than to any primitives. Certainly, for our purposes volume 4 of Mayhew's work is of the utmost significance, both for what it says and what it does not say.

Mayhew's articles on the London poor first appeared in the *Morning Chronicle* in 1849 (Neuburg 1985). A two-volume edition of *London Labour and the London Poor* appeared in 1852; the four-volume edition appeared in 1861–62. The first three volumes of the book contain vivid descriptions of traders, workers, children, entertainers, vagrants, cab drivers, and street cleaners. This is a panoply of social action, and the actors are given voice and often credited with all the agency they are capable of. The performer of Punch and Judy, Jewish street merchants, and the costermonger's wife address the reader directly. The middle-class readers of Mayhew may have learned for the first time how the other half lived. Volume 4 is entitled *Those That Will Not Work*. Its subject is "vice," as typified by thieves, swindlers, beggars, and prostitutes. It is the last of these that receives the most attention in the concluding volume of Mayhew's "Natural History of the London Poor." The actual section on prostitution in London was written not by Mayhew but by his collaborator, Bracebridge Hemyng, who was a barrister and novelist. Hemyng and Mayhew appear to have collaborated on a 120-page section on marriage and sexual practices in ancient Greece and Rome, the "barbarous nations" of Africa, Australia, the Americas, and Polynesia, the "semi-civilized" nations of Asia, and some northern European cultures. Although the work was written before most of the great works of evolutionary social anthropology appeared, the order of treatment roughly corresponds to the evolutionary hierarchies of the late 19th century. The images of alternative modes of sexuality and marriage are evidence of the strength of cultural and racial stereotypes. There are more than 130 sources cited in this catalog of alien practices. Most of them are accounts written by well-known travelers and explorers (e.g., John Barrow, George Catlin, Herman Melville, Edward Eyre).

In other words, Mayhew and Hemyng offer the modern reader a valuable review of British beliefs and "knowledge" concerning alien sexuality in the mid–19th century. Two salient facts about this discourse command our attention. Hemyng and Mayhew equate virtually every variation from mid-Victorian middle-class norms with prostitution – premarital sex and adultery as well as all sexual transactions with a material component are equated with the familiar "social evil." Second, the decision to include such a section is remarkable. Such use of the comparative method was not found necessary in the discussions of beggars and thieves, of entertainers and street traders. A certain section of the poor is uniquely associated with primitivity, to wit, the prostitutes and those who profited from them.

Two of the three images of primitive sexuality that we previously outlined are recapitulated by Mayhew and Hemyng, namely, the oversexed African (and Australian Aborigine) and the undersexed North American Native. The third image, the Polynesian paradise, is transmuted into the first. The antisensualist perspective typical of many mid-Victorian "progressives" (Mason 1994) did not accommodate any Tahitian utopia. According to Mayhew and Hemyng, "The hordes of Western Africa are the most gross and ferocious of savages, and their women are treated as reptiles" (Mayhew 1861–62:56). Matters do not necessarily improve when one ventures farther east. The female monkeys of Khartoum enjoyed "a far nobler and more natural position" than the women (Mayhew 1861–62:67). While the customs of the continent were not uniform, there was said to be an alternation between extreme patriarchal control and depravity. African patriarchy indicated the lack of respect shown by African males for their females, which was connected with their fear of the lasciviousness that might be unleashed were controls to be relaxed. In other words, Mayhew and Hemyng saw a link between female morality and men's treatment of women, and they believed that African cultures were at the bottom of the moral scale.

The Australian Aborigines were described as almost totally lacking in sexual morality. Women were brutalized. Despite the free-for-all, male jealousy was rampant. Indeed, the Australians were so primitive that prostitution had not made its appearance as a discriminable institution: "Of prostitutes as a class among the natives themselves, it is impossible to speak separately; for prostitution of that kind implies some advance towards the forms of regular society, and little of this appears yet to be made in that region. From the sketch we have given, however, a general idea may be gained of the state of women and the estimation of virtue among a race second only to the lowest tribes of Africa in barbarity and degradation" (Mayhew 1861–62:71).

The reign of debauchery also extended to Mayhew and Hemyng's picture of the South American continent, with rare exceptions such as the Abrifone of Paraguay. The indigenous people of South America were usually described as naked and depraved. The men lay in hammocks while their womenfolk suffered lives of "privation and labour." However, the women were a happier and more buoyant lot than their counterparts, "the squaws of North America," because "their spirit yields willingly to the yoke, which consequently does not pain them" (Mayhew 1861–62:93).

As we have mentioned, Mayhew and Hemyng's assessment of the sexual morality of North American Native peoples reflects the widespread idea that aboriginal North America was a region uniquely lacking in lust, though they are careful to draw a distinction "between the Indian of the seaport town corrupted in the dram-shop and the Indian of the woods, displaying the original characteristics of his race." Of the latter type of Native male they say: "He never, at any period of his history, condescended to voluptuousness. His sense of manly pride prevented him from becoming immodest or indecent. This feeling at the same time inspired him with the idea that everything except the hunt and the warpath was below the dignity of man. The sentiments, therefore, which saved the female sex from becoming the mere food of lust, consigned it to an inferior position. The Indian women formed the labouring class. . . . The wife is . . . her husband's slave" (Mayhew 1861–62:85).

Although Mayhew and Hemyng state that "no race is more peculiar than the North American Indian" (1861–62:84), the above remarks would seem to ground the perceived lack of licentiousness in cultural definitions of manliness rather than in racial characteristics. Because no mention is made of the berdache tradition, one of the major sources of "evidence" that led some earlier writers to see North American aboriginals as physiologically undersexed was absent from Mayhew and Hemyng's recension. In general, they do not discuss physical characteristics such as distribution of body and facial hair. In keeping with their portrayal of the cultural shaping of North American sexuality, they suggest that among most groups chastity is valued not as a good in itself but rather as a "test of Spartan endurance" (Mayhew 1861–62:88). They attribute to the North American Native a strong capacity for love but note that "with the Indian chief strong love is not inconsistent with his walking in lordly indolence along the forest path while she is bearing the heavy wigwam poles behind" (Mayhew 1861–62:87). They view at least some of the effects of European conquest of North America as negative, noting that in Canada, "particularly in areas dominated by the Hudson's Bay Company, Indians have learned European vices, and venereal disease and prostitution are rampant" (Mayhew 1861–62:89).

Concerning Polynesia, where sexuality attracted so much European contemplation, Mayhew and Hemyng recorded mixed assessments. The unconverted Maori of New-Zealand were relatively elevated in the moral scale. In Mayhew's ironic estimation they had attained an "advance in profligacy" that made them the moral equals of the most backward European peasants:

> Their immorality is on a plan, and recognised in that unwritten social law which among barbarians remedies the want of a written code. It is not the beastly lust of the savage, who appears merely obedient to an animal instinct, against which there is no principle of morals or sentiment of decency to contend; – it is the appetite of the sensualist, deliberately gratified, and by means similar in many respects, to those adopted among the lowest classes in Europe. We may, indeed, compare the Maori village, unsubjected to missionary influence, with some of the hamlets in our rural provinces, where moral education of every kind is equally an exile. (1861–62:71)

An example of that "unwritten social law" was the custom known as *tapu*: "Tyrone Power, in his observations on the immorality prevalent in New Zealand, remarks that some of the young girls, betrothed from an early age, are tapu, and thus preserved chaste. He regrets that this superstition is not more influential, since it would check the system of almost universal and indiscriminate prostitution, which prevails among those not subject to this rite" (Mayhew 1861–62:74).

As we have already remarked, Mayhew and Hemyng's Tahiti was the antithesis of Diderot's. There were a number of reasons for this shift. Conditions in Tahiti had changed in the interim. The form of the account is less overtly fictional, and the Victorians award a minus grade where their Enlightenment predecessor awarded a plus: "In few parts of the world could be discovered a more corrupt system of manners, a more complete absence of morals, than in Tahiti" (Mayhew 1861–62:79). The authors acknowledged that Tahitian custom had altered as a result of missionization. On balance, they felt that the missionaries had had a positive effect (Mayhew 1861–62:80).

In view of the recent controversy surrounding Derek Freeman's book on Margaret Mead and Samoa it is most interesting to read that Mayhew and Hemyng approved of the morality of the Samoans. Indeed, their most negative remarks refer to transactions between Samoans and Europeans: "Altogether their morals are of a superior order; and their libertine disposition exercises itself chiefly in the performance of lascivious dances. Everywhere, however, in these seas, except where the power of the missionaries is supreme, the whaling ships, on arriving at a port, attract numbers of prostitutes, who offer themselves to the sailors at various prices" (Mayhew 1861–62:83–84).

Among a number of cultures that Mayhew and Hemyng label "semi-civilized," India was one that figured importantly in subsequent debates about sex, race, and imperium. While they expressed negative opinions on the effects of Europeans on the morals of Native Americans and some Polynesians, Mayhew and Hemyng were confident that British rule had had a "wonderful" effect upon morality in India (Mayhew 1861–62:116).[7] On the whole, they believed that Hindu women had high status, lowered somewhat owing to Moslem influence. Concerning Bengal they wrote: "The timid effeminate Bengalee appears to be a sensual character and regards his wife as little more than the instrument of his pleasure. A better state of things is now beginning to prevail there, in consequence of the efforts made by the Company" (Mayhew 1861–62:117).

One tendency of Mayhew and Hemyng's writing that is especially evident in their treatment of India is that they equate "good" morals with high status for women. This is a tendency that can be found in the work of many 19th-century scholars. It supported women's entitlement to better treatment and assured readers that women in countries like England already had much to be satisfied about in comparison with others. Mayhew and Hemyng cite the abolition of suttee as "one among the innumerable blessings achieved for that region by the Company's administration" (Mayhew 1861–62:120). Considerable sensational detail about suttee is provided, including accounts of young children and 85-year-old women being thrown into the flames. "What 'Aborigines' Protection Society' can regret the revolution which has given India into the hands of England?" (Mayhew 1861–62:121). Female infanticide is also commented upon in some detail and its abolition credited to the Raj.

Child marriage is said to encourage prostitution, especially temple prostitution, because men were less likely to love wives acquired in this way (Mayhew 1861–62:123). This connection between prostitution and a lack of desire of men toward their wives is a theme that, we shall see, was very much in evidence later in the 19th century, though little else is said about it in Mayhew's work. Mayhew and Hemyng offer a long account of temple prostitution and dancer–prostitutes, and, here again, the British are credited with the decline of an institution the authors find undesirable (Mayhew 1861–62:123).

An alleged connection between the instillation of a work ethic and a decline in immorality in India is worthy of note, as the connection between willingness to work and other moral issues is an important theme in *London Labour and the London Poor*: "This decency of public manners appears of recent introduction, which is indeed a reasonable supposition, for the people have now aims in life, which they never enjoyed in security under their former rulers. It was for the interest of the princes that their subjects should be indolent and sensual. It is for the interest of the new government that they should be industrious and moral. Great efforts have been made with this object, and much good has resulted" (Mayhew 1861–62:123).

The relationship between lack of thrift and a deficient work ethic as characteristics of British prostitutes is mentioned by Hemyng in several contexts, although the subordinate position of lower-class women is also treated as a major factor. The general status of women, the significance of women's work, and the lure of money to be spent on ornament and amusement all figure in Hemyng's portrayal of prostitution as a social fact; variants of these themes have all figured in his treatment of foreign sexuality.

Anita Levy argues that Mayhew (actually Hemyng) dismisses all women who are engaged in working-class occupations as prostitutes and, in general, portrays *London Labour and the London Poor* as an example of a Victorian tendency, exhibited by anthropologists and social reformers alike, to see a fairly straightforward continuum, if not equivalence, between savage women, prostitutes, and working-class women in general (1991:42–57). In fact, we have seen that although Mayhew and Hemyng's treatment of other cultures fell within these broad demarcations, their portrayals were somewhat more textured. The same might be said for Hemyng's treatment of domestic prostitutes. While he suggests that factory workers, entertainers, and domestic servants were prone to prostitution, as were married women who needed money to supplement their husbands' wages, he does not imply that all women in these categories were prostitutes. As with primitives, however, the definitional boundaries of London "prostitution" are flexible and seem to include all sex out of wedlock where any form of compensation, including food, drink, or entertainment, is received.

The causes of prostitution listed by Hemyng reflect both sympathy for women who "fall" and criticism of their temperaments. Cultural and economic considerations mingle in descriptions of the context of female degradation. Prostitutes are said to be created by (1) low wages inadequate to the women's subsistence; (2) natural levity and the example around them; (3) love of dress and display, coupled with the desire for a sweetheart; (4) sedentary employment and want of proper exercise; (5) low and cheap literature of an immoral tendency; and (6) absence of parental care and the inculcation of proper precepts (Mayhew 1861–62:257). These elements might be said to constitute the main parameters of Victorian debates on prostitution. Insofar as Victorian representations of prostitutes, like those encountered in *London Labour and the London Poor*, displayed aspects of underdeveloped morality entwined with suggestions of environmental deprivation, they reflected much of the growing discussion about savages in which condemnation, sympathy, and hopes for improvement could all be found, though not necessarily in the same places.

Hemyng was not insensitive to the effects of the double standard in describing the context of prostitution and not unsympathetic to women. Of maidservants, for example, he said that they "live well, have no care or anxiety, no character worth speaking about to lose . . . are fond of dress, and under these circumstances it cannot be wondered that they are as a body immoral and unchaste" (Mayhew 1861–62:258). On the other hand, Hemyng is also compassionate concerning the poor treatment serving maids receive and blames some of their susceptibility to prostitution on their seduction by "men of the family, soldiers, shopmen and policemen." Moreover, he says that they are badly looked after by their mistresses, who are, however, quick to turn them out without notice for their lapses. He also speaks rather sarcastically about their "munificent" wages of eight pounds a year, including board and lodging (Mayhew 1861–62:257).

Hemyng is particularly sensitive to the plight of women whose ruin begins with a single lapse from chastity. One pathetic story concerns a curate's daughter who was seduced by the debauched son of a family for whom she worked as a governess. After he killed himself because of gambling debts, she felt that she might still have been forgiven had she returned home but was again seduced by a soldier friend of his. She ended her days as a syphilitic, drunken streetwalker, plying her trade by night in a park, wearing a veil to hide her facial disfigurement (Mayhew 1861–62:243–245). On the whole, Hemyng tends to be more condemnatory of the people who live off prostitutes and of middle- and upper-class male debauchery than of the prostitutes themselves. Issues of class, gender, disease, and the sexual secrets of "respectable" men touched several raw nerves for the Victorians, giving urgency to discourses, from the scholarly book to the music hall lyric, that threatened to expose them. It was in this context that the sexuality of primitives became a foil for debates that had their origin much closer to home.

CHAPTER 2

Sex and the Refuge for Destitute Truth

Our object of study being MAN *in all his relations, physical, moral, psychical, and social, it is impossible to treat the subject adequately without offending in general the* mauvaise honte, *the false delicacy, and the ingrained prejudices of the age. Without some such refuge for Destitute Truth as the rooms of the Anthropological Society, we should find it equally difficult to relate and to publish facts.*

Sir Richard F. Burton, "Notes on Certain Matters Connected with the Dahoman"

The strange career of Sir Richard Burton, to which we shall devote some attention, must surely caution us about any easy generalizations concerning Victorian society. Sexuality and gender were topics of debate and contestation throughout the period. However, it would be unwise to deny that those debates reveal the power exercised by "Mrs. Grundy" as well as the good queen herself.

In a recent volume Michael Mason has reminded us that the deprecatory use of the term *Victorian* originates in the writings of H. G. Wells, Lytton Strachey, and (to a degree) Edmund Gosse and that the consequent stereotype has inevitably diminished our understanding of a period that produced many rebels and critics (1994:8–16). Furthermore, he has stressed that, contrary to received popular belief, some of the more progressive forces of the era were on Mrs. Grundy's side, including some secularists who otherwise opposed Victorian religiosity.

In some measure the work of Mayhew and Hemyng that we considered in the last chapter illustrates the cogency of Mason's argument. It is obviously "Victorian" in its morality. Nonetheless, the discussion of prostitution is not devoid of sympathy, nor is it totally lacking in prurience. It is a work of journalism and is commonly said to be a founding work of social science.

It is an exemplary illustration of Michel Foucault's most compelling argument: rather than simply repressing sexual discourse, as the bourgeois society that succeeded the great 18th-century revolutions is supposed to have done, various agencies of 19th-century society required that a great deal of sexual information be made public. Public disclosure was required not only in order to bring the sexual behavior of women, children, patients, church members, and private citizens under the control of agents of authority (husbands, doctors, teachers, courts, etc.) but also to aid in the legitimation of that authority by providing, as a major justification of the hierarchy upon which it was based, evidence of a dangerous sexual depravity among the lower ranks (Foucault 1980). Granted, there was reticence about sex in some quarters, but it coexisted with noisy (Foucault would argue compulsory) discourse in others. There were indeed newlywed brides who were ignorant of basic physiology, while in both Britain and the United States there were a number of publications about the dangers of masturbation and how to prevent it (see Barker-Benfield 1976:163–188). However, the tracts that warned against unsanctioned forms of sexuality by their very nature required some discussion of the topic.

In this chapter we discuss a variety of anthropological writings that appeared between the years 1860 and 1890. It is our contention that these writings do not fail to reflect the social debates and issues of the time. These included the controversial Contagious Diseases Acts passed between 1865 and 1868, which empowered authorities in port towns to inspect prostitutes for venereal disease and to confine noncompliant women in lock hospitals.[1] This body of legislation did not address the responsibilities of the prostitutes' clients and was seen by Victorian feminist critics such as Josephine Butler as a reinforcement of the double standard. Coventry Patmore's famous paean to the "angel in the house," the sequestered, pampered, but disempowered middle-class antithesis of the "madwoman in the attic" and the "woman of the streets," was written in the 1860s. In the late 1870s a sex scandal led to the fall of Sir Charles Dilke, a prominent British politician. Charles Bradlaugh and Annie Besant faced prosecution in 1877 for publishing Charles Knowlton's 1842 pamphlet, *The Fruits of Philosophy*, which advocated barrier methods of contraception – condom, sponge, pessary, and so forth.

Despite such legal interference, contraceptive knowledge began to spread to all classes. In the 1880s a furor erupted over the white slave trade. Scandal also ensued from a police raid on a homosexual bordello in Cleveland Street that was frequented by a number of aristocrats, including, so rumor had it, a member of the royal family. The "moral panic" led to the passing of the Criminal Law Amendment Act in 1885, which endeavored to tighten controls over prostitution and which also contained new provisions, less draconian and, for that reason, perhaps more enforceable, against homosexuality between consenting adults. It was this legislation that was to be used against Oscar Wilde. A leading participant in the debate over the white slave trade was W. T. Stead, the influential and self-publicizing editor of the *Pall Mall Gazette*. Stead obtained the services of an adolescent girl by paying off her mother, shipped her to France, and published a pamphlet, *The Maiden Tribute of Modern Babylon*, to show how easy it was to export British virgins to sinister foreign places. Stead was supported by some feminists and Evangelical Christians and opposed both by those who disliked the brashness and frankness of his journalism and by many who quite simply opposed kidnapping, even if carried out in the service of higher moral interests. He was prosecuted and briefly imprisoned. Subsequently, Stead condemned the abuse of human rights by King Leopold in the Congo Free State and campaigned for several other causes, including marine safety. He drowned when the *Titanic* went down.

As the controversy over Stead raged on, Captain Burton's privately published and unexpurgated translation of the *Arabian Nights' Entertainments* (*The Book of the Thousand Nights and a Night*) came into print. (Ten volumes containing the 1,001 tales appeared between 1885 and 1887, and six additional volumes of *Supplemental Nights* were published between 1886 and 1888.) Perhaps because of the price of the volumes and the expectation of restricted circulation, only 1,000 copies were printed. Although the volumes contained vivid accounts of imaginary sexual encounters of all possible kinds, and the long section IV:D in the "Terminal Essay" in volume 10 consisted of a protracted survey of the nature and distribution of male homosexual practices, Burton was never prosecuted, though he and his wife feared he might be. These fears are evidenced in a series of newspaper clippings about such prosecutions that Burton pasted in his own copies of the *Arabian Nights*, which are now shelved in the Huntington Library. In fact, he was to receive his knighthood in 1886, the year following the publication of the first volumes of the *Arabian Nights*. Burton's fears were not without justification. Through the efforts of the National Vigilance Association and its supporters, including W. T. Stead, Henry Vizetelly was successfully prosecuted in 1888 for publishing a translation of Émile Zola's *La Terre*, which was deemed to be an "obscene libel."

Underlying all these events was a fundamental question concerning the balance of power in the Victorian family. The argument that was reflected in the Contagious Diseases Acts was that the monogamous Christian family was the preferable social form. Middle-class women were to be protected from a wicked world and their "baser instincts," and their future husbands were not to contract "the great scourge." However, as Mason (1994) observes, the Victorian idea of marriage did not exclude sexual pleasure within that union. Bachelors, moreover, unlike unmarried females, could not be expected to be chaste, although the influential physician William Acton advocated the avoidance of such premarital fantasies as might lead to sex. Prostitution was an unavoidable fact. The law could not prevent it, but its promulgators did hope to curb the threat to the health and welfare of British soldiers and sailors by controlling the bodies of the prostitutes.

The opposition to the Contagious Diseases Acts, which became the social purity movement, involved an alliance between Evangelical Christians, progressives, and feminists. (Butler and Stead fit all these descriptions.) This coalition argued that male liberties restricted women's safety and bodily integrity (see Walkowitz 1980; Kent 1990). Such critics considered Victorian sexual and marital institutions to be hypocritical at best. One might say that in a sense they considered them inadequately "Victorian," but their agenda challenged some of the emerging forms of control rather than simply demanding the suppression of impolite discourse. Butler was particularly scandalized by compulsory examinations of alleged prostitutes with a new gynecological instrument, the speculum, a procedure she characterized as an especially brutal variety of rape (Walkowitz 1980:109). She repeatedly encouraged middle-class women to join forces with their working-class sisters to resist such abuses.

If one set of radicals criticized Victorian sexuality because it hypocritically oppressed women, another influential group criticized it because it unrealistically restricted the sexual activity of men and imposed limits on the discussion of sexuality. Burton clearly belongs to this group; indeed, he was its most articulate spokesman. In other words, there were radical "men's" and radical "women's stories" and they frequently contradicted one another.

The picture is, in fact, a fairly complicated one. Opposition to Evangelical Christianity sometimes united male sexual libertarians with defenders of slavery and racial inferiority. There were feminist sexual libertarians such as Eleanor Marx, Karl Marx's daughter, who translated Zola, as well as the indefatigable Besant. There were alliances between ostensibly heterosexual advocates of sexual freedom such as Burton and closeted homosexuals such as J. A. Symonds.

If there was indeed a plethora of discourses, there were clearly rules as to where, with whom, at what time, and through what medium one could conduct any one of them: "Where and when it was not possible to talk about such things became more strictly defined; in which circumstances, among which speakers, and within which social relationships" (Foucault 1980:18). Some topics could be discussed in mixed company in the drawing room and addressed to a mixed audience in the form of fiction. Other topics could be addressed in serious monographs, and the "naughty bits" could be rendered in Latin, of which the masses could be presumed to be ignorant. The exclusively male world of the men's club and the usually exclusive world of the learned society constituted another kind of forum. And there was also the world of pornography, which, as we shall see, was not always fully distinct from all the other genres of expression.

The anthropological discussion of sexuality in mid-Victorian society fol-lowed precisely such a set of rules. Because the discourse often excluded women (in some cases intentionally) it privileged the discussion of male rather than female sexual concerns. Indeed, the conversations themselves sometimes served as a validation of manhood. At this critical period when the roots of institutional anthropology were planted and an influential body of evolutionary theory was published, the nascent discipline was involved in not one but several discourses on sexuality. The discussions concerning primitive promiscuity, matriliny or matriarchy, and marriage by capture in which John F. McLennan, Lewis Henry Morgan, Sir John Lubbock, and Johann Jakob Bachofen were involved are marked by a degree of reticence, indeed prudery, over sexual matters. There is an absence of explicit reference to genital sexuality; much is left to the imagination. The works of these authors were intended for a general but largely male scholarly readership. In the Anthropological Society of London (ASL), whose founders left the Ethnological Society in 1863 because the latter wished to admit women, members preferred that, "in the consideration of the subject, a spade is called a spade, and not a rake or hoe" (Sellon 1863–64:327). When the men of this learned society were not discussing the virtues of the proslavery po-sition in the United States or the connection of race and language, they had time on their hands to discuss the significance of phallic worship. (The ASL is discussed in Lyons 1974:224–261; Stocking 1971; Burrow 1966; and below.)

In all such discussions the "Other" or the "primitive" is conscripted in the service of pressing contemporary concerns, whether or not that con-scription is expressly acknowledged. As one of us has remarked concern-ing both the Victorian anthropologists and some of their successors: "One position, however, dominates anthropological discussions of sexuality. A truly instinctive sexual response, whether desired or deplored, is relatively absent from the bedrooms of modern Europe. One must seek (or avoid) it elsewhere. Science may be employed both to find it and to keep it at a safe distance" (Lyons 1996:348).

BURTON AND THE ANTHROPOLOGICAL SOCIETY OF LONDON

In *The Other Victorians* Steven Marcus makes some interesting remarks about nonfictional Victorian pornography: "By the mid-Victorian period the pornographic scene had established itself in very much the same modes, categories, and varieties as exist today. Alongside of works which fumbled toward a scientific account of sexuality were grouped volumes describing the 'rites' and 'practices' of certain curious sexual and religious cults, *volumes which purported to be anthropology of some kind, volumes of folklore,* and a whole range of sex and marriage manuals of differing inflammatory intensity but uniformly equal ineptitude and disingenuousness" (1966:66, emphasis added).

The ASL had been established to discuss what purported to be "anthropology of some kind." It was most certainly interested in curious rites and practices of a religious and sexual nature. Most accounts of this rather diverse body (e.g., Burrow 1966) have stressed its hard-line stance on racial issues. Its founder, Dr. James Hunt, was a polygenist, a supporter of the defeated American South, and a defender of Governor Edward John Eyre of Jamaica, who suppressed a rebellion with much brutality. Not all members of the society endorsed Hunt's political and scientific credos, but a majority probably did. Hunt firmly believed that physical type and culture were indissociable and that anthropological science should be grounded in comparative racial anatomy (see Lyons 1974).

Burton shared Hunt's racial prejudices and his dislike of Christian philanthropists. He had another axe to grind against Mrs. Grundy and the Evangelists of Exeter Hall. He wanted to be able to discuss sex with other men in the absence of women. He was on leave from the diplomatic service long enough to aid Hunt in establishing the ASL, which he served as vice president, but successive diplomatic postings in Fernando Póo, Brazil, and Damascus prevented him from playing an active role. Dismayed by the dissolution of the society after Hunt's death at the end of the 1860s (it merged with the Ethnological Society to form the Anthropological Institute), Burton was briefly active in the new London Anthropological Society in the 1870s. This society quickly folded, presumably leaving no refuge for destitute truth, no place to discuss topics such as phallic worship, which occupied that uncertain boundary between some Victorian anthropology and pornography.

Burton's own contributions to this rather curious discourse included a presentation to the Anthropological Society of London concerning clay figures of the phallic deity Legba in Dahomey (Burton 1863–64, 1865b): "Among all barbarians whose primal want is progeny, we observe a greater or less development of the Phallic worship."[2] A quarter of a century later he contributed verse translations of Latin poems and verse inscriptions to *Priapeia*. The volume was completed in the year of Burton's death (1890) and bore only the name of Leonard Smithers, who did prose translations. Burton was an unnamed coeditor and cotranslator. Isabel Burton, his widow, had made attempts to stop publication of the volume.

Burton always claimed that his work was addressed to scholars. It is impossible to know the precise motives of those who bought literature that hovered around this uncertain boundary. Some small publishers and bookstores still cater to both tastes. In 1865 the bookseller John Camden Hotten of 151b Piccadilly reprinted one of the earliest works on phallic worship, Richard Payne Knight's *A Discourse on the Worship of Priapus* (1786), together with a recent work by a Thomas Wright of the British Archaeological Society, *On the Worship of the Generative Powers in the Middle Ages* (Marcus 1966:70–71). Hotten also published *Aphrodisiacs and Anti-Aphrodisiacs* by John Davenport, whom Marcus describes as a "semi-learned pornographic hack" (1966:72), and a collection of seven works allegedly assembled by the historian Henry Buckle (*Library Illustrative of Social Progress*) dealing with the topic of flagellation. If we peruse the pages of *Ancient Symbol Worship: The Influence of the Phallic Idea in the Religions of Antiquity* by Hodder Westropp and Charles Staniland Wake, which reproduced two papers delivered before the ASL, we find a reference to Davenport (concerning phallic worship) in the introduction by the editor, Alexander Wilder (1875:21), a reference to the well-known Payne Knight by Wake (1875:33), and a reference to the seven works on flagellation by Wilder (1875:95). It should be noted that neither Westropp nor Wake refers to Davenport or the Buckle collection, though the editor does. We may presume, however, that both authors knew for what readership their work was intended, even if they did not themselves form part of it, and that the readership may have been more extensive than Hunt's motley crowd of "anthropologists."

Phallic objects were appropriate weapons for bashing church-inspired prudery, missionaries, and devout philanthropists. This was a time when the new German biblical criticism was challenging literal interpretations of the Bible. The challenge mounted by the ASL was surely much less subtle.

Capt. Edward Sellon, like Burton, was an Indian army veteran. His two papers, "On the Phallic Worship of India" and "Sacti Puja, the Worship of the Female Powers," aroused much discussion. Sellon's first paper dealt with the worship of the lingam (combined "linga" and "yoni") by various Hindu sects in India. "It has been the practice of missionaries to burke the question of linga puja, from a mistaken and false delicacy," remarked the author (Sellon 1863–64:327). The paper contains, inter alia, an interesting description of the idea of Sacti (generative force), an account of young maidens rubbing themselves on the linga at village temples in order to promote their own fertility, along with a description of Yonijas, Hindu sects who chose to worship the yoni rather than the linga and lingam (see also Sellon 1865–66:166). Lastly, we find an amazing assertion that Old Testament Judaism, along with all other religions of the ancient world, was based on the phallic cult: "The ark of the covenant, held so sacred by the Jews, contained nothing more nor less than a Phallus, the ark being the type of the Angha or Yoni" (Sellon 1863–64:334).

Wake's paper, "Influence of the Phallic Idea in the Religions of Antiquity," contained a refutation of Richard Burton's notion that phallic worship reflected the barbarian's "primal want of progeny" (1875:34). It was a more sober attempt to seek out the social correlates of such phenomena within an evolutionary context. Wake asserted that the roots of phallic worship lay in awe at the mysterious and the unknown (1875:34). Wake's text deals at some length with Indian and Egyptian religion but focuses mainly on the Old Testament Hebrews. "Circumcision, at its inception, is a purely phallic rite," proclaimed Wake (1875:37). It might be noted that G. Stanley Hall, whose work on adolescence is given a brief negative mention by Margaret Mead in *Coming of Age in Samoa*, also linked circumcision to phallic worship (1904, vol. 1:467–470).

According to Wake, the myth of the Fall contained a number of phallic and sexual symbols, including the phallic Tree of Life and the serpent. The idea of original sin was a later interpolation, derived doubtless from Mithraism, which opposed the spiritual and divine essence in the universe to the material elements that always threatened to corrupt it. The Mithraic notion of material corruption, of the tragedy of conception, is a major element in Christianity, but phallic elements such as the symbols of the fish and the cross and the notion of God the Father survive: "The fundamental basis of Christianity is more purely 'phallic' than that of any other religion now existing" (Wake 1875:77–78).

In a later work, *The Development of Marriage and Kinship* (1889), Wake had little to say about phallic worship as such but linked advanced forms of monogamy to developed forms of ancestor worship. He believed that in the future, the spiritual, chaste elements in Christianity, which had their roots in the Aryan religions of Zoroaster and Mithras, would predominate over the phallic elements and that the most advanced members of society would elect a life of virginity (Wake 1967:475).

One suspects that the members of the ASL were little interested in a future asexual paradise but that instead they were perhaps pleased to contemplate, between pipes and glasses of port, the vision of beautiful Hindu maidens prostrating themselves before a statue of an erect male organ. In fairness to Sellon, Wake, and his collaborator, Westropp, we must observe that they all noted that in its original cultural contexts, phallic worship was not obscene. In their own society the very talk of it would have been obscene in some circles, though not, presumably, in an all-male club devoted to "science."

The above might suggest that members of the ASL were incapable of developing a sustained critique of Victorian institutions that would go beyond their obsessions with genitalia, the baiting of organized religion and its sacred texts, and the goading of Mrs. Grundy. Captain Burton shared all these preoccupations, but he did have a more extensive agenda. He believed that the Victorian family was an unhealthy institution; however, his critique of it was inseparable from a pervasive racism and misogyny.

It would be interesting to discover how many contemporary anthropologists have ever taken Burton seriously *as an anthropologist*, although they are as likely as the rest of the population to have encountered him as a larger-than-life Victorian myth. It is generally known that he visited Mecca in disguise, discovered Lake Tanganyika, disputed with John Hanning Speke as to who had discovered the source of the Nile (Speke was right), and translated the *Kama-sutra* as well as the *Arabian Nights*. Less well known are his somewhat unsuccessful forays into the realm of poetry such as *Stone Talk*; his translation from the Portuguese of *The Lusiads* by Luis de Camões; and his Sufi elegy, the *Kasidah of Haji Abdu el-Yezdi*, which he passed off as a translation, although it was his own creation, a work that tried to bridge the cultural divide between the world of the Victorians and Persian Sufism (McLynn 1990:318–324). Burton was an accomplished linguist who mastered Hindi, Arabic, Urdu, Portuguese, Persian, French, and the usual classical languages. He also understood some Swahili and was acquainted with some other African languages.

Burton realized that as an army officer or diplomat he might never penetrate cultural worlds that were either distant or hidden from the typical untrained British observer. One solution he implemented would not accord with contemporary ethical standards, namely, disguise. He used this strategy both in his pilgrimage and in his researches in Karachi. It was a strange anticipation of participant observation, one in which European lack of understanding of "natives" is partly attributed to a decline in interracial sexual contact, a decline implicitly blamed on the Victorian social mores Burton so disliked: "The white man lives a life so distinct from the black, that hundreds of the former serve through what they call their 'term of exile' without once being present at a circumcision feast, a wedding, or funeral. More especially the present generation, whom the habit and means of taking furloughs, the increased facility for enjoying ladies' society, and, if truth be spoken, a greater regard for appearances, if not a stricter code of morality, estrange from their dusky fellow-subjects every day more and more" (Richard Burton's "Little Autobiography," in Burton 1893, vol. 1:155).

It is hardly surprising that Burton was often able to make astute, comparative observations concerning a number of customs, their diffusion, and their cultural rationality. Polygamy, we shall see, was a case in point. In a discussion of societies of sub-Saharan Africa that is contained in a review of a book by the explorer Paul Du Chaillu he notes that exogamy, the levirate, and matrilineal descent are widespread (he does not employ the modern terms), whereas cannibalism is not. He also observes a number of widespread cultural traits: the prevalence of elaborate greetings, the ritual abuse of a king about to ascend the throne, the attribution of illness to witchcraft, the general concern of religion with the fending off of death, as well as the belief in animated spirits rather than permanent ghosts (Burton 1861b). In other words, Burton was engaged in an attempt to define sub-Saharan Africa as a "culture area," to use the parlance of 20th-century anthropology.

Burton's observations of variations in sexual and gender relations in different cultures are often both comprehensive and informative. His interest in such matters cannot be considered aside from his own personal history, some of which is known and much of which is subject to surmise. Burton's sexual exploits included a dalliance with some prostitutes at a brothel in Siena when he was sixteen (Farwell 1963:16) and the attempted abduction of a Latin teacher at a convent in Goa. During his stay in Sind he not only completed his report on boy brothels but also collected information on female prostitutes, including their undergarments, and took comparative notes on the breast shapes of Sindi women. Later on, in England, he became acquainted with Richard Monckton Milnes, Lord Houghton, a collector of erotica who entertained a number of literary guests at Monk Fryston, including Thomas Carlyle, William Makepeace Thackeray, Charles Kingsley, and Coventry Patmore. The houseguests also included Fred Hankey, a disciple of the Marquis de Sade who liked to watch public executions from his home in Paris. When Burton left for Dahomey, he agreed to supply Hankey with a pelt taken from the skin of an African woman. Burton was joking, but Hankey was serious (McLynn 1990:178–179, 202). Burton's younger disciples included the Victorian journalist and man-about-town Frank Harris.

McLynn also argues that Burton was sexually humiliated because he was unable to satisfy his Indian *bubu* (mistress) and that his "abject failure as heterosexual lover" may explain an increasing homoeroticism in his writing and perhaps his behavior (1990:51, 52). This argument, apart from its assumption that homoeroticism is a consequence of heterosexual failure, is perhaps exaggerated inasmuch as Burton also enjoyed heterosexual conquests and appears to have married happily. Burton and the former Isabel Arundell, an adventurous but proper Catholic lady, remained together until Burton's death. Burton did express the belief that anal intercourse was "natural" and that the male nude was superior to the female nude (McLynn 1990:180). While Burton tended to admire beautiful young women of any "race," with the exception of most black women, he disliked the appearance of older women. Thus, when he encountered some "Prairie Indians" at the Platte River en route to Utah, he described a "belle savage" with "sleek, long black hair like the ears of a Blenheim spaniel, justifying a natural instinct to stroke or pat it," as well as a number of aged women: "The grandmothers were fearful to look upon – horrid excrescences of nature, teaching proud man a lesson of humility, and a memento of his neighbour in creation, the 'humble ape'" (Burton 1971:59). Burton's social attitudes, which were extreme even for their time, make much of his writing offensive to our sensibility. Nonetheless, they were integral to the structure of his thinking and to a racialist, anthropological discourse into which primitive Others were conscripted.

In Burton's writings a hierarchy of races emerges. The Australian Aborigines are probably at the bottom, but Burton has little to say about them. His remarks about Amerindians are ambivalent. He was impressed by the valor of the Sioux in fighting a losing battle: "They inflicted horrid tortures on their prisoners, as every child has read; but, Arab-like, they respected the honor of their female captives" (Burton 1971:102). Burton regarded the "pure negroes" of West and Central Africa as cruel and stupid (McLynn 1990:215–216). He thought that "the peculiar development of destructiveness in the African brain" was "the work of an arrested development, which leaves to the man all the bloodthirstiness of the carnivore" (Burton 1924:100). During discussion of his paper on Dahomey, which he read to the ASL in the mid-1860s, Burton agreed with Governor Henry Stanhope Freeman of Lagos that Islam had deservedly had better success than Christianity in converting blacks. He attributed Islam's success to the simplicity of the religion (Burton 1865b, 1924:132). In answer to a question he stated that he believed that the pure Negro "would be improved off the face of the earth" (Burton 1924:131). Paradoxically, Burton made one exception. He seems to have respected the Yoruba of Nigeria, who possessed "admirable forms and figures" (Burton 1967:127). He also conceded that blacks were often hospitable to strangers but in a manner that emphasized a preponderance of emotion over reason: they possessed "a peculiar power of affection," albeit "as in children, it is somewhat tempered by caprice" (Burton 1861b:318).[3]

Burton frequently observed that "negroids," by which category he meant populations that resulted from a mixture of blacks with more northerly stocks such as Arabs, Europeans, and Berbers, were racially superior to "pure negroes." In his book on *The Lake Regions of Central Africa* (1860) he noted that the proportion of Negro blood increased as one traveled inland from the East Coast. Sometimes he lumped Negroes and Negroids together as Africans. His description of Africans is an unusually stark example of the mutual construction of racial and moral stigmatization that is so characteristic of the era in general and Burton in particular: "He partakes largely of the worst characteristics of the lower Oriental types – stagnation of mind, indolence of body, moral deficiency, superstition and childish passion" (Burton 1995:490). East Africans, we are further informed, are cruel, selfish, untruthful, and characterized by "savage rudeness" (Burton 1995:496). Their culture is stationary: they are "unprogressive" in intellect (Burton 1995:497). Burton does acknowledge that there is variation and exception: "The Wanyamwezi bear the highest character for civilization, discipline and industry" (1995:498).

No systematic use of anatomical or physiological characteristics is present in Burton's writing. He was a racialist but not a raciologist. Race is primarily characterized in terms of inherited mental and cultural dispositions, subject to the influence of climate and topology.

In various ways, such as numerous assertions that Africans have an unpleasant odor, Burton, the one-time frequenter of Italian and Indian brothels, takes pains to convince his readers of his lack of sexual attraction to Africans while stressing the promiscuity of the latter. His characterization of African sexuality reflects both his ideas of racial superiority and a personal venom with perhaps deeper psychological roots. He speaks of the "malignant unchastity" of the race (Burton 1967:109). In Somaliland "both sexes are celebrated for laxity of morals" (Burton 1967:102). Throughout East Africa marriage was seen by Burton as an institution that particularly degraded women. One peculiarly Victorian irony was the tendency of some of the era's worst misogynists to castigate the "lower" races and classes for their mistreatment of women: "Marriage with these people – as among all barbarians and even the lower classes of civilized races[–]is a mere affair of buying and selling" (Burton 1995:493). African males were attractive to women of other races, Burton insisted, because their penises, which were particularly large even in the nonerect state, afforded women sexual pleasure. Regurgitating this old piece of racial gossip, Burton, like his 18th-century predecessor, Charles White, was content with a sample of one: "I measured one man in Somaliland who, when quiescent, numbered nearly six inches" (1885–87, vol. 1:6). Burton does not inform the readers of his translation of the *Arabian Nights* precisely how he conducted this measurement.

Burton's portrayal of the sexuality of West Africans was, for the most part, equally unflattering. He had heard many stories about the Amazon soldiers of Dahomey before he set out on the first of two trips to that kingdom, but, as he observed in a letter to Monckton Milnes in May 1863, he was most disappointed by what he saw: "The Amazons are bosh. I looked forward to seeing 5000 African virgins with the liveliest curiosity, having never in my life seen a negress in such a predicament. Imagine my disappointment at finding them to be chiefly wives taken in adultery and given to the king for soldiering instead of being killed. They are mostly old and all fearfully ugly, the officers are apparently chosen for the bigness of their bums" (McLynn 1990:202). Like many other travelers to Africa and again in accordance with an old polygenist tradition, Burton was intrigued by stories of apes making amorous advances to black women (1967:75, 76).

Burton believed that the expression of sexual feeling was linked to climate and terrain. He thought that in damp, hot, low-lying areas women were more amorous than men. This was not true of mountainous zones. As an officer in the British East India Company, Burton had ample opportunity to observe women in Sind – single women, prostitutes, and married women. In *Sindh and the Races That Inhabit the Valley of the Indus* (1851) Burton remarks that Sindi women differ from the women of most Islamic societies in that they are not particularly chaste and that their unchastity is publicized in "vernacular books." Koranic law was not adequate to deal with the debauchery of these women. Sindi men had, accordingly, developed the practice of chopping off the heads of their errant wives. Sir Charles Napier, Burton's commanding officer, had endeavored to end this practice, an unfortunate decision, in Burton's view, because it resulted in an epidemic of promiscuity on the part of married women.

As we have already remarked, Burton considered Indians and Arabs racially superior to Africans. His accounts of Eastern sexuality are, therefore, more measured than his depictions of Africa, inasmuch as he was a student of Indian sexual technique and an admirer of Arab polygamy – in its place. Burton had a particular loathing for Jews that became even more marked after hostile encounters with Jewish traders when he served as British consul in Damascus in the late 1860s. All of this should be borne in mind as we consider what Burton had to say on three topics that much interested him: genital mutilation, heterosexual relations (heterosexual freedom, prostitution, and polygamy), and homosexuality.

BURTON ON GENITAL MUTILATION

Burton had a lifelong fascination with genital mutilation. Before making his famous pilgrimage to Mecca, he underwent circumcision in the Moslem fashion in order to perfect his disguise. He was interested in eunuchry, circumcision, subincision, clitoridectomy, infibulation, and labial elongation. By the 1880s, when he translated and edited *The Book of the Thousand Nights and a Night*, he had accumulated a substantial amount of information.

Much of the 19th-century literature on genital mutilation, of which Burton's work is an exemplar, focused on the Australian Aborigines, Africa, the Jews, and the Arabs. This literature was founded on ethnographic fact as it was then known, but, as Harriet Lyons has noted, *the perceived provenance* of these customs, not to mention their absence among most Indo-European peoples, concurred exactly with then current notions of racial hierarchy (1981:501).

Both before and since the 19th century, explanations of male and female circumcision have dealt with a defined range of topics: the enhancement and prolongation of sexual pleasure; the diminution of sexual sensation, including castration; and cruelty and sadism. Issues of power – male versus female, senior versus junior – are addressed only in recent writings. Burton's work falls within this tradition. He is impressed by the cruelty of many of the operations, citing particular instances; one that involved the removal of portions of abdominal skin in addition to the foreskin was supposedly performed in a part of the Arabian Peninsula. Cruelty is clearly seen to be an index of primitivity (Burton 1886–88, vol. 2:90–93, in Burton 1967:156–162).

Burton noted that male circumcision was supposed to diminish sexual sensation, but he did not think that it diminished pleasure in the female, as the reduction in male sensation enabled intercourse to be prolonged (1886–88, vol. 2:90–93, in 1967:156–162; see also 1885–87, vol. 5:279). He claimed that clitoridectomy was deemed necessary by some societies that practiced male circumcision in order to forestall the unpleasant effects of too many orgasms in the female. Both operations had been traditional among Arab peoples for some time. Burton stated in a Latin footnote in his *Personal Narrative of a Pilgrimage to Mecca and Medina* that clitoridectomy was said to be universal in the area near Cairo and in the Hejaz region of Arabia and that a more radical operation involving labial excision was practiced in Somalia (1855–56, vol. 2:282). He also believed that clitoridectomy might be found among geographically remote groups of Jews (Burton 1885–87, vol. 5:279 n. 5).

If the purpose of such mutilations was to impose sexual control, it was assumed by Burton and his contemporaries that such control was all too necessary. This was the logic behind the occasional performance of clitoridectomy in Europe and America in the mid-Victorian era: women deemed to be incorrigibly promiscuous were forced to undergo the operation by a few gynecologists. Paul Broca, the French anatomist and raciologist, wrote of one such case: "Her mother's surveillance, a chastity girdle . . . nothing would help" (Schiller 1979:99). In England Isaac Baker Brown, who "invented" surgical clitoridectomy, was censured by his profession when he published his results in a popular journal in 1866. In America, after a few experiments with clitoridectomy, castration was sometimes performed on female masturbators, the last such case being in 1937 (Barker-Benfield 1976:120). More primitive peoples, who, unlike more respectable Victorians, supposedly could not control their sexuality by purely mental means, were thought to require physical restraints, which were imperfect. In other words, an argument that might otherwise seem to indicate that Africans, Jews, and Moslems were sexually controlled was turned against them: "The moral effect of clitoridectomy is peculiar. While it diminishes the heat of passion it increases licentiousness, and breeds a debauchery of mind far worse than bodily un-chastity, because accompanied by a peculiar cold cruelty and a taste for arti-ficial stimulants to 'luxury.' It is the sexlessness of the spayed canine imitated by the suggestive brain of humanity" (Burton 1885–87, vol. 5:279 n. 5).

Labial elongation is a less common practice than infibulation and cli-toridectomy; it too is found in some African societies. In the previous chap-ter we discussed the furor earlier in the 19th century over Saat-Jee, the so-called Hottentot Venus, and the controversy as to whether elongated labia were the product of cultural practice or an innate index of primitivity. Bur-ton found the practice in Dahomey, explained it as a form of sexual control, and dismissed it with a sneering remark: "The sole possible advantage to be derived from this strange practice is the prevention of rape, but the men are said to enjoy handling the long projections, whose livid slatey hue suggests the idea of the turkey-cock's caruncle" (1863–64:319).

The remarks we have just cited, which quite literally bestialize African and Asian peoples, illustrate above all else the difference between Burton's moral compass and ours and demonstrate too the yawning gap between his anthropology and our own. While the missionaries of Burton's and subse-quent eras may not have shared his fascination with genital mutilations, they shared his distaste for them. The legacy of such attitudes is clear: Africans and others are suspicious of the motives of Westerners who condemn tra-ditional forms of genital cutting.[4] (See chapter 9 for further discussion of these matters.)

HETEROSEXUAL RELATIONS

Burton believed that his contemporaries were pathetically uneducated about sexual matters, and their ignorance, particularly the ignorance of young women, led to poor marriages. In the East brides knew what to ex-pect, but this was not the case in England: "I have heard of brides over thirty years old who had not the slightest suspicion concerning what complaisance was expected of them: out of *mauvaise honte*, the besetting sin of the re-spectable classes, neither mother nor father would venture to enlighten the elderly innocents" (Burton 1886–88, vol. 4:42). Such ignorance inevitably led to trauma at the moment of defloration and a fear of the sex act that diminished the pleasure of both partners, although Burton also speculated that some women might be constitutionally incapable of sexual response (1886–88, vol. 5:233).

Despite his apparent attention to the sexual desires of Victorian females, Burton was no sexual egalitarian. He frequently, and more than merely conventionally, refers to women as "the weaker sex" or "the weaker vessel." His own conduct suggests that he did regard the double standard as inevitable, and there is much speculation about his knowledge of both female and male prostitutes in India. However, in the poem *Stone Talk*, which he published under the pseudonym Frank Baker, he strongly condemned the public spectacle of prostitution on London's streets:

Have you, I ask, no means to stop
The growth of such a poison crop –
To curb a scandal makes your name
Now and hereafter most infame?
(Burton 1865a:82)

Burton believed that women should not invade male domains, nor should they be cosseted as angels in the house. He was impressed by the degree of sexual segregation in polygamous societies. Obviously, a lesser but marked degree of sexual segregation was still the norm in 19th-century English society. Until his dramatically unsuccessful foray into Oxford undergraduate life, Burton had little or no experience of institutional, single-sex education. He and his brother Edward were educated by private tutors. However, he served in the military and the diplomatic service and participated in the world of the London clubs, both social and academic. In his last 20 years he was to share much of his time and most of his travels with his wife, Isabel, but by then most of his attitudes were fully shaped.

Polygamy flourished in Sind, Egypt, and Arabia, regions with which he became familiar as soldier, scholar, traveler, and pilgrim. Burton preferred the clear delineation of gender roles in these Islamic societies to the more hazily defined distinctions of Victorian England. It was possible, Burton argued, for Islamic males to develop a full association with one another, regardless of barriers of class. Women could enjoy each other's company and would not be tempted to cuckold their husbands. Wives could own property in their own right, which they could not yet do in England, and could leave home for a few weeks without seeking their husbands' permission. On some occasions, Burton denied some of the more patriarchal traits of Islamic cultures; on other occasions, he seemed to relish them (McLynn 1990:95, 96).

Burton did discover a sexual regime he admired in the most unlikely place, the wilds of Utah, where the Mormons had recently settled. Here both men and women struggled with raw nature, and there was polygamous marriage. Burton arrived in Salt Lake City on August 25, 1860, and stayed for just one month. He had an audience with Brigham Young, with whom he was greatly impressed. His book *The City of the Saints* (1861) was and still is regarded by Mormon scholars and writers as one of the fairest portraits of their society at an early stage in its history (Bishop 1993). Burton commented that in Utah "womanhood is not petted and spoiled as in the Eastern states; the inevitable cyclical revolution, indeed, has rather placed her below par, where, however, I believe her to be happier than when set upon an uncomfortable and unnatural eminence" (1861a:523). It is in the nature of Utopias that they are hard to descry and impermanent in nature, and Burton was well aware of this. Burton had also seen polygamous marriage at work among several nations and peoples on three continents, Asia, Africa, and North America. He was hardly disposed to suggest that polygyny in most of those societies could serve as a model for Europe. For one thing, such a recommendation would have been inconsistent with his disparaging views on moral conduct, intelligence, and sexual behavior among most nonwhite races. For another, he saw polygyny as inextricably linked to agrarian and pastoral socioeconomic systems, where labor rather than land is scarce and extra wives and children are a valued addition to the workforce. (See chapters 4 and 8 for discussions of the persistence of such characterizations of African sexuality.)

> To the unprejudiced traveller it appears that polygamy is the rule where population is required, and where the great social evil has not had time to develop itself. In Paris or London the institution would, like slavery, die a natural death; in Arabia and in the wilds of the Rocky Mountains it maintains a strong hold upon the affections of mankind. Monogamy is best fitted for the large, wealthy, and flourishing communities in which man is rarely the happier because his quiver is full of children, and where the Hetaera becomes the succedaneum of the "plurality-wife." . . . The other motive for polygamy in Utah is economy. Servants are rare and costly; it is cheaper and more comfortable to marry them. Many converts are attracted by the prospect of becoming wives, especially from places where, like Clifton, there are sixty-four females to thirty-six males. The old maid is, as she ought to be, an unknown entity. Life in the wilds of Western America is a course of severe toil: a single woman cannot perform the manifold duties of housekeeping, cooking, scrubbing, washing, darning, child-bearing,

and nursing a family. A division of labour is necessary, and she finds it by acquiring a sister-hood. (Burton 1861a:522)

Just a few years after his journey to Utah Burton was to describe polygamy in another region of the world, West Africa. He approved of some aspects of polygamy among the Egba Yoruba of Abeokuta. They observed postpartum taboos on intercourse until the child was two or three years old. This custom enabled the husband to enjoy legal marital relations with those wives who were not nursing babies. Monogamous Europeans entertained no such ban on sexual relations, to the detriment of their children: "Europeans, violating the order of the animal creation, lay to their souls the flattering unction that they are the largest and the strongest of races, forgetting that by conforming to this African custom they might become both larger and stronger. Besides, it would necessitate polygyny – that is to say, a love of offspring warmer than sexual feeling. The Mormons have tried it with success" (Burton 1967:128). There are a number of problems inherent to Burton's argument. Was he really so enamored of the Victorian family life he avoided by marrying late, so enamored of children?

Polygamy was clearly a sword (or, if one prefers, an overdetermined symbol) with which Burton might combat several foes, for he had now clearly gone so far as to advocate it. It was an instrument in a somewhat heterodox critique of Victorian morality, an argument that it was insufficiently patriarchal and divorced from the nexus of biology and the true bonds of kinship. Likewise, Burton used his new understanding to lambaste that most Victorian of professions, the missionaries. Burton hated most missionaries. He was not a Christian, and he had, if we may be excused the anachronism, a Nietzschean disdain for philanthropy.[5] Although he claimed to oppose the slave trade, he also loathed the very people who wanted to do something to stop it. Like the functionalist anthropologists of later years, Burton condemned those missionaries who were so keen to ban polygyny that they were willing to destroy family life and social structure in the process:

> During a missionary dinner at Abeokuta I was somewhat startled by an account of their treatment of polygamic converts. Having accidentally mentioned that a Protestant bishop in South Africa had adopted to advantage the plan of not separating husbands and wives, I was assured that in Yoruba the severe test of sincerity was always made a *sine qua non* before baptism. This naturally induced an inquiry as to what became of the divorcees. "We marry them," said the Rev. Mr. Collmer, "to some bachelor converts." This appeared to me the greatest insult

to common sense, the exercise of a power to bind and to loose with a witness, to do evil that good may come out of it, a proceeding which may make any marriage a no-marriage. (Burton 1967:134–135)

Burton's contempt for Victorian hypocrisy thus led him to understand the damage that Europeans were doing to African institutions, but his prejudices, which were strong even by the standards of his day, precluded any move toward relativism.

THE QUEST OF SIR RICHARD IN THE "SOTADIC ZONE"

It could be argued that Burton was an unlikely progenitor of the gay rights movement, but he has been claimed as such (Lauritsen and Thorstad 1974). His fascination with "the subject of unnatural crime" thoroughly perplexed Lady Isabel, who had burned his unpublished and unexpurgated translation of *The Scented Garden* shortly after his death; rumor had it that several hundred pages dealt with the topic of pederasty.[6] Writing to Burton's publisher and collaborator, Leonard Smithers, Isabel Burton wrote: "I wish you could answer me on one point. Why did he wish the subject of unnatural crime to be so largely aired and expounded – he had such an unbounded contempt for the Vice and its votaries? I never asked him this question *unfortunately*" (July 17, 1892, Burton Archive). Lady Burton's question has not been answered. Some of Burton's language in the famous "Terminal Essay" in the *Arabian Nights* is beyond doubt homophobic: "V. F. Lopez draws a frightful picture of pathologic love in Peru" (Burton 1885–87, vol. 10:242). However, the subject matter of the essay disturbed some of its readers and probably accounts for most of the controversy the translation caused.

Burton's academic interest in homosexuality can be traced to the report on lupanars, or male brothels, in Karachi that was prepared for Napier. Its arguments and some of its texts are apparently reproduced in the "Terminal Essay," which contains a description of pederasty, other homosexual acts, a discussion of varying cultural attitudes toward sodomy and bestiality in different parts of the world, a translation of Greek and Latin words and phrases describing homosexual acts, and, at various points of the text, lists of prominent homosexuals.

In the "Terminal Essay" Burton claimed that the frequency of homosexual acts as well as the tolerance extended toward them varied geographically. The greatest frequency was found in the area between longitude 30 and 40 degrees north. The area covered included the southern and, in pre-Christian times, the northern Mediterranean regions, Egypt, Turkey, the Fertile Crescent, Arabia, Mesopotamia, Persia (where it was treated as a "mere pecca-dillo"), and parts of the Indian subcontinent. Farther east, the zone widened to include all of China and Indochina, the South Seas, and both American continents. The "sotadic zone" thus encompassed a large part of the world's population. Burton claimed that "geographical and climatic, not racial," factors were responsible for the creation of a zone where "there is a blending of masculine and feminine temperaments, a crisis which elsewhere occurs only sporadically" (1885–87, vol. 10:207, 208). Here there was a suggestion that the "unnatural" might indeed be "natural" in certain ecological conditions. But Burton would hardly have dared suggest that such behavior would provide any sort of model for his own society, and it is unclear what his most private thoughts were. One might note that the sotadic zone corresponds to no reality. Perhaps because of the prudery of some African societies and perhaps because of the overwhelming fear of African heterosexuality, Burton and his contemporaries knew little about homosexuality in the pagan portions of sub-Saharan Africa (Bleys 1995:32–36).

However vague Burton's explanation may have been, he succeeded, quite literally, in naturalizing rather than demonizing same-sex sexual relations. This was the first major contribution toward the ethnographic study of this topic. It was perhaps no coincidence that one of the letters and reviews pasted into the front cover of Burton's own copy of the *Arabian Nights* was a letter to the *Academy* by John Addington Symonds that attacked the hypocrisy of the times and praised the "literary vigour, exact scholarship, and rare insight into Oriental modes of thought" that characterized Burton's magnum opus. Symonds was a well-known classical and Renaissance scholar who was later to produce a life of Michelangelo. He was also the author of a privately printed essay, *A Problem in Greek Ethics: Being an Inquiry into the Problem of Sexual Inversion* (1883), which was reprinted posthumously along with portions of *A Problem in Modern Ethics* (1891) as part of Havelock Ellis's *Sexual Inversion* (1897–98). Symonds sent a draft of *A Problem in Modern Ethics* to Burton shortly before the latter's death in 1890 because, though "not exactly sympathetic[,] he is a perfect mine of curious knowledge about human nature" (quoted in Grosskurth 1964:281).

Throughout his career Burton took, literally as well as metaphorically, the road less traveled. He was a racist, but he believed that anthropologists had to understand people in other societies. He was a sexist and misogynist who believed in women's right to sexual pleasure. He condoned and even advocated polygamy, an extraordinary stance for an eminent Victorian, but he stayed thirty years with the same wife. We can, in many ways, be grateful that his vision of anthropology, rather than that of Edward Tylor and Lewis Henry Morgan, was not victorious. However, as a pioneer in the anthropology of sex and as a defender of sexual liberation (primarily for men), Burton is without peer. His example should serve as a caution to modern scholars who might easily assume that a progressive attitude on other social issues uniformly accompanies advocacy of sexual liberation.

CHAPTER 3

Matriarchy, Marriage by Capture, and Other Fantasies

Apart from Charles Staniland Wake, whose book *The Development of Marriage and Kinship* achieved instant obscurity on publication and only received any real regard after its republication in 1967, no major evolutionary theorist regularly participated in the meetings of Dr. James Hunt's Anthropological Society of London (ASL). Edward Tylor, J. F. McLennan, Sir John Lubbock (who was active in the rival Ethnological Society as well as in the later Anthropological Institute), and Henry Summer Maine all published major works for a much wider audience. They were, to varying degrees, members of the Victorian establishment. Maine was a law professor; Lubbock a banker, popular writer, and politician; McLennan a somewhat unsuccessful lawyer; and Tylor a respectable, wealthy Quaker writer who became an academic. Their lives were, as far as we know, untainted by scandal. McLennan's disciple, William Robertson Smith, was, indeed, the subject of scandal because he dared to apply McLennan's theories to the study of Old Testament religion and linked the Hebrew patriarchs to Australian savages. This, however, was an intellectual and not a personal scandal (see Beidelman 1974). The American Lewis Henry Morgan was a deist and a willing subject of puritanical restraint by his wife and the Reverend Joshua McIlwaine, a family friend (see Stern 1931:2; Lyons 1974:291, 292). Johann Jakob Bachofen, the Swiss jurist, may have received some improper family preferment in his public career (Campbell 1967:xli) but was otherwise blameless. None of these men belong to Steven Marcus's category of "Other Victorians." Any reader who picked up Maine's *Ancient Law* or Tylor's *Primitive Culture* in search of salacious or titillating detail would be grimly disappointed.

Within these parameters, however, there was still considerable room in the writings of these scholars for the conscription of real or imagined savages into Victorian conversations about sexual morality. With all this in mind, let us turn to some well-known remarks by Sir Edmund Leach:

> The British nineteenth-century evolutionist anthropologists were mostly [sic] Presbyterian Scots, soaked in a study of the classics and sharing, as far as one can judge, most of the paternalist imperialistic values characteristic of the English ruling class of the period. Their theories reveal a fantasy world of masterly men who copulated indiscriminately with their slave wives who then bore children who recognized their mothers, but not their fathers [see also McLennan 1970:chap. 8]. This fantasy had some indirect resemblance to features of American chattel slavery, but it bears no resemblance whatever to the recorded behavior of any known species of animal. (1969:100)

Given the quintessential respectability of the scholars we have just mentioned (only two of whom were Presbyterian Scots) and the less than fantastic nature of so much of their writing, what substance is there in Leach's provocative remarks?

Leach was clearly not referring to Maine, who believed that patriliny and patriarchy had existed from the earliest times and that the family was the primal nucleus around which the gens had been built, nor to Darwin, who was inclined to doubt the truth of his friend Lubbock's assertion of the existence of primitive promiscuity on the basis of the sparse but significant evidence of the behavior of higher primates (1871, vol. 2:363). He was alluding to the theories of McLennan, Robertson Smith, Lubbock, Morgan, the Australian writers Lorimer Fison and A. W. Howitt, and Bachofen, who believed that the original human society was one that practiced virtually indiscriminate promiscuity. In Morgan's work we read of the "consanguine family" (1963:27, 393, 410), in Bachofen's of "hetaerism" (1967:94, 95), and in Fison and Howitt's of the "undivided commune" (1967:365). Morgan (1963:65), McLennan (1970:65), and Bachofen (1967:98) believed that descent in the female line occurred when the paternity of children could not be definitely determined.

All these writers believed that morality had evolved and that many primitives were in a less evolved state. There was assumed to have been a particular improvement in the status of women. McLennan (1970) and Lubbock (1978) believed that primitive promiscuity was succeeded by a stage of marriage by capture, which survives in a symbolic form as a reminder of the brutal past. It was also contended that prostitution in more developed societies may be a survival of earlier hetaerism (Lubbock 1978:86–88).

Several feminist scholars have noted that theories of the evolution of the family reinforced dichotomies conducive to maintaining the Victorian system of sex and gender. Rosalind Coward (1983) has noticed a reification of the essential antagonism between men and women in several evolutionist works. This tendency is noted in the works of authors who appeared to be sympathetic to women's plight as well as those who frankly supported male privilege. Because they did not consider the possibility of a cooperative relationship between equals, Coward argues, their arguments naturalize the socially constructed state of affairs that they are trying to explain.

Anita Levy (1991:48–74) has suggested that notions of a large gap between savage and civilized women strengthened distinctions between respectable, sexually controlled women and oversexed, savagelike, lower-class prostitutes (though we will see in the next chapter that this discourse coexisted with a tendency to see *all* female bodies as "savagelike" in their sexuality). This was significant at a time when activists like Josephine Butler sought support among middle-class women for repeal of the Contagious Diseases Acts of the 1860s. All the evolutionary theorists certainly linked modern prostitution to some events in the savage past.

The writings of the cultural evolutionists undoubtedly did invoke the same dichotomies deployed by Burton and his friends in the ASL. Oppositions between male and female, culture and nature, savagery and civilization, gratification and denial, mastery and subordination were mutually reinforced by their juxtaposition. The evolutionists differed from polygenists like Hunt and Burton in their insistence on progress. Burton, for example, opined that women were happier when they knew who was boss and that modern civilization placed too many restrictions on masculinity. On the other hand, he found primitives too distasteful to emulate. Insofar as all the admiring and deploring was more than an excuse for disclosure, it led to an aporia from which one could exit neither forward nor backward. Evolutionary theorists offered a way out. Moreover, they sought to assure their readers that even those things they did not like originated in some general move toward improvement. Nonetheless, they did think it necessary to postulate, or rather to invent, a zero point from which all such progress occurred. *Insofar as that zero point was characterized by an assumption of sexual promiscuity among the earliest humans and distance from it was gauged by the degree to which such license had been overcome, speculations about sex were at the core of evolutionary theory.* Accordingly, the first works universally accepted as the work of legitimate anthropologists co-opted the real and imagined sexual practices of surviving primitives to construct their histories of the emergence of civilization from savage beginnings.

In their discussions of the point zero of morality and in their interpretation of succeeding stages of moral development the evolutionists used language and styles of argumentation that were certainly more coy than those adopted by Sir Richard Burton, Edward Sellon, and other seekers of "destitute truth." Occasionally, the rhetoric of allusion is a little direct. The tableau of the *Australian Aboriginal Marriage Ceremony* in Lubbock's *Origin of Civilization* (figure 1) leaves not too much to the imagination (1970:75). The matrilineal or matriarchal theorists were participants in a wider domain of discourse than Burton and Sellon, a domain that could not permit discussion of the size of labia in Dahomey or phallic statues in India. However, we must remember that the Victorian novel, with its substantial female readership, was a still wider but much more restrictive field of discourse. A readership alarmed by *Madame Bovary* or *Tess of the D'Urbervilles* could not have endured a novel that incorporated lengthy narratives describing total promiscuity, brutal abduction, and exotic prostitutes. In other words, had Lubbock's *Origin of Civilization* been written as fiction rather than as a work of scholarship, large portions of it would never have seen the light of day.

McLennan, Lubbock, Morgan, and Bachofen all saw the unbridled gratification of male lust as the original state of humankind, although they differed in their notions of how it had been brought under control. As we have noted, both Lubbock and McLennan believed that marriage by capture had once been universal and that its remnants could still be found in some modern societies. Neither man credited primitive women with any desire to resist. Lubbock thought that the sentiment of love was absent from some primitive groups such as the Algonquin, basing his assertions on dubious missionary tales about difficulties in translating the Bible (1978:50). McLennan declared that "savages are not remarkable for delicacy of feeling in matters of sex. Again, no case can be cited of a primitive people among whom the seizure of brides is rendered necessary by maidenly coyness. On the contrary, it might be shown, were it worthwhile to deal seriously with this view, that women among rude tribes are usually depraved, and inured to scenes of depravity from the earliest infancy" (1970:12).

Believing that the point zero was a Hobbesian state of continual warfare, McLennan thought that a premium would inevitably be placed on male births. McLennan's *Primitive Marriage* (1865) had an elaborate plot: a scarcity of women caused by female infanticide led, in McLennan's scheme, both to polyandry and the practice of marriage by capture, which in turn was the forerunner of regulated exogamy. These earlier societies were so promiscuous that mothers could not always identify the male parent, hence the principle of mother right (matriliny). [1] As for Lubbock, he thought

1. *Australian Aboriginal Marriage Ceremony*, after Louis-Henri de Saulces de Freycinet, *Voyage autour du monde* (13 vols., 1824–44), pl. 104. From *The Origin of Civilization and the Primitive Condition of Man* (1870) by Sir John Lubbock.

that women were originally the communal property of males in the group. Subsequently, the desire to own women privately rather than communally led men to capture women from outsiders (Lubbock 1978:76–91). Thus, men's relations with other men led to the capture and control of women. According to McLennan, the Australian Aborigines, who represented a low stage in social evolution, still acted in this way: "Among the Australians, according to one account, when a man sees a woman whom he likes, he forces her to accompany him by blows, ending by knocking her down and carrying her off. The same account (somewhat suspiciously) bears that this mode of courtship is rather relished by the ladies as a species of rough gallantry" (1970:31–32). Through somewhat twisted paths, men came to regularize their sexual property rights. Once all the stages of exogamy, endogamy, polyandry, and so on had been worked through, it was no longer publicly acceptable to beat women about the head with clubs. Both female virtue and mechanisms for its protection had come into existence, at least among the respectable classes.

Lubbock's discussion of wife lending and temple prostitution in Babylonia and India is an exemplary illustration of those attitudes that have been regarded as archetypally Victorian. He considered both to have originated in remedies undertaken by the captors of brides to compensate their fellow males who might resent any exclusive claim to possession of an outsider female. His discussion was prefaced by an unctuous disclaimer: "The nature of the ceremonies by which this was effected makes me reluctant to enter this part of the subject at length; and I will have therefore merely to indicate in general terms the character of the evidence" (Lubbock 1978:86).

Lubbock claimed that his theory of marriage by capture explained "the remarkable subordination of the wife to the husband, which is so characteristic of marriage and so incuriously inconsistent with all our avowed ideas" (1978:90). Furthermore, it was a curious fact that men often preferred their captives to their original brides: "And even when this ceased to be the case, the idea would long survive the circumstances which gave rise to it" (1978:90). On the surface, this is an explanation of the prestige of Athenian and Indian courtesans, but it can also be read as an evolutionary apologia for the Victorian double standard.

Ancient Society (1877), Lewis Henry Morgan's major work on the evolution of the family, mentions only in passing anything so dramatic as marriage by capture (1963:443); he is, in fact, the most sober of the matriarchal theorists. Morgan was the only one of the grand theorists to visit and observe a functioning matrilineal society, namely, the Seneca. His construction of stages in the evolution of the human family incorporated not only his knowledge of the Iroquois but also his classical learning and his own interpretation of Mesoamerican prehistory. His speculations concerning primitive communism and promiscuity were based in part on his interpretation of Seneca kinship terminology and similar systems elsewhere. Morgan also had a genuine admiration for the Iroquois people as well as a commitment to democratic institutions and to the eventual equality of men and women (1963:499). All of these facts were consistent with a relative narrowing of the moral gap between savages and his contemporaries in Morgan's writings. Morgan saw a regrettable worsening in the position of women after the decline of matriarchy, for example (1963:481). This aspect of Morgan's argument was central to the incorporation of Morgan's work in the critique of the bourgeois family offered by Friedrich Engels in *The Origin of the Family, Private Property and the State* (1884).

Morgan concurred in the belief that matriarchy had originated in an era when sexual behavior made the determination of paternity impossible (1963:66), and he imagined the early existence of both promiscuous and incestuous intercourse (the consanguine family) and of group marriage. Morgan's archaeology of the human family was based largely upon the recognition that the kinship terms found in the world's languages fell into a small number of predictable patterns and that the distribution of these patterns was consistent with an Asian origin of New World populations. The consanguine family, as he imagined it, had developed from an earlier stage of generalized promiscuity to one in which intercourse was incestuous but restricted to members of the same generation. *Punaluan* marriage, the next stage, was a group marriage between two or more brothers from one kin group and two or more sisters from another. In other words, several men shared sexual access to several women, although these women were other people's sisters, not their own. He believed that the relationship terminology of the Iroquois reflected a former punaluan marriage practice that, he believed, had existed very recently in Pacific Islands such as the Hawaiian archipelago. In Morgan's schema the Iroquois themselves had advanced to "pairing marriages" in which a single man married a single woman or sometimes more than one woman. Marriage among tribal peoples, according to Morgan, created social links between clans, even after the disappearance of group marriage; indeed, such links were an important purpose of marriage. Morgan cautioned his readers against feeling moral disgust concerning Hawaiian marriage institutions. He criticized the missionary Hiram Bingham for picturing the people of the Sandwich Islands "as practicing the sum of human abominations" and for accusing them of "polygamy . . . fornication, adultery, incest, infant murder, desertion of husbands and wives, parents and children; sorcery, covetousness, and oppression" (Bingham 1847:21, quoted by Morgan): "Punaluan marriage, and the punaluan family dispose of the principal charges in this grave indictment and leave the Hawaiians a chance at a moral character. The existence of morality, even among savages, must be recognized, although low in type; for there never could have been a time in human experience when the principle of morality did not exist" (Morgan 1963:424).

Morgan accepted Bingham's account of incestuous marriages between full brothers and sisters at the upper reaches of Polynesian aristocracy (1963: 424), seizing upon it as evidence for survival of the consanguine family in the era of the punaluan, something for which he was criticized by Wake (1967:21). Despite this lapse, Morgan may thus be seen to have supported science against missionary delicacy for very different purposes than those of Burton and his friends. Morgan did, however, assent in general terms to the direction that others had discerned in the history of moral values: "Attention has been called to the stupendous conjugal system which fastened itself upon mankind in the infancy of their existence and followed them down to civilization. The ratio of human progress may be measured to some extent by the degree of the reduction of this system through the moral element of society arrayed against it" (1963:400).

Passages like this make it less surprising that Morgan had become an admirer of Bachofen, to whose thinking a scandalized attitude toward sexual license was central rather than peripheral and who saw an inclination to experience such distaste as a driving force in human history.[2] In Bachofen's writing there is an explicit equation between the conquest of sex and the triumph over nature. His primary sources are classical, specifically, Greek history, Greek and Roman myths, the *Oresteia* of Aeschylus, and speculative prehistory. Bachofen believed that matriarchy, or mother right (*Das Mutterrecht*, which is the title of his book), and marriage, which accompanied it, had replaced an earlier stage of "unregulated sexual relations" in which women were defenseless against abuse by men (1967:93). "Exhausted" by male "lusts," Bachofen declaimed, "woman was first to feel the need for regulated conditions and a purer ethic, while men, conscious of their superior physical strength, accepted the new constraint only unwillingly" (1967:93).

The era of mother right brought with it not only marriage but also agriculture, which, Bachofen believed, had had as ennobling an effect upon the sexual life of plants as marriage had had upon that of human beings. Although plants could not be imagined to have endured universal rape during the era of promiscuity, they had been subject to "the chaos of hetaeric generation" (Bachofen 1967:95). The reproduction of cultigens was far more seemly and ordered than that of the "swamp vegetation" that provided the subsistence of the earliest human beings.

Contemporary feminist theorists who have been attracted to Bachofen's portrait of an era of matriarchy characterized by the worship of Demeter and other goddesses of human and vegetable fertility would do well to consider carefully the place that Bachofen assigns the "Demetrian" principle in his total scheme of human evolution. The overall course of human development, as Bachofen discerned it from Greek and Roman myths, literature, and accounts of neighboring peoples, is a progression from domination by physical drives to a state in which spiritual and intellectual ideals govern human behavior.

Although the change from hetaerism to matriarchy was a major triumph over ungoverned sensuality, it occurred at a stage during which the central concerns of humanity, as manifested in religion, were still basically physical: marriage, motherhood, and the propagation of plants (Bachofen 1967:97). Moreover, Bachofen asserted, the era of mother right in ancient Greece did not pass without dangerous regressions, owing to the overwhelmingly physical nature of women. Bachofen argued that the phallic cult of Dionysus appealed to the weaker, sexual side of female nature and that for some time this atavistic religion threatened to undo the progress that had been achieved in the name of Demeter and motherhood (1967:100–102). The regression to which Bachofen objected was political as well as sexual. The Dionysian mysteries introduced a deplorable democracy along with their unfortunate debauchery. Indeed, the two trends were inextricably linked: "The Dionysian cult . . . loosed all fetters, removed all distinctions, and by orienting people's spirit toward matter and the embellishment of physical existence, carried life itself back to the laws of matter. This sensualization of existence coincides everywhere with the dissolution of political organization and the decline of political life. Intricate gradation gives way to democracy, the undifferentiated mass, the freedom and equality which distinguish natural life from ordered social life and pertain to the physical, material side of human nature" (Bachofen 1967:102).

The transition from hetaerism to maternalism, for Bachofen, was merely one of degree, a sometimes uneasy shift from a less disciplined to a more disciplined form of domination by the body. In the change from matriarchy to patriarchy Bachofen perceived a genuine qualitative difference in the nature of social and religious experience: for the first time the mind and the spirit are given precedence over the body. This occurs, says Bachofen, because the father's relationship to the child is not physically obvious but must be intellectually cognized. Indeed, he says, it possesses "a certain fictive character" (Bachofen 1967:109). Patriarchy and the Orphic religion, according to Bachofen, sought to conquer the physical and the sensual. Homosexuality, Bachofen points out, was regarded by some Greek thinkers as a higher form of love than the purely sensual feeling aroused by the opposite sex (1967:203). Arguing in this vein, Bachofen is particularly approving of Sappho's intentions concerning her circle of women on Lesbos. Sappho's fundamental goal was to "elevate" her sex, to accomplish "a purification and transfiguration of the feminine-material principle" (Bachofen 1967:204, 207). Sappho, says Bachofen, "deplored" the "strange, aimless striving peculiar to women," but, insofar as her inspiration came from Eros, she was never able to rid herself of the taint of Aphrodite; it was her fate to be trapped forever "on the dizzy heights where passion and reason are locked in eternal conflict" (1967:204, 207).

For a later-19th-century author like Bachofen, therefore, approval of homosexuality was not necessarily linked to sexual liberation, nor was it linked to liberal ideas on matters such as race and class; indeed, for Bachofen,

Egypt, India, and the plebs and helots of the ancient world represented matriarchal strongholds, intellectual and moral backwaters that had yet to feel the improving force of Orphic patriarchal religion (1967:178–200). Conquest and domination in the service of Orpheus, patriarchy, and spiritual improvement of the race were thus laudable human achievements. We may further note that Bachofen's theories are consistent with the widely held 19th-century view that women, the "angels in the house," might tame the brute in men, but, thus transformed, it is these civilized male creatures who must do the work of the intellect and the soul.

By the late 1870s, anthropological opinion was divided into three camps, the patriarchal theorists and the rival matriarchal schools of Morgan and McLennan. As we briefly noted, Maine and his followers believed that the patriarchal family had evolved into the larger patrilineal gens, which had formed the basis for early political and religious institutions. The head of the patriarchal family, who controlled his wife, children, and slaves from birth through marriage to death, gradually lost his patria potestas as small cities with a rural base evolved into multiethnic metropolises sustained by the commerce of individuals. Accordingly, states based on property, territory, and individual contract rather than kinship and group status were the final stage in social evolution. Maine's schema, based on his knowledge of the ancient world (Greece, Rome, and India), assumed that the family had existed throughout human history, although there had been changes in the legal status of its members.

The ideas of Morgan and Bachofen about the development of property institutions and the family differ from Maine's in that Morgan and Bachofen believed in the existence of a period of promiscuity, followed by matriliny, prior to the evolution of patriarchy. Both Maine and Morgan agreed that the mercantilist state was preceded by an earlier social stage in which political and property rights were invested in kin groups rather than individuals. Some of the sharpest disagreements were between Morgan and McLennan. Morgan accorded no significant role to marriage by capture in social evolution. McLennan insisted that exogamy was an evolutionary stage that preceded endogamy and that classificatory kin terminologies, the basis of Morgan's grand scheme, did not reflect present-day or past biological relationships based on marriage but were instead the product of etiquette, mere forms of address.

Until 1880 McLennan probably had the best of the argument. For instance, Morgan's primary evidence for the systems of group marriage was the existence in Asia and the Americas of what he called Ganowanian and

Turanian kinship terminologies, which he could document as a result of the questionnaires he had been distributing since the late 1850s.[3] However, inasmuch as groups like the Iroquois, the Omaha, and the Tamils had no institution comparable to Morgan's ideas of group marriage, clear evidence was needed of the concordance of Ganowanian terminology with actual group marriage or the visible vestiges of it. Just a few years before his death, Morgan received what he regarded as clinching evidence from his Australian correspondent, the Reverend Lorimer Fison, the roué son of a rich British landowner who had found religion and pursued a career as a missionary first in Fiji and then in Australia.

THE LIVING KINDERGARTEN OF THE HUMAN RACE

Prior to the publication of *Kamilaroi and Kurnai* (1880) by Fison and Howitt, there was very little in the way of systematic knowledge of Australian Aborigines and their social institutions. Fison and Howitt's book, their continuing work over the next couple of decades, and, above all else, the appearance in 1899 of *The Native Tribes of Central Australia* by Baldwin Spencer and F. J. Gillen had made Australian culture the focal topic of anthropology outside North America by the turn of the century. By this time, "real" primitives were no longer present in most parts of North America and Africa and were vanishing into barely accessible parts of the Amazonian jungle. Living proof of the past could still be found in Australia and parts of Melanesia, although even in those areas it was disappearing. The Tasmanians were gone, and most of Howitt's Kurnai spoke English. However, elements of the traditional culture still survived in the Australian Southeast, and it was still alive and well in other parts of the continent.

Australia was regarded as the living kindergarten of the human race. The technology was still Paleolithic. The boomerang was used in some places to hunt strange marsupials. There were no iron tools. There was no agriculture. Clothing was uncommon. There was little in the way of government apart from localized gerontocracies. Sexual and marital institutions certainly did not accord with the teachings of the Christian church. Circumcision, subincision (something previously unknown), and vaginal introcision were all common. Polygyny was preferred. There were reports of marriage by capture and ceremonial sexual license.

Although there were other pioneers (Samuel Gason, W. E. Roth, and T. G. H. Strehlow), the anthropological image of Australian primitivity owed most to the four scholars we have mentioned. Of the four only

Spencer, who was the Foundation Professor of Biology at Melbourne, was an academic. Howitt, the son of two British writers who immigrated to Australia, was a bushranger and herder who became a civil servant. Fison tried to enter academe as a lecturer in a Methodist college but did not succeed in doing so. Gillen, who was uneducated, was responsible for the mail and telegraph service in Alice Springs. He came to know the local Aborigines well in his capacity as a magistrate. All four pioneers were content or had to be content to play second fiddle to metropolitan masters of evolutionary theory.[4] When Morgan died, Tylor became the major sponsor of Fison and Howitt. Sir James Frazer read the proofs of both *The Native Tribes of Central Australia* by Spencer and Gillen and their second book, *The Northern Tribes of Central Australia* (1904) (see Ackerman 1987:155, 203). The theoretical work of McLennan and Robertson Smith in the 1880s and that of James Frazer, Andrew Lang, Northcote Thomas, Sidney Hartland, and Émile Durkheim in the 1900s was particularly informed by the new Australian data.

Morgan contributed a prefatory note to *Kamilaroi and Kurnai*. Fison was the author of the first part of the book. In the terms of what became known as "alliance theory" in 20th-century anthropology many of the societies discussed by Fison and Howitt (the Kurnai are an exception) were characterized by direct exchange and symmetric alliance. In these societies, as alliance theorists viewed them, men of one socially defined group relinquished sexual rights in their sisters to men of another similar group who in turn supplied them with wives. In chapter 9 we deal with feminist objections to some of the premises of alliance theory. Here we should note that Fison and Howitt prefigured alliance theory in noting the dependence of individual marriage upon group rights, though they downplayed the former more than 20th-century writers did and understood the latter in a more specifically sexual way than the alliance theorists.

Fison described at secondhand the moiety systems of the Mackay, Darling River, and Mount Gambier tribes (Fison and Howitt 1967:34) and also those of the Banks Islands and New Britain. The Mount Gambier tribe divided into two intermarrying, exogamous moieties. Kumite men had to marry Kroki women, and vice versa. Fison obtained information on the Kamilaroi from indigenous informants, who described four matrilineal marriage classes and six totems. Ipai and Kumbo were "brother" classes acting as alternate generations of the same unnamed moiety; their counterparts were Muri and Kubi.[5]

Fison discovered that the Kamilaroi relationship terminology matched

Morgan's Turanian type. In other words, it was not very dissimilar to the Iroquoian terminology typical of Ganowanian (or North American) systems of consanguinity and marriage. Fison noted that the older men tended to monopolize the women and that polygyny was desirable. However, elders sometimes had to allow young men access to their wives, if they were of the appropriate marriage class. Apparently, Fison had not discovered such a practice among the Kamilaroi with whom he was acquainted, but a Mr. Lance had observed it in another group. Furthermore, the same Lance had reported that Clarence River Kamilaroi Kubi men would address stranger Ipatha (feminine of Ipai) women as *spouse*. Membership in a moiety or marriage class acted as a kind of sexual passport (Fison and Howitt 1967:53, 54). A system of marriage class equivalences had been established throughout large parts of Australia. A visitor might be assigned temporary membership in a local class equivalent to his own and temporary sexual access to a woman of an appropriate group, even though he might be communicating by gesture language with foreigners a hundred miles from home. Armed with this body of facts and the template of Morgan's theory into which he could mold them, Fison determined that group marriage of a sort still existed in Australia: "*Marriage is theoretically communal. In other words, it is based upon the marriage of all the males in one division of a tribe to all the females of the same generation in another division*. Hence, relationship is not merely that of the individual to another but of group to group. By this it is not meant that present usage is hereby stated, but that this is the ancient rule which underlies present usage and to which that usage points" (Fison and Howitt 1967:51).

So considerable were the sexual opportunities thus afforded to the Australian Aborigines that paternity might well be in question, and matrilineal descent was accordingly the only logical mode of ascription to gens and marriage class: "For, when a man has no exclusive right to his wives; when even strangers from a distant tribe, who are of a class corresponding to his, may claim a share in his marital rights; when a woman is married to a thousand miles of husbands, then paternity must be, to say the least of it, somewhat doubtful. But there can be no possibility of mistake as to maternity, and therefore it seems natural enough that children should 'follow the mother,' as several of our correspondents put it" (Fison and Howitt 1967:73).

Albeit a woman might be "married to a thousand miles of husbands," such men did have to belong to the correct class and generation. Incestuous marriages and marriages in breach of the exogamy rules were abhorrent to the Aborigines. Although a residue of group marriage existed among them, they had progressed beyond Morgan's early stage of promiscuity (the consanguine family), a stage of which there was evidence in the Malayan terminology found among some tribes in which no terminological distinctions were made between fathers and any kind of uncles, between mothers and all aunts, and in which siblings were equated with all cousins of similar sex.

However, a tradition existed among the Dieri of South Australia that indicated that memories of sexual chaos were still fresh. Gason had received an account of the origin of totemic groups (the *murdus*) from his informants. "Evils" had resulted from an early period of promiscuity. The Dieri elders had beseeched the Good Spirit Muramura for assistance. He had created totemic classes based on animate and inanimate objects such as dogs, mice, emus, rain, and iguanas and assigned each branch of the Dieri to one of them. From that time forth they could intermingle but not intermarry (Fison and Howitt 1967:25; Morgan 1967:5).

Doubtless, the Dieri had such a tradition. The end of incest and other forms of indiscriminate sexuality is a feature common to origin myths. This was surely a fact known to Victorians who studied the classics as well as to modern readers of Claude Lévi-Strauss. Fison's ethnographic data were good enough that we can read them in our own way, but his own understandings were inextricably bound to the moral predispositions he shared with Morgan, and his analysis was therefore prone to ambitious deductions and leaps of faith. Both Fison and Howitt believed that the "undivided commune" (corresponding to Morgan's consanguine family), as described in the Dieri myth, had once existed throughout Australia. From it had been created the marriage-class systems for which Australian Aborigines are famous, although they are by no means universal (Howitt 1904).

The Kurnai of Southeast Australia had patrilocal territorial groups rather than moieties or marriage classes. Marriage took place between these groups subject to incest rules. Howitt thought that they were more socially advanced than the groups of the interior, although they had a Malayan kinship terminology (regarded by Morgan as a survival of promiscuity). Marriage was arranged individually. A boy would ask a girl to elope with him. These secretive arrangements often resulted in a physical confrontation between the couple and the bride's parents, and tempers were only gradually assuaged (Fison and Howitt 1967:201, 202). Adulterous wives were severely punished, and there was some evidence of strong sexual jealousy (Fison and Howitt 1967:205). Fison compared Kurnai marriage to the syndyasmian, or pairing marriage, of the Iroquois, although he thought that institutions such as the license surrounding marriage by elopement, occasional sororal polygyny, and the levirate were survivals of group marriage (Fison and Howitt 1967:317, 318). Fison thought that the Kurnai had once had a two-class system.

The importance of "totems" is taken for granted in Fison's discussion of the Kamilaroi. Anthropological interpretations of "totemism" are an important instance of the close interface between speculations about primitive sexuality and broader theoretical concerns. The notion that totemism was an early, albeit not the primal, stage in the evolution of religion had been developed by McLennan. He believed that totemism was a development of fetishism and that the worship of animals and plants (the totems) was historically coincident with matrilineal descent and a system of exogamous clans that were named after totemic species (McLennan 1970; Stocking 1995:48, 49). McLennan's discussion was focused on the Greeks, the Egyptians, and the Amerindians. In the 1880s McLennan's distinguished disciple, William Robertson Smith, decided that the original Semitic peoples were pastoral nomads organized into matrilineal, exogamous, totemic clans. Totemic affiliation enabled primitive people to determine who was and who was not kin to them and thereby regulate marriage. The totem was identified with the blood of the clan and might well have been ancestral to it. Because the totem was an object of veneration and worship, it was routinely avoided and only eaten at specific religious gatherings of the clan (Smith 1885, 1889). Smith believed that Jewish religion in the years prior to the exile still bore the traces of totemism. In one way or another, all Victorian theories of the origin of totemism link it to sex and theories of conception. After the appearance of *Kamilaroi and Kurnai*, Australia was to furnish the primary evidence for totemic practices among surviving primitives.

Although McLennan and Morgan both died in 1881, theories advocating the priority of mother right and its origins during a stage of promiscuity flourished for another couple of decades. However, they were subject to challenge. That the findings of the mother right theorists proceeded from prejudice rather than from an ineluctable reality bared by the probings of science was demonstrated by Wake in his 1889 work on *The Development of Marriage and Kinship*, a tour de force in which the theory of primitive promiscuity, McLennan's views on marriage by capture, the dogma that asserted the universal priority of matriliny, and Lubbock's ideas on hetaerism were all laid waste. For example, Wake noted that abduction and ceremonial marriage by capture were not necessarily connected. The latter was merely a jural institution that served to publicize marriage (Wake 1967:432). While Wake's book was not a success, the fact of its appearance does mark a turning of the tide. However, the notion of the oversexed primitive did not very quickly disappear. For all Wake's many reminders to his readers and to himself that primitive customs were not disgusting when viewed in their context, the author did believe (see our prior discussion) that the religion of the future should replace the love of procreation with the love of chastity and that Christianity had taken a step in that direction.

In the same year that Wake's book was published the Australian scholar John Mathew declared his opinion that group marriage was not to be found among the Aboriginal peoples and that there was no proof that it had ever existed on the Australian continent (Barnes 1975:28). In 1891 the Finnish scholar Edward Westermarck launched an even more radical attack on mother right theory and ideas of primitive promiscuity in the first edition of *The History of Human Marriage*, a book which in many respects forms a bridge between the Victorian period and the modernist writings of Malinowski.[6] Westermarck's career lasted until the 1930s, and he is accordingly one of a new generation of scholars whom we shall discuss in the next chapter. Later Victorian matriarchal theorists read his work (and argued against it), but they continued their own conversation about the role of primitive promiscuity in the origin of the family; it is this conversation that we shall discuss here.

In 1891 A. W. Howitt published a lengthy ethnographic account of the Dieri and related tribes of Central Australia with a special focus upon a marriage system that seemed to him to offer clues to the manner in which individual marital unions might have emerged from group marriage. In this work Howitt takes issue with McLennan, Maine, and Bachofen for their speculative reconstructions of the origin of marriage, arguing that his field research came much closer to settling the question. Key to the Dieri kinship system, as Howitt understood it, was the coexistence of two forms of marriage: *noa* marriage and *pirauru* marriage. Howitt said that noa was equivalent to the English "spouse" and that noa marriage united individual men of an appropriate marriage class with individual women of another. Pirauru marriage observed the same class rules but united many men with many women (Howitt 1891:53–55). Howitt clearly viewed pirauru marriage as the "missing link" between the "undivided commune" and individual marriage.

Pirauru marriage, in fact, was said by Howitt to account for the "unusual laxity" he observed in "intersexual relations" and "the freedom with which the Yantruwunta, Dieri, and other tribes proffered their women to friendly strangers" (1891:55–56). White settlers, he informed his readers, referred to the institution as "the paramour custom" (Howitt 1891:55). Pirauru couples were assigned to each other by the elders shortly before circumcision ceremonies, which involved a brief period of ceremonial license. At each circumcision ceremony, new pirauru partners were assigned, but men and women also kept their old ones (Howitt 1891:56). The end result was, effectively, a form of group marriage, though male and female pirauru partners did not form discrete corporate groups. Howitt argued that pirauru marriage is "clearly a form of group marriage" (1891:89). However, the picture that emerges from Howitt's description of the institution is one of crosscutting networks of sexual access rather than of groups of men having rights in corresponding groups of women. The pirauru partners of a man or woman were dispersed over a wide area and were available for sex, protection, and economic cooperation when movement through the territory created a need for them, but noa husbands maintained primary rights to their wives. The consent of a woman's noa husband, if he was present, had to be sought, except during periods of ceremonial license. Howitt remarked that paternity was often uncertain under this arrangement (1891:57, 58).

Howitt acknowledges that forms of capture and the jus primae noctis accompanied some marriages in this group of tribes. [7] He cites J. M. O'Donnell on the Kunandaburi to the effect that when a woman who had been promised to a man came of age, other men whose class membership would have made them potential husbands helped him drag her off, "biting and screaming, while the other women look on laughing." The men shared the woman for hours or days before she was claimed by her individual husband, who could punish her by "beating or by cutting [her] with a knife" if she attempted to run away (Howitt 1891:61).

Howitt took issue with some of his contemporaries on key issues of kinship theory. He disagreed with McLennan, for example, because McLennan saw the *origin* of marriage in the capture of women, whose scarcity had driven men to a form of polyandry. He described Bachofen's idea of a primitive gynocracy as "grotesque" and Maine's notion of primitive patriarchy, accompanied by polygyny, as more appropriate for ancient Aryans and Semites than for true primitives (Howitt 1891:103–104). Howitt saw exchange, not capture, as the force that impelled the evolution of marriage and saw group marriage, not the capture of individual women, as the original form. He argues that noa marriage is a late form of marriage that emerged out of group marriage as exchange became a more important feature of social life, just as group marriage replaced an even earlier period of promiscuity, of which only traces remained, for the same reason (Howitt 1891:103).

Howitt suggests that the peoples of Australia might be profitably seen as forming a continuum, with the Dieri near one end of the series and the Kamilaroi and Kurnai at the other. The Dieri group would be characterized as having group marriage "at all times, modifying the rights of the individual husband," while those groups at the Kamilaroi end of the spectrum gave the husband exclusive control over his wife's sexuality, except for "rare occurrences of extensive license." In between were tribes where periods of license were more frequent than among the Kamilaroi and Kurnai but where such license was, nonetheless, a "temporary reversion" to a group marriage that was no longer a permanent state of affairs (Howitt 1891:101–102). Howitt concluded that the social organization of Australian Aborigines was "based upon the relations of the sexes regulated according to their conception of morality" and that "the moral sentiment is as strong in its way with them as with us" (1891:88–89). Nonetheless, he believed that his work "proved conclusively" that "in Australia, at the present day, group marriage does exist in a well-marked form which is evidently only the modified survival of a still more complete social communism" (Howitt 1891:104).

In *The Native Tribes of Central Australia* Spencer and Gillen furnished further evidence in favor of the theory of group marriage. They discussed the *piraunguru* custom of the Urabunna, which was very similar to the pirauru marriage of the neighboring Dieri, although they furnished much less clear detail than Howitt (Spencer and Gillen 1899:62–64, 109). Their primary work was with the Arunta. Their findings were based in part on Gillen's acquaintance with the Arunta people and a short period of fieldwork during which they witnessed the *engwura* sequence of male initiation ceremonies. They had no doubt that the Arunta practiced some forms of group marriage. The Arunta had two patrimoieties, but it was their divisions (marriage classes or sections and subsections) that regulated marriage. The Southern Arunta had a four-section system, but an eight-section system was found among the Northern Arunta. Among the Arunta a marriageable man and woman (*unawa*) were usually classificatory cross-cousins but not first cousins. Prior to marriage to a single man who had to be an unawa an Arunta woman was taken out into the bush by a group of men that did not include her future husband (Spencer and Gillen 1899:92, 93). Her vulva was then cut.[8] Those members of the party of males who were members of appropriate kinship categories then had sexual access to the woman. After this ceremonial intercourse was complete the woman was given away to her husband, who was to exercise primary but not exclusive sexual rights over her (Spencer and Gillen 1899:92, 93).

Spencer and Gillen also note a form of license that was practiced at corroborees. A husband might allow a son-in-law (actual or classificatory) to have sexual access to his wife. In normal times rules of strict mother-in-law avoidance were in force (Spencer and Gillen 1899:97). For Spencer and Gillen, the premarriage ceremony was a living survival of group marriage and the license at corroborees was a ritual reenactment of ancestral conditions during the Alcheringa, or Dreamtime. They were dismissive of explanations for such customs that discounted group marriage.[9] However, they stressed that all forms of Aboriginal marriage were subject to rules and that marriages were arranged through peaceful negotiations, not violent abduction. Promiscuity "did not exist" as a normal feature of society, despite a lesser degree of sexual jealousy than existed in white society (Spencer and Gillen 1899:105, 99, 100).

Marriage classes among the Arunta did not own totems, which were assigned according to women's encounters with ancestral spirits at the time of conception. The Arunta believed that ancestral beings wandered the countryside and were transformed into natural objects such as stones, trees, witchetty grubs, emus, and frogs. Each totem had its own totem center. A woman passing through the territory associated with a particular totem might conceive a child as the result of a local totemic spirit's entering her body, regardless of her or her husband's affiliation. As there was considerable room for interpretation after the fact, children were often assigned to their fathers' totems, but there was no need for them to be. Thus, the Arunta provided a negative instance for the purported link between totemism and exogamy (Spencer and Gillen 1899:112–127).

The indigenous theory of totemism presented to Spencer and Gillen by their informants was one that clearly denied physiological paternity:

> Added to this we have amongst the Arunta, Kuritcha, and Alpirra tribes, and probably also amongst others such as the Warramunga, the idea firmly held that the child is not the direct result of intercourse, that it may come without this, which, merely, as it were[,] . . . prepares the mother for the reception and birth also of an already formed spirit child who inhabits one of the local totem centres. *Time after time we have questioned them on this point, and always received the reply that the child was not the direct result of intercourse.* (Spencer and Gillen 1899:265, emphasis added)

When one asks questions pertaining to potentially contested points of biology or cosmology, it is important that one frames the questions well, that communication is honest, and that one understands the replies. Spencer and Gillen did not inform their readers precisely how this question was asked, as such refinements of methodology had hardly developed. Gillen did understand some Arunta, but interpreters were used, and presumably not all were reliable. We cannot be sure of the reliability of their information in this instance, but that does not mean that it was false.

In keeping with this statement of native belief Spencer and Gillen denied that subincision could be a form of birth control. They note that the only barrier to an unsustainable increase in population was the frequent practice of infanticide. Following the suggestion of the physiologist (and occasional anthropologist) Edward Charles Stirling, they reject the depiction of subincision by Edward Micklethwaite Curr, Charles Sturt, and others as "the terrible rite." However, they do view it as "a most extraordinary practise" and are surprised to hear that opening the urethra along its entire length does not usually produce dire medical results (Spencer and Gillen 1899:263–265).

Although no product of the new science of ethnography, written in the colonial periphery, could yet command the reputation of armchair works like *The Golden Bough*, written by an esteemed scholar at Cambridge University, Sir James Frazer, *The Native Tribes of Central Australia* quickly became the late Victorian and Edwardian equivalent of a citation classic. The authors' style was graceful, the data were sometimes sensational, and the work had the imprimatur of their patron, Frazer himself. Furthermore, the work incorporated a new technology. Spencer and Gillen included more than 130 of their own photographs. They were mainly of Arunta ceremonial, but there were also prints of personal ornaments, stone axes, shields, boomerangs, knives, and decorative designs. Gillen had become an amateur photographer before his collaboration with Spencer.

In 1901 Spencer and Gillen went on a yearlong expedition on camelback through Central Australia. They took with them a Kinematograph (a movie camera) and an Edison concert phonograph with wax cylinders. Spencer, who had to learn the art of cinephotography from scratch in a desert environment with the cumbersome equipment of those early days, succeeded in producing footage of several Arunta rituals. He wrote articles for a Melbourne newspaper describing the expedition. He also gave public lectures on his return. In her excellent book *Wondrous Difference* Alison Griffiths tells us that Spencer found it necessary to warn his potential audience that he would be displaying photographs of naked savages. She speculates that this warning was perhaps also designed to attract an audience eager to encounter

visions of naked sexual alterity, although neither the lectures nor the photographs were remotely pornographic (Griffiths 2002:162–166). How the
Arunta would have felt had they known that Spencer was exhibiting images
of their secret ceremonies to large, unknown audiences is quite another
matter. As far as they knew, only Spencer's two friends, Fison and Howitt,
were to see them (Griffiths 2002:165).

It took more than a decade for the full impact of the work of Spencer
and Gillen to be appreciated. Even those who did not agree with some of
its arguments or disputed its data made much use of it. It informed not
only Frazer's *Totemism and Exogamy* (1910) but also Durkheim's *The Elementary Forms of the Religious Life* (1912) and Malinowski's first book, *The
Family among the Australian Aborigines* (1913). As we have indicated, some
of the book's most influential findings concerned the Arunta's ignorance
of physiological paternity, a notion that sharpened the image of Australian
primitivity, and their supposedly anomalous form of totemism, a pertur-
bation that contributed to the demise of totemism as a key problematic of
evolutionism.[10]

Within a few years of the publication of *Native Tribes*, W. E. Roth described ideas of conception similar but not identical to those of the Arunta
among the Tully River blacks far away in Queensland (Leach 1969:118–119;
Montagu 1974:141–149). However, the Tully River blacks did acknowledge
physiological paternity among animals as opposed to humans.

In *The Northern Tribes of Central Australia* Spencer and Gillen confirmed
that among the Northern Arunta there was no necessary connection between an individual's totem clan and the clans of his or her father or mother.
Accordingly, Frazer decided that it was time to revise his own theory of
totemism. In 1890 he had already expressed a view quite different from
that of Robertson Smith, that totemism arose because savages could not
imagine an immaterial rather than an embodied soul, and they accordingly
conceived of individual souls as deposited in plants and animals (Stocking
1995:141, 142). In 1899 Frazer had created a second theory, which envisaged
totemism as ceremonial collective magic dedicated to increasing the supply
of desired totemic species (Ackerman 1987:203). There was a division of
labor whereby each different group within the tribe was made responsible
for the increase of a particular species and accordingly built up a relationship of respect toward it. In an essay published in the *Fortnightly Review*
in 1905 Frazer claimed that Arunta conceptional totemism was the original
form of that institution and as such preceded magic aimed at increasing the
food supply. Frazer's third theory of totemism presupposed a philosophy of

evolution that saw the primitive mind as childlike or the primitive body as oversexed:

> So astounding an ignorance of natural causation cannot but date from a past immeasurably remote. Yet that ignorance, strange as it may seem to us, may be explained easily enough from the habits and modes of thought of savage man. In the first place, the interval which elapses between the act of impregnation and the first symptoms of pregnancy is sufficient to prevent him from perceiving the connection between the two. In the second place, the custom, common among savage tribes, of allowing unrestricted license of intercourse between the sexes under puberty has familiarised him with sexual unions that are necessarily sterile; from which he may not unnaturally conclude that the intercourse of the sexes has nothing to do with the birth of offspring. Hence he is driven to account for pregnancy and childbirth in some other way. . . . Nothing is commoner among savages the world over than a belief that a person may be possessed by a spirit. . . . Now, when a woman is observed to be pregnant, the savage infers with perfect truth that something has entered into her. What is it? And how does it make its way into her womb? (1905:455)

If one strips away the assumptions about "unrestricted license" and the patronizing language ("savages the world over"), and they are not merely incidental, one is left with assertions that someone born outside a culture with a scientific tradition might not connect initial intercourse with "the quickening" and might well conclude that, inasmuch as most acts of intercourse (particularly before full puberty) do not lead to pregnancy, intercourse is not causally linked to pregnancy or is certainly not the sole cause of it.

As for conception totemism itself, George Stocking has analyzed the version of the above text that appeared in the first volume of *Totemism and Exogamy* (Frazer 1910, vol. 1:139–172). With some irony, he observes that Frazer's primitive philosopher changes sex in midstream. A pregnant woman might identify her quickening with a natural event that catches her fancy, for example, a lizard jumps nearby, a butterfly flies above, a moonbeam shines. When the child is born, its physical features may bear the impress of spirit entry – it may be said to look like a lizard. The source of conception totemism is, therefore, the "sick fantasies of pregnant women" (quoted in Stocking 1995:144). The argument we have just reviewed is not typical of Frazer, who rarely wrote explicitly about sexual topics. Leach notes, for example, that "although 'fertility' is one of the central themes of Frazer's *The Golden Bough*, human sexual intercourse is mentioned only as a magical procedure for improving the crops!" (1984:6).

One of the most prominent defenders of the theory of primitive ignorance of paternity was the Gloucester solicitor Edwin Sidney Hartland, who was twice president of the Folklore Society in Britain. He had published work on the folklore of his native Gloucestershire as well as on the folklore of European peasants and the classical world. In volume 1 of *The Legend of Perseus* (1894) Hartland achieved a considerable reputation among literati by his exposition of the story of Perseus's birth through the miraculous fertilization of Danae by Zeus during a shower of rain. Using the comparative method, Hartland showed how this story was one of a body of *Märchen* that told of the miraculous birth of heroes. Sometimes the mothers were virgins. Often the mode of impregnation was irregular and involved an unusual part of the mother's body (an example was the common European tale that the Holy Ghost had impregnated the Virgin Mary through her ear).

Around the end of the 1890s Hartland decided that the traditions of primitive peoples were also part of folklore. During the first decade of the 20th century he defended anthropological folklore against detractors who believed that the new discipline should concern itself only with "Aryan" peoples, and he defended the Tylorian tradition against individuals such as Andrew Lang who sought to diminish the evolutionary distance between primitive and civilized peoples (Dorson 1968:238–248). In the two volumes of *Primitive Paternity* (1909, 1910) Hartland repeated much of the argument of *The Legend of Perseus* and then proceeded to deal with primitive morality and ignorance of physiological paternity. Some primitive beliefs concerning the birth of ordinary people resembled common folkloric accounts of the birth of heroes.

Hartland's argument is simple enough. He maintained that most primitive peoples throughout the world have low morals, although there is some degree of variation. He thought primitive men allowed other men more liberties with their wives than they would if they understood the facts of conception. The comparative rarity of pregnancy, as compared to intercourse, made it less likely that people of low intelligence would notice a connection between the two. The replacement of mother right by father right makes little difference unless there is some degree of social advancement. He spends 150 pages advancing this point. For example:

Among the Hurons Charlevoix reports that the young people of both sexes abandoned themselves without shame to all sorts of dissolute practices. (Hartland 1967:105)

Mr. Monteiro, writing of the Mussorongo Ambriz and Mushicongo tribes, says: "The Negro knows not love affection or jealousy . . . ." (Hartland 1967:116, ellipses in original)

[On the Malagasy:] Their sensuality "is universal and unconcealed." (Hartland 1967:153)

The Russian peasants . . . attach but too little importance to the sexual relations supposed to be safeguarded by their Church. (Hartland 1967:188)

Before she is handed over to him she has to undergo a cruel and revolting rite which is performed with the cognisance [of], but not among the Arunta, in the presence of the bridegroom (if we may dignify him by that name). (Hartland 1967:224)

Not surprisingly, Hartland mentions Howitt's Dieri and W. H. R. Rivers's Todas of southern India (see below) as well as the Arunta (1967:109–113, 158–160), but his language is always less guarded and markedly more pejorative than in the original accounts.

One compelling reason for primitive ignorance of paternity was the frequency of intercourse involving prepubertal children. Such unions would, of course, be sterile. Furthermore, sexual intercourse between young girls and adult men often caused "such injury to the sexual organs as may seriously affect the reproductive powers after maturity is reached" (Hartland 1967:254). It is not quite clear what Hartland means by this statement, but he did offer his readers a worldwide database of actual and alleged prepubertal sex and child marriage, noting that such practices were, "as might be expected, very common on the continent of Africa" (1967:263).

A mere 90 years separate us from *Primitive Paternity*. The modern reader finds it hard to separate sane but perhaps misguided statements about the possible, rational causes for ignorance of physiological paternity from the matrix of racial prejudice in which many of them are embedded. It is perhaps significant that the most extreme, value-laden statements concerning primitive sexuality, sexual knowledge, and social institutions come not from the early fieldworkers such as Howitt, Spencer, and Gillen, although they were all believers in group marriage and *ignorantia paternitatis*, but from two of the armchair theoreticians, Frazer and Hartland, who partially misread and exaggerated their findings.

Hartland bequeathed no intellectual legacy to anthropology because his ideas died with his generation. The same cannot be said of Rivers, the experimental psychologist who studied color perception in the Torres Strait Islands in 1898, the inventor of the genealogical method, the student of Toda polyandry, the prominent evolutionist who became a diffusionist, the medical psychiatrist of Craiglockhart, and, at the very end of his life, the socialist who decried the destruction of Melanesian culture. He is the subject of an acclaimed biography by Richard Slobodin (1978) and a protagonist in a fictional trilogy by Pat Barker based on his work with shell-shocked officers at Craiglockhart. He too believed in group marriage, after a fashion. He was able to study a people who actually combined female infanticide and polyandry and sometimes polygyny as well.

Rivers visited the Todas of the Nilgiri Hills in southern India for a total of five months in 1901–2. His fieldwork involved the use of an interpreter who was a Christian catechist (Stocking 1995:189). The Todas were and still are a cattle-keeping people, and much of Rivers's ethnography is occupied with a description of their sacred dairies. However, it is his brief account of their system of kinship and marriage (Rivers 1967:502–539) that has remained in the collective memories of anthropologists. The Todas are divided into two castelike endogamous moieties, each of which is subdivided into exogamous clans. Premarital sexual relationships were the norm, although girls were betrothed (and sometimes formally married) in early childhood. Cross-cousin marriage was preferred, and brother–sister exchange sometimes took place. Marriage was ideally polyandrous. The husbands were often real or classificatory brothers. When the wife became pregnant, the eldest brother presented her with a miniature bow and arrow (the *pursütpumi* ceremony), thereby legitimizing the future offspring. The brothers were not the only potential genitors of a child. Women had formal and informal, temporary and permanent sexual partners in addition to their legal husbands. Rivers said that the Todas had no concept of adultery and little in the way of jealousy. Casual lovers would therefore not even be noted. The formal extramarital unions included partnerships with males in the opposite half of the tribe who were forbidden as legal husbands by the endogamy rule. There were also approved liaisons with keepers of the sacred dairies. Men could also pass on their wives to others in exchange for a payment, but in these cases the new partner became a legal husband. Rivers observed that the Todas had a reputation for low morality among neighboring tribes and that their morality was indeed low by European standards. However, his analysis of 43 cases of color blindness demonstrated to Rivers that women were more faithful to their husbands than the Todas' reputation and self-image might lead one to expect. Familial color blindness followed patterns that indicated that a substantial portion of color-blind men were indeed the genitors of their wives' children (Rivers 1967:532–533).

Rivers was intrigued to note the coincidence between female infanticide and polyandry that McLennan might have led him to expect. However, he was unsure whether female infanticide was a cause or an effect of polyandry. In any case, he noted that the Todas might well have brought the institution of polyandry from elsewhere and that infanticide was declining because of missionary pressure. As the sex ratio changed, polygyny was occurring. Some marriages were simultaneously polyandrous and polygynous, leading to a state of de facto (but not institutionalized) group marriage. Rivers felt that this state of affairs might well be a transitional point on the way to monogamy (1967:519). The authorial tone with which Rivers discusses these matters is quite dispassionate for the period, considering the nature of his data. To some extent, the detached approach he takes is an artifact of the scientific method, which Rivers, the medical doctor, wished to impart to ethnographic research. The discussion of color blindness and sexual morality is one form of evidence for this, as is his famous use of formal genealogies, both to determine marriage rules and to document their relationship to actual practice. The Todas, in this early ethnography, are very much objects of the anthropological gaze rather than subjects in their own right, but they are not conscripted as counterexamples to Victorian or Edwardian sexual orthodoxy.

One year after *The Todas* appeared Rivers published his famous paper, "On the Origins of the Classificatory System of Relationships" (1907). He thus became active in two related debates concerning the referents of relationship terminologies and the place of "group marriage" in social evolution. The debate over the significance of kin terms begun by Morgan and McLennan could thus be resumed 30 years later by Rivers and Kroeber. What concerns us here is that, like Morgan, Rivers believed that relationship terminologies were not "mere forms of address" or artifacts of the psychology of language but rather referred to present or, more often, to past social forms. Rivers agreed with Morgan that contemporary relationship terminologies often encoded systems of consanguinity and affinity, but he noted that they could refer to factors other than biological kinship such as clan membership, age, and generational status, indeed, to a varied set of social rights, duties, and privileges. The Malayan terminology was not, as Morgan thought, a survival of that stage of "the consanguine family" where parent–child incest was banned but brother–sister relationships were permitted, but was instead a marker of relationships based on generational status. However, Rivers felt that terminologies of Morgan's Ganowanian and Turanian types (Iroquoian, Crow, Omaha, and Dravidian in our contemporary usage) were indeed survivals of the practice of group marriage, which he saw as the marriage of all the members of one moiety, class, or clan to all the members of another (Stocking 1995:195). In 1907 Rivers also published a review of Northcote Thomas's *Kinship Organisations and Group Marriage in Australia* (1906). In his review Rivers advanced the notion that pirauru marriage and allied institutions represented transitional forms, somewhere in between group marriage and individual marriage, suggesting that some term other than "marriage" be used for such customs. He also stated, however, that he believed it possible that more research on the Australian continent would turn up cases of genuine group marriage, still in existence at the time he wrote (Rivers 1907b:90–92).

At the beginning of the 20th century, both continuities and changes were evident in anthropological discussions of kinship and marriage. On the one hand, many still held the belief that human evolution had been accompanied by an increasing diminution of sexual license. On the other hand, that belief was increasingly one that needed to be defended. It was even beginning to be challenged by its equally distancing converse, a belief that primitives were less highly sexed than their civilized counterparts. As we shall see in the following chapters, as the 20th century moved on, those who drafted primitive sexuality into blueprints for social engineering were increasingly inclined to see or imagine in it things that modernity would do well to import rather than a simple list of dangers that the civilized were enjoined to eschew.

CHAPTER 4

The Reconstruction of "Primitive Sexuality" at the Fin de Siècle

In the eighteenth century, when savage tribes in various parts of the world first began to be visited, extravagantly romantic views widely prevailed as to the simple and idyllic lives led by primitive peoples. During the greater part of the nineteenth century, the tendency of opinion was to the opposite extreme, and it became usual to insist on the degraded and licentious morals of savages. . . .

In reality, however, savage life is just as little a prolonged debauch as a protracted idyll.

Havelock Ellis, *Analysis of the Sexual Impulse*

T he period we are now to examine is one in which anthropology is institutionalized in the United States (the American Anthropological Association is founded) and is taught in universities for the first time in the United States and Great Britain, ethnography in the true sense is first written, Australian kinship studies mature, and Durkheim's school flourishes in France. This is the time when the British imperium in Africa is solidified, and at home the welfare state is making its first tentative appearance during a period of class struggle. It is the period of jingoism, the Spanish-American War, the Boer War, and World War I. The eugenics movement flourished on both sides of the Atlantic, in the academy and in the halls of power. Psychoanalysis was born, and there also appeared several works of sexology or, as Michel Foucault would say, *scientia sexualis*. These included Richard von Krafft-Ebing's *Psychopathia Sexualis* (1886); *Das Weib* by Hermann Ploss (1885); John Gregory Bourke's *Scatologic Rites of All Nations* (1891); Havelock Ellis and John Addington Symonds's *Sexual Inversion* (1897); Ellis's *The Evolution of Modesty* (1899), *Analysis of the Sexual Impulse* (1903), and *Sex in Relation to Society* (1910); Edward Westermarck's *The*

History of Human Marriage (1891) and *The Origin and Development of Moral Ideas* (1906–8); Sigmund Freud's report of his analysis of "Dora" (1905); and Ernest Crawley's *The Mystic Rose* (1902). Crawley's *Studies of Savages and Sex* (1929) is a posthumous work that re-creates the Zeitgeist of the world preceding Mead and Malinowski.[1]

According to Foucault, discourse in this period validated and naturalized the status of the heterosexual, procreating couple and created a buzz around the figures of the perverse adult, the masturbating child, the Malthusian couple, and the hysterical woman (1980:105). In Britain there was doubtless less stigmatization of the Malthusian couple than in France, but contraceptive advice remained a matter of controversy. Foucault did not consider a fifth sexual Other, "the differently sexed savage," nor did he examine the place of the anthropologist in the structures of knowledge and power he so famously elaborated. In this chapter we shall attempt, among other things, to undertake these tasks.

Anthropologists' representations of the sexuality of primitives underwent radical changes in the years between 1885 and the Great War. Ellis, Westermarck, and Crawley did more than anyone else to revise widely held opinions on such matters. Andrew Lang and Northcote Thomas also made their contributions. Evolutionary fantasies about primitive promiscuity, marriage by capture, and exotic forms of sexual abuse were already suspect by the time the first classics of modern ethnography were written, though we have long since learned not to expect any simplistic replacement of fantasy by "truth." Historians of social anthropology have dealt relatively little with the circumstances that led to the disappearance of these illusions. To a degree, the works of these three thinkers were informed by new data, but they were also fictions of the fin de siècle, refractions of ideas concerning racial and sexual difference, sexual freedom, and restriction. Furthermore, the late Victorian and Edwardian eras saw a series of attacks on the familial institutions and gender concepts of the mid-Victorian era. It is our contention that those attacks, which came from both the advocates of social purity and the proponents of sexual liberty, paralleled a refashioning of the images of primitive strangers so that such images could continue to serve as foils for a new generation.

The reader of textbooks in anthropology, whether they are historical compendia or introductory surveys, will learn little of these five thinkers, whose contributions have been largely obliterated from our collective memory. Ellis, the author of the seven volumes of *Studies in the Psychology of Sex*, which originally appeared between the 1890s and the 1920s, is regarded as a quaint but interesting scholar, overshadowed by his great contemporary, Freud, and as such has been the subject of two excellent biographies (Brome 1979; Grosskurth 1980). He is not usually regarded as an anthropologist. Westermarck is known to regional specialists as an early ethnographer of Morocco and to most anthropologists as the inventor of one or two theories concerning incest that are dimly recalled from their oversimplified and garbled traduction in introductory textbooks. Most anthropologists today will complete their careers without reading a word he wrote. Brief summaries of *The Mystic Rose* appear in a few modern sources (Honigmann 1976:185–187; Evans-Pritchard 1965:35–37), but little is said of the book's author. During their lifetimes, both Ellis and Westermarck enjoyed intellectual celebrity and, in Ellis's case, some notoriety. Crawley, an Anglican churchman who briefly was headmaster of a public school and subsequently wrote articles of general scientific interest for *Nature*, received plaudits from many of his contemporaries, including Edwin Sidney Hartland, Arnold van Gennep, and Westermarck (Theodore Besterman in Crawley 1931:vii), and from one distinguished successor (Malinowski 1962). Crawley's primary success was outside academe. He was a player of lawn tennis and a sportswriter. His obituary notice in the *Times* (October 25, 1924) contains the remark: "He was also known as an anthropologist." As for Lang, he is best remembered as a folklorist. Thomas is remembered as an interesting footnote in the history of the armchair anthropology of kinship and social organization, though, as we shall see in the next chapter, he played a not dishonorable role as the first ever government anthropologist.

One can only surmise the reasons for such oblivion. The modern academic is easily bored by the lengthy compilations of data that were so beloved by both practitioners of the older physical anthropology and exponents of the comparative method. Yet many still read Lewis Henry Morgan and Edward Tylor. A more telling point is that historical memory is always shaped by current concerns, for example, intellectualist versus sociological theories of religion, the evolution of social organization, and, more recently, "the invention of kinship" as well as, for that matter, the invention of nearly everything else (see Kuper 1988). Only latterly did human sexuality and sexual or gender difference reemerge as *acknowledged* problematics within anthropology. Last but not least, transition points in the history of any discipline are notoriously difficult to comprehend. Paradigms erode slowly and in ways that often elude the consciousness of innovators. Transitional perspectives frequently appear as wrongheaded to modern readers as the paradigms they replace; nonetheless, they are both the products and the agents of changed intellectual and social climates. Sensitivity to the nuances of change can bridge the apparent chasms of difference that emerge when recent systems of truth and error are compared to older ones.

The movement from social evolutionism to historical particularism and cultural relativism has been well explored by some historians of American anthropology (e.g., Harris 1969; Stocking 1968). On the other hand, the parallel movement toward relativism and functionalism (as well as the hyperdiffusionist detour) in British anthropology has been less exhaustively detailed (apart from Stocking 1995 and Langham 1981). Insofar as this movement encompassed changes in our view of kinship and marriage, it both drew upon and contributed to changes in broad cultural understandings of sexuality. The very replacement of "sex" as a category of understanding by the more neutral "kinship and marriage" during the years when functionalism dominated British anthropology has helped to erase the importance of fin de siècle debates about primitive and modern sexuality from the collective memory of anthropologists. It is our contention that challenges to notions of sexual morality in fin de siècle society contributed to a tendency to replace fictive images of lascivious savages with representations of primitives as either less highly sexed than civilized men and women, less imaginative in their exercise of the sexual function, or blocked by taboo or environmental restraints from the full exercise of their libidos.

BACKGROUND

In earlier chapters we argued that there were not one but several discourses about sexuality in 19th-century anthropology but that the highly sexed primitive was a figure common to most of them. Iconography and popular culture also employed images of oversexualized primitives. Sander Gilman's brilliant essay "The Hottentot and the Prostitute: Towards an Iconography of Female Sexuality" (1985:76–108) commences with an account of Édouard Manet's painting *Olympia* (1862–63), which shows a naked white female attended by a black female servant. The reader is then introduced to other 19th-century images of oversexualized females, including the exhibitions involving Saat-Jee, the "Hottentot Venus," and photographs and plates from volumes by Pauline Tarnowsky and by Cesare Lombroso and Guglielmo Ferrero that depict genital anomalies and peculiarly atavistic facial features in both Hottentot females and modern European prostitutes. The images that Gilman analyzes are used to establish links between the sexualized female body, primitivity, behavioral excess, biological degeneracy, and the underclass of those times. Ideas of degeneracy and evolutionary atavism had become particularly prominent by the fin de siècle. A current of pessimism about urbanization, industrialism, and social instability was reflected in the belief that modern society could unwittingly defeat the forces of natural selection and allow the undesirable elements that flourished in its unhealthy cities to reverse the tide of progress. The equation between "savages" and real and imagined "enemies within" became even more specifically concerned with bodies and physiology as the new sciences of sexology and criminology were brought to bear on social crises and moral panics. Homosexuals, Jews, criminals, prostitutes, artists, and the insane were all seen as threats to the entire community (Gilman 1985).

Several feminist historians (see, e.g., Russett 1989; Levy 1991) have discussed the oversexualizing of the female body during the Victorian era, noting that wanton savage women were often depicted as warnings of the need to control all female sexuality. Such authors, however, pay little if any attention to the parallel treatment of primitive males. John and Robin Haller, in *The Physician and Sexuality in Victorian America* (1974), discuss 19th-century ideas of male sexual evolution but say relatively little about the treatment of primitive women. Susan Kingsley Kent, in *Sex and Suffrage in Britain, 1860–1914* (1987), provides an excellent account of the social and political ramifications of the Victorian double standard but is not concerned with the anthropological literature. In truth, the processes described by all of these authors reinforced each other in the creation of the tropic portrait of the oversexed savage.

Men of the Victorian middle classes were allowed more sexual indulgence than respectable women. Despite this, men were believed to be characterized by a higher mental development, making them less subject to the demands of their reproductive systems than their wives, provided they had not obstructed their mental development at an early age by indulgence in the "solitary vice." Images of primitive sexuality that saw male and female alike as debauched shored up a number of planks in the construction of the Victorian sexual and gender system. Such images underscored a belief in greater sexual differentiation the higher one went up the evolutionary ladder. Men, confronted with lecherous savage ancestors, might excuse their visits to prostitutes as inevitable expressions of male nature while at the same time congratulating themselves on hours spent in the study, the office, or the laboratory. Women, on the other hand, whose lives were centered mainly upon marriage and reproduction, might, as Levy suggests, be warned that their elevation above the primitive was tenuous at best and depended upon strict adherence to domestic norms. When norms came under attack at the fin de siècle, differentiations between men and women, savage and civilized remained salient, but some of the terms of the comparisons changed their value, and new tropes emerged.

There were early criticisms of the hypothesis of primitive promiscuity. That notion clearly contradicted Sir Henry Maine's opinions concerning the early patriarchal family, and, not surprisingly, he attacked it (1883:208). Others were more reserved as to their opinions. In correspondence with Westermarck Tylor requested that Westermarck, who was preparing a second edition of *The History of Human Marriage*, ensure that "I am put right in the Introduction, as an unbeliever in 'communal marriage'" (December 15, 1893, in Wikman 1940:12). His opposition had not been very public.

Sir Charles Darwin gave the theory a lukewarm endorsement in *The Descent of Man*. He was disturbed because his own reading suggested that higher apes (e.g., gorillas) were characterized by small families headed by jealous males. The gregarious, promiscuous commune conjured into being by the "matriarchal" theorists contradicted the principle of continuity in evolution. Furthermore, it would not allow for the individual choice on which his theory of sexual selection depended. However, Sir John Lubbock was his friend, neighbor, and ally, and Darwin did not regard himself as an expert in the new social anthropology. He thought that the marriage tie was very loose in many primitive societies and that there was much sexual license, but he doubted the necessity for "believing in absolutely promiscuous intercourse" (Darwin 1981:360).

In his discussion of sexual selection Darwin remarks that women, unlike men, do not delight in competition but are tender, unselfish, and nurturant. However, he noted: "It is generally admitted that with woman the powers of intuition, of rapid perception, and perhaps of imitation, are more strongly marked than in man; but some, at least, of these faculties are characteristic of the lower races, and therefore of a past and lower state of civilisation" (Darwin 1981:326, 327). Furthermore, as Francis Galton had noted, few women had excelled in the arts, history, philosophy, and science. *Overall*, "the average of mental power in man must be above that of woman" (Darwin 1981:327).

Charles Staniland Wake's book *The Development of Marriage and Kinship* (1889) laid waste to the theory of primitive promiscuity, John F. McLennan's views on marriage by capture, and Lubbock's ideas on hetaerism. Wake's book was neither a commercial nor an academic success. It was cited but seldom, and its author later died in Chicago, an obscure and forgotten figure.

It was Darwin rather than Maine or Wake who inspired a revival of "patri-archal" theory during the first decade of the 20th century. His views on the family organization of the higher apes furnished a model to J. J. Atkinson, whose *Primal Law* was published in 1903, at which time Sigmund Freud was beginning to develop the theory of psychoanalysis in Vienna. For many scholars during the first half of the last century and in some small circles even today, psychoanalytic theory is the primary source of speculation on the evolution of sexuality and the family. Few scholars of any kind and few devotees of psychoanalytical theory read *Primal Law*, the book that was the foundation stone of Freud's theory of the origin of religion, the incest taboo, and the Oedipus complex, as expressed in *Totem and Taboo* (1913). All of these phenomena, and with them culture itself, were imagined by Freud to have been born of the guilt felt by a horde of young men after an uprising during which they killed their fathers and subsequently married their mothers.

That Atkinson's work ever saw the light of day was due to his own cousin Andrew Lang, the distinguished folklorist, who published the work together with his own *Social Origins* after the author's death. Lang explained the origin of exogamy with reference to Crawley's theory of the need to avoid harmful contact with females and to his cousin's theory. Atkinson's argu-ment was a compote of patriarchal theory (but not Maine's version of it), common ideas of primitive brutality, Darwin's observations on gorilla fam-ily organization, as well as the projections of his own imagination. Atkinson postulated the existence of an archaic family, headed by a senior male, who had sole access to the women of the group, including his own daughters. Bands of exiled young males seized women by force from other family groups. Eventually, mothers demanded that their sons be allowed to remain in the group, but, in exchange, the patriarchs demanded that the sons re-nounce access to their own mothers. Émile Durkheim published a review of the Lang and Atkinson volume in the *Année Sociologique* in which he was somewhat sardonic about Atkinson's speculations about a past that was almost prehuman (1902–3:410–411).[2]

To Atkinson's theory, Freud added just a few key elements: parricide, mother–son incest, guilt, and totemism. Briefly, Freud argued that men invented totemism and the incest taboo out of guilt stemming from a mass slaying of fathers by sons followed by the sexual appropriation of the mur-derers' mothers. The memory of the father, displaced onto totemic animals, could be both honored and erased by taboos surrounding the killing and eating of the totems. Interestingly, Freud's theory of totemism is entirely based on male desire, male agency (parricide, war between the brothers, instigation of totemism). He does not consider why women in such societies also believe in totemism. In this he differs from Atkinson's original version of the primal horde theory: Atkinson thought that the driving out of the young males had ended because the mothers insisted on it once human ancestors had evolved enough for long, close relationships between mothers and children to develop. Atkinson's theory, though it is a crucial part of a general trend away from matriarchal theory (though some, like Robert Briffault, continued to believe in it), continues to allow female agency and affective relationships between men and women that are other than sexual. There is little if anything in Freud's version of patriarchal origins theory to explain why women should also believe in totemism. Matrilineally inherited totems (and hence exogamous matrilineal clans) are explained simply as a way of rendering the mother taboo.

When Freud adapted Atkinson's theory, he added to the notion of the primal, brutal primitive his own speculations concerning Australians, whose myths, he believed, revealed a more recent consciousness of incestuous desires than could be attributed to healthy, civilized adults. Adapting the popular recapitulation hypothesis ("ontogeny recapitulates phylogeny"), he compared totemism to childhood animal phobias. Such phobias are characterized by a psychic strategy whereby ambivalent sentiments toward the same-sex parent are displaced onto animals. By identifying totemism with childhood animal phobias, Freud was able to view primitives as being simultaneously childlike, irrational, guilt ridden, and closer to unsocialized sexuality than civilized adults. In this analysis of totemism lies the explanation for the fact that Freud saw primitives as simultaneously taboo ridden and sexually lascivious. This is exactly the position Freud attributes to the child late in the Oedipal phase, a point where significant limits have already been placed on the gratification of desire. It should be noted that the zero points of Atkinson's and Freud's stories of social evolution begin not with primitive promiscuity as such but with a "family" of sorts in which at least some restrictions on sexual access are maintained by the jealousy of the senior male. It requires little speculation on our own part to descry the link between Freud's assassinated patriarch, Atkinson's primal males, and, indeed, the corn god of Sir James Frazer's *The Golden Bough*, sacrificed annually only to rise again – they are all transformations of the discourse on phallic worship that we examined in an earlier chapter.

Lang died just a year before the appearance of *Totem and Taboo*, so we can only surmise what he would have thought of Freud's adaptation of

Atkinson's ideas. In *Social Origins* Lang suggested that the younger males who were cast out of the primal group (we must recall that in this version of the hypothesis the patriarchs stay alive and keep their women) obtained sexual partners by raiding other family groups. At some point members of such groups somehow got the notion of arranging themselves into pairs to facilitate the peaceful exchange of women. These newly created exogamous moieties would use animal sobriquets to insult each other, which eventually led to the emergence of totemic ideology. In *The Secret of the Totem* Lang, perhaps in an attempt to reach a compromise with some critics, suggested that phratry exogamy was given a religious meaning through the introduction of totemic taboos (1905:125). In short, instead of commencing with the "undivided commune" (which did not resemble "the family" in any sense we would recognize), social evolution commences with family bands dominated by patriarchs. Moiety and clan exogamy were thus not the product of an "unconscious reformation" that led to the dividing of the original group but were instead the product of conscious alliance between formerly warring groups. Given that Lang rejected the evolutionary sequence embraced by Morgan, Lorimer Fison, A. W. Howitt, and Baldwin Spencer, it is not surprising that he also rejected the idea of universal ignorance of paternity among primitives. He was willing to concede that the Arunta denied the father's role in procreation. However, he observed that other Australian groups who were as primitive as or more primitive than the Arunta were perfectly aware of physiological paternity. For this reason he suspected that such nescience was a unique product of Arunta dogmas about reincarnation rather than simple ignorance (Lang 1905:190–193). In no way did Lang wish totally to deny distance and differentiation between Australian Aborigines and ourselves, but he did see the differences as being less radical than did some of his contemporaries. His rejection of matriarchal theory accompanied a rejection of the Tylorian theory of animism. Lang insisted that there were residues of monotheism in Australian religion. This theoretical turn may have accompanied his interest in spiritualism.

Thomas was Lang's disciple as both an anthropologist and a spiritualist. There is, however, nothing esoteric or occult in *Kinship Organisations and Group Marriage in Australia* (1906). The book contained a long and precise exposition of what was known about Australian section systems. After completing this task Thomas launched an attack on assumptions that relationship terminologies referred to biological connection rather than "duties and status." Given that the Arunta term *unawa* covered a whole category of women whom a man might have married in addition to the person he did marry, it could not be translated into any single term in English such as "wife" (Thomas 1966:123). One would not say that "the fact that *femme* in French means both wife and woman is an argument for the existence of promiscuity in France in Roman or post-Roman times" (Thomas 1966:129). Thomas then reviewed all the Central Australian customs such as pirauru marriage and supposed variants of the jus primae noctis that had been adduced as evidence of the former practice of group marriage and concluded that each probably had a specific function and that all such customs, apart from saturnalian reversals, excluded intercourse between certain categories of people. His examination of Howitt's material on Dieri pirauru was particularly thorough, and he exposed a number of problems and contradictions in the narrative.[3]

After reviewing the work of Howitt and that of Spencer and F. J. Gillen, Thomas was hardly sure what the pirauru custom represented, but he was sure that it was not a survival of group marriage (1966:130–141). Indeed, he felt that descriptors such as "secondary marriage" were unhelpful. Thomas had previously discussed the advantages and admitted disadvantages of Westermarck's definition of "marriage" as "a more or less durable connection between male and female, lasting beyond the mere act of propagation till after the birth of the child" (1966:105). He felt that it was the best definition anthropologists had at that time. Many societies permitted forms of "gamic union" that were not perduring and did not impose the same rights and confer the same duties as marriage (Thomas 1966:106). Thomas appears to have endorsed Lang's views on Arunta nescience, but he has little to say about it (1966:12).

What Thomas displayed was an ability to talk about Australian Aboriginal sexual mores and marriage rules in a language that attempted "scientific" precision. Such language may indeed deprive Australian social life of flesh and blood, but it does try to avoid the ethnocentric excesses still so widespread in the first years of the 20th century. Such language was common in social anthropology 20 to 30 years later. By that time ideas of group marriage and primitive promiscuity were to be found only on the fringes of the discipline.

THE DEMISE OF PRIMITIVE PROMISCUITY

In 1889 Westermarck's doctoral thesis, which was to constitute the first six chapters of *The History of Human Marriage*, was accepted by his university in Finland. Two years later the complete book appeared in print. Nearly

40 years later the author described how his research led him to dispute the theory of primitive promiscuity.

> From Darwin's book I discovered that several scientists held the view that primitive man lived in a state of promiscuity – in other words, that in the earliest ages of our race individual marriage relations did not exist and all men had access to all women without distinction. He himself thought that in those times the men's jealousy would prevent such a condition, but took for granted – on the ground of Morgan's, McLennan's, and Lubbock's investigations – that promiscuity or something similar had, at a later date, been general amongst the human race. I went to the authorities he quoted, and thus at last – at twenty-five years of age – found it necessary to learn to read an English book. In the material I collected concerning the manners and customs of different peoples, I also thought I could trace remnants of earlier promiscuity; thus I began by supporting a theory which I was to dispute later on. But I had not got far before I found that I was on the wrong track. I perceived that marriage must primarily be studied in its connection with biological conditions, and that the tendency to interpret all sorts of customs as social survivals, without a careful investigation into their existing environment, is apt to lead to the most arbitrary conclusions. (Westermarck 1929:68)

Many of Westermarck's disagreements with the author of *The Descent of Man* arose from the simple fact that in many ways he was more Darwinian than Darwin himself. For instance, he felt that human racial variation could be adequately explained by natural selection and that the theory of sexual selection was at best redundant and at worst misleading. He firmly believed that some form of lasting pair bonding was part of the human inheritance from our primate ancestors. Such marriages had to last sufficiently long to ensure that children, few in number, might be nurtured until such time as they could fend for themselves. In that sense, "marriage" had a biological as well as a cultural base. He believed that monogamy was probably the prevalent form of marriage in primitive societies. Polygamous institutions were special adaptations. Polygyny was most common among advanced savages and barbarians; its causes included differentials in power, boredom on the part of men, barrenness, and the premature aging of females (Westermarck 1906–8, vol. 2:388–390). The "higher forms of civilization" favored monogamy, in part because the supply of animal milk reduced suckling time, the number of wars decreased, pregnancy taboos declined, and there was a less intense need for offspring. Additionally, civilization had made female beauty more durable. Social evolution had also resulted in changes that had favored women who benefited from monogamy: "Moreover, the sentiment of love becomes more refined, the passion for one more absorbing. The feelings of the weaker sex are frequently held in higher regard. And the better education of women enables them to live comfortably without the support of a husband" (Westermarck 1906–8, vol. 2:391). Later on we shall examine and dispute the contention that Westermarck's attitudes to monogamy constituted a defense of Victorian marriage. What concerns us now is that his Darwinian interpretation of human social history underpins and sustains his attack on theories of sexual communism.

Westermarck used several arguments to attack the theories of McLennan, Morgan, and Lubbock:

1. The theory of primitive promiscuity was based on unreliable reports by missionaries and travelers. Very often data were misinterpreted. The absence of a word for marriage in a foreign language did not entail that the institution did not exist among its speakers. New data from reliable sources, for example, E. H. Man on the Andamanese and John Mathew on the Australian Aborigines, indicated that supposedly promiscuous peoples were simply not promiscuous (Westermarck 1901:49–61).

2. Even if promiscuity did exist among some primitive peoples, no proof was available that it had always been present. Culture contact, slavery, and colonization often caused a collapse in morality and a decline in the birthrate (Westermarck 1901:66–69).

3. McLennan and Lubbock were wrong to suggest that the condition of women in very primitive communities was particularly degraded. The ethnographic evidence did not point in that direction (Westermarck 1901). Furthermore, if women had to labor hard in primitive communities, the same was true of their menfolk (Westermarck 1904:408–421).

4. The fact that a people permitted premarital sexual relations did not mean that they permitted promiscuity. The two concepts were not the same (Westermarck 1901:61–66).

5. Primitives tended to marry early in life, and few were left unmarried. More advanced peoples tended to favor late marriage, and a number of individuals were left on the shelf. For a variety of reasons the latter condition was more conducive to promiscuity than the former: "Irregular connexions between the sexes have on the whole established a tendency to increase along with the progress of civilization" (Westermarck 1901:69).

6. Lubbock had contended that institutions such as the lending of wives to

strangers and the jus primae noctis demonstrated that individuals asserting their own privileges had to make a ceremonial concession to the group. Such practices were, therefore, survivals of group marriage and primitive promiscuity. Westermarck suggested some more prosaic interpretations such as the observance of rules of hospitality (1901:72–81).

7. There was little evidence of ignorance of physiological paternity in any existing group (Westermarck 1901:105–107).

8. Morgan's analysis of relationship terminologies was faulty. McLennan had been correct to suggest that they were merely terms of address rather than accurate reflections of marriage patterns past or present (Westermarck 1901:82–96).

9. Ethnographic evidence did not indicate that matriliny inevitably preceded patriliny (Westermarck 1901:96–105).

10. Male jealousy was a biological and cultural universal in human societies. This very fact rendered it unlikely that systematic promiscuity could ever have been the rule (Westermarck 1901:115–133).

In *Analysis of the Sexual Impulse*, originally published in 1903 as volume 3 of his *Studies in the Psychology of Sex*, Ellis gave his loyal support to Westermarck on the question of primitive promiscuity. He observed that the conclusion that primitive peoples were "abandoned to debauchery" often rested on misunderstandings of customs such as wife lending and ritual intercourse (Ellis 1942a, pt. 2:260–262). Sometimes a genuine increase in promiscuity could be the consequence of interference by missionaries with established cultural practices: "Yet this dangerously unsettling process has been applied by missionaries on a wholesale scale to races which in some respect are often little more than children" (Ellis 1942a, pt. 2:261). Like Westermarck but in a much more cursory fashion, Ellis examined the ethnographic record of the time and claimed that it failed to support the hypothesis of primitive promiscuity. One of the examples he cites is particularly interesting to modern readers of J. Philippe Rushton's notorious writings. Although "the Negroid races of Africa" were reputed to be "particularly prone to sexual indulgence," a French army surgeon in his *Untrodden Fields of Anthropology* had remarked that "the negress is rather cold and indifferent to the refinements of love" (Ellis 1942b, pt. 2: 261). White men, the surgeon had noted, were particularly unlikely to satisfy black women because their penises were too small and they achieved ejaculation in too short a time.

Westermarck's Darwinism led him to consider that many features of human behavior, for example, marriage, maternal and paternal care, and maidenly coyness, were rooted in instinct and therefore "normal." In his review of the fifth edition of *The History of Human Marriage*, which was first published in 1928 in the seventh volume of *Studies in the Psychology of Sex*, Ellis was pleased to note that "the two main points in this [Westermarck's] method are its biological basis and its inductive collection of comparative facts" (1942b, pt. 2:495).

In the 1913 edition of *Analysis of the Sexual Impulse* Ellis cites Freud and Crawley. A gradual rapprochement developed between Crawley and Ellis, albeit they started from very different premises. Although Crawley was not among those who viewed primitives as slaves to excessive sexual drives, he did subscribe to that school of opinion that saw them as entrapped by superstition and taboo.

In *The Mystic Rose* Crawley developed a theory of marriage origins with highly individualistic premises. Primitive individuals lived in a state of fear. Contagion was a dreaded result of contact with any other thing or person. This net of primitive irrationalism was exemplified by the fear of sexual contagion, a terror on the part of each sex of that which was opposite and alien to it. Sexual intercourse was, needless to say, a requirement for the continued existence of any society. Accordingly, it was performed but at times and in a manner stipulated by taboo. Hedges were always necessary against the dangers caused by the crossing of ritual boundaries. Not surprisingly, Crawley was hostile to all theories of religion, kinship, and sexuality that were based in assumptions of human gregariousness. He devoted much of his time to attacking McLennan, noting that marriage by capture could well be the very thing McLennan said it was not, a cultural expression of sexual coyness.

Whereas Crawley's opinions may strike the modern anthropologist as somewhat quaint, it is easy selectively to read Ellis and easier still to read Westermarck and to conclude either that the modern, relativist view of primitive and modern sexuality is fully adumbrated in their writing or that they are, fundamentally, eminent Victorians at heart. To do the former, one must ignore many things, including frequent references to the "lower races" and progress in the refinements of love. With regard to the latter point of view, one must note Westermarck's annoyance at depictions of primitive lasciviousness. Second, his book *The Origin and Development of Moral Ideas* occasioned some outrage, inasmuch as it suggested that moral judgments were anchored in the emotions and not in reason and that there were no absolute moral truths. Third, by the 1920s (e.g., in *A Short History of Marriage* in 1926) Westermarck had adopted a more functionalist and less evolutionist style in his writing. Nonetheless, the writing of all three men on periodicity, Ellis's and Westermarck's opinions on the evolution of modesty, and Ellis's opinions concerning female neoteny all indicate that their thought world was very different from our own while revealing sharp breaks with their immediate past.

SEASONAL STORIES: PERIODICITY, COYNESS, AND "NO MEANS YES"

In an early conference paper (Lyons and Lyons 1981) we suggested that one consequence of the work of Ellis and Crawley was the substitution of the image of the "undersexed" for that of the "oversexed" savage. Those remarks were exaggerated, but they had a point. Westermarck, Ellis, and Crawley were all convinced that primitive humans had a mating season, a "rutting" time just like many other mammals. At other times they were sexually inactive.

Traces of periodicity were to be found even in civilized European countries: "In the eighteenth century Wargentin showed that in Sweden more children were born in one month than another" (Westermarck 1901:31). Statisticians had noted the same in other European countries. In general it appeared that conceptions peaked in May and June, which fact was reflected in a February–March peak in the birthrate (Westermarck 1901:32). While Westermarck did not adequately explore nonbiological explanations for the alleged phenomenon, his European data were at the very least more than anecdotal. However, when he endeavored to substantiate the existence of a rutting season among primitives, he relied on a kind of evidence that he would never have entertained from a proponent of primitive promiscuity: "Speaking of the Watch-an-dies in the western part of Australia, Mr. Oldfield remarks, 'Like the beasts of the field, the savage has but one time for copulation in the year. About the middle of spring . . . the Watch-an-dies begin to think of holding their grand semi-religious festival of Caa-ro'" (Westermarck 1901:28).

Westermarck entertained various reasons for the timing of rutting. It was noteworthy that among non-European as well as European peoples "we find . . . the sexual instinct increasing at the end of the spring" (Westermarck 1901:33). This was true, for instance, of India, and it was at this time that the festival of Holi was held. However, the main festival time in some parts of India was in January, a fact Westermarck found problematic, because he felt that saturnalian festivals and the mating season should coincide. Sexual periodicity could not be explained simply in terms of the position of the heavenly bodies. Nor was it adequate to suggest that the mating season occurred when there was a plenitude of food, because May and June in Scandinavia were "rather hard" months. Conditions at the time of birth and infancy were critical. Clearly, the mating season had to be timed so that births could take place during the season that was optimal for the survival of progeny (Westermarck 1901:34–35). The principle of natural selection was at work.

In Westermarck's opinion there was a simple reason why the mating season had nearly disappeared among civilized populations. Progress had enabled humans to escape the rigors of the seasons, thus permitting more "variations as to the pairing time," a pattern that was preserved and transmitted from generation to generation. A similar pattern was to be found among a few primitive groups such as the Yahgans of Tierra del Fuego, who had an adequate food supply all year round.

It is to be noted that Westermarck made no direct observations about the sexual potency of primitives, although the notion of periodicity implies such, and Ellis and Crawley were to make some very unambiguous remarks. Certainly, he did not believe that primitive peoples were always consumed by sexual desire, and that is perhaps one reason why he embraced a theory of incest that is the very opposite of Freud's inasmuch as he assumed that groups with an innate aversion to incest would have been favored by natural selection (Westermarck 1901:290–355). He thought that such an aversion did not come into play when close relatives were reared apart and were unaware of the relationship, so he was, in fact, speaking of a behavioral trait triggered by contiguity: "What I maintain is that there is an innate aversion to sexual intercourse between persons living very closely together from early youth, and that, as such persons are in most cases related, this feeling displays itself chiefly as a horror of intercourse between near kin" (Westermarck 1901:320).

Crawley at first eschewed biological explanations for primitive sexual restraint as surely as Westermarck rejected ritual determinism. The disagreement extended to the explanation of brief periods of license. Whereas Westermarck noted the coincidence of saturnalia and the supposed mating season and implied that nature in some way dictated its desires to culture, Crawley explained these festivals, which we would now call liminal rites or rituals of reversals, as magical ways to bridge the barriers that taboos had created between humans.

Ellis reconciled the biological and ritual positions on the origin of sexual restraint by suggesting that taboos could only take hold where the sexual instinct was fundamentally weak (1942a, pt. 2:263, 264). This weakness was often correlated with an underdevelopment of the sexual organs and certain psychic manifestations, for example, lack of jealousy (something Wester-marck would not have credited). The sexual urge, rather than being con-stant, ebbed and flowed. At its peak it burst forth in violent manifestations of sexual energy, feasts, orgies, and saturnalia (Ellis 1942a, pt. 2:266). Ellis accepted many of Westermarck's notions concerning periodicity and the rutting season and added more ethnographic data about their salience in primitive societies as well as statistical data that demonstrated that such phenomena were still significant in contemporary societies. He relied on some colorful and dubious travelers' tales such as the suggestion by Dr. Frederick Cook of the Peary North Greenland expedition that among the Eskimo, secretions, passions, and muscular activities diminish over the win-ter but that "soon after the sun appears a kind of rut affects the young population. They tremble with the intensity of sexual passion" (Ellis 1942a, pt. 1:126). Such violent but occasional outbursts of the sexual instinct were, in Ellis's opinion, the reason why so many mistakenly believed that savages possessed a particularly powerful sex drive.

Crawley accepted many of Ellis's arguments and modified others. Adding for good measure a dose of Anglican anti-Catholic sentiment, he wrote an essay on "Chastity and Sexual Morality" that appeared in a posthumous vol-ume edited by Theodore Besterman, *Studies of Savages and Sex*. This work is informed by a profoundly nonrelativist dogma. Crawley's intent in his essay was to write a minihistory of the "biological, economic and psychological causes of sexual morality" and, concomitantly, a study of "distribution of the habit of chastity, and the natural curve of its development" (1928:2). The reader is informed that, "roughly speaking, the sexual impulse is a psychical outgrowth from the nutritive, corresponding to it as physiolog-ical reproduction corresponds to physiological nutrition" (Crawley 1928:2). The undernourished primitive had "underdeveloped" sexual organs and manifested "difficulty in attaining sexual excitement" (Crawley 1928:3). Ac-cordingly, notions of primitive sexual communism were absurd. Crawley enthusiastically repeated some of the arguments of Ellis and Westermarck (1928:6–9). Unlike Ellis and Westermarck, Crawley was insistent that there was no primitive mating season in the strict biological sense. However, cultural institutions fulfilled the same role, inasmuch as they had a latent biological function. Group gatherings and festivals, whose overt purpose was merrymaking, were the occasions for sexual arousal and were often followed by long periods of natural chastity. "Thus we have a cultural as well as a physiological rhythm of periodicity" (Crawley 1928:10).

Overall, Westermarck's attacks on the promiscuity hypothesis served to elevate the primitive Other; Crawley's theories had a very different effect. He informed his readers that the higher races not only had greater sexual potency but could concentrate on higher things because their young took longer to mature and the "associational centres of the brain" could develop even after puberty. The savage child was as intelligent as the European up until puberty, but "subsequently he 'runs to seed,' or rather 'to sex'" (Crawley 1928:32).

The reader of the above account might be excused the thought that there is one human physiological process, menstruation, that is undeniably periodic but that is not directly linked to any mating season. Indeed, menstrual taboos commonly prohibit mating. A close reading of the texts, particularly Ellis's *The Evolution of Modesty*, leaves one with the feeling that Ellis confused menstruation with heat. He answered his own inquiry as to why intercourse was prohibited during menstruation with the remark that "the whole of religion is a . . . remolding of nature, a repression of natural impulses, an effort to turn them into new channels" (Ellis 1942a, pt. 1:98–99).

Thomas Laqueur has recently observed that the hormonal basis of ovulation was not understood until the 1930s and that women who read medical advice books were once told to restrict intercourse to the twelfth to sixteenth days after menstruation if they wished to avoid pregnancy (1990:9)! Furthermore, the relationship between menstruation and the cycle of ovulation was not understood. Nineteenth-century writers frequently confused menstruation with heat (Laqueur 1990:218–220).

The imagery involved in medical accounts of menstruation was quite vivid. According to Laqueur, Walter Heape, an antifeminist reproductive biologist who taught at Cambridge, used language "redolent of war reportage" to describe the "destruction" of the uterine lining, referring to it as a severe and devastating periodic action (1990:221). In *Man and Woman*, the first edition of which appeared in 1894, Ellis lamented that women were "periodically wounded in the most sensitive spot in their organism" (1930:335). The behavioral effects of menstruation, which allegedly included a rise in the suicide rate of females, were bemoaned: "They emphasize the fact that even in the healthiest woman a worm, however harmless and unperceived, gnaws periodically at the roots of life" (Ellis 1930:347). If one connects these remarks with Ellis's later comments about periodicity, particularly among primitives, one may make some inferences about the classificatory schemata that consciously or unconsciously directed his inquiries. In all fairness, one must remark that Ellis tentatively tried to extend the concept of periodicity to men, claiming that there was evidence of this phenomenon in the timing of nocturnal emissions (1942a, pt. 1:144). Of course, there is no suggestion of "wounds" or "disease" in his description of male periodicity.

The shift from presumed moral hierarchies to interpretations of partially understood physiological evidence left primitives both closer to lower animals than civilized folk and less sophisticated in their sexual attainments. It is fair to note, however, that Westermarck is far less pejorative in his descriptions of primitives than is Ellis, though the underlying logic of his arguments is similar, as both men see natural selection working its effects more clearly and directly upon the uncivilized.

Both Ellis and Westermarck modified the Darwinian model of courtship. Darwin assigned the male the active role and the female the passive role in this process. Ellis believed that women were naturally passive in sexual intercourse (Grosskurth 1980:231). Westermarck observed that, in point of fact, women in primitive societies sometimes played an active role in the choice of mates and frequently had the chance of refusing. Both Westermarck and Ellis drew attention to the role played by modesty in courtship. Westermarck observed that nudity was not a sign of immorality among those groups such as the Australians and Tasmanians who wore no clothing (Westermarck 1901:187–188). Clothing that might originally be adopted for several reasons, including decoration, warmth, a new sense of modesty, or perhaps the desire of husbands to hide their wives' bodies from rivals, served as a source of temptation or sexual excitement. Coyness and coquetry on the part of females now became possible (Westermarck 1901:195–198; Ellis 1942a, pt. 1:54–64).

In Ellis's view modesty was the concealment of sexual processes. It was prompted by fear, was particularly manifest in the behavior of the female sex, and was originally based in instinct (see Ellis 1942a, pt. 1). It was quite incorrect to assert that primitives were less modest, a fact that Ellis demonstrated by a review of over 50 ethnographical sources. Indeed, insofar as modesty was based in an instinct shared by some animals, it was hardly surprising that it should be exhibited most among those whose lives were closer to nature. Modesty might have developed to signal periods of sexual unavailability or, conversely, as a sexual lure (Ellis 1942a, pt. 1:39, 41). Ellis believed that modesty had ceased to be of much use to the most cultivated classes in Europe but was still important among just those lower-class individuals who, like primitives, were likely to be deemed immodest by popular opinion (1942a, pt. 1:67–68).

Ellis somewhat infamously (see, e.g., Jackson 1987:56–58) postulated that women might enjoy their own violation or feign reluctance, a speculation that offends current sensibilities to such an extreme degree that we forget that it also contained, implicitly, a new acknowledgment of female desire and sexual agency. Of marriage by capture, for example, Ellis says: "While this is sometimes a real capture, it is more often a mock capture; the lover perhaps pursues the beloved on horseback, but she is as fleet and as skillful as he is, cannot be captured unless she wishes to be captured, and in addition, as among the Kirghiz, she may be armed with a formidable whip; so that 'marriage by capture,' far from being a hardship imposed on women, is largely a concession to their modesty and a gratification of their erotic impulses" (1918:6). More radically, Ellis makes a similar observation of women of the middle class. Westermarck quotes him as repeating the following remark, made by one lady to another in front of a painting by Rubens of *The Rape of the Sabine Women*: "I think the Sabine women enjoyed being carried off like that" (1906–8, vol. 1:658).

The overall effect of much of the work we have been discussing was the rehabilitation of one term in the Victorian ranking of race, gender, and sexuality: sex itself gained in acceptability far more than did either primitives or women.

DISCOURSES AND SOCIAL MOVEMENTS: A CONTEXT FOR OUR AUTHORS

Much writing on the history of anthropology occurs as though the discipline existed in a social vacuum. The three scholars we have been discussing published their work during a period of considerable social turmoil. We question whether it is a coincidence that the smug image of the sexualized, promiscuous savage was replaced by another, more ambiguous image at a time when the institution of marriage and sexual relationships of all kinds had become a matter for public scrutiny. We should make it clear that we are not as convinced as Foucault (1980) was that discourses of reform and "shake-ups" in sexual attitudes merely served to shift the focus of constraint. We do think that there was some genuine groping toward liberalization of sexual norms at the period we were discussing, however fumbling and however guided by the emergence of new loci of power. There was also a very real repression of discussion of certain sexual matters.

It would be useful to acquaint the reader with some of the most important events of the period between 1877 and 1912. In February 1878 Charles Bradlaugh and Annie Besant won an appeal against their conviction for publishing a pamphlet on contraception by the American Charles Knowlton. In 1886 a Leeds dermatologist, Dr. Henry Allbutt, published a volume called

The Wife's Handbook, which instructed readers in the use of the Mensinga diaphragm. The General Medical Council of the British Medical Association struck his name from the medical register. By 1903 the volume had sold 390,000 copies (Fryer 1965:161–168).

The agitation of Josephine Butler and her supporters finally achieved the replacement of the Contagious Diseases Acts with the Criminal Law Amendment Act in 1885 (Bristow 1977:77–115). The Criminal Law Amendment Act raised the age of consent and attempted to control procuring and the white slave trade. It did not do a perfect job, and agitation continued until another bill, the Criminal Law Amendment White Slavery Bill, was passed in 1912 (Bristow 1977:191–194). Unfortunately, the 1885 bill outlawed, on pain of two years' hard labor, private as well as public homosexual acts between males. Flogging was also made a penalty for homosexual acts (Bristow 1977:115). The bill, as many have noted, may have intensified the persecution of homosexuals in England and abetted the social construction of a medicalized category of permanently and innately homosexual people. The 1890s witnessed the Oscar Wilde trial and the prosecution of George Bedborough, the bookseller who sold copies of Ellis's *Sexual Inversion*. That book was published by Watford University Press, an entirely fictional company, because no medical publisher would handle it.

It is generally known that the Victorians were both fascinated and repelled by masturbation. Booklets issued by the Church of England's White Cross Society dealt with its dangers, and Edward Littleton, headmaster of Eton, led a campaign against vice in the public schools (Bristow 1977:135–139). Soon after the Boy Scouts were created in 1908, Sir Robert Baden-Powell's Rovers (older Scouts) were given *Rovering to Success*, a guidebook whose chapter entitled "Woman" instructed the boys that the "rutting season" could be negotiated without loss of semen if they bathed their "racial organ" in cold water daily (Bristow 1977:140). Ellis thought that masturbation was not intrinsically undesirable and did not lead to blindness or psychiatric breakdown, but excessive indulgence was pathological and should be prevented (1942a, pt. 4:342–344). There were various attempts to stop the publication of supposedly corrupting materials. Efforts were made to clean up theatrical performances (Ellis 1942a, pt. 4:206–208).

As the above account implies, a number of social agendas, some with overlapping and others with conflicting aims, were being brought forward at this period. The groups founded to promulgate the agendas of social purity included the National Vigilance Association (whose secretary, William A. Coote, became Britain's answer to Anthony Comstock, secretary of the New

York Society for the Suppression of Vice, and whose head, Percy Bunting, was editor of the *Contemporary Review*), the Public Morality Council, and the aforementioned White Cross Society. It should not be assumed that the members of these associations were uniformly conservative in their aims. Bishop Winnington Ingram was active in the Oxford House settlement movement before heading the Public Morality Council. Some organizations included a number of feminists such as Josephine Butler, Ellice Hopkins, and Millicent Fawcett. Butler, however, resigned from the National Vigilance Association in 1886 because she was dismayed by its increasingly repressive turn under Coote's leadership. Feminism, in general, grew during this period. Some feminists sided with the social purity movement and some were against it. Discontent with the double standard took two forms: a demand for male chastity and a call for more freedom for women. The former was somewhat more common in the period before World War I (see Kent 1990:216–218 passim). Not all feminist demands for male continence were linked to a general desire for social purity, however. The transmission of venereal disease from profligate men to dependent women was a major concern that motivated, among other things, Christabel Pankhurst's famous slogan "Votes for Women, Chastity for Men" (Kent 1990:5).

Significantly, in the period between 1911 and 1913, Ellis published in a short-lived journal called the *New Freewoman*, founded by two active members of the Women's Social and Political Union. Many other feminists, including Millicent Fawcett and Ellis's friend Olive Schreiner, were infuriated by the *New Freewoman*'s frank discussions of "contraception, sexual pleasure, lesbianism and menstruation" (Kent 1990:217–218). A very different, small, and elite group supported a different kind of family reform. These were the eugenicists, led first by Francis Galton and then by Karl Pearson, who was an intellectual rival of Havelock Ellis as well as a temporary rival for the affections of Olive Schreiner. Eugenicists all supported positive eugenics, which would have encouraged the fit to breed while discouraging the unfit from breeding. Some, however, supported stronger measures such as compulsory birth control and sterilization for the unfit. All were terrified at the thought of families of degenerates who bred prolifically. There was much interest in the work of the Italian "criminal anthropologist" Cesare Lombroso, who believed that some individuals inherited a disposition to crime that was evidenced in certain bodily stigmata. Under the influence of Lombroso, Ellis wrote *The Criminal* (1890). One must observe that by the standards of the day many eugenicists were progressive. George Bernard Shaw, Sidney and Beatrice Potter Webb, and Pearson all thought of themselves as socialists. So too did Havelock Ellis – from time to time. Lastly, it should be noted that Francis Galton, the founder of eugenics, was a firm believer in the intellectual inferiority of women.

Ellis supported the "sterilization of the unfit" (1930:412) and also suggested in correspondence with Galton that individuals could be awarded Certificates of Eugenic Fitness based on physical examination (June 15, 1906, Ellis Papers). In 1904 he published *A Study of British Genius*, an analysis of some leading figures in the new *Dictionary of National Biography*, inspired by Galton's *Hereditary Genius* (Grosskurth 1980:26). Particularly proud of his Suffolk origins, Ellis also corresponded with the physical anthropologist John Beddoe (October 13, 1903, Ellis Papers), an author who had cataloged the racial types of England in great detail in *The Races of Britain*. Later in life, Ellis expressed approval of the racist American immigration laws of the 1920s, which were supported by American eugenicists on the grounds that they would limit the entry of those races that had a high ratio of population growth (Ellis 1957:152). However, he disapproved of attempts to legalize voluntary sterilization in Britain (Grosskurth 1980:413).

Another small group of individuals were freethinkers and libertarians, at least on certain issues. Sheila Rowbotham and Jeffrey Weeks (1977) have detailed the friendship of Havelock Ellis and Edward Carpenter. Ellis was also associated with John Addington Symonds. Both Carpenter and Symonds were homosexuals. Symonds was a distinguished biographer and literary scholar who specialized in the study of Renaissance poets and artists such as Sir Philip Sydney, Benvenuto Cellini, and Michelangelo. He corresponded with the German scholar Karl Heinrich Ulrichs, who created the term *Urning* to describe individuals who were innately homosexual. He collaborated with Ellis on the latter's work on homosexuality, supplying several of the case studies for Ellis's *Sexual Inversion*. (In the 1896 German edition that appeared before the work was published in England he was listed as coauthor.) His pamphlet *A Problem in Greek Ethics*, which examined *paiderastia* in ancient Greece, was posthumously reprinted at the end of Ellis's *Sexual Inversion* but removed from the second edition. In writings such as the privately circulated *A Problem in Modern Ethics* Symonds claimed that homosexuality was not a disease and that homosexuals had made valuable contributions to literature, government, and the military (Norton 1999, 2000; Grosskurth 1964:286–294).

Poet, mystic, nudist, anarchist, and socialist organizer Edward Carpenter lived much of his life with his working-class lover, George Merrill, on an estate he purchased in Derbyshire. He was the author of the epic poem

Towards Democracy (1883), *Love's Coming of Age* (1896), and *The Interme-diate Sex* (1908), which resumed the battle for gay dignity inaugurated by Symonds (Rowbotham and Weeks 1977; Dawson 2000). He also wrote *Intermediate Types among Primitive Folk* (1914), which we shall discuss in a little while. Eleanor Marx and her husband, Edward Aveling, were also part of Ellis's small circle. Edith Lees, who married Ellis, had several lesbian affairs and, like Ellis, preached a gospel of sexual freedom. James Hinton, a Yorkshire doctor who wrote about a vaguely spiritual dependence of organic processes on the laws of physics (Fortes 1933:73–74), exercised a posthumous influence over a diverse body of people, including Ellis, his wife, the novelist Olive Schreiner, and the social purity leader Ellice Hopkins.

Most of the eugenicists, most of the feminists, and virtually all of the supporters of social purity believed that some form of radical intervention in family life was essential because the status quo was scandalous. Thus, they justified the intervention of legal officers, settlement workers, churchmen, Boy Scout leaders, and teachers in people's private and family lives. Not all of these modes were confessional in the way that Foucault (1980) suggests. If the 1830s, 1840s, 1850s, and 1860s were an era when pious hypocrisy and the double standard kept a widespread license away from polite eyes, the period after 1870 was a period of exposure and attempts at intervention. Some of these interventions were designed to alter behavior; others took issue with sanctimoniousness and hypocrisy themselves.

It is fitting now that we say more about the extent to which the work of our three thinkers was influenced by the social currents of their day. Neither Ellis nor Westermarck had a conventional marriage. Ellis's marriage to Edith Lees was described by him as "semi-detached." Westermarck was a bachelor and may have been a homosexual. Westermarck (1929) avoids the issue of his personal sexuality in his autobiography, where he mentions no intimate relationships with women and describes several close friendships with men.

A dislike for certain varieties of Christianity is evident in the works of Crawley and Ellis. Crawley, as we remarked, condemned the Catholic Church's attitudes toward celibacy. Westermarck attacked the Catholic Church because its obsession with female impurity, from the time of the church fathers to the present, had resulted in the degradation of women (1906–8, vol. 2:661–666). Westermarck, indeed, was a thoroughgoing athe-ist who did not, like some agnostics, feel a need for substitute religious experience. In his autobiography he remarks, "Sometimes on Sundays I accompanied Mr. and Mrs. Coupland to South Place, a meeting place in Finsbury for those who wish for other Sunday fare than is offered them in churches. There I heard Charles Bradlaugh, Annie Besant, and other freethinkers. There was, in addition, some kind of hymn singing with 'Humanity' substituted for 'God.' I do not feel much attracted by such relics of ritual, and the last thing I should dream of worshipping is humanity – although I am glad I can be useful in its service" (Westermarck 1929:80).

Westermarck has been accused of being a defender of conventional Victorian monogamy (Coward 1983:57, 70, 72). If he helped to naturalize what Foucault has described as the heterosexual, procreating couple, it was because of an addiction to the Darwinian paradigm. In any event, he explicitly denied any conservative intent (Westermarck 1934:332). He believed that some sort of monogamy was part of our primate inheritance and that from the woman's point of view it was preferable to polygyny. He felt, however, that monogamy in its modern form was an institution in need of improvement. In *The History of Human Marriage* Westermarck remarks that the postponement of the age of marriage and the stresses of urban life have led to a decline in morality:

> Almost everywhere prostitution increases in a higher ratio than population. In consideration of these facts, it is almost ridiculous to speak of the immorality of unmarried people among savages as a relic of an alleged primitive state of promiscuity. . . . There are several factors in civilization which account for this bad result. The more unnatural mode of living and the greater number of excitements exercise, no doubt, a deteriorating influence on morality; and poverty makes prostitutes of many girls who are little more than children. But the chief factor is the growing number of unmarried people. . . . Free sexual intercourse previous to marriage is quite a different thing from promiscuity, the most genuine form of which is prostitution. But prostitution is rare among peoples living in a state of nature and unaffected by foreign influences. (1901:70–71)

Westermarck did not say that all primitive groups permitted premarital sex but rather showed that there was much variability in this respect. He did not advocate a return to primitive sexual institutions. He believed that conjugal love had probably grown more intense with the advance of civilization. He conclusively rejected the mid-Victorian equation between the primitive female and the prostitute. His position was not inconsistent with the advocacy of trial marriage, a position that was advanced for the time.

In the earliest years of the twentieth century trial or companionate marriage was championed by a number of sexual radicals, including Havelock Ellis and Elsie Clews Parsons (1906). Later on, its advocates included Bertrand Russell, Bronislaw Malinowski, and the American judge Ben Lindsey. They believed that marriages would be better preserved and children would be happier if couples were allowed to live together before making a long-term or lifetime commitment. Furthermore, Ellis stated that extramarital and premarital sexual intercourse need not be condemned unless the welfare of children was affected (1942a, pt. 1:249–259). In *The Future of Marriage in Western Civilization*, a very late work, Westermarck announced his support of Judge Lindsey (1936:112–118). Nonetheless, he was worried about allowing total freedom in premarital sex: "To sum up the gist of this lengthy discussion: however desirable it may be for a man to receive sex experience from a woman belonging to his own class as a prelude to his marriage, the acquisition of it is attended with such risks for the woman that he must consider whether he has a right to utilize her as a means of preparing him for his marriage – with another woman" (1936:150).

Westermarck felt that monogamous institutions should and would survive but that they would have to undergo a number of changes. Making divorce easier would make marriage more durable (Westermarck 1936:152). An increasing divorce rate was not a sign that marriage was no longer healthy. In the long term more diverse forms of marriage would be tolerated: "It seems to be very likely that this prediction will come true; that in questions of sex people will be less tied by conventional rules, and that they will recognize greater freedom for men and women to mould their own amatory life" (Westermarck 1936:201).

In his autobiography Westermarck notes that he was pleased to serve as vice president of two feminist societies during the 1890s, although, ironically, the reason for the invitation was something he had not written. Sime, his editor at Macmillan, added a final sentence so that *The History of Human Marriage* would end with a flourish. Its purport was that women were gradually triumphing over the prejudices, passions, and selfish interests of men (Westermarck 1901:550). Westermarck felt that this ending was far too optimistic and subsequently changed it.

Elsewhere, Westermarck expressed the opinion that the subjection of women seemed to be a constant in human history but that in primitive societies, because of the strong sexual division of labor, women had their own sphere of public influence (1906–8, vol. 2:629–646). Subsequently, they had lost it but in the future might regain it. He believed that the subjection of women had a number of causes. The ones he chose to list indicate a degree of conflict between his Darwinism and his feminism. They include the Darwinian contrast between the sexual impulses: the active male and the passive female, the male drive to exercise power, and "the natural inferiority of women in such qualities of body and mind as are essential for independence" (Westermarck 1906–8, vol. 2:657–658).

The contradiction between Havelock Ellis's "feminism" and his Darwinism has already been remarked. In *Man and Woman* he not only wrote about the terrible effects of menstruation but contrasted the two sexes in every conceivable way, listing body measurements, brain size, perception, and creative abilities. He thought that the smaller size of the female brain simply reflected the smaller stature and bulk of women; however, he believed that, inasmuch as mental ability varied more in men than in women, there were significantly more geniuses of the male than of the female sex and also more idiots. Men were more creative and independent; women were unoriginal, dependent, and nurturant. Some of these apparent weaknesses, however, were the consequence of the admirable maternal role that women performed. Ellis employed a contorted version of the theory now known as neoteny to show that women were, in fact, more evolved than men. This was not inconsistent with his other observations, for he believed that in evolutionary terms, if not cultural ones, nurturance was more important than variation and creativity. For all that, this aspect of Ellis's argument borders on the old Victorian notion of separate spheres. The angel in the house, beloved of Victorian sentimentalists, was also supposed to be nurturant and childlike. Ellis endeavored to demonstrate that in hominid evolution the more evolved forms retained a degree of paedomorphism, namely, all primate infants resemble each other; humans retain that form later in life and deviate less from it. Ellis said that women are more neotenic than men, Orientals are more neotenic than whites, and the Negro is the least neotenic of the human species. Despite Ellis's involvement with feminists and his marriage to one of them, he had strong reservations about suffragists who were noisy in their demands and indulged in violent public demonstrations (see Ellis 1912).

In *The Task of Social Hygiene* (1912), which was published under the auspices of the National Council for Public Morals, one of the social purity lobbies, Ellis advances a program for social hygiene and eugenics. He remarked that in the 19th century civil intervention had improved life in a number of ways: better sanitation, improved working conditions, the ending of child labor, and compulsory public education. The regulation of the family would complete this admirable process. It was necessary to improve both the quality and quantity of the stock. Ellis felt that "feminism," birth control, and other eugenic measures could achieve the same results. He particularly liked some of the German maternal feminists who stressed that women should enjoy equality in pursuit of their own gender-specific, nurturant instincts. He championed their campaign to remove the stigma attached to childbirth out of wedlock so that the maternal instinct might be freed from male control. He advocated birth control so that society might live free from degenerates and families could live free of hunger; however, he felt that sterilization of the unfit was an unnecessarily harsh measure. Wherever possible, eugenic controls should be exercised on a voluntary basis. Ellis also pointed to the folly of those who advocated Draconian measures to control prostitution, drinking, and other social vices. Inevitably, such measures had undesirable consequences and usually proved ineffective as well as unpleasant.

Ellis's views on birth control in no way justify Foucault's characterization of *scientia sexualis* and its practitioners as uniformly opposed to the Malthusian couple. Unlike some eugenicists who approved of birth control for obvious reasons but disdained its feminist supporters, and unlike others who feared it would lead to "suicide" of the fit rather than limitation of the unfit, Ellis strongly supported the campaigns and many of the campaigners of the early 20th century (1957:95–117, 152, 195). He maintained a 25-year friendship with Margaret Sanger, who may have fallen in love with him during her first visit to London (Grosskurth 1980:242–253 passim), and an acquaintanceship with Sanger's archrival, Marie Stopes (see chapter 6).

Westermarck and Ellis were both fascinated by the ethnography of homosexuality and the situation of the homosexual in Victorian and Edwardian society. Ellis believed that homosexuality was biological in base. In his study *Sexual Inversion*, coauthored with John Addington Symonds, Ellis cited a plethora of ethnographic data in order to demonstrate that homosexuality was common, indeed routine, behavior in many non-Western societies, particularly those that encourage late marriage and seclusion of military personnel. Where homosexuality was encouraged, many would engage in it. Ellis even included an appendix on schoolgirl crushes (1942a, pt. 4:368–384) as well as one on homosexuality among tramps written by "Josaiah Flynt" (1942a, pt. 4:359–367). However, in late Victorian respectable adult society, homosexuality was actively discouraged, and, accordingly, the person who practiced homosexuality in spite of all threats and dangers was likely, in Ellis's opinion, to be a congenital invert. Ellis did not wish to imply that homosexual behavior in later life was entirely determined by heredity; rather, he spoke of a "predisposition" that may or may not be triggered into action (1942a, pt. 4:302–324).

In the case of homosexuality hereditarian views led to liberal but not radical conclusions. Insofar as homosexuality was congenital, inverts could not and should not be cured. Insofar as they might be useful, indeed brilliant, members of society, they should not be persecuted. Rather, homosexual adults should enjoy the right to pursue sexual relationships in private. However, Ellis felt that public displays of homosexual behavior were unacceptable in the prevailing social climate (1942a, pt. 4:342–344). Doubtless, Ellis's collaboration with Symonds, the unhappy life of his own wife, Edith, and his friendship with Carpenter led him to appreciate the burden society inflicted on homosexuals.

Westermarck, for his part, felt that Ellis, along with Richard von Krafft-Ebing and Albert Moll, who were also authorities on homosexuality, had "underestimated the modifying influence which habit may exercise on the sexual instinct" (1906–8, vol. 2:468). Westermarck believed that if there was an inherited predisposition to homosexual behavior, it was "only a feature in the ordinary sexual constitution of man" (1906–8, vol. 2:468). All that was necessary to activate that predisposition was close and exclusive association in daily life with members of the same sex. In Morocco, a country where Westermarck had spent six years, homosexuality was common among certain single-sex groups such as the scribes who worked together from early childhood, but in other occupations and in certain neighborhoods homosexual practices were rare (1906–8, vol. 2). At the very end of his life Westermarck regretted that he had not given more stress to the congenital element in homosexuality. He felt that it was the reason for the persistence of homosexuality despite all attempts to ban it (Westermarck 1936:252).

Westermarck's ethnographic survey of homosexuality was contained in the second volume of *The Origin and Development of Moral Ideas*. Carpenter used it as a major source for *Intermediate Types among Primitive Folk*, a small but retrospectively significant volume that first appeared in 1914. In that volume Carpenter also cites Symonds, Sir Richard Burton, Père Joseph Lafitau, Hubert Howe Bancroft, and the German-Jewish sexologists Iwan Bloch and Magnus Hirschfeld. He argues that "intermediate types" often play important roles as priests, shamans, prophets, diviners, magicians, temple prostitutes, poets, and artists. They are suited for these roles because they combine features of both the male and female temperament. Ethnographic evidence from Siberia, Alaska, the southwestern pueblos, the North American Plains, Polynesia, and biblical Syria and Canaan is cited. In Carpenter's opinion sexually repressive cultures and religions such as Mosaic Judaism and Christianity were responsible for the deprecation of the rituals and ritual practitioners of those people whom they suppressed by force of arms (Carpenter 1975:1–83).

Carpenter also described two forms of military pederasty. Greek homoerotic practices were originally developed among the armies of the Dorian peoples. Dorian societies not only elevated homoerotic love, they also accorded equal status to women. Second, he discusses same-sex relations among the Samurai of Japan. His point was simple: where the "intermediate sex" was not repressed, its members made worthy contributions to society. *Intermediate Types* reflects the work of Carpenter's contemporaries such as Westermarck, Symonds, and Ellis, but it is itself an adumbration of current gay sociology and anthropology, particularly the work of Stephen O. Murray and David F. Greenberg. However, we must acknowledge that *Intermediate Types* conscripts the sexuality of others into European sexual politics, despite advancing an argument with which many contemporary readers are likely to have considerable sympathy. This is a reality we will encounter more frequently the closer our story moves toward the present.

CHANGING IMAGES OF THE PRIMITIVE AND THE CRISIS IN MASCULINITY

Prostitution was at the core of many of the discourses of both feminism and social purity. The old Victorian double standard, which saw men and women as having fundamentally different sexual natures and some women as being irretrievably fallen and thus acceptable vessels for male lust, was not tolerable to participants in the feminist, social purity, and social hygiene movements. Although many were content to concentrate on women's economic condition as a cause of prostitution, there was a growing belief that greater sexual satisfaction would have to be found within marriage if prostitution were to be combatted. There was thus a growing concern with the diagnosis and treatment of sexual blocks. Freud's work is a case in point, although he did not have much influence in England until after the Great War. Medical notions of mental and sexual inadequacy, whether labeled as hysteria, neurasthenia, neurosis, or perversion, represent an inward turning of the ideas of degeneracy we discussed earlier in this chapter. In *Sexual Anarchy* (1991) Elaine Showalter has examined the crisis in masculinity at the fin de siècle that was reflected in the writings of figures as diverse as Wilde, Rider Haggard, and Robert Louis Stevenson and in popular and scientific notions of degeneracy, perversion, madness, inadequacy, and neurosis.

The work of Ellis, Crawley, and Westermarck was certainly a part of this discourse, which may help explain the emergence of the "undersexed savage." "Primitive" sexuality was imagined in terms that either opposed or exaggerated the civilized condition. Hence, a society troubled by promiscuity and seduction had asserted a fundamental closeness between oversexed primitives and the seductive women and oversexed men of the lower classes. When men of the middle classes came to be troubled by their own perceived (or perhaps imagined) repressions and sexual disabilities, similar disorders, often in exaggerated form, began to crop up in their representations of primitives. Alternatively, insofar as primitives as well as sex itself rose in the Western estimation, primitives were portrayed as more natural and sensible than their civilized counterparts. Westermarck, more than Ellis and Crawley, inclined to the latter view.

CONTINUATIONS

While Crawley's work quickly passed into obscurity, the work of Ellis and Westermarck did exercise some influence on the direction of anthropology during their own later years and for a short time afterward. As we shall see, Westermarck's pupil, Malinowski, turned to Ellis after he became disillusioned with Freud, made detailed notes on Ellis's writings, and used themes from Ellis's *Studies in the Psychology of Sex* as chapter headings in *The Sexual Life of Savages in Northwestern Melanesia* (1929). Ellis was pleased to write the introduction to that work. If one reads it closely, one may notice references to periodicity, which Malinowski considered to be a purely cultural phenomenon, insofar as it existed.

We believe that the "undersexed savage" or "occasionally sexed savage" of Ellis and Crawley is best seen as a transitional model, bridging the gap between Victorian images of savage lechery and portraits that represent South Sea Islanders, whether Trobrianders or Samoans, as having passionless and boring but stable and sexually well-adjusted marriages.

CHAPTER 5

"Old Africa Hands"

A ustralia may have been seen as the zero point of cultural evolution, but Africa did not cease to be a locus for the stigmata of alterity. The British encounter with Africa was characterized by a number of prevailing stereotypes of "African" sexuality and such linked matters as sensual, even feral, ritual dances and the failure of Africans to benefit from education and civilization, even to be "spoiled" by it. Many of these tropes come together in a remarkable report of a ceremony in Elele, southern Nigeria, in 1921, prepared for his superiors by E. M. Falk, a district commissioner in the British colonial service:

CHRISTMAS 1921 (among the semi civilized)
A party of local drummers and singers with native made instruments then relieved the exhausted school band, a fire of logs blazed up in the darkening compound and a mass of villagers crowded around them, and commenced what is called a "play", more correctly described as a frenzied shuffle dance, known in Europe commonly as la danse du ventre. The most conspicuous feature of it is the prominence not of the stomachs but of the reverse portions of the performers' anatomy. The sexes dance separately, round and round in circles moving in opposite directions or in spirals to the rhythm of the drummers and chorus. Every muscle of the dancer vibrates. Many swing lighted lamps in their hands, and this and the fitful firelight made an indescribable impression of weirdness, a real witches' sabbath. A large crowd of spectators clad in every imaginable garment from the factories and old clothes dealers stores of Manchester throngs around. Gaudy loincloths jostle khaki breeches, tweed caps are cheek by jowl with brilliant silk handkerchieves tied around the heads of the fair, a dandy in immaculate white ducks ogles a dusky beauty naked to the waist, and

youths disport themselves in nothing but a ragged singlet and scant waistcloth. Such are the costumes of holiday makers in this part of Africa. (Falk Papers)

In Falk's narrative one can hear the echoes of countless conversations on the verandah after dinner during which colonial officials and their wives enunciated the stereotypical opinion of Africans, that they are sensual, over-sexed, not very intelligent, and childish and that they ineptly imitate their European superiors. These motifs in colonial writings about Africa have, of course, been noted by other writers. Philip Curtin (1964), Dorothy Hammond and Alta Jablow (1970), and Gustav Jahoda (1999) are among those who have alluded to such images. Brian Street (1975) and Marianna Torgovnick (1990) have paid particular attention to these and related themes in literature. Implicit in Falk's narrative is the old racist adage: "Take away the veneer of civilization and they're back in the bush." We heard it as recently as 1984 from an oil company employee who was seated next to us on a flight from Lagos to London.

As we shall see, Falk's opinions on the capacity of Africans to benefit from civilization, especially where matters of sex and gender were concerned, had more consequences than similar attitudes held by many other colonial administrators, as he happened to be in charge of the district of Calabar in 1929 at the time of the Igbo Women's Rebellion, an event that brought British attitudes to African sexuality and gender relations into sharp relief. This episode also increased demand for government anthropology in British Africa, though the divergence between administrators' and anthropologists' attitudes helps both to explain the temporary nature of such demands and to dispel any simplistic conceptions of anthropologists in Africa as hand-maids of colonialism.

At the outset, we must note that authors of fiction, journals of exploration, and government documents commonly used tropes similar to Falk's to describe African sexuality and intelligence, but in many cases such imagery was countered by remarks that sought some sympathetic understanding of Africans. Indeed, this is true of some writings much earlier than Falk's, particularly ones that presented some kind of ethnographic viewpoint. Travel narratives, missionary journals, popular fiction, administrators' reports, and some early ethnography are less far apart than we were taught in the last days of functionalism, as Mary Louise Pratt (1986) has made us well aware. [1] Accordingly, racist stereotypes are sometimes juxtaposed with a kind of protorelativism in writings about Africa produced during the last third of the 19th century. In matters of sex and gender, sensationalism, prurience, and familiar myths of oversexed Africans and their downtrodden and degraded women occasionally are interrupted by some more nuanced and perceptive accounts of kinship and marriage. Sexuality, kinship, and marriage are subjects of intense interest to ethnographers, regulators, and the general public. In the first third of the 20th century, when colonialism in Africa became bureaucratized and anthropology became professionalized, we can see a polarization in the writings of administrators and ethnographers that led the former to distrust the latter, even when they sought anthropological expertise. To explore these trends we shall look at the work of some 19th-century writers whose activities combined adventure and exploration with observation and intervention, the last two of which might be seen as laying the groundwork for administration and ethnography. We will then compare the writings and career of Northcote Thomas, in his role as a government anthropologist, with those of Falk. It is our contention that, whatever its shortcomings, anthropology did eventually become a counterforce to the more extreme forms of colonial discourse, though this very fact may have limited the degree to which anthropologists were taken seriously as players in the colonial game.

Winwood Reade belonged to the Anthropological Society of London (ASL) (see chapter 2). He was an admirer of Richard Burton. He was later to be known as a rationalist and humanist who wrote *The Martyrdom of Man*. In 1863 members of the ASL knew Reade as the young author of *Savage Africa* (1863), a description of his journeys in what are now Senegal, Gambia, Cape Verde, Ghana, Fernando Póo, Gabon, Congo, and Angola. The book is in part travelogue, in very small part ethnography, and in some measure political tract. It must be remembered that at the time when both Reade and Burton first described their African experiences the future of the "peculiar institution" of slavery was being decided in North America, and the European powers were still unsure whether and by what means their "civilizing mission" could be extended to the "Dark Continent." *Savage Africa* incorporates certain obligatory elements (or clichés) of writings about West Africa at this period. There is a description of human sacrifice in Dahomey that seems to be secondhand. In a short chapter on cannibalism it is revealed that people always accuse their neighboring opponents of such a practice. Reade's description of his role in Africa evokes a Jungian Shadow that anthropologists have struggled to bar from their collective consciousness: "I make, of course, no pretensions to the title of Explorer. If I have any merit, it is that of having been the first young man about town to make a *bona fide* tour of West Africa; to travel in that agreeable and salubrious country with no special object, and at his own expense; to *flaner* in the virgin forest; to flirt with pretty savages, and to smoke his cigar among cannibals" (Reade 1967:preface).

Reade's representations of African intelligence, sexuality, and ritual contained most of the stereotypes characteristic of his era as well as some equally characteristic contradictions. Africans were depicted as indolent people, drunkards, thieves, liars who possessed "no mental culture of any kind." The men were "frivolous and effeminate; they spend their nights in singing and dancing" (Reade 1967:447). (The dance, as we have seen and will continue to see, is a pervasive leitmotif in colonial portraits of Africans.) The seemingly contradictory portrayal of African men as debauched and effeminate was common in the writings of the era, perhaps designed to reassure Europeans, whose sense of their own virility was threatened by the chimera of the oversexed savage they themselves had created. In Reade's portrait both physical stigmata and behavioral traits were cited as evidence for an oversexed but fundamentally unmanly African male:

> The virile member is much larger than is found in Europeans, excepting in those who are idiotic. It is one of the chief seats of colour. When a negro child is born, it has a black ring round the virile member, a reddish mark on the nail, and another in the corner of the eye. These are the last signs by which the descendant of a negro can be distinguished.
>
> According to some writers, the same secretion forms the beard and propagates the human species. The negro seldom has any hair upon his face; it is never abundant; and he rarely has a great number of children. There is also a peculiarity in the negro's voice by which it can be distinguished. It is not unlike that of a eunuch. (1967:398)

Reade's portrayal of African women also employs contradictory tropes. They are portrayed, on the one hand, as unattractive (though relatively nonlascivious) drudges, drained of beauty by the "savage passions" of their menfolk, and, on the other, as dangerous cannibalistic seducers (Reade 1967:428, 49). Both images were widespread. Both can be found, for example, in Rider Haggard's *She* (1886), a best-selling novel of the 1880s that has never gone out of print. Haggard offers his readers stories of the wild dancing of the fictional Amahaggar people (chapter 19), a generally unattractive group, and an account of a cannibal feast during which a rejected female lover caresses an intended victim before he is seized and an attempt made to kill him with a heated pot (chapter 8).

Reade provides us with some similar set pieces in which African myth and colonial legend seem to merge so that African reality, if it is there at all, is totally submerged. Reade recounts the story of Tembandumba, queen of the Jaga, the "African Messalina," as related by Father Cavazzi. The Jaga of the Congo had a number of legends about Amazon warrior queens. The first was Shinga, but Tembandumba was the most ferocious. Reade's account is illustrated by a memorable engraving of *The Queen of the Cannibals* (figure 2) bearing shield and spear, surrounded by other Jaga warriors, one of whom (to her immediate left) is murderously dispatching an enemy, while speared corpses lie to her right (1967:293).

> Following in the footsteps of the great Zimbo, she would turn the world into a wilderness; she would kill all living animals; she would burn all forests, grass and vegetable food. The sustenance of her subjects should be the flesh of man; his blood should be their drink.
>
> She commanded that all male children, all twins and all infants whose upper teeth appeared before their lower ones, should be killed by their own mothers. From their bodies an ointment should be made in the way which she would show. The female children should be reared and instructed in war; and male prisoners, before being killed and eaten, should be used for purposes of procreation. (Reade 1967: 292)[2]

Reade's accounts of African sexuality are often contradictory. On the one hand, he claimed (in a passage specifically arguing against those claiming "equality" for Africans) that "the typical negro, unrestrained by moral laws, spends his days in sloth, his nights in debauchery" (Reade 1967:430). On the other hand, he admits that "during the whole time which I passed in Africa, I never saw so much as one indecent gesture pass between a man and a woman" and that "in many parts of Africa, no marriage can be ratified till a jury of matrons have pronounced a verdict of purity on the bride" (Reade 1967:424, 425).

Significantly, Reade made some attempts at applied anthropology, some of which, themselves, were or became tropes in the descriptive and administrative imaginations. An attempt, albeit condescending, was made to understand polygamy within its context. Accordingly, it is described as an institution that was "as great a benefit in Africa as in Europe it would be an evil" (Reade 1967:444). Polygamy was "one of Nature's necessities" in a

2. *The Queen of the Cannibals.* From *Savage Africa* (1863) by W. Winwood Reade.

land where sterility was common and infant mortality was high.[3] Reade's recommendations concerning education, unfortunately, were based on appraisals of African mentality that continued to inform the thinking of administrators like Falk. It is significant that these assessments have a sexual tinge. While Reade thought that there might be a benefit in teaching black children trades, he believed the missionaries' attempt to impart a European education to Negroes was futile, even dangerous, because of a precipitous decline in mental ability that, he believed, accompanied puberty in Africa (1967:445).

There were, of course, later explorers who were to become much more famous than Winwood Reade. Two of them, Sir Henry Morton Stanley and Sir Samuel White Baker, both of whom were active imperialists, conform much more to popular impressions of Victorian writers. In other words, they had very little to say about sexuality or sexual morality in Africa. Both of them did mention cannibalism, which was presumably thought to be a less dangerous topic and might act as a surrogate and index for unmentionable forms of savage immorality. Jahoda (1999) has noted that in discourses of cannibalism, food and sex are often in a metaphorical relationship. In *Through the Dark Continent* Stanley, describing Asama Island, observes that human skulls "ornamented the village streets of the island, while a great many thigh-bones, ribs and vertebrae lay piled at a garbage corner, bleached witnesses of their hideous carnivorous tastes" (1879:477). Baker was quite willing to extend the appellation "cannibal" to various peoples on the basis of hearsay, but he did claim to have witnessed one actual episode among his own troops, whom he called the "Forty Thieves." Some of them supposedly ate the liver of an enemy, believing that it would cause every bullet they fired to kill a Bunyoro (Baker 1875:411, 412).

In other respects, Stanley is at pains to portray Africans fairly by the standards of his time, which, of course, are not our standards. He believed that the societies of the Congo basin were at a disadvantage compared to Europe and America because of the hot African climate, inhospitable terrain, and prolonged periods of cultural isolation. "European pauperism planted among them would soon degenerate to the low level of aboriginal degradation" (Stanley 1885, vol. 2:376). One particularly "degenerate" group was the Uhombo, who lived about 100 miles west of Lake Tanganyika. Deciding that it was appropriate that the readers of *Through the Dark Continent* should know what a typical African village was like, Stanley described the conical grass huts that surrounded a circular common and then portrayed their inhabitants, the Uhombo. He did indeed see "a hundred beings of the most degraded, unpresentable type it is possible to conceive," but these villagers knew how to farm appropriate crops, built serviceable grass huts, had normal bodies and well-developed senses, and had some notion of property. "Only in taste and judgment, based upon larger experience, in the power of expression, *in morals and intellectual culture*, are we superior" (Stanley 1879:273, emphasis added).

Stanley, who had experienced poverty as the child of a fallen woman in Wales, believed that commerce and paternalistic direction would civilize Africans and that the endeavor was worthwhile for the white man because of the Dark Continent's immense riches. There is a bitter irony in Stanley's frequent professions of philanthropy. Apart from his discovery of Livingstone, Stanley's main legacy to history is his role in what he claimed was a philanthropic endeavor, the establishment of the International Association of the Congo on behalf of King Leopold II of Belgium, who was to turn that region into a private, predatory preserve.

Sir Samuel Baker, the son of a West Indian slave owner, was the discoverer of Lake Albert and from 1868 to 1873 performed an administrative function as governor-general of Equatoria for Khedive Ismail of Egypt. His role in the latter capacity was supposedly to stop the Arab slave trade, a task for which he claimed success, probably without justification. Baker's opinions reflected the "folk-polygenism" of the plantocracy. Both the stereotypes and the attempts at moderation described in *The Albert N'yanza* tell us something about an era in which exaggeration of difference could be conscripted as part of a plea for enlightened governance.

> A creature of impulse, seldom actuated by reflection, the black man astounds by his complete obtuseness, and as suddenly confounds you by an unexpected exhibition of sympathy. . . . When the horse and the ass shall be found in double harness, the white man and the African black will pull together under the same *régime*. It is the grand error of equalizing that which is unequal, that has lowered the negro character and made the black man a reproach.
>
> In his savage home, what is the African? Certainly bad; but not so bad as white men would (I believe) be under similar circumstances. He is acted upon by the bad passions inherent in human nature, but there is no exaggerated vice, such as is found in civilized countries. (Baker 1870:181)

Baker attempts some naturalism, with associated advice for administrators. He makes the familiar observation that the minds of African infants are precocious but that the brain soon ceases development. Baker, like many, believed that a too-easy climate causes "languor and decay" (1870:xxiii). Once formed, racial characteristics do not alter, even when the locality changes. The English remain the same the world over, and the Negro too retains his "natural instincts": "And these natural instincts being a love of idleness and savagedom, he will assuredly relapse into an idle and savage state, unless specially governed and forced to industry" (Baker 1870:183).

Baker also tried his hand at understanding polygamy and related anthropological staples. He blamed the climate for breeding sensuality, leading to polygyny and, in turn, to a lowered status for women. These were all pieces in prevailing collective representations of Africans. Baker does make the points that bridewealth enhances the value of daughters and that marriage in general has a strong economic dimension. These ideas were to appear later as key concepts in functionalist anthropology, though in Baker's formulation these insights hardly led to relativism. Women are seen as "slaves" of men's passion (though love is said to be nonexistent), and, most significantly, Baker concludes that "so long as polygamy exists, an extension of civilization is impossible" (1870:xxiii, xxiv).

By the end of the 19th century, colonial control in Africa was being solidified, and medical advances made travel safer. Mary Kingsley is perhaps the most well known of a number of female travelers who took advantage of these conditions. Mary Henrietta Kingsley (1863–1900) was a competent zoologist and an individual who, despite prejudices, laid some of the foundations for the social anthropology of West African societies. She wrote two books, *Travels in West Africa* (1897) and *West African Studies* (1899). In her work it sometimes appears that her intellect and experience (she liked most of the Africans she met) are at war with the collective representations of the colonial class that she could not wholly or was not yet willing to discard. "I own I regard not only the African but all coloured races, as inferior – inferior in kind not in degree – to the white races," remarked Kingsley in an appendix to her book (1982:669). In her opinion the African's greatest deficiency lay in a lack of technical prowess. She also believed in the polygenist notion that Africans and whites were separate species (Kingsley 1982:672). In her view social institutions such as polygyny and slavery constituted barriers to the kind of progress missionaries wished to achieve. Africans were not "keen on mountaineering in the civilisation range" (Kingsley 1982:680). The attempt by missionaries to civilize Africans by teaching them literary and clerical skills and a religion of "self-abnegation" was bound to have disastrous effects. Echoing Reade and Burton, Kingsley contemned the urban Negroes of Freetown (1982:660).

On the other hand, Kingsley was skeptical of claims that Negro brain development, while precocious in children, was arrested in later years, while European brains continued to develop (1982:672). She also believed that West Africans could be educated in the technical skills in which they were deficient and could be made by European culture into "a very good sort of man, not the same sort of man that a white man is" (Kingsley 1982:680). Kingsley downplays reports of cannibalism, though she does not deny that it exists. With regard to polygamy, Kingsley is critical of the obsession that missionaries had concerning the obliteration of this institution. She believed that polygamy might be compatible with being a good Christian and that African morality was made worse by attempts to suppress this institution. Kingsley, a spinster, was no admirer of Victorian marriage. She understood that women had both rights and agency within African marriage systems. For example, she noted that marriage among the Igalwa and the M'pongwe of Gabon involved a formal prestation to the bride's mother and mother's brother as well as several supplementary gifts. Although the main marriage payment had to be returned in the event of divorce, which was common, supplementary gifts were retained by the wife's kin. Igalwa and M'pongwe women nagged their husbands frequently and sometimes yelled at them in public "in a way that reminded me of some London slum scenes" (Kingsley 1982:425). The men might retaliate with violence. Were the blows to result in the drawing of blood, the wife would return to her kin, seek annulment, and soon be free to remarry. Her relatives would be glad enough to retain the supplementary gifts they had received at the time of her wedding (Kingsley 1982).

Kingsley was also aware that not all the pressure for polygynous marriage came from the male sex: "The African lady does not care a travelling white-smith's execration if her husband does flirt, so long as he does not go and give to other women the cloth, & c., that she should have. The more wives the less work, says the African lady; and I have known men who would rather have one wife and spent the rest of the money on themselves, in a civilized way, driven into polygamy by the women" (1982:212). Burton, of course, had made the same point but without the same stress on female agency.

There is no suggestion of primitive promiscuity in Kingsley's work. She believed informants who told her that love had existed in Africa before the coming of the white man. Her reaction to this idea, however, contains elements of the "primitive Africans are better than civilized ones" trope as well as being expressed in the language of evolutionary atavism: "*For we may here find a real golden age, which in other races of humanity lies away in the midst of the ages behind the kitchen middens and the Cambrian rocks*" (Kingsley 1982:226). We are now entering a period in the history of anthropology and exploration in which some of the cruder stereotypes of primitive sexuality were modified, moderated, or replaced by other, usually milder stereotypes (see chapter 6). In some measure, this was due to the growth of anthropological science and an increment in knowledge about the lives of tribal peoples. However, the development of modern fieldwork techniques was more than a decade away when Kingsley wrote. We shall suggest that it may be significant that very few of the individuals whose work helped to demolish the image of the oversexed savage (as Kingsley's short comments tend to do) were themselves involved in typical Victorian marriages. Edward Westermarck, to whose work Kingsley briefly refers (1982:435), was a confirmed bachelor with homosocial tendencies. He was also an atheist and moderately feminist. Havelock Ellis had a semidetached marriage with a lesbian writer. After years of obedience to her parents, Mary Kingsley was unprepared to be the angel in anyone's house. It would seem that in late Victorian society a certain positioning of oneself was necessary not only to escape or simply to avoid social constraints but also to see "others" in new ways.

Unlike the lady traveler Kingsley, Sir Harry Johnston was one of the leading imperialists of his time, ranking in importance behind only Cecil

Rhodes and Lord Frederick Lugard. He added some 400,000 square miles to Britain's East African empire (Stocking 1995:379). When he first visited Africa, he was also a botanist, a painter, and a journalist. He was briefly a traveler and an explorer in the Congo and Angola. He had a spell of military service in the Sudan and joined the British consular service in the 1880s. His first duties were in eastern Nigeria in administering the Oil Rivers protectorate. He then set up the British administration in Central Africa in 1889, acting as the first commissioner in Nyasaland (1891–95) before becoming consul general in Tunis and special commissioner in Uganda from 1899 to 1901. Johnston was a prolific writer: his many books and articles cover not only his period of service in Africa but also his opinions on woman suffrage in England and the condition of blacks in the United States. He wrote a number of volumes for young boys on British explorers in the colonies, including *Pioneers in West Africa* (1912), which propagated the imperialist gospel to the generation that came of age in the interwar years. Respected as a competent amateur anthropologist, he strongly advocated the teaching of anthropology as part of the training of colonial officials (Stocking 1995:379, 380).

Johnston believed that true Negroes were mentally and morally inferior to savannah-dwelling Islamic peoples such as the Fulani and the Hausa, who were partly Semitic or Caucasian. In other words, he subscribed to the body of ideas that became known as the Hamitic hypothesis (Lyons 1984), variants of which were promulgated by Charles Seligman and Elliot Smith. In his *A History of the Colonization of Africa by Alien Races* (1899) Johnston claimed that blacks were "born slaves," inasmuch as their mental and physical characteristics, which included a degree of docility, destined them for servitude. However, he believed that such racial differences could be lessened by education. His paternalistic approach was probably shared by a majority of missionaries and administrators.

In the following passage and footnote from Johnston's book *British Central Africa* (1897:408, 409) we see classic tropes of the colonial encounter as well as attempts to moderate their effects. Africans are said to be educable, though their mentality was alleged to diminish when puberty (and a highly developed sexuality) set in. Their dances are described as wild, but wild within limits. Little boys are portrayed as truly depraved and given to self-abuse (in an era when worry about self-abuse in England and America amounted to a moral panic). Few girls, it is claimed, remain virgins past the age of five. Adults, on the other hand, are acknowledged to be comparatively continent:

Still, taken as a whole, I think it must be admitted that the average negro of British Central Africa is not a born fool. His mental powers are not much developed by native training, but I am certain that he has in him possibilities in the present generation as great as those of the average Indian; and there is really no saying what he may come to after several generations of education. I think it is truly remarkable the way in which a little savage boy can be put to school and taught to read in a few months and subsequently become a skilful printer or telegraph clerk, or even book-keeper. The little boys are much sharper and shrewder than the grown-up male. When the youth arrives at puberty there is undoubtedly the tendency towards an arrested development of the mind. At this critical period many bright and shining examples fall off into disappointing nullity. As might be imagined, the concentration of their thoughts on sexual intercourse is responsible for this falling away.

This is the negro's genetic weakness. *Nature has probably endowed him with more than the usual genetic faculty. After all, to these people almost without arts and sciences and the refined pleasures of the senses, the only acute enjoyment offered them by nature is sexual intercourse.* Yet the negro is very rarely knowingly indecent or addicted to lubricity. In this land of nudity which I have known for seven years, I do not remember once having seen an indecent gesture on the part of either man or woman and only very rarely (and that not amongst unspoilt savages) in the case of that most shameless member of the community – the little boy. An exception must be made to this statement where the native dances are concerned, and yet here, also, the statement is really equally true, for although most tribes have initiation ceremonies or dances which are indecent to our eyes since they consist of very immodest gestures and actions, they can scarcely be called wantonly indecent, because they almost constitute a religious ceremony and are performed by the negroes with a certain amount of seriousness. Those dances are never thrust on the notice of a European; it is with the greatest reluctance that they can be brought to perform in his presence. . . . Our only knowledge is derived from the more or less trustworthy accounts of educated natives. So far as I know, the only dance of a really indecent nature which is indigenous to Central Africa and has not been introduced by low caste Europeans or Arabs, is one which represented originally the act of coition, but it is so altered to a stereotyped formula that its exact purport is not obvious until explained somewhat shyly by the natives. (Johnston 1897:408, emphasis added)

The following footnote occurs below the quoted passage:

Nevertheless, it is reported to me that after these dances (especially when a large quantity of native beer has been drunk) orgies of what are occasionally called a "shameful" character ensue. These, however, are seriously entered upon at certain seasons of the year just as they are at fairs in Egypt, a custom which has been handed down from remote antiquity through different forms of religion and under many different practices, but originating undoubtedly in the worship of the *phallus* [our emphasis], as a symbol of creative power. It may safely be asserted that the negro race in Central Africa is much more truly modest, is much more free from real vice than are most European nations. It is absurd to call misuse or irregularity of sexual intercourse "vice." It may be wrong, it may be inexpedient, it may conflict with the best interests of the community and *require control or restriction* [our emphasis again]; but it is not a "vice." And in this sense the negro is very rarely vicious after he has attained to the age of puberty. He is only more or less uxorious. Here, again, to give a truthful picture it must be noted that the children are vicious, *as they are amongst most races of mankind, the boys outrageously so.* A medical missionary who was at work for some time on the west coast of Lake Nyasa gave me information concerning the depravity prevalent among the young boys in the Atonga tribe of a character not even to be expressed in obscure Latin. These statements might be applied with almost equal exactitude to boys and youths in many other parts of Africa as almost any missionary who thoroughly understands the native character would know.

As regards the little girls over nearly the whole of British Central Africa chastity before puberty is an unknown condition. (Except perhaps among the A-nyanja). Before a girl becomes a woman (that is to say before she is able to conceive) it is a matter of indifference what she does and scarcely any girl remains a virgin after about five years of age. Even where betrothed at birth, as is often the case, or at a few months old, she will go to the family of her future husband when she is four or five years of age and although she will not formally cohabit with him till she has reached the age of puberty, it constantly happens that she is deflowered by him long before that age is attained. (Johnston 1897:408–409 n.)

The ostensible concern Johnston demonstrated for fairness and balance in accounts of Africa written for adult readers is not always present in the writings he directed at schoolboys, the overt purpose of which was the glorification of the imperial mission. The bravery of men like Mungo Park, Hugh Clapperton, and the Lander brothers was better dramatized by dire portrayals of the natural and human realities they tried to transcend. There is, of course, no mention of sexuality (apart from nudity), but cannibalism and witchcraft fulfill their usual roles in the absence of the former:

> Amongst the black people themselves there were terrible cannibals, poisoners, and even mesmerists. Some of the men and women . . . were possessed of horrible tastes. They not only liked to eat human flesh, and would waylay (as they do in the south-eastern part of Sierra Leone at the present day) lonely men and women and children at night, kill them, cook them, and eat them, and pretend afterwards that they had been slain by leopards or lions.
> . . . All the stories of ogres, witches, vampires, and ghouls, with which you have been thrilled from the age at which it was safe to let you read about such things – safe because you knew these creatures no longer existed in England, or wherever your comfortable home was – were not all imagination. They were based on real things which occurred within the experience of the prehistoric peoples of Europe . . . and also on what used to occur, and even still occurs in Africa. (Johnston 1912:64, 65)

Such was the comparative method specially retooled for the white schoolboys of the empire.

Johnston's peregrinations were not confined to Africa. He was also the author of *The Negro in the New World* (1910), a volume that met with the approval of Theodore Roosevelt. The educational programs at Tuskegee and Hampton not unsurprisingly met with his approval, as their educational philosophy accorded with the gradualism that he endorsed (Johnston 1929:272–278). In this book he claimed that the Negro was morally almost on a par with the white race, but he also stated his opposition to mixed marriages: "The white people in the United States will have to get used to the presence of the Negro in their midst, but not as a brother-in-law" (Johnston 1910, as quoted in Johnston 1929:272).

The period between Kingsley's writings and the end of Johnston's career saw the conclusion of the age of exploration. In the year that *Travels in West Africa* was published the city of Benin fell to a British punitive expedition. During the next decade the "pacification" of Nigeria was completed. As the whole continent apart from Liberia, Ethiopia, and, nominally, Egypt came under active European control, there was a change in race relations. One may make an exception of South Africa, where the Boer War was fought and where most of the social changes we now discuss had already occurred. We are referring to the installation of administrative bureaucracies, indirect rule in the British territories, direct rule in the French colonies, new settler colonies in Kenya and southern Rhodesia, and changes in the gender balance among colonists everywhere. The last point is worthy of our attention, because it solidified the color bar in all respects.

A number of writers who differ greatly in their method and theoretical approach to sexuality (e.g., MacCrone 1957 for South Africa during the 17th and 18th centuries; Cairns 1965 for southern and eastern Africa; Ballhatchet 1980 for India; Hyam 1990 for India, Africa, and elsewhere; and Stoler 1995 for Indonesia) have noted some similar historical dynamics with respect to the gender balance and the color bar.

In the early period of contact in India (during the 18th century) British officers took Indian wives as well as mistresses. Later on they took mistresses, or bibis. In the period after the Indian mutiny the officers rarely took mistresses, but caravans of prostitutes served the ordinary British soldiers, who came predominantly from lower-class families. By 1865 "lock hospitals (not so punitive in their regime as in Britain) were available in all cantonments to treat prostitutes suffering from venereal disease" (Hyam 1990:123). In addition, some officers and common soldiers availed themselves of homosexual contacts. After the Suez Canal opened, it became easier for administrators and senior officers (and eventually some even in the lower ranks) to bring their memsahibs to India. Sexual contact between British officers and Indian and Anglo-Indian women was increasingly frowned upon, although there were some willing to break the rules. The reasons for this change included the presence of wives and an enlarged European community, the rise of social purity in England, and stricter rules about abuse of authority and moral leadership. Without good reason, some fears developed about the security of British women, as readers of *A Passage to India* and *The Raj Quartet* are well aware. Obviously, the new barriers to sexual contact (which were never simply one-way) had the undesirable effect of increasing segregation, but we note with some amazement that one prominent modern historian

(Hyam 1990) seems single-mindedly to regard the impediments placed on the sexual contact between British men and Indian women and women of other colonized nations as merely the exportation of British prudery to nations that had a healthier attitude to sex!

There is a rough parallel between events in Africa and in India, except that there was no stage in which intermarriage was deemed permissible in Africa. Initially, traders, seamen, planters, and hunters availed themselves of some of the sexual opportunities that came their way. Missionaries did not do so, with a few notorious exceptions. Most of the explorers (Burton and possibly Reade being partial exceptions) were imbued with a sense of moral responsibility and caste loyalty and, in some cases (e.g., David Livingstone), feelings of repulsion toward African women (Cairns 1965:59–70). A notable exception was the German explorer Mehmed Emin Pasha (Eduard Schnitzer), who married an African and converted to Islam. In other words, the codes of sexual interaction were not unconnected with class demarcations in Europe. Until the very end of the Victorian era, the European presence in sub-Saharan Africa north of the Limpopo was overwhelmingly male, and that is why so much of what we have hitherto outlined is a "boy's story" of African sexuality. Some Victorian missionaries, particularly in South-central Africa, brought their wives with them, and there were a few redoubtable lady missionaries such as Mary Slessor in Calabar. Administrators and diplomats usually left their wives at home. Even the courageous Isabel Burton did not join her husband when he became consul in Fernando Póo. Tropical disease, difficulty of travel, and frontier hardships were obvious reasons for the absence of women, but fear of African males was another. Sir Samuel Baker reluctantly consented to his wife's desire to accompany him on his African travels: "I shuddered at the prospect for her, should she be left alone in savage lands at my death" (1870:2).

Improved travel, an increasing ability to treat tropical disease, and the imposition of Pax Britannica by conquest enabled women to travel and reside more freely in Africa. There was also a feeling that the "white man's burden," the moral incumbencies of imperialism, might be better discharged if administrators and missionaries were to bring their wives with them. Missionaries in particular could present an example of monogamous, Christian family values. Wives could nurse, teach in schools, and instruct African women in practical skills such as needlework. There were, of course, continued concerns about the white women's safety and even moral integrity when exposed to "rude contact with coarse animal natures" and "depraved" language (Sir Harry Johnston, quoted in Cairns 1965:61).

In Africa, as in India, the coming of women has been blamed for an intensification of the color bar. In both cases that closure was accompanied by occasional outbreaks of panic about the rape of white women. In both cases such fears had little justification. Inevitably, there were just a few cases on which such fears could be built. In Kenya "the Legislative Assembly set up a commission of enquiry, which reported that from 1910 to 1920 there had been only sixteen cases of sexual assault against Europeans, and of those only one was the rape of an adult woman. Seven were against children, and these were in every case committed by African boys aged between ten and fifteen employed as servants in European households. The age of the victims was between two and seven, and what particularly outraged the settlers was that in some cases the children had contracted venereal disease" (Gill 1995:16). Had these women and children stayed in Britain, of course, many would not have been able to afford servants at all. Moreover, among British families who did keep servants, cases of sexual abuse of young girls were far from rare. In Britain, however, it was the servants who were the victims, and respectable people passed over such matters in silence. In British Africa male house servants were the rule.

Meanwhile, other events in Kenya put a temporary stop to the practice of concubinage by colonial officials in Africa and elsewhere. In the Sudan Sir Reginald and Lady Wingate had already taken steps against this practice, but it was common elsewhere until 1909. Hubert Silberrad was an assistant district commissioner who "inherited" two African wives from his predecessor, who had paid bridewealth for them. One of them was a girl of about twelve who did not like the arrangement. Silberrad also came to an arrangement with an askari, or native police officer, to acquire a third girl age twelve or thirteen. There was some dispute over the deal, and Silberrad locked up the askari. A neighboring white farmer and his wife removed two of the girls and complained to the governor. Upset by the mild punishment Silberrad received (he was placed last instead of first on a list of 28 assistant district commissioners eligible for promotion), the farmer, Routledge, blew the scandal wide open. The secretary of state at the Colonial Office, Robert Offley Ashburton Crewe, issued an official circular warning that grave consequences would ensue for officials involved in "immoral relations with native women," and it was distributed to most of the colonies except the West Indies, where racial intermarriage was not discouraged (Hyam 1990:160–168). As we have already noted, such measures were bound to have a few undesirable as well as the obvious desirable effects, inasmuch as the officials became more remote from the communities over which they presided.

We examined a small sample of files containing the reports, correspondence, and journals of colonial officials in Africa (mainly Nigeria) covering the period 1910–35 in the Rhodes House library at Oxford. We noted that some of the officials were accompanied by their wives and that in all cases the expatriate social world was very narrow. Most of the officials were imbued with a sense of imperial duty, but their attitudes toward African institutions, intelligence, and morality were at best paternalistic and at worst contemptuous. Falk and his wife were typical in this regard.

Among the many materials we examined were some boxes pertaining to Lord Lugard, Nigeria's first governor-general and author of *The Dual Mandate* (1922); to Hubert Mathews, who spent 19 years in the Nigerian colonial service and received a certificate in anthropology from Oxford in 1912 and a diploma in 1925; and to Falk himself. In addition, we examined some of the reports of Northcote Thomas, whose career included a tour of duty as the first government anthropologist in Nigeria. There is, as we will demonstrate, a contrast between the attitudes of Thomas, who had already gained a reputation for his anthropological writings on Australian kinship, and the career administrators.

By the time of Thomas's appointment in 1910 there had been sporadic lobbying in anthropological circles for some 15 years both to establish an Imperial Bureau of Ethnology and to train officers in the colonial service in anthropology. Although the Colonial Office was not fully convinced of the benefits of anthropological training, a few leading administrators, including Johnston and Sir Richard Temple, were in the anthropologists' camp. By this time Oxford, Cambridge, and London were offering limited programs in anthropology. In 1913 R. R. Marett of Oxford told the anthropological section of the British Association that in the six years that Oxford had offered its diploma and certificate courses its 60 students had included 21 colonial officers, there being ten from West Africa, nine from Sudan and Egypt, one from British East Africa, and one from India (Marett in Temple et al. 1913:192; Stocking 1995:380).

It would be as wrong to assume that there was anything like an institutional culture in anthropology at this time as it would be anachronistic to assume relativism in its practitioners. Professionalization was merely beginning. Most anthropologists were still evolutionists of one stamp or another, except for W. H. R. Rivers and Elliot Smith, who had embraced diffusionism; additionally, many of Sir James Frazer's disciples were more interested in Britain or in Greece and Rome than in the colonial territories. On the other hand, a strong camaraderie as well as a common ethos of paternalism and racial superiority pervaded the colonial service. It was a world in which one changed for dinner, was served drinks on the verandah, and socialized only with those one regarded as one's peers. A year or two's exposure to evolutionist anthropology would not be designed to break or tamper with such an ethos.

In contrast, Northcote Thomas was a member of the Society for Psychical Research as well as the Anthropological Institute. He shared interests in folklore, the occult, and the family with Andrew Lang, who was his intellectual mentor and collaborator. As we have seen, Thomas's writings on Australian marriage and mating customs were devoid of Victorian moral presumption. In those writings he had delivered a devastating critique of Morgan and Spencer and Gillen and had denied the existence of group marriage. Later remembered in colonial circles as a "recognized maniac" who "lived on vegetables" and wore sandals even back in England, Thomas seems to have alienated local colonial officials from the moment he began work in southern Nigeria (Stocking 1995:377). Lugard, who became governor of the newly united Nigeria in 1912, disliked Thomas and had him transferred to Sierra Leone, where he got into further trouble for refusing to disclose to the authorities the names of presumed murderers in the Human Leopard Society. It is interesting to contrast Thomas's views of Edo and Igbo marriage and sexual morality with those of his contemporaries such as Falk and Mathews.

Other colonial administrators regarded premarital sexuality among traditional southern Nigerian peoples as immoral. Bride-price was seen as a form of outright purchase and marriage accordingly as a form of slavery. The difficulty of obtaining divorce in many Nigerian societies was viewed as an impediment to the freedom of women. This, of course, does not mean that the male colonial elite was feminist or necessarily in favor of easy divorce. Rather, it signifies that they used and exaggerated the patriarchy of traditional institutions in Africa as a distancing device. Falk, significantly, regarded the premarital arrangements of the Igbo of Aba as the social product of the institution of bride-price and the natural product of their primitivity. High bride-price, he suggested, led to immorality, not restraint: "As soon as he has attained the age of puberty an adolescent will be allowed to have connection with the girl for whom his parents or guardian have paid a bride price. Restraint is quite unknown among so primitive a people. If lack of funds prevent early marriage, the growing boy will find another man's wife or daughter with whom to gratify his instincts."[4] An alleged absence of homosexuality and incest among the Igbo and Ibibio is seen by Falk to be merely the result of animalistic, heterosexual indulgence.[5]

Sometimes social institutions were observed that did not fit the prevailing stereotypes. In such cases, a writer's style of reportage could, nonetheless, be used to make native custom appear to support prevailing views of African character. In the following assessment by Mathews the author notes the relative freedom conferred upon Nungu women by the fact that wives were difficult to obtain in this region of central Nigeria. However, the resulting situation is shaped by diction and irony into evidence of the unruliness of women and the inability of men to maintain order:

> There always are numbers of men who have no wives, but are trying by hook or crook to get them. This makes the women very independent. If a sufficient inducement is offered a woman, or if she is moved by a desire for change, she will desert one man for another. She is, of course, careful to choose a man who lives in another village, for it would be too risky both for her and for her new consort to be within easy reach of the previous and now aggrieved husband. The first result of such a desertion is that the abandoned husband wanders round the countryside loudly bemoaning his loss to the accompaniment of a drum, and trying to get the woman to take pity on him and return. If this is of no avail, and the man is sufficiently daring, he will lie in wait, perhaps with the other men of his village, near the farms, or on the edge of the village to which the woman has run away, and will shoot or kidnap the first member of the village who appears. In this way the responsibility of the private quarrel devolves upon the community and an inter-village feud arises.[6]

Most European "experts" on Africa were of the opinion that some undesirable outcomes had resulted from the suppression of slavery, the introduction of general purpose money, and changes in law and custom induced or forced by government and the churches. It was assumed that many changes in family structure and family law had adversely affected the morals and status of African women. It is, of course, entirely possible that a general anomie was expressed in changing sexual behavior, but it is entirely certain that there were some who were inclined to prejudge these outcomes. Falk felt that the efforts of missionaries "to incul[c]ate the virtues of chastity" and the ease with which the native courts granted divorce under the new colonial dispensation had damaged the institution of marriage in Nigerian tribal society. In some cases, Falk remarked, men sold their wives and young daughters. In other cases, women "emancipated" by divorce drifted into concubinage and prostitution. Reformers failed when they did not take proper account of the "native mind" and the "negro character" and its "inherent vices."[7]

Falk was not sure that he knew the remedy for the "moral chaos" that supposedly surrounded him. He recommended an ordinance restricting child marriage and, for each district, a codification of the law of marriage, divorce, and custody that native courts would apply. He regretted the unwillingness of native leaders and native courts to permit the registration of marriages. In general terms, he felt that the colonial administration should take a more active supervisory role in the everyday lives of the Igbo and Ibibio.

To the reader of modern accounts of the AIDS epidemic in southern Africa, Falk's remarks on gonorrhea are most interesting. It would appear that both the surveyors of morality and those whom they survey have their own folklore. It would be of interest to know from which body of folklore the following tale (now displaced to Zambia and Zimbabwe, not to mention Nepal and Thailand) originated:

> Most District Officers have probably come across cases of violation of children and immature girls by men afflicted with gonorrhea. Such cases are more common among the Ibibios than among the Ibos. It is said that the offence is based on the belief that to have connection with a virgin is a cure for the disease, but the evidence on this point is conflicting. The strongest proof of the existence of this belief lies in the fact that no native lacks the opportunity to gratify his sexual passions with mature females, and that the crime seems otherwise inexplicable among a population who lead natural lives as the people do. All persons ever arraigned before the writer for this crime were pagan bushmen.[8]

Northcote Thomas was perhaps unique among government officials working in Nigeria in the early decades of the century inasmuch as he was not disturbed by any of the sexual and marital customs of the peoples among whom he was resident. Although he gives considerable information about premarital sex and adultery among the Edo and the Ibo, his tone in writing about these matters is, for the most part, matter-of-fact, neither alarmed nor ironic. His reports make it clear that although members of these societies may act differently from Europeans, they are, in fact, bound by clear rules. He describes what payments must be made or gifts given between lovers or to the parents or husband of a sexual partner in various localities. He notes under what conditions sexual relations are permitted, when they are not, and when local custom dictates that sexual freedom must end. Moreover, he recognizes differences between groups. "The women of Okpe," he remarks in his work on the Edo, "seem to be far more moral, according to European lights, than those of the tribes of the south. It seems to be exceedingly rare for a girl to bear a child before marriage." Reporting on the marriage of very young girls at Soso, in the extreme north of the Edo area, he states that he "could not, however observe the slightest ill-effects of this premature marriage, on the contrary, both young and older wives, appeared to be particularly healthy, and the standard of physical development was a good one." Attitudes such as these, as well as his propensity for wearing sandals and his interest in the occult, were reasons why Northcote Thomas's anthropology had little appeal in the circles of colonial power. Thomas did not do intensive fieldwork in the Malinowskian mode, but his detailed work implied an intimacy with African custom that transcended the color bar.

In 1929 events occurred that led the British Colonial Office to reconsider its attitudes toward anthropology and, in particular, to recognize a need for more accurate information about women, marriage, and the family. The patterns of colonial social relations made it inevitable that as little direct knowledge British administrators had of the motives and emotions of African men, those of women were even more of a mystery. These circumstances meant that resistance by women to colonial rule, when it occurred, was met with a level of misunderstanding sufficient to provoke both public and bureaucratic responses from London.

In 1929 riots erupted in several communities in the south of Igboland and in nearby Ijaw coastal towns. The protests were led by women traders who anticipated that their inclusion in a census indicated the imminent imposition of government taxation. Other possible causes of the protests included the converting of farmland from the cultivation of food crops to cash crops and the women's indignation at the male-dominated native court system. Mrs. Falk, whose husband was now resident in Calabar, described in her diary the conditions that pertained among colonial wives during the rebellion: "Outwardly we still lead a fairly normal life, except for a number of strange women in the station. We drive about, play tennis and go to one another's houses and to the club, and pretent [sic] that all is well. We are not going to show the natives that we are alarmed or nervous. But we are preparing for the worst."[9] In the meantime, her husband was engaged in fighting the women's insurrection in Opobo District. On December 9, 1929, he wrote to her about an encounter during which police deflected an attack on a government office by defying the Nigerians' expectation that British troops would not fire on women who "wrecked" government offices: "Total death 40. Since then all quiet at Opobo. Factories reopened. The war fleet paddled away as soon as it realized that the plan had failed." Mrs. Falk wrote proudly of her husband's firmness of purpose: "I have just heard a lovely joke, which is being told along the coast. People say that Daddy saved the situation in this province by quick and firm action. The only real punishment for the natives is to burn their villages and to seize their goats, chickens and yams. Daddy ordered the police to burn an abandoned village to make the chiefs sue for peace. So people say that Daddy's latest slogan is 'A village a day, keeps the riot away.'"[10]

Both the Falks speculated on the causes of the disturbances and the character of Africans. Their conclusions were informed by many of the stereotypical assumptions we have been documenting, especially those concerning the treatment of African women and the ability of Africans to benefit from the "improving influences" of colonialism. Both Falks denied that the rebellion was the result of Igbo women acting independently to redress their own grievances. Assumptions about the intelligence and status of local women made such a possibility appear unlikely. In Falk's official report and "Plan for the Government of Calabar" (1933) he expressed the certainty that the women were encouraged to riot by the men, who hoped that British consideration for women would undermine colonial authority.[11] Mrs. Falk blamed the riots on agitation from "American negroes," whom she believed to be both "far more civilized than the African negroes" and eager to start a worldwide black revolution. She worried about the effects of civilization on Africans: "It is already obvious that this country will go the way of India if we continue to educate the natives as fast as it has been done during the last few years. We certainly do not make them happier. . . . The half-educated negro is a disgusting specimen. The real pagan is the best of the lot."[12]

It must be stressed that the Falks were not regarded by their associates as eccentric (as Northcote Thomas was) or as extreme or excessive in their views. When Falk left Calabar in 1934 to become acting administrator of the colony in Lagos, a testimonial praised the Falks' admirable work on behalf of local welfare. It congratulated Falk for heading the Leprosy Relief Commission and for work in road building and other public works and in teacher training. Mrs. Falk, according to the testimonial document, "is known and admired by all classes for her common sense, a trait rare in these days." She served as president of the Calabar branch of the Ladies Association of Nigeria, and the testimonial said that her excellence at needlework would be attested to by that body.[13]

The Igbo Women's War and its suppression had immediate repercussions in London. The Colonial Office was disturbed and, furthermore, faced criticism. Shortly thereafter (in 1930), Lugard received a letter from the National Council of Women (a British body that is still in existence) urging that a woman be appointed in the Colonial Office as a consultant on women's issues. Lugard replied that this would be inadvisable but that the International African Institute, which included women researchers (Audrey Richards and others are mentioned), were looking into such matters. He also stated that he did not think a woman in the Colonial Office could have prevented the 1929 women's riots (1930, Lugard Correspondence).

The events of 1929 did indeed result in the employment of anthropologists such as Charles Kingsley Meek (previously government anthropologist in northern Nigeria) and G. T. Basden, who concentrated most on the role of men among the troublesome Igbo. Most important, two female scholars were asked to study Igbo women. They were Margaret Green, who wrote *Ibo Village Affairs* (1947), and Sylvia Leith-Ross, who wrote *African Women* (1939). The studies by Meek and Green are solid, functionalist works that do not promote the racial or sexual stereotypes of the preceding century. (They are concerned with the delineation of social structure.)

In the end, the misrecognition of African sexuality and gender roles that was itself the complex product of the colonial practice of racial distancing and gender separation had produced political consequences that called out for investigation. The studies were undertaken at the behest of a colonial government that thought that the women's war indicated that sex and gender among the Igbo posed a peculiar problem in surveillance that anthropologists might help them solve. The divergence we have seen between bureaucratic and anthropological attitudes may help to explain why this project, in British Africa at least, never was as successful as either its proponents or its detractors claimed and continue to claim.

CHAPTER 6

Malinowski as "Reluctant Sexologist"

I n *The Sexual Life of Savages in Northwestern Melanesia* (1929) Bronislaw Malinowski derides 19th-century sensationalism concerning primitive sexuality and emphasizes the stable marital relations that succeed
youthful promiscuity among Trobrianders. [1] His work appealed greatly to
Havelock Ellis and Bertrand Russell, who were endeavoring to develop the
foundations of a new secular sexual morality. This chapter discusses the uses
made of anthropological data by the pioneering advocates of companionate
marriage, contraceptives, and sex education and assesses the degree to which
their views were shared by Malinowski. It also explores the limits of any new
"objectivity" concerning "primitive" sexuality.

Malinowski, in a witty essay written during the 1920s but not published
until 20 years after the author's death, remarks upon the tendency of anthropologists to report data concerning primitive behavior in such a way
as to transform primitives into models of "an ideal human state" (1962:112).
In this essay, which was intended as a statement of the role scientific anthropology might play in debates of the 1920s concerning sexual reform,
Malinowski dismisses as "junk" attempts to assimilate psychology and behavior to modes of existence advocated by apologists for diverse ideologies (1962:112–113). He gave as an example the discovery of a "puritanically
chaste" primitive by Father Wilhelm Schmidt, Elliot Smith, and William
J. Perry, while W. H. R. Rivers had "advanced Socialism in England because he imagined that Melanesian savages were Communists" (Malinowski
1962:112). "One or two quite intelligent writers on feminism," Malinowski
chides, "have based their reformatory conclusions on the fact of primitive
mother right, while . . . [f]ree love has been advocated for the last fifty years
all over the world by pious references to primitive promiscuity" (1962:112–
113).

Despite this vociferous rejection of distortions of the data to fit ideological requirements, Malinowski does not refrain from offering his contemporaries a number of very specific prescriptions for sexual reform. The "stratified morality" advocated by Malinowski would involve the retention of marriage, said to be universal among primitives, as a central social institution. Those married couples who willingly and responsibly take on the role of parents are to be suitably rewarded with both the "greatest human happiness" and "special social privileges." Bachelors and spinsters are to be tolerated, even permitted sexual expression, but might be subjected to deterrents imposed by the system of taxation (Malinowski 1962:130). Homosexuals, Malinowski suggests, should be provided with some "arrangements" by which they may gratify their desires without risk of persecution and without the danger that they might "infect" others (1962:131). In the article, which was published under the title "Aping the Ape" (although the draft copy in the Yale University library indicates that he had not selected a title for it), Malinowski mentions a number of contemporary advocates of sexual reform as persons who have been misused by defenders of free love and argues that their positions are really more compatible with his own. These figures include Havelock Ellis, Bertrand and Dora Russell, and Judge Ben Lindsey, an American famous at the time for his advocacy of "companionate marriage." Marie Stopes, the English birth control crusader, is not mentioned by name but figures in the essay as "The Sensible Woman (Birth Control Expert)." Malinowski further argues that the true facts of primitive sexuality are much closer to the state of affairs he advocates than to the ways of life championed by either traditionalists or advocates of free love. Thus, Malinowski believed, the reforms he proposed were dictated not by utopian vision but by objective science.

It is perhaps unfair to hold a scholar to opinions expressed in an article he chose not to publish during his lifetime. We shall, however, attempt in this essay to demonstrate that "Aping the Ape" is merely an unusually clear and forthright statement of positions taken by Malinowski elsewhere in published sources and public statements, a statement particularly valuable because it is explicit in its acknowledgment of the common ground shared by Malinowski with leading sexual reformers of his day. We hope that by examining Malinowski's work, especially *The Sexual Life of Savages*, in the context of the ideas of some of these thinkers, particularly Ellis and Russell, we can understand better the importance of contemporary political and social debate in shaping the thinking of this staunch advocate of empiricism.

Michel Foucault argued that sexuality is an area in which scientific discourse can be seen with particular clarity to have been shaped, indeed necessitated, by political considerations. Foucault (1980) includes the work of Ellis in the *scientia sexualis* he examines in his *History of Sexuality* but does not consider any empirical research among primitives under that category. To what degree, we shall ask, do Foucault's characterizations of sexual scholarship accurately describe the work of some of Malinowski's contemporaries, and how well do they apply to Malinowski's own work?

ANTHROPOLOGY AND THE COMPULSION TO CONFESS

Anthropology was and is, or so we were all once told, a science based on participant observation. Malinowski has been regarded as the pioneer of this technique, although he was not, in fact, its first practitioner (see Hinsley 1983; Stocking 1983). Now what, precisely, is participant observation? The anthropologist gains entry to the stranger community, sits, watches, and, above all else, listens to what the strangers tell him or her about themselves. Confession, Foucault (1980) informs us, emerged as a technique of power during the 13th century. Employed for centuries by the Catholic Church, the technique later entered the secular realm. The lawyer, doctor, social worker, and alienist all hear confessions. The manifest aim of such procedures is the eliciting of truth and the remedying of disease or disorder; their latent function is to reinforce the unequal power structure that compels and conducts discourse.

It is a paradox of modern civilization, Foucault asserts, that the need to tell the other(s) about oneself is perceived as a mechanism of individuation, whereas it is, in fact, a method of socialization and subordination. In other words, the confessional strategy is embedded in mystification. A patient with a sexual problem discusses it with a psychiatrist, who judges, consoles, reconciles the patient perhaps to this situation, and, having elicited the requisite number of statements, converts them into a truth useable by patient and interlocutor and compatible with the ideology of the power structure. The patient's behavior is triply determined by outside forces: (1) there is a personal secret that results, in fact, from an implicit or explicit injunction to hide things so that (2) a satisfaction is gained from "self-revelation" and "self-discovery," which are perceived to be voluntary but, in fact, emerge out of a social compulsion to confess, and (3) a truth is elicited and a cure effected by a socially approved agent. Malinowski's anthropology is surely a confessional art, but does it accord with Foucault's description of confession?

From his Trobriand informants, Malinowski gained detailed knowledge of folklore, "tribal" economics, garden magic, sexual theories, and sexual behavior. His very claim to fame rested on his ability to elicit detailed and reliable information. Confession is not absent from primitive praxis. We find it associated with curing and witch-finding cults, for example, often with considerable sexual content in the confessed material. The Trobriand practice of exhumation and examination of corpses for signs of sorcery, followed by general discussion concerning the sorcerer's possible motives, often led to the revelation of significant sexual misconduct. Misconduct, thus confessed, would normally have been broadcast to all interested parties, typically an entire village. Margaret Mead, writing about the introduction of Christianity to Peri Village (Manus), notes that villagers chose Catholicism over Protestantism partly because of the attraction of auricular confession: the confession of sin to a single individual promised a desirable gain in privacy to a community that, like the Trobriands, was used to public exposure of private indiscretion (1956:94, 324–325). If similar pressures were at work in the agrarian village communities served by the early Catholic Church, Christian confession might well have helped to establish the value placed on privacy in Europe, whatever it may have done later to threaten its achievement. Of course, it is a paradox of privacy that a good deal of it is necessary to create a guilty secret so burdensome that one feels a compulsion to confess.

At any rate, Malinowski was not collecting Trobriand secrets in the privacy of the confessional. His express purpose was to share them with the world, a purpose that critics of social science have long insisted is more easily accomplished with the secrets of those who wield little power – primitives, the poor, women, and children. Malinowski seized upon indigenous compulsions to confess as a source of data in *The Sexual Life of Savages* (1929:458–461) and elsewhere.

Trobrianders, however, were not accustomed to making confessions to scientists, hence the need for participant observation. Much of Malinowski's scientific evidence is drawn from the spontaneous confidences of friends (1929:329). He also employs such projective systems as myth and dramatic performance (notably, the disparaging public imitation of white men's sexual ineptitude [1929:338]) as guides to sexual attitudes and behavior. Where self-revelation is not available, Malinowski listens to gossip or asks questions of white traders and administrators. He makes ordinary Trobriand language disclose sexual information by the careful interlinear translation of texts, verbatim transcriptions of conversations, and glosses of lexical items. These multiple methodologies are employed with such seeming ease that the skill and imagination involved are easy to overlook. It is even easier to overlook the fact that, once subject to the hermeneutic operations of the ethnographer, these disparate fragments assume for Malinowski's European reader, albeit not for his Trobriand informants, something of the character of a psychiatric case history – a constructed portrait of the sexual, emotional, and familial experience of a composite Trobriander, offered to readers with an implicit invitation to compare it with their own case histories and those of their friends. If the confession as existential experience is absent from Malinowski's fieldwork, its transformation into its characteristic literary form is certainly present in his ethnography.

If Malinowski's informants were not offered therapy, as one presumes to have been the case with the subjects of published psychiatric reports, certainly the possibility is there that another therapeutic purpose of case histories may have been served – the "healing" of the reader or of those over whom the reader may have professional influence. Moreover, there is evidence, to be discussed later, that Malinowski intended his work to be used in this way.

Throughout two of his three periods in the field, two of them in the Trobriands and the first in Mailu, Malinowski practiced a form of self-confessional autotherapy by keeping a field diary, "keeping the diary as a form of psychological analysis" (1967:247). There is only one diary entry for his first trip to the Trobriands, a visit that resulted in his first publication on that culture, examining myths of reincarnation and advancing the idea of Trobriand ignorance of physiological paternity (Malinowski 1916). The posthumously published *A Diary in the Strict Sense of the Term* (1967) contains very little data on Trobriand sexuality and, unsurprisingly in a personal account, next to nothing on the intellectual influences that informed Malinowski's field research. The diary's notoriety in anthropological circles arose from Malinowski's repeated revelations of antipathy rather than admiration toward his subjects, especially his use of the word "nigger," whether in Polish or English. In such a context his reports of sexual attraction to male and female Trobrianders, including two instances in which such attraction progressed to "pawing" (Malinowski 1967:256, 282), inevitably appeared exploitative to readers in the 1960s and beyond.

George Stocking has drawn attention to the noticeable link between Malinowski's not infrequent periods of depression and personal sexual frustration and his explosions of revulsion toward his Trobriand hosts (1986:26). In our own reading we have noted expressions of regret about a perceived betrayal of his fiancée that often follow Malinowski's accounts of sexual arousal (e.g., 1967:268). The overall impression is one of someone strug-gling with the sexual constraints of his own culture while recording the apparently greater freedoms of another. Most of the relevant diary entries occur between mid-April and the end of May 1918, a time when Malinowski was undergoing a conflict, reminiscent of some Victorian fiction, over the need to write a letter to a former object of his affections, Nina Stirling, so that he might be free to become engaged to Elsie Masson. A diary entry of April 19, in particular, reveals that he anticipated that a respectable marriage, whether to Nina or Elsie, would entail limitations on sexual expression that contrasted to the experience of the Trobrianders: "A pretty, finely built girl walked ahead of me. I watched the muscles of her back, her figure, her legs, and the beauty of the body so hidden to us, whites, fascinated me. Probably even with my own wife I'll never have the opportunity to observe the play of back muscles for as long as with this little animal. At moments I was sorry I was not a savage and could not possess this pretty girl" (Malinowski 1967:255). One of the "pawing" episodes took place on the evening of the same day. The next day, Malinowski was overcome with guilt, both about this incident and his rejection of Nina Stirling. His response was reminiscent of the sexual culture we discuss in earlier chapters, insofar as it incorporated both the sexualizing of a primitive woman and a vow of purity as a condi-tion of his projected engagement: "Resolve: absolutely never to touch any Kiriwina whore. To be mentally incapable of possessing anyone except E. R. M. [Elsie Masson]" (Malinowski 1967:256). Two days later, on April 22, Malinowski collected information about Trobriand positions during sexual intercourse (1967:260). Returning to his tent, he had what he described as a *"flash of insight"* (emphasis his): "Physical intimacy with another human being results in such a surrender of personality that one should unite only with a woman one really loves" (Malinowski 1967:256). Three days later, Malinowski was assuring himself that Elsie Masson was the only woman he "really" loved while acknowledging that in his "sensual apperceptions" Nina Stirling "corresponded . . . better" to his "emotional longings" (1967:256).

By the time Malinowski published an ethnographic account of the data on sexuality he had collected from the Trobriands, they had been con-scripted, for better or worse, into a discourse that challenged the social and cultural norms that informed the conflicts Malinowski experienced in the field. In that discourse the Trobrianders were not "niggers," "little animals," or "whores" but, in many ways, admirable examples.

Malinowski knew and corresponded with some of the leading sexual reformers in England during the 1920s and 1930s, met some of their counterparts (e.g., Margaret Sanger) in the United States, and corresponded with
European members of the psychoanalytic movement, including Princess
Marie Bonaparte, who was a personal friend, and Wilhelm Reich, whose
work he encouraged but never endorsed. Malinowski's English contacts
included Marie Stopes, Havelock Ellis, and Bertrand Russell. The four reformers were as unlike in personality as they were in background, yet they
shared some (but not all) political aims in common.

Stopes, well known as the founder of the first birth control clinic in England, wrote a number of popular books (e.g., *Married Love* and *Wise Parenthood*, both published in 1918) that advocated sex education, sexual satisfaction for both marriage partners, a "spiritual" love relationship based on
mutual companionship, birth control, and eugenics. No libertarian, Stopes
believed that marital fulfillment, family spacing, and birth control were
moral imperatives that should be implemented by education and example.
She was saddened by the failure of her gospel to penetrate to those who
most needed it, the ignorant and the poor, who should be discouraged from
breeding both for the amelioration of their own hardship and for the good
of the race. The full title of the organization Stopes founded, the Society for
Constructive Birth Control and Racial Progress, clearly reveals its founder's
ethos.[2] One of the vice presidents of Stopes's organization in the 1930s was
Bronislaw Malinowski. At an earlier period, in the 1920s, Bertrand Russell
had also served in this capacity. However, he resigned in 1923 in protest
against Stopes's decision to support the prosecution on grounds of obscenity of the English distributors of Margaret Sanger's *Family Limitation* (Kerss
1977:73). Russell later remarked that Stopes's books, written in the language
of the educated classes, were immune from prosecution, while Sanger's publications for working women were banned because working women could
understand them (1929:90–91). Unlike Russell, Stopes loved the applause of
the Establishment, and by the 1930s, when she gained the endorsement of
the Church of England's Lambeth Conference and the Prince of Wales, she
had received the support of the Establishment's more "progressive" members.

Russell, the grandson of a prime minister, the godson of John Stuart Mill,
and the heir to a peerage, could more readily afford the Establishment's
disdain and was ideologically and temperamentally inclined toward the role

of mischievous social gadfly. A diehard libertarian individualist, Russell was more open about his extramarital relationships than was conventional in his day. The author of *Principia Mathematica* noted that "societies that have been conventionally virtuous have not produced great art. Those which have, have been composed of men such as Idaho would sterilize" (Russell 1929:96). Russell condemned the church's traditional support of celibacy and asceticism, advocated sex education and the abolition of obscenity laws, supported the idea of trial marriage (see below), upheld the right of women to enjoy sexual and social equality within and without marriage, and favored freer divorce laws. All these opinions were lucidly and forcefully proclaimed in *Marriage and Morals* (1929).

Rebel though he was, Russell's program for sexual reform did not differ much from those proposed by less scandalous figures of the period. He argued that casual sex that did not create an emotional bond between the partners was socially and personally detrimental; trial marriage might diminish the need for it (Russell 1929:159). In principle, he approved of some intrusion by the state in the affairs of the household. It was desirable that the state and its agencies should enhance the health and welfare of the family by providing education and sanitation and by relieving the working-class father of much of his financial and social burden. However, Russell was aware that the intrusion of state power was potentially dangerous, insofar as the destabilization of the working-class family might have unforeseen consequences and a militaristic nation-state might educate a nation of soldiers. Russell also gave qualified support to the eugenics movement. He believed that positive eugenics, that is, promoting the breeding of the more intelligent, was desirable, albeit politically impractical, in a democratic society. Surprisingly, he also supported a negative eugenic measure, the sterilization of the mentally retarded, although he noted that sterilization of the morally incompetent, epileptics, and others deemed socially unfit was unjustifiable and dangerous, given the present state of knowledge (Russell 1929:204–220, 254–273).

Raised in the 19th century, Russell, not surprisingly, adopted an evolutionary schema in *Marriage and Morals*, albeit he did not consider that sexual morality had exhibited any unilinear progress. Rather, he appears to have believed that a review of human evolution and social history might reveal what had gone wrong. Given that human sexual behavior, family organization, and sexual education were the products of nurture as well as instinct, such a review might suggest precisely what rational humans could do in order to create sexual enlightenment.

No anthropologist himself, Russell utilized the works not only of Malinowski but also of Robert Briffault, whose latter-day beliefs in primitive matriarchy and sexual communism were challenged by Malinowski. Russell's library, now housed at McMaster University in Hamilton, Ontario, contains a copy of Malinowski's *Father in Primitive Psychology* with half a dozen annotations as well as an unmarked copy of *The Sexual Life of Savages*.

On November 8, 1929, Russell dispatched the following letter to Malinowski: "I have been reading with a great deal of interest not only *Sex and Repression in Savage Society* but also *Argonauts of the Western Pacific* and your little book on Paternity in the Psyche series. I found your observations on paternal affection divorced from power and inheritance very interesting psychologically and throwing a great deal of light on the nature of the paternal sentiment" (Russell Archive). Russell utilized Malinowski's data to demonstrate that paternal care developed from an instinctive bond that grew out of cohabitation, that it was present even when physiological paternity was an unknown concept, and, insofar as it flourished before patriarchy began, that patriarchy was not necessary to support it. The Trobrianders thus demonstrated to Russell that the structure of the Victorian family was neither a biological nor a moral necessity (1929:14–24).

Both Russell and Malinowski shared an admiration for Havelock Ellis. Writing in the *New Statesman and Nation* in 1933, Russell lauded Ellis for his "unprejudiced" scholarship:

> Havelock Ellis' most notable quality is a kindly sanity. Almost all writers on sex have some axe to grind; they want to prove that people hate their fathers, or love their mothers, or ought to know all about sex at the age of three, or ought to know nothing about sex till the age of twenty-one. Some wish to prove that sex covers the whole of life; others that it is nothing but an unimportant and temporary aberration from which well-regulated persons are immune. Havelock Ellis holds none of these theories: on each subject he knows what is to be known, and draws the conclusions of a sensible, unprejudiced person who likes people to be happy. (1933:325–326)

Ellis was indeed a kindly recluse, disinclined toward polemic. One nonetheless suspects that when scholar A says of scholar B that he has no axe to grind, both scholars wish to grind the same axes. As we shall see, this was to some extent true.

Box 2 of the Malinowski Papers at Yale University contains a substantial correspondence (38 items in all) between Malinowski and Havelock Ellis, mostly letters from Ellis to Malinowski. Writing in the *Birth Control Review*, the journal of the American Birth Control League, Malinowski had this to say of Ellis: "To me in my earlier youthful enthusiasm, Havelock Ellis was first a myth, fraught with artistic and moral significance; later he was an intellectual reality in shaping the plastic phase of my mental development; finally he became a great personal experience when I met him and saw realized in life the anticipation of a great personality" (1931a:78). In what ways, then, did Ellis shape the "plastic phase" of Malinowski's development? In what ways did the two men agree, and on what subjects did they differ?

MALINOWSKI AND *SCIENTIA SEXUALIS*

In 1910, as a young Polish student, Bronislaw Malinowski came to England to study with Leonard Hobhouse, Edward Westermarck, and Charles Seligman at London University. He quickly adopted Westermarck's position that the individual family was a universal human institution and that accounts of group marriage were spurious (see Lyons and Lyons 1986; Stocking 1986). This position was sustained in Malinowski's thesis, which was published in 1913 as *The Family among the Australian Aborigines*, his first book (Firth 1957:7, 158). Utilizing Westermarck's definition of marriage as a "more or less durable connection between male and female, lasting beyond the mere act of propagation until after the birth of the offspring" (1901:19, 20), Malinowski asserted that Australian Aborigines most certainly possessed the institution. He further endorsed the attacks of Andrew Lang, Northcote Thomas, and Ernest Crawley on interpretations of the pirauru institution as group marriage. In an appendix to his book he stated his approval of the argument of Crawley's *The Mystic Rose,* which he had read while his own book was in press (Malinowski 1963:305–309). He appeared to endorse the key notion that sexual contact in primitive societies was beset by magical danger and that marital rites were designed to remove such perils. Furthermore, customs such as the couvade and brother–sister avoidance were also the consequence of such beliefs. The name of Havelock Ellis does not occur in the index. However, according to Grosskurth, intellectual contacts between Ellis and Westermarck increased around this time (1980:384). This fact may not be insignificant, given the close ties between Westermarck and Malinowski. Perhaps it was around this time that Malinowski's "youthful enthusiasm" first directed him to Ellis's work.

Malinowski's admiration of Ellis was passed on to his students and some members of his seminar. Ashley Montagu told us that he read much of

Ellis's work and greatly admired him (personal communication, 1989). It is not uninteresting to note that in 1933 Malinowski's student Meyer Fortes wrote a review for *Man* of *Life in Nature* by the obscure Victorian thinker James Hinton solely because "any document which helps us to understand the mental evolution of so redoubtable a social thinker as Havelock Ellis cannot be lightly dismissed" (1933:73). In 1937 Ellis, who always avoided the public gaze, declined an invitation to be Huxley Memorial Lecturer at the Royal Anthropological Institute (Grosskurth 1980:429). By the 1930s the old physical anthropology and the Victorian comparative method were no longer in vogue. Both had informed Ellis's thinking.

We have observed in Ellis's analyses of primitive sexuality the rejection of notions of primitive licentiousness and immodesty and the substitution for them of an assertion that the sexual urge is weak and sporadic among savages. Malinowski did not endorse all of these views, but his reaction to them greatly informed his thinking on Trobriand sexuality. Our knowledge of Malinowski's reaction to Ellis's work is based on an undated notebook on Ellis's *Studies in the Psychology of Sex* that forms part of the Malinowski papers at Yale University. It was certainly written after Malinowski's return from the field and, in all likelihood, before Malinowski invited Ellis to comment on early drafts of *The Sexual Life of Savages*.

MALINOWSKI'S CRITIQUE OF ELLIS

Malinowski's notes cover five volumes of Ellis's *Studies in the Psychology of Sex*, namely, volume 1 (renumbered volume 2), *Sexual Inversion*; the title essay, "The Evolution of Modesty," in volume 2 (renumbered as volume 1); the essay "The Sexual Instinct among Savages" in volume 3; *Sexual Selection in Man* (volume 4); and *Sex in Relation to Society* (volume 5). In all, there are some 23 pages, not all of which are legible.[3]

On homosexuality, Malinowski had this to say: "In my conclu. Nothing to learn ? ab. hosox. from Trobs. Except that when great freedom perversion ? doesn't exist. As to pract. hints of moral cond. thrghly in symp with H. E. (except VII concl.)" (3). Although the notebook contains no direct statement concerning Ellis's assertion that, insofar as homosexuality is congenital, it could not be cured, the above extract indicates a belief that if the Trobriand institutions produced a low incidence of homosexuality, greater heterosexual freedom in Western society might effect a similar result.

Some seven pages of the notebook deal with "The Evolution of Modesty." Malinowski appears to have approved of the gist of Ellis's argument.

Malinowski's remarks concerning "The Sexual Instinct among Savages" reveal the extent to which his own later argument may have resulted from his reaction to Ellis. He doubts Ellis's claim that the sexual instinct has increased rather than diminished with the growth of culture: "I'd say: it has become diff., plastic, more varied with individuals (comp. to gustatory instinct)" (15). Interest in sex per se and passion need not be equated; passion, but not sexual interest, had increased with the growth of civilization.

Ellis's argument that the existence of penalties for unchastity was evidence of a low sex drive is dismissed with a witticism: "You could as well argue that a *ceinture de chaste* was a sign of chastity" (17). If, indeed, primitives were, as Ellis suggested, horrified by the sight of genitals, how then could he explain the prominence of genitals in primitive art?

Malinowski concludes his notes on Ellis's essay with the following observation: "I cannot agree fully with his general conclusion that while . . . restrictions on sexual intercourse are very numerous, there is underlying these restraints a fundamental weakness of the sexual instinct" (19).

Malinowski's notes on *Sex in Relation to Society* consist of very brief notes on each chapter. In a couple of cases it is not clear whether he is merely summarizing Ellis or indicating his own agreement with the latter's argument. The following are some of Malinowski's notes on the first five chapters:

1. *On the mother and her child*: "We can learn but little from savages about this. Except to see how badly they do it."

2. *Sex Education*: "Here I am firmly impressed by the fact that H.E. and all those who are for sex education are right."

3. *(Sexual education and) Nakedness*: "Learn a great deal of healthy stuff from savages."

4. *The Valuation of Sexual Love*: "By studying savages we may also gain an insight into the real position of love."

5. *The Function of Chastity*: "Trobr . . . have no chastity. Are there any expressions of [it?] there at all?" (21, 22)

A consistent thread runs through Malinowski's meditations on the Trobrianders and Ellis. Savage sexuality is free, healthy, and somewhat monotonous. Civilization, affecting the pliant individual in many ways, has brought with it better maternal care, more variation, and more passion, but this sophistication has clearly exacted a toll in the form of unsuccessful and unhappy experiments. Ellis has underestimated the role played by environment as against instinct and has mistaken sexual monotony for low sexual drive. For all their disagreements, the two men seem to agree on one very important point: "Learn a great deal of healthy stuff from savages."

We may ask to what extent *The Sexual Life of Savages* was concerned with the lessons we might learn from primitives. In the introduction Malinowski denies that "the native–European parallels of the present book are meant to provide a homily on our own failings or a paean on our virtues" (1929:xxv). He stresses at several points that his is a "scientific" treatment (Malinowski 1929:xxiii, xxiv, xxvi). Are we, then, to discount the possibility that anything of the reformer's zeal might have motivated the ethnographer? There are, we suggest, some good reasons not to do so.

Malinowski certainly did take a visible part in the debates of the 1920s concerning sexual reform. His lectures on the subject included an address to the First International Congress on Sexual Questions held in Berlin in 1926. As we have seen, he wrote a number of articles stating his views on sexual behavior. He was a friend and supporter of Stopes and, of course, admired and was admired by Ellis. What of *The Sexual Life of Savages*? To what degree was the ethnographer informed by developments at home?

One fact that must be remembered in assessing the relative importance of "objective" and "reformist" postures in *The Sexual Life of Savages* is that, for the period under discussion, the opposition is, to some degree, a false one. There was not yet a tendency on the part of reformers and radicals in Britain and America to see science as one of the tools of a controlling establishment, a tendency for which the current popularity of Foucault's work is itself an important piece of evidence. Rather, to expose such controversial questions as sexual behavior to the cold, clear light of science was seen, in itself, as a liberating procedure. If there had been, as Foucault asserts, a loud and compulsory discourse about sexuality taking place since the 18th century, the reformers of the first third of the 20th century were certainly unaware of the fact. Ellis was haunted by the 1898 prosecution of George Bedborough for distributing the first volume of Ellis's *Studies in the Psychology of Sex* (Grosskurth 1980:201–202). Both Ellis and Malinowski, despite important theoretical differences with Freud, viewed him as a great liberator for his open and scientific discussion of sexuality. Science, by revealing and publicizing the objective truth about human sexuality, would, in the minds of reformers such as Ellis, Russell, and Malinowski, lead to social arrangements more in tune with what science was best equipped to discover: the real facts about human nature. In the important area of birth control, what was specifically being fought for was the right to seek and disseminate scientific knowledge.[4] Ellis, who certainly regarded himself as an objective scientist, described late in life the motives that had led him at 16 to resolve upon his life's work: "I determined that I would make it the main business of my life to get to the *real natural facts* of sex apart from all would-be moralistic or sentimental notions, and so spare the youth of future generations the trouble and perplexity which this ignorance had caused me" (1942a:ix, emphasis added). Malinowski, on page 1 of *The Sexual Life of Savages*, asserts, "That which means supreme happiness to the individual must be made a fundamental factor in the scientific treatment of human society" (1929:1).

We can, however, see in *The Sexual Life of Savages* evidence of reformist concerns beyond the legitimation of a science of sexuality itself. Ellis, who supplied an introduction for the work, wrote to Malinowski on March 18, 1927 (Box 2, BMPY), that he believed him to be a moralist in spite of himself. By a close examination of the text we hope to demonstrate that the "scientific" questions Malinowski asks of the Trobriand data reflect many concerns raised by reformers, particularly Ellis and Russell.

Certain themes in Malinowski's writings on sexuality may be said to serve the purposes of demythologizing widely held views concerning marriage and the family in primitive society and providing models for reform. A repeated theme in these writings, as we have noted, is Malinowski's insistence upon the universality of marriage and the nuclear family in human society.[5] In particular, as a fieldworker in a matrilineal society, he is at pains to demonstrate that clan organization can coexist with the nuclear family. Malinowski frequently criticized both his forebears and his contemporaries for insisting on the exclusive priority of either the communal family or the monogamous heterosexual pair; his debates with Briffault concerning matriarchal communalism are well known (see Briffault and Malinowski 1956).[6] He was equally opposed to what he termed the "Adam and Eve" theory (Malinowski 1962:109); that is, the belief that the monogamous couple was the sole original social unit. In a 1928 review of Briffault's *The Mothers* (1927) and a posthumous edition of Crawley's *The Mystic Rose* Malinowski states that the "black and white," "yea or nay" attitude on this subject is distorting (1962:142).[7] Similarly, he rejected the notion of primitive promiscuity and the experiments in the abolition of the conjugal family that were then being tried in the Soviet Union and advocated by some at home, with clan communism and free love as charter myths. He also scorned the opinion of John Broadus Watson and his followers, whom he described as "misbehaviourists" (Briffault and Malinowski 1956:26), that the institution of marriage was doomed to disappear within 50 years. Central to Malinowski's accounts of Trobriand sexuality is the repeated insistence that premarital license and respect for the institution of marriage were not mutually exclusive phenomena. The brakes put on license by the centrality of marriage are evident in many of the accounts of specific aspects of Trobriand sexuality offered in *The Sexual Life of Savages*.

Infantile sexuality is a topic that Freudian theory had made a subject for wide debate by the 1920s. Malinowski had already argued in a 1924 paper republished in *Sex and Repression in Savage Society* (1927) that among Trobrianders the transfer of disciplinary functions from the father to the mother's brother had prevented the development of the Oedipus complex, with its associated repression of childhood sexuality by a threatening, potentially castrating father.

In his magnum opus on Trobriand sexuality Malinowski has moved beyond the critique of Freud for which he appears to be best known by writers interested in his views on culture and personality. In *The Sexual Life of Savages* there is no direct engagement with Freud. In his preface Ellis contends that by 1929 Malinowski was "neither Freudian nor anti-Freudian" but recognized "the fertilizing value of Freud's ideas" (Malinowski 1987:liv). In a brief remark on Freud at the beginning of the chapter "Erotic Dreams and Fantasies" Malinowski remarks that he had to reject more of psychoanalytic theory than he could accept but acknowledges that his findings "showed beyond all doubt how even a theory which has, in the light of investigation, to be partly rejected can stimulate and inspire" (1987:325).

In *The Sexual Life of Savages* Malinowski documents the lively interest in sex shown by children in the Trobriands, thus validating the claim, still shocking to many in 1929, that children had such interests, but he also stresses that these interests are guided and channeled not by a stern father but by a consciousness, even at this early age, of the importance of custom. Children's sex games are regarded with amused tolerance by adults, but the games consist of imitations of sexual intercourse *within* contexts where such behavior would be acceptable for their elders: pretended marriages and imitations of the amorous expeditions of adolescents (Malinowski 1929:58).

Adolescence in the Trobriands, as is now well known, is a period associated with considerable sexual freedom. If there were any stage in the Trobriand life cycle that could provide evidence for some notion of "primitive promiscuity," it would be this one. Malinowski's treatment of Trobriand adolescence in *The Sexual Life of Savages* stresses both the lack of repression (and the resulting satisfaction and emotional health) and the clear presence of controlling rules. Moreover, Trobriand adolescent freedom is portrayed as a period leading inexorably, if gradually, to marriage.

Like Ellis and Crawley and despite his seemingly contradictory comments in the notebook quoted above, Malinowski stresses the need for external stimuli to erotic passion, even during the period of adolescent "license": "Early acquaintances take fire, as it were, under the influence of music and moonlight, and the changed mood of the participants, transfigure the boy and girl in each other's eyes. Intimate observation of the natives and their personal confidences have convinced me that extraneous stimuli of this kind play a great part in the love affairs of the Trobrianders" (1929:67). Echoing Ellis and Stopes (1918a:58–74), Malinowski does not fail to point out that there appears to be a periodic element in Trobriand dalliances: "Such opportunities of mutual transformation and escape from the monotony of everyday life are afforded not only by the many fixed seasons of festivity and permitted license, but also by that monthly increase in the people's pleasure-seeking mood which leads to many pastimes at the full of the moon" (1929:67).

It is of some interest to note that the topics Malinowski considers worthy of discussion in *The Sexual Life of Savages* are in many cases subjects that had engaged Ellis's particular attention in the *Studies in the Psychology of Sex*. We have already mentioned external sexual stimuli and periodicity of stimulation; other topics include "modesty," to which Ellis devotes a volume and Malinowski a chapter; the connection between love and pain (a section in Ellis, several pages in *The Sexual Life of Savages*); and sexual dreams (a chapter in Ellis, a chapter on "Erotic Dreams and Fantasies" in Malinowski). Ellis devotes a volume to the psychic state in pregnancy; Malinowski provides a long account of Trobriand pregnancy customs, although little of the material in it seems very directly related to the "sexual life." In fact, it would not be an exaggeration to say that there is strong evidence, here and in the notebook, that it was Ellis's work that provided Malinowski with a model to use in investigating sexuality in a primitive society.

A subject that was much discussed during the 1920s was "companionate marriage." Ellis (1942b, pt. 2:499–500) and Russell (1929:155–167) both advocated variants of it. Malinowski included a section entitled "Husband and Wife as Companions" in *The Sexual Life of Savages* (1929:109–114). The term "companionate marriage" was most prominently associated with Judge Ben Lindsey, who was hounded out of his position in the family relations courts of Denver because of his advocacy of it (Russell 1929:162). In an article for the *Birth Control Review* (1931) Lindsey offered a summary of the principal arguments of his 1927 book *Companionate Marriage*. The arrangements that he advocated included ready access to contraception and sex education, divorce by mutual consent for the childless, counseling by experts to help couples with children stay together (though they might be granted divorces if counseling failed), and alimony laws that reflected the growing economic independence of women (Lindsey 1931:79). Lindsey argued that contraception and divorce by consent were already available to those with knowledge and means to circumvent hypocritical laws and that information about sex was widely available to young people, although its clandestine nature guaranteed that it would be inferior information.

Despite the continued opposition of Fundamentalists and a resulting lag in legal changes, Lindsey's beliefs are now so common among ordinary middle-class people in England and North America that it is difficult to appreciate how controversial they once were. Indeed, it is the very "taken-for-grantedness" of easy access to contraception, divorce, and sexual information that gives their current opponents a sense of urgency. Despite a good deal of rhetoric, then and now, to the effect that companionate marriage would lead to happier marital unions and better relations between parents and children (Lindsey and Russell are among those who argued in this vein), the fact remains that easy divorce for the childless combined with ready access to the means to remain childless implied official acknowledgment of acts of sexual intercourse not intended or expected to lead to lifelong monogamous relationships. Moreover, it implied that both partners might seek sexual pleasure for its own sake and postpone or even avoid procreation altogether.

Whether or not it was so labeled, the period of childlessness during which marriage could be terminated at will constituted a form of "trial marriage," and some, including Russell, viewed companionate marriage largely in this light. Others, including Ellis, whose wife described their marriage as semidetached (Grosskurth 1980:249), argued for greater freedom for couples *within* a redefined marital union as a goal in and of itself (Ellis 1942b, pt. 2:499–500). The basic tenet that sexual intercourse might be acceptable without exclusive, lifetime commitment made these positions logically possible and was undoubtedly the reason for the opposition to companionate marriage. Bertrand Russell, arguing that acceptance of trial marriage would lead to more open communication between parents and their adolescent children, cites as an example of such communication the matter-of-fact statement of a Trobriand father to his daughter's lover: "You sleep with my child; very well, marry her" (1929:161).

In the Trobriand milieu described by Malinowski such a statement would be made at the end of a long period of sexual experimentation and growing sexual knowledge, culminating in an increasing commitment to one individual. The marriages resulting from such commitment, according to Malinowski's account, typically stressed companionship, cooperation, and mutual concern for children more than erotic passion, though the partners' premarital experience guaranteed a reasonable measure of sexual satisfaction to both of them (1929:77–83, 109–114, 342, 343 passim). These features of Trobriand marriage and the preparation for it come close to the state of affairs advocated by Russell, who believed in trial marriage, easy separation for the childless, and a rational, companionable effort on the part of couples with children to stay together after passion waned. Indeed, some of Russell's most "libertarian" positions, for example, his insistence that extramarital sexual relations should be accepted both by society and by the spouses of those who took lovers or mistresses, were offered in part as measures to insure that children were raised in stable, strife-free homes (1929:142–143). Even the advocacy of sexual pleasure for women, an important plank in Russell's platform for reform, was justified by him partly because of its supposed influence upon the mental health of children: "If the mother's sexual life is satisfying to her, she will not look to her child for a type of emotional satisfaction which ought to be sought only from adults" (1929:191).

Ellis, like Russell, thought that trial marriage could be followed by a permanent marriage in which responsibilities were taken more, not less, seriously. Of trial marriage, he said: "The open recognition of a kind of relationship which already exists secretly on a large scale cannot but be a steadying and ennobling influence" (Ellis 1931:40). With regard to extramarital sexuality, Ellis suggests that couples who confide in each other about their love affairs are better equipped to cooperate in controlling and containing them so as to neutralize their threat to the marital bond (1942b, pt. 2:528, 529). Moreover, Ellis cites Malinowski as proof that sexual relations outside marriage need not have any effect upon the endurance and usefulness of that institution (Ellis 1931:40). Malinowski discusses divorce, jealousy, and adultery in the Trobriands, notes that all occur and that jealousy may even lead to suicide, but is also at pains to detail the economic advantages that fall to men who keep their marriages intact despite dissatisfaction and the number of cases in which a breach is, indeed, avoided (1929:113–131).

Companionate marriage, as it was advocated by reformers, and Trobriand marriage, as it was described by Malinowski, were institutions that restricted as much as they liberated. In both cases those freedoms that were permitted served to support marriage either by providing training for it or by tolerating nonmarital sexual activity and thus isolating it where it could do marriage no harm. Moreover, despite the advocacy of birth control by Ellis and Russell, Malinowski's support of Stopes, and the frequently asserted Trobriand ignorance of physiological paternity, the separability of sexuality and procreation is seen by all three men as conducive to greater, not less, concern of marital partners for the welfare of their offspring.[8] One of the conclusions that Malinowski draws from his insistence upon Trobriand ignorance of the facts of conception is the importance of parental sentiment as a human emotion sui generis.

The advocates of companionate marriage did not doubt that the Foucauldian figures, the hysterical woman, the Malthusian couple, the masturbating child, and the adult pervert populated the sexual landscape. For them, hysteria, masturbation, and perversion were better dealt with by neutralization than suppression. Ellis and Russell were confident that perversion and onanism posed a lesser threat to marriage and the family if they were recognized and tolerated than if they were actively suppressed. Female hysteria could be prevented by sex education and greater attention to women's sexual needs. They viewed birth control (the Malthusian couple) as an asset to responsible parenthood, not a threat to it.

The habits of primitive people could be cited, as Malinowski's work *was* cited, as evidence for all these facts. That Malinowski supported all these positions is beyond doubt. The degree to which the Trobrianders depicted in *The Sexual Life of Savages* were constituted by the discourse on companionate marriage is a complicated question; Malinowski may have done no more than describe the facts that were there. Apart, however, from the similarity between Trobriand sexual life, as he depicts it, and certain elements of companionate marriage, we may find evidence of his possible motives in the facts that he didn't find, the matters on which his texts are silent. Later studies, most notably the work of Annette Weiner (1976), have demonstrated the economic and political advantages to the father's *dala*, or matrilineal subclan, of debts incurred by sons for the care and preference they receive from their fathers, an aspect of parent–child relations Malinowski slights in stressing the purely sentimental aspects of fathers' attachments to their sons. Moreover, Weiner and others have detailed a rich sexual symbolism linking marriage and property exchanges, a symbolism at which Malinowski barely hints, despite his interest in sexuality. Dala politics and the symbolism of the *kula* and the *sagali* are part of the Trobriand sexual discourse; could Malinowski have failed to hear some of the things the Trobrianders were saying to each other about sex because he was too concerned to make them speak to us?

As we have remarked, the collecting of anthropological data in the field is a confessional art, but it is peculiar in that it is the reader of ethnography who normally receives "therapy." The reader of a work like *The Sexual Life of Savages*, if he or she were not a professional anthropologist, might be a social reformer who saw in Trobriand daily life a justification for companionate marriage or an intelligent layman who sought guidance for his or her own life in Trobriand practice. However, the author intended that his books and ideas should have a wider audience than this. Malinowski believed that his new functionalist anthropology should be of practical use to the colonial administrator and the missionary and that functionalism could therefore engender a more careful and enlightened colonialism. Insofar as this project could be implemented, of course, the "therapeutic" focus of anthropology would be redirected, at least in part, toward the peoples anthropologists studied.

The movement toward applied anthropology seems to have slowly gained momentum within Britain in the period after the establishment of the International African Institute by Frederick Lugard and others in 1926. Applied anthropology thus only came into being in the last decades of British imperialism, and, as is well known, its appeal to the wielders of colonial power was limited. In a sense, it was the anthropologist's response to the depiction of him as a collector of sensationalist curios rather than a bearer of practical advice. Insofar as he had rejected the trait collecting of diffusionism and the survivals of evolutionism, Malinowski could have felt immune from many such charges, but he must have felt sensitive to one particular kind of criticism. One of his adversaries, according to Ian Hogbin, was Sir Philip Mitchell, who remarked a decade after Malinowski's death: "Anthropologists, asserting that they only were gifted with understanding, busied themselves with enthusiasm about all the minutiae of obscene tribal and personal practices, especially if they were agreeably associated with sex or flavored with obscenity" (1951:57, quoted in Hogbin 1957:257).

Malinowski clearly felt that his data on Trobriand sexuality were anything but irrelevant and obscure. In 1928 and 1930 he participated in special conferences organized by the British Social Hygiene Council and the Board of Study for the Preparation of Missionaries in order that scientists and missionaries might discuss the desirability and practicality of intervention (or nonintervention) by church representatives and colonial officials in the sexual and family life of colonial peoples. The first conference took place at High Leigh in Hoddesdon in October 1928. On January 10, 1930, there was a one-day conference at Livingstone House, Westminster, to discuss "The Contact of Modern Civilizations with Ancient Cultures and Tribal Customs." In March 1931 Malinowski gave six lectures on problems of sex life and morality at a vacation school for missionaries. The following remarks made at the Livingstone House conference clearly indicate Malinowski's feelings concerning both the relationship between sexual behavior and a variety of social institutions and the relevance of the functionalist Verstehen to the missionary as well as the anthropologist: "The anthropologist's function at High Leigh was really to desexualize the sexual problem. To a slight extent the title of our subject today is euphemistic. Very boldly, very graciously, Mr. Paton, Canon Spanton and others have approached the problem from the sexual side; but one of the first things I did was to urge that it is not possible to discuss problems arising out of pre-nuptial licence, continence, higher development of conjugal morality without discussing social questions as to the organization of the family, or marriage law, and the importance of bringing up children."[9]

It should be remarked that the merging or dissolving of data on sexuality within the context of a broader discussion of marriage and the family, that is, "desexualizing the sexual problem," is an important component of Malinowski's functionalist approach in *The Sexual Life of Savages*. Moreover, the approach is consistent with the importance Malinowski attaches to the family. The notion of the interconnectedness of institutions is employed to demonstrate the danger that an attack on a single institution may cause damage to the whole social fabric. With respect to the third point, we have already mentioned Malinowski's advocacy of a more careful and enlightened colonialism. It behooves us to examine the matter in greater detail.

Malinowski noted some of the negative effects of colonialism. However, he greatly admired Lord Lugard. If Lugard's "dual mandate" were properly executed, then the colonial enterprise might prove successful. In other words, government would serve the interests of both colonizers and colonized. Malinowski feared the destabilization of tribal culture and opposed racial prejudice, though he thought the latter inevitable when the races were in close contact. Most important, in this context he was wary of missionaries' attempts to improve pagan Africans.[10] Malinowski never advocated the overthrow of colonialism; rather, he was concerned that it be administered in as informed a manner as possible.[11] A confessed agnostic, Malinowski was always careful in his dealings with missionaries. Occasionally, he confesses a prejudice. His correspondence indicates that he was irritated by Roman Catholic missionaries who sought either to stop native contraceptive practices or prevent the spread of contraceptive information.[12] He was, of course, himself a Catholic by birth and perhaps felt more comfortable passing judgment on institutions to which he was not foreign. As the proceedings at High Leigh and Livingstone House indicate, he maintained a good relationship with members of the Anglican hierarchy.

Malinowski was invited to submit a memorandum for discussion by delegates to the conference at High Leigh. The memorandum consisted of a series of questions, interspersed with Malinowski's own comments, elucidations, and explications of anthropological matters. The questions dealt with topics such as premarital, marital, and extramarital sex; forms of ceremonial license; polygamy; and polyandry. The memorandum stressed that there were certain universals in sexual conduct; parenthood was an institution that all societies favored, whereas bestiality and sadism were universally proscribed; and homosexuality was said to be forbidden by most but not all societies.[13] In many other respects, rules of sexual conduct differed. Accordingly, Malinowski advised a degree of relativism in sexual matters; indeed, he incorporated it into his questionnaire to such a degree that many of the questions are "loaded." The following is our summary of the arguments included in the questionnaire and Malinowski's comments:

1. Sexual morality has changed and does vary within our own society. Just as we tolerate divergence within our own society, so too should we tolerate it elsewhere.[14]

2. Missionaries must not dismiss traditional sexual codes as "heathen immorality"; to encourage disrespect for any rules was to encourage the rejection of rules in general.

3. Certain customs that were repugnant to the missionaries might nonetheless possess important functions within the social fabric as a whole. They might even act as a safety valve for urges that might otherwise be expressed in ways that both Malinowski and his audience would find unacceptable. In Melanesia, for example, missionary-inspired segregation of boys and girls had been known to lead to homosexuality. Polygamy was another practice that often had functional links with important economic and social institutions. It was not even clear that there was an inherent opposition between polygamy and Christian doctrine. In general, Malinowski warned, natives were "unable to cope with regulations which frequently appear to them unintelligent and always unpleasant and exacting."[15]

In the discussions of Malinowski's memorandum that occupied the larger part of the weekend meeting several different positions were taken by the delegates. Some of those present clearly disagreed with the tenor of Malinowski's argument, for example, Mrs. Donald Frazer, who argued that many "native" practices such as premarital sexuality were, in an absolute sense, degrading to women. Others, however, seemed to agree with him. The Reverend Canon E. Spanton, secretary of the Universities' Mission to Central Africa, described an attempt to retain as much as possible traditional initiation rites among the East African Malakonda in newly introduced Christian initiation camps, a version of the idea of "functional substitution."[16]

Malinowski seemed to approve of Spanton's experiment, remarking that "he had shown how necessary it is to make the Christian ideal more plastic to find out what it really means."[17] It would appear that Malinowski maintained an exemplary patience, even though some of the missionaries' remarks may occasionally have irked him (e.g., the comment of a Mrs. Hopper that the initiation rites in her district were so appalling that the church could have nothing to do with them). Malinowski only once took issue with the fundamental sexual attitudes of his audience, gently urging them to embrace the new companionate ideal. In this instance, he remarked that the "positive development of sexual ethics" depended upon a "conscious appreciation by the Missionaries of the beauty of sexual relations within married life."[18]

How, then, do we interpret Malinowski's incursion into the world of the missionary? Earlier on, we discussed the relationship between the native informant, the ethnographer, and the sexual reformer. Although he warned the missionaries of excessive interference in the lives of others, at High Leigh Malinowski was perhaps exploring a closer relationship between power and knowledge. The anthropologist receives "confession" from the native informant. As a result, he acquires knowledge, which he passes on to the priest (or administrator), who must hear of and watch the "sins" of the native and, in accordance with the best anthropological advice, suffer them, subtly alter them, or proscribe them. Such a relationship between power and knowledge would, of necessity, have entailed an indirect anthropological supervision of the daily lives of indigenous populations, a mode of conduct hardly compatible with Malinowski's individualism, unless one could say that the alternative was wholesale interference by the ignorant. In any event, there were too few anthropologists, too many missionaries, and far too many other preoccupations to permit development of an applied functional anthropology dealing with the intimate details of everyday life. Insofar as applied anthropology developed in Britain, it concerned itself with land tenure, clan structure, and warfare and tended to leave the missionaries and their concerns alone.

The question of whether precontact Trobriand Islanders and Australian Aborigines understood the role of the father in conception is a conundrum that surfaces in several contexts over a time span covering much of the 20th century. The matriarchal theorists as well as Malinowski and Edmund Leach are among those whose opinions we consider in this book. The following discussion, which concentrates on Malinowski and his student, Ashley Montagu, offers some observations on a debate that has never really ceased.

In the third edition of *The Sexual Life of Savages* Malinowski offered the following opinion: "The Trobrianders do not suffer from a specific complaint *ignorantia paternitatis*. What we find among them is a complicated attitude towards the facts of maternity and paternity. Into this attitude there enter certain elements of positive knowledge, certain gaps in embryological information. These cognitive ingredients again are influenced by beliefs of an animistic nature, and influenced by the moral and legal principles of the community" (1987:21). This was a somewhat qualified statement of a position that Malinowski had been defending throughout his professional career. In *The Family among the Australian Aborigines* he had accepted Baldwin Spencer and F. J. Gillen's authority concerning Arunta spirit children, though, as we have seen, he was no defender of matriarchal theories of human origins, which linked ignorance of physiological paternity to universal promiscuity and group marriage. Indeed, when he reported that Trobrianders were ignorant of physiological paternity, he used this "fact" to argue against those very theories. Malinowski insisted that the existence of individual marriage and strong father–child ties among matrilineal Trobrianders was proof that neither matriarchy nor communal marriage was a necessary corollary to either matriliny or ignorance of the father's role in conception.

Malinowski's essay on *baloma* spirits in the Trobriands appeared in 1916. This was his first account of Trobriand theories of conception. Although some details in his account were to vary over time (did or did not the Trobrianders understand the facts of life with respect to pigs and other animals?), the essential details remained the same. Trobrianders believed that the dead go to the isle of Tuma. Periodically, they tire of life in Paradise and are transformed into spirit children, who are washed ashore on Kiriwina. A spirit child enters the body of a woman, impregnating her and assuring the perpetuity of the dala. The father's intercourse with the mother merely "prepares the way" for the entry of the spirit child. Sperm does not fertilize. The father can mold the form of the child by sleeping with the mother during pregnancy. Although the biological role of the father is not acknowledged, his social role in raising the child is very important. He is the object of affection for both female and male children. Because the mother's brother is the locus of jural authority and paternity is not acknowledged, there is no place for the Oedipus complex (Malinowski 1927).

An alleged ignorance (or "nescience," as Ashley Montagu called it) of physiological paternity suited Malinowski's theoretical positions, insofar as it was consistent with an intertwining of kinship, myth, and political economy. Matrilineal descent, belief in baloma spirits, and the rules of exchange and inheritance could all be shown to be interlinked and to be consistent with a father who was tied to his offspring by sentiment, not substance. The existence of a strong father–child bond in the absence of knowledge of physiological paternity was also consistent with some of the goals of 1920s sexual reformers, insofar as it might alleviate fears that sex divorced from procreation, as a result of birth control and greater sexual freedom, would inevitably lead to the breakdown of the family.

Malinowski may have had more immediate reasons for insisting on Trobriand ignorance. At the time of his fieldwork the Massim region was subject to considerable surveillance and intervention by administrators and missionaries. The latter were concerned with morality, the former with venereal diseases and a problem that was later proven to be linked to them, what Rivers had called the "depopulation of Melanesia" (see Reed 1997; Rivers 1922; Riley 2000). In its annual report for 1906–7 the colonial administration announced plans to open lock hospitals in Losuia and Samarai in the Trobriands (Riley 2000:3). Reyner Bellamy, medical officer and magistrate in the Trobriands, decided to examine every adult in the 156 villages in that territory for venereal diseases. Between 1908 and 1915 he conducted 50,900 genital examinations and claimed that he had reduced the incidence of venereal disease from over 5 percent to somewhere between 1 and 2 percent (Riley 2000:4). The government had outlawed adultery but left to the missionaries the task of actually changing sexual behavior (Reed 1997).

Malinowski told his readers little of this immediate history. It is clear from his writing, however, that he and his Trobriand informants saw a connection between the alien sexual system that the missionaries were trying to impose and the insistence on the role of a genitor in the creation of children (see, e.g., Malinowski 1987:158–159). Some of Malinowski's doggedness in affirming Trobriand nescience concerning physiological paternity was doubtless intended to warn off those who wished to impose a regime of continence and churchgoing on the Trobrianders, whether in the interests of morality or the cause of public health.

Malinowski's most bitter dispute was with the administrator Alex Rentoul, whose brief note in *Man* (Rentoul 1931) evoked rage and annoyance. Rentoul, who had clearly not read all of Malinowski's writings on the subject, claimed that his court experience in adultery cases clearly demonstrated that Trobrianders knew all too well where babies came from. Malinowski responded that statements in court did not properly represent Trobriand attitudes. Parties to a dispute could be expected to frame their testimony in terms they knew would impress European authorities, and they would also be likely to lie (Malinowski 1932a:34). The issue became divisive. Support for Rentoul from Jack Driberg and Edward Evans-Pritchard became the excuse for a lasting professional schism.[19] (In Evans-Pritchard's case there was also the matter of a defection to A. R. Radcliffe-Brown; see Stocking 1995:425.) Malinowski poured particular scorn on Rentoul's account of the inadequate contraceptive measures supposedly utilized by Trobriand women. Rentoul had claimed that Trobriand women possessed unusual muscular powers: "I have been informed by many independent and intelligent natives that the female of the species is specially endowed or gifted with ejaculatory powers, which may be called upon after an act of coition to expel the male seed. It is understandable that such powers might be increased by use and practice, and I am satisfied that such a method does exist" (1931:153). Alex Rentoul did not reveal his confidential sources, nor did he state the reasons for his (intellectual) satisfaction. A subsequent letter to *Man* revealed that this particular piece of "anthroporn" or colonial folklore had a long-lasting and widespread currency. More than half a century before Rentoul, Sir Richard Burton had salaciously recounted stories of the strength of the *constrictor vaginae* muscle among Hindu maidens (Bothwell 1931:280).

What we have said may adequately indicate that Malinowski's remarks about Trobriand nescience occurred in a specific and new political context. In other words, his account of Trobriand nescience was placed in a frame very different from that which encased the assertions of John McLennan, Baldwin Spencer, and James Frazer. What Trobriand men and women actually believed is another question that may never be adequately answered. Surely Tilapoi, the legendary Trobriand woman of *The Sexual Life of Sav-*

ages, who had many children despite the fact that her ugliness supposedly repelled all men, knew that this alleged repugnance could be overcome. Doubtless, she had female friends who shared her secrets. The possibility that Trobriand men and Trobriand women did not share the same form of knowledge was not entertained by Malinowski. Many years later, and therefore in a different context, Weiner (1988:55) was to note that a resort to beliefs in "magical" pregnancy could prove useful to adulterous Trobriand women.

In his Columbia University doctoral thesis, which became his first book, *Coming into Being among the Australian Aborigines* (1937), Montagu, who became best known as a physical anthropologist, sought to defend his undergraduate teacher, Malinowski, against those who challenged his statements about Trobriand theories of conception. Montagu argued, as others had before him, that the delay between intercourse and pregnancy made their connection less than obvious. Unlike figures such as Edwin Sidney Hartland, however, Montagu did not see the failure to recognize the connection to be a result of a combination of licentiousness and lack of intellect; rather, he saw it as a perfectly rational response to social and physiological circumstances.

Malinowski had noted that despite the very considerable freedom they enjoyed, unmarried Trobriand girls very seldom became pregnant. He presumed that they knew nothing of contraception and confessed his ignorance about any resort to abortion, although he suspected it happened at best infrequently (Malinowski 1929:166–168; Montagu 1957:8, 9). Other ethnographers had reported similar data: Hogbin from Wogeo, Rivers from Eddystone, Verrier Elwin on the Baiga of Central India, Roy Franklin Barton on the Ifugao (see Montagu 1957:9–22). Montagu was aware that some studies of primate behavior and reproductive physiology indicated that there was a gap between first estrus and successful pregnancy among some nonhuman primates (1957:50–70). Utilizing demographic data, Montagu advanced a strong case for the occurrence of a period of adolescent sterility among human populations. A book incorporating this hypothesis appeared in 1946 under the title *Adolescent Sterility* and in 1957, in revised form, as *The Reproductive Development of the Female*. Montagu's notion of delayed fertility in at least some human populations has not been proven, but it is consistent with some known facts. Delayed onset of fertility might be particularly likely where diets are relatively low in animal protein or in conditions of great physical activity (e.g., some young women athletes stop menstruating altogether during periods of intensive training).

Montagu reiterated Malinowski's position concerning the interrelatedness of social organization, religion, and theories of conception (1974:230). He went further and claimed that among some Australian groups there was no idea of physiological maternity (Montagu 1974:326–336; Montagu 1942a). As evidence that maternity was merely social or sociological, he cited narratives concerning southeastern and Cape York groups in which it was asserted that the mother was merely an incubator for the child.

In the absence of knowledge about Trobriand and Australian inner understandings, as opposed to elucidations of some of their collective representations by outsiders, their beliefs have been construed in ways that fit the agendas of the interpreters. For the matriarchal theorists, Aboriginal "ignorance" of paternity was evidence of promiscuity and backwardness. For Malinowski, it was evidence of interconnection of belief and social structure and proof that love for the father needn't be based upon knowledge of his role in conception. For Rentoul and other administrators, Trobriand denials of paternity were part and parcel of attempts to evade colonial authority. For Montagu, the biologist and antiracist, nescience was consistent with those aspects of scientific fact accessible to Australian Aborigines and Trobriand Islanders. It was also relative: Montagu pointed out that the facts of conception weren't fully known by European scientists until 1850 (1974:271). Many 20th-century fieldworkers in Australia reported that there was knowledge of physiological paternity, at least by some people some of the time (see Berndt and Berndt 1942; Goodale 1971:136, 137; Warner 1958:23, 24). Their statements on the topics supported one or more of several agendas, among them a desire to combat stereotypes about Aborigines with careful fieldwork. For Leach (1966), ignorance of paternity was something invented by anthropologists as a device to distance primitives from themselves. The Freudian agenda added a third possibility to the question, Did they know or didn't they? For Spiro (1968), "ignorance" is really "denial," born out of the very same Oedipus complex that Malinowski so vociferously denied in the Trobriands – and it is not only the Trobrianders, Spiro implies, who are in a state of denial.

For some anthropologists influenced by feminist thought, dogmas about paternity are really dogmas about patriarchy. In 1986 *Man* published two articles in its ongoing debate on the issue of "virgin birth" (Delaney 1986; Merlan 1986) that argued, among other things, that in both Aboriginal Australia and European societies theories of conception, particularly as they are understood by men, have been such as to enhance male control over women. This can be done by stressing the importance of the male role of begetter, which Delaney sees at the core of European beliefs, both physiological and religious, or by stressing the nonphysical aspects of conception, in which men's role is not limited by their anatomy, as the Australians do. The "virgin birth" controversy might well be described as an illustration of the old adage that to a hammer, the whole world is a nail. In other words, it is a case study in conscription.

FUNCTIONAL ANTHROPOLOGY AND THE DEPRESSION

The 1930s saw the fall of the second Labour government in Britain, the start of the Great Depression, and the gloomy sequence of events that led to World War II. Some of Malinowski's students, like Meyer Fortes, turned to the Durkheimian functionalism of Radcliffe-Brown, which neglected individual sentiments, including most expressions of sexuality.

During a conservative and despondent era, there is little time for "frivolity." It is an interesting fact that many anthropologists, although hardly unaware of sexuality, regard the discussion of culturally variable ideologies and practices that continually affect the daily lives of all peoples everywhere as frivolous. This may be one reason why the volume of anthropological literature (journal articles as well as books) on sexuality diminished somewhat in Britain during this period. Significantly, in his special foreword to the third edition of *The Sexual Life of Savages*, Malinowski expressed his concern that readers were ignoring his demonstration of the utility of the functional method: "I wanted to show that only a synthesis of facts concerning sex can give a correct idea of what sexual life means to a people." Unfortunately, too many readers had misunderstood the book and instead picked out "sensational details" to wonder or laugh at. These details included "the notorious ignorance of physiological paternity, the technicalities of lovemaking" (Malinowski 1987:xix–xx, xxi). However, work did not cease, as we shall see in chapter 8. As for Malinowski himself, having "desexualized" the sexual problem, he turned his attention elsewhere in a way most appropriate to the hungry thirties: "It is extraordinary what an uneven treatment has been meted out in all studies to the twin impulses of sex and hunger respectively . . . We are enjoying now a surfeit of sex – I alone have to plead guilty to four books on the subject, two of which have the word sex on the title page" (Malinowski 1932b:x). This passage is from Malinowski's introduction to his student Audrey Richards's *Hunger and Work in a Savage Tribe*. Apart from the new political and economic climate, there may have been other, more personal reasons why Malinowski turned his attention elsewhere. His initial interest in sexuality had resulted not only from the examination of the Trobriand data, which was now nearly completed, but also from a flirtation with psychoanalysis that had diminished appreciably after the publication of *Sex and Repression in Savage Society*, in which he still accepted some of Freud's basic premises. Nonetheless, he still cared sufficiently for Freud's work to campaign for his nomination for the Nobel Prize in medicine in 1938.[20]

At a time when the Nazis were triumphant in Central Europe, Malinowski may also have been concerned about the fact that he was being internationally labeled as a "sexologist." Sexology has seldom been regarded as a respectable academic discipline. Politics, of course, played a role here too. The Nazis had condemned sexology and burned the books of Havelock Ellis. In the summer of 1938 Lidio Cipriani, director of the Florentine Museum, writing in *Corriere della Sera*, described Freud, Adler, and Malinowski as "Jewish sexologists." Malinowski wrote letters to Richard Thurnwald in Germany and to Kazimierz Stolyhwo, president of the Polish Academy, among others, asking them to make it public that he was neither Jew, nor anti-Semite, nor sexologist.[21]

In the United States a small minority of anthropologists continued to be interested in the cause of sexual reform and associated studies of sexuality. As for companionate marriage, the focus of the reforming zeal of Malinowski and his contemporaries, it was doomed to become the orthodoxy attacked by the next wave of sexual liberators, though birth control and sex education became the targets of a new surge of reaction. Perhaps the lesson anthropology can best teach us about sexuality concerns the universal tendency of human beings, including anthropologists, to approach the "real, natural facts" about sex through a heavy wrapping of cultural clothing, clothing that simultaneously conceals and reveals and that is subject to change when alterations occur in the factors that determine cultural hegemony.

CHAPTER 7

Margaret Mead, the Future of Language, and Lost Opportunities

Anthropology lectures were full of references to Evans-Pritchard, Radcliffe-Brown and Margaret Mead. The set books had titles like Growing Up in New Guinea, Structure and Function in Primitive Pago-Pago *and* Having It Off in Hawaii.

Clive James, Unreliable Memoirs

Nina's mother also had a huge collection of "sex books," among which we included Coming of Age in Samoa *and* Sex and Temperament; *any book with the word puberty in it was O.K.*

Erica Jong, Fear of Flying

The regime of professional authorities on sexuality, as Foucault understood it, had the effect of constructing sexuality so that incidents that might otherwise be defined as isolated fantasies, sensations, or behaviors were deployed to fit those who experienced them into reified categories. These included the heterosexual adult, the hysterical woman, and the homosexual. People were persuaded to perceive themselves as possessing single identities and consistent sexual desires. It remained only for the incentive of "cure" to be put forward for these sexual "subjects" to participate in their own ranking and the ranking of others according to standards of "health" and "normalcy" that reflected the needs and conditions of the culture that produced and rewarded the experts. As we have argued so far, a parallel process of reification of the sexual subject took place when entire races and whole cultures or even categories of cultures were ranked by experts not according to the sexual natures of individuals but according to the supposed sexualities of entire groups.

Foucault suggests that the monogamous, heterosexual, reproducing couple, essential both to the stability of the labor force and to the orderly transmission of capital, was little studied by sexual scientists. He argues that this was the one silence the new discourse of diagnosis allowed and that this absence of scrutiny privileged heterosexual reproductive marriage as the only locus of sexual expression that did not require explanation. We have seen thus far that heterosexual, reproducing couples in primitive societies *were* studied, though in ways that focused upon their "difference" from the norm – the bourgeois European or North American married couple. In fact, even in studies of primitives, the fascination with "primitive promiscuity" meant that the data under scrutiny were often drawn from the behavior of the unmarried, whether authors were aware of this or not.

If ever there was, in the popular mind, an "expert" on sex, it was, for more than a generation, Margaret Mead. Many of the facts about Mead's life are well known, from biographies, autobiographies, and published letters (see Howard 1984; Bateson 1984; Grosskurth 1988; Lapsley 1999; Mead 1972, 1977). Margaret Mead was born in Philadelphia in 1901 and died in New York in 1978. She received her bachelor of arts from Barnard College in 1923 and her doctorate from Columbia University in 1925. Her anthropology professor at Barnard, Franz Boas, had part of his contract bought out cheaply by the women's undergraduate college of Columbia because his disagreement with the racist, anti-immigrant sentiments prevailing in the United States in the 1920s made him appear, to the president of Columbia University, a dangerous radical not to be entrusted with the molding of young men who were to be America's future leaders (see Rosenberg 1995 for a discussion of this episode). Thus, anthropology, somewhat unusually for the time, acquired a generation of notable female scholars, the most famous of whom was undoubtedly Margaret Mead. A recent article notes that Columbia produced 29 male and 22 female anthropology doctorates before 1940, a period during which Harvard graduated no women with a doctorate in anthropology and the University of Chicago but two (Wallace 1999:427).

In the decades since Mead died her work has been the subject of much controversy, most notably, that which followed the famous attacks by Freeman (1983, 1999) on her Samoan ethnography. There have been symposia centered on those attacks (Brady 1983; Caton 1990) as well as restudies of her field sites (for Samoa, see Holmes 1987; Côté 1994) and of her field materials (Orans 1996; Grant 1995). It is not our intention to review this voluminous literature here, still less to reinvent the wheel and start afresh on all of the issues raised by previous authors. What we hope to do is to offer some ideas of our own about Mead's treatment of sexuality and its place in the story this book has been telling.

The anthropological community, during Mead's lifetime and after her death, sometimes defended her, sometimes distanced itself from her views, and was often divided over the value of her contribution. What anthropology has never been able to do is free itself from her spell. She still, for example, merits a few paragraphs, usually accompanied by a photo, in most introductory anthropology textbooks, though these notices usually mention some defects in her work. In 2001 the American Anthropological Association annual meeting celebrated the centennial of her birth with a number of symposia and other well-attended events. Nonetheless, for some this chapter will doubtless represent an unwonted degree of attention to a discredited figure. To them we can only say that, like many of the authors we have discussed, Mead is indubitably part of the *history* of anthropology's encounter with sexuality, whatever value current practitioners of the discipline place on her work.

For people like the adolescent invoked by Erica Jong in the epigraph to this chapter, anthropology *was* sex, and Mead was its mouthpiece. The anthropological profession was never very comfortable with either of these characterizations. Nancy Lutkehaus, in a 1995 volume devoted to increasing the recognition of women's texts within the anthropological canon and exploring the reasons for their relative invisibility in the past, suggests that anthropologists were embarrassed by Mead's status as a figure who could speak to a mass audience, particularly an audience of women. She observes that Mead's writing was dismissed as "feminine" and/or "unscientific" by a number of critics, including A. C. Haddon, E. E. Evans-Pritchard, and Peter Worsley (Lutkehaus 1995:193–194). She notes that Clifford Geertz, among others, has seen Mead's writing as "undisciplined, loose limbed, and improvisational" (Lutkehaus 1995:201). Above all, Lutkehaus suggests, anthropologists have found sex, marriage, and infant care, especially when seen from a woman's perspective, to be embarrassing topics for discussion (1995:200).[1]

Mead's politics (or lack of them) have been criticized by both the Left and the Right. Partly this is because Mead approached "primitives" with a particular constellation of attitudes, consciously critical of some varieties of hierarchy but apparently tolerant of others. She was more concerned with challenging popular assumptions about the "nature" of sexual difference than with investigating other forms of inequality. Even on the issue of race, despite a famous "rap" on the subject with the black author James Baldwin toward the end of her life (Mead and Baldwin 1970), during which she congratulated herself on her lack of racist sentiment (see Walton 2001 for a less sanguine viewpoint), she had far less to say than Boas or Ruth Benedict, for example. She frequently appeared oblivious to class difference when discussing "American" society. In her accounts of Samoa she certainly does note the connections between rank and sexual norms but pays little attention to such matters when comparing "Samoan" and "American" mores.

When Mead argued that sexual norms and experience were variable across cultures, she was striking a blow against the tendency to generalize about "primitive" sexuality and to contrast it with "civilized" practice. Mead argued that there was no uniform "primitive" sexuality and no sexual regime that was "natural" to all human beings. She believed that sexual behavior was a product of the interaction between individual inclination and cultural rules. She did not deny biological sex drives but did not assume that they were universal in their expression. She also denied that such drives were differentially distributed according to race or degree of civilization. In this sense, her work can be seen as relativist. On the other hand, when she diagnosed members of her own and other cultures as "satisfied," "frustrated," "prudish," "normal," or "free" she was helping to promulgate a new classification of supposed sexual health and disease with its own forms of inequality and constraint.

The book that thrust Mead to fame, *Coming of Age in Samoa*, was published in 1928. It was based on fieldwork done in Manu'a, American Samoa, between 1925 and 1926. The topic of her study had been approved by her teacher Franz Boas as a test of an alleged universality of emotional stress during adolescence, an idea that Mead and others attributed to the recently deceased psychologist G. Stanley Hall. It should be noted, in this regard, that Stephen O. Murray and Regna Darnell have suggested that Derek Freeman and his supporters have overemphasized the importance of Mead's work to Boas's critique of biological determinism, noting that this critique was well established by the time Mead went to Samoa. Interestingly, they suggest that *Coming of Age in Samoa* bears more resemblance to Malinowski's work than to the writings of Boas (Murray and Darnell 2000:562). They do acknowledge that Boas's interest in Mead's topic may have been fed by resentment at his treatment by Hall at Clark University some years earlier (Murray and Darnell 2000:564).

An interesting sidelight on this choice of topic is that Boas, Mead, her admirers, and her critics all seem to have operated under a misapprehension, or at least an oversimplification, of Hall's argument, insofar as they assumed that a relatively untroubled Samoan adolescence would constitute a disproving "negative instance." Ironically, the critique of Hall contained in *Coming of Age in Samoa* could actually be read as confirmation of some of his opinions of primitive adolescence, albeit a denial of the underlying evolutionary assumptions of his work. Hall was characterized by Mead, in a single brief sentence at the opening of *Coming of Age in Samoa*, as having said that adolescence is universally a time of storm and stress (1928:2); supporters and critics of Mead's work have since assumed that this was Hall's position and that it was contrary to Mead's.[2] Mead's attribution of the notion of adolescent storm and stress to Hall has become part of the folklore of the discipline (see, e.g., Orans 1996:1).

In fact, Hall had argued that adolescence, in the sense of a difficult period of transition from childhood to adulthood, was largely the product of an evolution from savagery to civilization that was as much biological as it was cultural. In 1904, when Hall's book *Adolescence* was published, as well as in the 1920s, when Mead did her fieldwork, many people believed that primitive adults resembled the children of civilized nations. On the one hand, Hall argued that primitives had recognized the importance of the transition from childhood to maturity with ubiquitous puberty rituals. On the other hand, he argued that the transition between childhood and adulthood was more protracted among civilized peoples than among primitives (Hall 1904, vol. 2:232). Primitive puberty ceremonies, upon which he wrote at length, seemed to him to effect a rapid but incomplete transition to adulthood, which the civilized struggled lengthily to obtain through the religious, educational, and medical establishments (Hall 1904, vol. 2:232–249). In any case, Hall believed that mature primitives, in their natural state, had less of a transition to make, being essentially "adolescents of adult size" (1904, vol. 2:649). He provided a lengthy litany of authors who had warned of the dangers of educating Africans and other members of the "adolescent races" (Hall 1904, vol. 2:649–707). These ideas smack of an evolutionist distancing far more specific than the generalized biological determinism implicit in the notion of universally difficult adolescence.

Further, insofar as Mead was given the specific problem of studying *female* adolescence, it is worth noting that many of Hall's comments about adolescent girls concern the special difficulties placed upon them by civilization. It was common in Hall's time to believe that gender differentiation had increased with evolution. Émile Durkheim, for example, had actually used Samoa as an example of the similarity between the sexes among primitives (1964:57–58). Hall cites such notions with apparent approval and argues at great length that modern women and girls suffer because of attempts to bring them to the level of civilized men, developing their intellects at the expense of their nurturing capacities (1904, vol. 2:561–636). Interestingly, among Hall's many proposals for appropriate female education, which included the development of maternal qualities, were suggestions that girls should be trained in zoology and anthropology because women were particularly fit to understand animals and primitives (1904, vol. 2:642–643).

It is not clear to what degree Mead recognized all the complexities in Hall's argument. Although in her autobiography she made a brief reference to Hall's belief in recapitulation and attributed the notion of adolescent storm and stress to "German theory" (Mead 1972:139), in the text of *Coming of Age in Samoa* Mead implied that she had contradicted Hall by the simple demonstration that adolescence was not a difficult time for Samoan girls. If it were not, the travails of adolescence could not be biologically determined. In emphasizing the differences between civilized and primitive adolescence, however, Mead echoed a key feature of Hall's argument, though she would not have endorsed his evolutionary scheme. Moreover, the call for a special education for women that did not slight their maternal needs (which was by no means unique to Hall) found increasing resonances in Mead's work as her career progressed.

Mead attributed what she believed to be a relatively easy Samoan adolescence to the few choices girls (and boys) were called upon to make about their future and to the society's relatively casual attitude toward sexual experimentation. Women and men alike were said to approach marriage secure in the knowledge both of their own and of their partners' sexual competence. Moreover, Mead asserts that both sexes knew that appropriate partners would eventually be found and that Samoans did not believe in deep personal differences between individuals to which only true love could cathect. Mead presents a picture of Samoan sexual health that must have seemed remarkable to the legions of marriage counselors, writers of advice manuals, psychiatrists, urologists, gynecologists, social workers, and others busy in the work of diagnosing and remedying sexual malaise in America and Europe: "Familiarity with sex, and the recognition of a need of a technique to deal with sex as an art, have produced a scheme of personal relations in which there are no neurotic pictures, no frigidity, no impotence, except as the temporary result of severe illness, and the capacity for intercourse only once in a night is counted as senility" (1928:151). In an essay on sex and the unmarried adult Mead says of sex in Samoa that it is a skill in which one becomes adept and to which personality is felt to be as irrelevant as it might be to a consideration of table manners. Within the appropriate social class, one expects virtuosity from one's partner, in the same way that one expects any other form of graceful social adequacy.

. . . The emphasis is laid not upon sex as a dangerous and powerful force, but as a pleasant aptitude of the human race at which it is suitable that those for whom it has no serious social consequences shall play and become proficient with no fear that it will develop desires which cannot be easily channeled within a not too burdensome marriage bond. (1934:63)

The long postscript to *Coming of Age in Samoa*, in which Mead discusses the lessons America can learn from Samoa, was suggested by her publisher as a device to attract a wider audience (Lutkehaus 1995:190; Côté 2000:582–583). It is not clear whether or not this was Mead's sole motive; her field notes do not suggest such a concern, though she had given public lectures on the topic shortly before adding the section (Lutkehaus 1995:190; Mead 1972:165). Whatever her initial motive, for the rest of her career Mead was only too delighted to draw lessons for her own milieu from the cultures she studied. Further, the text of *Coming of Age in Samoa*, and not just the postscript, is full of diagnostic and prescriptive asides. What were the lessons Mead thought Americans could learn from Samoa, particularly as they concerned sexuality?

In some ways, Mead's account of Samoan sexuality could be seen by a contemporary scholar as a prime example of the applicability of several of Foucault's principles. On the one hand, Mead staked part of her claim to professional expertise on the diagnosis of sexual health and disease, at home and abroad. On the other, somewhat ironically, the Samoan material could be read as a demonstration that it is not only in the West that sex is a transfer point of power.

Sexual behaviors were named, scrutinized, and regulated by Samoans to the degree to which they affected or effected the acquisition and transmission of power and property. Masturbation or homosexual behavior among the young or among temporarily unattached adults was said by Mead to be of little concern to anyone, so long as reasonable discretion was observed (1928:136). Some young people, both boys and girls, formed relatively intense homosexual attachments, but these were temporary in nature (Mead 1928:70, 147). Identified categories of heterosexual relationships included properly arranged marriages; elopements, which might or might not lead to marriages legitimated by property exchange; casual nighttime rendezvous between unmarried, usually young partners; *moetotolo* (sleep crawling), a highly specific form of sexual assault; and adultery. Of these, only moetotolo, a boy gaining access to a girl's sleeping mat under cover of darkness by disguising his identity, was said by Mead to have consistently negative consequences, and those for the boy, not the girl (1928:95). On the one hand, elopement might cause a stir for a while and might cause permanent problems for the couple if the families did not agree to a marriage, but it could be used by young people to get their own way. On the other hand, elopement, in Mead's account, was the one really risky sexual adventure for girls, especially if they retained even nominal claims to virginity and their lovers refused to marry them. In earlier times punishments for such girls had been severe, and the value of high-ranking girls in the marriage stakes could be seriously compromised (Mead 1928:102–104).

Unlike the Trobrianders, whose institutionalized adolescent sexual experimentation Malinowski had not yet fully described at the time Mead did her fieldwork, Samoans did not categorically sanction premarital sex. Mead describes Samoa as a society that had embraced strict Protestant Christianity and that valued virginity but in which most adolescent girls could, nonetheless, amass considerable sexual experience without incurring either guilt or social disgrace. This was possible, in Mead's opinion, because certain kinds of sexual expression, notably, youthful homosexual activity and masturbation, existed outside the sphere of social interest and, therefore, of social control, while heterosexual contact attracted such interest only in the minority of cases where familial status was at stake. Such status, Mead suggested, was compromised only if a liaison was indiscreet, incestuous, or involved a woman of a high-ranking family, especially a ceremonial virgin, known as a *taupou*. The higher a family's rank, the more closely its girls would be chaperoned and the more likely that their marriages would have involved a public defloration ceremony, a custom that, Mead said, was only slowly dying out at the time of her visit (1928:98).

For most young people, according to Mead, casual love affairs, involving late-night visits or meetings under the palm trees when the rest of the village was asleep, carried few risks and many benefits. Adolescent males were told about sexual techniques by older men and then taught them to their young female partners (Mead 1928:150). Women thus learned, at an early age, that sex could be pleasurable and how such pleasure could be attained. Above all, Mead argued, unlike American girls, Samoan girls learned not to overestimate sex, either as an evil to be avoided or an overwhelming, life-controlling experience (1928:222).

Sexual pleasure was predictable and not dependent upon any particular relationship. The marriages that followed the years of experimentation were portrayed by Mead as largely practical affairs. Sexual adjustment in marriage was not seen by Mead as problematic for Samoans. She suggested that most couples took it for granted and eventually turned their minds to village politics and economic pursuits (Mead 1928:105–106). Adultery, she reported, was common and usually a cause for divorce only in instances where a chief had been dishonored by the adultery of his wife. If feelings were strong, in other situations the lover might undergo a ritual humiliation, followed by reconciliation. On the other hand, divorce and remarriage were said to be easily accomplished when married couples were unhappy with each other (Mead 1928:106–108).

We have noted the irony implicit in the fact that it is possible to see in Mead's Samoan data, as in the historical European cultures described by Foucault, close links between the surveillance of sexual behavior and the structures of power. Surveillance was both an artifact of those structures and a powerful reinforcer of them. Girls were more likely to be guarded the higher one went in the social structure. Even when surveillance was temporarily eluded, as in the case of elopement, self-regulation made consummation less likely to take place if the eloping girl was a high-ranking virgin and the boy of good enough family to have a chance of gaining her relatives' consent to a proper marriage. On the other hand, Mead reported that disgracing less well connected girls by eloping with them and not marrying them was a popular route to status among young men (1928:103–104). The world of Mead's informants does not seem to have been exempt from a tendency also common in the West: an expectation that suitors will be more respectful of the chastity and reputation of high-ranking girls than of those of low status. Mead, however, did not investigate the possibility that rank could be a cause of psychological conflict for Samoan girls. In fact, she views the predetermined nature of rank as a deterrent to inner strife.

As we shall see in chapter 9, a later generation of anthropologists was to analyze Samoan attitudes to premarital sex as a manifestation of social, economic, and even religious hierarchy. Mead, meanwhile, whose best-selling work contained many of the materials necessary for such an analysis, has been seen even by friendly critics as oblivious to issues of class (see, e.g., Lutkehaus 1995:203 n. 26).

There are a number of possible reasons for this apparent obliviousness.

The most obvious is that Mead was asked to study the emotions of adolescent girls, not Samoan hierarchy. Mead, like some of the other scholars interested in culture and personality, was relatively unconcerned with matters of class, an omission to some degree characteristic of American culture's tendency to personalize phenomena that elsewhere might be seen as social or political. Moreover, it is by now a cliché to say that the bourgeoisie often sees the whole world when it is really looking at its own image. When Mead speaks of "American culture" in *Coming of Age in Samoa* she is really speaking about white middle-class culture. When she speaks of the experience of "average" Samoan girls she is simply extending this practice abroad. Another factor was Mead's decision to present her data as a "negative instance" to disprove what she took to be Hall's assertion that adolescence was universally a time of storm and stress. If one is disputing alleged universals, it really doesn't matter whether one's conclusions apply to all or only some of the young women of Samoa.

In any case, regulation of sex according to rank need not necessarily lead to emotional conflict, so long as both the rules and the paths for evading them are clear, at least in Mead's opinion. Mead reminds us often of the ludic elements of premarital sex in Samoa: "Sex is a game, played according to one's age and rank; only the taupou, the daughter of the high chief, is supposed not to play at all, but to marry as a virgin. If she is not a virgin, she must have the courage to confess the fact, so that her virginity test may be gracefully faked" (1934:63).[3]

Although at the time of its publication *Coming of Age in Samoa* was received as advocating a new sexual freedom, from a current perspective the work appears surprisingly nonpermissive. The latitude accorded Samoan adolescents is blamed for a "poverty of conception of personal relations" (Mead 1928:221). Although the Samoans are praised for accepting a wide range of sexual techniques within the marital relationship, the beneficial results of such acceptance are said to include the avoidance of "unsatisfactory marriages, casual homosexuality, and prostitution" (Mead 1928:149). The undesirability of these phenomena is taken for granted. Mead seems to approve of Samoans' tolerance toward adolescent homosexual behavior, but her approval is largely based upon the fact that such tolerance seemed to her to discourage the development of fully fledged homosexuals (1928:148–149). Dorothy Counts (personal communication, 2002), when working on a United Nations–sponsored project in contemporary independent Samoa, a place admittedly removed in space and time from American Samoa in the 1920s, was told by Samoans that, unlike Westerners, Samoans don't make an issue out of homosexuality but simply accept it. Counts's acquaintances in Samoa used the English word "homosexual" to refer to someone who answered to the description of a *fa'afafine*, the Samoan version of the widespread Polynesian institution of gender crossing.

It is unclear to what degree Mead may have missed or ignored this aspect of adult Samoan life. Nowadays, fa'afafines are apparently much more common than they were in the past (Mageo 1998:207–208). It has, however, been rightly observed that the absence of this institution in missionaries' and travelers' accounts, in contrast to the frequency with which similar figures were mentioned elsewhere in Polynesia, need not mean it was absent or even rare on the ground (Besnier 1994:294–295). Mead notes that Samoan "native theory and vocabulary" recognized "the real pervert who was incapable of normal heterosexual response" (1928:147, 148), but she does not tell the reader what Samoan word(s) and theories she has in mind. The single instance of such a person she claimed to have observed certainly fits several of the criteria by which modern authors define fa'afafine and its equivalents. Sasi, a 20-year-old boy preparing for the ministry, is described as "pronouncedly feminine in appearance," "skilled at women's work," and unusually comfortable and easygoing in the presence of girls (Mead 1928:148). Mead could find "no evidence that he had ever had heterosexual relations" (1928:148). Girls regarded him as "an amusing freak," and the men whom he had approached sexually looked at him "with annoyance and contempt" (Mead 1928:148). In 1961 Mead wrote that in Samoa, preference by men for feminine occupations produced no more than "a mild amount of amusement" (1961:1452). Mead also suggested in *Coming of Age in Samoa* that the very small population in the area in which she worked might account for the presence of only one such individual (1928:148). Nonetheless, despite this glimpse of a potentially interesting exception to the rule, Mead's discussion of homosexuality in Samoa centers upon the reasons why for most people same-sex eroticism is but a passing phase.

Interestingly, Mead gives, as one reason for the alleged near-absence of adult homosexuality, the "use in heterosexual relations of all the secondary variations of sex activity which loom as primary in homosexual relations," thus "minimizing their importance" (1928:149). In this observation Mead does several things. She breaks down what we would now call "sexual preference" into technique, on the one hand, and the sex of one's partner, on the other. We shall see a similar breakdown of "sex" into its component parts in *Growing up in New Guinea*. She implies that there are some sources of pleasure that are missing from American heterosexual relations, leading Americans to seek them in homosexuality. Although she closes down what could be read as an encouragement of sexual variation by viewing it as an inoculation against perversion, such encouragement might still be found by those who sought it.

Subsequently, in her work on the Omaha, whom she calls "The Antlers" in *The Changing Culture of an Indian Tribe*, first published in 1932, Mead credits early homosexual experience for the pleasure adult women take in heterosexual activity. She says that without the knowledge gained from homosexual experience, one would expect that the negative attitudes toward sex and the antagonism between men and women that she believed to prevail among the Omaha would result in a high level of frigidity (Mead 1966:188).

Although Mead suggests that Samoan girls are missing something significant as a result of their culture's lack of emphasis upon romantic love, she blames the Western emphasis upon such love for the "huge toll of barren, unmarried women who move in unsatisfied procession across the American and English stage" (1928:211). Offering a potentially radical critique of her culture's sexual ideology, evidence that sexual desire and love can be uncoupled in female as well as male experience, Mead blunts its impact by the suggestion that Samoan experience is thereby impoverished and that at home the unmated and the nonprocreative are "unsatisfied."

Mead's work on Manus, conducted in 1929–30 and published in 1930 as *Growing up in New Guinea*, is regarded by many anthropologists (who, as a profession, have always tended to be skeptical of Mead's sweeping assertions) as her most successful work. If *Coming of Age in Samoa* might have offered unintended support to some of what Hall actually said about primitive adolescence, then Mead's work on Manus was designed specifically to deny the equation between primitive adults and civilized children. This equation, found in the work of Freud among many others, involved both cognitive and emotive components. Cognitively, it was asserted that primitive adults thought magically rather than rationally, like Western children. Emotively, primitives were thought to be either less given to repression of their impulses, including their sexual impulses, or so afraid of sex that they hedged it round with taboo and superstition.

Sexually, Manus contrasted in every way with the easygoing tolerance Mead had found on Samoa: Manus adults, according to Mead, did not enjoy any consensual form of heterosexual copulation. The ghosts of deceased ancestors were believed to punish severely any heterosexual activity other than marital intercourse or forced sex with captive women, and no expectation of affection or knowledge of sexual technique existed to sweeten marital sex, particularly for women.

Mead actually describes a situation in Manus that might form the basis of a critique of Western assumptions more radical than anything she found on Samoa. The Samoans had merely failed to develop an ideal of romantic love, at least as an observer from the United States understood that term, not an unusual omission, according to much of the literature on kin-based societies. The Manus, as Mead described them, seemed to have organized normative sexuality in a manner that was quite distinctive. According to her account, Peri villagers routinely expected that love, sexual play, and reproduction were to be found in three separate relationships (Mead 1968a:162–164). The bond between brother and sister was expected to be both loving and chaste. Sex between husbands and wives was directed toward reproduction only, while children of opposite-sex siblings engaged in various forms of verbal sexual teasing as well as forms of nongenital sexual play that were never found in marriage.

The discovery that the affective, reproductive, and ludic functions of sex could be uncoupled in collective representations might have led Mead to deconstruct the notion, described in our opening remarks about Foucault, of a unified sexual being, an assumption central to such "advanced" notions of sexual functioning as Freud's concept of the genital adult. Instead, Mead insists that the people of Manus had impoverished sex lives (1968a:165), a warning to her compatriots reinforced by the strong similarities she noted between Manus prudery and some aspects of American culture. In both cases she implied that there was an association between a deemphasis on grace and sensuousness and an overemphasis on economic competition (Mead 1968a:164, 173–174, 215–218).

It would be a mistake, however, to see in Mead's characterization of Manus simply an endorsement for the stereotype of the *naturally* undersexed, taboo-ridden savage. Although Manus ghosts certainly were believed to keep a stern and disapproving eye out for the sexual peccadilloes of the living, Mead notes that violations did take place and forgiveness could be immediately obtained by confession (1968a:167). Mead blamed women's lack of sexual fulfillment on very local conditions, a combination of male incompetence and women's traditions, both things that could, conceivably, be remedied. When C. G. Seligman wrote to her to ask if Manus women were frigid in the "medical sense," she replied that "tumescence" was absent among Manus women and blamed this upon Manus culture and the fact that Manus men lacked sexual technique.[4]

Mead's early writings on sexuality (later she was to remark that the public overestimated the amount of attention given to sex in *Coming of Age in Samoa*), insofar as they are informed by assumptions about sexual health and disease, may be seen as part of the Western discourse about sex described by Foucault. Insofar as they deal specifically with the sexuality of the Manus and the Samoans they exhibit several of the tendencies we have observed in other writings on primitive sexuality during the first third of the 20th century. We have argued that a view of primitives as excessively chaste, whether through superstition or physiology, was compatible with racial hierarchy, just as the notion of primitive promiscuity had been. Despite some pleas for skepticism about sexual theories from Edward Westermarck and about racial theories from Franz Boas, this was the intellectual baggage the generation of anthropologists who became prominent in the 1920s carried with them as they interpreted their data. Some of them, most notably Mead and Bronislaw Malinowski, devoted a good deal of effort to casting it off, which is not to say that at the end of the process they did not continue to labor under other burdens.

Mead's writing on sexuality differs, however, from both contemporary and earlier treatments of the subject in a crucial respect: the desires attributed to the primitive "Other" have been envisioned within the light of female experience. The writers we have discussed in earlier chapters can fairly be said to be telling a "men's story." Whether they believed primitives to have been licentious, continent, inhibited, or sensible in matters of sex, the modal savage of their imagination was decidedly male. Female sexuality was generally ignored or else treated as either a replica or an artifact of male desire.

Richard Burton and his all-male colleagues at the Anthropological Society of London in the 1860s imagined a phallus-worshiping savage, refined in the arts of love in his Asian manifestations, crudely but abundantly priapic in his African ones. Evolutionary theorists like Morgan, Engels, Bachofen, Lubbock, and McLennan differed in their attitudes to gender and class, but all of them assumed a certain male insatiability to be part of the landscape of human origins. When the undersexed primitive replaced the oversexed savage in the fantasies of some evolutionary theorists in the late 19th and early 20th centuries, it was the arousal of male desire that was the imagined object of various cultural or biological ruses. Female sexuality, if it was not assumed to mirror that of men, was thought to develop largely as an enticement to its male counterpart, as in Havelock Ellis's treatment of female modesty. In Mead we have a writer who sees lack of *female* tumescence as a problem to explain, though the use of the word "tumescence" to describe female sexual response is indicative of a difficulty in writing about female sexuality that we will discuss shortly.

It is a curious fact that Mead acquired far greater fame (or notoriety) as a sexual reformer than Malinowski, despite his involvement with the birth control movement, his correspondence with Ellis, and the citation of his work by Bertrand Russell. Mead certainly shared many of the positions of the sexual reform movements with which Malinowski was associated. She approved of birth control, sex education, and greater attention to the physical pleasure of women. She never spoke in favor of promiscuity, although she supported a lessening of sexual restrictions, and she endorsed neither the persecution of homosexuals nor the unqualified acceptance of homosexuality. She may have had to steer a very careful course on both topics, of course. Gossip about her divorces and at least one extramarital affair would have done her far more harm than Malinowski's reputation as a womanizer ever did him. Moreover, her lesbian relationships with Benedict and others have only become public knowledge since her death. During most of her lifetime, Mead's professional survival would certainly have been imperiled had this aspect of her life been revealed; at the same time, she is unlikely to have been inclined to condemn homosexuality entirely. Samoan homosexual expression is treated as a sensible safety valve for desires that might otherwise get out of hand and, more interestingly, as a training ground in techniques that made heterosexual relations more pleasurable. As we have seen, she treated Euro-American manifestations of homosexuality as an artifact of sexual repression. She may even have believed this; in a culture that teaches that one's desires are unhealthy, one may accept at least part of that diagnosis. If one is a student of culture, what more logical place than culture itself to seek a cause for parts of one's own experience one has been taught to regard as perverse?

Mead saw many of the same desirable features in Samoan marriage that Malinowski did in its Trobriand counterpart; both descriptions were compatible with the promotion of the ideal of companionate marriage. Having worked in a variety of cultures, however, Mead was far more concerned than Malinowski to document the variety in human sexual practice, both primitive and contemporary. In "The Sex Life of the Unmarried Adult in Primitive Society" she suggests that if a society succeeds in enforcing any general sexual regime it must be congenial to some human individuals. She argues that dysphoria is a likely result not of the prescription or prohibition of any particular behavior but rather of inconsistency within the system of sexual expectations. In the case of Manus she says that stress results from a society that views males as inherently sexually aggressive but forbids them access to local females while training females to be frigid. With regard to the Omaha, she argues that traditional Omaha culture had dealt with a conflict between an emphasis on female chastity and comparatively weak controls on men by training women to be bashful and modest but not frigid (Mead 1934:71–73). In 1930, when she visited the Omaha, strict chaperonage was still required, though actual sexual behavior was changing rapidly. In *The Changing Culture of an Indian Tribe* Mead suggests that a widespread consternation concerning the rates at which women and girls become sexually "delinquent" resulted from the fact that by 1930 a generational change in sexual mores, similar to that which had affected American society at large, had occurred among the Omaha. Unlike the situation that Mead believed to exist in white culture, Omaha culture had not adjusted to recognize this shift, leaving the old and the young at odds with each other. She also suggests that such adjustment might have been impeded by the fact that Omaha blamed whites for this dysphoria, which provided them with a cognitive and emotional coping mechanism without solving the basic problem (Mead 1966:192–193). Of course, the Omaha may have been quite correct in their assessment of the situation.

Moreover, Mead undoubtedly overestimated the degree to which American culture at large had accommodated changes in sexual mores by 1932. This was an instance in which Mead's failure to take issues of class and ethnicity into account led her to a false generalization about American sexuality. Outside the elite, avant-garde circles in which Mead moved (see, e.g., Stocking 1992:307–309 for a description of Mead's social milieu), Americans in the 1930s were far from coming to terms with a more permissive sexual culture. This situation may even have affected Mead's own writing and the positions she took.

Although Mead shares many interests and positions with 1920s sexual reformers, she does not appear to have been actively involved with them in the way that Malinowski was. Moreover, her specific concern with the emotional experiences of women and children gave her positions on sexuality a significantly different cast from those of Malinowski and Russell. In Samoa Mead found people she deemed to be more sexually adjusted than many of her compatriots, as Malinowski did in the Trobriands. Like Malinowski, she links some of her subjects' sexual equanimity to an absence of romantic love and has some regrets about that lack. Where Malinowski, however, has some qualms about the limits a lack of romantic passion places on the development of male character, Mead notes the trade-offs she believes Samoan women make in exchanging love for emotional security and reliable sexual technique: "The Samoan girl never tastes the rewards of romantic love as we know it, nor does she suffer as an old maid who has appealed to no lover or found no lover appealing to her, or as the frustrated wife in a marriage which has not fulfilled her high demands" (1928:211).

Lowell Holmes, who revisited Mead's field site in the 1950s with the intention of reevaluating her data, suggests that Mead underestimated the level of emotional attachment that may develop between men and women in Manu'a: "Custom dictates that displays of affection between spouses and lovers not take place in public, but expressions of love and affection were often observed in the families of informants, and many of these same people spoke of feelings for their wives that involved much more emotional depth than mere compatibility or economic convenience. The folklore of Manu'a contains notable examples of fidelity and expressions of deep emotional attachment between spouses and between lovers" (1987:120). The absence of love in primitive culture is, in fact, a remarkably persistent trope in ethnographic accounts of courtship and marriage. It has had varied uses, from diagnosing primitives as suffering from a lack of finer feelings to expressing admiration for efficient social structures not dependent upon messy human emotions for their continuity. Malinowski, for example, saw the absence of romantic love in the Trobriands as, on the one hand, contributing to healthy sexual adjustment and, on the other, as depriving young men of "the feeling of mystery, the desire to worship at a distance" (1929:261).

William Jankowiak, the editor of *Romantic Passion*, a recent volume devoted to the cross-cultural study of love, sums up the situation as follows: "The study of romantic passion (or romantic love) as it is experienced in non-Western cultures is virtually nonexistent. Why bother to explore what is, according to historical conception, supposedly not there? After all it is a given that romantic passion and its companion, affection, are unique to Euro-American culture" (1995:1). On the other hand, it is not uncommon for ethnographers like Holmes to report that individuals fall in love even where social norms don't favor it. The loving couples who provide exceptions to cultural norms are almost as much of an ethnographic staple as statements that this or that primitive society favors marriages arranged on pragmatic grounds. Where the issue of love in non-Western societies is addressed, as in Jankowiak's volume, the emphasis is generally on the question of whether love is a universal emotion. The authors represented in that volume present a convincing case for the existence of love in a wide variety of cultures, including, significantly, Polynesian societies like Samoa. Helen Harris's essay in *Romantic Passion* is primarily aimed at refuting statements made by Donald Marshall concerning the Mangaians of the Cook Islands. Harris asserts, contrary to Marshall, that the Mangaians possess an extensive vocabulary of terms for romantic and passionate love. Moreover, she says that such love, even to the death, is a recurrent theme in myth and that the Mangaians' accounts of their own experiences bear many resemblances to descriptions of love in Western psychological literature. Although the Mangaians (who will be discussed at greater length in chapter 8) aren't Samoans, Harris cites Mead as a prime contributor to an image of all Polynesians as "emotionally stunted yet exuberantly sexual people whose uninhibited libidos set them apart from the rest of humanity" (1995:96).

If writers like Holmes and Harris are correct, then Mead was almost certainly wrong about the absence of emotional intensity in Samoan heterosexual relationships on the part of both men and women. This much said, however, it is worth asking what led her to write as she did and how one should evaluate her work within the history of anthropology's encounters with sexuality. Even seriously flawed works may hold important historical lessons. Indeed, error may be more illuminating than accuracy when one is trying to determine how "facts" were constructed and conscripted to fit into an ongoing story.

Derek Freeman, who published two volumes after Mead's death seeking to discredit her work in Samoa, argued that Mead underestimated the intensity of Samoan emotions and overestimated the degree of sexual freedom enjoyed by Samoan girls (1983, 1999). He believed that Mead made errors partly because, as a loyal student of Boas, she was determined to make a case for culture as a determinant of personality and partly because she allowed herself to be hoaxed by some of her informants (Freeman 1999:139–140 passim). Harris suggests that Mead's work "shaped" anthropological perceptions of Polynesia in a manner that made them consistent with existing images in literary and other sources (1995:96). Freeman, similarly, notes that Mead listed in the bibliography of her 1925 dissertation fiction and travelers' reports describing the supposedly great sexual freedom enjoyed in Polynesian societies (1999:73). Interestingly, Harris makes a similar claim to Freeman's about hoaxing as a source of information about Polynesian sexuality. In her case it is Marshall who is said to have been the victim of "recreational lying" by bragging members of a "drinking group" (Harris 1995:108). Martin Orans, who has performed a close comparative reading of Mead's field notes and the text of *Coming of Age in Samoa*, does not think her data warranted the conclusions she drew about Samoan adolescence (1996:156–157). Nonetheless, he suggests that Mead's conclusions on sexuality were not based upon the alleged hoaxing and, in any case, were far more nuanced in their claims concerning Samoan adolescent freedom than either Freeman or the majority of Mead's reading public believed (Orans 1996:33–100).

For Freeman, the major problem with Mead's work is her loyalty to Boasian cultural determinism. Freeman's own view is that sexuality and family relations are largely the result of biological patterning. For Harris, the problem is somewhat different; she takes exception to the distancing of Polynesians from members of Western cultures by denying them the capacity to love. By Freeman's own account, ironically, Mead was not as committed to Boas's project as his characterization of her argument might lead one to suspect. Indeed, he suggests that she was subject to hoaxing because she had devoted too much of her time to assembling an ethnological collection and not enough to solving the problem of whether Samoan girls suffered storm and stress during adolescence (Freeman 1999:151–152). James Côté disputes this, producing evidence that Boas was fully apprised of Mead's ethnographic work for the Bishop Museum, which, according to Côté, was complementary to her main project (2000:578–579). Mead, perhaps more significantly, did not adopt a totally cultural determinist position elsewhere in her work, for example, in "The Sex Life of the Unmarried Adult in Primitive Society."

Mead did have to work hard to persuade Boas to allow her to go to Polynesia at all, and the project she had been handed was not her first choice. She had wanted to work on issues of social change. In order to get to a more distant field site than Boas normally thought appropriate for his female students Mead had to agree to concentrate her studies on young women like herself. Moreover, in order to get the work published, she had been required to further concentrate upon "feminine" issues, specifically, a disquisition on what parents and educators concerned with adolescent girls in America might learn from Samoa. Once she accepted this particular form of conscription (of both herself and her Samoan informants), this comparison became the real subject of her book and women's experience a major focus of her work for the rest of her life. In this context, her remarks on love take on meanings distinct from either an "Othering" of Polynesians or an argument for cultural determinism. Specifically, she argues that American sexual culture places pressure on girls that Samoan culture does not. This pressure results from the fact that love is presented to them, on the one hand, as a highly desirable experience and the only justifiable motive for sex and marriage and, on the other, as an arena in which they must prove their worth and at which they may fail (for examples of this argument, see especially Mead 1928:211, 222). Mead was one of many writers to note the hazards that the Western linking of love, sex, and marriage poses for women: it is still a major topic in feminist writing and research. Francesca Cancian (1987) and Carol Tavris (1992), for example, argue that one effect of modernity has been a "feminization" of love, a transformation of love into a form of "work" for women. Tavris says: "The female domain of emotional expression is part of women's general responsibility to keep their relationships humming along and deal with any problems that occur. Marriage is the wife's territory; her domain of expertise. It is her *job* to know how everyone is feeling in order to head off problems at the pass. Naturally, she is motivated to talk; she needs to know if anything in the relationship needs fixing, because she will be blamed if she doesn't fix it" (1992:265).

Even if we allow that Mead was wrong in denying that Samoans experience strong emotional attachments to their partners, there was a valid contrast to be drawn between Samoan and American culture concerning the matter of love. Harris herself argues that the Polynesian culture she observed does differ from Euro-American culture in one respect: love is seen not as a duty, as a measure of success in personal relations, but rather as "an emotional state that arises involuntarily, sometimes intensely – and often unfortunately – as it overturns the plans of parents and disturbs the web of relationships that binds individuals to their family and community" (1995:109).

The other authors and cultures represented in Jankowiak's volume similarly present a picture of love outside modern Western culture as something that happens, often (though not always) in violation of cultural norms. Love is not described as a cultural requirement, let alone one particularly exercised with regard to women, though some authors see a development in this direction as a concomitant of modernization. *Coming of Age in Samoa* was part of a cultural temperature taking on matters of love and marriage that has been a characteristic of modernity in the West. Mead's comparison of Samoan and American sexual cultures may best be seen in this light rather than as an argument about the presence or absence of biological determinism or love as a universal emotion.

If Mead did not see American girls as being made especially happy by their culture's emphasis on romantic love, neither was she entirely willing to relinquish it. If love were women's work, to take it away would be to undermine what women, by Mead's time, had come to believe to be essential to their happiness. Mead's objection to what she perceives to be Samoan emotional economy is one that Benedict raised concerning advocates of free love in a journal entry made between 1923 and 1926 and later published by Mead in *An Anthropologist at Work* (1959:149): too much sensible sexual hygiene is the enemy of belief in the possibility of an enduring love and thus destroys the "dignity" of sex. It is significant that the one criticism Boas made of *Coming of Age in Samoa* is that Mead failed to distinguish between passionate and romantic love (Mead 1972:121; Murray and Darnell 2000:563). "Passion" (which implies a strong sexual component) in Western culture has largely been the province of men, "romance" of women; indeed, the language of passion is one that women were often barred from speaking. Boas's observation was astute, and we believe Mead's failure can be explained by the fact that she was attempting to define, through cross-cultural comparison, not merely a sensible sexuality but a female sexuality as well.

Mead sometimes supplied other scholars with suggestions about female experience that might expand their male-centered formulations. In a letter to Malinowski she recommended several ways in which he might have taken more account of the female perspective in his writings, including paying more attention to daughters' perspectives in *Sex and Repression in Savage Society*.[5] Ten years later she wrote to Erik Erikson that his notion of an "intrusive" stage in childhood sexual development privileged male experience at the expense of the female's receptive role in sexual intercourse.[6]

In *Sex and Temperament in Three Primitive Societies* (1935) Mead compares three societies in terms of their valuation and assignment of personality traits labeled "masculine" and "feminine" in the West. The "feminine" Arapesh; the "masculine" Mundugumor, whose women do not try to comfort crying babies and float infants down the river when they do not want to be bothered with child rearing; and the "masculine" women and "feminine" men of the Tchambuli have been much debated among anthropologists and others. For our purposes, it is instructive to note that Mead does not load the dice evenly with regard to these three variations on the patterns of gender. She speaks in the warmest tone about the nurturant Arapesh, although her time among them appears, from biographies and her autobiography, to have been an unpleasant one because of an injured foot and heavy rains, which could not be blamed on Arapesh passivity, and a growing boredom, which could. Reo Fortune, from whom she became permanently estranged on this field trip, accuses her of underestimating Arapesh aggression (1939:36–38).[7]

A comparison between a claim Mead made in *Sex and Temperament* and a statement in her field notes reveals at least one instance in which Mead contradicted some of her own data. She makes much of the fact that Arapesh men "grow" their wives; that is, they participate in the care and feeding of little girls obtained for them by their fathers and brought up in their households to be their wives. There is a belief that premature intercourse will cause both members of the couple to be stunted in physical development; in *Sex and Temperament* Mead suggests that "slight unobtrusive chaperonage" (1963:97) keeps them apart, along with a generally passive attitude toward sex. Her field notes state that a father may beat his son to prevent premature intercourse.[8]

In "The Sex Life of the Unmarried Adult in Primitive Society" Mead uses the Arapesh to argue that a strong male libido is not an inevitable fact of nature. Of their sexual culture she says:

> Of the insistent sexuality of man, which so many peoples take for granted, they know nothing; of the innate aggressiveness of the male they are equally ignorant. Sex is conceived of as a response to an appropriate situation. The mere presence of an unprotected woman is not regarded as a stimulus to sex activity, and women go about and sleep unchaperoned in houses with male friends or relatives of their husbands. The lengths to which such an attitude may lead a people is well illustrated in the tabu during lactation when a man must sleep beside the mother of his child, but have no intercourse with her. He may not even have intercourse with another wife if he has one, for his presence is necessary to make the child grow. It must be enclosed in the rounded circle of its parents' affection from which sex is temporarily and painlessly banished. With the lack of interest in sex, it is not surprising that homosexuality is practically unknown among the Arapesh. Sex is conceived of as play, play meaning in Arapesh any gentle, pleasantly toned activity. When a child is desired, however, sex activity is conceived as work. The Arapesh have pregnancy magic which they sometimes use, for it is said "if people get tired of copulating, they can use pregnancy magic to help out." (1934:64–65)

In *Male and Female*, published in 1949 during the early stages of the postwar glorification of domesticity, Mead revisits the Sepik River valley in New Guinea in order to argue more explicitly not merely for recognition of the cultural malleability of gender but also for a need to value distinct but complementary qualities attributed to women and men. This seeming inconsistency is explained by an assertion that, though culture can and does define gender roles, the cultural imagination does not create out of nothing; it takes its models from inborn temperaments. Caring and nurturance can be instilled in either males or females, members of both sexes may be born with a talent for them, but it is easier and therefore probably more common to train women to be completely fulfilled by reproduction and nurturance than men (see, e.g., Mead 1949:149). Indeed, at one point Mead asserts that childbearing is an experience so real and so valid that "only very few and very sick women who are bred in societies that have devalued maternity are able wholly to disavow it" (1949:158).

The Mundugumor cultural configuration is invoked to stack the dice against a culture whose women are not encouraged to love children:

THE CANNIBAL MUNDUGUMOR OF THE YUAT RIVER
These robust, restive people live on the banks of a swiftly flowing river, but with no river lore. They trade with and prey upon the miserable, underfed bush peoples who live on poorer land, devote their time to quarrelling and head-hunting, and have developed a form of social organization in which every man's hand is against every other man. The women are as assertive and vigorous as the men; they detest bearing and rearing children, and provide most of the food, leaving the men free to plot and fight. (Mead 1949:54)

By contrast, Arapesh women, gently nurtured and fed by their mothers, fathers, and adolescent husbands, are said to acquire sexual, among other, benefits, accomplishing an "easy" transfer of "pleasant expectancy from mouth to vulva, of soft, optimistic retentiveness" (Mead 1949:66). Arapesh men, Mead acknowledged, did not fare as well. They had some difficulties asserting themselves and considerable fear of strange women. They did not, however, become homosexual, an outcome Mead attributed to a lack of desire to dominate that made them uninterested in performing the "active" homosexual role (1949:67). On the whole, Mead claimed, Arapesh sex roles were more congenial to women than to men, except, she admitted, for the occasional woman who was still "positively sexed and interested in a climax for herself" (1949:68).

Betty Friedan (1963) characterized Mead as pursuing a "feminine protest," a fairly tireless advocacy of sexual attitudes that value nurturance and motherhood as much as genital gratification. In particular, Friedan believed *Male and Female* had played a significant role in creating the cultural atmosphere that drove American women back to the kitchen and the nursery after World

War II. In fairness, Mead does argue, when prescribing for her compatriots, that this female tendency toward nurturance should be balanced with an encouragement for women to find fulfillment in other careers and to allow for individual variation, though she warns against "masculinizing" women and "feminizing" men (1949:366–384). As in Mead's treatment of love in *Coming of Age in Samoa*, her discussion of motherhood in *Male and Female* recognizes the constraints that motherhood (especially in the American nuclear family) can place on women (1949:325–341), but she does not advocate that women be encouraged to sacrifice its supposed joys.

In 1939 Mead complained to Erikson that no one was writing about sex anymore, except in the context of sexually determined aggression (an observation that is only partially consistent with our findings concerning this period). [9] In the postwar world Mead was still seeking some way of assuring that love and pleasure could be linked with marriage and procreation. While she continued to favor sex education, birth control, a more open attitude toward premarital experimentation, and the relatively liberal attitudes toward divorce she had advocated twenty years previously, she was still worried, as she had been in 1928, about the anxiety caused by too much freedom. Her solution to the question of divorce was permissiveness coupled with surveillance in the form of social science expertise applied to help people to divorce with dignity or work to preserve their marriages. She also suggested that anthropologists were uniquely qualified to help devise ritualized ways of handling the new freedoms and providing advice, like the advice in her book, based on the experience of other cultures (Mead 1949:354–366).

This therapeutic role for anthropology is not one that other anthropologists have been sure they wanted. Malinowski's unfulfilled dream of an applied anthropology was limited to advising missionaries and administrators on the proper management of the colonies. Mead continued to offer advice on the matters she had touched on in her early work, in *Redbook* magazine, in public lectures, and on government commissions. Her focus on women and children doubtless played a role in making these forums available and congenial to her – there is a long tradition of experts' advice to women on sex, marriage, and child rearing, partly linked to and partly independent of the culture of professional expertise. Though John Haller and Robin Haller (1974) record the correspondence in the 19th century between males, both boys and men, and doctors who offered advice on matters such as the effects and prevention of masturbation, the popular advice genres have been aimed largely at a female audience. Mead's use of this tradition, a use that included the addenda to *Coming of Age in Samoa*, assured her a wider audience than

Malinowski but also made her vulnerable to criticism. As Lutkehaus (1995) notes, critics have included not only the anthropologists who disliked the popular, "feminine" tone of her writing but also feminists like Friedan who lament Mead's association with a tradition that has generally supported traditional sex roles.

Mead's advice changed with changing times, though with a continuing passion for the nurturance of children and the fuller expression of masculine and feminine natures. In 1963 she wrote in *Redbook* that "bisexual potentialities are normal" (Metraux 1979:73). In 1974 (by which time such things were becoming less dangerous) Mead acted as one of the discussants at the first panel at an American Anthropological Association conference devoted to the study of homosexuality. Clark Taylor, who, some years earlier, had urged a somewhat stunned association membership to actively pursue such studies, has reported of the 1974 occasion: "That was Margaret Mead at her best, she was there with her transsexual secretary, and relatively open about her bisexuality, absolutely tremendously supportive" (Amory n.d.).

Mead's failure to develop a truly radical anthropology of female sexuality in the years when she was a public expert on the topic was, in large part, a political one. Her claim to authority would certainly have been compromised by too radical a critique of an America in which political loyalty was increasingly being measured by sexual conformity. Micaela di Leonardo has offered us a trenchant account of the "fit" between Margaret Mead's change of position on gender malleability and the new political realities of the postwar world. *Male and Female* "fit well the anxious, sexist postwar Weltanschauung, and Mead's own statements in publicizing the book reveal her nervous skittering to establish simultaneously her scientific credentials and her inoffensive 'femininity,' all the while ducking to avoid a stigmatizing sexualization" (Leonardo 1998:208).

In her memoir of her parents Mary Catherine Bateson, Mead's daughter, discusses the need her mother felt to keep her bisexuality (and some aspects of her heterosexual attachments) secret in the atmosphere of 1950s America and her own sadness, tempered with at least partial forgiveness, at discovering she had been kept in the dark (1984:115–127). Returning from her final year of high school, spent in Israel, Bateson entrusted her mother with a confidence concerning a brief (and unconsummated) romance she had with a young woman there, expecting her mother to be pleased to be taken into her daughter's confidence. Instead, Mead (who later gave her daughter a novel that cast bisexuality in a favorable light) launched into a lecture on the damage it could do to her career were her daughter to become involved in scandal (Bateson 1984:124).

Jean Walton, in a book on racial subtexts in feminist psychoanalytic writing, is less forgiving than Bateson. She sees Mead as concealing her sexuality in order to claim an authority over the sexuality of racial "Others" that would only be granted to a white heterosexual, whatever public pronouncements Mead may have made in favor of racial tolerance (Walton 2001:169–176). Certainly, if Mead had a more subversive message for American women than she delivered in the surface texts of her work, it became increasingly necessary, during the cold war period, to deliver it in innuendo and to reserve parts of it for later.

In a rather curious appendix to *Male and Female* Mead claims the role of doctor, prescribing for the social "patient" (1949:449). For several pages Mead tortures a peculiar metaphor about maintaining the right tautness on the rope by which Americans have been taught to hitch their wagons to a star (1949:427–439) and explains why she doesn't discuss "deviations" like prostitution and "promiscuous homosexuality." Precisely because she sees these things as systematically related to the "healthy" aspects of American sexuality, she says, healthy readers need to be protected from discussion of them. Otherwise, they might either reject her arguments out of hand or, instead of being inspired to show "mercy" toward deviants, launch "a destructive crusade against those whose strength has been less than their own" (Mead 1949:448–449). One of those people, of course, might have been Mead herself.

There is, one might suggest, another problem of communication, quite aside from any political considerations, that prevented Mead from developing a more explicit anthropology of female sexuality. It is a problem to which feminist writers have repeatedly referred: the absence of a language in which to write (or speak) about sex as women experience it. Adrienne Rich (1979) and Marilyn Frye (1988) are among the many writers who have either commented upon this problem or written works that tried to correct it or both. Frye, for example, says that the term *sex* in English is inextricably linked to notions of penile penetration and ejaculation rather than female pleasure. Lesbians, she argues, may not know what to say when asked by researchers how often they have "sex," and heterosexual women may, in effect, be reporting the frequency with which their *partners* have "sex."

In the feminist science fiction classic *Native Tongue* (Elgin 1984) the women of a future caste of linguists, seeking to evade the control held over them by male linguists, who constitute the new ruling class because of their control of interplanetary communication, secretly conspire to develop a women's language, Láadan. Suzette Hayden Elgin, the author of *Native Tongue*, is herself a linguist. A group of feminist linguists in the United States spent some time in the 1980s enlarging and refining the Láadan vocabulary, but, in a recent online interview, Elgin expressed disappointment that more women had not expressed interest in learning the language. She says, perhaps ironically, that she concluded after ten years that women did not find ordinary English or French or Spanish inadequate for their purposes (Glatzer 1999). Perhaps the "failure" of Elgin's invented language to catch on is a result of the fact that its lexemes are disproportionately concentrated in two semantic fields: that of emotion and that of sex. Láadan, for example, contains separate words for desired and undesired pregnancy and welcome and unwelcome menopause as well as a lexeme for those menstrual periods that come as a relief. Such locutions seem designed to express the entwining, for women, of sex, reproduction, and their social consequences, a subject about which Mead had much to say. To label this intertwining is, on the one hand, to recognize its existence. On the other, it is a way of reifying and naturalizing cultural expectations that many women might wish to change.

The conceit of a women's language was a striking way to draw attention to the fact that the lexicon of public discourse lacked descriptors for women's experiences. Such a language, however, would not really have been a more useful writing tool for Mead than the idiom she adopted, the one that the arbiters of anthropological taste found so cloying. Although female sexual experience involves bodily and emotional states shared by only part of the population, Mead wanted to disseminate her thoughts about it as widely as possible, contributions to such "female" venues as *Redbook* and *Parents Magazine* notwithstanding. Accordingly, she had to speak and write in some version of ordinary language, with certain problems attendant upon that decision.

When Mead set out to write about sexuality from a female perspective and/or a culturally relativist one, she had available several vocabularies, all of which reified the prevailing ethos of Western culture. She suggested to Erik Erikson that he would profit from devising a term for "female genital behaviour" that did not encompass the male anatomical assumptions of his "intrusive" stage of sexual development. [10] She also objected to the medicotechnical discourse of Kinsey (Mead 1948) and the earlier sexual reformers. Certainly, to a public for whom male models of sexuality such as Erikson's seem "natural," descriptors such as "soft, optimistic retentiveness" to describe aspects of Arapesh female sexuality were bound to seem saccharine.

Both Mead and Erikson were speaking in metaphors, but Erikson's locution slipped past the radar of a culture that marked Mead's talk as egregious. If one rejects the language of the clinic and the smoking room to describe sex and forgoes the escape routes of professional jargon, native terminology, and flights into Latin that were already beginning to look dated, one's alternatives are limited. Apart from anything else, there are some things one cannot say clearly. In 1928 it is unlikely that a publisher would have allowed, in a publication for a mass audience, a straightforward statement of the "techniques" for pleasing women that Samoan men were said to possess and Manus men to lack. Even if William Morrow would have allowed a word like "clitoris," it is almost certain that many women (and men, for that matter) would have had to reach for their dictionaries to find out what it meant. Even after doing so, a fair number would have remained unenlightened, given the injunctions of the time against masturbation and sexual exploration. Our mothers, who married in 1936 and 1941, would almost certainly have fallen into this category.

Stocking reports that Mead possessed, at the time of her field research in Samoa, a "lengthy and highly explicit list" of Samoan sex terms compiled by George Pratt, a missionary (1992:312). He also observes that her notes include "a long and vividly detailed interview with one adult male informant covering all aspects of Samoan sex life, including techniques of masturbation and foreplay, sexual positions, frequency of married and premarital intercourse, and female behavior at the height of orgasm" (Stocking 1992:312). Significantly, this explicit discussion did not find its way into *Coming of Age in Samoa*. Indeed, a reader could be excused for a certain level of mystification. What, precisely, were the "techniques" that Samoan men were said to possess with such satisfying results? What exactly were the "secondary variations of sex activity" (Mead 1928:149) that Samoans allegedly transferred from youthful homosexual play to adult heterosexuality? Mead seems either to trust that her readers will have the knowledge to fill in the blanks or to fear that they will be scandalized or uncomprehending were she to do so for them.

Mead's lack of explicitness in describing Samoan sexual techniques has led one contemporary commentator, Nicole Grant, to conclude that "sex" for the unmarried, at the time of Mead's visit to Manu'a, meant "oral and manual" stimulation rather than intercourse. This interpretation is seen to solve two mysteries: the low pregnancy rate and the seeming contradiction between premarital freedom and the high value placed on virginity (Grant 1995:678–682). The chief evidence for this interpretation is drawn from Mead's field notes, in which she recorded that "boys proceed from breast, navel, abdomen, clitoris, vagina, using hands and lips," and that cunnilingus and fellatio were "both frequent as preliminary to intercourse" (Grant 1995:679).

Grant interprets "preliminary" as meaning that oral and manual sex were the norm before marriage, though she acknowledges that a reader could also conclude that they were used as foreplay (1995:678–682). Grant suggests that it was missionaries and American sailors who introduced to Samoans the notion that intercourse was the only activity that fully counted as sex, which might even account for the disparity between what Mead's informants told her and what they told Freeman many years later (1995:679–680). Unfortunately, since Mead does not carry the explicit language of her notes into her text, Grant's suggestions must remain but an interesting hypothesis. We have tried to suggest here some possible reasons why Mead's published text left her readers so unenlightened.

With regard to one of the puzzles Grant believes she has solved, the low premarital pregnancy rate in Samoa, Mead in 1961 offered a solution of her own that is very much in keeping with a focus on female sexual sensibilities. This solution also indicates that she did think that at least some Samoan premarital sexual encounters included vaginal penetration. Citing the findings of C. S. Ford and F. A. Beach (1951) and the Kinsey Report on *Sexual Behavior in the Human Female* (Kinsey et al. 1953), Mead suggests that women may be sexually most responsive at the point in the menstrual cycle when they are least fertile. She argues that before marriage "the male is dependent on the willingness of the female to yield to his advances, so he may be refused at those periods when she is unreceptive." Along with a period of adolescent sterility this pattern is said to be a likely factor in low premarital pregnancy rates in societies that allow a period of sexual freedom before marriage. After marriage, the balance of power changes, and the pregnancy rate rises (Mead 1961:1465).

One of the few alternative vocabularies open to Mead was that of sentiment and domesticity, already devalued in contrast to the "serious" (masculine) business of life. We have, many times in the course of a 30-year anthropological career, heard the opinion expressed that *Growing up in New Guinea* was a (marginally) better book than Mead's other works because of its extensive attention to cognition as opposed to babies and breast-feeding. We have even been known to say something like this ourselves.

In the matter of language, as in the topics she addressed, Mead's choices left her open to attack and dismissal from both conservative and radical positions. Mead attempted to validate and valorize, as both a serious subject of study and a mode of sexual expression, some of the components of what the Victorians had called women's "separate sphere." It appeared to some as if she were invading public space to conduct a conversation best held in a kitchen, a bathroom, or a boudoir. On the other hand, when a later generation finally addressed the problem of how to speak about sexual experience not encompassed by the categories of male heterosexual hegemony, it developed not a solution but a blanket suspicion of all ordinary language in the description of sex and gender. To a generation we shall meet later in the book to whom terms such as "woman" and "homosexual" are as problematic as "savage" and "primitive," Mead could not help but sound cloying, simplistic, and conservative.

Of course, the problem that we (and others) have called a problem of "language" is, more accurately, a problem of culture, if, indeed, it is possible to separate the two. When experiences are difficult to label, it is often because culture does not provide a space for them. An alleged problem with "language" may, indeed, result from a lack of lexemes, but it may also result from an interdiction against using the lexemes that exist or engaging in the behaviors to which those lexemes refer. Mead's difficulties may well have been mainly of the latter variety. Both Walton (2001) and Bateson (1984) suggest that Mead, in *Blackberry Winter*, jumped from an account of the dissolution of her marriage at about the same time that *Male and Female* was published to an account of her experiences as a grandmother some 20 years later. Both suggest that this was done to submerge the inconvenient details of her sexual life. Both of them also imply that her lifelong equation of female experience with maternity was, in part, a way of deflecting attention from other experiences that might not have been met with sympathy had they received closer scrutiny. In this textual practice Mead was not alone.

It is significant that Simone de Beauvoir's *The Second Sex* (1949) was published in the same year as *Male and Female*. Although the work seems to later generations far more revolutionary in its challenge to conventional categories, in some ways it addresses the same problem. Beauvoir argues that "women" as a class have been created by men to fill the role of the "Other" and that there is no discourse in which they may express themselves *as themselves*. In other words, she was aware of the problem of language and, accordingly, is regarded as a foundation theorist by those contemporary writers who attempt to address this issue, although her book was largely forgotten during the years in which Mead was enjoying a huge influence on popular opinion. Nonetheless, Beauvoir tried to come to terms with some of the same issues as Mead. Where Mead says motherhood needs to be positively valued as an integral part of the female sexual experience, Beauvoir (1963:456–497) offers a lengthy discussion of women's ambivalence toward their children, documented by extensive allusions to literary, clinical, and archival sources, rooting this ambivalence in a discussion of the fuzziness of the self/other boundary that is part of French existentialist thought. Beauvoir, like Mead, argues that children will benefit if their mothers are freer to pursue other interests (1963:495), employing a trope that has long been a part of liberal, as opposed to radical, feminist discourse.

By using ordinary language words for what she may have intended as thoroughly revamped experiences, Mead made it hard to tell how much of a change she was advocating in the conceptualization of female sexuality. Certainly, her apparently enthusiastic presence on government committees and in the pages of mainstream women's magazines in the 1950s indicates that she was, at the very least, "co-optable"; we think, however, that there are some clues that she occasionally had glimpses of possibilities of more penetrating critiques than she ever produced. At the very least, she assured that anthropology became a discipline in which women could encounter texts that took seriously women's experience of childbearing, lactation, menstruation, and love (or the lack of it) long before other disciplines routinely did so and during a time when a feminist framework for speaking about such things was largely in retreat. Moreover, we shall see in the next chapter that other neo-Freudian apologists for the maternal imperative were far more uncompromising than Mead in their conscription of the primitive into a discourse that glorified and idealized maternity but bemoaned the failure of actual mothers, at home and abroad, to achieve it.

CHAPTER 8

The "Silence"

Until a few years ago sex was a subject usually avoided in anthropological monographs. This omission was due partly to sheer prudery, the legacy to the science of
our peculiar type of social and moral code, and partly to the difficulty of obtaining
information on this most intimate side of man's personal life. But as the modern
anthropologist developed his technique of collecting data, lived in native villages,
talked with the people in their own language, and shared their daily life, on the
one hand it became obvious that a dismissal of sexual matters would really falsify
the whole perspective of the native culture, and on the other the collection of data
became easier. . . . What is needed in this field is more work of the elaborately
analytical objective character given in Professor Malinowski's Sexual Life of Savages, where the subject is set with the greatest care against its background of social
institutions.

Sir Raymond Firth, We, the Tikopia

At the beginning of a discussion of sexuality in Tikopia that, all told,
occupies nearly a quarter of a lengthy book, Sir Raymond Firth
commented on the history and the prospects for the anthropological study of sexuality. His remarks about the paucity of monographs until
the late 1920s must be taken in context. He was referring to ethnographic
writing in the modern sense and not the Victorian and Edwardian modes
of writing we have already discussed. His hope that his work would be
a precedent for future publications on sexuality was not to be realized.
Significantly, Daryll Forde's review of We, the Tikopia does not mention
the section on sexuality, concentrating entirely on Firth's detailed data on
kinship, economics, and various aspects of ritual (1938:27–28).

There is a common consensus that sex retreated from the center stage of anthropology sometime during the 1930s. It was more than 30 years before it reemerged as a major concern. We are hardly arguing that *nothing* about sex appeared for an entire generation. In fact, quite a bit of useful, probably more or less correct factual information can be gleaned from the ethnographies of this period. However, anthropologists did not make sexuality as such a subject of grand theory as it showed signs of becoming in the late 1920s. Sexuality did not so much disappear as become subsumed in other discourses: kinship and marriage, child socialization, gender and aggression, even environmental adaptation. A few monographs appeared that did feature sexuality as a major theme, but the discipline tended to treat these discussions as sidelines. Only a minority of anthropologists wrote about sex at all during this period, and most of them limited their remarks to a few paragraphs. As late as 1971 Robert Suggs and Donald Marshall remarked upon "the suppression of a good deal of information on sexual behavior which will remain forever locked in the heads (and in some personal field notes) of anthropological investigators" (1971a:221).

The "silence" about sex in anthropology as well as the things that *were* said about the topic were almost certainly overdetermined. In these four decades the discipline underwent accelerated professionalization on both sides of the Atlantic. As Henrika Kuklick (1991) has emphasized, most of the new generation of anthropologists were no longer upper class or upper middle class in origin. Until the 1960s jobs were hard to find. Anthropologists avoided publications that might detract from their professional status or that of an insecure discipline. Despite changes in societal attitudes that occurred during the era of sexual reform, sex was still not entirely respectable as a topic of serious scientific study. The Great Depression, World War II, and the onset of the cold war presented "progressive" thinkers with issues for discussion that seemed to be far more pressing than sex.

Theoretical developments within anthropology played their part in directing attention away from sex. Radcliffe-Brown's Durkheimian anthropology made individual motivation a forbidden topic of discussion for many British and South African social anthropologists, including some former students of Malinowski such as Meyer Fortes and Evans-Pritchard (Stocking 1995:422–426). The Durkheimian program excluded biological and psychological data from its agenda. Inasmuch as sex was personal and individual or universal and natural, it was not pertinent to sociology, though its transformations in institutions such as marriage and the family were of central concern to the unsexed new science of kinship (see Borneman 1996 for a provocative discussion of this issue).

In the United States there is a less radical discontinuity between the anthropology of the 1920s and subsequent developments. The sociological method made inroads at the University of Chicago during Radcliffe-Brown's sojourn there in the 1930s but had much less impact elsewhere. American anthropologists continued to take Freud seriously, whether they accepted his sexual theory, modified it, rejected it, or subsumed it in new syntheses. Individual psychology, including sexuality, continued to be discussed, but adult sexual behavior was rarely the subject of primary interest. We shall consider some significant exceptions, including a few anthropologists professionally employed in psychoanalytic practice. Many other anthropologists of the "culture and personality" school rejected Freudian orthodoxies concerning infantile sexuality, even when they discussed oral, anal, and genital socialization. Nursing, toilet training, masturbation, and Oedipal desire (or the lack of it) were seen as both products and antecedents of diffuse "modal personalities." The sexual routines of early childhood were likely to be seen as rooted in environment and ecology rather than as independent variables or cultural universals. The majority of American anthropologists of this period, like their British counterparts, did not discuss sex (or culture and personality) very much at all. On both sides of the Atlantic there was a tendency to disparage concern with childhood bodily regimes and romantic sentiments as "feminine," making them unattractive objects of study for many men and some women.

Until the 1970s British social anthropology and the variant forms of American cultural anthropology were decidedly distinct national traditions. However, both were founded on the rejection of the excesses of their 19th-century evolutionary heritage. For Boas and his associates, opposition to racism and the salvaging of traditional cultures were explicit goals, both morally and theoretically. In Britain the rejection of racism was rarely a dominant objective of social anthropologists, though we have seen that their attitudes sometimes tended to diverge from other British participants in the colonial encounter. British functionalists, whether followers of Malinowski or Radcliffe-Brown, often saw themselves as advocates for tribal peoples against colonial mismanagement. As believers in the organic interdependence of social institutions, they decried the disruptive effects of bans against bridewealth, enforced monogamy, interference with initiation ceremonies, and disregard of the rules of inheritance.

At the High Leigh conference, it may be recalled, Malinowski had advocated an applied anthropology of sexuality. Anthropologists would train missionaries in the principles of care and respect for indigenous institutions. However, anthropologists' perceived interest in sexuality could detract from the seriousness with which colonial administrators received their claims of expertise. We recall that one of the most influential of administrators and one of those more supportive of anthropology, Sir Philip Mitchell of New Guinea, criticized the obsession of anthropologists "with minutiae of obscure tribal and personal practices, especially if they were agreeably associated with sex or flavored with obscenity" (1951:57).

Donna Haraway has noted an important similarity between British functionalism and American studies of culture and personality (1991:20–44). Both, she says, were focused on the organization of human raw material into well-running systems, colonial societies in one case, a healthy American citizenry in the other. Gilbert Herdt has made a similar point (1999:224). For Haraway such social and psychological engineering was part of the discipline of capitalism. Sex, she argues, was something that required not repression as such but transformation into the reproduction of labor and the production of capital as a means of supporting healthy families. Haraway's points are intriguing and to some degree certainly valid, but the politics of the "silence" in the anthropology of sex were somewhat more complex (and sometimes more benign) than she allows. Whatever their visions of the social applications of anthropology, both the Boasians and the British functionalists were increasingly concerned to portray the people they studied in as positive a light as possible. For many practitioners, this concern led either to active challenges to paradigms of oversexed savages or to discreet silence about what had become an embarrassing topic. However, we shall draw attention to a number of American writers who spurned the relativist project and conscripted the sexuality of "primitive Others" as fodder for their own antimodernist social agenda.

SOME VOICES FROM BRITAIN AND THE COMMONWEALTH

Malinowski's third edition of *The Sexual Life of Savages* was published in 1932. It was his last word on the subject apart from posthumous publications. The political struggle against totalitarianism preoccupied Malinowski during the last years of his life, eclipsing sex in his priorities. His posthumously published *Freedom and Civilization* (1944) is an impassioned defense of liberalism against totalitarianism. After the fall of Poland in 1939 Malinowski, who had taken up an appointment at Yale, became involved with the Polish partisan cause.

Among those who attended Malinowski's seminars at the London School of Economics or worked with him at the new African Institute were the Oceanists Ian Hogbin and Raymond Firth and the Africanists Meyer Fortes, E. E. Evans-Pritchard, and Isaac Schapera. Three of these scholars gathered ethnographic data about sexuality within a few years of the publication of *The Sexual Life of Savages*. Firth's *We, the Tikopia* (1936) and Schapera's *Married Life in an African Tribe* (1940) were major monographs that reported these findings. Hogbin's monograph on the Wogeo, *The Island of Menstruating Men*, did not appear until 1970, though he published several significant articles in *Oceania* during the 1930s and 1940s on sexuality in societies in the Solomons and New Guinea. With the exception of an early paper on Zande ideas concerning conception, the soul, and the fetus and some information in an article on the Zande royal court published in a specialist regional journal in 1957, Evans-Pritchard chose not to publish data on Zande sexuality that he gathered in the 1920s until the early 1970s.

We, the Tikopia contains a detailed description of supercision (an operation during which a long cut is made through the top of a young or adolescent boy's foreskin), Tikopian terms for the genitalia, discussions of infantile sexuality, indigenous theories of reproduction, folktales on sexual themes, and data on menstruation, courtship, marriage, and marriage exchanges. Firth describes the most common sexual positions and techniques employed by Tikopians and the use of coitus interruptus, infanticide, and abortion as modes of population control. Firth explicitly counters images of Polynesia as a sexual idyll (1957b:513). Although he frankly portrays the violence and "crudity" as well as the romance in Tikopia premarital and marital relations, Firth is always careful to point out parallels between European and Tikopian practice, sometimes in ways that question Europeans' assumptions about their own sexual morality: "Chastity in Tikopia is not a moral issue; the physical state is interpreted consciously and traditionally solely in terms of social advantage. This is so for the girl as well as for the man. On reflection one wonders if this is not largely true of our own society as well" (1957b:520).

Firth describes among the Tikopia both courtship and romance as a prelude to marriage and marriages that began with abduction and rape. The overall impression is that neither images of "love among the palm trees" nor pictures of high status elders brutally imposing their will upon the young offer an adequate portrait of Tikopia courtship and marriage. Each of these stereotypes has some basis in truth, as Firth depicts it, but only a partial basis. Relationships between sweethearts commonly led to marriage in Tikopia and often involved premarital sex. On the other hand, Firth's informants told him that marriage by capture had recently been frequent; indeed, some of them had married in this way. Firth offers correctives to both popular and anthropological representations of marriage by capture that, as we have already noted, played a significant role in evolutionary anthropology. The "modern scientist," Firth tells us, finds "ludicrous" the descriptions in the popular press of "the savage who goes courting with a club instead of a nosegay of flowers" (1957b:534). On the other hand, Firth rejects both general anthropological wisdom, which would suggest that Tikopia capture was a mere formal survival of some ancient, "real" form of capture between hostile clans or tribes, and Ernest Crawley's particular suggestion that capture was primarily a mode of overcoming female reluctance.

Firth thus offers his readers rare data on a widely discussed practice that has seldom been described in detail. The fighting that occurred during and immediately after the abduction of a Tikopian woman was real enough to lead to injury and occasionally to death, although it was circumscribed by some social rules. Indeed, situating marriage by capture within its social context is the key point of Firth's analysis, as one might expect from Malinowski's student. It occurred between neighboring kin groups who previously and subsequently coexisted in relative harmony. It occurred among Tikopians of noble rather than commoner rank. Ideally, the bride, who was usually unaware of the wedding plans, would be abducted from her house in the middle of the night. Otherwise, she might be seized on a pathway outside her residence (such seizures were regarded as a strong insult to her lineage). Sometimes the groom too would be an unwilling partner to these plans, inasmuch as his elders and betters might decide on their own choice of spouse in order either to overcome his reluctance to marry or to substitute their good choice of bride for his own poor one. If the bride did not consent to sexual intercourse with the groom, she might face rape. Usually, the parties settled down and accepted the fait accompli. An elaborate etiquette governed the long series of visits and ceremonial food exchanges that secured social peace. Firth adopts a matter-of-fact approach in the description of abduction and rape. This is obviously upsetting to the modern reader. It should be reiterated, however, that the sensationalism and ethnocentrism he was endeavoring to counter were serious problems in their own right.

Most but not all Polynesian societies have a form of institutionalized homosexuality. Firth found nothing of the kind in Tikopia, although he was told that pederasty did occur (1957b:495). Neither he nor his informants are portrayed as being very interested in the topic.

Firth's primary goal is to demonstrate the links between sexuality, kinship, and the economic system in a functioning Tikopian society. The final paragraphs of *We, the Tikopia* discuss the practical uses to which anthropology might be put and the limits to such deployment. Though Firth introduces these conclusions with comments on the relevance of kinship studies for those managing changes in land tenure in Polynesia, he insists on a distinction between the role of the scientist and that of the social engineer: "Social anthropology should be concerned with understanding how human beings behave in social groups, not with trying to make them behave in any particular way by assisting an administrative policy or a proselytizing campaign to achieve its aims more easily" (1957b:599). It would seem that Firth is opposed to the practices we have defined as "conscription" and committed to the relativity of moral truth:

> Missionary, government officer and mine manager are free to use anthropological methods and results in their own interests, but they have no right to demand as a service that anthropology should become their handmaid. Nor can the standards which they invoke – "civilization," "humanity," "justice," "the sanctity of human life," "Christianity," "freedom of the individual," "law and order" – be regarded as binding; the claim of absolute validity that is usually made for them too often springs from ignorance, from an emotional philanthropy, from the lack of any clear analysis of the implications of the course of action proposed, and from confusion with the universal of what is really a set of moral ideas produced by particular economic and social circumstances. (1957b:599)

Firth goes on to acknowledge that scientists will inevitably have their own biases and to suggest that they must be aware of these prejudices and allow for their possible effects. This is not in any sense an appeal for self-reflexivity; that is prevented by the fact that one "claim of absolute validity" is not questioned – the claim of science itself. That is precisely the claim that Haraway has suggested requires interrogation. We recognize the dangers of reifying "systems" and the authority of those who study them. Many critics have found in functionalism a potential for blindness to issues of power and resistance. We give an example of such an instance in our discussion of Firth's treatment of marital rape and abduction. Nonetheless, *We, the Tikopia* offers a significant achievement in what Kath Weston (1998:149–156) was later to call the "ethnocartography" of sexuality, at least of heterosexuality. Such rich, layered descriptions, we argue, turned out to be surprisingly rare.

Married Life in an African Tribe is Schapera's study of the Kgatla people of Botswana (then Bechuanaland) who were both horticulturalists and
pastoralists. Its author had taken his bachelor of arts as Radcliffe-Brown's
student in Cape Town, studied with Charles Seligman, and assisted Malinowski as a doctoral student at the London School of Economics (Kuper
2001). Schapera's account of married life and heterosexual relationships
was crafted for the general intelligentsia rather than for a specifically academic audience. Consequently, the style is fluid, often anecdotal. Schapera
acquired a plethora of data concerning intimate sexual relations, including
love letters between unmarried and married couples. Although at the time
of publication Schapera had become a practitioner of Radcliffe-Brown's
more austere structural functionalism, there are many echoes of Malinowski's *The Sexual Life of Savages* evident in this book. Once again, there is
detail on love magic, courting techniques, positions in intercourse, theories
of conception, standards of beauty, and tolerance of adultery, at least within
limits.

However, Schapera was much more concerned than Malinowski with
presenting a contemporary picture of a society undergoing rapid change
(see Kuper 2001). He was clearly aware of the political and economic realities
faced by the Tswana peoples. The Kgatla had settled in Bechuanaland in
the mid–19th century in order to get away from the Boers in the Transvaal.
Missions began their work in the 1890s, and, in the early 1900s, the king,
Lentswe, adopted Christianity. By the early 1930s a substantial minority of
Kgatla had become Christians. Missionaries preached against traditional
forms of marriage and ceremonial. Accordingly, Christians, at least in theory, did not practice polygyny. The initiation ceremonies for both young
men and young women were greatly simplified and no longer contained
rites that were offensive to Christians. The missionaries also succeeded in
securing the abolition of bride-price (*bogadi*), but that policy was reversed
just before Schapera did his fieldwork in the early 1930s. By that time, too,
there was substantial labor migration, particularly by young males, to the
towns and mining camps of South Africa. As Schapera portrayed them, the
Kgatla of the 1930s stood between two different worlds. Those who did not
venture to the cities pursued their livelihoods in the way their ancestors had
done for a century or two, albeit many of them had received some primary
education and were increasingly reliant on a small number of consumer
goods. There was much poverty. A minority of Kgatla married according
to the rites of the Dutch Reformed Church, but traditional marriages were
more common, although often with reduced ceremonial. Labor migration,

however, eroded the authority of the elders, who had once organized marriages.[1] Young men who went back and forth to the cities acquired a degree of financial independence that enabled them to subvert the power of the elders.[2] Accordingly, some marriages were still arranged, but others were the result of individual choice. According to Schapera, premarital continence had been a strict rule in the 19th century, but by 1930 a degree of premarital license prevailed.

Schapera does not question the reliability of assertions about the morality of the old days; presumably, they are based on the consensus of his informants. Such assertions are commonplace in anthropological accounts of elders' recollections of past times. Schapera includes several case studies of individuals whose path to marriage involves challenges to or compromises with their elders' wishes. In some cases the elders are brought round to the young people's point of view. Sometimes the couples elope and defy the elders.

Trained in a tradition that saw kinship as the key to coherence of tribal societies, Schapera was presented with a society in which families had lost some of their functions, not least in the organization and regulation of sexual behavior. Although Schapera is subtly critical of the colonial reality that produced this situation, in his conclusions he tries to paint as favorable a picture of Kgatla family life as possible: "Despite the many factors making for disruption, the Kgatla family has therefore not broken down to any considerable extent" (1966:355). One must observe that the positive images Schapera presents (and, for that matter, the negative ones) incorporate the assumption that social organization founded on heterosexual marriage and reproduction is the norm, and a desirable norm at that, in preindustrial societies. Where Schapera finds some room to praise the new freedoms for individuals, especially women, that praise is based partly on their potential contribution to a more satisfying married life (1966:356). Nonetheless, he blames the changes introduced by Western civilization for a "lack of happiness" and contentment that, he says, characterized many Kgatla marriages (Schapera 1966:355).

Doubtless, Schapera's choice of subject matter (his title, after all, refers to functionalism's key institution) is not conducive to discussion of homosexual relationships. One wonders whether his evident concern to portray Kgatla in as "good" a light as possible in a society where homophobia was pervasive led him to neglect same-sex relationships. There is an isolated reference (Schapera 1966:185) to homosexual play between women.

In an earlier chapter we discussed the curious history of speculations about the alleged peculiarities of Khoi and San genitalia. As we noted, the elongation of the labia and steatopygia in the buttocks were seen as markers that placed these peoples at an infrahuman level on the Great Chain of Being. In his early monograph *The Khoisan Peoples of South Africa*, which was not based on intensive fieldwork but rather on secondary sources, Schapera had expressed the opinion that the apron was a physiological feature and not the product of manipulation (1930:59). He had noted that it was found not merely among the Khoi and San but also among "various East African peoples." However, in *Married Life in an African Tribe* Schapera recounted that Kgatla girls, at the onset of puberty, regularly manipulated the labia in order to lengthen them and, further, that the practice continued after marriage (1966:47). Kgatla informants told Schapera that elongated labia were seen as sexually attractive by both genders and were manipulated in sexual play. In fact, as one informant said, elongated labia were a sign of adult status (Schapera 1966:188). These statements provided an alternative view of a bodily characteristic that had been seen as an index of racial inferiority and natural depravity. In *Married Life in an African Tribe* the elongation of the labia was described as an innocuous cultural practice.

Ian Hogbin, who was taught by both Malinowski and Radcliffe-Brown, conducted fieldwork in many places, most notably in New Guinea (among the Wogeo and the Busama) and in the Solomon Islands (Guadalcanal and Malaita). In 1931 he published a description of the sexual practices of the people of Ontong Java, whom he saw as resembling Trobrianders and Samoans in some ways, though he describes a less permissive society than either Malinowski or Mead, at least with regard to premarital sex. Infantile sexuality was not restricted. While premarital sex for women was technically prohibited, it seems to have gone on discreetly; girls could be shamed for promiscuity or quickly married off if they were discovered. Ugly or disabled women became prostitutes, who were supposed to be the sole outlet for unmarried youth and, at that time, for white men, who could previously marry local women. Adult male masturbation was tolerated, female masturbation was said to be unknown. Some men snuck in to have intercourse with married women, pretending to be their husbands; they faced severe shaming if caught. The only cases Hogbin observed involved widowers in two cases and a known wife beater whom no one would marry in another. There were a couple of cases of known homosexuality. In one the man was regarded as rather comical, though many heterosexual men were said to have had sex with him. Another homosexual man had committed suicide. Homosexual men were said to use women's oils to attract men. Female homosexuality was said to be unknown. Oral sex was performed within marriage as foreplay or as an alternative to intercourse (Hogbin 1931:23–34). Physiological paternity was only partially understood: semen from many acts of intercourse was believed to form a plug to stop the menstrual flow. Women who had had intercourse only once were said not to be afraid of becoming pregnant (Hogbin 1931:32–33).

During World War II Hogbin was advisor on civilian morale to the prime minister of Australia (1942–43) and subsequently advisor to Governor Sir Philip Mitchell on the rehabilitation of Melanesian populations first in the Solomons and later in mainland New Guinea in the aftermath of the Japanese invasion and defeat. He was also an expert on land tenure and its applications in anthropology and government. Perhaps more than any of Malinowski's students, he fulfilled Malinowski's program for an applied anthropology of personal life. In a series of articles in *Oceania* in 1946 and 1947 Hogbin discussed sexual behavior, morality, and social change among the Wogeo and Busama of New Guinea. Just as Mead had done in Manu'a and Manus, Hogbin drew a contrast between sexual morality in two Pacific communities (1947b:282). Despite fears of female genital impurity the Wogeo were portrayed as sexually permissive, encouraging premarital sex, and laughing at bawdy jokes and at myths and tales with a strong sexual and scatological content (Hogbin 1946). The Busama, however, regarded any premarital or extramarital sex within their community as shameful. Some of Hogbin's informants made it clear that they experienced shame about adultery only when they were caught and that a fair amount of transgression did occur. Whereas the Wogeo encouraged individual choice in marriage (provided that the union was not incestuous or did not involve members of the same moiety residing in the same village), the Busama expected that all marriages would be arranged by older kin. In practice, the wishes of the boy or girl were sometimes taken into account. Nonetheless, "romantic attraction . . . receives no official recognition: indeed, the Busama bear out the truth of La Rochfoucauld's assertion that people would not fall in love if they had not read about it" (Hogbin 1947a:133).

The Wogeo male cult, like others on the nearby Sepik River and elsewhere in New Guinea, involved the use of a men's house, secret ritual flutes, and bloodletting. Specifically, Wogeo men made incisions on the penis in order to purify it from female contamination. They explicitly compared this procedure with menstruation, which they saw as the female's natural, periodic mode of purification. The title of Hogbin's book, *The Island of Menstruating Men*, was therefore ethnographically accurate. Significantly, Hogbin does not explicitly refer to the psychoanalyst Bruno Bettelheim's well-known theory (1952) that suggests the universal importance of male jealousy of female fertility, reversing Freud's ideas of penis envy. Hogbin does note that such cults and the ideology that supports them often accompany forms of ritual homosexuality, but he found no evidence of this among the Wogeo. He said that homosexuality in the Wogeo village was uncommon, apart from mutual masturbation by youths (Hogbin 1970:90). The Wogeo accepted the homosexual practice that was routine among labor migrants isolated from the opposite sex. They compared such sexual satisfactions to the experience of eating tinned meat away from home. They liked it well enough, but pork was preferable (Hogbin 1946:206).

Labor migration also resulted in homosexual contacts between Busama males and other migrants. The Busama regarded homosexual practices as deviant and were concerned about these developments. Hogbin discusses the case of Ki'dolo', a thief from a problem family who prostituted himself to army employees and was subsequently involved in two incidents in the village. He was said to have introduced homosexual practices to the village. Three other young men were also involved in similar incidents. In all four cases there was either a financial transaction or an element of force or a substantial age difference (Hogbin 1947a:128). The Busama, according to Hogbin, dismissed Ki'dolo' as beyond shame, though he also reports that they applied this diagnosis to Ki'dolo''s brother's heterosexual pandering and adultery.

The Busama thought that many contemporary youths were lacking in shame. The experience of other cultures that followed labor migration tempted them to break the rules of premarital chastity even at home. Although Hogbin did question whether the elders were idealizing a mythical golden age, he notes an increasing volume of bawdy discourse on masturbation in the community and a somewhat increased (though still low) incidence of seduction and illegitimacy. He blamed the prudery of the missionaries for developing an obsession with sex among the Busama.

Missionaries misunderstood Busama culture and therefore misrepresented it. Hogbin strongly disagreed with the views of an acquaintance, Stephen Lehner, a missionary who had been the head of a Lutheran teachers college in Bukawa, which was close to Busama. The two communities shared the same language and culture. Hogbin took particular exception to remarks made by Lehner that he quotes in his article on shame in Busama. Lehner wrote of sex as "the pivot" of Bukawa existence, of a lack of moral principles, of feminine resistance to males covering their genitals: "All the physical needs were satisfied in any place, and dances imitative of carnal lusts were extremely popular and anchored in phallic religious views" (Hogbin 1947b:281). In response, Hogbin remarked that morals were "relative":

> Thus in the Trobriands promiscuity before marriage is accepted as normal, whereas in Manus, the girls are expected to be chaste. . . . I would prefer to say that the native code is at some points different from ours. . . .
>
> It is relevant to mention here an incident which I witnessed some years ago in the Solomons. No clothing was worn in the community concerned, and when a young man whom I already knew returned after completing a period of indenture he immediately divested himself of his loincloth. He would have been ashamed, he said, to call attention to his genitals by covering them. (1947b:282)

Hogbin has some interesting things to say about the effects of Christian ideology on Melanesian communities. He suggests that Christian notions of sin may have provided an added sanction to reinforce Busama morality: God was believed by some to watch even acts successfully concealed from fellow villagers. On the other hand, the cessation of severe physical punishment for seducers, another result of Christian teaching, had probably had the opposite effect. Hogbin notes with some irony that Busama were quick to quote New Testament prohibitions on fornication to counter a remark that premarital sex was not banned in the Commandments but that when the same texts were brought to the attention of Trobrianders they shrugged them off with the remark, "That's only Paul."

Hogbin, like other anthropologists of this period, worried about missionary meddling and ethnocentrism. On the other hand, he diverged from the usual anthropological practice of his time when he wrote of Christianity as an integral part of 1940s Busama culture, with its own local meanings, rather than a mere accretion.

The role of missionaries was addressed, with a less nuanced disapproval, in some of the writings of Geoffrey Gorer, Verrier Elwin, and Ronald and Catherine Berndt, all of whom had much to say about other aspects of the anthropology of sexuality. Gorer was a travel writer who received some training in anthropology from Margaret Mead and Ruth Benedict in the late 1930s and was referred to as an anthropologist for the rest of his life. Elwin was an amateur anthropologist with a long and complicated career in India. His work on adolescent sexuality among the Muria is cited in many anthropology textbooks. The Berndts were professional anthropologists who did extensive fieldwork in many areas of Australia and New Guinea.

Gorer came to the attention of the anthropological community with *Africa Dances* (1935), a book that received some considerable favorable notice in the quality press, where it was considered a work of anthropology. Gorer was 30 years old when the book was published. He had received a degree in English from Cambridge and had no anthropological training at that time. He received a "crash course" in New York City in 1935–36 from Margaret Mead and Ruth Benedict, who had read and admired his book (Caffrey 1989:314). By the time he completed his first proper field study of the Lepcha of Sikkim (discussed below) he was certainly aware of some of the deficiencies of his earlier work, which was somewhat ethnocentric and filled with applications of half-digested evolutionary theory about fetishism and matriarchy.

The book begins with Gorer's meeting with Féral Benga, a Wolof dancer at the Folies Bergère in Paris and popular young man about town. Gorer and his new friend traveled for three months in Senegal and other parts of French West Africa as well as Ghana (then the British-ruled Gold Coast). The purpose of the trip was to see different forms of African dance and to recruit some dancers who would form Benga's ballet troupe. Gorer possessed an acid wit, a degree of misanthropy, a large measure of ethnocentrism, and proper moral indignation against French colonial administrators, traders, and missionaries. Lebanese traders are portrayed as swindlers who nonetheless make a real contribution to the Senegalese economy. There are quite unsympathetic portraits of two Jews whom Gorer met. According to Gorer, French administrators and their lackeys routinely humiliated and sometimes beat Africans, traders shortchanged them, and missionaries tried to deprive them of much that was valuable in their lives.

In *Africa Dances* Gorer sometimes but by no means always attempts to debunk some of the myths about African sexuality we discussed in chapter 5, especially those that concerned the dances he came to Africa to see. He acknowledged an erotic element in African dance but noted such an element in European dance as well (Gorer 1949:176). Indeed, Gorer's remarks on African sexuality err on the side of incorporating the rival stereotype of the "undersexed savage" to which we referred in chapter 4: "Dances which seem to us violently erotic are to the negro the equivalent of the Victorian sitting in the conservatory. Far from being oversexed they are by European and Asiatic standards frigid" (1949:176). In a review of *Africa Dances* in *Man* S. F. Nadel took Gorer to task for describing one dance performance as "a mixture of Breughel and Bedlam, semi erotic, semi ecstatic and quite cuckoo" (1936:125). Gorer acknowledged his own impression of African dance as sexual and chaotic but seems also to have been aware that his perceptions may have been conditioned by his own cultural background.

Gorer directs considerable venom at the results of missionary attempts to alter African sexual mores:

> The missionaries are changing all that. They have succeeded in making sex as overwhelmingly important and as filthy in the minds of their converts as it is in their own. With the obvious result that they either indulge their natural instincts and lie about it, or become neurotic and perverted. Anyone in the police department of the English colonies will tell you that the aggressors in the fairly numerous cases of rape, especially against small girls, are almost inevitably prominent churchgoers. In the Ivory Coast the missionaries put their young male converts to sleep in dormitories to avoid the occasion of sin, with surprisingly successful public-school results. They all turned pederasts (so one of the converts told me). (1949:176)[3]

Himalayan Village (1938) was Gorer's study of the Lepcha of Sikkim, then an independent state in the Himalayas but now part of India. Gorer did preparatory work among urban Lepcha, but his actual stay among the rural Lepcha was a mere three months. The ethnography, for all that, is quite detailed. Gorer has much to say about the Lepcha marriage system. Most significantly, he noted that a form of anticipatory levirate and sororate was prevalent. Both men and women, married and unmarried, had legitimate sexual access to partners they might someday inherit from senior relatives. There was in practice a great deal of sexual freedom despite a strict incest taboo and a belief that illegitimate pregnancy could cause hailstorms. Talk about sex, including bawdy jokes, was frequent in mixed company, although some restrictions applied when certain in-laws were present. Like Malinowski on the Trobrianders and Mead on Samoa (and numerous writers on other non-Western societies) Gorer insisted that passionate love was rare among the Lepcha and, where it occurred, was singularly disruptive (1967:169). In general, the Lepcha downplayed differences between individuals. It is this lack of stress on individual affect, including jealousy, which, in Gorer's opinion, made it possible for the Lepcha to have access to numerous sexual partners without arousing an aggression that their society explicitly condemns.

Some Lepcha sexual usages described by Gorer may serve to remind readers that what counts as "aggression" is itself a culturally defined matter. The Lepcha believed that, in the absence of supernatural intervention, girls would not begin menstruating until copulation had taken place. Accordingly, Gorer informs us, there is "no stigma attached to grown men forcing little girls of nine or ten," though he reports that this occurs only "occasionally" (1967:315). Gorer also mentions that it sometimes happens that either the male or female partner to an arranged marriage may refuse the other sexual access; in such cases the reluctant partner "may be thrashed by his or her uncle to make him like his partner" (1967:317–318). Gorer notes, in this regard, that such thrashings contradict Lepcha notions of proper deportment and are, accordingly, more likely to be threatened than administered (1967:318).

In a foreword to the second edition of *Himalayan Village* Gorer linked the whole emotional complex to the late introduction of weaning and toilet training in an argument likely to appeal mainly to those who came to it already convinced of the validity of some version of Freud's psychosexual stages. Because toilet training occurred in the early genital stage of development (in Freud's chronology), the Lepcha, Gorer argued, did not learn to associate renunciation and loss or, conversely, the overvaluing of sexual objects with desire (1967:8, 9). Gorer's neo-Freudian gloss on Lepcha affect was clearly influenced by his long association with Mead, Benedict, and a number of psychoanalytically oriented anthropologists. He explicitly relied on George Devereux, who (as we shall see) had developed similar ideas regarding Mohave sexuality.

The Lepcha regarded sodomy as very antisocial. Breach of the taboo on sodomy was thought to result in a yearlong disaster for the village. However, the Lepcha encouraged special friendships between pairs of young men who worked and hunted together. These relationships were close but did not involve physical intimacy. In fact, Gorer cites this institution as evidence for the divorce between love and sex in Lepcha culture (1967:120). Homosexuality, he said, was a "meaningless concept" for the Lepcha (Gorer 1967:120).

Verrier Elwin is most remembered today as the author of *The Muria and Their Ghotul* (1947). He is the subject of a recent biography by Ramachandra Guha (1999). Elwin's own sexual career and his shifts of political and religious allegiance are the subtext of much of his writing and were overtly discussed or covertly suggested by critics, some of whom doubted for these reasons the veracity of his ethnographic writing.

Elwin's father, who died when he was eight, was bishop of Sierra Leone. His mother raised him to follow a somewhat joyless, Low Church Anglican Evangelical tradition. At Oxford Elwin came under the influence of a don who believed in ministering to the poor in the slums. He obtained a degree in English literature and then proceeded to take a degree in theology. Elwin then became principal of Wycliffe Hall, a theological college. However, he surrendered this position in the late 1920s in order to join the Christa Seva Sangh, an Anglican community in Poona that was modeled on Hindu ashrams and sought to mediate the cultural contradiction between Hinduism and Anglican Christianity. Elwin developed an admiration for Mahatma Gandhi and the Congress cause. He visited Gandhi on a number of occasions, protested against repressive British policies in India, and supported the Congress's goal of *swaraj* (independence). He converted other members of the ashram to his viewpoint. The British administration and his superiors in the church regarded him as a thorn in their flesh. Having left Christa Seva Sangh, Elwin and his ashram friend Shamrao Hivale set up a new ashram among the tribal peoples of the central provinces. In the ensuing five years Elwin became more and more identified with the tribal peoples and ever more opposed to those he perceived to be neglectful of their interests. He left the church in 1935 and also became increasingly disenchanted with Hindu supporters of caste and tribal assimilation. He also became critical of Gandhi's stipulations on chastity, vegetarianism, and celibacy. He no longer sought to convert the tribals to celibacy and temperance; rather, they taught him an appreciation of sex, liquor, and the hunt. He was appalled by colonial and, subsequently, postcolonial interference with the life of the tribals.

Elwin's self-identification and self-education as an anthropologist occurred in the late 1930s. By the 1940s he had made some sort of peace with the administration and occupied honorary positions as government ethnographer in parts of Central and East India (Central Provinces, Orissa), but his primary influence stemmed from his power as a speaker and writer.

Unlike many other British residents, Elwin did not leave India after independence. He took Indian citizenship in 1954, just before taking up a position as tribal advisor to the Northeast Frontier Agency. As a senior civil servant and a personal friend of Nehru, he influenced the peaceful development of the agency, which is now Arunachal Pradesh. He was no longer (if he ever had been) an advocate of total noninterference. He successfully advocated a philosophy of gradual change. Tribal land rights were to be respected at all costs (Guha 1999:234–277).

In his posthumously published autobiography, *The Tribal World of Verrier Elwin,* Elwin notes some contrasts between his own history and that of the tribal people with regard to sexuality, an aspect of his work that is as often remembered as his efforts to defend the rights of India's autochthonous populations: "Until I was twenty-one I knew nothing about women and certainly never would have anticipated that one day I would be mentioned half-a-dozen times as an authority on the sexual behaviour of the human female in the Kinsey Report. Tribal children know all about a woman's anatomy, the rules of menstruation and – whatever Malinowski may have said – how babies come, before they are five years old. I knew nothing when I was four times that age" (1964:16).

In the early 1930s, as a follower of Gandhi's teachings on celibacy, Elwin twice rejected opportunities for marriage. Shortly thereafter, he changed his views on celibacy. By 1935 Elwin and his friend Hivale both had female friends among the tribals. In 1940 Elwin married a Gond woman named Kosi. She was beautiful, sexually experienced, and relatively uneducated. She traveled with Elwin and aided him in his Muria fieldwork. However, they were unfaithful to one another and were divorced in 1949 after she left him. Subsequently, Elwin married a Pardhan woman named Lila. This marriage was successful. Elwin's marriages caused some controversy. Guha quotes a remark made by a Delhi sociology professor around 1990: "Elwin – you mean the anthropologist who married his fieldwork" (1999:124). Elwin's alma mater, Merton College, funded his wartime research. The principal of Merton at that time was supportive of Elwin and claimed that he had married Kosi "in the interests of science"! However, the warden's successor, appalled by the thought of entertaining Kosi at high table, suggested that Elwin should look elsewhere for funding or return to England (Guha 1999:135).

Elwin's first ethnography, *The Baiga* (1939), contained a protracted account of a relatively uninhibited sexuality. The Baiga did not, like the Muria and most other Indian peoples, have arranged marriages. Individual preference (which often shifted) played a major role in their sexual choices. Elwin suggested that the only rest they took from sexual activity was provided by the menstrual taboo. In a rare departure from his normal primitivism he remarked that the menstrual taboo was the "one thing that saves the tribe from complete sexual degradation" (Elwin 1939:215). Elwin argued that the Baiga possessed a form of romantic love that he labeled "phallic consciousness," following D. H. Lawrence (1939:253).

The information on Baiga sexuality was placed in two chapters. The first consisted of sixteen life histories (chapter 4). Most of Elwin's argument on Baiga sexuality was placed in chapter 8, in the middle rather than at the front or end of the book, and there was some censoring of the content. John Murray, Elwin's publisher, apparently requested such changes because the contents of the book were likely to offend female and lay readers (Guha 1999:112–113). A reviewer of the book in a missionary journal accused Elwin of an unethical breach of the Baiga's privacy. He remarked that it was customary then to cover chimpanzees' cages when they engaged in intimate acts, whereas Elwin's Baiga confidantes were accorded less respect than chimpanzees (Guha 1999:117).

Elwin's work on the Muria has been much more widely read by anthropologists and others than his work on the Baiga. His vision of the Muria as having formed a sexual utopia may have been conditioned by the unusual repression from which he was quite suddenly liberated – by them and other tribals. The criticisms of his work are in part directed to his failure as a fieldworker to stay put in one place and his neglect as an anthropological autodidact adequately to consider theory. There is a consequent absence of structure in prolonged ethnographic narratives in which factual narrations of minutiae alternate with lyrical ethnography, poetry, folklore, and life history.

However, the strongest reasons for skepticism are his fervid portrayals of adolescent sexual freedom, which do not always accord with others' ethnographic experience (see Gell 1992). "The Muria," he wrote in 1947, have

> a simple, innocent and natural attitude to sex. In the ghotul this is strengthened by the absence of any sense of guilt and the general freedom from external interference. The Muria believe that sexual congress is a good thing; it does you good; it is healthy and beautiful . . . it is the happiest and best thing in life.
>
> This belief in sex as something good and normal gives the Muria a light touch. Nari's saying that the penis and vagina are . . . in a "joking relationship" to each other, admirably puts the situation. Sex is great fun; it is the best of ghotul games; it is the dance of the genitals; it is an ecstatic swinging in the arms of the beloved. It ought not to be too intense; it must not be degraded by possessiveness or defiled by jealousy. It is believed that the best and most successful sex relations are to be had in the modern ghotul where partners often change. (Elwin 1991:419)

The assertions of the naturalness of Muria sexuality as well as the emphasis on lack of intensity, possessiveness, and jealousy are among the tropes we have noted in some other accounts of premarital sexual freedom, but the lyricism of Elwin's description goes beyond anything in, say, Malinowski and Mead, who were themselves sometimes criticized for their flowery language.

The *ghotul* is a dormitory where young people among the Muria spend each night from puberty until shortly before the time they marry. The ghotul is a religious as well as a social institution: according to Muria myth it was founded by Lingo Pen, the local culture hero, and ghotul members dance on ritual occasions, especially marriages. In the ghotul members are initiated into sexuality and live according to the rules laid down by members who hold traditional titles of authority. Depending on the regimes of particular houses, Elwin tells us, members may be obliged to change sexual partners every few days or may have one particular partner over a long period. In the latter case it is, at least formally, the girl who makes the choice. When ghotul members travel to other communities to perform and visit they may have sexual encounters with members of other ghotuls, apart from any partners they may have in their home ghotul. Muria marriages are arranged by parents, and members of the same ghotul are not supposed to marry each other. Sometimes ghotul partners do manage to convince their elders to let them marry, though often this is absolutely precluded by exogamy rules. Women, once they marry, must never enter the ghotul again. Elwin says that women sometimes long for their ghotul partners, though most marriages are happy. Men are allowed to visit the ghotul after they marry, and some do, though they may be resented if they do so too much or for too long.

All in all, Elwin sees the ghotul as an admirable institution where young people receive not only valuable sexual experience but also training in leadership and social cooperation. There are strong echoes of Mead's Samoa and Malinowski's Kiriwina in Elwin's portrayal of adolescent sexuality among the Muria, though his account is a description of a full-blown institution, with its own rules and structure, rather than a simple report of permissiveness. These parallels are noted by Maria Lepowsky in a 1998 article on adolescence on Vanatinai, an island in the Massim region. She suggests that institutions like the ghotul and the Trobriand *bukumatula* (bachelor hut) may, as Elwin had suggested, be fairly common in the Asian and Pacific region (Lepowsky 1998:145). Lepowsky argues that such institutions are found in areas of relative gender equality, especially where there are no religious encodings of male superiority. In such societies, she suggests, allowing adolescents a private place to explore their sexuality is more significant than maintaining female chastity before marriage.

Pregnancy before marriage is frowned upon and occurs in only about 4

3. Chelik of Toinar with his *ghotul* wife. From *The Muria and Their Ghotul* (1947) by Verrier Elwin.

percent of cases. The Muria believe that pregnancy is less likely to occur where ghotul partners do not become too attached to each other, and in some ghotuls frequency of actual intercourse (as opposed to nongenital sexual contact) is restricted by the rules (e.g., there may be a rule that girls only stay in the ghotuls on Friday nights). Elwin's data suggest that ghotul partners have sex less frequently than married couples, among whom the fertility rate is high, though he cites Ashley Montagu concerning a likely period of adolescent sterility. The Muria have a belief that pregnancy only occurs after repeated intercourse between a couple who are attached to one another; Gell, in her more recent study, suggests that sexual intercourse rarely occurs between ghotul partners who are not closely attached (1992:219). Where pregnancy in the ghotul does occur, the couple as well as the ghotul officials are reprimanded about their irresponsibility, and, in most cases, the girl's arranged marriage to someone outside the ghotul is rushed forward. In a minority of cases, if there is no incest barrier, a pregnant girl and her ghotul partner will elope and succeed in altering their parents' marriage arrangements.

Elwin's assertions about the "happiness" of Muria marriages were based on statistics that showed that only 59 out of 1,941 marriages ended in divorce (1991:200), a rate of 3 percent. The divorce rate, however, was above 10 percent among those who married their ghotul wives. Though his political agenda was very different from the one outlined by Haraway (1991), Elwin was most concerned to show that the Muria social system was particularly coherent. Divorce rates, however, tell us only so much, inasmuch as "stability" and "happiness" are subjective and culture-bound qualities. *The Muria*, a 1982 BBC film on the Muria ghotul, clearly demonstrates that many Muria women are unhappy at their families' choice of partner and make attempts to run away or elope with their ghotul "husbands." The men may be unhappy too, but the culture offers them more compensations. In the film an older Muria woman advises a prospective bride that Muria women usually have to defer to the wishes of the males who negotiate contracts. Although Elwin mentioned several cases of flight and attempted elopement, he did not speak of a fundamental gender inequality. Gell (1992) stresses that most arranged marriages do settle down after an initial period of stress. In fact, this initial period, in her opinion, has elements of ritualized courtship – wives repeatedly run away, the husbands run after them and bring them back. In later life the husband loses influence to the son, whereas the wife gains influence through her children. This is a new source of stress.

Elwin asserts that homosexuality is virtually unknown among the Muria apart from sexual play between adolescents (1991:446, 447, 656). Even in jails natives evince no interest in same-sex relations (Elwin 1991:447). This assertion carries some ideological baggage. On the one hand, Elwin wished to counter the claims of racists such as Franz Muller-Lyer and evolutionists such as Robert Briffault who had claimed that more "vices" were to be found among primitives than in "Babylon and London" (1991:446). On the other hand, Elwin argued for heterosexual permissiveness by acquiescing in the prevailing homophobia. Moreover, his language was more extreme than that found in the works of other anthropologists like Malinowski and Mead who suggested correlations between adolescent freedom, stable marriage, and an absence of adult homosexuality: "Sexual deviations are almost unknown. Bestiality is regarded as a crime of civilization, unworthy of a Muria. The devious course of modern European sexuality would seem horrible to so straightforwardly heterosexual a tribe. Homosexuality, which Stekel has called 'the insoluble problem of modern civilized man' is no problem to the uncivilized Muria. 'Jealousy and homosexuality are the two primary causes of the disorder of our passions,' says this same scientific observer of the European scene. Will not even the reformer admit the advantage of a tribe which is so largely free from these two evils?" (Elwin 1991:656). This passage, no less than Elwin's lyrical invocations of the pleasures of the ghotul, is a clear instance of what Firth called "emotional philanthropy." In his praise of Muria heterosexual practices as well as in his assertion that heterosexual outlets protect young people from perversion Elwin was conscripting the Muria into personal, intellectual, and political conversations that may have had little to do with their own concerns.

Within the anthropological profession the names of Ronald and Catherine Berndt were largely associated with studies of sexuality. The married couple who lived until the 1990s conducted extensive ethnographic work on many aspects of native culture in both Australia and New Guinea, including work in folklore and political anthropology. When we began this study a former colleague suggested that if we were not careful, we'd become known as "the new Ronald and Catherine Berndt." There was a somewhat disparaging undertone to the remark.

Ironically, it was a reading of Ronald Berndt's *Djanggawul* (1952), assigned for an undergraduate course in folklore, that attracted Harriet Lyons to anthropology. For all that, *Sexual Behavior in Western Arnhem Land* (1951), which was originally a Viking Fund publication, is a rather disturbing book, because a superficial perusal would easily confirm many 19th-century stereotypes of Australian Aboriginal sexual behavior. This is more than a little ironic, given the authorial declaration of intent with which the monograph concludes: "By appreciating the natives' point of view, we are materially contributing to inter-racial understanding, and assisting gradually to break down the barriers of intolerance and illogical thought and accumulated misapprehensions which retard human welfare and the peaceful assimilation of peoples" (Berndt and Berndt 1968:243).

Members of more than a dozen linguistic groups resided near the Oenpelli and Goulbourn Island missions in Arnhem Land. Ronald Berndt relied heavily on information from about three dozen male informants. Catherine Berndt worked with the women, but we are not told how many informants she had (Berndt and Berndt 1968:187 n. 8). Marriage in the region followed the rules of a social organization based on moieties and subsections. The Berndts report "some understanding" of the physiological aspects of conception, though fathers were thought to "bring" spirit children into the camp (Berndt and Berndt 1968:81).[4] Polygyny was common, and cousin marriage was the norm (Berndt and Berndt 1968:75). The Berndts report substantial opportunities, sanctioned and unsanctioned, for premarital and extramarital sexual relations. In particular, they describe the 'ma:mam relationship, a variety of secondary marriage similar to the pirauru relationship that Howitt had described, for a different part of Australia, in the previous century, though they do not label it a form of group marriage.

The Berndts stressed that sexual behavior was a constant topic of conversation and of so-called gossip songs. The Dreamtime myths and related ritual performances enshrined fertility (Berndt and Berndt 1968:109–138). Following a classic functionalist agenda, the Berndts sought to place sexual behavior in a social and ritual context and to explicate its mythological charter. It was normal for a female age 9 or 10 and a male of 12 to be initiated into sex by a more mature adolescent or adult. The Berndts' description of children's sexual desires seems to cry out for some more specific documentation, since it discusses not just observable behavior but highly contentious interior states, including "indiscriminate coitus with any stranger, relative, etc., such as promiscuous little girls are apt to indulge in, particularly just after their first and second menstruation when they are anxious to try all the men they can. On marriage, this tendency (in all but the more promiscuous) is diverted to more or less legal extra-marital mates" (Berndt and Berndt 1968:93 n. 43). Premarital sex was expected, though the authors acquiesce in some of their informants' opinions that this was largely due to missionary bans on infant betrothal and early marriage. Abductions of married women often occurred, sometimes with the consent of the abducted woman. Jealousy often led to fighting, particularly after abductions (Berndt and Berndt 1968:180). Several of the Berndts' narratives involve episodes of alcohol abuse preceding sexual misconduct.

The authors were concerned to dismiss reports of abuse of Aboriginal women by their menfolk as ethnocentric. However, their justifications for some of the conduct they report employ another sort of stereotype we have encountered, for example, in the work of Ellis, an assertion that women derive pleasure from such treatment (Berndt and Berndt 1968:53). Women were also portrayed as acquiescing in physical punishment if their behavior warranted it (Berndt and Berndt 1968:53), another functionalist convention.

Apart from youthful masturbation, the Berndts report an absence of homosexuality in western Arnhem Land. These observations resemble the remarks of Elwin and Malinowski on the effects of heterosexual freedom on homosexual desire, albeit with a caution expressed in somewhat revealing diction: "Perhaps the comparatively free association between the sexes has almost eradicated any of these tendencies; but on the other hand, cultures of somewhat similar structure have institutionalized sexual perversion, that is, sodomy and homosexual practices within one sex group" (Berndt and Berndt 1968:67). Bestiality was said to occur in the Liverpool region of Arnhem Land. The authors reported that in the absence of their husbands women would often masturbate a male dog and place the penis in the vagina until the dog ejaculated (Berndt and Berndt 1968:68). They give no source for this information but vaguely defined common opinion. One wonders about the inclusion of such data in an account that seeks "to break down the barriers of intolerance" surrounding a people whose sexuality had already been inscribed in more than the usual number of stigmatizing fantasies. The Berndts reported other data on female sexuality that evoked the very image of the oversexed savage they sought to discredit: "It is said that some women are satisfied only after a number of ejaculations – one insertion being 'too quick' for them to enjoy completely. This probably explains why some native women desire the attentions of more than one man during a night, or have extra-marital coitus during the day or evening when their husbands are busy and later enjoy the sexual act with their own spouse" (1968:57).

In fairness, it should be noted that the Berndts did attempt to protect their informants from negative impressions that might result from the publication of data on Arnhem sexual culture. Ronald Berndt withdrew the original manuscript of *Love Songs of Arnhem Land*, which had been accepted for publication in 1950, partly because he was "not sure that its frankness and its erotic content would be appreciated by non-Aboriginal readers"

(1978:xi). In the version of *Love Songs of Arnhem Land* that was eventually published in 1976 Ronald Berndt took pains to demonstrate that attitudes toward sexuality varied within the region; such variation would make a racial explanation far less credible. He contrasted the direct approach to sexuality of western Arnhem Land with a more sublimated discourse in eastern Arnhem Land, where sexual matters were more highly symbolized and romanticized (Berndt 1978:xviii–xv). He also noted that in both regions whatever license existed did so within a context of rules of behavior and demands for modesty and propriety (Berndt 1978:5–12), an argument also advanced in the earlier version. *Love Songs of Arnhem Land* is largely given over to texts in which sexual matters are imbued with religious meanings. In that work as well as in *Djanggawul*, a collection of stories of creation, more emphasis is placed upon the positive value Aboriginal culture placed upon sex as a manifestation of generalized fertilizing power.

In *Sexual Behavior in Western Arnhem Land* there is often a puzzling segueing of authorial narrative, indigenous reportage, and myth and folk-tale. Sometimes there is a blurring of the ethnographic present, the imputed past, and the frankly mythological. This idiosyncratic chronicity makes it difficult for the reader adequately to resolve issues of factuality.[5] It is not clear, moreover, whether the Berndts were describing traditional morality or contemporary anomie, since they made contradictory statements about the degree of missionary influence on their informants' sexual practices. For example, they say that the traditional moral code had not been interfered with to any great degree (Berndt and Berndt 1968:42) but, as we have noted, attributed premarital promiscuity to bans on early marriage.[6] Moreover, they noted a degree of depopulation and an 80 percent incidence of venereal disease, mainly gonorrhea (Berndt and Berndt 1968:44).

Although the Berndts conceded that there were some good missionaries, particularly those who had anthropological training, they were highly critical of the missionary enterprise. They accused male missionaries of masking their own attraction to the breasts and buttocks of native women with an overt concern for women's rights. They charged female missionaries with a desire created out of their own frustrated fantasies disguised as a wish to protect their "dark sisters" from older Aboriginal men (Berndt and Berndt 1968:56). The Berndts do record at least one instance of missionary influence upon a sexual encounter. Without authorial comment, they note that a woman made persistent sexual approaches to one of their informants, all the while singing "Walking with Jesus" (Berndt and Berndt 1968:185).

The Berndts wrote candidly about sexuality at a time when very few anthropologists in the British tradition were willing to do so. Their stated goal was to counter prejudice and harmful interference with native custom by studying sex in its proper context. Unfortunately, the anecdotal, loosely documented format of *Sexual Behavior in Western Arnhem Land* seems to sensationalize as much as it desensationalizes and at times appears to give an impression opposite from that which its authors intended. Of course, it would be a legitimate, if still controversial, argument to state that questions of morality and "normality" were simply irrelevant to the study of sexual matters. The Berndts do not make this argument, though, at least so far as morality was concerned, it may have been their private opinion. It is highly unlikely in any case that such an argument would have carried much weight with readers in 1951, even with the professional anthropologists who would have formed most of the audience for a Viking Fund monograph.

Another possible approach to Arnhem sexuality at the time of the Berndts' fieldwork would have been a consistent statement of cultural disintegration. They do not follow this route either, though they were certainly highly critical of the colonial enterprise and its effects. In a world still pervaded by negative attitudes both to sexuality and to native peoples, challenges to collective representations concerning "primitive" sexuality carry an almost unavoidable danger of reinforcing them where local sexual cultures allow practices officially forbidden by Judeo-Christian norms. The dangers we perceive in *Sexual Behavior in Western Arnhem Land* are dangers created not by the Berndts but by the attitudes of potential readers of their work.

SEXUALITY, CULTURE, AND PERSONALITY

Most of the authors we have discussed so far wrote mainly about heterosexuality among ethnographic subjects in various locales that were at some time within the British Empire or Commonwealth.[7] The anthropologist, psychoanalyst, and ethnopsychiatrist George Devereux was rare, if not unique, in publishing, during the 1930s, 1940s, and 1950s, a great deal of specific information about sexual practices other than vaginal heterosexual intercourse based upon data gathered during several visits to the Mohave people of California and Arizona during the 1930s. He discussed Mohave masturbation, homosexuality, alleged anal fixations, adultery, prostitution, and gang rape. Later in his life, at a time when abortion was illegal in virtually all Western countries, Devereux (1955) published a lengthy study of abortion in 400 preindustrial societies.[8]

Devereux came from the borderlands of Hungary and Rumania. He came to Paris in 1926, started but did not complete medical school, studied ethnology with Marcel Mauss and Paul Rivet, and came to the United States in order to study the Mohave. About this time he changed his surname from Dobo to Devereux. Under Alfred Kroeber's direction he received a doctorate from Berkeley in 1935 for a dissertation on Mohave sexuality. Devereux was not initially sympathetic to Freud, but his views gradually changed. His earliest publication on the Mohave, which concerned homosexuality (1937), coincides with the beginning of his Freudian move. In the late 1940s Devereux worked with Karl Menninger at Topeka as a therapist with World War II veterans. Because he had not completed medical training and received a negative recommendation from his first training analyst, Marc Schlumberger, Devereux's recognition as a psychoanalyst was delayed, but he was eventually admitted to the Philadelphia Psychoanalytic Institute (Fermi 1998). His works were and continue to be well regarded among both French and American scholars interested in psychoanalytic anthropology. He is regarded by many as the founder of ethnopsychiatry. His approach to much of his data on Mohave sexuality, however, was contentious from several perspectives. There was a considerable contradiction between the ethnographer's obvious fascination with his Mohave friends' pleasures, desires, and entertainments and the diagnostician's compulsion to chart and explain alleged deviations from the Freudian ideal.

Devereux, like many in the American culture and personality movement, was aware that the Freudian timetable of oral, anal, and genital sexuality was not invariant but was, rather, influenced by local practices of weaning and toilet training. Moreover, the Mohave accepted many adult sexual practices that did not conform to Freud's notion of mature genital sexuality. The picture that Devereux paints of Mohave sexual attitudes is one of humorous acceptance of many avenues of sexual expression. He does note disapproval of behaviors such as incest, excessive masturbation, and the deliberate provoking of jealousy that were likely to disrupt the social fabric.

In a series of articles on various aspects of Mohave sexuality Devereux explored the results of the bodily regimes associated with early childhood among the Mohave. There is a great deal of redundancy in this corpus. Where repetition occurred, we have selected the statements that seem to us to reflect most clearly consistent strands in Devereux's views of sexuality rather than following strict chronological order.

In Western society, Devereux argued in a 1951 article, "early, strenuous and severely moralistic sphincter training" led to "fixation on the phase of anal mastery with traits of compulsiveness" (1951:406). The Mohave showed no evidence of this, as would be expected in a society where toilet training was so lenient, but they did show, in Devereux's opinion, considerable evidence of "anal-expulsive" tendencies, proof that the Freudian complexes cannot be entirely avoided. Devereux attributes this not to "phylogenetic" uniformity but to the ability of small children to detect even low levels of discomfort with excretory matters on the part of adults (1951:406).

In this article and elsewhere Devereux described instances of anal penetration recounted to him by Mohave informants as well as considerable verbal and practical joking and nickname formation, all centered upon this theme. Sometimes these genres coincided. One man whose nickname, Amayk itcerktce, was translated as "Defecated Upon," got the name from a mishap that occurred after anal intercourse with a virgin "too young for vaginal intercourse," a common practice among the Mohave, according to Devereux, "because the rectum of a girl ten to fourteen years of age is larger than her vagina" (1951:409, 411). In the episode that led to Amayk itcerktce's nickname he had to withdraw suddenly when he was discovered by the girl's grandparents, causing her to defecate on his penis (Devereux 1951:409–410). The man in question was said to be "rather proud of it because it refers to the kind of scurrilous sexual exploit in which the Mohave take a great deal of pride" (Devereux 1951:410).

Devereux attributed to the Mohave a variety of "anal–penis fantasies" and "anal–child fantasies" as well as tendencies toward "analization of the vagina" and "vaginalization of the anus" (1951:410–414). Anal–penis fantasies were said to be present in mythical material, insults, and an account of people spying on a defecating man, known for the size of his penis, and pretending to confuse his descending feces with a penis about to drop off (Devereux 1951:410). Anal–child fantasies were reported to manifest themselves in a practice associated with institutionalized transvestism. An *alyha*, as a male transvestite was called, sometimes induced severe constipation by drinking an infusion of mesquite beans, giving "birth" eventually to a huge stool that he called a "stillborn child" (Devereux 1951:411). Analization of the vagina was the interpretation Devereux put on stories of vaginal noises resembling flatulence, a "well-known" tendency of women to "relax all sphincters" after intercourse and a tendency of both boys and girls to use mud, "a very common fecal symbol," as a masturbatory tool (1951:411–412).

Vaginalization of the anus was Devereux's diagnosis of the reported Mohave proclivity to anal intercourse, both homosexual and heterosexual. One drunken husband was said not to object when his inebriated wife had vaginal intercourse with his drunken companion but threatened violence when his friend attempted anal intercourse, claiming exclusive ownership of his wife's anus, which, Devereux said, represented a "supervagina" (1951:412–413). Moreover, Devereux jumped from this narrative to a claim that an association between "regressive," "cloacal," and "homosexual" conceptions of the vagina and episodes of inebriation "supports the interpretation that cannibalistic fantasies and intense preoccupations with the body content of women play a significant role in the psychology of Mohave alcoholism" (1951:413). This assertion contains two arguments highly likely to disturb a contemporary reader concerned with either gay or Native issues: Devereux's assumption that "homosexual" ideation is regressive and his claim that Mohave alcoholism, which most students of Native affairs would see as the product of colonization and culture loss, had a significant basis in sexual fantasy.

Of Mohave sexual culture in general, Devereux said that sexual activity was "felt to be an enjoyable and humorous sport" (1969:xii). Overall, he said that "sexual activity was limited solely by the incest taboo, which only witches were prone to violate. The only conspicuously absent sexual practices were cunnilingus, fetishism, and sado-masochism" (Devereux 1969:xii).

Devereux acknowledged a supernatural aspect to "even the most casual coitus," since souls as well as bodies were believed to cohabit, and noted some "not overly meticulous" taboos on puberty, menstruation, pregnancy, childbirth, and lactation (1969:xi–xii). In *Mohave Ethnopsychiatry* (1961), in particular, Devereux supplied considerable information about collective representations concerning connections between sexuality and spirituality, but such data were presented as clues to the Mohave unconscious, including pathologies said to reside there, rather than as part of a cosmology interesting in its own right.

Devereux's descriptions (1950, 1937) of Mohave heterosexuality featured frequent partner changes, including alternating periods of cohabitation with alyhas and *hwame*'s (institutionalized female transvestites) and ordinary opposite-sex partners. No premium was placed on virginity (Devereux 1950:111). "Mohave promiscuousness," Devereux said, "was only slightly curbed by the institution of marriage" (1950:85). The latency period was described by Devereux as "conspicuous by its absence" (1950:xiii). "Many children," Devereux reported, "cohabited with adults long before puberty" (1950:xiii). This particular statement is an example of a tendency we have already noted to report, as normative behavior, features of Mohave life that might well have been regarded by them as social problems resulting from poverty and related impediments. Indeed, Devereux's informants told him that current conditions might have been responsible for the young age at which sexual experience (and venereal disease) began and expressed some concern about it: "In aboriginal times people had their first sexual experiences at a much later date. That is why our young people do not remain potent until they die" (1950:113).

The exploitative relationship between white men and Native Americans and the social dislocation that was its consequence are disturbingly evident, though not commented upon by Devereux, in his report of narratives about a "practical joke" carried out under the influence of alcohol and the victims' revenge. A white man was said to have taken 15 shinney-players and "two women who were to be the team's concubines" to Los Angeles, where he housed them in a Pullman car parked on a railway siding. When the white man went off, the Mohave brought a case of hard liquor, which "someone" had given them, into the Pullman car. When everyone was thoroughly drunk and the women had passed out, the men took turns having sex with them. Afterward, they threw mud at the women's genitals and set fire to their pubic hair. This story was told to Devereux by one of his main informants, who claimed to have taken part in the sex but not the subsequent activities. The women, for their part, told him of their revenge some time after returning to Needles, California. They claimed to have come upon two of the guilty men, passed out near the ice plant, and to have seized the opportunity to tie back their foreskins and paint the men's penises red, black, and yellow, leaving the results for passers-by to admire (Devereux 1950:118–119). Devereux says that "Americans" would be angrier at the sexual assault than the mud slinging and burning but that his Mohave informant thought that only the practical joke violated Mohave custom (1950:118–119). That the whole incident could be seen as a result of "American" interference with such custom is very far in the background of Devereux's account, if it can be said to be there at all.

Many of the stories that comprise so much of Devereux's data on sexuality were told to him by informants who were obviously amused by the stories' salacious content. The story above is one such example, as was the story of how Defecated Upon got his nickname. Motifs such as fecal smearing and burned genitals are frequent in North American Trickster tales. Interestingly, in a 1948 article on Mohave Coyote tales, Devereux suggested that real events or individual dreams might have been absorbed into narratives told to him as folktales by his informants, but he did not consider the possibility of a reverse process of attribution (Devereux 1948:237). Although Devereux recognized that a "case history" approach was likely to "record primarily unusual incidents" (1950:126), we must also address the issue of what sorts of narratives Devereux's informants believed they were telling. For psychoanalysts, narratives, including myths and fictions, are at least as valuable as behavior in revealing the workings of the unconscious. Those interested in comparative sexuality, however, are likely to want to know what sort of "truth" they are dealing with.

Devereux's account of Mohave heterosexuality, for all its explicit detail, ends with a reprise of the trope of the sexually unimaginative (though non-neurotic) savage, surprising but not inconsistent with the Freudian paradigm. "The routine sexual life of the average Mohave Indian," Devereux concludes, "while considerably less inhibited than that of Western man, is probably a rather simple one, precisely because it carries a smaller load of anxiety, and is therefore less likely to become a stage for the testing, or acting out, of various neurotic fantasies" (1950:126).

Devereux's (1937) account of the Mohave berdache was probably the most extensive exploration of this common North American institution at the time it appeared and for some decades thereafter, although it has been subject to scathing criticism recently (e.g., Roscoe 1998:92–97, 137–165). The appropriate term for institutions of this kind is itself the topic of a debate that will be discussed in the next chapter. Devereux's work, of course, preceded the partial replacement of "berdache" with "two spirit." Devereux, in any case, tended to refer to Mohave alyhas and hwame's simply as "homosexuals," thereby begging several essential questions.

According to Roscoe, it was Alfred Kroeber who was responsible for the standardized usage of the term *berdache*, although it had been used on a couple of occasions in earlier anthropological literature (1998:8). Kroeber also heard the myth connected with the origin of the Mohave alyha, the male berdache, from the shaman Nyadarup (Roscoe 1998:137). The Mohave are unusual in that they held initiation ceremonies for both alyhas and perhaps for their biologically female counterparts, hwame's (Roscoe 1998:139–140). According to Devereux, individual election was involved in entry into the alyha or hwame' role. Boys who behaved like girls and girls who behaved like boys were obvious candidates. Dreams were also strong indicators, and, to some extent, the roles were said to be predestined. Initiation acted as a ritual test to confirm that the role had been properly selected. Devereux notes that alyhas and hwame's often possessed shamanic powers and were believed to be especially lucky in love and gambling (1937:503). The hwame's were thought to be particularly adept at the curing of venereal disease.

For all his awareness of the religious implications of the berdache institution among the Mohave, Devereux concentrates more on their sexual status. Despite noting that such a status is a recognized and accepted one among the Mohave, Devereux still sees many elements of deviance in their position. Among the Mohave, as among the Cheyenne, those who were unfit for warfare were often said to become berdaches. Devereux etymologically relates the word "alyha" to the Mohave word for "coward" (1937:517), though Roscoe cites evidence that this was not correct (1998:268).

Central to Devereux's account of Mohave homosexuality are narratives about the alyha wives of a man named Kuwal and the ultimately tragic career of the hwame' Sahaykwisa. Although Kuwal's alyha wives seem to have been treated with some respect, Kuwal himself was the butt of some jibes for marrying alyhas, who could not give him offspring (Devereux 1937:521–523). Although Sahaykwisa's career is discussed in Devereux's early work, a particularly cogent account may be found in his later compilation, *Mohave Ethnopsychiatry*. Sahaykwisa and her wives, we are told, were subject to considerable teasing and occasional humiliation. Despite economic success (at least enough to buy shoes, a luxury good for the Mohave) and a formidable reputation as a shaman, Sahaykwisa was abandoned by three wives in succession, though one of them returned to her temporarily. Devereux was told that Sahaykwisa satisfied her wife more than her male husband. Sahaykwisa stopped taking wives after the husband of her third wife raped her when it was rumored she was bewitching him. After this incident she was said to have taken to drink and had numerous affairs with men. Eventually, Sahaykwisa was murdered when she boasted that her witchcraft had killed a man who refused to have intercourse with her (Devereux 1969:416–420).

Devereux compared Sahaykwisa's ultimate fate to that of figures in Greek tragedy: "The harder these tragic personages struggle against their character, which is also destiny, the deeper they sink into the quicksand of their fate" (1969:421). Devereux said that Sahaykwisa's tragedy could be explained either as the "downward spiral of psychiatric illness" or as the "culturally mandated career of a Mohave witch," concluding that the "sociocultural and psychological explanations of a given act are perfectly complementary and lead to identical conclusions" (1969:421). Devereux's linking of mental illness with witchcraft is something that many anthropologists would contest. Roscoe suggests that Sahaykwisa attempted a series of identities at a time when her culture was under strain (1998:96).

Memory of the hwame' institution had eroded more than that of the alyha by the time Devereux did his research, though his sources for both, as for so much else, were narratives rather than direct observation. There were neither alyhas nor hwame's alive in the late 1930s. On the basis of this evidence, Devereux opined that, with regard to homosexuality, "Mohave civilization acted wisely perhaps in acknowledging the inevitable" (1937:520). He was one of several scholars who offered a "safety-valve" theory of the berdache role, pathologizing homosexuality while suggesting that its institutionalization may have been functionally useful. In this sense, we may see Devereux's account of Mohave homosexuality as part of the discourse of social engineering described by Haraway. Mohave institutions, according to Devereux, provided "reserved quarters" for "permanent" homosexuals while providing those whose attraction to same-sex partners was merely a "passing whim" a door that was "wide open for a return to normalcy" (1937:520).

Devereux claimed to harbor no moral objection to Mohave sexual culture. Despite describing a considerable amount of binge drinking and other problems consistent with a lack of economic opportunities and loss of traditional lifeways, Devereux described the Mohave as efficient farmers, comfortable in their world (1969:x). In the preface to the second edition of *Mohave Ethnopsychiatry* Devereux remarked that he "felt more at home amongst them than anywhere else on earth" and that their "flaws and foibles" seemed to him "part of their humanity," which troubled him no more than "the smoke of a great and luminous flame" (1969:xvi). He was, however, concerned in this edition to correct what was, in the psychoanalytic milieu, a damning charge of relativism made by a reviewer of the first edition, published in 1961. He rejected as "preposterous" the notion that psychological normality might be a culture-bound notion. Firmly asserting that "normality" had only one definition, the psychoanalytic one, he nonetheless offered an alternative state, "adjustment," which he defined as "sociological" and thus subject to legitimate variation (Devereux 1969:viii). In a volume written after the first publication of the work we have discussed Devereux (1967) suggested that anthropologists might gain considerable insight into other cultures by focusing on the material they found most disturbing. He was, it should be noted, invoking the Freudian notion of countertransference, which refers to the projection onto patients of analysts' own inner conflicts. In an article we published in 1997 we discussed a long-standing debate among psychoanalysts over whether countertransference is best regarded as a mine of useful insights or as noisy interference to the analytic endeavor. Either way, a full psychoanalytic approach would require an interrogation and acknowledgment of possible countertransference issues in an analyst's approach to his or her data.

In ethnography countertransference might well lead an author either to reticence or to disclosure concerning sexual matters, particularly those that the anthropologist or his or her audience are disposed to regard as deviant. Devereux analyzed gang rape, homosexuality, and alleged anal fixations as symptoms of the Mohave psychic condition. To do so he had, of necessity, to put certain constructions on his informants' statements, many of which concerned the distant past. Given Devereux's later statement concerning the importance of countertransference, it is worth noting that in his early fieldwork reports he manifested little proclivity for introspection. For the most part his choice and rendition of informants' narratives were simply presented as "fact," and Freudian interpretations of such data were simply assumed to be appropriate. A contemporary reader might be forgiven for a sense of a great opportunity missed as well as for a temptation to extend an imaginary analysis of countertransference issues in Devereux's work to the psychic baggage his audiences were likely to bring to his startling revelations.

Ruth Benedict wrote much less about homosexuality or, indeed, about sexuality in general than Devereux. Her comments, when she did discuss the topic, stressed the desirability of acknowledging and respecting cultural difference and sometimes included an implied critique of American sexual culture. In *The Chrysanthemum and the Sword*, a study of Japan published shortly after World War II, Benedict suggests that America's recent enemies may have had a less hypocritical attitude toward sexuality than her compatriots (1974:184). The Japanese, she argued, made provisions for "human feelings," both heterosexual and homosexual, in ways that kept them separate from and unthreatening to the serious business of marriage (Benedict 1974:183–188). Benedict does not dwell on the fact that these arrangements seem mainly designed for the comfort of men, though that is clear from her account. She acknowledges but does not interrogate the unhappiness a wife in Japan might feel when paying the bill for her husband's evening out. "That," Benedict says, "is her own affair" (1974:186). However, Benedict implies that a Japanese wife may be at least as satisfied as an American wife raised to hold unrealistic expectations of the power of love (1974:184).

Benedict's (1935) firsthand work on the Zuni focused on mythology and folklore, not on contemporary sexuality. She was well aware that the institution of the berdache had been found among the Zuni (it was already in eclipse), the artistic, placid, sober "Apollonians" of *Patterns of Culture* (Benedict 1934). Her few statements about homosexuality have, quite understandably, aroused the attention of biographical writers such as Margaret Caffrey (1989) and Hilary Lapsley (1999) as well as leaders of gay anthropology such as Gilbert Herdt (1999). Alone among her contemporaries, Benedict did not stigmatize homosexuals in the ways that were fashionable. She did not see homosexuality as a safety valve to defuse tensions in single-sex sodalities; she did not view homosexuality as a sign of regression, as a pathology associated with alcoholism (Devereux); she did not see it merely as a misfortune that would disappear were heterosexual life in the West to become freer, as attested by its supposed absence among the Trobrianders and the Muria.

Benedict's relationships with women such as Natalie Raymond and Ruth Valentine were known to her circle but not her reading public. Her brief pleas for tolerance are concerned with male homosexuality, more subject than lesbianism to such extreme sanctions as criminal prosecution. The context of these pleas is significant: gender rights and homosexuality are key subtexts of the configurationist theory at the core of her work.

"Anthropology and the Abnormal," published in 1934 and based on a 1932 conference paper, was one of Benedict's early theoretical statements. A condensed version of the argument appeared in the last chapter of *Patterns of Culture*, and the essay was reprinted by Mead in *An Anthropologist at Work* (1959). Configurationism's point is simple. The range of human temperament may be seen as a vast but finite arc. A continuum stretches from placidity to aggression, from easy tolerance to suspicion, from calm contemplation of the numinous to frenzied trance and self-mutilation, from behavioral traits the West considers feminine to those it considers masculine. Each culture makes a different selection of desirable traits from the arc of temperament, guided by a core configuration or pattern of cultural values consistent with its particular *Geist*, or spirit. Individuals were pressured through socialization and social sanctions to express those parts of their temperamental makeup consistent with their culture's values and to suppress those parts that did not fit. Inevitably, some individuals could not make such an adjustment. Inescapably, one culture's normality was another's deviance or creative genius. In "Anthropology and the Abnormal" Benedict observed that in some places trance and possession are honored as indices of spirituality, whereas in others they are stigmatized as manifestations of disturbance. Benedict may have been one of the first to make such an observation. (Her doctoral dissertation, completed in 1923, was on the differential distribution of the vision quest.)

This powerful example provided a context for her remarks on Plato's *Republic* and the berdache, strengthening their impact and embedding them so that they did not stand out too starkly:

Cataleptic and trance phenomena are, of course, only one illustration of the fact that those whom we regard as abnormals may function adequately in other cultures. Many of our culturally discarded traits are selected for elaboration in different societies. Homosexuality is an excellent example. . . . Homosexuals in many societies are not incompetent, but they may be such if the culture asks adjustments of them that would strain any man's vitality. Wherever homosexuality has been given an honorable place in any society, those to whom it is congenial have filled adequately the honorable roles society assigns to them. Plato's *Republic* is, of course, the most convincing statement of such a reading of homosexuality. It is presented as one of the major means of the good life, and it was generally so regarded in Greece at that time.

The cultural attitude toward homosexuals has not always been on such a high ethical plane, but it has been very varied. Among many American Indian tribes there exists the institution of the berdache, as the French called them. These men–women were men who at puberty or thereafter took the dress and the occupations of women. Sometimes they married other men and lived with them. Sometimes they were men with no inversion, persons of weak sexual endowment who chose this role to avoid the jeers of the women. The berdaches were never regarded as of first-rate supernatural power, as similar men–women were in Siberia, but rather as leaders in women's occupations, good healers in certain diseases, or, among certain tribes, as the genial organizers of social affairs. In any case, they were socially placed. They were not left exposed to the conflicts that visit the deviant who is excluded from participation in the recognized patterns of his society. (Benedict 1959:267–268)

In *Patterns of Culture* Benedict painted pictures of the Apollonian Zuni, the Dionysian and "megalomaniac" Kwakiutl, as well as the "paranoid" Dobuan, pictures that have been criticized as overdrawn. Ironically, Benedict, the advocate of relativism, an opponent of racism and homophobia, used the language of pathology to describe the normative behaviors and emotions of other cultures.

Five years after the publication of *Patterns of Culture*, Benedict refined her position on the relativity of deviant and normal sexual roles. She observed that the Dakota differentiated sharply between male and female gender roles. The role of the berdache was institutionalized, and there was some lesbianism. In contrast, the Ojibwa, who allowed women to become shamans and warriors without adopting a special gender role, had no institutionalized homosexuality. This showed that the social roots of homosexuality were more significant than its physiological derivation (Benedict 1939; Caffrey 1989:254).

We are grateful to Gilbert Herdt for an essay in which he draws attention to a lesser-known paper by Benedict entitled "Continuities and Discontinuities in Cultural Conditioning" (1938; Herdt 1999:222–242). Its premise is that each society has to deal with discontinuities and continuities in the life cycle, some of which are imposed or suggested by "nature," others of which reflect technology or religious dogma. It is natural that people will move from infantile dependency to adult leadership roles, but there are many ways of marking points in the transition. Some societies encourage three-year-old children to copy adult roles and even to undertake adult tasks, whereas we sharply separate the world of children from the realities of adult labor. In some cultures children indulge freely in genital play, and there is no obvious latency period (albeit biology imposes a limitation inasmuch as children are sterile). However, Benedict's America was appalled by infantile sexuality, and attitudes have changed little since her day.

Sexual object choice too might have a temporal aspect. Referring to descriptions of male cults in *Papuans of the Trans-Fly* by F. E. Williams, Benedict noted: "The life cycle of the Keraki Indians [sic] includes, therefore, in succession, passive homosexuality, active homosexuality and heterosexuality" (1938:166). In other words, in addition to societies in which "homosexuals" occupied a special social niche, there were groups in which the male initiate's separation from the mother–child tie was symbolically emphasized in a protracted liminal period during which homoerotic behavior was normative.

Like her broader political position, Benedict's configurationist approach to homosexuality was anomalous in its time. It anticipated contemporary discourse on the topic. One might contrast Benedict's assertion that those whose temperaments did not fit well into their cultures might become innovators and creators with Alexander Goldenweiser's contribution to V. F. Calverton and S. D. Schmalhausen's 1929 volume, *Sex in Civilization*. Goldenweiser, an earlier student of Boas, provided later generations of readers with at least three causes for complaint. He allows homosexuality a brief one-and-three-quarter-page mention in an 18-page article in a section with the dismissive title "Sex Byways" (Goldenweiser 1929:60–62). A large part of that discussion is given over to ridiculing Edward Carpenter's suggestion that people who felt their sexuality to be at odds with the values of their culture often became innovators in fields ranging from art to religion to medicine (Goldenweiser 1929:61–62). Although Goldenweiser's overall goal was said to be a desire to narrow the distance between "primitive" and "civilized" sexuality, as it was perceived in 1929, in this section he offers a singular example of "Othering" the primitive: "A quaint fantasy this – homosexual men and women as culture heroes of mankind! And it has a delightfully primitive flare about it. Primitives think this way. Unusual people do unusual things. Those marked by the gods become responsible for great events. The Indian, Australian and African Negro would readily accept Carpenter's theory as a creation myth" (1929:62). Benedict's biographer notes that it was not until 26 years after Benedict's death that the American Psychiatric Association finally removed homosexuality from its list of pathological conditions (Caffrey 1989:255).

The writings of Benedict's close friend and erstwhile pupil, Margaret Mead, are examined in chapter 7. Configurationism was a theory they developed together. In general terms, we may remark that Mead's much more detailed writings on sexuality are somewhat less relativist than Benedict's, and we should reiterate that her public approach to homosexuality was more guarded. This silence may have stemmed from fear of public exposure; another explanation for it is that she herself absorbed some of the stigma of homoerotic relationships into her own thinking, despite her personal experience.

Both Benedict and Mead became part of the seminar group led by the psychoanalyst Abram Kardiner at the New York Psychoanalytic Institute in the late 1930s.[9] Mead had become more sympathetic to Freudian theories after conversations with John Dollard of Yale in 1934. The young Cora Du Bois was a key aide to Kardiner. Ralph Linton, Geoffrey Gorer, and Esther Schiff Goldfrank (later Wittfogel) were also participants in the seminar. Edward Sapir and Dollard came down periodically from Yale to participate (Manson 1986:78–86). At the Psychoanalytic Institute and at Columbia, where the seminar later moved, generations of social workers and psychoanalysts received an introduction to lessons other cultures supposedly had to teach them about the problems presented by their clients and patients.

Kardiner adhered to a theory of personality developed by revisionist psychoanalysts, especially Karen Horney. This approach differed from classical Freudian theory in that the ego, the part of the psyche associated with conscious control, was looked to as the core of personality. Freudian orthodoxy assumed direct, though masked, manifestation of the infantile libido in the dreams, symptoms, sexual choices, and creative accomplishments of adults. For Kardiner, libido was superseded by the culturally normative personalities resulting from its control. Ego formation involved an intersection between environment and cultural values such as frugality or cooperativeness or obedience, which themselves were grounded in environmental adaptation. Abundant or scarce natural resources, for example, might affect the availability of food. A set of "primary institutions" developed in response. These institutions included subsistence techniques, economics, and social structure as well as culturally specific management of "basic disciplines" such as nursing, weaning, toilet training, and early childhood sexuality. From these resulted a "basic personality structure" composed of a list of prevailing emotional states, for example, "food anxiety." The basic personality was expressed in secondary institutions such as food taboos and cannibalism and projective systems such as folklore and myth.

The core of Kardiner's book *The Individual and His Society* contains ethnographic descriptions of the Tanala of Madagascar and the Marquesans of Polynesia by Ralph Linton as well as Kardiner's analyses of Linton's data on the two cultures (1939:137–354). It should be noted that Linton worked primarily on archaeological rather than ethnological research in the Marquesas but that he was confident he understood the contemporary culture of the islands. We shall examine the Marquesan case because of a significant critique by Robert Suggs (1971) and because of its centrality to Kardiner's position.

The following are the claims Linton made about the Marquesans. They did not enjoy an abundance of food. There were periodic prolonged droughts, and there was no rainy season. Taro and yams were seldom cultivated. There was little irrigation and a generally low level of technology. At the time of Linton's visit (1920–22) "race suicide" (his term) in the aftermath of colonialism had led to a substantial decline in population (Linton 1939b:137). In all probability selective infanticide was practiced, hence there was a demographic ratio of seven males to every three females (Linton 1939b:155). Polyandry was institutionalized. Men had to compete for the favors of women, but, strangely enough, there was little jealousy between them. There was considerable sexual freedom and lax childhood discipline. Women did little useful work and neglected to breast-feed their children in order to preserve the erotic shape of their breasts. Indeed, the raison d'être of the Marquesan woman was erotic attractiveness and her own sexual gratification. In sexual relations women had the upper hand. Men had to ensure adequate stimulation of their partners (e.g., by cunnilingus) before intercourse.

According to Kardiner (1939:197–250), the deprivation of breast milk and maternal attention caused a lifelong feeling of anxiety among Marquesans, a particular manifestation of which was a fear of being eaten up or consumed. Men hated women, and, although there was little jealousy between men, relations between women were poor. Women feared that their children would be stolen from them. Evidence of neurotic conflict was to be found in the projective systems that were produced by the basic personality structure. There were false pregnancies. Women feared sorcery, inflicted by *fanaua*, the spirits of dead males conjured by female rivals. A body of myths described female ogresses who kidnapped men for intercourse, a form of sexual feeding, or cannibalism. Male heroes could then triumph in the sexual act (i.e., by a redeeming rape). The hero's loss of body parts (which were eaten by relatives or strangers) was a recurring mytheme.

Suggs, who did extensive ethnographic fieldwork in the Marquesas and other parts of Polynesia, notes one particular problem with Linton's report and Kardiner's analysis: most of the facts appear to be wrong. Therefore, the analysis is more than suspect. The Marquesas do not suffer from periodic drought, and the shift of the trade winds brings on a rainy season. Yams and taro are cultivated, and there is extensive terracing. The demographic ratio is close to 50:50, and there is no evidence to indicate that it was ever skewed in the way described by Linton, though population decline has certainly occurred. Women make a considerable economic contribution, do nurse their babies, and are not overly concerned about the appearance of their breasts. There was no polyandry but rather a form of secondary marriage available to both sexes. Females were not dominant in the sex act, and there was little foreplay. The fanaua were female spirits, not male. Some of the "ogresses" in Marquesan myth were, in fact, helpers and benefactors. Motifs present throughout Oceania were related to allegedly specific and localized traits of Marquesan sexual personality. Overall, Suggs's account of the Marquesas agrees with Linton and Kardiner only on certain very broad points: there is a lot of adolescent sexual freedom, some extramarital sex, and some homosexuality. Although we shall take issue with some of Suggs's conclusions about sexuality in general, his refutation of Linton and Kardiner seems to be based on a generally accurate statement of the facts. While such things as degree of maternal nurturance may be subject to interpretation, annual rainfall is an easily verifiable matter about which Suggs appears to be right. Moreover, ecology is the key independent variable in the work of

Kardiner and those influenced by his work. The online edition of the journal *Plant Talk*, published by the British National Tropical Botanical Garden, says of the Marquesan climate: "During most of the year the south-east trade winds moderate the temperatures and supply rain. Rainfall ranges from about 1000 to over 3000 mm per year, with windward slopes and crests being the wettest" (Lorence 2001). Linton definitely seems to have been wrong in his statement that the Marquesas lie outside the climatic influence of the trade winds. On the other hand, droughts do sometimes occur during the El Niño cycle (Male 2001).

Distortions in Linton's ethnography were significant because both of Linton's reports were used to sustain a theoretical corpus that expanded over 25 years, culminating in the work of John Whiting and his associates. We may make three observations here. First, adult sexuality has become buried in a mass of sometimes tenuous and tenuously connected data concerning ecology, breast-feeding, weaning, and myth. Second, *The Individual and His Society* is the first of a body of neo-Freudian ethnological analyses deploying the language of mental illness to characterize normality in other cultures. Third, the analysis places exceptional blame upon women for the personality characteristics that the text pathologizes. This tendency is repeated in many other works of this school, from Cora Du Bois's *The People of Alor* (1944) to Jules Henry's *Pathways to Madness* (1971). Psychoanalytic practice in the United States during this period and derivatives of that practice such as popular advice manuals and psychology textbooks have frequently been criticized for a tendency to "blame the mother" for personal and social ills. The Marquesans were the first of a series of societies whose enculturation and sexuality were negatively conscripted and clinically pathologized through the unquestioned extension of a therapeutic agenda that itself was a reaction to changes in gender roles in the United States.

In *Feminism and Its Discontents: A Century of Struggle with Psychoanalysis* (1998) historian Mari Jo Buhle discusses the era of mother blaming in the history of psychoanalysis in detail, including the uses made of anthropology. Buhle sees the discourse begun by Mead and Malinowski as one in which primitive sexuality was employed to argue for greater sexual freedom and fulfillment for women. Buhle's critique of the culture and personality movement is directed not at these figures or at Benedict but at Kardiner, Linton, and a number of other anthropologists, including the later Gorer, who, she says, used ethnographic data to argue that changes in women's sexual and domestic roles had had deleterious effects on psychosexual adjustment (1998:85–164). She is particularly critical of a number of writers, including

John Dollard of Yale (another member of Kardiner's seminar), for creating the figure of the African American matriarch. Though these writers recognized that the Negro mother was forced into the role of family breadwinner by racism, such women were blamed, according to Buhle, for many alleged failings on the part of their male offspring, including, significantly, a lack of control of sexual impulses (1989:153).

Du Bois's initial contributions to Kardiner's seminar consisted of analyses of the ethnographic literature in the terms Kardiner and his associates were developing. The field research she undertook between 1937 and 1939 in Alor, which was then part of the Netherlands Indies, was planned to test and refine Kardiner's insights against empirical data specifically gathered for the purpose (Du Bois 1960:viii–ix). In 1939 and 1940 she submitted her field data for discussion at the seminar, publishing *The People of Alor* in 1944. She selected Alor partly because she expected that the "gross pathologies" of *lata* and *amok* (so-called culture-bound syndromes reported in the literature on this region) would be present among the population (Du Bois 1960:ix). At the time, she believed that "by the very grossness of its manifestations pathology could be more clearly understood than normality"; however, she encountered neither of these syndromes on Alor, and her preconceptions were "swept aside" (Du Bois 1960:ix).

Rather than studying overt pathologies, Du Bois turned her attention to what she termed "modal personalities," constellations of characteristics not present in all Alorese but rather ones that turned up at a high level of frequency under multiple modes of observation: normal ethnographic methods, collection of autobiographies, analysis of religion and other projective systems, and, most innovatively, administration of Rorschach and other personality tests. To control for possible ethnographer bias, the Rorschach tests were interpreted "blind" by Dr. Emil Oberholzer, who was an expert in their interpretation but had no direct knowledge of the Alorese. The autobiographies were interpreted by Kardiner. If Kardiner had ascribed Marquesan personality partly to an alleged failure of Marquesan women to perform useful labor, the modal personality that Du Bois ascribed to the Alorese was said to be conditioned by the primary responsibility of women for agricultural work, while men devoted their efforts to amassing property for exchanges and feasts. Women spent most of their days in the garden, so that infants born during the season when garden labor was heavy endured many hours of hunger during the period between early morning and their mothers' late-afternoon return (unless their mothers were lazy). Mashed vegetable foods and nursing by women other than the mother provided some nourishment during the day, but Du Bois says that they were unreliable (1960:34–35).

Du Bois, in a manner consistent with Kardiner's approach, notes connections between sexual practices and economics (1960:36). As the primary garden workers, women might delay resuming intercourse with their husbands in order to reduce the number of people their labor would have to feed. Until parents resumed intercourse (and sometimes after they did) children slept on the same mat as their mothers; Du Bois notes a village scandal concerning a child who died when its parents crushed it during intercourse. Moreover, hungry infants' genitals were often massaged to stop them from crying (Du Bois 1960:37).

Du Bois is careful to note that individuals' experiences in early childhood differ considerably from person to person (1960:38). Nonetheless, the story that she tells of life during and after infancy would read like a history of severe pathology if it were reported in the case file of a Western social service agency. Once they had learned to walk, with little adult assistance, Alorese toddlers might be left to roam the village during the day, dependent on grudging handouts from older children unless they had a grandmother who was too old for garden work. [10] At this period children were likely to be weaned because another child was expected (Du Bois 1960:40). Du Bois suggests that many children suffered protein deficiency, though vitamins were plentiful (1960:42). Toddlers were given cold baths, which were said to be especially painful for children whose skin was sore from yaws. Children's earliest attempts at speech are described as "rhythmic wails" directed to their mothers and curses directed at relatives who displease them (Du Bois 1960:46–47).

Masturbation is said to be freely practiced in early childhood, and children are described as having full knowledge of the sexual activities of their parents (Du Bois 1960:45). Toilet training is gradual and gentle (Du Bois 1960:42). These alleged laxities in repression are implicated by Du Bois in creating a child prone to temper tantrums, as children are alleged to suffer "hunger, desertion and discomfort" and are not subject to the libidinal discipline that would give them "mechanisms of defense or mastery" (1960:54).

Later in childhood a pattern of petty theft, mainly of vegetable foods, and anxiety about theft is said to set in, particularly for boys and men (Du Bois 1960:56–58). Corporal punishment "may be meted out by any irritated adult who cannot even theoretically claim to be nurturing" (Du Bois 1960:65). Lying is said to be "taken as a matter of course" among children and adults (Du Bois 1960:65). Social standards are said to exist as a prerequisite for social life but to be "not so rigid or so deeply rooted as they are in our middle class" (Du Bois 1960:79). On the other hand, the culture is described as "less harsh" in respect to sex, with masturbation and childhood exploration being generally expected to diminish but no special punishments applied. "Again," we are told, "as in earlier developmental periods, the activities of the instincts seem to be less destructively handled than those of the ego" (Du Bois 1960:79).

In adult life, Du Bois argues, sex is seen by men as something women can give or withhold in exchange for property. There are fairly arduous marriage payments to be made, and women are said to cite delinquencies in such payments when they deny sex to their husbands for reasons of their own (Du Bois 1960:94). There are taboos on sex from the time that pregnancy is noted until the child can sit up, and men are supposed to abstain from sex when accumulating wealth for feasts, though these rules are often broken. In general, Du Bois sees sex, food, and wealth as areas in which women are seen as frustrating stand-ins for the denying mothers of infancy.[11] Du Bois considers it significant that several items in the sexual vocabulary have links with food and digestion: the word for penis means "intestine," while that for orgasm means "heart from it tasty" (1960:101). In general terms, symbolic associations between food and sex may well be linked to early childhood experience, though their presence needn't be evidence of an etiology as specific as the one Du Bois suggests. Metaphors linking food and sex are found in many cultures with a wide range of childhood regimes.

Du Bois, though acknowledging some stable and loving marriages, stresses the high divorce rate (1960:97). Of the carryover from childhood to adult emotions she comments, concerning the inhabitants of the village where she did her fieldwork, "In both sexes the striking thing brought out in the autobiographies is the ease with which loved persons may be surrendered. It is a character trait consistent with the supposition made at the end of the section on late childhood, namely, that there are few opportunities in Atimelang life for the establishment of secure and permanent relations and little expectation of, or insistence upon, them" (Du Bois 1960:93).

A lack of interest in incest, even as a topic of mythology, is interpreted by Du Bois as a consequence of the rarity of deep relationships among the Alorese; shallow relationships, she argues, reduce the likelihood of incestuous fixations (1960:105). In this case, a lack of interest in pathology is itself pathologized. This maneuver is repeated by Kardiner in a chapter on personality determinants in Alorese culture that he contributed to *The People of Alor* (Kardiner 1960). Kardiner's consulting room diction is, in fact, more extreme than Du Bois's language. Alorese boys are said to have a "strong fetishistic attachment to the mother's breast" and to carry "fears and hostilities" associated with the mother–infant relationship into their relations with adult women. The resultant "shyness and anxiety" are said to result, among other things, in a scarcity of rape (Kardiner 1960:184–185). An absence that might, to the untutored, appear desirable thus becomes a symptom.

Some reviewers of *The People of Alor* questioned whether Du Bois had drawn inferences from her data beyond those mandated by the facts she reported. Brenda Seligman, writing in *Man*, noted that Mead reported adult personality characteristics and cultural emphases on Manus similar to those Du Bois found on Alor with very different child-rearing patterns (1950:67). Conversely, Hortense Powdermaker, in a review published in the *American Anthropologist*, remarked that she had observed similar child-feeding practices in New Ireland, with markedly different adult outcomes (1945:160).

The People of Alor appeared when the various forms of mother blaming alluded to earlier were at their height. In particular, the groundwork was being laid for the "expert" opinion that was later going to be used to encourage women to return to the home at the end of World War II. Although "Momism," popularized by Philip Wylie in *A Generation of Vipers* (1942), was characterized by overprotective rather than neglectful mothers, who were blamed for an alleged lack of manliness among American men, Wylie and his admirers also blamed women for being unresponsive sexual partners to their husbands and for making excessive financial demands on them. In *The People of Alor* Du Bois did not make direct comparisons to American culture, was careful to note that there were some successful marriages, and conceded that efforts were made to care for children when their mothers were working in their gardens. No such limits applied to the rhetoric employed by Abram Kardiner when he conscripted the Alorese for his own particular contribution to America's campaign against working mothers in the 1950s.

In a 1955 book, *Sex and Morality*, Kardiner blamed feminism and the liberal philosophy that gave rise to feminism for a "flight from masculinity" and the surprisingly high rate of homosexuality revealed by the Kinsey Report (see below). "The most conspicuous feature" of Alorese society is said to be "the problem of the working mother." Children are said to receive "unsystematic care from anyone who happens to be around" (Kardiner 1955:205). In Alor, according to Kardiner, "everyone" is "greedy, deceitful and selfish," and "their intellectual capacity is slight." "Their marriages," we are told, "are discordant. Divorces are frequent." "In sum," Kardiner admonishes, "the people of Alor present an appalling picture of almost total social and emotional incapacitation" (1955:207). In case we miss the lesson, Kardiner warns that "identical results can be found in poorer levels of any people where working mothers are numerous" (1955:209).

In *Sex and Morality* Kardiner turns some of the central tenets of Boasian anthropology against the relativist project itself. He is careful to disabuse his readers of any notion that racial difference may account for social dysfunction of the sort he describes among the Alor as well as the Marquesans, who are also revisited in this book (Kardiner 1955:208, 111–115). As previously, he insists that culture, in the form of family structure, causes personality. "In every society," he acknowledges, "'morality' consists of living up to the stipulations of established custom" (Kardiner 1955:98). However, he takes specific issue with "several anthropologists," most notably Benedict, for suggesting that "anything goes" with regard to cultural patterning (Kardiner 1955:94). Some cultural patterns, he argues, are inferior to others and may even be lethal, citing a casual remark attributed to Charles Wagley about population decline among the Tapirape (Kardiner 1955:95).

Not all attempts to relate food and sex were psychoanalytic or prescriptive. Allan Holmberg's *Nomads of the Long Bow* (1950), an ethnography of the Amazonian Siriono, is a case in point. Before visiting the Siriono, Holmberg had been associated with the Cross-Cultural Survey at Yale (1969:xvii). It is unclear to us whether the Siriono of the early 1940s could be said to constitute a "culture" or a "society." They were refugees without the title, the sparse remnants of a Tupi–Guarani group that had been overwhelmed by more powerful neighbors, doubtless displaced by the population migrations that had followed colonial contact elsewhere. The small nomadic band that Holmberg visited lived in an inhospitable part of the eastern Bolivian jungle, riddled with disease and tormented by insect pests. Their technology was very rudimentary, and food was scarce.

Like George Peter Murdock and Malinowski, Holmberg believed that humans were governed by primary innate physiological drives that were further expressed in variant secondary cultural drives (1969:244–247). Although psychoanalysts had assumed the universal primacy of the sex drive, the Siriono case proved for Holmberg that the drive for food could be significantly more important in some cases. The quest for food dominated not only the Siriono workday but also their dream life (Holmberg 1969:241–242). Food was a major cause of social tension. Furthermore, for long periods the demands of hunger repressed the sexual urge: "Actually, when food is scarce, there is little expression of sex. On one expedition which I made into the forest with the Siriono for a period of about six weeks, I observed that my informants indulged in little or no sexual activity during periods of food deprivation but engaged in sexual orgies following periods of food satiation" (Holmberg 1969:255). These observations bring to mind Havelock Ellis's observations about sexual periodicity, although Siriono periodicity is based in cultural rather than evolutionary difference.

THE KINSEY REPORT AND ITS LEGACY

Three major compendia of survey research on sexuality appeared between 1948 and 1953. Two of the volumes, *Sexual Behavior in the Human Male* (Kinsey, Pomeroy, and Martin 1948), based on 12,000 case histories, and *Sexual Behavior in the Human Female* (Kinsey et al. 1953), based on 8,000 case histories, were published under the auspices of the Institute of Sex Research at Indiana University (the Kinsey Institute) and are commonly known as the Kinsey Report. *Patterns of Sexual Behavior* by Clellan Ford and Frank Beach appeared in 1951. It analyzed ethnographic data from 190 societies around the world in addition to American society. Two of the authors of these three works (Paul Gebhard and Clellan Ford) were anthropologists, but the others were not. Alfred Kinsey and Frank Beach were biologists. Wardell B. Pomeroy was a psychologist. Clyde E. Martin had been Kinsey's student. The reader can find little in these reports about sexual meanings, the place of sexuality in cultural systems, and the relationship between sexual meanings and systems of power. That surely was not their aim. Kinsey and his associates eschewed totalizing assumptions in favor of hard (if imperfect) statistics and people's reports of their actual experiences. Moreover, their accounts succeeded in developing a position that had not always been consistently present in the ethnographic tradition: a relativist approach to all human sexual behavior.

Born in Hoboken, New Jersey, in 1894, Kinsey was raised by religious parents. He became an entomologist, specializing in taxonomy. In 1917 he began to study the family Cynipidae, or gall wasps, receiving his doctorate from Harvard in 1919. Members of this family exhibited a high degree of phenotypic variation. In some species the first generation resembled the third but not the second or fourth, which resembled each other. Taxonomically, Kinsey was a splitter, creating many new species, subspecies, and so on. His taxonomy has been subject to attack. Most saliently for us, he concluded that variation was normal in nature. Individual difference was part of the evolutionary program. These views were a template for his later findings on human sexuality (see Jones 1997:141, 148).

Kinsey married in 1921; at this time his sexual knowledge and experience appear to have been consistent with his conventional religious upbringing. Over the next couple of decades Kinsey began to resent the repression that had enveloped him and so many others of his generation. He expressed his "anti-Victorian" opinions in a popular and extremely frank lecture course on marriage at Indiana University. His research now shifted from insects to human subjects. He interviewed many students and recorded case histories. His research into homosexuality in Chicago included a study of the tearoom trade. In 1942 he sought funds for his new Institute of Sex Research and received them in 1943.

Kinsey felt that human dignity could be upheld in many kinds of relationship. His case studies revealed the enormous variation in sexual behavior in the United States. He believed that established morality was the creation of members of the upper middle class, who endeavored to impose their standards on the rest of the population. The attempt was unsuccessful because of the power of the sex drive, but much guilt and unhappiness resulted. Proper sexual education, involving an awareness of simple biological facts and the inevitability of variation from the supposed norm, would serve as a liberating force.

On the first page of *Sexual Behavior in the Human Male* the authors note that "human sexual behavior represents one of the least explored segments of biology, psychology and sociology" (Kinsey, Pomeroy, and Martin 1948:3) and that religion, social taboo, and formal legislation have restricted scientific investigation of the subject. In an often-quoted paragraph the authors discuss the reasons why sexuality in most societies is a more likely object of taboo than other bodily processes: "There are cultures which more freely accept sexual activities as matters of everyday physiology (e.g., Malinowski 1929), while maintaining extensive rituals and establishing taboos around feeding activities. One may wonder what scientific knowledge we would have of digestive functions if the primary taboos in our own society concerned food and feeding" (Kinsey, Pomeroy, and Martin 1948:4). The authors argue, nonetheless, that the strong emotional content of sexual behavior makes it a far more likely object of taboo in cross-cultural terms than excretion, eating, or any other physiological process.

The overture to the book promises more anthropology than the performance delivers, though where anthropology is used it is in support of relativism. Accordingly, an argument that premarital intercourse need not

necessarily be harmful is prefaced by a statement that most "so-called primitive peoples" have no problems with such relations. The authors cite Bronislaw Malinowski, Richard Thurnwald, Margaret Mead, Reo Fortune, Ruth
Landes, Isaac Schapera, Gladys Reichard, Ralph Linton, George Peter Murdock, Beatrice Blackwood, and Clark Wissler (Kinsey, Pomeroy, and Martin
1948:547).

In *Sexual Behavior in the Human Female* Kinsey and his group, which now
included the anthropologist Paul Gebhard, delivered a scathing attack on
anthropological studies of sexual behavior. They remarked that anthropologists usually relied on information from a few trusted informants, group
discussions, and public sexual behavior. As a result, they were ill placed
to discover the "covert" culture. Because of their own "cultural conditioning" many anthropologists were ill equipped and reluctant to inquire about
"specific aspects of sex." "Only too frequently he excuses himself on the
grounds that sexual questioning would spoil rapport with his subjects, but
the success of those few explorers who have seriously attempted to gather
sexual information indicates that valid and reasonable extensive data may
be collected without undue difficulty, provided that the interviewing is well
done" (Kinsey et al. 1953:92). Insofar as the process of data collection was
flawed, secondary compilations such as the Human Relations Area Files
were also unreliable (Kinsey et al. 1953:93).

Kinsey's remarks (were they Gebhard's?) could well apply to many forms
of "covert culture" besides sexuality, and there is much to say for them.
Ignored, nonetheless, are issues of privacy, power, and responsibility in representation. Where privacy is desired, is it appropriate to breach it in defense
of sexual "freedom" elsewhere? However, as Stephen Murray has pointed
out to us (personal communication, 2002), anthropologists may well project
their own reluctance to discuss sexual matters onto others. Greenberg has
remarked that fear of being suspected of being a participant or of being
denied permission to return to the research site may add to this reluctance
to investigate stigmatized sexualities (1988:77).

Kinsey and his associates disagreed with some Freudian and neo-Freudian doctrines that they saw as little more than reifications of conventional
morality. Nonetheless, they did acknowledge the contributions of Freud,
Ellis, and other pioneers in the study of sex, inasmuch as they opened the
conversation that their own work continued. Above all else, Kinsey and his
associates rejected Freud's idea of sexual normality, the mature, genital adult
capable of successful heterosexual object relations, the product of an appropriate socialization process or, in lieu of that, a productive transference

on the psychoanalyst's couch (Kinsey et al. 1953:447–448). Kinsey, Pomeroy, and Martin quote Ruth Benedict in support of the notion that culture determines what is defined as "abnormal" (1948:202).

While they were well prepared to accept the existence of sexuality in humans from the earliest infancy, Kinsey and his associates felt there was no evidence for Freud's "pre-genital stage of generalized pre-erotic response" (Kinsey, Pomeroy, and Martin 1948:180) and there was no necessity for a latency period. Unlike Freud, they did not endorse ideas of healthy repression or sublimation. Rather, sublimation was rejected as an absurd religious doctrine that masqueraded as science in Freudian writing. Freudian theory was contradicted by obvious fact: "It does not suffice to cite artists, or statesmen, or other busy persons as cases of sublimation, merely because they are energetic in the pursuit of their non-sexual professions. Certainly no one who knew the sexual histories of particular artists would have thought of using them as examples of sexually sublimated people" (Kinsey, Pomeroy, and Martin 1948:207). Last but not least, Kinsey rejected a key article in the Freudian creed, the preeminence of the vaginal orgasm: "Histologic studies show that there are essentially no tactile nerve ends in the surfaces of the cervix" (Kinsey et al. 1953:584).

Readers of Kinsey were informed that "worry frequently does damage, while masturbation itself does none" (Kinsey et al. 1953:170 n. 49), and a multitude of sources were cited in support of that opinion. To say that homosexuality was unnatural behavior and that heterosexuality was instinctive was absolutely false. "Such interpretations are, however, mystical" (Kinsey et al. 1953:448). They contradicted physiological fact and observed behavior in most mammalian species.

The Kinsey Report achieved its greatest impact through the power of statistics, which astonished many of those who read it or read of it, revealing a contradiction between the case histories, on the one hand, and "official" morality and representations of normality, on the other.

> Kinsey reported that more than 90 per cent of the males he had interviewed had masturbated, about 85 per cent had engaged in premarital intercourse, something between 30 and 45 per cent had had extramarital intercourse, another 59 per cent had indulged in mouth-genital contacts, some 70 per cent had patronized prostitutes, and finally (and most disturbing to many) no less than 17 per cent of farm boys had had sexual relations with a lower animal. Because he abhorred the hypocrisy and deceit that were the stock-in-trade of

middle-class morality, Kinsey made certain his readers would never be able to look at each other again in quite the same way. "The persons involved in these activities, taken as a whole," he declared with a flourish, "constitute more than 95 per cent of the total male population." (Jones 1997:528)

The publication of *Sexual Behavior in the Human Male* brought instant celebrity to Kinsey. The book was favorably reviewed in *Time* and the *New York Times*. The Kinsey Report was discussed on the airwaves, it was saluted in the lyrics of popular songs, and it became the subject of jokes by popular comedians. Not surprisingly, it annoyed conservative critics (Jones 1997:564–574). However, there was also an adverse reaction from well-known academic figures, including the theologian Reinhold Niebuhr, the literary critic Lionel Trilling, and two anthropologists about whom we have had much to say, Geoffrey Gorer and Margaret Mead (Jones 1997:577). Gorer discussed supposed inadequacies in Kinsey's sampling method in a review in the *New York Herald Tribune* (Jones 1997:578, 579). Mead launched a full-scale assault on Kinsey at a meeting of the American Social Hygiene Association in April 1948. As neo-Freudians, Gorer and Mead were dismayed by Kinsey's criticisms of psychoanalysis. Mead attacked Kinsey's theoretical position and the atomistic, mechanistic descriptions of sexual organs, sexual feelings, masturbation, and coitus that resulted from it. She asserted that Kinsey's description of sexuality removed from it any sense of fun and deprived it of its interpersonal context (Jones 1997:579). Mead remarked that the volume was devoid of advice on building successful sexual relations with one's fellow humans: "The book suggests no way of choosing between a woman and a sheep" (Mead 1948:69). (Perhaps the avoidance of such judgments was Kinsey's precise point!)

It is arguable that Kinsey's impact on popular American attitudes was greater than Mead's and much greater than Gorer's, however apt some of their criticisms may have been. Even though his statistics were indeed flawed, inasmuch as the number of male prisoners in the 1948 volume and volunteers in both volumes biased his sample, Kinsey's numbers were powerful arguments for sexual liberation. The social changes that led to homosexual law reform in the United States, Canada, and Britain in the 1950s and 1960s may in part be the product of his work. These changes did not occur without resistance. During the McCarthy era, Kinsey was denounced as an atheistic Communist. A special committee of the House of Representatives was set up to investigate the activities of tax-exempt bodies such as the Rockefeller Foundation, which had funded Kinsey through a committee of the National Research Foundation. Kinsey was a particular target of the Reece Committee. Exhibiting a singular lack of courage, the Rockefeller Foundation cut off Kinsey's funds in 1954. They had been only partially restored when Kinsey died in 1956 (Jones 1997:722–737).

Patterns of Sexual Behavior appeared in 1951, between the publication of the first and second volumes of the Kinsey Report. It attempted to add a cross-cultural dimension to the statistical study of sexual behavior and, inter alia, to summarize and tabulate anthropological knowledge on that subject. The authors were Clellan Stearns Ford, who had done fieldwork among the Kwakiutl and was an expert on cross-cultural methodology, and Frank Beach, a psychologist who had studied the effects of hormones and cortical changes on sexual behavior in rats. In their study Ford and Beach used data from 191 societies: 47 from Oceania, 28 from Eurasia, 33 from Africa, 57 from North America, and 26 from South America. Much of their data was from primary sources, but they relied heavily on the Human Relations Area Files. (Ford was later to become president of HRAF Inc.) They also frequently cited *Sexual Behavior in the Human Male* as evidence from contemporary American society. Lastly, they introduced extensive data on sexual behavior among the higher and lower primates and other mammals. Although the authors claimed they were explicitly eschewing all questions of moral value (Ford and Beach 1951:14), the study, like Kinsey's, has been viewed as supportive of sexual relativism.

The authors admit to a number of self-imposed limitations. Sexual behavior was "behavior involving stimulation and excitation of the sexual organs" (Ford and Beach 1951:4). Although the authors fully understood that language, intentionality, social rules, socialization patterns, and symbolism accounted not only for the difference between human sexuality and that of other mammals but also for differences in sexual behavior in the societies in their sample, they did not attempt to explore the domain of sexual symbolism. They explicitly refused to investigative expressive symbolism in the form of myth and dream (Ford and Beach 1951:14). Furthermore, although they admitted that their findings might have implications for the psychiatrist and psychoanalyst, they felt they lacked the specialist knowledge necessary for an exploration of these questions.

The authors observed that "men and women in our own society who wish to understand their own sexual tendencies and habits cannot reach this goal merely by introspection" (Ford and Beach 1951:4). Kinsey had provided the curious with some answers. However, contemporary American society could not furnish such a student with "a comprehensive understanding of human sexuality." Inasmuch as human sexual behavior "takes different forms in different social conditions," an analysis of different cultures was essential. It was necessary to explain not only differences but universals in sexual behavior. Similarities could be explained by commonalities in life experience, but they could also be the product of the species' common heredity (Ford and Beach 1951:5). Furthermore, because humans were mammals, they shared "certain basic behavioral traits" with other mammals. This was the rationale for the authors' interpolation of anthropological and zoological data. The authors admitted that information on human as well as mammalian sexuality was often hard to obtain and "disappointingly incomplete" (Ford and Beach 1951:16). It could therefore be said that they were all too aware of the shortcomings of their research project.

Among the topics examined in the book are the physiology of sex, techniques of coitus, duration and frequency of intercourse, foreplay and stimulation (including grooming, delousing, kissing, genital stimulation, and stimulation through biting and scratching), rules and regularities concerning the time and place of coitus, standards of sexual attractiveness and behaviors designed to attract a mate, forms of heterosexual partnership, masturbation, homosexuality, intercourse with other species, sexual maturation and the life cycle, and feminine fertility cycles. Because of the authors' programmatic alternation of data from comparative anthropology and comparative zoology, *Patterns of Sexual Behavior* has a certain flavor or piquancy that may strike some modern social anthropologists as amusing and slightly inappropriate, although this may merely reflect our profession's acquired aversion to any biological reduction of social behavior. Thus we find on page 56 a statement that "Choroti women spit in their lover's face during coitus, and the Apinaye woman may bite off bits of her partner's eyebrows" and shortly thereafter ascertain that "the normal pattern of the mink, marten and sable begins when the male springs on the female and seizes the skin of her neck in his mouth" (Ford and Beach 1951:59). The discussion of "Relations between Different Species" is enhanced by R. M. Yerkes's account of his experience of a sexual approach from a female gorilla (Ford and Beach 1951:148, 149).

Although the authors state that in most societies etiquette dictates that the male should make the first sexual advance, the ethnographic record exhibits some cases where the contrary is the case (Ford and Beach 1951:102). In the course of their examination of premarital sex the authors categorize societies as "restrictive," "semi-restrictive," and "permissive" with respect to behaviors permitted to each sex (Ford and Beach 1951:178–192). There are roughly as many societies in their "permissive" as in their "restrictive" category (approximately 30 in each case). Ford and Beach cite evidence that there are societies that encourage childhood sexuality. The Chewa believe that children who do not practice sexual behavior "will never beget off-spring" (Ford and Beach 1951:190). The authors repeat Gorer's assertion that the Lepcha believe that girls will not mature without sexual intercourse and that, accordingly, girls of 11 and 12 frequently engage in coitus (Ford and Beach 1951:191).

Comparative zoological data indicated that masturbation to orgasm and same-sex coupling, more commonly between males than between females, were found in several mammalian species. They were not, therefore, "un-natural." The ethnographic record indicated that societies listed by the Human Relations Area Files varied in their attitudes toward masturbation by children and adolescents. Attitudes toward homosexuality exhibited considerable variance. Ford and Beach listed 76 societies for which information was available. In 28 out of the 76 groups homosexual behavior was absent, prohibited, or carried out in secret (Ford and Beach 1951:129). However, in 49 groups in the sample "homosexual activities of one sort or another are considered normal and acceptable for certain members of the community" (Ford and Beach 1951:130). The Tswana accounted for the apparent numerical discrepancy because they allowed homoerotic behavior between females only. The authors concluded that there was a "basic mammalian capacity" for same-sex behavior, although in human societies there is much variation in the degree to which that capacity is expressed (Ford and Beach 1951:143). [12] Though now this seems like a middle-of-the-road position, between innatism and cultural determinism, it did, like the Kinsey Report itself, contribute to making homosexual behavior both more visible and more acceptable within the culture of its time.

Human Sexual Behavior: Variations in the Ethnographic Spectrum, edited by Donald Marshall and Robert Suggs, was published as part of a series, Studies in Sex and Society, sponsored by the Kinsey Institute. Both editors had done extensive fieldwork in Polynesia. Marshall had also worked in Southeast Asia. In 1971, when *Human Sexual Behavior* was published, he was "a member of the International Security Affairs staff in the Office of Secretary of Defense" (Marshall and Suggs 1971:vii). Marshall was best known for his work in the Cook Islands (Ra'ivavae and Mangaia). Suggs, who has been employed both in the academy and in the service of the U.S. government (Marshall and Suggs 1971:ix), is both an archaeologist and a cultural anthropologist. His publications include *Marquesan Sexual Behavior* (1966) and a well-known piece of popular anthropology, *The Island Civilizations of Polynesia* (1960).

With the exception of Alan Merriam's contribution, all the chapters in *Human Sexual Behavior* were based on papers originally submitted to the 1961 conference of the American Anthropological Association and the 1965 meeting of the Central States Anthropological Society. Not all the conference papers were included. The contribution of William Masters was presumably part of *Human Sexual Response* (Masters and Johnson 1966), and Mead's paper on "Incest" appeared as an article in the *International Encyclopedia of the Social Sciences* (1968b). The omission of Mead's paper was significant. All of the authors who contributed to *Human Sexual Behavior* were male, although one author, John Messenger, was accompanied and assisted by his wife. Several of the papers clearly reflect a masculine bias. Despite the volume's imprimatur and the inclusion of a piece by Paul Gebhard, the Kinsey Institute's president, that updated and summarized cross-cultural findings concerning sexuality, *Human Sexual Behavior* is a markedly more conservative collection than either the Kinsey Report or the volume by Ford and Beach. Two articles (by Messenger and by Milton Altschuler) adhere to the uninspiring ethnographic tradition of mother blaming, and the epilogue by Suggs and Marshall is marked by a pronounced homophobia. Indeed, insofar as the essays have a common focus it is the perceived threat to male identity, which, we have noted, has been a recurrent theme in the social science literature since the First Wave of feminism.

Messenger's account of "Inis Beag" is probably the best-known piece in the Marshall and Suggs collection. Messenger described a bleak community off the Irish coast where people did not remove their underclothes during their infrequent performances of sexual intercourse and where shame and anxiety surrounded most bodily processes (1971:16–19). The breast-feeding of infants was rare because of "its sexual connotations" (Messenger 1971:29). Women, who were particularly restricted in their life chances and were even more prudish than their menfolk, exercised a central role in household affairs and day-to-day authority over their children. Although Inis Beag could hardly be described as a feminist Utopia, Messenger nonetheless attributed male sexual anxiety, in part, to excessive female power, which, he thought, might have been the result of a weakening of the male role in response to economically straitened circumstances. In the family constellation the father was a shadowy figure, and women took control. In consequence, males suffered from sexual anxiety and inadequacy, hostility toward women, latent homosexuality, and other "distortions" of personality (Messenger 1971:25, 26).

Male anxiety and mother domination were also supposed features of Cayapa life in lowland Colombia and Ecuador. In the second chapter of *Human Sexual Behavior* Altschuler discussed the severe trauma caused by the denial of the mother's breast as a reinforcement mechanism for harsh toilet training. Applying established concepts of neo-Freudian "childhood determinism," Altschuler declared that an oral fixation resulted from the trauma. Such a fixation is said to cause sexual anxiety and alcoholism, vagina dentata stories, and latent homosexuality, especially in men.

In a chapter on the Basongye of Kasai the ethnomusicologist Alan Merriam contributed some observations on berdache figures called *kiteshas* (1971:93–98). This is one of the few moderately detailed descriptions of such an institution in a central Bantu society, although there are isolated reports going back to the 16th and 17th centuries (Bleys 1995:33). Among biologically male kiteshas, there are both "male" and "female" types. Merriam tells us that kiteshas don't like work, wiggle their hips, wear women's clothing, and play a kind of thumb piano. Musicians as a category are said to be sexually anomalous. There are also biologically female kiteshas who primarily associate with other women. One of Merriam's informants was a male kitesha married to a woman. This informant denied that kiteshas performed homosexual acts. Other accounts asserted the opposite. Merriam does not offer much theoretical interpretation of his data or any moral or psychological assessments of homosexuality per se.

Harold K. Schneider's essay on romantic love among the Turu is a discussion of *mbuya*, a relationship between adult men and women outside the bonds of marriage. Romantic love did indeed exist among this patrilineal Tanzanian people, but it was rare in arranged marriages. The Turu practice both circumcision and clitoridectomy. Schneider claims that clitoridectomy does not seem greatly to diminish the Turu woman's sexual pleasure and capacity for orgasm (1971:62 n. 2). He learned this from his male informants.

The most controversial chapters in *Human Sexual Behavior* were written by the two editors, Marshall and Suggs. We have already mentioned the scathing critique by Suggs of the Linton–Kardiner account of the Marquesas. However, if Marquesan sexuality is a matter of contention, so too is Marshall's exposition of sexuality in the Cook Islands.

Marshall's first foray into the topic was his book about Ra'ivavae, *Island of Passion* (1962). Harry Shapiro had drawn Marshall's attention to some rather sensational accounts of sexuality in pagan Ra'ivavae that had been written by J. Frank Stimson. Marshall mounted an expedition to the small island in order to ascertain the veracity of Stimson's stories about phallic cults and ritual copulation between warriors and maidens and occasional sodomy during ceremonies on the temple grounds, or *marae*, that preceded the commencement of battle. In order to excavate evidence of phallic sculpture and the like Marshall undertook an exhaustive exploration of the mountainous island. He became obsessed with stories of the bygone practice of clitoral elongation, something that has been reported of other Polynesian islands. His assistant refused to accompany him on any "clitoris-hunting" expedition. On the very last day of his trip, Marshall became acquainted with an old woman who said that her great-grandmother had possessed the sort of organ Marshall had in mind. Certainly, Marshall's image of an orgiastic past consoled him when he contemplated the relative boredom of quotidian existence among the contemporary Christian inhabitants of the "island of passion." In a scathing review Derek Freeman (1964) condemned Marshall for producing a lurid account for a popular audience based on fragments of information. The real question for study was why there was a market for such books.

In his chapter in *Human Sexual Behavior* Marshall described sexuality in Mangaia, which is not far from Ra'ivavae. In Mangaia young men were said to have 21 orgasms a week (1971:123), but there was no such thing as "love" in the European sense: to say "I love you" in English to another person was tantamount to saying "I want to copulate with you" (1971:157). In addition to participant observation Marshall elicited information about sexuality through discussions of the topic with "work groups," a methodology similar to the focus groups now commonly used in various forms of social research. Marshall's all-male work group on sexuality met weekly and included teachers, a planter, a pastor, and "others." Each session began with a prayer and included the sharing, by Marshall, of general biological information as well as information about American sexual customs (1971:106).

In some ways Marshall's account resembles those of sexuality in many Polynesian societies. There was a great deal of sexual segregation in everyday life. Couples could not embrace in public. It was improper for strange men, including Marshall, to talk about sex in front of Mangaian women. The custom of *motoro*, or sleep crawling, was a desirable way of attracting a mate, provided the girl's parents approved of these secret visitations. Although marriage was theoretically arranged, in most cases the consent of both parties was a determining factor. Though information such as this is unremarkable, much of what Marshall said about Mangaia conveyed the impression of a society that was absolutely obsessed with genitalia and heterosexual intercourse. Sex was said to be a constant topic of conversation; even the pastor told dirty jokes. After the supercision operation the initiate was offered sexual intercourse by an older woman. A period of premarital sexual freedom followed. The Mangaians were said to be less concerned with a potential partner's secondary sexual characteristics than with the size and shape of the genitals, for which an elaborate lexicon existed. Marshall says that there was "no trace whatsoever of the active practice of homosexuality or of homosexual relations" (1971:161), although there were men who liked cooking, the company of women, and cutting out clothes for women to sew. Some of these incipient berdaches were effeminate. These individuals did not suffer from any social disapproval.

It is possible that much of this information is true, although we have learned to be skeptical of complete denials of homosexual practices in any locale. With regard to the reports of orgasmic frequency alluded to above, the veracity of which cannot be checked, Helen Harris is right when she states that "the effect of this report has been to confer almost legendary status on Mangaians, distinguishing them as the most sexually motivated people in the world" (1995:96). Harris, who visited Mangaia many years after Marshall, offers statements by many informants as evidence that the Mangaians experience love, contrary to Marshall's assertions.

The sensibility of Donald Marshall's writing is ostensibly "sex-positive" but, in fact, very conservative about expressions of sexuality other than male-centered heterosexual practices. These attitudes are clearly expressed both in his essay on Mangaia and in the epilogue to the book, which he co-wrote with Suggs. Marshall believed that the incidence of homosexuality was not constant in human societies. Inasmuch as Mangaians tolerated minor manifestations of transvestism and effeminacy, they may have prevented the emergence of "confirmed homosexuals" (Marshall 1971:161). Here, Marshall and Suggs employ the trope of "tolerance" as inoculation against the disease of homosexuality. Marshall and Suggs felt that homosexuality was indeed a form of mental illness: "Just as the homosexual advertisements in the *Berkeley Barb* appear with those of the voyeur, the sadist, the masochist, and the fetishist, so is it difficult to interpret such behavioral manifestations as the 'fairy balls' or the transvestite 'beauty contests' of some urban areas as anything more exalted than sociopathic manifestations of personality disturbances *complicated by membership in a pervasive subculture*" (Suggs and Marshall 1971a:235).

Marshall and Suggs had already noted that the "variant subculture" had spread to the military, where homosexual social groups, or "hominterns," had formed. Homosexual officers and senior noncommissioned officers sometimes recruited more of their kind to form homosexual "rings" (Suggs and Marshall 1971a:234). In their view nothing less than the survival of society itself was at stake if homosexuality was allowed to make further inroads: "Social approval of active homosexuality is tantamount to declaring that society has no interest in, or obligation to make well, the sociopsychologically deviant so as to prevent a disturbing behavior pattern from spreading in its midst – or that the society is not concerned with its own survival!" (Suggs and Marshall 1971a:236). Elsewhere in their epilogue Suggs and Marshall condemn the "puritanical approach of anthropology to human sexuality" (1971a:221) as manifested in the unwillingness of anthropologists to publish field data on human sexuality in Polynesia. One person's freedom is another's Puritanism, and discourses that "liberate" in one respect demarcate and control in others. For Marshall and Suggs, heterosexual liberation in America would surely involve better sex education, but nothing as radical as "trial marriage," as had been advocated by Havelock Ellis, Elsie Clews Parsons, Judge Ben Lindsey, Bronislaw Malinowski, and Bertrand Russell some four or five decades earlier: "Although the institution of trial marriage, or formal premarital experimentation, could increase the probability of marital success *if sex were the major dimension of marriage*, the fact remains that sex is *not* the major dimension. Such a simplistic view, in addition to neglecting the psychological impact of sexual intercourse, overlooks the fact that the marital relationship is neither exclusively nor mainly sexual, nor is it solely interpersonal (between the two partners); *all society is involved*" (Suggs and Marshall 1971a:239).

The epilogue by Suggs and Marshall was presumably conceived a few years after the drafting of the other chapters in *Human Sexual Behavior*. The intervening years had seen the birth of the "permissive" society, the antiwar movement in the United States, the hippies, the first glimmers of gay liberation (e.g., Stonewall in 1969), and the Second Wave of feminism. Historians and cultural commentators may still dispute how "real" these changes were, but our analysis leaves little doubt that Marshall and Suggs did not like what they saw. Their writing marks the end of the period many perceive as "the silence" in the anthropology of sexuality.

Our scrutiny of the literature has shown that in some ways there was no silence at all. The Kinsey volumes appeared in 1948 and 1953. In anthropology there was hardly a lack of explicit detail about sexual practices (particularly heterosexual practices) in non-Western societies, although one sometimes has to search for it. Nonetheless, certain topics (e.g., homosexuality and female heterosexual emotion) were rarely discussed, and some theoretical statements exhibit elements of concealment (e.g., those of Benedict). The project envisioned by Firth, of an "objective" and "analytical" account of sexuality, had not transpired. It is doubtful it was ever possible. Much that was said about the anthropology of sex between 1935 and 1970 was swiftly forgotten. In a period of professionalization the central theoretical developments of the discipline were taking place well away from discussions of sexual behavior. The sexuality of the periphery continued to be conscripted to serve metropolitan social agendas, ranging from mother blaming to homophobia to pleas for liberation grounded in the romanticization of primitive sexual idylls. People in remote places who never sought psychoanalytic attention became evidence for Freudian, neo-Freudian, and anti-Freudian positions. There is some continuity in the use of tropes from an earlier period. The "oversexed savage" returns in extravagant descriptions of the variety and frequency of the sexual exploits of primitives. A new image, arguably a transformation of the "undersexed savage," namely, the "sexually sick savage," appears in the anthropology of an American society in which sexuality has become the focus of medical attention as well as continuing moral concern. In the British Empire a few anthropologists continue to offer cautionary advice about the disruptive effects of externally induced change on the misunderstood moralities of subject populations. Their writing attracted much less popular and official attention than that of their American contemporaries.[13]

Within a year or two of the publication of *Human Sexual Behavior*, the voices of those who had been silent, including some of the voices of those Suggs and Marshall pretended to "tolerate," combined to produce a new anthropology of sexuality. Most saliently, by the end of the 20th century, issues raised by the study of sexuality had become part of theoretical endeavors at the core of the discipline.

CHAPTER 9

Sex in Contemporary Anthropology

S ince the 1970s sexuality has reemerged as a focus of anthropological theorizing, leading to the widespread perception that anthropology has, in fact, "rediscovered sex." In anthropology, as in the wider intellectual culture, the notion of "sex," along with the related category "gender," has been subject to scrutiny and redefinition. "Commonsense" definitions of "man," "woman," "homosexual," and "heterosexual" have been contested and reformulated within and outside of anthropology. The social context of this revived theoretical focus has included much flux and debate with regard to sexual mores as well as a renegotiation of the relationship both between men and women and between the peoples who in other times were called "primitive" and "civilized." Anthropology itself has undergone considerable dislocation as a result of these debates, much of it reflected in recent formulations about sex and gender.

Although at least a formal adherence to the precepts of relativism has characterized contemporary anthropological discussion of sex, gender, and sexuality, variants of many of the stances we have described earlier may be discerned within current debates. There are echoes of specific discussions of bygone eras. There remains a tension between a simple desire to set the "record" straight by including fresh data on human sexual behavior and sexual meanings and the continued conscription of constructions of others' lives in the service of Western political and academic agendas. It is perhaps impossible to divorce them. Such agendas include those of feminists and their opponents, different wings within the feminist movement, proponents of emergent "gay" understandings of sexuality, sociobiology and its constructionist opponents, Freudians and anti-Freudians, heterosexual libertarians and conservatives, defenders of extreme relativism who are opposed by universalists, and, at the outer fringes of anthropology, those who wish to revisit old debates about the relationship between race, sex, and intelligence. In recent years ethnographers have often turned their attention away from the sexuality of "primitive Others" to participant observation in sexual subcultures in Western societies. Indeed, the nature and degree of ethnographers' participation in near and distant sexual fields, once a subject of silence and gossip, has become a focus of discussion and examination.

The notion that human sexuality is primarily a social construct appeared for a while to be on its way to dominance in contemporary cultural anthropology. Feminist anthropologists and "queer theorists" have sometimes fostered this position and sometimes argued against it. Recently, there has been something of a revival of interest in "essentialist" interpretations of human sexuality, a project akin to Ellis's search for "the real, natural facts" about sex. Although some scholars working in this vein take the familiar heterosexual couple, with a dominant male, as the "normal" outcome of human evolution, by no means all do so. Indeed, one current line of argument suggests that the widespread recognition of "third genders" may indicate that such social categories and sexual variation in general have a natural basis. A minor revival (mostly outside anthropology) of theories that link sexual to racial determinism has made many suspicious of the naturalist trend, but naturalism continues to appeal to those who would defend anthropology's position as a "scientific" discipline. Whether they argue for essentialism or constructionism, for the constraint of facts or the positional nature of "truth," contemporary anthropologists continue, in significant ways, to construct the sexuality of the "Other" in images that mirror contemporary debates.

Present discourse on the anthropology of sex also includes topics that might be recognized as descendants of "applied anthropology," as Malinowski envisaged it. Ritual alteration of the sexual organs was the subject of an attempt by Malinowski to reconcile reform with cultural sensitivity. Debate on this topic continues, but issues of health and female empowerment are more likely to provide the stimulus for discussion than the theological considerations that engaged Malinowski's audience at High Leigh.

While the issue of sexually transmitted diseases informed important debates in the history of European and North American sexuality, it was not an issue that anthropologists tended to examine in field situations. The prevalence of AIDS among some populations traditionally studied by anthropologists as well as among gay men in the West has made that disease an important focus of medical anthropology. Medical anthropology is a field rife with issues of power, knowledge, and relativism, all of which must be balanced against a deceptively simple concern to promote human health.

Inevitably, the epidemiology of AIDS brings all these issues to center stage, as they are in most contemporary discussions of sexuality.

The mention of power and knowledge obviously brings Foucault into the conversation. Foucault inspires us in this chapter, as elsewhere, though we remain mindful of the issues of relativism that must be addressed when applying Foucault in a cross-cultural context. Nonetheless, it is impossible to discuss any contemporary sexual discourse without reference to Foucault's identification of sex as an important transfer point of power. In this chapter readers will find evidence of Foucault's influence on the anthropology of sex as well as markers of limits to that influence.

SEX: GOOD TO THINK WITH?

Transitions are best viewed in hindsight; it is only from that vantage point that they are clearly visible. In retrospect, certain key works of the late 1960s and early 1970s invited sex into the house of theory, though it entered through a back door. Although French and British structuralist anthropology was little concerned with the question, how do people do sex? its practitioners were frequently willing to consider, as a serious subject for anthropological inquiry, the related issue, how do cultures think about sex? Victor Turner, who favored a processual, experiential approach over the formalism of his British and French contemporaries, considered bodily experience to be an important dimension of symbolic meaning, although he rarely discussed sexual acts. Later on, through a process that was highly overdetermined, the generation of anthropologists who emerged in the 1980s and 1990s linked questions of sexual meanings to questions of sexual practice, which demanded embodied and experiential answers. In the postmodern, poststructuralist world, however, the question of interpretation is rarely ignored, even by the most "naturalist" of writers. What is meant by "body" and "experience" has itself become a matter of controversy, and there is not always agreement on where sex is to be found. Some anthropologists have argued that their colleagues have been too ready to find "sex" in situations whose sexual aspects may be more significant for the ethnographer than the participants. The emergence of sexuality as a "hot topic" in anthropological theory has not eradicated a lingering uneasiness that the reputation of anthropologists or their subjects will be compromised by discussions of sexuality not subordinated to some "larger" or "higher" concern. For all of these reasons, "sex" and "symbol" have remained intricately linked in recent anthropological considerations of sexuality.

Although structural anthropology has been widely criticized as an apolitical movement, structuralism did encompass a political agenda, particularly in its analyses of myth and totemism, specifically to prove that primitives could think rationally. Claude Lévi-Strauss, after all, participated, along with Ashley Montagu and E. Franklin Frazier, in a UNESCO symposium to address issues of racism and published *Race et histoire* (1958) under UNESCO auspices. This is significant to us because the trope of the oversexed savage, which survives in the work of J. Philippe Rushton and in the collective representations of much of popular culture, includes a deficiency of intellect along with libidinal superfluity. Donna Haraway has remarked tellingly that despite pious statements about the need for a *simultaneous* critique of race, sex, class, and gender, successful integration of these concepts has proved elusive in practice (1991:146–148). Certainly, Lévi-Strauss did not attempt such integration. Indeed, later in this chapter we will quote some startlingly condescending remarks about homosexuals in *Tristes tropiques,* published in 1955. What he did accomplish, for better or worse, was a disarming, at the level of theory, of the trope of the oversexed, irrational savage. Although Lévi-Strauss did not comment specifically about the role played by sex in the devaluing of primitive intellects, his reassessment of primitive thought involved a systematic desexualization of ethnographic problems, notably totemism and the origin of the incest taboo, that had been approached in ways that inextricably linked sexual excess with intellectual lack. John Borneman, in a general critique of the desexualization of kinship studies, notes that sexuality was, at most, a topic of "secondary concern" to structuralists (1996:221), but he does not link this observation to a consideration of the purposes that such a deemphasis on sex might have served.

Although evolutionary theorists had differed as to how and why the incest taboo was instituted, their theories converged in the assumption that this taboo marked both the beginning of a long process of mental improvement and a major check on unrestricted sexuality. Theories about totemism had been linked to theories of group marriage and often to ideas about ignorance of the nature of conception (see our discussion in chapters 3 and 4). Sharing a common totem and a common pool of marriageable women had, though the specifics of particular arguments varied, been widely assumed to be synonymous with extensive sexual access and consequent confusion (or denial) of the facts of conception. If sexual excess made it impossible to know for sure who one's father was, that father might well be an eagle or a frog. If one had recently stolen one's own mother, as Freud thought humans on the verge of culture had done, it might be comforting to pretend that

Dad was really a kangaroo. Such ideas about totemism and the incest taboo depended upon highly sexualized assumptions about the origin of culture. In Lévi-Strauss's *Totemism* (1962) the presumed link between animal ancestors and human descendants was displaced from its position at the center of an anthropological conundrum. Totemic relationships, as Lévi-Strauss refigured them, were not about exotic theories of conception; instead, they were part of elaborate classificatory systems in which a series of species and a series of human clans each defined the other and imparted order to the natural world.

In *The Elementary Structures of Kinship* (1949) Lévi-Strauss deeroticizes the whole issue of incest by virtually dropping women from the discussion except as objects of men's exchanges among themselves. Rather than seeing the incest taboo as an innate or behaviorally acquired mechanism for defusing erotic tension within the family, Lévi-Strauss focuses on the practical benefits of men giving away their sisters and daughters. Women as objects of desire became almost incidental benefits in the quest for brothers-in-law, who might help a man in the serious business of life. As Gayle Rubin rightly noted in her influential essay "The Traffic in Women" (1975), women disappeared from Lévi-Strauss's view altogether as potential *subjects* of desire or as social actors in their own right. Women's loss of agency in Lévi-Strauss's story of the origin of the incest taboo was a casualty of the gains in rationality and continence made by primitive men and, perhaps by implication, primitive women as well. The project to which Haraway alludes, rewriting the texts of race and sex and gender simultaneously, was not on Lévi-Strauss's agenda. Sex was not erased from structuralism, of course; like written-over text on a palimpsest, it simply changed position. No longer the sole obsession of primordial man or a dirty secret hidden away in the unconscious of civilized ones, sex, like food, had become something to "think with."

Sex, for Lévi-Strauss, was a particularly powerful medium for making symbolic statements because it lay at the juncture between the bodily and the social, as, in its own way, did the preparation and consumption of food. Sex was a signifier; for Freud (and Freudian anthropologists) it was the ultimate signified. As a signifier sex had a place in structuralist texts: in myth, in art, in the rules of kinship. Moreover, despite Rubin's critique, the structuralist turn in anthropology deserves a considerable portion of the credit for calling attention to the arbitrariness of gender categories, insofar as it focused attention on the arbitrariness of categories in general.

In terms of its overt argument Edmund Leach's essay "Virgin Birth" (1966) would appear to be an extreme case of the dissolution of the sexual in the cerebral. Leach proposes that the debate that followed Malinowski's assertion that Trobriand belief in impregnation by spirit children demonstrated ignorance of the human male's contribution to conception was best settled by reframing the question. Instead of asking whether the Trobrianders knew where babies came from, Leach argued, we would do better to assume that all collective representations of sex and reproduction are essentially cosmologies. As cosmologies, they might be expected to reflect on some planes empirical observation, on others social structure, and, overall, to meet a need for order and consistency in the world. Such world pictures reflect neither "knowledge" nor "ignorance" but social constraints on what is knowable. Leach implicitly criticizes Malinowski for singling out Trobriand "ignorance" in a world in which few individuals of any culture think about conception without the obfuscation of religious dogma. Ironically, Leach's framing of the question was a logical development from the approach used by his erstwhile teacher. Malinowski, after all, sought to explain Trobriand "ignorance" in terms of the matrilineal social structure and its associated eschatology.

For academic audiences in the 1960s an irrational primitive posed a greater challenge to relativism than a licentious one, and it was in these terms that Trobrianders' "ignorance" made them and all primitives candidates for rehabilitation. Leach made a valiant try at such reputational reconstitution. In good Durkheimian fashion he argued that all religions were rational, insofar as they modeled social reality, and irrational, insofar as they were at odds with scientific fact. As we noted in an earlier chapter, in "Virgin Birth" Leach also takes a step toward the analysis of links between anthropological theories about sex and their social contexts when he links notions of primitive promiscuity and archaic matriarchy to the Victorian milieu (1966:42). Indeed, a main theme of "Virgin Birth" is the puzzling willingness of anthropologists to believe in the oddity of primitive sexuality. This book was, in part, inspired by Leach's example.

Some years before "Virgin Birth" Leach had published an article entitled "Magical Hair" (1958) in which he suggested that widespread, if not universal, patterns in the symbolism of hair and hairdressing were evidence of some underlying psychosexual universals. He argued that a Freudian equation between hair and genitalia might indeed be expressed in many symbolic systems. He took issue, however, with the psychoanalytic assumption that such symbolism rarely emerged at a conscious level and with the allied assumption that once one had discovered phallic symbolism in collective representations the task of decoding was complete. Although both "Magical Hair" and "Virgin Birth" instigated lengthy debates, in which Leach was accused by Christopher Hallpike (1969) of being unnecessarily Freudian and by Melford Spiro (1968, 1979) of not being Freudian enough, Leach had forced anthropologists more comfortable with symbols and social structure to consider sex as well as to examine the origins and nature of their own thoughts on the subject.[1] Such projects are now a significant focus of study, encompassing recognizable tropes, traditions, and points of disagreement. One such point of argument is whether human sexuality can meaningfully be said to exist in isolation from the symbols through which we encounter it.

Robert I. Levy's *Tahitians: Mind and Experience in the Society Islands* (1973) is a remarkable work that sets out to apply psychoanalytic methodology to an ethnographic study without describing its subjects in terms of Western disease categories. In some ways the book bridges a gap between the period we discussed in the last chapter and the types of analyses we discuss in this one. "Mind," as it is discussed in this book, encompasses both emotion (conscious and unconscious) and cognition. Psychodynamic interviews, archival research, and inquiries into both traditional and Tahitian Christian cosmologies are among the sources of the data presented. Sexuality is one of the many aspects of Tahitian experience that Levy discusses. This discussion is exceptionally rich, largely because of the wealth of data Levy furnishes. These data include the images of Tahitian eroticism that have been instilled in the European consciousness since the 18th century. Levy describes childhood sexuality, the *taure'are'a* period of premarital sexual freedom, the establishment of marital relationships and attitudes toward adultery, as well as the beliefs and practices surrounding the *māhū*, the local mode of institutionalized transgendered identity. Although some interviews were done in urban neighborhoods, for the most part *Tahitians* describes conditions as they existed in a rural village in the early 1960s and during the lifetimes of the preceding generation.

What is particularly interesting about this volume (perhaps a product of the author's version of the psychoanalytic method) is that Levy pays close attention to how his informants talk – about their bodies, their beliefs, their satisfactions and dissatisfactions. Prevailing opinions as well as disagreements and contradictions are duly noted, as are apparent discrepancies between informants' reports and likely behavior. With regard to sexuality, where such slippages are undoubtedly common in most, if not all, societies, this type of reporting is particularly important and seen surprisingly rarely.

Levy's discussion of masturbation is an example of the sort of layered, textured account that his methodology produced. Levy's informants tended to report very little of it, and that in early childhood. On the other hand, one taure'are'a was cynical about older men who denied masturbating as adolescents: "There were people in those days who had intercourse with horses" (Levy 1973:116). Levy suggests that actual sexual opportunities, particularly for a taure'are'a, might have declined in the years immediately prior to his study, leading to the discrepant report. Whatever the reality, the discussion of masturbation is an illustration of the way in which Levy's methodology lays a foundation for a processual and interpretive account of sexuality, in contrast to the generalizing pictures usually presented by earlier ethnography.

Like many writers on Polynesia, Levy describes a world where deep affect is discouraged, in sexuality as in other areas of life, though Levy describes an avoidance of deep emotion more than an absence of it. Adultery, for example, was disapproved of mainly because of the anger and recrimination likely to result (Levy 1973:330–331).

Levy remarks in a number of contexts on a tendency of Tahitians to distance themselves from unpleasant feelings. The language of sexuality seemed to shield people from experiencing a sense of internalized failure. People spoke to Levy of "a fit" between the bodies of couples who got along well and who had settled into a long-term relationship, with an implied "misfit" rather than any personal defect afflicting those who didn't (1973:192). Instead of talking about an inability to achieve an erection, Levy's informants said that they sometimes discovered that they didn't really want intercourse at all (1973:129, 224).

The portrait Levy presents of the māhū foreshadows conceptions of sexual identity that we shall discuss later in this chapter, insofar as gender, biological sex, sexual desire, and sexual behavior are seen as separable and variable components of a life history rather than as part of a comprehensive and fixed identity. The māhū, as Levy described them, were biological males who, in the past and occasionally in the present, dressed as women and who, at the time of his study, still performed women's work. As is common in the case of such institutions worldwide, māhū were viewed as destined for this role. According to Levy, it was believed that one person in each village was supernaturally called to occupy the māhū role, though this was not always the precise reality (1973:132, 472). The role could be given up if the person no longer felt called to it (Levy 1973:133). Some informants said that māhū did not necessarily engage in sexual activities with other men, an aspect of their presumed role that had attracted much comment from foreign observers. Others said that all māhū performed fellatio on other men, who said they went to the māhū either for variety or because no woman was available at the time. Levy reports that only a minority of his male informants reported engaging in sex with māhū, and those only a few times (1973:139). Such men did not have their sexual or gender status altered in any way. Men said that sex with the māhū was equivalent to sex with a woman, though some said the sensation was stronger (Levy 1973:134–135).

Tahitian attitudes toward the māhū were described as somewhat mixed, even contradictory (Levy 1973:139). Divergent attitudes reported by Levy include acceptance of the māhū role as "natural," repugnance for fellatio, but not the assumption of female dress and occupations and, conversely, an acceptance of māhū sexual practices but not of men doing housework (1973:138–139). The māhū figure, Levy suggested, may have acted as a boundary marker to avoid a totally permeable border between male and female sexual identities in a society where gender roles were not sharply defined. Men, he proposed, knew they were men because they were "not māhū" (Levy 1973:471–473). It is not entirely clear whether Levy viewed this situation as a structuralist or a psychoanalyst. The former would see in this situation a reinforcement of arbitrary conceptual categories. The latter would see an inherent need to bolster male identity, a more essentialist interpretation consistent with Levy's claim that Tahitian women were more secure in their sexual identity than males and that it was considered improper to apply the term *māhū* to "female homosexuals." Levy denied hearing reports of homosexual behavior among women in Piri, though incidents of it were said to be frequent in Papeete (1973:141).[2]

The volume *Sexual Meanings: The Cultural Construction of Gender and Sexuality*, edited by Sherry Ortner and Harriet Whitehead and published eight years after *Tahitians*, can fairly be said to be a benchmark work in what Carole Vance (1991) called the "rediscovery" of sex by anthropologists. The editors understood "sex" "in the double English sense," as encompassing both gender and the erotic, and maintained that sex could be treated as "a symbol, or system of symbols, invested with culturally variable meanings" (Ortner and Whitehead 1981:ix). They claimed that a symbolic approach could "liberate" the study of gender and the erotic from "constraining naturalistic assumptions" but that a symbolic analysis of sex, incorporating gender, might offer correctives for a propensity of structuralists to view women primarily as objects for men's games of symbol making and ceremonial exchange. Using the phrase current among feminists at the time, they argued that the study of sexual meanings had the potential to link the analysis of "the personal and the political." The essentially political nature of the study of gender and the impossibility of avoiding consideration of individual experience when studying the erotic would, in their opinion, avoid the pitfalls of excessive relativism and extreme social determinism (Ortner and Whitehead 1981:ix).

In this statement of purpose Ortner and Whitehead position their undertaking in relation to a number of dialogues that were unfolding within anthropology at the time and that encompassed issues that were part of a much broader discussion. In 1981 the "sexual revolution" and the many changes brought about by the Second Wave of feminism of the 1960s and 1970s were still controversial. It was, however, also assumed that new cultural patterns were well on the way toward broad acceptance in North America and, to a slightly lesser degree, in England. At the time *Sexual Meanings* was actually being assembled (during the late 1970s), legal and social transformations affecting sexuality and the status of women were occurring at a rapid rate. In the days just before the AIDS epidemic, it appeared to many (at least to those who did not have to experience directly the enormous amount of homophobia that still prevailed) as if sexual freedom for homosexuals was a goal well on its way to accomplishment. Of course, such widely publicized events as the assassination of Harvey Milk in San Francisco and police raids on gay bathhouses in Toronto show how deep the resistance to societal acceptance really was. These developments informed the opinions of those who considered themselves au courant, both inside and outside the academy. The respectability that the Reagan–Thatcher era would give to conservative opinion on sex and gender as well as other issues was not foreseen. Women became more visible on university faculties to a greater degree than their actual increase in numbers. Some of them demanded curricula that reflected women's experience. The emerging field of women's studies explored the ways in which the newly problematized "gender system" enforced what the feminist poet Adrienne Rich (1980) labeled "compulsory heterosexuality" in an influential essay published in *Signs*, the first major academic journal devoted entirely to feminist scholarship. To some degree feminists, both gay and straight, were suspicious of the new sexual freedom, arguing that it privileged male, genitally focused response over female sexuality. The latter was said by many to be more somatically diffuse, more dependent on sentiment, and more concerned with mutual "nurturance" than the desires and behavior that male-dominated culture – now labeled "phallocentric" – had understood by "sex." Within the lesbian community, many believed that lesbian identity was characterized more by a "woman-centered" emotional economy than by sexual practice, and many women who had formerly considered themselves heterosexual were declaring themselves lesbian, at least in these terms.

Concurrently with these challenges to the culture of gender and sexuality, anthropology was "reinventing" itself, particularly with regard to its perceived relationship to the colonized and formerly colonized people usually studied by anthropologists (see, e.g., Asad 1973; Hymes 1972). In the early and mid-1970s there had been a lively debate, especially in the United States, between anthropologists who located culture in systems of symbols and those who felt it important to retain the traditional concern with evolutionary adaptation. Cultural anthropologists of the latter persuasion argued that attention to matters such as the relationship between ecology, hierarchy, and the rise of the state provided a better basis for a politically committed anthropology than did the study of symbolism. Studies of various types of "mental culture" were perceived by materialists as tautological at best, since they ignored the question of causality. At worst, they were seen as reifications of ideologies that sustained inequality, ideologies tolerated by liberal anthropologists under the banner of cultural relativism.

In the 1980s these concerns were, to some degree, subsumed by new developments in symbolic anthropology. Anthropologists began to consider systems of thought from the perspective of those placed at different social positions. It was recognized that the conventional practice of seeking information from those whom ethnographers perceived to be "authoritative" privileged the interpretations of male elders, especially those of high status. The connection between symbolic systems and the maintenance of hierarchy moved into the foreground as a focus of analysis. Moreover, anthropologists, like scholars in other disciplines, began to question the relationship between their own social placement and their understandings of the "data" they reported. In view of the cultural developments we have discussed above it is not surprising that sexuality and gender were among the first subjects to be interpreted in this way. Two of the earliest contributions to the literature on homosexual topics that university presses began to publish in the 1970s were anthropological monographs that began as doctoral dissertations. *The Lesbian Community*, published in 1979, was an ethnographic study of the lesbian feminist community in San Francisco by Deborah Wolf, a straight feminist. It was based on research for her doctoral dissertation at Berkeley. Esther Newton's University of Chicago dissertation on female impersonators was originally published in 1972 by Prentice-Hall as *Mother Camp: Fe-*

male Impersonators in America. It was reissued by the University of Chicago Press in 1979. Newton remarked in 1973 that most of her professors at the University of Chicago did not regard her topic as a legitimate field of study (Newton 2000c:106).

Sexual Meanings applied some of the emerging theoretical perspectives discussed above to the cross-cultural study of sexuality. In their introduction, subtitled "Accounting for Sexual Meanings," Ortner and Whitehead, members of Newton's cohort at Chicago, argue that understandings of gender relations as well as conceptions of "permitted," "forbidden," "natural," and "unnatural" sexual behaviors and desires are closely articulated with cultural "prestige systems." They assert that relations between these systems are not unidirectional. Prestige, gender, and eroticism interact in ways that provide more than mutual reinforcement. Their intersection makes the commonsense world of a culture appear an inevitable part of the order of things. The most abstract public values are inseparable from the most concrete individual experience. The connections between prestige, gender, and eroticism define nuances of motivation and performance mentally and practically accessible to actors at all levels of prestige. Since the prestige system is also imagined to be linked but not reducible to power and control over material production, Ortner and Whitehead are able to envision an analysis that is both profoundly political and unashamedly symbolic in its orientation. It is, perhaps, less explicitly concerned with eroticism than one might expect. In this regard, *Sexual Meanings* might be said to continue the tendency we have already noted to link a certain amount of desexualization to attempts to achieve a nonjudgmental understanding of the sexuality of non-Western cultures.

One of the most widely quoted essays in *Sexual Meanings* is Harriet Whitehead's article "The Bow and the Burden Strap: A New Look at Institutionalized Homosexuality in Native North America." In it she argues that those who have interpreted institutionalized homosexuality and transgender phenomena in terms of bodily desire or psychological predisposition are missing the point. In an argument reminiscent of remarks we have made in earlier chapters, she suggests that "a good many of the cross-cultural investigations have been, explicitly or implicitly, aimed at mustering support for one or another interpretation of 'our' homosexuality rather than at laying bare the meaning of 'theirs'" (1981:80).

Whitehead's own interpretation is dependent upon two assertions. She claims that "spontaneous" desire must be considered separately from institutionalized practice and that culturally prescribed acts are best understood in terms of the meanings assigned to them in their particular contexts (Whitehead 1981:80). Whitehead's consideration of the berdache tradition in North America is directed much more toward occupational specialization than to sexual behavior or even to cross-dressing, commonly said to be the central feature of this class of customs.[3] She argues that gender-crossing complexes in Native North America exist where a number of phenomena intersect: a tendency to define gender largely in terms of occupation; a need to recruit workers from within kinship groups, where the gender balance may be skewed; and relatively prestigious occupational niches to which cross-dressers may aspire. Since most cross-dressers are biological males, Whitehead pays particular attention to occupations associated by some groups with women (e.g., pottery making) or assigned specifically to transgender individuals (e.g., ceremonial performance). Ortner and Whitehead suggest that Whitehead's analysis demonstrates the articulation of sexuality, gender, kinship, and economics within the prestige system. The analysis of "sexuality" in "The Bow and the Burden Strap" relegates desire and sexual acts primarily to an introductory section. Whitehead notes that most people who have written on Native American "homosexuality" have been more concerned with Western conceptions of the topic than with those of Native American cultures (1981:80–84). The effect is to desensationalize a topic that had led to considerable pathologizing of Native Americans and, if Whitehead is right, to correct ethnographic error as well. However, as we shall see, the argument about the role of homoeroticism and sexual identity in berdache-type institutions is by no means closed.

Fitz-John Porter Poole's article on female ritual leaders in a New Guinea Highland society links gender malleability to the symbolic construction of both sexuality and social status. It also provides us with a detailed analysis of a model of the human body, whose sexual identity is perceived as multiple, not unified. Drawing upon a characteristic of New Guinea cosmologies that has attracted much interest in recent years, Poole notes that the Bimin–Kuskusmin view the body as a composite of male and female influences produced by the complementary effects of male and female fertilizing fluids, the latter of which, apart from polluting menstrual blood, are believed to be of male origin. The orientation of the fetus in the womb is believed to determine sexuality and to be subject to change at least until the beginning of labor. A central focus of Poole's analysis is the *waneng aiyem ser*, a ritual specialist who is physically a postmenopausal woman but whose symbolically ambiguous gender attributes are said by Poole to be "good to think" (1981:154). The waneng aiyem ser enjoys a high (if lonely) status in a society in which women are symbolically and socioeconomically at a disadvantage relative to men. It must be reiterated, however, that leaving aside the wa-neng aiyem ser, whose identity is particularly defined by gender ambiguity, females and males come in several different varieties in the society Poole describes. Initiated, uninitiated, virgin, and experienced statuses are socially and symbolically marked by different combinations of male and female fluids and tissues.

Fluids also figure in Stanley Brandes's account in *Sexual Meanings* of a sexual system far removed from the South Pacific, one that is characteris-tic of other oceans altogether: the Mediterranean and the Mediterranean-influenced Caribbean and South Atlantic. In "Like Wounded Stags: Male Sexual Ideology in an Andalusian Town" Brandes describes an ideology in which milk and semen are symbolic equivalents and women are seen as inadequate suppliers of the first and thieves of the second. Brandes recounts a folk belief that has it that a serpent, analogous to the one in the Garden of Eden, comes to women at night and inserts itself between the breast and the nursing baby, so that the serpent is sucking on the nipple and the baby on the serpent's tail. As breast milk is believed to be in short supply, the babies of mothers thus deceived slowly die, though they can nurse nor-mally during the day. In addition to linking the failure of women to pro-vide adequate nourishment to their role in the biblical Fall, men interpret the serpent sucking at the breast as equivalent to women draining men of semen during sexual intercourse. Men in Andalusia and throughout both the Christian and Islamic Mediterranean are said to share an ideology in which the site of male power lies in the genitals, and its potential loss is a subject of high anxiety. Women are both feared for their power to rob men of their masculinity, particularly through cuckolding them, and kept under strict control lest that power be realized. Anal penetration is viewed as the epitome of feminization, dreaded by males, to the degree that men refuse medical suppositories, a common way to administer medication in Spain. (In an ironic comment on this assertion Stephen O. Murray noted that one might wonder how a practice could remain "common" if half the population refused to participate in it [personal communication, 2002].)

The receptive position in anal intercourse is the extreme signifier of male feminizing and dishonoring. Few men would go so far as to accuse each other in person of preferring it, though some men may do so in conversa-tions with third parties. By contrast, a reference to performing the inserter role is a boast of masculine power. Brandes discusses these possibilities mainly as elements of verbal culture rather than as actual behavior, but the associated attitudes, as he reports them, are typical of sentiments surrounding actual anal penetration in many sexual cultures, ancient and modern, in the Mediterranean and the Mediterranean diaspora. Many writers on sexual cultures in these regions have stressed that "normal" and "homosexual" male sexualities are determined not by the sex of one's partner but by the acts performed and the positions assumed or sometimes by fictions about who may penetrate and who is penetrated (see Lancaster 1995; Parker 1991; Carrier 1995; Kulick 1998; Murray 1995). This topic was to become an important theme in the emerging anthropology of homosexuality in the 1980s and 1990s.

Sexual Meanings contributed in other ways to what were to become important conversations in the anthropological literature. It provided some rich analyses of Polynesian sexuality, including that of Samoa, two years before Derek Freeman (1983) was to offer the challenge to Mead's classic account that we have discussed in connection with Mead's work. Unlike both Mead and Freeman, Bradd Shore and Sherry Ortner suggest that the important question concerning sexual permissiveness in Polynesia is not whether it exists but what permissiveness and restriction mean in their contexts. In her article Ortner highlights apparent contradictions in reports of Polynesian sexual mores. In particular, she points out that observations of great sexual freedom coincide with reports of a high premium placed on virginity among unmarried females. Rather than attribute this apparent discrepancy to faulty data, as Freeman does in his criticism of Mead, Ortner argues that both the virginity complex and the supposed premarital license are part of a complex ranking system in which consanguinity, marriage, and sexual connections all may act to increase or decrease prestige.

High-ranking families, Ortner asserts, use their daughters' and sisters' sexual attractiveness and virginity to lure the best-connected males into desirable marriages. High-ranking men assert both their masculinity and their power to influence others, both marks of rank, by sleeping with as many girls as possible, with virgins being especially desirable. Unmarried young women of low rank and their families may feel that their status would be enhanced by a liaison with a higher-ranking male, who would not, in any case, court a virgin of inferior rank with a view toward a parentally sanctioned marriage. This theme, in its specifically Samoan application, was taken up in several studies by Jeannette Mageo, who worked in Samoa for many years. Mageo's writings on this topic include an ethnography, *Theorizing Self in Samoa: Emotions, Genders, and Sexualities* (1998), and an article in *Man* contributing to the discussion begun in "Magical Hair." In "Hairdos and

Don'ts: Hair Symbolism and Sexual History in Samoa" (1994) Mageo argues that Samoan girls signaled their participation in this system (or might be punished for improper performance of their roles) by the styles in which their hair was cut and adorned. In these works Mageo argues that girls did not always accept the role of sexual lure in their parents' games of status and that some girls found advantages in the chastity that became an increasingly pervasive concomitant of Samoan Christianity. In particular, Mageo argues that the role of village princess (taupou, the ceremonial virgin) has become democratized in modern Samoa (1998:202, 215), particularly with regard to dance performances and the widening of the range of the cultural ideal of virginity.

In his article in *Sexual Meanings*, "Sexuality and Gender in Samoa: Conceptions and Missed Conceptions," Shore suggests that for Samoans, spiritual value (*mana*) inhered in women to varying degrees, depending upon how closely they approached the status of chaste sisters. The taupou was at the top of this scale, the legitimately married wife in the middle, and the common-law wife (the largest category) at the bottom. Since high family rank was closely linked to arranged marriage and premarital chastity, Ortner's analysis of practical sexual politics is not inconsistent with Shore's formulation in terms of symbol manipulation. Both argue that sexual practice is comprehensible largely in terms of social inequality and that both are the products of a discourse favorable to those in a privileged position. In the process the Samoan sexual ambience comes to seem much more like the 19th-century England described by historians such as Steven Marcus and much less like stereotypes of uninhibited Polynesia or the prudish society imagined by Freeman and his supporters.

While the contributions to *Sexual Meanings* are consistent with a political position favorable to increased social equality, greater flexibility in gender roles, and acceptance of a wider variety of sexual behavior, these implications are mainly implicit rather than explicit. This is true despite the claim in the introduction that close analysis of sex and gender ideologies is inevitably a political exercise. The ethnography of "systems" of sexuality and gender was soon to be put to more explicitly political uses.

QUEERING ANTHROPOLOGY

One goal of the growing body of ethnographic literature on homosexuality that has appeared in recent years is simply to make visible a dimension of human experience that had, in the past, generally been ignored or granted brief remarks in works dedicated to other subjects. We have seen that the denial of homosexual practices has been deployed in ethnographic texts as justification for alleged heterosexual freedom. Alternatively, institutionalized homosexuality has been treated as pathology, albeit sometimes as a safety valve that avoided even worse pathology – uncontrolled homosexuality driven by individual desire.

Insofar as gay anthropologists have undertaken the work of disclosing submerged truths about same-sex eroticism and seen their own sexual orientation as relevant to it, the project of presenting data in some respects resembles the process known in feminist studies as "claiming a voice." This has been a genuine change in ethnographic practice, at least so far as sexuality is concerned. Although Mead and some other women of an earlier era had made female experience a central part of their fieldwork, they did not generally claim to be crusaders for a female voice in anthropology. Indeed, Mead made clear that the study of adolescent girls had been assigned to her by Boas. We do not deny the existence of what came to be called "silencing." Indeed, such a phenomenon undoubtedly influenced the decision of pioneering female anthropologists not to make claims for a distinctly female idiom. In the excellent collection edited by Ruth Behar and Deborah Gordon entitled *Women Writing Culture* (1995), which *is* part of an attempt to discover and claim a female voice in anthropology, the motivations of women of an earlier period are discussed in some detail. In her introduction to the work Behar speaks of "erasures" of female (and ethnic) identities that it is her goal to undo and to avoid for future generations and future texts.

On the other hand, personal "voice" may be less important to some female anthropologists who have studied women and many gay anthropologists who have studied same-sex eroticism than the salient fact that these topics, of compelling interest to them, were largely ignored by others.

What was true of gender in the foundational texts of modern anthropology was undoubtedly even truer of sexual preferences and behaviors. Although we have argued that anthropologists have long been influenced in their interpretations by personal and social sexual issues, such matters were generally handled obliquely, if they were acknowledged at all.

Anthropologists who contributed to the surge in cross-cultural studies of homosexuality during the 1980s and 1990s attempted to write this topic into the anthropological record from two perspectives, either or both of which may motivate a given author or a given work. One stated purpose has been simply to make information available that was once avoided or distorted. The other goal has been the use of cross-cultural studies to directly address contemporary gay political issues. Several authors who began writing from the first position during the early years of anthropology's "rediscovery" of sex have, more recently, produced texts compatible with the second goal. To some degree this shift (or expansion) of interests is reflected in the name change in 1987 of the organization within the American Anthropological Association concerned with the study of gay issues from Anthropology Research Group on Homosexuality to Society of Lesbian and Gay Anthropologists (Amory n.d.).[4]

Gilbert Herdt's *Guardians of the Flutes* (1981), published in the same year as *Sexual Meanings*, was the first widely read ethnography to deal at length with the homosexual practices associated with male initiation in a New Guinea society, though there had been significant references in earlier literature. These practices, found in a number of New Guinea societies, are a manifestation of the broader tendency, noted above, for cultures in this region to link masculinity and femininity to bodily fluids. In some of these cultures it was thought necessary to supply boys with the semen of postpubertal males in order to insure their development into men. Among the "Sambia," the pseudonym for the culture studied by Gilbert Herdt, insemination was accomplished by compulsory fellatio over the course of several years in secret ceremonies conducted in the men's house. Some societies in the area employed anal intercourse for this purpose; others rubbed semen into initiates' skin. In all these cases erection and ejaculation within an all-male environment were employed to insure a new generation of male warriors. There are salient divergences between these customs and northern European and North American conceptions of male homoeroticism, apart from the compulsory nature of the Melanesian practices, though their associated ideology bears some resemblance to the Mediterranean beliefs discussed above. The age-specific nature of Sambia same-sex eroticism and its association with the training of warriors have also been said to parallel some aspects of ancient Greek and Roman practice. In New Guinea neither adult heterosexual desire nor masculine gender identity was believed to be threatened by same-sex contact during initiation. Indeed, the point of the exercise was to create masculinity and strengthen boys so that they would eventually be able to withstand the polluting influence of female fluids and thus render them fit for marriage to women. Some New Guinea societies, particularly in the north of the island, accomplished the latter goal solely through ritual bleeding, designed to remove female pollution from men and boys. Others practiced various forms of semen transfer without ritual bloodletting. Herdt reports the presence of both practices.

Herdt appears not to have intended to make the study of homosexual behavior per se the object of his investigations. The young men who became his friends and confidants in the field first made him aware of the presence of this aspect of initiation some five months into his study (Herdt 1981:xv). However, Herdt's account of his original motives in undertaking the study and their reflection in the text that resulted does signal the incorporation of a new dimension to the cross-cultural study of sexuality when compared to the analyses we have been discussing so far in this chapter. Herdt states in his preface that his book "began with a dream," that he "wanted to learn something new about the meaning of individuals' experiences in ritual initiation, a discarded problem in anthropology" (1981:xiii). The resulting work certainly provides the reader with a detailed account of the social system that defines and creates gender and sexuality among the Sambia of Papua New Guinea, but its focus upon informants' personal accounts of their feelings and perceptions during and after initiation necessitates a more individualized and corporealized account of sexuality than Durkheimian or classic structuralist models allowed for. At various points in the work Herdt expresses a debt to Victor Turner, whose studies of ritual among the Ndembu and elsewhere incorporated multiple poles of symbolic meaning, including the corporeal and the antistructural. Most specifically for Herdt, Turner recognized the importance of informants' own exegesis of symbolic meanings, including personal ones, though Herdt states that he has emphasized individual, as opposed to shared, meanings to a greater degree than Turner did in most of his work (1981:328–329). In this regard, Herdt, throughout his career, has employed Freudian and neo-Freudian models alongside insights drawn from symbolic anthropology. The discussion of ritualized homoeroticism within such potentially pathologizing frameworks has unsettled some critics (see, e.g., Whitehead 1986). Psychoanalytic models of identity, like Turner's analyses of ritual, were processual. Freud, like the Sambia, saw gender identity and erotic object choice as the outcome of a lengthy and punctuated developmental process. The notion of a changing temporal dimension to sexuality has been a cornerstone of Herdt's work.

Where sexuality and gender intersect, Herdt's account had the potential to unsettle Western readers secure in their notions of the "natural" and the "unnatural" in human desire in much the same way that Mead's early work did, as Robert A. LeVine observes in his foreword to *Guardians of the Flutes* (LeVine 1981:ix). For many people in Europe and North America in 1981, common sense dictated that homosexual practice and disturbance in gender identity were inextricably linked. The Freudian legacy, and the continuing influence of the various sexual reform movements we have discussed, did little to challenge this assumption. Gay rights advocates of the 1970s had contested the presumption that homosexual males were effeminate and lesbians were masculinized. On the other hand, most believed sexual identity to be a fairly permanent and internally consistent phenomenon. The "coming out" stories of the 1970s and early 1980s tended to stress childhood awareness of difference, although typically this difference was neither named nor understood at the time. *Guardians of the Flutes* provided a glimpse of a world in which homosexual fellatio was an essential part of imparting masculine, heterosexual adult identity to boys believed to be congenitally feminized by the processes of birth and maternal care in early childhood. [5]

Guardians of the Flutes marks a significant departure from the position taken by Evans-Pritchard 11 years earlier on homosexual relationships among Zande adolescents, though that work also was instrumental in drawing attention to a culture in which both homosexual and heterosexual object choice was expected within a single lifetime. Evans-Pritchard (1970) employed the functional approach of his earlier work in viewing Zande boy wives as a convenient and temporary substitute for women in a warrior society. Herdt's approach is certainly not unmindful of the social (and cosmological) structure in which Sambia initiation unfolds, but he sees it as necessary but not sufficient for the kind of understanding he wishes to achieve. Cognitive and erotic readings of Sambia experience, he emphasizes, must not be seen as alternatives but as mutually constitutive of Sambia sexuality.

Deborah Elliston (1995) has argued that Herdt and others may have been too ready to interpret the insemination of Melanesian initiates as "ritualized homosexuality" (a term that Herdt had, in any case, rejected by the time her article appeared). She suggests that focusing analysis on the exchange of symbolic fluids rather than the orgasmic experience necessary for semen transfer to take place may better serve to contextualize New Guinea initiations in the symbolic systems of a region where many liquids, including milk and coconut juice, may carry heavy loads of meaning. Herdt has dismissed critiques like Elliston's as "cultural hygiene," causing writers to "deodorize accounts of the sexual" (1999:26). Dorothy Ayers Counts (1985), who provides data cited by Elliston on fluid exchanges in a West New Britain community, is the coauthor of another article that contains an extensive account of Kaliai beliefs concerning conception, pollution, and sexuality in general (Counts and Counts 1983). [6] The authors imply throughout that the people they worked with certainly did value the purely physical pleasure of sexual experience, quite apart from the equivalent symbolic value assigned to semen, breast milk, and the milk of green coconuts and the fears that intercourse could drain essential life forces. (The group in question, the Kaliai, do not inseminate boys as part of initiation.) Elliston accuses Herdt of co-opting the Sambia into Western discourses of homosexuality. One could counterargue that a stress on the symbolic at the expense of erotic physicality is another form of conscription, in this case into a Western discourse that has frequently privileged the cerebral over the corporeal.

In his subsequent work Herdt has explored more deeply the construction of gender and sexual desire in individual Sambia, including a hermaphrodite he studied for many years. He has also edited an extremely influential volume, *Third Sex, Third Gender* (Herdt 1994), a compilation of work concerned with manifestations of more than two genders in diverse cultural settings. In this book Herdt takes a somewhat more political tack than in his early work on the Sambia, arguing that a culture that recognizes only two genders imposes an arbitrary dichotomy upon a reality capable of supporting multiple categories, if not a continuum. This collection is another massive contribution to the project of presenting information that had previously constituted a major "absence" from the cross-cultural data.

In *Same Sex, Different Cultures: Gays and Lesbians across Cultures*, a 1997 book intended for a general audience though aimed particularly at gay and lesbian readers, Herdt has stressed the cultural specificity of particular understandings of "homosexual" identity and practice. He notes that the Sambia are as puzzled by his choice of a man as his life's companion as many Westerners are about Sambia men's sequential progress from homosexual to heterosexual erotic practice (Herdt 1997:xiv). Herdt has also written and edited numerous volumes on anthropology and AIDS research (Herdt and Lindenbaum 1992; Brummelhuis and Herdt 1995) and on the lesbian and gay experience in North America (Herdt 1992, 2000; Herdt and Boxer 1996). The book-launching party for the 1992 book was held at a gay bookstore in Chicago while the American Anthropological Association was meeting in that city and was announced in the meeting program, a rare attempt to physically move anthropologists into the public arenas of sexual politics.

One topic that may fairly be said to act as a sort of litmus test of opinion in the history of writings on sexuality in a cross-cultural context is the berdache. Discussion of institutionalized cross-dressing among Native people has exhibited a strong tendency to reflect the temper of the age in which it has occurred. Perhaps the most persistent question that has been asked concerning this phenomenon is whether these transgendered individuals were given to the performance of homosexual acts or were, in other ways, equivalent to Western "homosexuals." We have already seen, in Whitehead's "The Bow and the Burden Strap," a highly influential argument against assigning such culturally specific labels to Native North American gender categories. Other contemporary writers on the anthropology of sexuality, including some gay activists, think it is important that berdache institutions not be lost to the history and ethnography of same-sex eroticism. Early observers had assumed that berdaches were sodomites and condemned the practice, although at least one Spanish priest opined that male berdaches took carnal advantage of the access to women they enjoyed because of their female attire (Roscoe 1988:50). As discussed earlier, racial speculations linked to this practice had not been lacking from the time of conquest onward.

As we have seen in discussing the work of Devereux, one mode of interpretation tried to shed a positive light on Native traditions by suggesting that providing a culturally recognized niche for homosexuals and others unable to meet their "normal" gender roles avoided some of the suffering experienced by such individuals elsewhere. The assumption of pathology implicit in this approach is resented by many contemporary authors. Even Benedict was not able to entirely avoid a "safety-valve" approach, despite her insistence that normality is relative. During the 1980s and 1990s gay activists and others in both the anthropological and Native communities attempted their own reframing of the berdache question, even giving the new name "two spirit" to such intermediating genders. This textual practice is consistent with a tendency among such scholars to emphasize the religious aspects of such institutions, even when such an emphasis is coupled with a celebration of two-spirit eroticism.

Walter Williams's 1986 book, *The Spirit and the Flesh: Sexual Diversity in American Indian Culture*, won the Gay Book of the Year Award from the American Library Association and the Ruth Benedict Award from the Society of Lesbian and Gay Anthropologists.[7] In large measure, *The Spirit and the Flesh* is simply an attempt to make information about the incidence, meaning, and history of alternative gender roles in Native cultures available to as broad a reading public as possible. In this sense, the work may be said to be part of what Kath Weston has characterized as the "ethnocartographic" phase in the anthropological study of homoeroticism, a development that preceded later theorizing (1998:149–156).[8] Williams documents the variety and distribution of berdache traditions and the history of suppression first by outsiders and, in response, by some Natives, a suppression that is to some degree responsible for scholars' difficulties in understanding such practices. The book is based partly on archival research and partly on fieldwork with diverse communities and individuals. Williams is especially interested in the meanings the berdache tradition holds for contemporary gay Natives. For Williams, who helped to found the Committee on Lesbian and Gay History of the American Historical Association, berdaches are part of gay history and deserve to be recorded and honored as such. While his account is not lacking in sociological and symbolic analysis of the sort we have described in discussing *Sexual Meanings*, Williams does not slight the physical: he compiled a considerable body of information on the sexual techniques and sexual responses of berdaches past and present, and pleasure is very much part of the "insider's" experience he attempts to access. The outspoken coupling of erotics, history, ethnography, and politics made *The Spirit and the Flesh* a significant departure within the anthropological scholarship of sex. In one respect, though, it is very much part of that tradition – its subjects' sexual experience is offered as part of an argument for the transformation of Western sexual hegemony.

As Weston, Vance, and others have noted, the documentation of homosexuality (Weston's ethnocartographic phase) gave rise to a recognition that the subject being uncovered changed its form as soon as scholars approached it. "Gayness" was not the same thing when encountered across temporal and spatial boundaries; in fact, there didn't seem to be such a thing as "homosexuality" at all.

Barry Adam (1986) and Stephen O. Murray have produced influential works that argue that there is some order in this apparent chaos. Adam identified a few broad patterns into which local understandings of same-sex eroticism may usefully be grouped for purposes of comparison, though "homosexuality" is still understood in the plural. Murray's adaptation of Adam's types is described in numerous publications (e.g., 1995:3–16, 2000:1–13). Murray's categories include age-structured homosexualities, gender-stratified homosexualities (where a gender distinction is created between partners of the same biological sex, e.g., by cross-dressing), and egalitarian homosexualities. Murray notes that he differs from Adam insofar as Adam views occupation-related homosexuality as a separate class, one that Murray subsumes under gender-stratified forms (2000:202). Murray has authored and contributed to a formidable collection of work that documents and compares homosexual ideology and practice in North America, Oceania, Latin America, Africa, and the Islamic world (e.g., Murray 1992, 1995, 2000; Murray and Roscoe 1997, 1998), using these categories to organize the diverse materials. He and his collaborators paint a picture of an aspect of human experience that is both highly culturally mediated and recognizably similar in different places and times. Murray's data challenge Foucault's assertion of a break between contemporary Western understandings of homosexuality and everything that preceded it while acknowledging the power of culture to shape, if not determine, sexualities (2000:11–12).

There were, at various times and places, sexual acts between men or between women, men and/or women who experienced desire for the same sex, and a wide range of injunctions or prohibitions concerning such acts and desires. Foucault argued that the West, for the last century and a bit, has seen homoeroticism as definitive of a particular kind of person, the "homosexual." Murray is among those who have concluded from historical evidence that modern Western representations of homosexuality are not unique.

Though classification of behaviors and desires (and those who act and desire) varies from culture to culture, the embodiment of such behaviors and desires is not confined by social categories. Manuel Fernández-Alemany and Murray, for example, have written of considerable slippage between people's actual experience and the categories applied to male–male sexuality in Central America (2002:50–52; Murray 1996:238–239). Kulick has made similar observations for Brazil (1998:165–166, 193–194).

Same-sex eroticism might form the basis for the formation of subcultures or characterize subgroups linked in other ways, for example, age or stage in the life cycle. "Same-sex" could itself be a problematic notion, given the various forms of cross-dressing and transgender phenomena encountered across cultures and across history. As many have noticed, the search for gay history led inescapably to the notion that "sex," "sex acts," and "sexual desire" are social constructions at the same time that feminist theory was exposing the arbitrariness of gender categories. [9] This was the context in which anthropologists began to reexamine "third gender" phenomena.

Many of the leading works of gay anthropology use cross-cultural examples of multiple genders to argue that not only gender but also sex and sexuality are social constructions. A good example of this trend is the 1997 collection *Two-Spirit People: Perspectives on the Intersection of Native American Gender Identity, Sexuality, and Spirituality*, edited by Sue-Ellen Jacobs, Wesley Thomas, and Sabine Lang. *Two-Spirit People* is based upon a sequence of memorable symposia held at and shortly after the 1993 meetings of the American Anthropological Association, involving anthropologists and members of the Native American community, some of whom presented an avowedly gay perspective.

Elizabeth Lapovsky Kennedy and Madeline Davis's *Boots of Leather, Slippers of Gold: The History of a Lesbian Community* (1993) is an ethnohistorical work that argues that the butch–femme roles that characterized working-class lesbian culture in the 1950s may have presented as much of a challenge to dualism as the lesbian feminist culture of the 1970s and 1980s that strived for more androgynous gendering. Butches and femmes may have come in pairs, but those pairs challenged the inevitability of the heterosexual couple.

There is, we should note, a conundrum built into contemporary anthropological arguments for valorizing nondualistic gender classification. On the one hand, this body of work tends to insist upon the *cultural* construction of gendered personae: males, females, and those who are neither male nor female. Conversely, writers in this tradition frequently argue that multi-gender systems provide enhanced flexibility for the expression of individual temperaments. Herdt's introduction to *Third Sex, Third Gender* (1994), a massive collection of ethnographic studies of third-gender phenomena, seems to argue both of these somewhat contradictory points, possibly because it attempts to bring order to a heterodox collection of materials.

Multiple genders certainly offer more alternatives to choose from than two-gender systems, though in many cases it is parents or other authority figures who make the assignment. On the other hand, arguing that more gender slots increase the likelihood of an appropriate choice implies that some aspects of gender and sexuality have an existence prior to their cultural production. It is difficult to insist upon the social construction of gender and sexuality and, at the same time, to argue that some societies offer opportunities for the freer expression of preexisting desires and identities.[10] Sometimes this contradiction is recognized; sometimes it is not. Where it is not acknowledged, recent studies sometimes bear an uncomfortable resemblance to the earlier, rejected practice of praising "other" cultures for allowing "outlets" for deviant impulses. Insofar as poststructuralist gender studies insist on the arbitrariness of "male" and "female" as categories of thought, the presence of additional categories may provide welcome evidence for the illusory nature of dualism, but to use these constructs in this way tends to obscure the fact that triads and tetrads may be as arbitrary as dyads.

Kath Weston (1998:159–160) and Gilbert Herdt (1997:8–10), among others, suggest that this problem may be reformulated, albeit not solved, in a manner that might take discussion in a more productive direction. These authors propose that anthropology incorporate a central premise of the intellectual movement known as "queer theory": the interpretation of same-sex eroticism and transsexual identification as transgressive *performance* rather than deviant *identity*.[11] This analytical practice is rooted in the gender theory elaborated in the works of Judith Butler (1990, 1993), who sees gender roles in general as performances. Queer theorists characterize same-sex eroticism and gender behavior inconsistent with "male" or "female" designations as a critique "from the margins" of the "naturalness" and inevitability of dualistic gender categories.

Belief systems that designate more than two gender categories or that, like the Sambia, the Azande, and the inhabitants of the ancient world, assign a temporary intermediate gender and erotic status to pubescent and adolescent boys become evidence for the noninevitability of the modern Western assumption that both one's gender identity and the object of one's sexual desire should follow "naturally" from the possession of a penis or vagina. Thus, the documentation of the normative beliefs and practices of other cultures may have transgressive uses for modern Westerners, though such use may represent yet another manifestation of conscription.

Saskia Wieringa and Evelyn Blackwood point out a somewhat related problem in the cross-cultural comparison of "homosexualities." Anthropologists, they warn, may be more ready to offer "validation" and "naturalization" to the collective representations of their informants than to the sex and gender categories of their own cultures (Wieringa and Blackwood 1999:13). Such a tendency might either lend undue support to constructionism, insofar as it stressed variability, or lead to new essentialisms, in which the "essence" of homosexuality (or heterosexuality, for that matter) could be seen in the definitions prevailing in the field site of a particularly prolific or persuasive anthropologist.

If cross-cultural comparison lends some support to a constructionist position concerning sexuality and gender, it may also suggest critiques of such a position. Wieringa (1999) has noted strong similarities between butch–femme cultures in North America and Europe and similar modes of gender presentation among lesbians in Indonesia and Peru. For Wieringa, the emergence of analogous patterns of dress, behavior, and social interaction in very different cultures is particularly telling, because in all her examples the practices she describes occur despite strong opposition from the dominant culture. She argues that it is difficult to see social construction as a sufficient explanation for behaviors and self-understandings that surface repeatedly in cultures whose only similarity is their persecution of those who manifest them. She suggests that the position of Havelock Ellis and the sexologists concerning innate tendencies toward inversion, though overly reductionist, may well have been describing a real phenomenon rather than simply help-ing to constitute the reified class "homosexual," as Foucault and others have accused the sexologists of doing (Wieringa 1999:213–214).

Furthermore, insofar as the anthropologists doing work of this kind rep-resent a close-knit group of people with common political goals, criticism from within the group may be difficult. A broadly favorable review of *Two-Spirit People* in the *American Anthropologist* credits the volume for its "gentle but firm" contradiction of Williams's " 'romanticization of purported posi-tively sanctioned pan-Indian gender or sexual categories that do not fit the reality of experiences faced by many contemporary . . . two-spirit Native Americans'" (McMullen 1999:210). The reviewer offers her own "gentle con-tradiction" when she suggests that the "somewhat" uncritical acceptance of the term *two spirit* may subordinate historically, culturally, and individually diverse experiences through the priority it implicitly accords to one aspect of Native American transgender statuses (McMullen 1999:210).

Such strategies as emphasizing the spiritual aspects of Native American transgendered roles or defining same-sex eroticism as resistance may actu-ally reinforce some "antisex" attitudes. To foreground "spirituality" and "re-sistance" while deemphasizing "bodies" and "sex" is to participate in a cul-tural system in which there is still a fundamental incompatibility between "sex" and "respectability." As Stephen O. Murray (1997) has observed, the new anthropology of sex retains some silences. We would suggest that this situation may result in part from the difficulty inherent in making sexuality itself and "strangers" both near and distant simultaneously more acceptable in a social milieu that remains suspicious of sexual "deviance" and in which racism and ethnocentrism have hardly disappeared. How does one write, without apology, about desire and its fulfillment?

The new anthropology of homosexuality does make some refreshing excursions into documenting the enjoyment gay people have experienced from their sexuality and their communities. The women who had been part of the working-class lesbian culture in Buffalo, New York, in the 1950s, the subjects of Kennedy and Davis's *Boots of Leather, Slippers of Gold*, talk about parties and sexual pleasure as well as class and gender politics. In-deed, "pleasure" for many of these women was the vehicle through which the power relations were quite literally embodied as well as challenged. Femmes dressed according to female convention and, in some ways, de-ferred to butches, who were, in turn, expected to defend them in public settings that could sometimes be dangerous. The authors suggest that the butches actually claimed a certain amount of public space for lesbians, since their appearance made it impossible to hide, and that this space became, to some degree, permanently available. On the other hand, in this community removed from the centers of arts and fashion where significant numbers of gay people could obtain employment, conventionally dressed women often found it easier to find work than women with a more masculine appearance. Accordingly, it was frequently the "fem" (this is the spelling used by Kennedy and Davis) who earned a living for the couple. Even where this was not the case, flexibility in work and domestic responsibilities within butch–femme couples presented a sharp contrast to the gender roles expected of heterosexual couples during this period (Kennedy and Davis 1993:283–293). Kennedy and Davis argue that later lesbian feminists who rejected butch–femme roles as replications of heterosexuality missed some of the modes of defiance lesbian "roles" of the 1950s actually offered to the gender system (1993:183–190). Not the least of these challenges was enacted within the production of pleasure itself. A highly masculinized lover, or "stone butch," was expected during this period to be the dominant partner in sexual relations, but a stone butch's dominance took the form of stimulating and giving pleasure to her "fem," who was not allowed to reciprocate. Although a later generation (including many of Davis and Kennedy's informants at a different stage of their lives) rejected both the denial of pleasure to one partner and the apparent replication of the dominant culture's association of femininity with passivity, Davis and Kennedy suggest that this economy of pleasure was, in fact, a double inversion of the heterosexual norm. Passive "feminine" figures received pleasure, while active "masculine" ones gave it at a time when companionate marriage's unrealistic demand that women be gratified through vaginal penetration by a penis, the source of men's pleasure, was perhaps at its strongest (Kennedy and Davis 1993:204–214).

Boots of Leather, Slippers of Gold is an ethnohistory and, as such, very much a work in Weston's ethnocartographic mode. As a work of history, it makes visible a community that was "hidden in plain sight" and, in doing so, implicitly raises some interesting questions about the nature of the anthropological study of sexuality. It is on the basis of their sexuality as opposed, for example, to their class status that these working-class lesbians are defined by the authors (and defined themselves) as a community.

Indeed, in this and similar studies, anthropologists are not so much studying the "sexuality of the Other" as implicitly diagnosing "otherness" on the basis of sexuality, even though they have, in many cases, been attracted to their field subjects because of a "sameness" of sexual orientation. For Davis and Kennedy, who are lesbians themselves, their subjects were a link to a past that, they frankly state, was to them alien territory. In their combination of sameness and otherness, with regard to both straight society and contemporary gay communities, the subjects of gay ethnohistory, like earlier subjects of the anthropology of sex, provide a refracting mirror for current visions of pleasure, gender, and desire.

Esther Newton's history of life in a gay beach resort, *Cherry Grove, Fire Island: Sixty Years in America's First Gay and Lesbian Town* (1993), does not slight the politics of pleasure. Indeed, Newton argues that the pleasure and the politics were inseparable. Cherry Grove is depicted as a place of play, plays, and parties, but issues of class, race, gender, and the larger society's sometimes violent homophobia are the subtexts of many of these performances and encounters. Once an escape for aristocratic and avant-garde people who were attracted to members of their own sex or who enjoyed the company of those who were so attracted, Cherry Grove later attracted summer residents and short-term visitors from a much broader range of social milieus. These changes did not take place without tensions, which Newton documents. In the 1970s many visitors to Fire Island, like much of the rest of gay male society, acted out their post-Stonewall defiance of American sexual norms through an insouciant kind of promiscuity. Despite the fact that this moment in gay history was painfully ended by the AIDS epidemic and despite recognizing that many residents of Cherry Grove, including many lesbians, did not entirely approve of promiscuity, Newton is unapologetic. On the one hand, she repeats her informants' pastorally and spiritually tinged articulations concerning the "naturalness" and childish innocence of anonymous sex in the dark with strangers in an unspoiled wilderness, describing the result, in the language of anthropology, as "pure *communitas*" (Newton 1993:186). On the other hand, although Newton says that as a female she finds this sexual culture "at times . . . frenzied and frantic," she is not afraid to claim rights for it *as sex*: "It is far too facile in our Judeo-Christian, sex-hating society to condemn gay male promiscuity. In every way *but* its vulnerability to venereal disease transmission I see far less social and personal harm, and more potential good in it than in the repressive double-standard monogamy preached by the dominant heterosexual culture" (1993:181). There are more echoes of Malinowski and Ellis than of Foucault in this language, though the freedoms Newton defends are precisely the ones deferred by champions of a regime of enlightened, companionate marriage.

Interestingly, Newton does not mention Lévi-Strauss's comments in *Tristes tropiques* about male couples on Fire Island, a locale that he presents, on the basis of both its topography and its inhabitants, as a contender for the title of "the weirdest spot one could hope to find on the face of the earth" (1974:162). The need for work like Newton's is underscored by the casualness with which Lévi-Strauss adopts an ironic stance toward the homosexual "Other":

> To complete the picture, I must add that Cherry Grove is chiefly in-habited by male couples, attracted no doubt by the general pattern of inversion. Since nothing grows in the sand, apart from broad patches of poisonous ivy, provisions are collected once a day from the one and only shop, at the end of the landing-stage. In the tiny streets, on higher ground more stable than the dunes, the sterile couples can be seen returning to their chalets pushing prams (the only vehicles suitable for the narrow paths) containing little but the weekend bottles of milk that no baby will consume. (1974:163)[12]

Lévi-Strauss makes Cherry Grove seem as far away as possible. Newton anchors it to the New York urban milieu by offering herself as a link between them, even describing her attraction (never physically consummated) to a senior member of Cherry Grove's lesbian community in an article that was published in the journal *Cultural Anthropology* shortly before the appear-ance of *Cherry Grove, Fire Island* (1993:3–23).

Weston (1998) has described the stance of "native ethnographer" as a risky one in a profession that expects its subjects to occupy distant spaces and times, particularly if their customs are the sort that still make some anthro-pologists uncomfortable. Under these circumstances, what is perhaps most remarkable about the literature we have been discussing in this section is that despite the barriers the work continues to appear and to increase in quantity, indeed in greater quantity than ethnographic or theoretical dis-cussions of heterosexual experience. This leads one to ask another question, itself very much a part of queer theory: why are there not more scholars who treat heterosexuality as a problem worthy of study?

BEYOND CONSTRUCTIONISM? *SEXUAL NATURE, SEXUAL CULTURE* AND *THE TIME OF* AIDS

While we have discussed several scholars who may be said to be the Meads and Malinowskis of gay anthropology, heirs to these figures have been sur-prisingly slow to appear and to stake out territory in the study of heterosex-uality. There has been little recent ethnography with heterosexual behavior as a central theme as opposed to the studies mentioned earlier in this chapter that view sex through the lens of some other concern, for example, ritual, cosmology, hierarchy. There are a few contenders for such a disciplinary space. One of them, Donald Tuzin, has even worked in Arapesh country, one of the "sacred sites" brought into the anthropological conversation by Mead. He is the author of *The Cassowary's Revenge: The Life and Death of Masculinity in a New Guinea Society* (1997). Another ethnographer concerned with sexuality is Thomas Gregor, author of *Anxious Pleasures: The Sexual Lives of an Amazonian People* (1985), a work that studies the erotic and emotional side of Amazonian kinship and cosmology. These two writers are among those to be found in the collection *Sexual Nature, Sexual Culture*, edited by Paul Abramson and Steven Pinkerton (1995), which, as its title suggests, contains articles that explore the limits to the construction of sexuality by discourse. The emphasis in many of the articles is on physiology and evolutionary adaptation. Also worthy of note is the attempt by some of the authors to integrate discussions of heterosexuality and homosexuality.

The objective of the volume, as stated in the introduction, is to apply "theoretical approaches towards the problem of assessing the relative importance of procreation and pleasure to human sexuality" and to "highlight the mutual and interdependent contributions that nature and nurture render to an understanding of human sexual behaviour" (Abramson and Pinkerton 1995:x). It promises us views of sexuality from "anthropological, biological, psychological, and sociological vantage points" as well as something of a redress for the "paradoxically anemic" stature of the study of sexuality within the academy (Abramson and Pinkerton 1995:x). Insofar as the volume maintains a consistent theoretical orientation, that orientation involves two positions. On the one hand, many of the authors attempt to steer a course in between biological determinism and pure constructionism. Several articles as well as the introduction are specifically dedicated to exploring the effects of nature and culture upon each other in the constitution of human sexual behavior and experience. The other consistent and relatively innovative approach of *Sexual Nature, Sexual Culture* is a focus on sexual pleasure as both an evolutionary mechanism and a source of social and cultural meaning. The degree to which these goals are met varies from article to article. The articles differ even more in the degree to which they observe another theoretical premise of the introduction: the insistence that "natural" and "normative" are not interchangeable notions.

Sexual Nature, Sexual Culture does not, for the most part, fulfill its promise to integrate the physiological with the cultural. Some articles are based entirely in physiology or evolutionary psychology. For instance, Donald Symons, in "Beauty Is in the Adaptations of the Beholder: The Evolutionary Psychology of Human Female Sexual Attractiveness," hypothesizes an evolutionary base for an allegedly universal male preference for narrow-waisted, clear-skinned women that takes little account of cultural influences on standards of beauty.[13]

In "The Evolution of Female Sexual Desire" Kim Wallen offers a caution against reductionism, despite seeing human–primate comparisons as potentially fruitful lines of inquiry. She suggests that ovarian hormones may play a role in human females' desire to engage in copulation as they do in nonhuman primates. She notes that some women in some studies report increased sexual desire around the likely time of ovulation. Nonetheless, if they live in a contemporary industrial society, women are most likely to report sexual activity at the weekend, whatever message they may be getting from their hormones (Wallen 1995:69–70). This observation might serve as a model (or a warning) for those who wish to integrate the biological and the cultural in studies of sexuality.

Mary Pavelka's "Sexual Nature: What Can We Learn from a Cross-Species Perspective?" reviews a large body of primate evidence and concludes that primatology supports both the naturalness of a wide range of human sexual practices and the potential for cultural influence on the forms those practices take.

The article "Sex as an Alternative to Aggression in the Bonobo" by Frans de Waal summarizes some of de Waal's well-known research, which suggests that evolutionary adaptations may be social rather than directly reproductive. Bonobo chimpanzees of both sexes have become somewhat famous for the wide variety of partnerings and positions they employ in their frequent sexual activities, including same-sex and adult–juvenile couplings. Many of these encounters seem to help neutralize potentially tense situations. The bonobo evidence has been used by de Waal and others to argue both that a wide range of sexual behaviors is found in at least one species of higher primate and that sex may be a peacemaking activity as well as an avenue for the expression of aggression and male dominance.

To some degree it might be fair to say that nonhuman primates have joined women, primitives, and homosexuals in the space assigned to "Others" in the discussion of sexuality, as Susan Sperling (1991) suggests has been the case for gender. The pleasures and desires of apes and monkeys are not immune from conscription into the social agendas of those privileged to analyze and report them.

Sexual Nature, Sexual Culture pays more attention to heterosexual expression than many other contemporary studies; indeed, its avowedly evolutionary perspective would seem to demand that it do so. Thomas Gregor's contribution to this volume, "Sexuality and the Experience of Love," suggests that anthropologists have paid too little attention to the role of love in other cultures and that among the Mehinaku of Brazil sexual pleasure can create strong bonds between couples, both spouses and extramarital partners, despite considerable sexual antagonism at the ideological level.[14] Donald Tuzin's article in the volume, "Discourse, Intercourse, and the Excluded Middle: Anthropology and the Problem of Sexual Experience," stresses that we need to know a lot more about sexual behavior, as opposed to sexual norms, in other cultures. He gives the example of cunnilingus as a practice that most of his New Guinea informants would claim to find repulsive but, on closer questioning, that several of them acknowledged enjoying (Tuzin 1995:265). Gregor and Tuzin do not claim to possess general theories of sexuality; they mainly call for more field ethnographers to pay attention to the quotidian manifestations of sex, which they discuss largely in terms of heterosexual, male experience. In his book *Anxious Pleasures* (1985) Gregor discusses Mehinaku sexuality from a psychoanalytic perspective; he suggests that misogyny and men's fear of sexual pollution are the result of envy of female reproductive power on the part of Mehinaku males.

Interestingly, both *Sexual Nature, Sexual Culture* and recent anthropological literature contain little cross-cultural comparison of heterosexual *female* pleasures and desires; this is, perhaps, the silence that has lasted longest. Possibly, a relative lack of successors is one of the reasons why Margaret Mead's work remains so controversial.

David Greenberg's article, "The Pleasures of Homosexuality," takes a more constructionist stance than many essays in this volume. Its ultimate reference, however, is to physical realities: sexual acts and the pleasure to be gained from them. Greenberg's argument is that specific forms of sex may be good to do precisely because culture has made them good to think. Greenberg starts from the premise that "the meaning someone attaches to a sexual encounter will play an important role in determining whether that encounter will be experienced as pleasurable" (1995:225). Greenberg postulates a causative connection between sexual meanings and the frequency of specific sexual acts: he speaks of oral sex, for example, as being not only less esteemed but actually rare during certain historical periods (1995:236).

As we have seen, the relationship between "sex" and "gender," like sexual orientation, has been a topic of contention in the debates between essentialists and constructionists. Indeed, the link between the two has itself been a topic for debate. The *hijra*s of India, biological males who dress as women and, at least normatively, submitted to castration, have been an important case in the literature on third genders. Through the writings of Serena Nanda (see especially 1990) they have become well known to nonanthropologists. Like berdaches or two-spirit people, they fill important ceremonial roles; like the *xanith*s of Oman (see Wikan 1977), they sometimes act as male prostitutes. Lawrence Cohen's article in *Sexual Nature, Sexual Culture*, "The Pleasures of Castration: The Postoperative Status of Hijras, Jankhas, and Academics," suggests that this widespread interest in the hijras may have eclipsed, for most audiences, other forms of male cross-dressing and homosexual identities in India. *Jankha*s and *saheli*s, for example, may wear women's clothes and have sex with men, but they do not submit to castration. The male husbands and customers of all types of cross-dressers as well as Western-style gays and lesbians must be added to the list of available sex and gender statuses. Cohen suggests that extreme constructionism may falsely downplay the importance of corporeality to the sexual personae he describes. He notes that both hijras and jankhas view their sexuality as located in their bodies, with castration adding an extra dimension of embodiment and "authenticity" to hijra sexuality. Cohen also argues that the long fascination of the West with the most exotic gender forms ethnography can offer, like hijras, is part of an Orientalizing strategy that maximizes racial and cultural difference.

The issue of Orientalism is also taken up in another article in *Sexual Nature, Sexual Culture* – Lenore Manderson's "The Pursuit of Pleasure and the Sale of Sex," which deals with the representation of (mainly) prostitutes' bodies in Thailand. Manderson argues that the famed sex shows in the Bangkok district of Patpong as well as Western documentary films like *The Good Woman of Bangkok* both draw upon and reinforce stereotypes of Asian sexuality that distance the Western viewer or foreign sexual consumer from Thai realities. The stereotypes in question are not unlike those we have discussed in our chapter on Burton and other Victorians.[15]

The dangers inherent in cross-cultural research on sexuality, which have been a main subject of our book, can occur in both essentialist and constructionist approaches. That is one lesson we can learn from *Sexual Nature, Sexual Culture*.

The AIDS epidemic has contributed to an intensified concern among anthropologists studying sexuality with the physicality of sex. The urgency of AIDS has led to renewed demands for an applied anthropology of sexuality and to impatience with disembodied forms of constructionism that see sex as primarily something that is "good to think." On the other hand, perhaps paradoxically, acquiring accurate information requires an awareness that "sex" exists in a matrix of culturally mediated representations and practices. *The Time of* AIDS: *Social Analysis, Theory, and Method*, edited by Gilbert Herdt and Shirley Lindenbaum (1992), contains several articles that delineate the barriers that stand between anthropologists and the "facts" of sexuality. Ethnocentrism, differential cultural understandings of "sex" and particular sexual practices, and the universal tendency to perform sexual acts in private were among the more familiar research problems discussed at the 1990 conference that inspired this widely read volume. What is most significant about this volume is that several of the authors attempt to use arguments widely associated with social constructionism to argue that there are realities to be described and that local cultural understandings are part of those realities, not evidence of their absence – a point made particularly strongly by Lindenbaum in her summary of the papers presented at the conference (1992:328). The treatment of the material world as "imaginary," Lindenbaum argues, is inadequate to deal with the reality of death. In this section we shall discuss *The Time of* AIDS as a theoretical and methodological contribution to the anthropology of sexuality.

The broader work of several of the 1990 conference participants has already been discussed in this or previous chapters or will be discussed below. Sander Gilman, who presented a paper that was not published in the collection, discussed the significance of historical links between diseases and modes of stigmatization in the construction of the public face of the HIV/AIDS epidemic (Lindenbaum 1992:326). Richard Parker's paper, "Sexual Diversity, Cultural Analysis, and AIDS Education in Brazil," discussed the importance of understanding collective representations about sexuality, both homosexual and heterosexual, in Brazil and elsewhere for designing AIDS education programs that could address local behaviors and desires. "Erotic ideologies" and "erotic scripts," including scripts and ideologies of transgression, were, in this formulation, vital clues to on-the-ground realities (Parker 1992:228–236).

In a paper that was controversial at the conference and that has remained so in several subsequent iterations, "Mapping Terra Incognita: Sex Research for AIDS Prevention – An Urgent Agenda for the 1990s," Ralph Bolton argued that the truth about sexual practice could only be learned in bed, citing his own participant observation in gay sex in Belgium as an example. We will discuss the controversial issue of sex in the field in our conclusions. In this context the important point to be made is that Bolton's argument, if not his practice, is consistent with the general direction taken by *The Time of* AIDS. Much of Bolton's argument rests upon the premise that definitions of sex in general and of particular sexual practices are mediated both by culture and by individual respondents' particular understandings, making questionnaires and other modes of verbal reporting suspect, but the physical facts of sex are real and at least potentially knowable through participant observation. On the other hand, as Paul Abramson's contribution to the volume, "Sex, Lies and Ethnography," argues, participant observation is not immune from the distorting effects of the lies, partial truths, and misunderstandings (all aspects of the social construction of sex) that cloud our knowledge of our own and others' sexual practices. Abramson's solution is intensive ethnographic triangulation – the use of multiple sources of information and longitudinal follow-up.

The cultural construction of notions of disease is an issue as relevant to the management of the AIDS epidemic as the cultural construction of sexuality; both involve important questions of the relationship between nature and culture. Paula Treichler, in "AIDS, HIV, and the Cultural Construction of Reality," suggests that effective treatment delivery will depend upon recognizing and validating the conceptual schemes within which AIDS and other diseases are encoded in affected communities. Several of the contributors to *The Time of* AIDS advocate an applied anthropology of AIDS in which local cultural constructions of both sex and disease are made a part of strategies for intervention. Paul Farmer and Brooke Schoepf, whose work we discuss below in some detail, discuss the intersection between economic realities and cultural understandings of sexuality and HIV/AIDS in Haiti and in Zaire. The social and political agendas of contributors to *The Time of* AIDS are centered upon combating the inequalities that have contributed to the AIDS epidemic and/or made it difficult to manage: homophobia, racism, sexism, economic disparities between the First and Third Worlds, and stigmatization of various urban subgroups. As we shall see next, discussions of AIDS also possess the potential for conscription to serve very different agendas.

"OLD AFRICA HANDS" REVISITED: SOME CONTEMPORARY ISSUES IN AFRICAN SEXUALITY

If information about the sexuality of others has been deployed in diagnosing and prescribing for real and imagined dysphorias at home, similar data have also been cited and sometimes collected in connection with attempts at curing or preventing death, illness, and suffering abroad. The portraits of target populations that have accompanied such attempts at intervention have frequently been problematic. During the last quarter century, two major health issues, HIV/AIDS and female circumcision, have focused attention on African sexuality, the object of so much stereotyping in earlier eras. With the stated goals of slowing the spread of a deadly disease and protecting the health and well-being of women, much has been said that revives earlier images of Africans as differently and usually excessively sexed when compared with other population groups. Ethnographic reports have been cited as evidence in the discussion of these problems. Anthropologists have expressed disquiet at the potential for their work to be used in this way, though some have, intentionally or not, written in potentially stereotyping ways.

One contemporary field of research particularly prone to reviving the image of the oversexed other is research into AIDS and other sexually transmitted diseases. In their article in *Sexual Nature, Sexual Culture* entitled "Sexuality, Infertility, and Sexually Transmitted Disease among Farmers and Foragers" Robert C. Bailey and Robert V. Aunger conclude that the pleasure motivation for sex is sufficiently strong among all humans that campaigns that seek to counter disease transmission by reducing sexual activity are doomed to failure. They suggest that promoting the use of condoms and antibiotics and research directed toward the discovery of vaccines are likely to prove more effective. Although this argument is probably quite a sensible one, and the authors are careful to stress that its conclusions apply to all human populations, a great deal of the article is given over to statistics on behaviors and sexual attitudes supportive of the notion that there is an entity called an "African sexuality" characterized by frequent intercourse and a low value placed upon either premarital or extramarital continence (Bailey and Aunger 1995:214). If, indeed, sexual pleasure is as powerful a motivator for all human and primate populations as many articles in *Sexual Nature, Sexual Culture* seem to suggest, then it is puzzling that "African sexuality" is singled out for special attention. Bailey and Aunger explicitly rely on writings by the demographers John and Pat Caldwell (Caldwell, Caldwell, and Quiggin 1989), who argue that such a complex exists, although they concede that variants of it exist in other parts of the world that do not have plough agriculture and where labor is in shorter supply than land. A similar position is advanced by Patricia Draper (1989), who has worked with the Herero. She argues that African marriage systems are characterized by a specific constellation of features, including premarital sex, polygyny, early marriage for women and late marriage for men, truncated parental nurturance and extensive fostering, and a low paternal involvement in the family. The Caldwells would add to this list a tendency to see sex as a service to be offered in exchange for goods and other services (Caldwell, Caldwell, and Quiggin 1989:203–205). On the other hand, they differ from Draper insofar as they have suggested that extramarital sex and polygyny facilitate lengthy postpartum sexual taboos and a concomitantly lengthened nursing period (see, e.g., Caldwell and Caldwell 1977:195).

Suzette Heald, who has studied the Gisu in East Africa, argues against such depictions of African sexuality. She points out that religions in Africa often stipulate periods of supernaturally sanctioned control and abstinence and that married love and family loyalty are prominent features of Gisu life (Heald 1999:128–145). Other scholars have questioned the accuracy and the representativeness of the Caldwells' data and noted that "African sexuality" varies greatly (see Le Blanc, Meintel, and Piché 1991:498–500). Although the Caldwells carried out extensive research in West Africa, much of their data for East Africa was gleaned from a collection of short pieces on sexual and family life contributed by anthropologists to a 1973 resource book for family planners. As the Caldwells acknowledge, these pieces were written from memory, and in most cases sexuality was not a primary focus of the authors' research. We are, of course, disturbed by any claims or inferences that Africans are more highly sexed than other populations, given the history of the uses to which images of African hypersexuality have been put. The Caldwells (Caldwell, Caldwell, and Quiggin 1991) are sensitive to criticisms of their work that have been made on precisely these grounds and are vociferous in denying that they impart either moral or racial inferiority to Africans. It is certainly true that nowhere in their work do they assign a racial basis to the attitudes and behaviors they believe to exist. They claim they are simply interested in providing data that may be of use in family planning and the management of sexually transmitted disease (Caldwell, Caldwell, and Quiggin 1989:186).

Unfortunately, J. Philippe Rushton has placed heavy reliance on Draper's arguments in constructing his argument for subspecific racial differences between Caucasoids, Negroids, and Mongoloids that are said to correspond neatly with differences in AIDS infection rates (1997:156–157).[16] Other stories about AIDS transmission in Africa that surface repeatedly in the media describe traditional custom and belief in ways that make Africans appear ignorant and superstitious to Western readers. Reports of widow inheritance as a vector for the spread of HIV/AIDS and men seeking sex with virgins in the hope of being protected have been featured far more frequently than their likely importance in disease transmission would seem to warrant.

Of course, not all atavistic images of Africans and people of African descent involve sex. The AIDS epidemic in Haiti began in the 1980s. Within a short time there were reports in the American press that the disease was being spread by ingestion or inhalation of or dermal contact with human sacrificial blood during voodoo rituals. Paul Farmer, who, like Brooke Schoepf, was a contributor to *The Time of AIDS* and who has worked as a physician and medical anthropologist in Haiti, cites an article from the *Journal of the American Medical Association* that propagates this myth (2001:106). Folklore about AIDS is, in fact, a global product. Within Africa a number of popular etiologies for AIDS exist. It has been said to have been developed in American laboratories. Ideas of its accidental African origin are dismissed as racist. Because the disease was first noted among gay men in North America and because homophobia is hardly absent in Africa, some political leaders have been vociferous in their denial that same-sex practices occur in Africa except as products of Western contamination. Winnie Madikizela-Mandela has described same-sex relations as "utter filth" and "alien to our culture" (Murray and Roscoe 1998:11). Robert Mugabe's decision to close the exhibit of GALZ (Gays and Lesbians of Zimbabwe) at the Zimbabwe International Book Fair in 1995 received worldwide press coverage (Murray 1998:247–252). However, south of the Limpopo, Nelson Mandela's South Africa became one of the first nations to include gay and lesbian rights in its constitution.

Denial of same-sex practices in Africa can be doubly dangerous. Educational efforts that do not include information about safe and unsafe homoerotic sex practices ignore a mode of disease transmission that is real, whatever politicians may say. Furthermore, such denial contributes to distancing African sexuality from that of the West. The myth of oversexed Africans, which we documented earlier in this book, often featured reports of an absence of homosexuality alongside accounts of excessive heterosexual activity. Both of these were used to make Africans seem more "animal-like" in their libidinal constitution (see Murray and Roscoe 1998:12–13; Bleys 1995:34–35). Rushton does not claim that homoeroticism is absent in Africa, but he does claim that a disproportionate amount of heterosexual transmission of HIV/AIDS among African Americans is evidence that African Americans are more heterosexually promiscuous than whites (1997:178–183). He says that this "racially-distinct mode of AIDS transmission" bears significant similarities to the African pattern of epidemiology, because biologically based African family patterns are found throughout the diaspora (Rushton 1997:183, 154–183).

The urgency of the AIDS crisis both interrupted and penetrated another discourse on African sexuality in which anthropologists (e.g., La Fontaine 1970; White 1980) and some others had been involved during the 1970s and early 1980s: the discussion of "free women," that is to say, unmarried, divorced, or widowed women who lived in African cities and who received various levels of assistance and support in exchange for sexual services. These services were performed within relationships that ranged from straightforward commercial transactions to relatively long-term associations not limited to sexual exchanges. In a period when scholars in many fields were discovering women's power in contexts where they had previously been thought to be passive and subordinate, "free women" appeared to some to be exemplars of female agency. A decade into the AIDS epidemic, Brooke Schoepf, who worked for many years in Kinshasa, wrote that the strategies of such women, with a few exceptions, were for the most part the only means open to them of achieving bare subsistence and that, with the coming of AIDS, "what once appeared to be a survival strategy has been transformed into a death strategy" (1988:629).

Schoepf's portrait of the harsh lives of women migrants in the cities of the Republic of the Congo and the Democratic Republic of the Congo (Zaire) parallels recent descriptions of the effects of "structural violence" on Third World populations. In some parts of Africa AIDS has become known as "Acquired Income Deficiency Syndrome" (Schoepf 2001:342–346). Structural violence may be defined as the effect of the inequities of the global economic system on those who occupy the bottom rungs of the economic ladder. Schoepf (2001) and Farmer (2001) have observed that differences in the incidence of AIDS have everywhere become clearly tied to differences in economic status and that this variance is far more significant than AIDS education (which is nonetheless desirable), ideological resistance to scientific explanation (which is seldom impermeable), and any cultural variation in sexual practices or the frequency of intercourse. Poor women and men in Third World towns and members of impoverished minorities in rich countries suffer from economic stresses that destroy families, encourage drug abuse, and promote migration to cities where there may be no stable networks of support and where prostitution may be the only reliable income supplement. In addition, other untreated venereal diseases may weaken the immune system before contact with an AIDS carrier. Condom use is infrequent because of either ideological opposition to birth control or the compensatory machismo of males. The antiretroviral drug cocktails that have diminished AIDS mortality and prevented the infection of fetuses in developed countries are too expensive in undeveloped countries. In *Infections and Inequalities* (1999) Farmer narrates the life histories of poor Haitian women who move back and forth between the countryside and Port-au-Prince in a determined but unsuccessful search for a livelihood and a coprovider for themselves and their children. Their reward is the AIDS virus. Sex tourism, another consequence of economic inequality, offers opportunities to shift the blame to both individual tourists and their Third World sexual partners (see Lyons 1998 for a discussion of this issue with regard to Thailand).

Schoepf (2001) suggests that anthropologists have sometimes contributed to discourses that are both distancing and unhelpful to current and potential AIDS patients in Africa and the rest of the Third World. For example, she says, anthropologists have sometimes endorsed, on the grounds of cultural sensitivity, programs to encourage the use of traditional medicine rather than investing in a biomedical infrastructure. Schoepf notes that in 1979 some medical anthropologists supported USAID's adoption of the slogan "Primary Health Care (PHC): Traditional Healers Are Already There." Such schemes, she argues, are all too often a way of both denying optimal care to people in need and conscripting them into the primitivist fantasies of the elite (Schoepf 2001:352). On the other hand, in a comment reminiscent of the fate of anthropologists like Northcote Thomas who were at odds with "old Africa hands," Schoepf notes the frequent marginalization of anthropologists who have, to their credit, often offered critiques of the stigmatizing and reductionist practices of those who fund and control AIDS research and prevention efforts. Nonetheless, she notes that some, like Farmer, have managed to make valuable contributions to a critical literature. She notes that she herself and a few others "worked on small grants, without salaries," in order to be independent of such gatekeepers (Schoepf 2001:340).

Another focus of current controversy that raises difficult issues for those concerned about the future and reputation of sub-Saharan Africa is female circumcision, a generic word for a set of practices found in every African country though absent in many individual societies. The term *female circumcision* may describe operations ranging in extensiveness from the removal of the tip of the clitoris, to the excision of the entire clitoris, to the removal of the clitoris and the labia minora, accompanied by the sewing together of the labia majora, leaving only a small aperture for menstruation and urination. These operations may be performed on females of various ages, from infancy to young adulthood. Like two spirit or berdache, the term *female circumcision* represents a political choice. Such alternative locutions as clitoridectomy, excision, infibulation, genital cutting, and female genital mutilation occupy different locations on the political map. *Female genital mutilation* is a term used mainly by those who wish to emphasize the very real health problems these practices pose for women. Those who prefer this term warn against sanitizing women's sufferings in the interest of relativism (or nationalism). *Female circumcision* is the term used by those whose main concern is desensationalizing the practice and lessening the stigma and exoticism imparted both to cultures that practice these operations and to the women who have them, some of whom object to having their genitals described to the world at large as "mutilated." *Excision* and *clitoridectomy* have sometimes been used as generic terms for all the operations rather than the removal of the clitoris, which is what they specifically describe. Using them in this way has sometimes led to descriptions of excision or clitoridectomy that in fact should be applied only to infibulation, the most extensive form of surgery and the one that most Western attention has focused on, though it is not the most common. The term *genital cutting* has also been used as an alternative to the more controversial concepts of circumcision and genital mutilation (James and Robertson 2002), though some activists see even this term as excessively sanitized.

At issue for anthropologists in this discussion is the question of relativism versus activism. More specifically, this question appears to many to involve a hard choice between feminism and antiracism as foci for advocacy. More than 20 years ago, Harriet Lyons (1981) wrote one of the first articles by an anthropologist articulating the difficulty of this particular choice. She was moved to write this piece by a series of feminist writings (e.g., Daley 1978; Hosken 1976) that seemed to single out Africa as a continent both peculiarly sexed and especially brutal to women. In her article Harriet pointed to anthropologists such as Sarah and Robert LeVine (1979) and Rose Oldfield Hayes (1975) who attempted to discuss these practices from the point of view of African women themselves. She tried to draw anthropologists' attention to another episode in the history of the West during which genital operations had been invoked in the service of stigmatization, namely, the uses made of Jewish circumcision in the history of anti-Semitism. Nonetheless, she acknowledged the validity of the issues raised by those, many of them Africans, who campaign against the practice.

In the intervening years a large literature has burgeoned on this topic. Some African countries, like Kenya, have banned the practice, though with far from total compliance. Countries with a large African migrant population have debated the appropriate attitude to take toward immigrants who continue to circumcise their daughters, and some have prosecuted such people, under either new statutes or existing legislation governing child abuse, which has prompted further debate. African women and women of the African diaspora have conducted an impassioned debate among themselves between those who, like Alice Walker (1992, 1993), have fervently attacked female circumcision in the name of sisterhood and those who have been opposed to the racial overtones of some of the opposition to the practice. Anthropologists have continued to write works that attempt to examine female circumcision from an emic perspective. One of the most prominent among these is Janice Boddy, whose book *Wombs and Alien Spirits: Women, Men and the Zār Cult in Northern Sudan* (1989) provided a counterargument to the assumption that removal of the clitoris was inherently desexualizing, an issue raised by feminists, along with the health risks, as a reason to oppose the operation. Boddy reported that Sudanese women viewed the operation not as destroying their sexuality but as transferring its focus from genital excitement to reproduction, from the clitoris to the womb. Another writer who has worked with circumcised women in the Sudan, Ellen Gruenbaum, reports that her informants held some disturbing images of Western women's bodies. They asked her, with some horror at the prospect, if uncircumcised women took the entire male sexual apparatus, including the testicles, into their vaginas during intercourse (Gruenbaum 2001:140). Circumcised Sudanese women also told Gruenbaum that they experienced sexual pleasure, including orgasm; Gruenbaum concluded that the degree to which female circumcision impeded female sexual response was a more debatable matter than had hitherto been thought (2001:133–157).

Boddy has also been involved with the publication of a truly unique work, *Aman, the Story of a Somali Girl* (Aman, Barnes, and Boddy 1994), which, among many other things, offers a multilayered portrayal of one Somali woman's experience with infibulation. "Aman" is the pseudonym of a Somali woman who taped much of her life story for Virginia Lee Barnes. When Barnes died, Boddy took over the project and brought the book to publication. In telling her story Aman does not slight the pain of the surgery, the fear and pain associated with her husband's reopening her vagina after her marriage, or the difficulties she had in childbirth as a result of being infibulated. On the other hand, she tells us that she and her friends were proud of their circumcisions and regarded uncircumcised women as dirty. She also describes her anger and feelings of humiliation when staff at the hospital where she delivered her first child made negative comments about her intimate body parts that to her were also negative comments about her culture.

One outstanding article, written by Claudie Gosselin (2000), offers a way out of the aporia entrapping anthropologists strongly committed to both feminism and Africa as well as to cultural relativism. Gosselin worked in Mali during the 1990s. She points out that in Mali it would be naive in the extreme to see a "traditional" position or a "feminist" position concerning excision (the usual term for the practice employed by Malians speaking in French). Rather, she points out that in Africa, as anywhere, there are multiple perspectives on important issues and conflicting definitions of both tradition and women's interests. Urban and rural, young and old women have their own ideas of what it means to be Malian or Dogon or Bambara and their own ideas of how these identities articulate with female circumcision. Some women defend the practice, and some are members of organizations that seek to ban it. Some Malian activists do not seek legislation but wish to combine medical treatment for women whose health has been compromised by the operation with educational efforts designed to encourage the eventual rejection of the practice by Malian mothers. Others are not enamored of excision but see it as an enduring condition of existence, as the English are reputed to see the weather. Gosselin argues that the best thing that anthropologists can do, concerning this and other matters, is to capture the many voices so that their dialogue can be heard and better understood by the world at large. If they do this, then in future debates anthropologists may have a role to play that integrates their specific skills, some values that have become central to their professional tradition, and their personal moral commitments.

OTHER RECENT THEMES: PLAY AND REPRODUCTIVE TECHNOLOGY

In our discussion of gender studies and queer theory we noted that Herdt and others have argued that "gender" is, in fact, a mode of performance, an argument made familiar outside anthropology in Judith Butler's widely cited works *Gender Trouble* (1990) and *Bodies That Matter* (1993). Performance is a concept that, in the work of Victor Turner, added a bodily, temporal, and experiential dimension to the anthropological study of symbols. Earlier in this chapter, we remarked upon the relative lack of such a perspective in the treatment of sexuality by some structural anthropologists. One current body of work in the anthropology of sexuality draws on the legacy of Victor Turner's concepts of liminality and antistructure to explore the play functions of sex, both homosexual and heterosexual. A remarkable ethnography in this genre is Richard G. Parker's *Bodies, Pleasures, and Passions: Sexual Culture in Contemporary Brazil* (1991). On the one hand, this book details many of the overt themes in Brazilian collective representations concerning sex, including the ideology of machismo, the somewhat conflicting Christian doctrines of purity, and the guilty history of miscegenation between Europeans, aboriginal populations, and African slaves. Underlying all of these "official" discourses, however, Parker notes a paradoxical validation of the transgressive aspects of sexuality. This is most pronounced during Carnaval, a liminal performance that, as is well known, was studied by Victor and Edith Turner (see Turner 1983). During Carnaval cross-dressing, near-nudity, and embracing in the street are accepted, even encouraged. Roger Lancaster notes that in Nicaragua, where most same-sex relationships reinforce the norms of machismo, some men are experimenting with a "subversive" equality. Lancaster may well overemphasize the potential of Carnaval to challenge the social system in a poor and repressive culture: "This spirit of play has been growing and developing inside *carnaval* for the better part of five centuries. And when that spirit of play escapes *carnaval*, it will remake the world" (Lancaster 1995:155). Nonetheless, if one can avoid excessive enthusiasm, there are some interesting uses for the study of play in the context of sexuality.

Beyond the public liminality of Carnaval, Parker discerns in Brazilian sexual culture a pervasive attitude that rules are made to be broken, that it is naughtiness that gives sex much of its pleasure. This is true of same-sex contacts, premarital sex, and adultery but also of experiments with positions and techniques by married couples, and it may even refer simply to an attitude that one is flirting with sexual danger whatever one happens to be doing. This is an aspect of sexuality that, we suspect, resonates with the personal experience of many students of sexuality, indeed, of many human beings, but it has been surprisingly little studied by anthropologists.

"Play" appealed to Turner and many of his associates precisely because it was a point where the ideological, social, and corporeal aspects of human existence seemed to meet. It is, therefore, a dimension of sexuality that deserves more attention by those seeking an exit from the essentialist–constructionist aporia. One might note that Herdt employs Turnerian models to argue that the formation of sexual identity is a process embedded in ritual, whether the rituals in question are performed in New Guinea men's houses or "coming-out" workshops in Chicago (Herdt and Boxer 1996). Jeannette Mageo (1998:210–217) and Niko Besnier (1994) discuss at length the liminality implicit in Polynesian transsexualism, both in public performances and in lived identities.

Reproduction is another domain in the study of sexuality where culture and nature inevitably meet. We have seen some earlier results of this intertwining in the debates over Trobriand ideas about physiological paternity that formed a bridge between earlier chapters and this one. Technological interventions in the reproductive process, whether in the ending of pregnancies or in their creation, are obvious points of interest for anthropologists schooled in this disciplinary tradition. It is not surprising, then, that Rayna Rapp (2000), Faye Ginsburg (1987), and others have written from an anthropological perspective about the cultural frameworks within which abortion, genetic manipulation, and the new reproductive technologies are understood and interpreted. Ginsburg, for example, has argued that women on both sides in American debates over abortion cite cultural ideals about motherhood in support of their position. Rapp has examined the intersection and clashes between amniocentesis, genetic counseling, gender and variant class, and ethnic cultures in the United States. An outstanding ethnography by Susan Kahn, *Reproducing Jews: A Cultural Account of Assisted Conception in Israel* (2000), places the cultural interpretation of reproductive technologies by Orthodox and secular Jews in Israel squarely within the anthropological context. Kahn cites, among other comparative sources, Malinowski's accounts of the Trobrianders and Weston's (1991) work on "chosen" families in gay and lesbian communities when trying to come to terms with, among other things, rabbinic interpretations that make artificial insemination of a married woman by a Jewish donor adulterous but the use of the sperm of a German Christian kibbutz volunteer permissible. The overall effect is to call into question all preconceptions of the "familiar" and the "exotic," the "modern" and the "archaic," not to mention the "cultural" and the "natural."

In this chapter we have traced something of a circle: from an intensification of anthropological interest in sex, accompanied by a notion that sex is a matter of meaning, to occasional glimmers of a concern with bodies and pleasure.[17] These recent episodes in the history of the anthropology of sex, compared with writings of earlier periods, have been characterized by increased esteem both for ethnographic subjects and for sex itself. Some of the issues of relativism that we raised in earlier chapters have found their way into the research questions and methodologies of the cross-cultural study of sexuality. Homosexuality and gender have become topics both highly theorized and the foci of intense debate. The issues of nature versus nurture, essence versus construct have been raised again, and once again no clear answer is in sight. To some degree the question has changed from, why do humans do sex the way they do? to, is there sex outside of the way humans talk about it? This reformulation of the question, we have suggested, may reflect a lingering reluctance to admit to an interest in sex without a "higher" purpose. Where one's subjects have been the victim of oppression, there may be a desire to extend this loftier purpose to them. On the other hand, in many ways the question is a valid one, and its posing represents an important advance.

When questions about nature and nurture are raised nowadays in contested areas of human experience, it is frequently insisted, as in the introduction to *Sexual Nature, Sexual Culture,* that "nature" and "nurture" are mutually and reciprocally constructed in human society, that neither makes sense without the other. In some cases, this insistence is a screen for biological reductionism and an associated apologia for the status quo. In other instances, the mantra "culture and nature cannot be separated" has been a screen for ignoring biology in favor of various forms of cultural determinism. Some writers simply feel that our knowledge is as yet inadequate to make a choice, particularly in a climate where a choice might have serious social and political consequences. One point made by many of the authors we have discussed remains indubitably true. For all its prominence in the broader intellectual culture, the study of sexuality is still a minority interest in anthropology, and its importance in earlier eras is only just beginning to be acknowledged.[18] It remains to be seen whether this interest will grow and how future anthropologists will venture to speak about sex in a territory still haunted by the ghosts of oversexed savages, undersexed savages, and those whose admission to a status no longer savage was at least partly conditional upon the usefulness of their pleasures and desires to the sexual agendas of others.

CHAPTER 10

Conclusions and Unfinished Business

I n the introduction to this book we remarked that a mere absence of
knowledge did not suffice to prevent scholars and "experts" in Western
countries from forming strong opinions about non-Western forms of
sexuality. Sex as an issue was always laden with a lot of baggage. Our extensive review of literature covering more than two centuries clearly demonstrates that anthropologists have perhaps learned a little about sexuality
in other cultures in the last 80 years of intensive fieldwork and extensive
ethnographic writing, and we can thus dispel some of the myths of earlier
eras. However, we too are positioned as players and not merely observers in
the events we describe and as involved interlocutors in ideological dialogue.
Most assuredly, there is a lot we still do not know or understand about
sexuality in our own and other societies. In the last chapter, we noted the appearance of much new literature on homosexualities in non-Western as well
as Western societies as well as the relative dearth of literature dealing with
heterosexuality. Ethnographic studies that consider both together are even
rarer, despite a few notable exceptions, like Levy's *Tahitians* and Parker's
Bodies, Pleasures, and Passions. Is that so simply because there is nothing
much to relate (a position we don't endorse), or are there other reasons for
relating little or nothing? Perhaps an anecdote will provoke some argument.

Our first foray into this area was in the years 1979–82 before we were dis-
tracted by an opportunity to do a study of mass media in Nigeria in 1983–84.
An article Harriet Lyons wrote on clitoridectomy (1981) was the springboard
for our project, and we organized a session on anthropology and sexuality
for the 1981 meetings of the American Anthropological Association. At the
session one learned commentator was clearly discomfited by the explicitness
of some of the papers. Back at the university where we both taught, a senior
administrator who had heard of Harriet Lyons's article on clitoridectomy
snickered and smuttily remarked that many colleagues would protect their

crotches when she walked into the room. From all this we learned that work on sexuality still carried a risk of marginalization within the academy and even within anthropology, one of the most liberal of academic disciplines. Even a noted figure such as Foucault addressed sexuality after he had secured a reputation by writing about other subjects and did not publicize the fact that he had written articles for the *Advocate*, a gay newspaper. Although in this writing Foucault had used the symbolism of consensual sadomasochism to explore the relationship between sex and power, this fact was unknown to most readers of his philosophical work. The invisibility of these articles could be maintained only because few readers of the *Advocate* were particularly eager to invite speculation concerning their own interest in this paper. When Foucault's homosexuality became more generally known, we heard several conversations that indicated that for some scholars, at least, his whole oeuvre was now tainted as "homosexual apologetics." Outside the academy, in Reagan-era Middle America, intolerance thrived. On the March night in 1982 when we completed a short lecture tour, one of our closest friends who was gay and a former anthropologist was brutally murdered in St. Louis. The police conducted only a cursory investigation. They told one of our friends, "A lot of those people die that way." On our lecture tour, during which we discussed some of the data included in this book, a senior member of a major anthropology department accused us of engaging in "titillating" research. We reminded him that titillation was a perceptual category.

Our temporary abandonment of this work was caused by what we saw as a last, belated chance to do "real" anthropology, having both written historical and theoretical dissertations. Although we are pleased with our Nigerian work, it is obvious that a whole set of institutional rewards, punishments, and values made us see our historical work on anthropologists' attitudes toward sexuality as less "real" than our field study abroad.

During the past 17 years, some of the work we discussed in our last chapter may have made our own interest in sexuality seem more acceptable within the anthropological community. The courage of a small group of gay anthropologists has had a lot to do with whatever change in values there may have been. In their work homosexualities and genders have been problematized, and hidden histories have been made visible. Writers like Weston, however, have issued an invitation to anthropologists at large, which few have yet accepted, to return sexuality to a more visible position in our discipline, a position it has not held since the 1920s, if it can be said to have held it even then.

This time around, it is hoped that we will be able to talk about sex without assuming that there is a hierarchy of sexual practices or, worse, a hierarchy of individuals or peoples who engage in them. Minimally, this will require us to decide what questions are worth asking in an anthropology of sex that doesn't seek to separate the "normal" from the "abnormal," the "primitive" from the "civilized." It may also be possible, at last, to study sexuality in an atmosphere in which we don't need an excuse to talk about it. In such a milieu, we can admit to an interest in something that gives pleasure to many of us and that, we assume, is pleasurable to at least some of our informants some of the time!

We believe that several important projects remain uncompleted. While there is a plethora of recent work that examines female gender roles and dissolves sexuality into broader topics, the most neglected project of all is the one that Margaret Mead essayed, the cross-cultural study of female sexuality. Should the cross-cultural study of sexuality assume its proper place as a core topic in anthropology, it will still provoke unusual difficulties. Ethical issues that are normal in any anthropological fieldwork assume particular importance here. They include privacy of the subject and safeguards against the power of the published word. *Informed* consent, problematic enough in some sexual encounters at home, is even more difficult to ensure in many fieldwork situations. Different cultures and different people have different ideas about the contexts for disclosure as well as its propriety. The fieldworker presumably will usually report discourse more than behavior, but that need not always be the case.

Inasmuch as we do see ourselves as players in the same social field as our informants, we cannot avoid seeing ourselves, seeing them, and being seen by them as sexual beings, whether we are there to study sexuality, folk medicine, or ethnic conflict. Sometimes that fact will have no effect whatsoever on our findings and the accounts we give of them, but on other occasions we may be aware or totally unaware that sexual cues recognized or misrecognized, relationships fulfilled or unfulfilled, may dramatically affect field results. In just the same way, it has long been acknowledged that the decision whether or not to bring children to the field may both restrict and in other ways enlarge anthropologists' social networks.

Presumably, some anthropologists have always slept with their informants (relationships that may or may not be exploitative) and also sometimes formed stable partnerships with them based on respect. More often than not (at least since the time of Burton and Reade) they have felt ethically compelled to maintain a "respectable" social and sexual distance. Not surprisingly, this problem was rarely discussed in textbooks or histories of the discipline. All this could have changed with the posthumous publication of Malinowski's *A Diary in the Strict Sense of the Term* (1967), a chronicle of frustrated desire, loneliness, longing, guilty thoughts and guiltier occasional gropings, violent ethnocentrism alternating with empathy, ennui oscillating with excitement, courage, and physical suffering. (See Torgovnick 1990: 232–234 for an ironic account of Malinowski's body as an object of female desire.) However, it was the so-called postmodern turn that brought a new sexual frankness into intentionally published accounts of human relationships in the field, beginning with Paul Rabinow's (1977) account of his encounter with a prostitute in Morocco and Manda Cesara's (otherwise Karla Poewe's) (1982) account of her love affair in Namibia.

Recently, three edited volumes, *Taboo* (Kulick and Willson 1995), *Sex, Sexuality, and the Anthropologist* (Markowitz and Ashkenazi 1999), and *Out in the Field* (Lewin and Leap 1996), have emphasized sexual intersubjectivity and communication between anthropological strangers and their hosts. Some of the contributors to the volumes describe voluntary sexual encounters in the field (Blackwood, Bolton, and Gearing in *Taboo*; Salamone, Chao, Markowitz, and Lumsing in *Sex, Sexuality, and the Anthropologist*; Bolton and Murray in *Out in the Field*). A Swedish anthropologist (the pseudonymous Eva Moreno), who contributed an essay to *Taboo*, was raped by her research assistant. Andrew Killick, who was the only white male heterosexual anthropologist to contribute to *Taboo*, succeeded in avoiding any sexual relationship.

The ethnographic insights of these authors vary in the degree to which they are convincing evidence of the value of paying attention to one's own sexual positioning in the field, whether or not that positioning involves any actual sex with informants. All of the authors are convinced they acted morally, though it is likely to be some time before the gatekeepers who bestow ethical approval on proposed research give advance approval to sex with informants *as part of a research methodology*. Some of the pitfalls of research about sex apply to all such studies, whether or not one chooses to make one's own sexuality an instrument through which one records the sexuality of others. These pitfalls are what we understand by the term *conscription*, the linking theme that runs through the story we have told. Doing fieldwork with one's body may comprise an especially concentrated mode of conscription. On the other hand, by putting one's body on the line, one may be evening the score a bit, allowing some conscription of oneself in return. One wonders what stories are told about sex with the anthropologist after the anthropologist has gone home.

Murray's contribution to *Out in the Field* is specifically directed toward an assessment of what can and can't be learned from sexual encounters. He writes of being told that informants never engaged in certain sexual practices when, in fact, they had participated in those very practices with the anthropologist. He does not conclude from this, however, that the "truth" he learned from informants' sexual relations with him was more privileged than the things they communicated in interviews and conversations. People's behavior with a visiting ethnographer, he warns, may not reflect their usual experience when the ethnographer is absent and may, indeed, be motivated by factors intrinsic to the ethnographic encounter itself, such as a wish to please a potential sponsor for immigration to Europe or North America (Murray 1996:242–251).

Some of the most interesting insights in *Taboo* and *Sex, Sexuality, and the Anthropologist* concern difficulties in communication about sexual codes. Both books contain cautionary tales of missed messages or, occasionally, deceptions on both sides. People say they are married when they are not and vice versa, choose to hide or reveal whether they are gay or straight, make mistakes with respect to etiquette, give true or false signals of sexual availability. However, all these things are likely to happen whether or not one sleeps with one's informants. In large measure, the problems of sex in the field are simply the problems of fieldwork itself.

In most human relationships, including those of fieldworker and informant, adolescent and adult inquisitor, sexual partners of all kinds, there are secrets and lies. Georg Simmel (1950) knew this piece of common sense and expressed it well. If Margaret Mead's Samoan adolescents indeed tried to deceive her, they were hardly unique in so doing. There is no doubt she deceived them about her marital status. We shall never know how many lies inform the texts of our greatest ethnographies.

We have described several different forms of conscription of the sexuality of ethnographic subjects. Racial hierarchy was supported by 18th- and 19th-century writings that viewed "savages" as oversexed as well as by some who advocated the inverse image. Primitivist views of sexual Arcadias and Utopias, which appeared most often in the 18th century and sometimes later on, were often connected with the critique of industrial modernity and postfeudal morality. Burton wished to overthrow Victorian prudery in the interests of a clearly defined sexual as well as racial hierarchy and accordingly defended Mormon and African polygamy while linking it firmly with a precivilized past. Most of his contemporaries used descriptions of sexuality in non-Western societies to reaffirm their faith in social progress and what we now call Victorian values, albeit they differed in their views of gender relations in their own time. The critique of the theory of primitive promiscuity was advanced by individuals such as Ellis, Westermarck, and (to some degree) Crawley, who believed in increased gender equality and a variety of changes in sexual norms. All of these men, of course, supported the retention of some established institutions and rules such as a companionate version of heterosexual marriage. Their interpretation of ethnographic data was consistent with the requirements of an argument that demanded that marriage be seen as primordial but flexible in its definition. Malinowski's advocacy of a moderate increase in heterosexual freedom was informed by his field data: "Learn a lot of healthy stuff from savages." Mead's accounts of Samoan sexuality were used not merely to combat hereditarian theory but to offer positive and negative examples for those concerned with the education of young women in America. Freeman's critique of Mead clearly articulates with several contemporary debates, involving sociobiologists and their critics, about the malleability of gender roles, family structure, and hierarchy. Increasing knowledge of the sexuality of our primate relatives has resulted in their conscription in recent debates, and our hominid ancestors are not exempt either. We have also discussed the incorporation of Mohave alyhas and hwame's, Omani xaniths, Indian hijras, and Sambia homoerotic initiation practices in the discourse of gay liberation alongside working-class lesbians in Buffalo and wealthy homosexuals summering on Fire Island. In this case, writers such as Herdt, Newton, and Weston have been well aware of the nature of their undertaking and the possible dangers of conscription. Their writings, accordingly, have to some degree been treated as theoretical contributions to our own analysis.

Conscription is a procedure that hardly conforms to the positivist norms many of us once believed in. It can, of course, be morally wrong. It can also be harmless. It can even be beneficial. Obviously, the dangers involve infringement of privacy and the possible reconscription of one's data by those with other agendas. For example, data offered in support of increased tolerance might be used by those who favor suppression. At the other extreme, anthropological texts might be read as a form of literary sexual tourism or even as roadmaps for the real thing. Accuracy of representation is another complex issue, particularly insofar as sexuality is a subject about which men and women, young and old, gay and straight may know different truths. This is a problem that goes beyond the issue of concealment and deliberate distortion, which we have already discussed. Even in the unlikely event that a consensus of anthropologists could agree on the desirability of some form of conscription or other, the results might bear little relation to the understandings and aspirations of the conscripted. Most modern forms of conscription serve the purposes of a moral relativism, a position to which only a minority in any human society subscribes. In fact, the moral absolutism of their informants may present a strong challenge to anthropologists who believe in sexual relativism.

We cannot offer an easy escape from these dilemmas. To add to the difficulty, selective silence may itself be a form of conscription. We have written this book as a record of the historical context of acts of conscription so that readers may better understand the problems inherent in making representations of the sexuality of "Others." As we have already made clear, we hardly think that these quandaries should prevent anthropologists from studying sexuality in their own and other societies, and we think it is naive to believe that conscription can be avoided. Anthropologists who study sexuality should acknowledge their own moral compass and make an informed judgment concerning the effects of their revelations on the lives of their subjects and their publics (which nowadays are more likely than not to include their subjects). Of course, as Weston reminds us, the subject, the anthropologist, and the readership may be one and the same. Alternatively, as our discussion of gender crossing among North American Native peoples suggests, attempts to capture the cross-currents of dialogue about sexuality may guide us through some but not all of the perils of conscription.

Indeed, we often read that anthropology should be dialogic and polyvocal. We have not yet fully considered all the implications of allowing other voices and other anthropologies into our discussion. As we have already indicated, we may not always like what we hear, but we are surely bound to represent it in our work. During our own fieldwork in Benin City, Nigeria, we did not encounter any particularly unusual forms of sexuality and marriage. Polygyny was undergoing a modest revival, although it was the butt of joking in television shows and was opposed by those who saw it as a sign of paganism, corruption, and backwardness. Most marriages in the city were monogamous. Southern Nigerian sexual mores would not appear particularly exotic to most North Americans. Clitoridectomy might tax the relativism of some of us, but it was rarely discussed in Benin City, although it was quite common. In fact, the only people who discussed this topic with us were Nigerian anthropologists. It was also mentioned once in a television documentary. A number of our informants were quite homophobic, as too were the Nigerian mass media. In fact, they saw same-sex eroticism as a sign of Western decadence. Some southern Nigerian Christians thought that it might be an unfortunate custom of Islamic northerners. There was a common feeling that Westerners were oversexed and that, where sexual excess existed in southern Nigeria, it was a Western import. The killing of the singer Marvin Gaye by his father was described both by one of our informants, a senior television executive, and by the press as the inevitable result of American laxity in matters of filial respect and the decline of patriarchal authority. The American comedy *Sanford and Son* was specifically blamed for encouraging moral decadence, although foreign media in general were seen as evidence of pervasive Western immorality. Here is an irony: a mere 80 to 90 years after E. M. Falk and others wrote so disparagingly of the morals of the Nigerian peoples whom Britain had colonized, Nigerians who are now part of the global Establishment are making similar judgments about the cultures of America and Britain. Insofar as there was fear that Western immorality was spreading in Nigerian cities and corrupting the traditional values of the countryside, Nigerian interpretations of British and American television programs represented a form of conscription of the presumed sexuality of "Others" into a new national discourse.

We are curious as to why Western anthropologists have shown so little interest in the opinions of non-Western "Others" concerning our own sexual behavior, sexual codes, and discourses. Here, perhaps, is a fitting power inversion in the time and space of global culture: Foucault's panopticon will be turned on its former keepers.

When anthropologists study sexuality in other cultures, a possibility exists that informants may conscript anthropological work for their own moral and political purposes. Ronald Berndt noted that the inhabitants of Arnhem Land, with whom the Berndts worked for many years, were pleased that their vanishing culture was being recorded, that some continuity might be preserved, and that clear memories of their lives and customs would be passed on to their descendants (Berndt 1978). Conscription by one's informants may be seen as a form of payment for one's own conscription of them. Such an exchange might appear to be a clear resolution of the ethical dilemmas we have presented, but reflection reveals that it poses further conundra. Anthropologists may flatter themselves that they benefit the peoples they study. They may invest so much emotion in their informants that a form of countertransference occurs (Lyons and Lyons 1997). However, such countertransferences may reflect a one-way process, a fiction whose utility is to serve as a salve for the ethnographer's conscience. In such cases, anthropologists may be engaged in a form of self-deception or may even be deceiving their subjects. Furthermore, the facts ethnographers record may represent sectional interests in the communities they study, such as the preservation of male power in Amazonian or New Guinea societies where the traditional men's house culture is in decline. These are truths, but they are, in a double sense, *partial* truths.[1]

To unravel hidden agendas, to prepare a map of a maze of representations, of "truths," partial truths, distortions, untruths, and downright lies, is the task of the historian of anthropology of sex. If discussions about sex are indeed discussions about power, there probably will always be elements of conscription when such discourses cross cultural lines. In battles for power people seek allies. Historical knowledge may grant us awareness of the sorts of conscription others have engaged in and the gains and losses that resulted. This may improve our chances of recognizing processes of conscription at work in our own inquiries and gauging the likely risks and benefits. Acknowledging conscription is an important facet of the writing of disciplinary history. We think it is particularly important when a topic like sex is concerned. In this book we have endeavored to map multiple plots of conscription. The dominant theme has been one of conscription of the sex lives of so-called primitives into the history of sex in Europe and North America. Entwined in this tale has been a story of the conscription of anthropologists themselves, as possessors of exotic sexual knowledge, into this same history and into the histories of the cultures they have studied. Anthropologists have varied in the degree to which they colluded in this conscription or even sought it, but it is unlikely that anyone in Europe or America has written about sex in the last few hundred years without some awareness of entering contested territory. This book is meant to encourage, not discourage, further explorations of the uncertain and troubled though potentially delightful domain of comparative sexuality. However, it is also intended to encourage reflection on past engagements so that present ones may be informed by a sensibility of who is being brought into the lists, why, and with what effect.

Notes

INTRODUCTION

1. Neither Malinowski nor his publishers ever faced prosecution. However, Routledge did have some worries about *The Sexual Life of Savages* (1929). In an obituary published in *Isis* Malinowski's former student Ashley Montagu noted that "the publishers anticipated some difficulty with the police about the content of this book and so the price was made deliberately high" (1942b:148).

2. Gobineau was the author of the *Essai sur l'inégalité des races humaines* (1853–55, translated in 1966). Gobineau believed that there were three major races, the white, the black, and the yellow. There were also many subraces. Although the "law of repulsion" acted as a barrier to miscegenation, superior white racial groups were less subject to it. When they interbred among themselves, a successful race such as the English might be the product. However, there was a repetitive historical tendency for superior groups to dilute their blood by interbreeding with inferior stock. For this reason the Aryan race was probably doomed. Among those influenced by Gobineau were the American polygenist Josiah Clark Nott, the composer Richard Wagner, and the fin de siècle racial theorist Houston Stewart Chamberlain. Although Gobineau would have deplored many aspects of Nazism, the Nazis regarded him as their precursor. For a useful account of Gobineau, see Biddiss 1970.

1. IMAGES OF PRIMITIVE SEXUALITY AND THE DEFINITION OF SPECIES

1. Nous suivons le pur instinct de la nature, et tu as tenté d'effacer de nos âmes son caractère. Ici tout est à tous, et tu nous a prêché je ne sais quelle distinction du tien et du mien. Nos filles et nos femmes nous sont communes, tu as partagé ce privilège avec nous, et tu es venu allumer en elles des fureurs inconnues. . . . Nous sommes libres, et voilà que tu as enfoui dans notre terre le titre de notre futur esclavage. . . . Si un Otaïtien débarquait un jour sur vos côtes et qu'il gravât sur une de vos pierres ou sur l'écorce d'un de vos arbres: Ce pays est aux habitants d'Otaïti, qu'en penserais-tu?

2. *L'aumônier.* Qu'est-ce que votre mariage?

Orou. Le consentement d'habiter une même cabane et de coucher dans un même lit, tant que nous nous y trouvons bien.

L'aumônier. Et lorsque vous vous y trouver mal?

Orou. Nous nous séparons.

3. One point worthy of our attention is the precise degree of sexual prudery exhibited by scholars in the 18th and early 19th centuries and the motivations, scientific or political, that sometimes enabled them to surmount it. Blumenbach prefaced the remarks cited here with a wry comment: "*Genitals.* Linnaeus says in the prolegomena of his *Systema Naturae,* 'that a too minute inspection of the genitals is abominable and disagreeable.' It is evident however that in process of time he came to think otherwise, and above all we find it so from the *Venus Dione,* depicted by him in a sufficiently licentious metaphorical style" (1969:249).

4. Subsequently, from the late 19th century on, scholars also renewed their attention to supposed anomalies in the male genitalia: the penis in adult San is said to be almost horizontal when not erect. There was an argument as to the reason for reports of monorchidism among Cape Hottentots. Some 18th-century writers believed that the left testicle was ritually excised, but 19th-century writers such as Gustav Fritsch claimed that "the scrotum is often drawn up close to and under the root of the penis, and appears to contain only one testicle, the other not having descended into the scrotal sac" (Schapera 1965:71). Schapera believed that excision may well have been performed at one time, but the practice had completely disappeared (1965:71).

5. For the influence of ideas of ignoble Amerindian savagery on the Scottish Enlightenment, see Meek 1976. In a recent book, *The Myth of the Noble Savage,* Ter Ellingson (2001) endeavors to show that pure primitivism never existed and that the idea that it once had was an invention of the mid-19th century. We would rather say that pure primitivism is rare. However, noble savagery is a concept with much slippage, encompassing myths of a golden age, hypothetical states of nature, real and hypothetical peoples or individuals, devout imaginings, and rhetorical conceits. We would agree with Duchet (1971) that representations of the noble or *bon sauvage* and the ignoble or "rude" savage often incorporate the same or similar negations of European civility. Sometimes arcadian notions inform narrations of first contact, as was the case with Columbus. Other times, supposed advocates of noble savagery from Lescarbot in the early 17th century to Rousseau *ironically* assign a positive value to such negations as a strategy in cultural advocacy or cultural critique.

6. After they ceased to threaten European power, the San became noble savages and harmless people. Guenther (1980) and Gordon (1992a) deal convincingly with these mythic transformations. Gordon tells us much about elaborations of Euro-

pean stereotypes of Bushman and Hottentot sexuality by German scholars prior to World War I.

7. Although Mayhew and Hemyng mention European relations with Indian women, they tend to minimize its prevalence and significance.

2. SEX AND THE REFUGE FOR DESTITUTE TRUTH

1. The first lock hospital in London was opened in the middle of the 18th century. These hospitals were used to segregate and treat patients infected with venereal disease. The lock hospitals established under the Contagious Diseases Acts were used to confine prostitutes who were proven or suspected carriers of these infections. Lock hospitals were subsequently established in many parts of the British Empire, including, for example, India and the Trobriand Islands.

2. The "Dahoman Priapus" was described by Burton as a clay figure of varying size: "A huge penis, like the section of a broom-stick, rudely carved as the Japanese articles which I have lately been permitted to inspect, projects horizontally from the middle. I could have carried off a donkey's load had I been aware of the rapidly rising value of Phallic specimens among the collectors of Europe" (1863–64:320).

3. It is somewhat perplexing that in 1865 Burton published a collection of West African proverbs under the title *Wit and Wisdom of West Africa* and remarks on the common good sense displayed in them. (McLynn 1990:218 has also made this observation.)

4. Genital mutilations, particularly clitoridectomy and infibulation, are often condemned as cruel and sexist by Western feminists as well as by some feminists in countries such as the Sudan and Ethiopia (see Hosken 1976; Daly 1978). Unfortunately, there is a thin line between well-intentioned criticism and racism. Accordingly, the anthropologist, inclined perhaps to antiracism and relativism as well as feminism, faces an intellectual and moral dilemma (see Lyons 1981).

5. Burton's wife, Isabel, claimed to have converted her dying husband to Catholicism and secured for him the last rites and a Catholic burial. She convinced few apart from herself. One recent biographer, Edward Rice (1991), claims that Burton was a closet Sufi, but his arguments prove only that Burton was intellectually interested in mystical forms of Islam.

6. This translation is not to be confused with an earlier, less complete version, privately published in 1886 as *The Perfumed Garden of the Cheikh Nafzaoui*.

3. MATRIARCHY, MARRIAGE BY CAPTURE, AND OTHER FANTASIES

1. McLennan does utilize some "ethnographic" illustrations to demonstrate the

existence of "modern examples of promiscuity and of practices which have the same effect in rendering uncertain male parentage" (1970:72 n. 9). Nineteen sources are cited; most of these are travelers' monographs, the greater part of which were not more than 100 years old and some of which were as recent as Livingstone's *Missionary Travels* and Reade's *Savage Africa*. Incredibly, however, Marco Polo is cited three times, and so is Mandeville. As Hodgen (1964:69–70, 101–103) has observed, some of the writings of Marco Polo and a large part of Mandeville belong to the realm of mythology rather than ethnography.

2. Morgan was unaware of Bachofen when he wrote *Systems of Consanguinity and Affinity of the Human Family* (1870). They exchanged letters on a number of occasions between 1874 and 1881, as Leslie White noted in his edition of Morgan's *Ancient Society* (1964:297 n. 5).

3. In such relationship terminologies the following equations are made: mother = mother's sister, father = father's brother, brother = father's brother's son = mother's sister's son, sister = mother's sister's daughter = father's brother's daughter. The mother's brother is not equated with the father or father's brother. Cross-cousins (mother's brother's and father's sister's children) are distinguished from siblings. There is usually a distinction between older and younger siblings.

4. See Stocking for an excellent short account of the careers of all four men (1995:17–34, 87–98).

5. Readers unfamiliar with four-class systems may find the following helpful:

Were we to designate members of the four Kamilaroi classes so that Ipai is A1, Kumbu is A2, Kubi is B1 and Muri is B2, we can see that the system might work as follows:

(1) A1 Male must marry a B1 Female;

(2) Their children are B by the rule of matrilineal descent and 2 in terms of alternate generational grouping, i.e., B2;

(3) If a B2 Male (according to rule) marries an A2 Female, the children will be A1, and so on.

It should be noted that under these rules an A1 cannot marry either another A1 or an A2 because of exogamy rules, and generational propriety dictates that the partner must be of the appropriate Kubi marriage class (B1) rather than being a Muri (B2). In addition, all Ipai and Kumbu belong to one of three matrilineal totemic groups, which are Kangaroo, Opossum, and Iguana; the corresponding Muri-Kubi groups are Emu, Bandicoot, and Blacksnake (Fison and Howitt 1967:42).

6. "Modernist" has become something of an "odd-job" word. When we apply it to Malinowski's anthropology, we are referring to a rejection of Victorian certainties coupled with a faith in the liberating power of a professionalized and institutionalized "science."

7. The jus primae noctis most properly refers to a supposed medieval custom whereby the lord of the manor might demand the sexual services of the serf's bride prior to the marriage ceremony. There is little historical evidence that such practices ever occurred, although payments were made by serfs to their lords as recompense for permission to marry. There are other well-known fables of this kind respecting other periods of history. One is central to *The Epic of Gilgamesh*. The evolutionists deployed the notion of the jus primae noctis in a nontraditional sense to refer to customs whereby the groom and/or the abductor or reclaimer of a woman had to grant specified individuals sexual access to her before he could claim primary sexual control. In these anthropological writings the jus primae noctis is often viewed as a survival of group marriage.

8. Spencer and Gillen were presumably referring to the practice of vaginal introcision. It was thus described by their contemporary, John Mathew, in the context of a discussion of male subincision: "But the most horrible of all the mutilations is that which Mr. Sturt designated 'the terrible rite' [male subincision]. This bloody concision is done within the area where circumcision occurs, but is not widely practised. . . . I accept the view of Westermarck that the object is ornamentation and increased virility of appearance. . . . Where subincision is practised vaginal introcision becomes inevitable. No mutilation is more horribly cruel or disabling, but savages have little or no compunction with respect to their treatment of women" (1899:121; see also Lyons 1981:501). Although it was not as extensive as circumcision, subincision was more extensive than Mathew suggested. Presumably, the custom is no longer practiced by Aboriginal peoples.

9. The explanations Spencer and Gillen rejected included phallic worship, hospitality to strangers, forms of wife lending, varieties of the jus primae noctis. These alternatives were suggested by Westermarck (1901:51–133, esp. 76–78), who did not believe in group marriage. Westermarck's work will be discussed in the next chapter.

10. Indeed, *The Native Tribes of Central Australia* contained a statement that should have made Frazer aware of the need to jettison all grand theories of totemism until much more analysis was done. In the introduction to the book Spencer and Gillen address the differences as well as the commonalities of forms of social organization in Australia: "In some tribes totems govern marriage, in others they have nothing to do with the question. . . . In some tribes there is a sex totem, in others there is no such thing; and in isolated cases we meet with an individual totem distinct from the totem common to a group of men and women" (Spencer and Gillen 1899:34–36).

4. THE RECONSTRUCTION OF "PRIMITIVE SEXUALITY"

1. All dates in this paragraph are the dates of first publication rather than the dates of the cited editions.

2. Durkheim also expressed considerable skepticism about ideas of primitive ignorance of paternity, pointing out that Europeans saw both body and soul as being involved in the birth of a child, but that did not mean that Christians were ignorant about physiology (1912:413).

3. The data collected by Spencer and Gillen on Urabunna piraunguru were sparse, in Thomas's view, and unhelpful. He noted that among the Dieri the *tippa-malku* (primary marriage) betrothals were arranged by the mothers of the parties with the consent of the girl's mother's brother. Pirauru relationships were created at certain ceremonies by the heads of the totem kin of the individuals concerned, and the moiety and section groups were not involved. The individual males who were pirauru to an individual's tippa-malku wife were a very small minority of males in his section; most members of it were excluded. Pirauru husbands and wives did not constitute a class, moiety, or any kind of major kin group. A woman's pirauru husband might be the brother of her tippa-malku husband, but it was unclear from the sources whether this was normally the case. The unions appeared to be temporary rather than permanent, and sexual relationships occurred when the tippa-malku husband was absent or on ceremonial occasions. The sources were unclear as to the question of consent. On the one hand, it was said that the tippa-malku husband's consent was not necessary. On the other hand, there were cases in which a widower gave presents to his brother so that he could establish a pirauru relationship with the brother's wife, and there were rare occasions when visitors could arrange to have pirauru wives through payment. Such transactions were not suggestive of group rights and group marriage.

5. "OLD AFRICA HANDS"

1. The representation of Africans in the writings of missionaries could be the subject of another whole book. Indeed, it has been discussed in several excellent ones already (see, e.g., Ajayi 1965; Ekechi 1972; Beidelman 1982; Comaroff and Comaroff 1991; Comaroff and Comaroff 1997).

2. Some contemporary feminists, including some anthropologists (see Wieringa and Blackwood 1999:4), have argued that scholars like Ifi Amadiume (1987) have been too quick to dismiss all notions of African warrior queens. On the other hand, even the strongest of such champions of African Amazons would be repelled by Reade's account. Indeed, accounts like Reade's are undoubtedly one of the reasons for denial of such traditions by Africans like Amadiume.

3. In 19th-century discourse sterility is not necessarily a sign of sexual lack. Indeed, it was often blamed upon promiscuity.

4. E. M. Falk, "Memorandum on the Superstitions and Customs of the Population of Aba Division" (1920), 13, Falk Papers.

5. Falk, "Memorandum," 42.

6. Hubert Mathews, "Memorandum on Nungu Women" (1917), 85–86, Mathews Memoranda.

7. Falk, "Memorandum," 42, 15, 16, 56, 58, 59, 71.

8. Falk, "Memorandum," 71.

9. Diary of Mrs. E. M. Falk, December 17, 1929, Falk Papers.

10. Diary of Mrs. E. M. Falk, December 15, 1929.

11. E. M. Falk, "Plan for the Government of Calabar" (1933), 16/200, Falk Papers.

12. Diary of Mrs. E. M. Falk, December 9, 1929.

13. E. M. Falk, 1934 testimonial, 3–4, Falk Papers.

6. MALINOWSKI AS "RELUCTANT SEXOLOGIST"

1. The following passage exemplifies such opinions: "The matrimonial knot, once tied, is firm and exclusive, at least in the ideal of tribal law, morality, and custom. As usual, however, ordinary human frailties play some havoc with the ideal. The Trobriand customs again are sadly lacking in any such interesting relaxations as *jus primae noctis*, wife lending, wife exchange or obligatory prostitution. The personal relations between the two partners, while most illuminating as an example of the matrilineal type of marriage, do not present any of those 'savage' features, so lurid, and at the same time so attractive to the antiquarian" (Malinowski 1929:76).

2. For details of Stopes's life, see Hall 1977. Other, somewhat hagiographic, accounts may be found in Briant (1962) and Aylmer (1924).

3. Our discussion of Malinowski's notes on Ellis's *Studies in the Psychology of Sex* (folder 214, box 26, BMPY) is reproduced from Lyons and Lyons (1986), the article on which most of this chapter is based. We are grateful to Mrs. Helena Wayne (Malinowska) for permission to publish this information. The notes are hereafter cited in the text by page number.

4. Ellis once chided Malinowski for his fear of a "holocaust" if he published certain comments on sexuality and olfaction in *The Sexual Life of Savages*. The scientist must not suppress information, said Ellis, though he must take care to present it in a scientific, not a salacious, manner (Havelock Ellis to Bronislaw Malinowski, December 26, 1926, BMPL).

5. Raymond Firth describes Malinowski as a "pioneer in the advocacy of what may be called modern, enlightened sex values" (1981:115). For Firth, Malinowski's moder-

nity and enlightenment consist in a rejection of unnecessary repression combined with a view that "the full attainment of sexual satisfaction cannot be realized except in a permanent union of deep love and mutual sacrifice" (1981:115).

6. Robert Briffault (born in the 1870s) was the son of a Scotswoman and a senior French diplomat who had become a British citizen after a disagreement with Napoléon III over the latter's subversion of the French constitution. Briffault was a doctor who became a writer after World War I, during which he suffered from shell shock. In *The Mothers* (originally published in 1927) Briffault revived the idea of primitive communism. Group marriage and sexual communism were the expressions of the primitive economic system. Group marriage gave way to institutions such as sororal polygyny and the levirate. Following Morgan and Bachofen, Briffault believed that primitive societies were originally matriarchal. He was inconsistent as to whether "matriarchy" signified female rule or merely the social predominance of women. Matrilocality was the key to matriarchy inasmuch as patriarchal institutions could not prevail when the husband had to reside with his wife's kin. Matriarchal societies were characterized by goddess worship. The movement from pastoralism to agriculture caused the rise of private property, patrilocal marriage, and patriarchy (see Briffault 1977; Rattray Taylor 1977; Briffault and Malinowski 1956). Although Briffault was very much an amateur anthropologist, his rancorous attacks on Westermarck caused some concern in Malinowski's circle. Ashley Montagu introduced Malinowski and Westermarck to Briffault, and a temporary suspension of hostilities occurred. Malinowski invited Briffault to discuss the future of marriage with him in a series of six radio broadcasts published in the *Listener* in 1931 and reissued by Montagu in 1956. During the broadcasts Malinowski annoyed Briffault by making remarks about primitive communism that the latter saw as "Red-baiting." Briffault responded by saying that communists and behaviorists were not the only foes of modern marriage: the most cogent opposition to contemporary marriage came from "the women of England," and it was occasioned "by certain features of our marriage institutions which, while they make husband and wife one, seem to provide that the husband shall be that one" (Briffault and Malinowski 1956:30). Malinowski responded by saying that he was "not yet an antifeminist" (Briffault and Malinowski 1956:40). In 1946 Briffault, who was dying of tuberculosis, sought permission to join his American wife, who was also ill and had returned to New York. He was refused entry into the United States on political grounds (Rattray Taylor 1977:22).

7. In a letter to Margaret Mead, Malinowski warns against *any* extreme assertion concerning primitive sexuality (March 29, 1930, BMPL).

8. Malinowski and Stopes exchanged frequent letters and a number of visits. For a while in the 1930s Malinowski was a vice president of Stopes's Society for Constructive Birth Control and Racial Progress.

9. Bronislaw Malinowski, "Remarks Made to Conference on the Contact of Modern Civilizations with Ancient Cultures and Tribal Customs, Livingstone House, London" (1930), folder 29, box 11, BMPY.

10. See Malinowski, "Remarks Made to Conference," and 1931b.

11. See Malinowski to Jack Driberg, October 12, 1931, BMPL. It might be noted that the colonial authorities also were aware of the delicate balance between the needs of the missionaries and the practical requirements of Indirect Rule (see Fields 1982:567–594).

12. Bronislaw Malinowski to Rev. E. L. Morgan, November 23, 1933, folder 445, box 6, BMPY.

13. Bronislaw Malinowski, "Memorandum to Joint Conference of British Social Hygiene Council and Board of Study for the Preparation of Missionaries, High Leigh" (1928), 20, folder 28, box 11, BMPY.

14. Malinowski, "Memorandum," 20.

15. Malinowski, "Memorandum," 13, 19.

16. High Leigh Conference, "Report of the Joint Conference of the British Social Hygiene Council and the Board of Study for the Preparation of Missionaries" (1928), 6, folder 28, box 11, BMPY.

17. High Leigh Conference, "Report," 11.

18. High Leigh Conference, "Report," 23.

19. See Jack Driberg to Bronislaw Malinowski, October 7, 1931, and Malinowski's response of October 12, both in file B, BMPL.

20. Malinowski wrote to Marie Bonaparte on September 6, 1938, to solicit her support in this campaign (folder 63, box 1, BMPY).

21. See Bronislaw Malinowski to Marie Bonaparte, September 6, 1938; to Eugen Fischer, September 11, 1938, folder 191, box 3, BMPY; to Richard Thurnwald, September 10, 1938, folder 605, box 8, BMPY; and to Kazimierz Stolyhwo, Polish Academy, September 11, 1938, folder 191, box 8, BMPY.

7. MEAD, THE FUTURE OF LANGUAGE, AND LOST OPPORTUNITIES

1. Early in her postgraduate studies at Oxford University, Harriet Lyons was asked to read and compare *Coming of Age in Samoa* with Marcel Mauss's remarks on Samoan property exchange in *The Gift* (1967). It was made clear that the intellectual sophistication, discrimination, taste, and even intelligence of a reader who could find anything positive to say about Mead's work were in serious doubt. This reaction was sufficient to cause at least one ambitious young woman, for most of her life, to regard Mead's writings and other work concerned with "emotional" issues as a shameful addiction, best indulged in secret. Esther Newton sums up some of Mead's

appeal when she says of her encounter with *Coming of Age in Samoa* as a college student that "through Margaret Mead I grasped that my adolescent torments over sex, gender, and the life of the mind could have been avoided by different social arrangements" (2000a:1).

2. Mead's application for funding for the Samoa study had cited not Hall but the doctoral thesis of Miriam Van Waters, a student at Clark University where Hall was president. As Murray and Darnell note (2000:564), Van Waters cited Boas with approval; in fact, she maintained a strongly relativist position throughout her thesis. In *Coming of Age in Samoa*, Van Waters is mentioned only in an appendix, where she is said to have "exhausted the possibilities" of a comparative as opposed to an ethnographic approach to the topic (Mead 1928:259–260).

3. Of course, in 1928 Mead was not to know the seriousness with which a future generation of anthropologists would regard the notion of "play." Mageo (1998) and Besnier (1994) have discussed aspects of liminality in contemporary Samoan sexual culture.

4. Charles G. Seligman to Margaret Mead, November 13, 1930, and Margaret Mead to Charles G. Seligman, December 1, 1930, container C4, Mead Papers.

5. Margaret Mead to Bronislaw Malinowski, January 4, 1929, container N40, Mead Papers.

6. Margaret Mead to Erik Erikson, June 23, 1939, container B5, Mead Papers.

7. Fortune's account of Arapesh aggression is not totally at odds with Mead's general argument. He noted that warfare (which had been suppressed since 1914) was limited to situations in which men attempted to abduct consenting women from other groups and that the casualty rate was low (Fortune 1939:24). Fortune stated that the primary purpose of such abduction was to acquire increased reproductive potential. Most interestingly, in the light of Mead's assertion that Arapesh men abhor violence, is a comment by Fortune to the effect that Arapesh men enticed women from other groups by getting them to admit that their husbands beat them, with an implied promise of better treatment (1939:28).

8. Margaret Mead, field notes on Arapesh, March 25, 1932, container N97, Mead Papers.

9. Margaret Mead to Erik Erikson, May 25, 1939, container B5, Mead Papers.

10. Mead to Erikson, June 23, 1939.

8. THE "SILENCE"

1. At the behest of the government of Bechuanaland, Schapera wrote a book, *Migrant Labour and Tribal Life* (1947), that describes labor migration and its impact on family life.

2. In a 2002 ethnography on the Kgatla, David Suggs notes that "serial monogamy" has become a more viable option for men in recent years and that women are now able to attain full adult status while avoiding marriage altogether. Nonetheless, he points out that Kgatla today talk about continuities as well as discontinuities in the norms governing kinship and marriage, emphasizing that women have "always" put motherhood first and "always" managed their households (Suggs 2002:41–42).

3. Lest this remark be thought homophobic, it should be noted that a South African website dedicated to "gay and lesbian affairs" describes *Africa Dances* as a "pink travelogue" (http://www.mask.org.za/Sections/ArtsAndCulture/library .html). There are, of course, no direct references in this mass-market book to Gorer's own sexual interests, though Hilary Lapsley (1999:268) indicates that Gorer was homosexual.

4. The Berndts imply that this knowledge of the physiological aspects of conception may be the result of contact (1968:80). In *Love Songs of Arnhem Land* Ronald Berndt states that "north-eastern Arnhem Land Aborigines did not doubt that there was a causal, sequential connection between sexual intercourse and childbirth, and for that matter saw the growth and renewal of nature generally in those terms" (1978:9).

5. In a review of Ronald Berndt's *Excess and Restraint* (1962), Cyril Belshaw (1964) noted precisely the same problems in that book. *Excess and Restraint* is notable not only for its treatments of warfare and sorcery but also for its account of ritual nose bleeding and penis bleeding during the male initiation process (Berndt 1962:94–105).

6. In *Love Songs of Arnhem Land* Berndt suggests that in the 1950s western Arnhem Land had experienced more cultural interference than the eastern region (1978:xvi).

7. Somewhat later than the period we have been considering, in 1966 Geoffrey Gorer published a survey of sexual behavior within England itself.

8. Harriet Lyons recalls that this work was one of the most borrowed books in the Barnard College Library in the early 1960s. It appeared revolutionary to a young woman terrified of the risks of violating the sexual restrictions of this period just before the "sexual revolution."

9. Benedict left the seminar after Linton, who was to become a key collaborator of Kardiner, came to Columbia in 1937. Linton supplanted Benedict, who had been acting chair of the Columbia anthropology department after Boas's retirement (Manson 1986:81). Mead was later to downplay the originality of Kardiner's contribution, while Kardiner opposed Mead's and Benedict's Research in Contemporary Cultures project, which was a continuation of their wartime work on the comparative study of national characters through the use of literature, art, and other material drawn from projective systems (Manson 1986:88, 91).

10. Du Bois recounts an incident that links even walking to the dominant theme of oral deprivation. One child whose development she studied with particular attention is described as learning to stand by "pulling himself up on his mother's leg in an effort to get her attention so that she would pick him up and nurse him" (Du Bois 1960:37).

11. Du Bois's interpreter seemed to confirm the wife–mother equation while contradicting Du Bois's central theme of denial: "Wives are like our mothers. When we were small our mothers fed us. When we are grown our wives cook for us. If there is something good, they keep it in the pot until we come home. When we were small we slept with our mothers; when we are grown we sleep with our wives. Sometimes when we are grown we wake in the night and call our wives 'mother'" (1960:96). Du Bois immediately negates this with the assertion: "In many cases this sentiment is more the expression of a hope than a reality. The mother is indeed the provider, but as we have seen she is an uncertain and unreliable figure" (1960:96).

12. David Greenberg has expressed some doubts about the validity of these codings. Indeed, Greenberg has described the quantitative study of such matters as generally "problematic" (1988:81).

13. Robert A. LeVine, an American anthropologist whose early work was done in Kenya toward the end of British rule, published a study of rape among the Gusii in 1959. LeVine attributed a high level of rape partly to colonial interference with traditional methods of social control. LeVine's analysis interestingly combined elements reminiscent of British anthropology of the colonial period with a Whiting-influenced culture and personality orientation. LeVine argued that Gusii heterosexuality, about which he provides considerable information, had always involved some elements of force and male aggression. This, LeVine said, was partly reflective of hostility between intermarrying clans and partly a result of the training of women and girls to be reluctant sexual partners. Colonialism was said to have made early marriage economically prohibitive at the same time that the Pax Britannica greatly reduced the possibility of violent retribution for unsanctioned sex. LeVine argued that while in some societies colonial interference led to female promiscuity, in societies like the Gusii the combination of heightened male frustration, female sexual reluctance, and a decreased likelihood of serious consequences led to an increase in rape (1959:987 passim).

9. SEX IN CONTEMPORARY ANTHROPOLOGY

1. If one weren't bothered by the speed with which novel and useful locutions have become clichés, one might say that "Virgin Birth" "problematized the anthropological gaze."

2. Deborah Elliston (1999), who worked in Papeete in the 1990s, believes that the māhū role was available to women in the past as well as the present. She argues that stigmatization of transgendered behaviour in the contemporary period applies to men and women who display nontraditional forms of gender crossing, especially where these are seen as foreign imports.

3. In 1981 there was little reliable data available, in any case, concerning the sexual behaviour of berdaches, a fact that has not altered much.

4. In 1997 this group received formal recognition as a "section" within the American Anthropological Association, a status dependent upon the size of a group's membership.

5. Links between war, homosociality, and notions of masculinity have more recently become a staple of modern gender studies. In an interesting photo-essay, available on the World Wide Web (http://users.lanminds.com/~sonyarap/index .html), Sonya Rappoport has provided an extended comparison of Sambia belief and practice concerning masculinity and Western representations, ancient and modern, of the production of "men."

6. This article is, in its own right, a significant contribution to our knowledge of New Guinea conception beliefs and collective representations concerning heterosexuality. Also worthy of note in this regard are the contributions of Ann Chowning (e.g., 1989) and Jane Goodale (e.g., 1980).

7. Williams (1995) delivered the welcoming address at "Queer Frontiers: 1995 and Beyond," a landmark conference of lesbian, gay, and bisexual graduate students hosted by the University of Southern California. The brochure for the conference describes him as a 1960s civil rights activist who, in the 1970s, "was so angered by the Anita Bryant anti-gay campaign that he came out of the closet, and became an activist again, this time for gay and lesbian liberation" (Sipe 1995).

8. Carole Vance (1991) has described this phase in the anthropology of homosexuality as analogous to the first stage of gay historiography, in which authors searched for gay people who had been "hidden from history." Foucault, of course, saw the emergence of a discourse created by homosexuals in support of their own cause as an artifact of the production of "homosexuality" as a category for diagnosis, treatment, and control (1980:101). The possibility that in finding a voice oppressed minorities are reifying and contributing to their own "Othering" creates a dilemma that is not easily solved.

9. In "Anthropology Rediscovers Sex" Carole Vance (1991) notes that there is a tendency to attribute to Foucault the establishment of a constructionist stance in intellectual discourse regarding homosexual identity, a position that in fact had emerged before the publication of *The History of Sexuality*.

10. In a presentation to anthropology department chairs at the American An-

thropological Association, Esther Newton raised a similar question. How, she asked, could gay and lesbian anthropologists combat homophobia in the academy given the diversity within the gay community? Her conclusion, that gay people are oppressed "as if" they belonged to a "real" category and that oppression must therefore be fought on these terms (Newton 2000b:241), is probably an adequate political compromise. She made a similar remark in an article on the general topic of anthropology and homosexuality, in which she directly denied essentialism (Newton 2000d:235).

11. Transsexual individuals are more likely to perceive their status as intrinsic to their natures rather than as performance and to deny their deviance rather than celebrate it.

12. The vehicles actually used for this purpose are children's toy wagons.

13. Symons portrays reluctantly monogamous males supplying provisions to females whose physiognomy is an index of their fertility. His argument has drawn considerable criticism when published elsewhere. Meredith Small, for example, has suggested that Symons's claims owe more to stereotypes of male and female sexuality than to either observed primate behaviors or genetic reality (1993:200). She presents an alternative picture of human evolution in which both males and females must limit the expression of strong libidos in order to care jointly for their progeny, noting that infants who died because of lack of male care would compromise the reproductive success of their fathers as well as their mothers (Small 1996:198). Of course, Small's argument may be influenced as much by the feminist ideal of male–female cooperation and shared parenting as Symons's is by collective representations of lustful males and females who demand commitment, a point that underscores our fundamental argument that debates about the sexuality of others are in large measure conditioned by the sexual conflicts of the milieu in which they are conducted.

14. William Jankowiak's edited volume *Romantic Passion: A Universal Experience?* (1995) was published in the same year as *Sexual Nature, Sexual Culture*. Although applying the label "love" to all of the experiences described by the authors in the volume presents considerable definitional problems, cases are made for heightened emotional attachments to sexual partners in a wide variety of cultures, and, as we have seen, challenges are offered to anthropologists who have linked sexual permissiveness, especially in Oceania, to a devaluation of strong feelings. On a slightly different tack, Pamela Stern and Richard Condon's contribution to this volume suggests that wife exchange, a staple of popular images of the Inuit, may serve female desires as well as male political and economic ends.

15. In early 1996 Harriet Lyons was asked to contribute a paper to a symposium, "Trafficking in Persons in South Asia," organized by the Shastri Indo-Canadian In-

stitute. At the time, neither of us had read *Sexual Nature, Sexual Culture*, which was then newly published. Not being an expert on the sex trade in South Asia as such, she chose to concentrate on the tropes employed in representing it. In her paper (Lyons 1998), which has since been published in a volume of papers presented at the Shastri conference, she made similar points about Orientalist discourse to those raised in Manderson's article, placing more emphasis than Manderson does upon the similarity of the tropes used in advertisements for the sex trade and arguments for its abolition. As a historian of sexuality, she also was more explicit than Manderson about the historical lineage from which current cultural representations have evolved.

16. Rushton argues that polygyny, deficient pair bonding, excessive sexuality, and indifferent nurturance characterize populations that rely (relatively speaking) on r rather than K selection. Among tropical populations r strategies involve a maximization of mating opportunities for men and childbirth for women, and they are aided by large genitalia, strong sexual drives, and a high number of multiple births. Prolonged nurturance in such populations is less important. Rushton believes that natural selection has provided Negroids with all of these evolutionary adaptations. He also claims that populations with r strategies are more violent and less intelligent than cold-region populations with K strategies characterized by prolonged and intensive parental investments in children, birth spacing, small families, and a relatively low sexual drive. Rushton ignores modern social anthropology (apart from references to Draper and Freeman) and relies on an idiosyncratic use of the r–K model that was devised to explain the difference between the reproductive strategies of species as different as rabbits and gorillas rather than alleged variations within single species.

17. One might question whether such a concern had ever been present in anthropological writings about sex. Certainly, most authors have had other agendas. Nonetheless, we can catch glimpses of such an interest in the works of some authors, notably Mead and Malinowski, whatever one may think of their conclusions.

18. For example, in the 2002 collection *Out in Theory: The Emergence of Lesbian and Gay Anthropology*, edited by Ellen Lewin and William Leap, Gayle Rubin "excavated" a substantial tradition of ethnographic studies of gay and lesbian communities, carried out mainly by scholars trained as sociologists, that had been largely ignored by anthropologists.

CONCLUSIONS AND UNFINISHED BUSINESS

1. In a 1994 article published in *Ethos* Bruce Knauft suggests that sexual understandings and practices throughout New Guinea, particularly the South Coast, were

both central to indigenous systems of power and knowledge and extremely diverse. He further suggests that such practices have been deployed to further the interests of observers as diverse as nineteenth-century missionaries and late-twentieth-century anthropologists seeking evidence for both the malleability of human sexuality and gender identity and, somewhat contradictorily, the worldwide provenance of same-sex eroticism. Knauft argues that sexuality has been used by members of South Coast New Guinea societies, before and after colonial incursion, both to inscribe hierarchy and authority on human bodies and to resist such authority. Such resistance is attributed to Asmat men who give a new meaning to the close homosexual bonds forged in the men's house as a substitute for the ritualized heterosexual adultery forbidden by Catholic priests (Knauft 1994:416). In the case of the inland Gebusi, Knauft sees resistance, both to the authority of elders and to the enforced heterosexuality which followed initiation, in voluntary homosexual relations between fellow initiates, carried out alongside the insemination from their seniors to which they are required to submit (417). Knauft suggests that the New Guinea data support the cross-cultural applicability of the Foucauldian regimes of power and knowledge and the creation of subjectivity and resistance through sexuality. At the same time, he warns against applying such notions without careful attention to multiple local, historical, and individual variations in the ways in which sexual desire and performance have been deployed.

References Cited

MANUSCRIPT COLLECTIONS

Burton, Sir Richard, Archive. Huntington Library, San Marino CA.

Ellis, Havelock, Papers. Sterling Library, Yale University.

Falk, E. M., Papers. MSS. Afr. S. 1000. Bodleian Library of Commonwealth and African Studies at Rhodes House, Oxford University.

Lugard, Lord Frederick, Correspondence. Lugard MSS., box 14, file 5. Bodleian Library of Commonwealth and African Studies at Rhodes House, Oxford University.

Malinowski, Bronislaw, Correspondence. London School of Economics and Political Science (BMPL).

Malinowski, Bronislaw, Papers. Boxes 1, 2, 3, 6, 8, 11, 26. Sterling Library, Yale University (BMPY).

Mathews, Hubert, Memoranda. MSS. Afr. S. 783. Bodleian Library of Commonwealth and African Studies at Rhodes House, Oxford University.

Mead, Margaret, Papers and the South Pacific Ethnographic Archives. Containers B5, C4, N40, N97. Manuscript Division, Library of Congress, Washington DC.

Russell, Bertrand, Archive. Folder 239c. Bertrand Russell Research Centre, McMaster University, Hamilton, Ontario.

Thomas, Northcote W., Miscellaneous Manuscripts. MSS. Afr. series, 1910–12. Bodleian Library of Commonwealth and African Studies at Rhodes House, Oxford University.

BOOKS AND PERIODICALS

Aarmo, Margrete. 1999. How Homosexuality Became "Un-African": The Case of Zimbabwe. In Evelyn Blackwood and Saskia E. Wieringa, eds., *Same-Sex Relations and Female Desires: Transgender Practices across Cultures*, 255–280. New York: Columbia University Press.

Abler, Thomas. 1992. Scalping, Torture, Cannibalism and Rape: An Ethnohistorical Analysis of Conflicting Cultural Values in War. *Anthropologica* 34(1):3–20.

Abramson, Paul R. 1992. Sex, Lies and Ethnography. In Gilbert Herdt and Shirley Lindenbaum, eds., *The Time of AIDS: Social Analysis, Theory and Method*, 101–123. Newbury Park CA: Sage Publications.

Abramson, Paul R., and Steven D. Pinkerton. 1995. Preface. *Sexual Nature, Sexual Culture*, ix–xvii. Chicago: University of Chicago Press.

Ackerman, Robert. 1987. *J. G. Frazer: His Life and Work*. Cambridge: Cambridge University Press.

Adam, Barry. 1986. Age, Structure and Sexuality: Reflections on the Anthropological Evidence on Homosexual Relations. In Evelyn Blackwood, ed., *The Many Faces of Homosexuality: Anthropological Approaches to Homosexual Behavior*, 19–34. New York: Harrington Park Press. Originally published in 1985 in *Journal of Homosexuality* 11(3–4).

Ajayi, J. F. Ade. 1965. *Christian Missions in Nigeria, 1841–1891: The Making of a New Elite*. Evanston IL: Northwestern University Press.

Altschuler, Milton. 1971. Cayapa Personality and Sexual Motivation. In Donald S. Marshall and Robert C. Suggs, eds., *Human Sexual Behavior: Variations in the Ethnographic Spectrum*, 38–58. Studies in Sex and Society. New York: Basic Books.

Amadiume, Ifi. 1987. *Male Daughters, Female Husbands: Gender and Sex in an African Society*. London: Zed Books.

Aman, Virginia Lee Barnes, and Janice Boddy. 1994. *Aman: The Story of a Somali Girl*. By Aman as told to Virginia Lee Barnes and Janice Boddy. Toronto: Alfred A. Knopf Canada.

Amis, Kingsley. 1965 [1960]. *Take a Girl Like You*. Harmondsworth: Penguin Books.

Amory, Deborah. N.d. A Brief History of the Society of Lesbian and Gay Anthropologists. Electronic document, http://homepage.mac.com/ctgrant/solga/history.html, accessed May 9, 2003.

Angelino, Henry, and Charles Shedd. 1955. A Note on Berdache. *American Anthropologist* 57:121–126.

Asad, Talal, ed. 1973. *Anthropology and the Colonial Encounter*. London: Ithaca Press.

Atkinson, J. J. 1903. *Primal Law*. Published with *Social Origins* by Andrew Lang. London: Longmans, Green and Company.

Aylmer, M. 1924. *The Authorized Life of Marie C. Stopes*. London: Williams and Hogarth.

Bachofen, Johann Jakob. 1967 [1861]. *Myth, Religion and Mother Right: Selected Writings of J. J. Bachofen*. Trans. Ralph Manheim. Bollingen Series 84. Princeton NJ: Princeton University Press.

Bailey, Robert C., and Robert V. Aunger. 1995. Sexuality, Infertility, and Sexually Transmitted Disease among Farmers and Foragers. In Paul R. Abramson and Steven D. Pinkerton, eds., *Sexual Nature, Sexual Culture*, 195–222. Chicago: University of Chicago Press.

Baker, John R. 1974. *Race.* New York: Oxford University Press.

Baker, Sir Samuel White. 1870. *The Albert N'yanza, Great Basin of the Nile. New Edition.* London: Macmillan.

—. 1875. *Ismailia: A Narrative of the Expedition to Central Africa for the Suppression of the Slave Trade.* New York: Harper and Brothers.

Ballhatchet, Kenneth. 1980. *Race, Sex and Class under the Raj: Imperial Attitudes and Policies and Their Critics, 1793–1805.* London: Weidenfeld and Nicholson.

Banton, Michael. 1967. *Race Relations.* London: Associated Book Publishers.

Barker-Benfield, G. J. 1976. *The Horrors of the Half-Known Life: Male Attitudes toward Women and Sexuality in Victorian America.* New York: Harper and Row.

Barnes, R. H. 1975. Editor's Introduction. In *On the Prehistory of Marriage by Joseph Kohler (1897),* 1–70. Trans. R. H. Barnes and Ruth Barnes. Chicago: University of Chicago Press.

Barzun, Jacques. 1965. *Race: A Study in Superstition.* 2nd ed. New York: Harper and Row.

Bateson, Mary Catherine. 1984. *With a Daughter's Eye: A Memoir of Margaret Mead and Gregory Bateson.* New York: William Morrow.

Beauvoir, Simone de. 1963 [1949]. *The Second Sex.* Trans. H. M. Parshley. New York: Bantam Books.

Behar, Ruth. 1995. Introduction: Out of Exile. In Ruth Behar and Deborah A. Gordon, eds., *Women Writing Culture,* 1–32. Berkeley: University of California Press.

Behar, Ruth, and Deborah A. Gordon, eds. 1995. *Women Writing Culture.* Berkeley: University of California Press.

Beidelman, Thomas O. 1974. *W. Robertson Smith and the Sociological Study of Religion.* Chicago: University of Chicago Press.

—. 1982. *Colonial Evangelism.* Bloomington: Indiana University Press.

Belshaw, Cyril S. 1964. Review of *Excess and Restraint: Social Control among a New Guinea Mountain People* by Ronald M. Berndt. *Man* 64:31.

Benedict, Ruth. 1934a. *Patterns of Culture.* Boston: Houghton Mifflin.

—. 1934b. Anthropology and the Abnormal. *Journal of General Psychology* 10:59–82.

—. 1935. *Zuni Mythology.* 2 vols. New York: Columbia University Press.

—. 1938. Continuities and Discontinuities in Cultural Conditioning. *Psychiatry* 1:161–187.

—. 1939. Sex in Primitive Society. *American Journal of Orthopsychiatry* 9:570–573.

—. 1959 [1934]. Anthropology and the Abnormal. Reprinted in Margaret Mead, *An Anthropologist at Work: Writings of Ruth Benedict,* 262–283. Boston: Houghton Mifflin.

———. 1974 [1946]. *The Chrysanthemum and the Sword: Patterns of Japanese Culture*. New York: New American Library.

Berndt, Ronald M. 1952. *Djanggawul: An Aboriginal Religious Cult of North-Eastern Arnhem Land*. London: Routledge and Kegan Paul.

———. 1962. *Excess and Restraint: Social Control among a New Guinea Mountain People*. Chicago: University of Chicago Press.

———. 1978 [1976]. *Love Songs of Arnhem Land*. Chicago: University of Chicago Press.

Berndt, Ronald M., and Catherine H. Berndt. 1942. A Preliminary Report of Fieldwork in the Ooldea Region, Western South Australia. *Oceania* 13:243–280.

———. 1968 [1951]. *Sexual Behavior in Western Arnhem Land*. New York: Johnson Reprint.

Besnier, Niko. 1994. Polynesian Gender Liminality through Time and Space. In Gilbert Herdt, ed., *Third Sex, Third Gender: Beyond Sexual Dimorphism in Culture and History*, 285–328. New York: Zone Books.

Besterman, Theodore. 1931. Introduction. In *Dress, Drinks and Drums* by Ernest Crawley, i–x. London: Methuen.

Bettelheim, Bruno. 1952. *Symbolic Wounds: Puberty Rites and the Envious Male*. New York: Collier Books.

Biddiss, Michael D. 1970. *Father of Racist Ideology: The Social and Political Thought of Count Gobineau*. London: Weidenfeld and Nicholson.

Bingham, Hiram. 1847. *A Residence of Twenty-One Years in the Sandwich Islands*. 3rd ed. Hartford CT: Huntington.

Bishop, M. Guy. 1993. "The Captain Has Seen Utah without Goggles": The Mormons and Richard Burton. In Alan Jutzi, ed., *In Search of Richard Burton: Papers from a Huntington Library Symposium*, 61–79. San Marino CA: Huntington Library.

Blackwood, Evelyn, and Saskia E. Wieringa. 1999. Sapphic Shadows: Challenging the Silence in the Study of Sexuality. In Evelyn Blackwood and Saskia E. Wieringa, eds., *Same-Sex Relations and Female Desires: Transgender Practices across Cultures*, 39–63. New York: Columbia University Press.

Bleys, Rudi. 1995. *The Geography of Perversion: Male-to-Male Sexual Behavior outside the West and the Ethnographic Imagination, 1750–1918*. New York: New York University Press.

Blumenbach, Johann Friedrich. 1969 [1795, 1865]. *On the Natural Varieties of Mankind (De Generis Humani Varietate Nativa)*. Trans. and ed. Thomas Bendyshe. New York: Bergman Publishers.

Boddy, Janice. 1989. *Wombs and Alien Spirits: Women, Men and the Zār Cult in Northern Sudan*. Madison: University of Wisconsin Press.

Bolton, Ralph. 1992. Mapping Terra Incognita: Sex Research for AIDS Prevention –

An Urgent Agenda for the 1990s. In Gilbert Herdt and Shirley Lindenbaum, eds., *The Time of* AIDS: *Social Analysis, Theory and Method*, 124–158. Newbury Park CA: Sage Publications.

————. 1996. Coming Home: The Journey of a Gay Ethnographer in the Years of the Plague. In Ellen Lewin and William L. Leap, eds., *Out in the Field: Reflections of Lesbian and Gay Anthropologists*, 147–168. Urbana: University of Illinois Press.

Borneman, John. 1996. Until Death Do Us Part: Marriage/Death in Anthropological Discourse. *American Ethnologist* 23(2):215–234.

Bothwell, A. 1931. Letter. *Man* 31:280.

Bourke, John Gregory. 1891. *Scatologic Rites of All Nations*. Washington DC: W. H. Loudermilk.

Brady, Ian, ed. 1983. Speaking in the Name of the Real: Freeman and Mead on Samoa. *American Anthropologist* 85(4):908–947.

Brandes, Stanley. 1981. "Like Wounded Stags": Male Sexual Ideology in an Andalusian Town. In Sherry B. Ortner and Harriet Whitehead, eds., *Sexual Meanings: The Cultural Construction of Gender and Sexuality*, 216–239. Cambridge: Cambridge University Press.

Briant, K. 1962. *Marie Stopes: A Biography*. London: Hogarth Press.

Briffault, Robert. 1977 [1927, 1931, 1959]. *The Mothers. With an Introduction by Gordon Rattray Taylor*. Reprint of the 1959 abridged ed. by arrangement with Humanities Press. 1st single-vol. ed. published 1931. Original 3-vol. ed. published in London by George Allen and Unwin, 1927. New York: Atheneum.

Briffault, Robert, and Bronislaw Malinowski. 1956. *Marriage: Past and Present: A Debate between Robert Briffault and Bronislaw Malinowski*. Ed. and with an introduction by M. F. Ashley Montagu. Boston: Procter Sargeant.

Bristow, Edward J. 1977. *Vice and Vigilance: Purity Movements in Britain since 1700*. London: Gill and Macmillan.

Broca, Paul. 1864. *On the Phenomena of Hybridity in the Genus Homo*. Trans. C. Carter Blake. London: Publications of the Anthropological Society of London.

Brodie, Fawn. 1967. *The Devil Drives: A Life of Sir Richard Burton*. New York: W. W. Norton.

Brome, Vincent. 1979. *Havelock Ellis, Philosopher of Sex: A Biography*. London: Routledge and Kegan Paul.

Brummelhuis, Han ten, and Gilbert Herdt, eds. 1995. *Culture and Sexual Risk: Anthropological Perspectives on* AIDS. Luxembourg: Gordon and Breach.

Buffon, Georges Louis Leclerc, Comte de. 1791. *Natural History (Histoire naturelle)*. Trans. William Smellie. 3rd ed., 9 vols. London.

Buhle, Mari Jo. 1998. *Feminism and Its Discontents: A Century of Struggle with Psychoanalysis*. Cambridge: Harvard University Press.

Burbank, Victoria Katherine. 1988. *Aboriginal Adolescence: Maidenhood in an Australian Community*. New Brunswick NJ: Rutgers University Press.

Burbank, Victoria Katherine, and James S. Chisholm. 1998. Adolescent Pregnancy and Parenthood in an Australian Aboriginal Community. In Gilbert Herdt and Stephen C. Leavitt, eds., *Adolescence in Pacific Island Societies*, 55–70. Pittsburgh: University of Pittsburgh Press.

Burrow, J. W. 1966. *Evolution and Society*. Cambridge: Cambridge University Press.

Burton, Isabel. 1893. *The Life of Captain Sir Richard F. Burton*. 2 vols. London: Chapman and Hall.

Burton, Sir Richard F. 1851. *Sindh and the Races That Inhabit the Valley of the Indus*. London: W. H. Allen.

———. 1852. Postscript. In *Falconry in the Valley of the Indus*. London: John van Voorst.

———. 1855–56. *Personal Narrative of a Pilgrimage to Mecca and Medina*. 3 vols. London.

———. 1861a. *The City of the Saints, and across the Rocky Mountains to California*. London: Longmans, Green and Company.

———. 1861b. Ethnological Notes on M. Du Chaillu's "Explorations and Adventures in Equatorial Africa." *Transactions of the Ethnological Society of London*, n.s. 1:316–326.

———. 1863. A Day amongst the Fans. *Anthropological Review* 1:43–54.

———. 1863–64. Notes on Certain Matters Connected with the Dahoman. In *Memoirs of the Anthropological Society of London* 1:308–321.

———. 1865a. *Stone Talk. Being Some of the Marvellous Sayings of a Petral Portion of Fleet Street, London, to One Doctor Polyglott, Ph.D., by Frank Baker, D.O.N.* London: Robert Hardwicke.

———. 1865b. Discussion of "Notes on the Dahoman." *Journal of the Anthropological Society of London* 1 (February):vi–xi.

———. 1865c. *Wit and Wisdom of West Africa: Or, a Book of Proverbial Philosophy, Idioms, Enigmas, and Laconisms, Compiled by Richard F. Burton*. London: Tinsley Brothers.

———. 1885–87. *A Plain and Literal Translation of the Arabian Nights' Entertainment, Now Entitled the Book of the Thousand Nights and a Night. With Introduction, Explanatory Notes on the Manners and Customs of Moslem Men and a Terminal Essay upon the History of the Nights*. 10 vols. London: Kamashastra Society.

———. 1886–88. *Supplemental Nights to the Book of the Thousand Nights and a Night. With Notes Anthropological and Explanatory* by Richard F. Burton. 6 vols. Printed by the Kama-Shastra Society for Private Subscribers Only.

————. 1924. *Selected Papers on Anthropology, Travel and Exploration* by Sir Richard Burton; ed. and with an introduction and occasional notes by N. M. Penzer. London: A. M. Philpot.

————. 1967. *The Erotic Traveller. Selections.* Ed. Edward Leigh. New York: Putnam.

————. 1971 [1862]. *The City of the Saints, and across the Rocky Mountains to California.* 1st American ed. New York: AMS Press.

————. 1978a [1863]. *Abeokuta and the Camaroons Mountains.* 2 vols. Authorized facsimile of vol. 1. Ann Arbor MI: University Microfilms International.

————. 1978b [1864]. *A Mission to Gelele, King of Dahomey, with Notices of the So-Called "Amazons," the Grand Customs, the Yearly Customs, the Human Sacrifices, the Present State of the Slave Trade and the Negro's Place in Nature.* 2 vols. Ann Arbor MI: University Microfilms International.

————. 1995 [1860]. *The Lake Regions of Central Africa. An Unabridged and Slightly Altered Republication of the Work Originally Published by Harper & Brothers, New York.* Mineola NY: Dover Publications.

Butler, Judith. 1990. *Gender Trouble: Feminism and the Subversion of Identity.* New York: Routledge.

————. 1993. *Bodies That Matter: On the Discursive Limits of "Sex."* New York: Routledge.

Caffrey, Margaret M. 1989. *Ruth Benedict: Stranger in This Land.* Austin: University of Texas Press.

Cairns, H. Alan C. 1965. *Prelude to Imperialism: British Reactions to Central African Society, 1840–1890.* London: Routledge and Kegan Paul.

Caldwell, John C., and Pat Caldwell. 1977. The Role of Marital Sexual Abstinence in Determining Fertility: A Study of the Yoruba in Nigeria. *Population Studies* 31(3):193–217.

Caldwell, John C., Pat Caldwell, and Pat Quiggin. 1989. The Social Context of AIDS in Sub-Saharan Africa. *Population and Development Review* 15(2):185–234.

————. 1991. The African Sexual System: Reply to Le Blanc et al. *Population and Development Review* 17(3):506–515.

Campbell, Joseph. 1967. Introduction to Myth, Religion and Mother Right. In *Myth, Religion and Mother Right: Selected Writings of J. J. Bachofen* by J. J. Bachofen, xxiv–lvii. Trans. Ralph Manheim. Bollingen Series 84. Princeton NJ: Princeton University Press.

Cancian, Francesca M. 1987. *Love in America: Gender and Self-Development.* Cambridge: Cambridge University Press.

Carpenter, Edward. 1930 [1916]. *The Intermediate Sex: A Study of Some Transitional Types of Men and Women.* Reprint of 4th ed. 1st ed. published 1908. London: George Allen and Unwin.

————. 1975 [1919]. *Intermediate Types among Primitive Folk: A Study in Social Evolution*. Reprint of 2nd ed., originally published in London by George Allen and Unwin. 1st ed. published in London by George Allen and Unwin, 1914. New York: Arno Press.

Carrier, Joseph. 1995. *De los Otros: Intimacy and Homosexuality among Mexican Men*. New York: Columbia University Press.

Caton, Hiram, ed. 1990. *The Samoa Reader: Anthropologists Take Stock*. Lanham MD: University Press of America.

Cesara, Manda. 1982. *Reflections of a Woman Anthropologist: No Hiding Place*. London: Academic Press.

Chowning, Ann. 1989. Sex, Shit, and Shame: Changing Gender Relations among the Lakalai. In Mac Marshall and John L. Caughey, eds., *Culture, Kin and Cognition: Essays in Honor of Ward H. Goodenough*, 17–32. Special Publication no. 25. Washington DC: American Anthropological Association.

Claridge, Elizabeth. 1982. Introduction. In *Travels in West Africa* 5th ed., by Mary Kingsley, ix–xviii. London: Virago Books.

Cohen, Lawrence. 1995. The Pleasures of Castration: The Postoperative Status of Hijras, Jankhas, and Academics. In Paul R. Abramson and Steven D. Pinkerton, eds., *Sexual Nature, Sexual Culture*, 276–304. Chicago: University of Chicago Press.

Comaroff, Jean, and John Comaroff. 1991. *Of Revelation and Revolution: Christianity, Colonialism and Consciousness in South Africa*. Chicago: University of Chicago Press.

Comaroff, John, and Jean Comaroff. 1992. *Ethnography and the Historical Imagination*. Boulder CO: Westview Press.

————. 1997. *On Revelation and Revolution: The Dialectics of Modernity on a South African Frontier*. Chicago: University of Chicago Press.

Côté, James E. 1994. *Adolescent Storm and Stress: An Evaluation of the Mead–Freeman Controversy*. Hillsdale NJ: Lawrence Erlbaum.

————. 2000. The Implausibility of Freeman's Hoaxing Theory: An Update. *Journal of Youth and Adolescence* 29(5):575–585.

Counts, Dorothy Ayers. 1985. Infant Care and Feeding in Kaliai, West New Britain, Papua New Guinea. In Leslie B. Marshall, ed., *Infant Care and Feeding in the South Pacific*, 155–169. New York: Gordon and Breach.

Counts, Dorothy Ayers, and David R. Counts. 1983. Father's Water Equals Mother's Milk: The Conception of Parentage in Kaliai, West New Britain. In *Concepts of Conception: Procreation Ideologies in Papua New Guinea*. Special issue of *Mankind* 14:46–56.

Coward, Rosalind. 1983. *Patriarchal Precedents: Sexuality and Social Relations*. London: Routledge and Kegan Paul.

Crawley, Ernest. 1902. *The Mystic Rose: A Study in Primitive Marriage*. London: Macmillan.

———. 1929. *Studies of Savages and Sex*. Ed. Theodore Besterman. London: Methuen.

———. 1931. *Dress, Drinks and Drums: Further Studies of Savages and Sex*. Ed. Theodore Besterman. London: Methuen.

Curtin, Philip M. 1964. *The Image of Africa: British Ideas and Action, 1780–1850*. London: Macmillan.

Daly, Mary. 1978. *Gyn/Ecology: The Metaethics of Radical Feminism*. Boston: Beacon Press.

Darnell, Regna. 1998. *And Along Came Boas: Continuity and Revolution in American Anthropology*. Amsterdam: John Benjamins Publishing Company.

Darwin, Charles. 1871. *The Descent of Man, and Selection in Relation to Sex*. 2 vols. New York: Appleton.

———. 1981 [1871]. *The Descent of Man and Selection in Relation to Sex*. Reprint of 1st English ed. published in London by J. Murray, with an introduction by J. T. Bonner and R. M. May. Princeton NJ: Princeton University Press.

Dawson, Simon. 2000. The Edward Carpenter Archive. Electronic document, http://www.simondsn.dircom.co.uk/ecindex.htm, accessed May 7, 2002.

Delaney, Carol. 1986. The Meaning of Paternity and the Virgin Birth Debate. *Man*, n.s. 21(3):494–513.

Devereux, George. 1937. Institutionalized Homosexuality of the Mohave Indians. *Human Biology* 9:498–527.

———. 1948. Mohave Coyote Tales. *Journal of American Folklore* 61:233–255.

———. 1950. Heterosexual Behavior of the Mohave Indians. In Géza Róheim, ed., *Psychoanalysis and the Social Sciences*, 2:85–128. New York: International Universities Press.

———. 1951. Cultural and Characterological Traits of the Mohave Related to the Anal Stage of Psychosexual Development. *Psychoanalytic Quarterly* 20:398–422.

———. 1955. *A Study of Abortion in Primitive Societies: A Typological, Distributional, and Dynamic Analysis of the Prevention of Birth in 400 Preindustrial Societies*. New York: Julian.

———. 1967. *From Anxiety to Method in the Behavioral Sciences*. The Hague: Mouton.

———. 1969 [1961]. *Mohave Ethnopsychiatry: The Psychic Disturbances of an Indian Tribe*. Washington DC: Smithsonian Institution Press.

de Waal, Frans B. M. 1995. Sex as an Alternative to Aggression in the Bonobo. In Paul R. Abramson and Steven D. Pinkerton, eds., *Sexual Nature, Sexual Culture*, 37–56. Chicago: University of Chicago Press.

Diderot, Denis. 1989. Le Supplément au voyage de Bougainville. Written ca. 1772, posthumously published in 1796. In *Le Neveu de Rameau (oeuvres complètes)*, 12:577–647. Paris: Hermann.

Dorson, Richard. 1968. *The British Folklorists: A History*. Chicago: University of Chicago Press.

Draper, Patricia. 1989. African Marriage Systems: Perspectives from Evolutionary Ecology. *Ethology and Sociobiology* 10:145–169.

Du Bois, Cora. 1960 [1944]. *The People of Alor: A Social-Psychological Study of an East Indian Island*. Cambridge: Harvard University Press.

Duchet, Michèle. 1971. *Anthropologie et histoire au siècle des lumières*. Paris: François Maspero.

Durkheim, Émile. 1902–3. Review of *Social Origins* by Andrew Lang and *Primal Law* by J. J. Atkinson. *Année Sociologique* 7:407–411.

———. 1912. Review of *Primitive Paternity* by E. S. Hartland. *Année Sociologique* 12:410–414.

———. 1915 [1912]. *The Elementary Forms of the Religious Life*. Trans. J. Swain. London: George Allen and Unwin.

———. 1964 [1893]. *The Division of Labor in Society*. Trans. George Simpson. New York: Free Press.

Dykes, Eva Beatrice. 1962. *The Negro in English Romantic Thought*. Washington DC: Associated Publishers.

Ekechi, Felix M. 1972. *Missionary Rivalry and Enterprise in Igboland, 1857–1914*. London: Frank Cass.

Elgin, Suzette Hayden. 1984. *Native Tongue*. New York: DAW Books.

Ellingson, Ter. 2001. *The Myth of the Noble Savage*. Berkeley: University of California Press.

Ellis, Havelock. 1890. *The Criminal*. London: Walter Scott.

———. 1910a [1899]. *The Evolution of Modesty*. 3rd ed. Vol. 1 (originally published as vol. 2) of *Studies in the Psychology of Sex*. Philadelphia: P. A. Davis.

———. 1910b. *Sex in Relation to Society*. Vol. 6 of *Studies in the Psychology of Sex*. Philadelphia: P. A. Davis.

———. 1912. *The Task of Social Hygiene*. London: Constable.

———. 1913 [1903]. *Analysis of the Sexual Impulse*. Vol. 3 of*Studies in the Psychology of Sex*. 2nd ed. Philadelphia: P. A. Davis.

———. 1918. *The Erotic Rights of Women and the Objects of Marriage: Two Essays by Havelock Ellis*. Publication no. 5, British Society for the Study of Sex Psychology. London: Battley Brothers.

———. 1930 [1894]. *Man and Woman: A Study of Human Secondary Sexual Characters*. Reprint of 6th ed., published in 1926. London: A. and C. Black.

————. 1931. *More Essays of Love and Virtue*. Garden City NY: Doubleday, Doran.

————. 1942a. *Studies in the Psychology of Sex*, vol. 1. Pt. 1 is a reprint of the 3rd ed. of *The Evolution of Modesty* (previously vol. 1, originally published in 1899 as vol. 2). Pt. 2 is a reprint of the 2nd ed. (1913) of *Analysis of the Sexual Impulse* (previously vol. 3). Pt. 3 is a reprint of *Sexual Selection in Man* (1905, previously vol. 4). Pt. 4 is a reprint of the 3rd ed. (1910) of *Sexual Inversion* (previously vol. 2, originally published in 1897 as vol. 1 by the so-called Watford University Press). Pages of these 4 pts. are separately numbered. 2 vols. New York: Random House.

————. 1942b. *Studies in the Psychology of Sex*, vol. 2. Pt. 1 is a reprint of the 3rd ed. (1910) of *Erotic Symbolism* (originally vol. 5). Pt. 2 is a reprint of the 1st ed. (1928) of *Eonism and Other Supplementary Studies* (originally vol. 7). Pt. 3 is a reprint of the 1st ed. (1910) of *Sex in Relation to Society* (originally vol. 6). Pages of these 3 pts. are separately numbered. 2 vols. New York: Random House.

————. 1957 [1922]. *On Life and Sex*. Containing *Little Essays of Love and Virtue* and *More Essays of Love and Virtue*. New York: New American Library.

Ellis, Havelock, in collaboration with John Addington Symonds. 1897. *Sexual Inversion*. London: Wilson and Macmillan. Withdrawn from publication. Reissued (without mention of Symonds) by Watford University Press, November 1897.

Elliston, Deborah A. 1995. Erotic Anthropology: "Ritualized Homosexuality" in Melanesia and Beyond. *American Ethnologist* 22(4):848–867.

————. 1999. Negotiating Transnational Sexual Economies: Female *Māhū* and Same-Sex Sexuality in "Tahiti and Her Islands." In Evelyn Blackwood and Saskia E. Wieringa, eds., *Same-Sex Relations and Female Desires: Transgender Practices across Cultures*, 232–252. New York: Columbia University Press.

Elwin, Verrier. 1939. *The Baiga*. Foreword by J. H. Hutton. London: John Murray.

————. 1964. *The Tribal World of Verrier Elwin*. Bombay: Oxford University Press.

————. 1991 [1947]. *The Muria and Their Ghotul*. Delhi: Oxford University Press for Vanya Prakashan.

Engels, Friedrich. 1986 [1884]. *The Origin of the Family, Private Property and the State*. London: Penguin Books.

Evans-Pritchard, Sir E. E. 1940. *The Nuer*. Oxford: Clarendon Press.

————. 1957. The Zande Royal Court. *Zaïre* 5:495–511.

————. 1965. *Theories of Primitive Religion*. Oxford: Clarendon Press.

————. 1970. Sexual Inversion among the Azande. *American Anthropologist* 72(6): 1428–1434.

————. 1974. *Man and Woman among the Azande*. London: Faber and Faber.

————. 1975. Some Notes on Zande Sex Habits. *American Anthropologist* 75(1):171–175.

Farmer, Paul. 1992. New Disorder, Old Dilemmas: AIDS and Anthropology in Haiti.

In *The Time of* AIDS: *Social Analysis, Theory and Method*, 287–318. Newbury Park CA: Sage Publications.

———. 2001 [1999]. *Infections and Inequalities: The Modern Plagues*. 1st paperback ed., updated. Berkeley: University of California Press.

Farwell, Byron. 1963. *Burton: A Biography of Sir Richard Francis Burton*. London: Longmans, Green and Company.

Ferguson, Adam. 1995 [1767]. *An Essay on the History of Civil Society*. Ed. Fania Oz-Salzberger. Cambridge: Cambridge University Press.

Fermi, Patrick. 1998. Georges Devereux (Suite). Electronic document, http://perso .wanadoo.fr/geza.roheim/html/devereu1.htm, accessed March 8, 2003.

Fernández-Alemany, Manuel, and Stephen O. Murray. 2002. *Heterogender Homosexuality in Honduras*. San Jose CA: Writers Club Press.

Fields, K. 1982. Political Contingencies of Witchcraft in Colonial Central Africa: Culture and the State in Marxist Theory. *Canadian Journal of African Studies* 16(3):567–594.

Firth, Sir Raymond, ed. 1957a. *Man and Culture: An Evaluation of the Work of Bronislaw Malinowski*. London: Routledge and Kegan Paul.

———. 1957b [1936]. *We, the Tikopia: A Sociological Study of Kinship in Primitive Polynesia*. 2nd ed. London: George Allen and Unwin.

———. 1981. Bronislaw Malinowski. In S. Silverman, ed., *Totems and Teachers: Perspectives on the History of Anthropology*, 101–137. New York: Columbia University Press.

Fison, Lorimer, and A. W. Howitt. 1967 [1880]. *Kamilaroi and Kurnai: Group Marriage and Relationship, and Marriage by Elopement, Drawn Chiefly from the Usage of the Australian Aborigines; Also the Kurnai Tribe, Their Customs in Peace and War*. Oosterhout: Anthropological Publications.

Ford, C. S., and F. A. Beach. 1951. *Patterns of Sexual Behavior*. New York: Paul B. Hoeber.

Forde, Daryll. 1938. Review of *We, the Tikopia* by Raymond Firth. *Man* 38:27–28.

Fortes, Meyer. 1933. Review of *Life in Nature* by James Hinton. *Man* 33:73.

———. 1957. Malinowski and the Study of Kinship. In Raymond Firth, ed., *Man and Culture: An Evaluation of the Work of Bronislaw Malinowski*, 157–188. London: Routledge and Kegan Paul.

Fortune, Reo F. 1939. Arapesh Warfare. *American Anthropologist* 41:22–41.

Foucault, Michel. 1980 [1976]. *The History of Sexuality*. Vol. 1, *An Introduction*. Trans. Robert Hurley. New York: Vintage Books.

Frazer, Sir James G. 1899. Observations on Central Australian Totemism. *Journal of the Anthropological Institute of Great Britain and Ireland* 28(3–4):281–286.

———. 1905. The Beginnings of Religion and Totemism among the Australian Aborigines. *Fortnightly Review* 84:452–466.

————. 1910. *Totemism and Exogamy: A Treatise on Early Forms of Superstition and Society*. 4 vols. London: Macmillan.

Freeman, Derek. 1964. Review of *Island of Passion* by Donald Marshall. *Man* 64:31–32.

————. 1983. *Margaret Mead and Samoa: The Making and Unmaking of an Anthropological Myth*. Cambridge: Harvard University Press.

————. 1999. *The Fateful Hoaxing of Margaret Mead: A Historical Analysis of Her Samoan Research*. Boulder CO: Westview Press.

French Army Surgeon (Jacobus X). 1898. *Untrodden Fields of Anthropology*. 2 vols. Paris: Carrington.

Freud, Sigmund. 1953 [1905]. Fragment of an Analysis of a Case of Hysteria. In *The Standard Edition of the Complete Psychological Works of Sigmund Freud*. Ed. James Strachey, 7:130–243. London: Hogarth Press.

————. 1959 [1913]. *Totem and Taboo*. In *The Standard Edition of the Complete Psychological Works of Sigmund Freud*. Ed. James Strachey, 13:ix–162. New York: Macmillan.

Friedan, Betty. 1963. *The Feminine Mystique*. New York: Norton.

Friedl, Ernestine. 1994. Sex the Invisible. *American Anthropologist* 96(4):833–844.

Frye, Marilyn. 1988. Lesbian "Sex." *Sinister Wisdom* 35 (Summer–Fall):46–54.

Fryer, Peter. 1965. *The Birth Controllers*. London: Secker and Warburg.

Gallagher, Catherine. 1994. *Nobody's Story: The Vanishing Acts of Women Writers in the Marketplace, 1670–1820*. Berkeley: University of California Press.

Gebhard, Paul H. 1971a. Foreword. In Donald S. Marshall and Robert C. Suggs, eds., *Human Sexual Behavior: Variations in the Ethnographic Spectrum*, xi–xiv. Studies in Sex and Society. New York: Basic Books.

————. 1971b. Human Sexual Behavior: A Summary Statement. In Donald S. Marshall and Robert C. Suggs, eds., *Human Sexual Behavior: Variations in the Ethnographic Spectrum*, 206–217. Studies in Sex and Society. New York: Basic Books.

Gell, Simeran M. S. 1992. *The Ghotul in Muria Society*. Chur: Harwood Academic Publishers.

Genovese, Eugene. 1974. *Roll, Jordan, Roll*. New York: Pantheon Books.

Gill, Anton. 1995. *Ruling Passions: Sex, Race and Empire*. London: BBC Books.

Gilman, Sander L. 1985. *Difference and Pathology: Stereotypes of Sexuality, Race, and Madness*. Ithaca NY: Cornell University Press.

————. 1989. *Sexuality: An Illustrated History; Representing the Sexual in Medicine and Culture from the Middle Ages to the Age of* AIDS. New York: Wiley.

Ginsburg, Faye. 1987. Procreation Stories: Reproduction, Nurturance, and Procreation in Life Narratives of Abortion Activists. *American Ethnologist* 14:623–636.

Glatzer, Jenna. 1999. Interview with Suzette Hayden Elgin. Electronic document, http://www.absolutewrite.com/novels/suzette_haden_elgin.htm, accessed January 4, 2002.

Gobineau, Arthur, Comte de. 1966 [1853–55]. *The Inequality of Human Races*. Trans. Adrian Collins. Los Angeles: Noontide Press.

Goldenweiser, Alexander. 1929. Sex and Primitive Society. In V. F. Calverton and S. D. Schmalhausen, eds., *Sex in Civilization*, 53–66. Garden City NY: Garden City Publishing Company.

Goodale, Jane. 1971. *Tiwi Wives*. Monographs of the American Ethnological Society 51. Seattle: University of Washington Press.

———. 1980. Sexuality and Marriage: A Kaulong Model of Nature and Culture. In C. MacCormack and M. Strathern, eds., *Nature, Culture and Gender*, 119–143. Cambridge: Cambridge University Press.

Gordon, Robert J. 1992a. *The Bushman Myth: The Making of a Namibian Underclass*. Boulder CO: Westview Press.

———. 1992b. The Venal Hottentot Venus and the Great Chain of Being. *African Studies* 51(2):185–201.

Gorer, Geoffrey. 1949 [1935]. *Africa Dances*. 2nd ed. London: John Lehmann.

———. 1967 [1938]. *Himalayan Village: An Account of the Lepchas of Sikkim*. 2nd ed. New York: Basic Books.

Gosselin, Claudie. 2000. Feminism, Anthropology and the Politics of Excision in Mali: Global and Local Debates in a Postcolonial World. *Anthropologica* 42(1):43–60.

Gould, Stephen Jay. 1982. The Hottentot Venus. *Natural History* 91:20–27.

Grant, Nicole J. 1995. From Margaret Mead's Field Notes: What Counted as Sex in Samoa? *American Anthropologist* 97(4):678–682.

Green, Margaret M. 1947. *Ibo Village Affairs*. London: Sidgwick and Jackson.

Greenberg, David F. 1988. *The Construction of Homosexuality*. Chicago: University of Chicago Press.

———. 1995. The Pleasures of Homosexuality. In Paul R. Abramson and Steven D. Pinkerton, eds., *Sexual Nature, Sexual Culture*, 223–256. Chicago: University of Chicago Press.

Greene, J. C. 1959. *The Death of Adam: Evolution and Its Impact on Western Thought*. Ames: Iowa State University Press.

Gregersen, Edgar. 1983. *Sexual Practices: The Story of Human Sexuality*. New York: Franklin Watts.

Gregor, Thomas. 1985. *Anxious Pleasures: The Sexual Lives of an Amazonian People*. Chicago: University of Chicago Press.

———. 1995. Sexuality and the Experience of Love. In Paul R. Abramson and Steven

D. Pinkerton, eds., *Sexual Nature, Sexual Culture*, 330–350. Chicago: University of Chicago Press.

Griffiths, Alison. 2002. *Wondrous Difference: Cinema, Anthropology and Turn-of-the-Century Visual Culture*. New York: Columbia University Press.

Grosskurth, Phyllis. 1964. *The Woeful Victorian: A Biography of John Addington Symonds*. New York: Holt, Rinehart and Winston.

———. 1980. *Havelock Ellis: A Biography*. Toronto: McClelland and Stewart.

———. 1988. *Margaret Mead: A Life of Controversy*. London: Penguin Books.

Gruenbaum, Ellen. 2001. *The Female Circumcision Controversy: An Anthropological Perspective*. Philadelphia: University of Pennsylvania Press.

Guenther, Mathias G. 1980. From "Brutal Savages" to "Harmless People." *Paideuma* 26:123–140.

Guha, Ramachandra. 1999. *Savaging the Civilized: Verrier Elwin, His Tribals, and India*. Chicago: University of Chicago Press.

Guillaumin, Colette. 1995. *Racism, Sexism, Power and Ideology*. London: Routledge.

Haggard, H. Rider. 1886. *She*. New York: Harper and Brothers.

Hall, G. Stanley. 1904. *Adolescence: Its Psychology and Its Relations to Physiology, Anthropology, Sociology, Sex, Crime, Religion and Education*. 2 vols. New York: D. Appleton.

Hall, R. 1977. *Passionate Crusader: The Life of Marie Stopes*. New York: Harcourt Brace Jovanovich.

Haller, John, and Robin Haller. 1974. *The Physician and Sexuality in Victorian America*. Urbana: University of Illinois Press.

Hallpike, Christopher. 1969. Social Hair. *Man*, n.s. 4(2):256–264.

Hammond, Dorothy, and Alta Jablow. 1970. *The Africa That Never Was: Four Centuries of British Writing about Africa*. New York: Twayne.

Haraway, Donna J. 1991. *Simians, Cyborgs, and Women: The Reinvention of Nature*. New York: Routledge.

Harris, Helen. 1995. Rethinking Heterosexual Relationships in Polynesia: A Case Study of Mangaia, Cook Island. In William Jankowiak, ed., *Romantic Passion: A Universal Experience?* 95–127. New York: Columbia University Press.

Harris, Marvin. 1969 [1968]. *The Rise of Anthropological Theory*. London: Routledge and Kegan Paul.

Hartland, Edwin Sidney. 1894. *The Legend of Perseus*. Vol. 1, *The Supernatural Birth*. London: David Nutt.

———. 1967 [1909, 1910]. *Primitive Paternity: The Myth of Supernatural Birth in Relation to the History of the Family*. 2 vols. reprinted in a single-vol. ed. Nendeln: Kraus Reprint Ltd.

Hayes, Rose Oldfield. 1975. Female Genital Mutilation, Fertility Control, Women's

Roles and the Patrilineage in the Modern Sudan: A Functional Analysis. *American Ethnologist* 2(4):617–633.

Hays, H. R. 1972. *Birds, Beasts and Men: A Humanist History of Zoology*. Baltimore MD: Penguin Books.

Heald, Suzette. 1999. *Manhood and Morality: Sex, Violence and Ritual in Gisu Society*. London: Routledge.

Henry, Jules. 1971. *Pathways to Madness*. New York: Random House.

Herdt, Gilbert. 1981. *Guardians of the Flutes: Idioms of Masculinity*. New York: Mc-Graw-Hill.

———, ed. 1992. *Gay Culture in America*. Boston: Beacon Press.

———, ed. 1994. *Third Sex, Third Gender: Beyond Sexual Dimorphism in Culture and History*. New York: Zone Books.

———. 1997. *Same Sex, Different Cultures: Gays and Lesbians across Cultures*. Boulder CO: Westview Press.

———. 1999. *Sambia Sexual Culture: Essays from the Field*. Chicago: University of Chicago Press.

———. 2000. *Something to Tell You: The Road Families Travel When a Child Is Gay*. New York: Columbia University Press.

Herdt, Gilbert, and Andrew Boxer, eds. 1996 [1993]. *Children of Horizons: How Gay and Lesbian Teens Are Leading a New Way out of the Closet*. Boston: Beacon Press.

Herdt, Gilbert, and Stephen C. Leavitt, eds. 1998. *Adolescence in Pacific Island Societies*. Pittsburgh: University of Pittsburgh Press.

Herdt, Gilbert, and Shirley Lindenbaum, eds. 1992. *The Time of* AIDS: *Social Analysis, Theory and Method*. Newbury Park CA: Sage Publications.

Herdt, Gilbert, and Paul Stoller. 1989. *Intimate Communications: Erotics and the Study of a Culture*. New York: Columbia University Press.

Hinsley, Curtis. 1983. Ethnographic Charisma and Scientific Routine: Cushing and Fewkes in the American Southwest, 1879–1893. In George W. Stocking Jr., ed., *Observers Observed: Essays on Ethnographic Fieldwork*, 53–69. Madison: University of Wisconsin Press.

Hodgen, Margaret. 1964. *Early Anthropology in the Sixteenth and Seventeenth Centuries*. Philadelphia: University of Pennsylvania Press.

Hogbin, H. Ian. 1931. The Sexual Life of the Natives of Ontong Java (Solomon Islands). *Journal of the Polynesian Society* 40(1):23–34.

———. 1946. Puberty to Marriage: A Study of the Sexual Life of the Natives of Wogeo, New Guinea. *Oceania* 16(3):185–209.

———. 1947a. Sex and Marriage in Busama, North-Eastern New Guinea. *Oceania* 17(2–3):119–138, 225–247.

————. 1947b. Shame: A Study of Social Conformity in a New Guinea Village. *Oceania* 17(4):273–288.

————. 1957. Anthropology as Public Service and Malinowski's Contribution to It. In Raymond Firth, ed., *Man and Culture*, 245–264. London: Routledge and Kegan Paul.

————. 1970. *The Island of Menstruating Men*. Scranton PA: Chandler Publishing Company.

Holmberg, Allan R. 1969 [1950]. *Nomads of the Long Bow: The Siriono of Eastern Bolivia*. New York: Natural History Press.

Holmes, Lowell D. 1987. *Quest for the Real Samoa: The Mead/Freeman Controversy and Beyond*. South Hadley MA: Bergin and Garvey.

Honigmann, John. 1976. *The Development of Anthropological Ideas*. Homewood IL: Dorsey Press.

Hosken, Fran P. 1976. *Genital Mutilation of Women in Africa*. Munger Africana Library Notes 36. Pasadena: California Institute of Technology.

Howard, Jane. 1984. *Margaret Mead: A Life*. New York: Simon and Schuster.

Howitt, A. W. 1891. The Dieri and Other Kindred Tribes of Central Australia. *Journal of the Anthropological Institute of Great Britain and Ireland* 20:30–104.

————. 1904. *The Native Tribes of South-East Australia*. London: Macmillan.

Hunt, James. 1863. On the Negro's Place in Nature. *Memoirs of the Anthropological Society of London* 1:1–64.

Hyam, Ronald. 1990. *Empire and Sexuality: The British Experience*. Manchester: Manchester University Press.

Hymes, Dell, ed. 1972. *Reinventing Anthropology*. New York: Pantheon Books.

Jackson, Margaret. 1987. "Facts of Life" or the Eroticization of Women's Oppression? Sexology and the Social Construction of Heterosexuality. In Pat Caplan, ed., *The Cultural Construction of Sexuality*, 52–81. London: Tavistock Publications.

Jacobs, Sue-Ellen, Wesley Thomas, and Sabine Lang, eds. 1997. *Two-Spirit People: Native American Gender Identity, Sexuality, and Spirituality*. Urbana: University of Illinois Press.

Jaenen, Cornelius. 1982. "Les Sauvages Amériquains": Persistence into the 18th Century of Traditional French Concepts and Constructs for Comprehending Amerindians. *Ethnohistory* 29:43–56.

Jahoda, Gustav. 1999. *Images of Savages: Ancient Roots of Modern Prejudice in Western Culture*. London: Routledge.

James, Clive. 1981 [1980]. *Unreliable Memoirs*. London: Pan/Picador.

James, Stanlie, and Claire C. Robertson, eds. 2002. *Genital Cutting and Transnational Sisterhood: Disputing U.S. Polemics*. Urbana: University of Illinois Press.

Jankowiak, William, ed. 1995. *Romantic Passion: A Universal Experience?* New York: Columbia University Press.

Jefferson, Thomas. 1944 [1784]. Notes on Virginia. In *The Life and Selected Writings of Thomas Jefferson*. Modern Library ed. New York: Random House.

Johnston, Alex. 1929. *The Life and Letters of Sir Harry Johnston*. London: Jonathan Cape.

Johnston, Sir Harry Hamilton. 1897. *British Central Africa*. London: Methuen.

―――. 1899. *A History of the Colonization of Africa by Alien Races*. Cambridge: Cambridge University Press.

―――. 1910. *The Negro in the New World*. London: Methuen.

―――. 1912. *Pioneers in West Africa*. London: Blackie and Son.

Jolly, Margaret. 2001. Damming the Rivers of Milk? Fertility, Sexuality and Modernity in Melanesia and Amazonia. In Thomas A. Gregor and Donald Tuzin, eds., *Gender in Amazonia and Melanesia: An Exploration of the Comparative Method*, 175–206. Berkeley: University of California Press.

Jones, James H. 1997. *Alfred C. Kinsey: A Public/Private Life*. New York: W. W. Norton.

Jong, Erica. 1973. *Fear of Flying*. New York: Holt, Rinehart and Winston.

Jordan, Winthrop D. 1969 [1968]. *White over Black: American Attitudes toward the Negro*. Baltimore MD: Penguin Books.

Kahn, Susan. 2000. *Reproducing Jews: A Cultural Account of Assisted Conception in Israel (Body, Commodity, Text)*. Durham NC: Duke University Press.

Kardiner, Abram. 1939. *The Individual and His Society: The Psychodynamics of Primitive Social Organization*. New York: Columbia University Press.

―――. 1955. *Sex and Morality*. London: Routledge and Kegan Paul.

―――. 1960 [1944]. Some Personality Determinants in Alorese Culture. In *The People of Alor*, 176–190. Cambridge: Harvard University Press.

Keen, Benjamin. 1971. *The Aztec Image in Western Thought*. Rutgers NJ: Rutgers University Press.

Kennedy, Elizabeth Lapovsky, and Madeline D. Davis. 1993. *Boots of Leather, Slippers of Gold: The History of a Lesbian Community*. New York: Routledge.

Kent, Susan Kingsley. 1990 [1987]. *Sex and Suffrage in Britain, 1860–1914*. London: Routledge.

Kerss, D. M. 1977. Russell, Stopes, and Birth Control. *Russell: The Journal of the Bertrand Russell Archives* 25–28:72–74.

Killick, Andrew P. 1995. The Penetrating Intellect: On Being White, Straight, and Male in Korea. In Don Kulick and Margaret Willson, eds., *Taboo: Sex, Identity, and Erotic Subjectivity in Anthropological Fieldwork*, 76–106. London: Routledge.

Kingsley, Mary. 1982 [1897]. *Travels in West Africa*, 5th ed. London: Virago Books.

Kinsey, Alfred C., W. B. Pomeroy, and C. E. Martin. 1948. *Sexual Behavior in the Human Male*. Philadelphia: W. B. Saunders.

Kinsey, Alfred C., W. B. Pomeroy, C. E. Martin, and P. H. Gebhard. 1953. *Sexual Behavior in the Human Female*. Philadelphia: W. B. Saunders.

Knauft, Bruce M. 1994. Foucault Meets South New Guinea: Knowledge, Power, Sexuality. *Ethos* 22(4):391–438.

Krafft-Ebing, Richard von. 1892 [1886]. *Psychopathia Sexualis*. Philadelphia: F. A. Davis.

Kuklick, Henrika. 1991. *The Savage Within: The Social History of British Anthropology, 1885–1945*. Cambridge: Cambridge University Press.

Kulick, Don. 1998. *Travesti: Sex, Gender and Culture among Brazilian Transgendered Prostitutes*. Chicago: University of Chicago Press.

Kulick, Don, and Margaret Willson, eds. 1995. *Taboo: Sex, Identity, and Erotic Subjectivity in Anthropological Fieldwork*. London: Routledge.

Kuper, Adam. 1988. *The Invention of Primitive Society*. London: Routledge.

———. 2001. Isaac Schapera – A Conversation (Part 1: South African Beginnings). *Anthropology Today* 17(6):3–7.

La Fontaine, Jean S. 1970. *City Politics: A Study of Leopoldville: 1962–63*. Cambridge: Cambridge University Press.

Lancaster, Roger N. 1995. "That We Should All Turn Queer?": Homosexual Stigma in the Making of Manhood and the Breaking of a Revolution in Nicaragua. In Richard G. Parker and John H. Gagnon, eds., *Conceiving Sexuality: Approaches to Sex Research in a Postmodern World*, 135–156. New York: Routledge.

Lang, Andrew. 1903. *Social Origins*. Published with *Primal Law* by J. J. Atkinson. London: Longmans, Green and Company.

———. 1905. *The Secret of the Totem*. London: Longmans, Green and Company.

Langham, Ian. 1981. *The Building of British Social Anthropology: W. H. R. Rivers and His Cambridge Disciples in the Development of Kinship Studies, 1898–1931*. Dordrecht: D. Reidel.

Lapsley, Hilary. 1999. *Margaret Mead and Ruth Benedict: The Kinship of Women*. Amherst: University of Massachusetts Press.

Laqueur, Thomas. 1990. *Making Sex: Body and Gender from the Greeks to Freud*. Cambridge: Harvard University Press.

Lauritsen, John, and David Thorstad. 1974. *The Early Homosexual Rights Movement (1864–1935)*. New York: Times Change Press.

Le Blanc, Marie Nathalie, Deidre Meintel, and Victor Piché. 1991. The African Sexual System: Comment on Caldwell et al. *Population and Development Review* 17(3):497–505.

Leach, Sir Edmund. 1958. Magical Hair. *Journal of the Royal Anthropological Institute of Great Britain and Ireland* 88(2):147–164.

———. 1966. Virgin Birth. *Proceedings of the Royal Anthropological Institute of Great Britain and Ireland*, 39–49.

———. 1969. Virgin Birth. In *Genesis as Myth and Other Essays*, 85–112, 117–122 (notes). London: Jonathan Cape.

———. 1984. Glimpses of the Unmentionable in the History of British Social Anthropology. *Annual Review of Anthropology* 13:1–23.

Leith-Ross, Sylvia. 1939. *African Women: A Study of the Ibo of Nigeria*. With a foreword by Lord Lugard. London: Faber and Faber.

Leonardo, Micaela di. 1998. *Exotics at Home: Anthropologies, Others, American Modernity*. Chicago: University of Chicago Press.

Lepowsky, Maria. 1998. Coming of Age on Vanatinai: Gender, Sexuality and Power. In Gilbert Herdt and Stephen C. Leavitt, eds., *Adolescence in Pacific Island Societies*, 123–147. Pittsburgh: University of Pittsburgh Press.

LeVine, Robert A. 1959. Gusii Sex Offenses: A Study in Social Control. *American Anthropologist*, n.s. 61(6):965–990.

———. 1981. Foreword. In *Guardians of the Flutes* by Gilbert Herdt, ix–xi. New York: McGraw-Hill.

LeVine, Sarah, and Robert A. LeVine. 1979. *Mothers and Wives: Gusii Women of East Africa*. Chicago: University of Chicago Press.

Levy, Anita. 1991. *Other Women: The Writing of Class, Race and Gender, 1832–1898*. Princeton NJ: Princeton University Press.

Levy, Robert I. 1973. *Tahitians: Mind and Experience in the Society Islands*. Chicago: University of Chicago Press.

Lewin, Ellen, and William L. Leap, eds. 1996. *Out in the Field: Reflections of Lesbian and Gay Anthropologists*. Urbana: University of Illinois Press.

———. 2002. *Out in Theory: The Emergence of Lesbian and Gay Anthropology*. Urbana: University of Illinois Press.

Lévi-Strauss, Claude. 1963 [1962]. *Totemism*. Trans. Rodney Needham. Boston: Beacon Press.

———. 1968 [1958]. *Race et histoire*. Paris: UNESCO.

———. 1969 [1949]. *The Elementary Structures of Kinship*. Ed. Rodney Needham, trans. James Harle Bell, John Richard von Sturmer, and Rodney Needham. Rev. ed. London: Eyre and Spottiswoode.

———. 1974 [1955]. *Tristes tropiques*. Trans. John and Doreen Weightman. New York: Atheneum.

Lieberman, Leonard. 2001. How "Caucasoids" Got Such Big Crania and Why They Shrank: From Morton to Rushton. *Current Anthropology* 42(1):69–95.

Lindenbaum, Shirley. 1992. Knowledge and Action in the Shadow of AIDS. In Gilbert Herdt and Shirley Lindenbaum, eds., *The Time of* AIDS: *Social Analysis, Theory and Method*, 319–334. Newbury Park CA: Sage Publications.

Lindsey, Ben. 1931. The Companionate Marriage. *Birth Control Review* 15(3):78–80.

Linton, Ralph. 1939a. Foreword. In Abram Kardiner, *The Individual and His Society: The Psychodynamics of Primitive Social Organization*, v–xviii. New York: Columbia University Press.

———. 1939b. Marquesan Culture. In Abram Kardiner, *The Individual and His Society: The Psychodynamics of Primitive Social Organization*, 137–196. New York: Columbia University Press.

Long, Edward. 1774. *History of Jamaica*. 2 vols. London.

Lorence, David. 2001. Paradise Lost? The Magical Marquesas. *Plant Talk Online: The Bulletin of the National Tropical Botanical Garden*. Electronic document, http://www.plant-talk.org/Pages/25marq.html, accessed February 2, 2002.

Lubbock, Sir John. 1885. On the Customs of Marriage and Systems of Relationship among the Australians. *Journal of the Anthropological Institute of Great Britain and Ireland* 14:292–300.

———. 1978 [1870]. *The Origin of Civilization and the Primitive Condition of Man*. Ed. and with an introduction by Peter Riviere. Chicago: University of Chicago Press.

Lutkehaus, Nancy C. 1995. Margaret Mead and the "Rustling-of-the-Wind-in-the-Palm-Trees School" of Ethnographic Writing. In Ruth Behar and Deborah A. Gordon, eds., *Women Writing Culture*, 186–206. Berkeley: University of California Press.

Lyons, Andrew P. 1974. The Question of Race in Anthropology. PhD diss., University of Oxford, Bodleian Library, University of Oxford.

———. 1984. Hamites, Cattle and Kingship: An Episode in the History of Diffusionist Anthropology. *Canadian Journal of Anthropology* 4(1):57–64.

Lyons, Andrew P., and Harriet D. Lyons. 1981. The History of Sexuality Is the History of Anthropology. Paper presented at the Annual Meeting of the American Anthropological Association, December, Los Angeles.

———. 1986. Savage Sexuality and Secular Morality: Malinowski, Ellis, Russell. *Canadian Journal of Anthropology* 5:51–64.

———. 1997. Savages, Infants and the Sexuality of Others: Countertransference in Malinowski and Mead. Seriatim Symposium on Countertransference in the Humanities. *Common Knowledge* 6(3):73–98.

Lyons, Harriet D. 1981. Anthropologists, Moralities and Relativities: The Problem of Genital Mutilations. *Canadian Review of Sociology and Anthropology* 18(4) November:499–518.

———. 1996. Sex, Race and Nature: Anthropology and Primitive Sexuality. In Larry T. Reynolds and Leonard Lieberman, eds., *Race and Other Misadventures: Essays in Honor of Ashley Montagu in His Ninetieth Year*, 347–364. Dix Hills NY: General Hall.

———. 1998. The Representation of Trafficking in Persons in South Asia: Orientalism and Other Perils. In Hugh Johnston and Sona Khan, eds., *Trafficking in Persons in South Asia*, 100–119. Calgary: Shastri Indo-Canadian Institute.

MacCrone, Ian D. 1957. *Race Attitudes in South Africa: Historical, Psychological and Experimental Studies*. Johannesburg: Witwatersrand University Press.

Mageo, Jeannette. 1994. Hairdos and Don'ts: Hair Symbolism and Sexual History in Samoa. *Man*, n.s. 29(2):407–432.

———. 1998. *Theorizing Self in Samoa: Emotions, Genders, and Sexualities*. Ann Arbor: University of Michigan Press.

Maine, Sir Henry. 1883. *Dissertation on Early Law and Custom*. London: John Murray.

Male, Tim. 2001. Marquesas Tropical Moist Forests. Electronic document, http://www.worldwildlife.org/wildworld/profiles/terrestrial/oc/oc0108_full.html, accessed February 2, 2002.

Malinowski, Bronislaw. 1916. Baloma; The Spirits of the Dead in the Trobriand Islands. *Journal of the Royal Anthropological Institute* 46:353–430.

———. 1927. *Sex and Repression in Savage Society*. London: Routledge and Kegan Paul.

———. 1929. *The Sexual Life of Savages in Northwestern Melanesia*. With a Preface by Havelock Ellis. London: Routledge and Kegan Paul.

———. 1930. Race and Labour. *Special Supplement to the Listener*, July 16.

———. 1931a. Havelock Ellis. *Birth Control Review* (March).

———. 1931b. A Plea for an Effective Colour Bar. *Spectator*, June 27.

———. 1932a. *Pigs, Papuans, and Police Court Perspective*. Man 32:33–38.

———. 1932b. Introduction. *Hunger and Work in a Savage Tribe* by Audrey Richards. London: Routledge and Kegan Paul.

———. 1944. *Freedom and Civilization*. New York: Roy.

———. 1962. *Sex, Culture and Myth*. Ed. A. Valetta Malinowski. London: Rupert Hart-Davis.

———. 1963 [1913]. *The Family among the Australian Aborigines*. New York: Schocken Books.

———. 1967. *A Diary in the Strict Sense of the Term*. Trans. Norbert Guterman. Preface by Valetta Malinowski, introduction by Sir Raymond Firth, index of native terms by Mario Bick. London: Routledge and Kegan Paul.

———. 1987 [1932]. *The Sexual Life of Savages in North-Western Melanesia*. Preface by Havelock Ellis. With a new introduction by Annette Weiner. Reprint of 3rd ed. Boston: Beacon Press.

Manderson, Lenore. 1995. The Pursuit of Pleasure and the Sale of Sex. In Paul R. Abramson and Steven D. Pinkerton, eds., *Sexual Nature, Sexual Culture*, 305–329. Chicago: University of Chicago Press.

Manson, William C. 1986. Abram Kardiner and the Neo-Freudian Alternative in Culture and Personality. In George W. Stocking Jr., ed., *Malinowski, Rivers, Benedict and Others: Essays on Culture and Personality*, 72–94. *History of Anthropology* 4. Madison: University of Wisconsin Press.

Marcus, George E., and Michael M. J. Fischer. 1986. *Anthropology as Cultural Critique: An Experimental Moment in the Human Sciences.* Chicago: University of Chicago Press.

Marcus, Steven. 1966. *The Other Victorians: A Study of Sexuality and Pornography in Victorian England.* London: Weidenfeld and Nicholson.

Markowitz, Fran, and Michael Ashkenazi, eds. 1999. *Sex, Sexuality, and the Anthropologist.* Urbana: University of Illinois Press.

Marshall, Donald. 1962. *Island of Passion: Ra'ivavae.* London: George Allen and Unwin.

———. 1971. Sexual Behavior on Mangaia. In Donald S. Marshall and Robert C. Suggs, eds., *Human Sexual Behavior: Variations in the Ethnographic Spectrum*, 103–162. Studies in Sex and Society. New York: Basic Books.

Marshall, Donald S., and Robert C. Suggs, eds. 1971. *Human Sexual Behavior: Variations in the Ethnographic Spectrum.* Studies in Sex and Society. New York: Basic Books.

Mason, Michael. 1994. *The Making of Victorian Sexuality.* Oxford: Oxford University Press.

Mason, Peter. 1990. *Deconstructing America: Representations of the Other.* London: Routledge.

Masters, William H., and Virginia E. Johnson. 1966. *Human Sexual Response.* Boston: Little, Brown.

Mathew, John. 1899. *Eaglehawk and Crow.* London: David Nutt.

Mauss, Marcel. 1967. *The Gift: Forms and Functions of Exchange in Archaic Societies.* Trans. Ian Cunnison, with an introduction by E. E. Evans-Pritchard. New York: W. W. Norton.

Mayhew, Henry. 1861–62. *London Labour and the London Poor: A Cyclopaedia of the Condition and Earnings of Those That Will Work, Those That Cannot Work, and Those That Will Not Work.* 4 vols. London: Griffin, Bohn.

McClintock, Anne. 1995. *Imperial Leather: Race, Gender and Sexuality in the Colonial Contest.* New York: Routledge.

McLennan, John F. 1970 [1865]. *Primitive Marriage: An Inquiry into the Origin of the Form of Capture in Marriage Ceremonies*. Ed. and with an introduction by Peter Riviere. Chicago: University of Chicago Press.

McLynn, Frank. 1990. *Burton: Snow upon the Desert*. London: John Murray.

McMullen, Ann. 1999. Review of *Two-Spirit People: Native American Gender Identity, Sexuality, and Spirituality*, ed. Sue-Ellen Jacobs, Wesley Thomas, and Sabine Lang. *American Anthropologist* 101(1):210–211.

Mead, Margaret. 1928. *Coming of Age in Samoa: A Psychological Study of Primitive Youth for Western Civilization*. New York: William Morrow.

————. 1934. The Sex Life of the Unmarried Adult in Primitive Society. In Ira S. Wile, ed., *The Sex Life of the Unmarried Adult*, 53–73. New York: Vanguard Press.

————. 1948. An Anthropologist Looks at the Report. In *Proceedings of a Symposium on the First Published Report of a Series of Studies of Sex Phenomena by Professor Alfred C. Kinsey, Wardell B. Pomeroy and Clyde E. Martin*, 58–69. New York: American Social Hygiene Association.

————. 1949. *Male and Female*. New York: William Morrow.

————. 1956. *New Lives for Old*. London: Victor Gollancz.

————. 1959. *An Anthropologist at Work: Writings of Ruth Benedict*. Boston: Houghton Mifflin.

————. 1961. Cultural Determinants of Sexual Behavior. In William C. Young, ed., *Sex and Internal Secretions*, 2:1433–1479. 3rd ed. Baltimore MD: Williams and Wilkins.

————. 1963 [1935]. *Sex and Temperament in Three Primitive Societies*. New York: William Morrow.

————. 1966 [1932]. *The Changing Culture of an Indian Tribe*. New York: Capricorn Books.

————. 1968a [1930]. *Growing up in New Guinea: A Comparative Study of Primitive Education*. New York: William Morrow.

————. 1968b. Incest. In David L. Sills, ed., *The International Encyclopedia of the Social Sciences*, 7:115–122. New York: Macmillan and the Free Press.

————. 1972. *Blackberry Winter*. New York: William Morrow.

————. 1977. *Letters from the Field, 1925–1975*. New York: Harper and Row.

Mead, Margaret, and James Baldwin. 1970. *A Rap on Race*. Philadelphia: J. B. Lippincott.

Meek, Ronald. 1976. *Social Science and the Ignoble Savage*. Cambridge: Cambridge University Press.

Merlan, Francesca. 1986. Australian Aboriginal Conception Beliefs Revisited. *Man*, n.s. 21(3):474–493.

Merriam, Alan P. 1971. Aspects of Sexual Behavior among the Bala (Basongye). In

Donald S. Marshall and Robert C. Suggs, eds., *Human Sexual Behavior: Variations in the Ethnographic Spectrum*, 71–102. Studies in Sex and Society. New York: Basic Books.

Messenger, John C. 1971. Sex and Repression in an Irish Folk Community. In Donald S. Marshall and Robert C. Suggs, eds., *Human Sexual Behavior: Variations in the Ethnographic Spectrum*, 3–37. Studies in Sex and Society. New York: Basic Books.

Metraux, Rhoda, ed. 1979. *Margaret Mead: Some Personal Views*. New York: Walker and Company.

Midnight Sun. 1988. Sex/Gender Systems in Native North America. In Will Roscoe, ed., *Living the Spirit: A Gay American Indian Anthology*, 32–47. New York: St. Martin's Press.

Mitchell, Sir Philip. 1951. Review of *Native Administration in the British Territories in Africa* by Lord Hailey. *Journal of African Administration* 3:55–65.

Molnos, Angela. 1972. *Cultural Source Material for Population Planning in East Africa*. Vols. 1–4. Nairobi: East African Publishing House.

Montagu, M. F. Ashley. 1937. *Coming into Being among the Australian Aborigines*. London: Routledge and Kegan Paul.

————. 1942a. Ignorance of Physiological Maternity in Australia. *Oceania* 12:75–78.

————. 1942b. Bronislaw Malinowski (1884–1942). *Isis* 34, pt. 2(94):146–150.

————. 1946. *Adolescent Sterility*. Springfield IL: C. C. Thomas.

————. 1957. *The Reproductive Development of the Female*. New York: Julian Press.

————. 1974. *Coming into Being among the Australian Aborigines: A Study of the Procreative Beliefs of the Native Tribes of Australia*. Foreword by Bronislaw Malinowski. 2nd rev. and expanded ed. London: Routledge and Kegan Paul.

Moreno, Eva. 1995. Rape in the Field: Reflections from a Survivor. In Don Kulick and Margaret Willson, eds., *Taboo: Sex, Identity, and Erotic Subjectivity in Anthropological Fieldwork*, 219–250. London: Routledge.

Morgan, Lewis Henry. 1870. *Systems of Consanguinity and Affinity of the Human Family*. Washington DC: Smithsonian Institution.

————. 1963 [1877]. *Ancient Society*. Ed. and with an introduction and annotations by Eleanor Burke Leacock. Cleveland: World Publishing Company.

————. 1964 [1877]. *Ancient Society*. Ed. and with an introduction by Leslie A. White. Cambridge: Belknap Press of Harvard University Press.

————. 1967 [1880]. Introduction. In *Kamilaroi and Kurnai* by Lorimer Fison and A. W. Howitt, 1–20. Oosterhout: Anthropological Publications.

Mort, Frank. 1987. *Dangerous Sexualities: Medico-Moral Politics in England since 1830*. London: Routledge and Kegan Paul.

Murray, Stephen O. 1992. *Oceanic Homosexualities*. New York: Garland.

————. 1995. *Latin American Male Homosexualities*. Albuquerque: University of New Mexico Press.

————. 1996. Male Homosexuality in Guatemala: Possible Insights and Certain Confusions from Sleeping with the Natives. In Ellen Lewin and William L. Leap, eds., *Out in the Field: Reflections of Lesbian and Gay Anthropologists*, 236–260. Urbana: University of Illinois Press.

————. 1997. Explaining Away Same-Sex Sexualities: When They Obtrude on Anthropologists' Notice at All. *Anthropology Today* 13(3):2–5.

————. 1998. Sexual Politics in Contemporary Southern Africa. In Stephen O. Murray and Will Roscoe, eds., *Boy-Wives and Female Husbands: Studies of African Homosexualities*, 243–254. New York: St. Martin's Press.

————. 2000. *Homosexualities*. Chicago: University of Chicago Press.

Murray, Stephen O., and Regna Darnell. 2000. Margaret Mead and Paradigm Shifts within Anthropology during the 1920s. *Journal of Youth and Adolescence* 29(5): 557–573.

Murray, Stephen O., and Will Roscoe. 1997. *Islamic Homosexualities: Culture, History and Literature*. New York: New York University Press.

————. 1998. Africa and African Homosexualities: An Introduction. In Stephen O. Murray and Will Roscoe, eds., *Boy-Wives and Female Husbands: Studies of African Homosexualities*, 1–18. New York: St. Martin's Press.

Nadel, S. F. 1936. Review of *Africa Dances* by Geoffrey Gorer. *Man* 36:143.

Nanda, Serena. 1990. *Neither Man nor Woman: The Hijras of India*. Belmont CA: Wadsworth Publishing Company.

Neuburg, Victor. 1985. Introduction. In *London Labour and the London Poor (Selections)* by Henry Mayhew, xiii–xxiii. London: Penguin Books.

Newton, Esther. 1972. *Mother Camp: Female Impersonators in America*. Englewood Cliffs NJ: Prentice-Hall.

————. 1979. *Mother Camp: Female Impersonators in America*. Reprint ed. Chicago: University of Chicago Press.

————. 1993. *Cherry Grove, Fire Island: Sixty Years in America's First Gay and Lesbian Town*. Boston: Beacon Press.

————. 2000a. Introduction. In *Margaret Mead Made Me Gay: Personal Essays, Public Ideas*, 1–8. Durham NC: Duke University Press.

————. 2000b [1993]. Lesbian and Gay Issues in Anthropology: Some Remarks to the Chairs of Anthropology Departments. In *Margaret Mead Made Me Gay: Personal Essays, Public Ideas*, 238–242. Durham NC: Duke University Press.

————. 2000c [1973]. Marginal Woman/Marginal Academic. In *Margaret Mead Made Me Gay: Personal Essays, Public Ideas*, 103–112. Durham NC: Duke University Press.

———. 2000d [1988]. Of Yams, Grinders and Gays: The Anthropology of Homosexuality. In *Margaret Mead Made Me Gay: Personal Essays, Public Ideas*, 228–237. Durham NC: Duke University Press.

Norton, Rictor. 1999. The Life and Writings of John Addington Symonds. Electronic document, http://www.infopt.demon.co.uk/symonds.htm, accessed May 7, 2002.

———. [John Addington Symonds.] 2000 [1997]. A Problem in Modern Ethics, the John Addington Symonds Pages. Electronic document, http://www.infopt.demon.co.uk/modern.htm, accessed May 7, 2002. Selection copyright 1997.

Orans, Martin. 1996. *Not Even Wrong: Margaret Mead, Derek Freeman and the Samoans*. Novato CA: Chandler and Sharp.

Ortner, Sherry B. 1981. Gender and Sexuality in Hierarchical Societies: The Case of Polynesia and Some Comparative Implications. In Sherry B. Ortner and Harriet Whitehead, eds., *Sexual Meanings: The Cultural Construction of Gender and Sexuality*, 359–409. Cambridge: Cambridge University Press.

Ortner, Sherry B., and Harriet Whitehead. 1981. Introduction: Accounting for Sexual Meanings. In Sherry B. Ortner and Harriet Whitehead, eds., *Sexual Meanings: The Cultural Construction of Gender and Sexuality*, i–xxvii. Cambridge: Cambridge University Press.

Ortner, Sherry B., and Harriet Whitehead, eds. 1981. *Sexual Meanings: The Cultural Construction of Gender and Sexuality*. Cambridge: Cambridge University Press.

Parker, Richard G. 1991. *Bodies, Pleasures, and Passions: Sexual Culture in Contemporary Brazil*. Boston: Beacon Press.

———. 1992. Sexual Diversity, Cultural Analysis, and AIDS Education in Brazil. In Gilbert Herdt and Shirley Lindenbaum, eds., *The Time of AIDS: Social Analysis, Theory and Method*, 225–242. Newbury Park CA: Sage Publications.

Parsons, Elsie Clews. 1906. *The Family*. New York: Putnam.

Pavelka, Mary S. McDonald. 1995. Sexual Nature: What Can We Learn from a Cross-Species Perspective? In Paul R. Abramson and Steven D. Pinkerton, eds., *Sexual Nature, Sexual Culture*, 17–36. Chicago: University of Chicago Press.

Ploss, Hermann H. 1935 [1885]. *Woman: An Historical, Gynaecological and Anthropological Compendium*. Originally published in German as *Das Weib*. Ed. E. J. Dingwall. London: Heinemann Medical Books.

Poole, Fitz-John Porter. 1981. Transforming "Natural" Woman: Female Ritual Leaders and Gender Ideology among Bimin-Kuskusmin. In Sherry B. Ortner and Harriet Whitehead, eds., *Sexual Meanings: The Cultural Construction of Gender and Sexuality*, 116–165. Cambridge: Cambridge University Press.

Porter, Roy. 1990. The Exotic as Erotic: Captain Cook at Tahiti. In G. S. Rousseau and Roy Porter, eds., *Exoticism in the Enlightenment*, 117–144. Manchester: Manchester University Press.

Porter, Roy, and Lesley Hall. 1995. *The Facts of Life: The Creation of Sexual Knowledge in Britain, 1650–1950*. New Haven CT: Yale University Press.

Powdermaker, Hortense. 1945. Review of *The People of Alor: A Social Psychological Study of an East Indian Island* by Cora Du Bois. *American Anthropologist*, n.s. 47(1):155–161.

Pratt, Mary Louise. 1986. Fieldwork in Common Places. In James P. Clifford and George E. Marcus, *Writing Culture: The Poetics and Politics of Ethnography*, 27–50. Berkeley: University of California Press.

Prichard, James Cowles. 1826. *Researches into the Physical History of Mankind*. 2 vols. 2nd ed. London: John and Arthur Arch.

Rabinow, Paul. 1977. *Reflections on Fieldwork in Morocco*. Berkeley: University of California Press.

Rainwater, Lee. 1971. Marital Sexuality in Four "Cultures of Poverty." In Donald S. Marshall and Robert C. Suggs, eds., *Human Sexual Behavior: Variations in the Ethnographic Spectrum*, 187–205. Studies in Sex and Society. New York: Basic Books.

Rapp, Rayna. 2000. *Testing Women, Testing the Fetus: The Social Impact of Amniocentesis in America (The Anthropology of Everyday Life)*. New York: Routledge.

Rattray Taylor, Gordon. 1977 [1959]. Introduction and Biographical Notes. In *The Mothers* by Robert Briffault, 9–25. New York: Atheneum.

Reade, W. Winwood. 1967 [1863]. *Savage Africa: Being the Narrative of a Tour in Equatorial, Southwestern and Northwestern Africa; with Notes on the Habits of the Gorilla; on the Existence of Unicorns and Tailed Men; on the Slave Trade; on the Origin, Character and Capabilities of the Negro; and on the Future Civilization of West Africa*. New York: Johnson Reprint.

Reed, Adam. 1997. Contested Images and Common Strategies: Early Colonial Sexual Politics in the Massim. In Lenore Manderson and Margaret Jolly, eds., *Sites of Desire, Economies of Pleasure: Sexualities in Asia and the Pacific*, 48–71. Chicago: University of Chicago Press.

Rentoul, Alex. 1931. Physiological Paternity and the Trobrianders. *Man* 31:152–154.

Rice, Edward. 1991. *Captain Sir Richard Francis Burton*. New York: Harper Perennial.

Rich, Adrienne. 1979. *On Lies, Secrets, and Silence: Selected Prose, 1966–1978*. New York: Norton.

———. 1980. Compulsory Heterosexuality and Lesbian Existence. *Signs: Journal of Women in Culture and Society* 5(4):631–660.

Riley, Ian. 2000. It's Everyone's Problem: HIV/AIDS and Development in Asia and the Pacific. Lessons from Sexually Transmitted Disease Epidemics. Paper prepared for the Australian Agency for International Development (AusAID) special seminar, November 22. Electronic document, http://www.ausaid.gov.au/publications/pdf/riley.pdf, accessed May 4, 2003.

Rivers, W. H. R. 1907a. On the Origins of the Classificatory System of Relationships. In Northcote W. Thomas, ed., *Anthropological Essays Presented to Edward Burnett Tylor in Honour of His 75th Birthday*, 309–323. Oxford: Oxford University Press.

———. 1907b. Review of *Kinship Organisations and Group Marriage in Australia* by Northcote Thomas. *Man* 7:90–92.

———, ed. 1922. *Essays on the Depopulation of Melanesia*. Cambridge: Cambridge University Press.

———. 1967 [1906]. *The Todas*. Oosterhout: Anthropological Publications.

Róheim, Géza. 1932. Psycho-Analysis of Primitive Cultural Types. *International Journal of Psychoanalysis* 12(1–2):1–224.

Roscoe, Will. 1988. Strange Country This: Images of Berdaches and Warrior Women. In Will Roscoe, ed., *Living the Spirit: A Gay American Indian Anthology*, 48–76. New York: St. Martin's Press.

———. 1998. *Changing Ones: Third and Fourth Genders in Native North America*. New York: St. Martin's Press.

Rosenberg, Rosalind. 1995. The Legacy of Dean Gildersleeve. *Barnard Alumnae Magazine* (Summer):16–21.

Rowbotham, Sheila, and Jeffrey Weeks. 1977. *Socialism and the New Life: The Personal and Sexual Politics of Edward Carpenter and Havelock Ellis*. London: Pluto Press.

Rubin, Gayle. 1975. The Traffic in Women: Notes toward a Political Economy of Sex. In Rayna Reiter, ed., *Toward an Anthropology of Women*, 157–210. New York: Monthly Review Press.

———. 2002. Studying Sexual Subcultures: Excavating the Ethnography of Gay Communities in Urban North America. In Ellen Lewin and William L. Leap, eds., *Out in Theory: The Emergence of Lesbian and Gay Anthropology*, 17–68. Urbana: University of Illinois Press.

Rushton, J. Phillippe. 1988. Race Differences in Behavior: A Review and Evolutionary Analysis. *Personality and Individual Differences* 9:1009–1024.

———. 1992. Contributions to the History of Psychology: xc. Evolutionary Biology and Heritable Traits (with Reference to Oriental–White–Black Differences). The 1989 AAAS Paper. *Psychological Reports* 71:811–821.

———. 1994. *Race, Evolution and Behavior: A Life History Perspective*. New Brunswick NJ: Transaction Books.

———. 1997. *Race, Evolution, and Behavior: A Life History Perspective*. 1st paperback ed., with a new afterword by the author. New Brunswick NJ: Transaction.

Rushton, J. Philippe, and A. F. Bogaert. 1987. Race Differences in Sexual Behavior: Testing an Evolutionary Hypothesis. *Journal of Research in Personality* 21:529–551.

Russell, Bertrand. 1929. *Marriage and Morals*. New York: Horace Liveright.

———. 1933. Havelock Ellis on Sex. *New Statesman and Nation*, March 18.

Russett, Cynthia Eagle. 1989. *Sexual Science: The Victorian Construction of Woman-hood*. Cambridge: Harvard University Press.

Schapera, Isaac. 1947. *Migrant Labour and Tribal Life: A Study of Conditions in the Bechuanaland Protectorate*. London.

————. 1965 [1930]. *The Khoisan Peoples of South Africa*. London: Routledge and Kegan Paul.

————. 1966 [1940]. *Married Life in an African Tribe*. 2nd ed. London: Faber and Faber.

Schiebinger, Londa. 1993. *Nature's Body: Gender in the Making of Modern Science*. Boston: Beacon Press.

Schiller, Francis. 1979. *Paul Broca, Founder of French Anthropology, Explorer of the Brain*. Berkeley: University of California Press.

Schneider, Harold K. 1971. Romantic Love among the Turu. In Donald S. Marshall and Robert C. Suggs, eds., *Human Sexual Behavior: Variations in the Ethnographic Spectrum*, 59–70. Studies in Sex and Society. New York: Basic Books.

Schoepf, Brooke Grundfest. 1988. Women, AIDS and Economic Crisis in Central Africa. *Canadian Journal of African Studies* 22(3):625–644.

————. 1992. Women at Risk: Case Studies from Zaire. In Gilbert Herdt and Shirley Lindenbaum, eds., *The Time of AIDS: Social Analysis, Theory and Method*, 259–286. Newbury Park CA: Sage Publications.

————. 2001. International AIDS Research in Anthropology: Taking a Critical Perspective on the Crisis. *Annual Review of Anthropology* 30:335–361.

Seligman, Brenda Z. 1950. Review of *The People of Alor* by Cora Du Bois. *Man* 50:66–67.

Sellon, Edward. 1863–64. On the Phallic Worship of India. *Memoirs of the Anthropological Society of London* 1:327–334.

————. 1865–66. Some Remarks on Indian Gnosticism, or Sacti Puja, the Worship of the Female Powers. *Memoirs of the Anthropological Society of London* 2:264–282.

Shore, Bradd. 1981. Sexuality and Gender in Samoa: Conceptions and Missed Conceptions. In Sherry B. Ortner and Harriet Whitehead, eds., *Sexual Meanings: The Cultural Construction of Gender and Sexuality*, 192–215. Cambridge: Cambridge University Press.

Showalter, Elaine. 1991. *Sexual Anarchy: Gender and Culture at the Fin de Siècle*. New York: Penguin.

Simmel, Georg. 1950 [1908]. The Secret and the Secret Society. In Kurt H. Wolff, ed., *The Sociology of Georg Simmel*, trans. K. H. Wolff, 307–378. New York: Free Press.

Sipe, Lynn. 1995. Introduction of Dr. Walter Williams. In *Queer Frontiers: 1995 and Beyond*. Electronic document, http://www.usc.edu/isd/archives/queerfrontiers/, accessed April 8, 2002.

Slobodin, Richard. 1978. *W. H. R. Rivers*. New York: Columbia University Press.

Small, Meredith F. 1993. *Female Choices: Sexual Behavior of Female Primates*. Ithaca NY: Cornell University Press.

Smith, William Robertson. 1885. *Kinship and Marriage in Early Arabia*. Cambridge: Harvard University Press.

———. 1889. *Lectures on the Religion of the Semites*. Edinburgh: Black.

Smithers, Leonard, and Sir Richard F. Burton. 1995 [1890]. *Priapeia Sive Diversorum Poetarum in Priapum Lusus, or Sportive Epigrams on Priapus by Divers Poets in English Verse and Prose*. Original ed. published privately in 1890 with the translation attributed to "Neaniskos." Latin text omitted from 1995 ed. Ware, Hertfordshire: Wordsworth Editions.

Soemmering, Samuel Thomas von. 1799. *Essay on the Comparative Anatomy of the Negro and European*. Translated selections from *Über die körperliche Verschiedenheit des Negers von Europäer*, 1785. Published as an appendix. In *An Account of the Regular Gradation in Man* by Charles White. London.

Spencer, Baldwin, and F. J. Gillen. 1899. *The Native Tribes of Central Australia*. London: Macmillan.

———. 1904. *The Northern Tribes of Central Australia*. London: Macmillan.

Sperling, Susan. 1991. Baboons with Briefcases vs. Langurs in Lipstick: Feminism and Functionalism in Primate Studies. In Micaela di Leonardo, ed., *Gender at the Crossroads of Knowledge: Feminist Anthropology in the Postmodern Era*, 204–234. Berkeley: University of California Press.

Spiro, Melford. 1968. Virgin Birth, Parthenogenesis and Physiological Paternity: An Essay in Cultural Interpretation. *Man*, n.s. 3(2):242–261.

———. 1979. Whatever Happened to the Id? *American Anthropologist* 81(1):5–13.

Stanley, Sir Henry Morton. 1879 [1878]. *Through the Dark Continent*. Single-vol. ed. London: Sampson Low, Marston and Company.

———. 1885. *The Congo and the Founding of Its Free State*. 2 vols. New York: Harper and Brothers.

Stanton, William. 1960. *The Leopard's Spots: Scientific Attitudes toward Race in America, 1815–1859*. Chicago: University of Chicago Press.

Stern, Bernhard J. 1931. *Lewis Henry Morgan: Social Evolutionist*. Chicago: University of Chicago Press.

Stern, Pamela R., and Richard G. Condon. 1995. A Good Spouse Is Hard to Find: Marriage, Spouse Exchange, and Infatuation among the Copper Inuit. In William Jankowiak, ed.,*Romantic Passion: A Universal Experience?* 196–218. New York: Columbia University Press.

Stocking, George W., Jr. 1968. *Race, Culture and Evolution*. New York: Free Press.

———. 1971. What's in a Name? The Origins of the Royal Anthropological Institute (1837–1871). *Man*, n.s. 6:369–390.

———. 1983. The Ethnographer's Magic: Fieldwork in British Anthropology from Tylor to Malinowski. In George W. Stocking Jr., *Observers Observed: Essays on Ethnographic Fieldwork*, 70–120. Madison: University of Wisconsin Press.

———. 1986. Anthropology and the Science of the Irrational: Malinowski's Encounter with Freudian Psychoanalysis. In George W. Stocking Jr., ed., *Malinowski, Rivers, Benedict and Others: Essays on Culture and Personality*, 13–49. *History of Anthropology* 4. Madison: University of Wisconsin Press.

———. 1987. *Victorian Anthropology*. New York: Free Press.

———. 1992. The Ethnographic Sensibility of the 1920s and the Dualism of the Anthropological Tradition. In George W. Stocking Jr., ed., *The Ethnographer's Magic and Other Essays in the History of Anthropology*, 276–341. Madison: University of Wisconsin Press.

———. 1995. *After Tylor: British Social Anthropology 1888–1951*. Madison: University of Wisconsin Press.

Stoler, Ann Laura. 1995. *Race and the Education of Desire: Foucault's History of Sexuality and the Colonial Order of Things*. Durham NC: Duke University Press.

Stopes, Marie. 1918a. *Married Love*. London: G. P. Putnam's Sons.

———. 1918b. *Wise Parenthood*. London: G. P. Putnam's Sons.

Street, Brian. 1975. *The Savage in Literature: Representations of "Primitive" Society in English Fiction, 1858–1920*. London: Routledge and Kegan Paul.

Suggs, David N. 2002. *A Bagful of Locusts and the Baboon Woman: Constructions of Gender, Change and Continuity in Botswana*. Fort Worth TX: Harcourt College Publishers.

Suggs, Robert C. 1960. *The Island Civilizations of Polynesia*. New York: New American Library.

———. 1966. *Marquesan Sexual Behavior*. New York: Harcourt, Brace and World.

———. 1971. Sex and Personality in the Marquesas: A Discussion of the Linton–Kardiner Report. In Donald S. Marshall and Robert C. Suggs, eds., *Human Sexual Behavior: Variations in the Ethnographic Spectrum*, 163–186. Studies in Sex and Society. New York: Basic Books.

Suggs, Robert C., and Donald S. Marshall. 1971a. Epilogue: Anthropological Perspectives on Human Sexual Behavior. In Donald S. Marshall and Robert C. Suggs, eds., *Human Sexual Behavior: Variations in the Ethnographic Spectrum*, 218–243. Studies in Sex and Society. New York: Basic Books.

———. 1971b. Appendix II: The Anthropological Study of Sexual Behavior: Definitions, Outline, and a Critique of Method and Theory. In Donald S. Marshall and Robert C. Suggs, eds., *Human Sexual Behavior: Variations in the Ethnographic Spectrum*, 250–294. Studies in Sex and Society. New York: Basic Books.

Symonds, John Addington. 1883. *A Problem in Greek Ethics: Being an Inquiry into the Problem of Sexual Inversion*. Privately printed.

————. 1891. *A Problem in Modern Ethics*. Privately printed.

Symons, Donald. 1995. Beauty Is in the Adaptations of the Beholder: The Evolutionary Psychology of Human Female Sexual Attractiveness. In Paul R. Abramson and Steven D. Pinkerton, eds., *Sexual Nature, Sexual Culture*, 80–118. Chicago: University of Chicago Press.

Tavris, Carol. 1992. *The Mismeasure of Woman*. New York: Simon and Schuster.

Temple, R. C., et al. 1913. Suggestions for a School of Applied Anthropology. *Man* 13:185–192.

Thomas, Northcote W. 1966 [1906]. *Kinship Organizations and Group Marriage in Australia*. New York: Humanities Press.

Torgovnick, Marianna. 1990. *Gone Primitive: Savage Intellects, Modern Lives*. Chicago: University of Chicago Press.

Treichler, Paula A. 1992. AIDS, HIV, and the Cultural Construction of Reality. In Gilbert Herdt and Shirley Lindenbaum, eds., *The Time of AIDS: Social Analysis, Theory and Method*, 65–100. Newbury Park CA: Sage Publications.

Trexler, Richard C. 1995. *Sex and Conquest: Gendered Violence, Political Order, and the European Conquest of the Americas*. Ithaca NY: Cornell University Press.

Turner, Victor. 1968. *The Drums of Affliction*. Oxford: Clarendon Press.

————. 1983. Carnaval in Rio: Dionysian Drama in an Industrializing Society. In Frank Manning, ed., *Celebration of Society*, 103–124. Bowling Green OH: Bowling Green University Popular Press.

Tuzin, Donald. 1991. Sex, Culture and the Anthropologist. *Social Science and Medicine* 33:867–874.

————. 1994. The Forgotten Passion: Sexuality and Anthropology in the Ages of Victoria and Bronislaw. *Journal of the History of the Behavioral Sciences* 29:114–137.

————. 1995. Discourse, Intercourse, and the Excluded Middle: Anthropology and the Problem of Sexual Experience. In Paul R. Abramson and Steven D. Pinkerton, eds., *Sexual Nature, Sexual Culture*, 257–275. Chicago: University of Chicago Press.

————. 1997. *The Cassowary's Revenge: The Life and Death of Masculinity in a New Guinea Society*. Chicago: University of Chicago Press.

Vance, Carole. 1991. Anthropology Rediscovers Sex. *Social Science and Medicine* 33(8):865–907.

Virey, Julien. 1824. *Histoire naturelle du genre humain, nouvelle édition – augmentée et entièrement refondue par J. J. Virey*. 2 vols. Paris.

Wake, Charles Staniland. 1875. Influence of the Phallic Idea in the Religions of Antiquity. In Charles Staniland Wake and Hodder Westropp, eds., *Ancient Symbol*

Worship: The Influence of the Phallic Idea in the Religions of Antiquity, 33–78. London: Trubner.

———. 1967 [1889]. *The Development of Marriage and Kinship*. Ed. and with an introduction by Rodney Needham. Chicago: University of Chicago Press.

Walker, Alice. 1992. *Possessing the Secret of Joy*. New York: Harcourt Brace Jovanovich.

———. 1993. *Warrior Marks: Female Genital Mutilation and the Sexual Blinding of Women*. New York: Harcourt Brace.

Walkowitz, Judith. 1980. *Prostitution and Victorian Society: Women, Class and the State*. Cambridge: Cambridge University Press.

Wallace, Lee. 1999. Academic Recognition: Margaret Mead, Ruth Benedict and Sexual Secrecy. *History and Anthropology* 11(4):417–435.

Wallen, Kim. 1995. The Evolution of Female Sexual Desire. In Paul R. Abramson and Steven D. Pinkerton, eds., *Sexual Nature, Sexual Culture*, 57–79. Chicago: University of Chicago Press.

Walton, Jean. 2001. *Fair Sex, Savage Dreams: Race, Psychoanalysis, Sexual Difference*. Durham NC: Duke University Press.

Warner, Lloyd. 1958 [1937]. *A Black Civilization: A Social Study of an Australian Tribe*. Harper Torchbooks version of the rev. ed. New York: Harper and Row.

Weiner, Annette. 1976. *Women of Value, Men of Renown*. Austin: University of Texas Press.

———. 1988. *The Trobrianders of Papua New Guinea*. New York: Holt, Rinehart and Winston.

Wekker, Gloria. 1999. "What's Identity Got to Do with It?": Rethinking Identity in the Light of the Mati Work in Suriname. In Evelyn Blackwood and Saskia E. Wieringa, eds., *Same-Sex Relations and Female Desires: Transgender Practices across Cultures*, 119–138. New York: Columbia University Press.

Westermarck, Edward. 1901 [1891]. *The History of Human Marriage*. 3rd ed. London: Macmillan.

———. 1904. The Position of Women in Early Civilization. *American Journal of Sociology* 10:408–442.

———. 1906–8. *The Origin and Development of Moral Ideas*. 2 vols. London: Macmillan.

———. 1929. *Memories of My Life*. London: George Allen and Unwin.

———. 1934. *Three Essays on Sex and Marriage*. London: Macmillan.

———. 1936. *The Future of Marriage in Western Civilization*. London: Macmillan.

———. 1968 [1926]. *A Short History of Marriage*. New York: Humanities Press.

Weston, Kath. 1991. *Families We Choose: Lesbians, Gays, Kinship*. New York: Columbia University Press.

———. 1998. *Longslowburn: Sexuality and Social Science*. New York: Routledge.

Westropp, Hodder M. 1875. Phallic Worship. In Charles Staniland Wake and Hodder Westropp, eds., *Ancient Symbol Worship: The Influence of the Phallic Idea in the Religions of Antiquity*, 23–32. London: Trubner.

Westropp, Hodder M., and Charles Staniland Wake. 1875 [1874]. *Ancient Symbol Worship: The Influence of the Phallic Idea in the Religions of Antiquity*. 2nd ed. London: Trubner.

White, Charles. 1799. *An Account of the Regular Gradation in Man and in Different Animals and Vegetables and from the Former to the Latter*. London.

White, Luise. 1980. *Women's Domestic Labor in Colonial Kenya: Prostitution in Nairobi, 1909–1950*. Working Paper no. 30. Boston: Boston University African Studies Center.

Whitehead, Harriet. 1981. The Bow and the Burden Strap: A New Look at Institutionalized Homosexuality in Native North America. In Sherry B. Ortner and Harriet Whitehead, eds.,*Sexual Meanings: The Cultural Construction of Gender and Sexuality*, 80–115. Cambridge: Cambridge University Press.

————. 1986 [1985]. Review of Gilbert Herdt, ed., *Ritualized Homosexuality in Melanesia*. In Evelyn Blackwood, ed., *The Many Faces of Homosexuality: Anthropological Approaches to Homosexual Behavior*, 201–205. New York: Harrington Park Press.

Wieringa, Saskia E. 1999. Desiring Bodies or Defiant Cultures: Butch–Femme Lesbians in Jakarta and Lima. In Evelyn Blackwood and Saskia E. Wieringa, eds., *Same-Sex Relations and Female Desires: Transgender Practices across Cultures*, 206–231. New York: Columbia University Press.

Wieringa, Saskia E., and Evelyn Blackwood. 1999. Introduction. In Evelyn Blackwood and Saskia E. Wieringa, eds., *Same-Sex Relations and Female Desires: Transgender Practices across Cultures*, 1–38. New York: Columbia University Press.

Wikan, Uni. 1977. Man Becomes Woman: Transsexualism in Oman as a Key to Gender Roles. *Man*, n.s. 12(2):304–319.

Wikman, K. R. V., ed. 1940. *Letters from Edward B. Tylor and Alfred Russell Wallace to Edward Westermarck*. Åbo: Acta Academiae Aboensis.

Wilder, Alexander, M.D. 1875. Introduction and Appendix. In Hodder M. Westropp and Charles Staniland Wake, eds., *Ancient Symbol Worship: The Influence of the Phallic Idea in the Religions of Antiquity*, 1–21, 79–98. London: Trubner.

Williams, Walter. 1986. *The Spirit and the Flesh: Sexual Diversity in American Indian Culture*. Boston: Beacon Press.

————. 1995. Academics and Activism: Future Directions for Gay, Lesbian, Bisexual and Transgender Studies. Keynote Speech, Queer Frontiers: 1995 and Beyond. March 23. Electronic document, http://www.usc.edu/isd/archives/queerfrontiers/, accessed August 4, 2002.

Wolf, Deborah. 1979. *The Lesbian Community*. Berkeley: University of California Press.

Wylie, Philip. 1942. *A Generation of Vipers*. New York: Farrar and Rinehart.

Young, Robert J. C. 1995. *Colonial Desire: Hybridity in Theory, Culture and Race*. London: Routledge.

Index

in, 103, 148, 174; disciplinary boundaries of, 15–16, 18; Durkheimian, 217–18, 282; evolutionary, 74, 148–49, 174, 218, 221; feminist, 4, 278, 287; and "fictions," 12, 19, 101, 103, 293; fin de siècle, 103; foundational texts of, 293; functionalist, 17, 103, 113, 132, 138, 154, 174–78, 183–84, 218–19, 221–22, 239–40; gay, 129, 251, 293–94, 300, 306, 325; government, 102, 132, 154, 232; and the Great Depression, 183–84; history of, 17, 101, 140, 187, 202; and homoeroticism, 298; of homosexuality, 11, 287, 291; Kinsey Report attack on, 256; liberal, 287; and marginalization, 10, 325; medical, 278–79, 315; modernist, 88, 336n6; and 19th-century debates, 52, 103; physical, 27, 28, 37, 102, 165, 181; and pornography, 3, 17, 56–57; postmodern, 8; professionalization of, 4–5, 11, 16, 55, 100, 133, 148, 217, 276; processual, 279, 284, 295, 321; "queering," 292–306; and questionnaires, 312, 176–77; and racism, 218; and rediscovery of sex, 11, 277, 285, 294; and relativism, 8, 15, 103, 219, 277–79, 287; roots of, 55; as science, 155, 157, 278; of sexuality, 4, 11, 102, 216, 218–19, 276, 279, 298–99, 303, 304–5, 311, 322, 326, 332; and silence on sexuality, 9–11, 216–19, 275–76, 303, 320; structural, 279–83, 295, 320; symbolic, 285, 287–88, 295; as therapy, 159, 174, 208–9, 257; as voyeurism, 1; women in, 186. *See also* applied anthropology; fieldwork; participant observation; psychoanalytic anthropology; symbolic anthropology

Anthropology Research Group on Homosexuality, 294

anthropometry. *See* body measurement

"anthroporn," 180

anti-Semitism, 184, 318; of Burton, 64

"Antler" tribe. *See* Omaha

anxiety, 8, 9, 134, 256, 259, 266; male sexual, 28, 271–72, 290

applied anthropology, 135, 174, 177–78, 208, 218, 226, 278

Arabs, 142; Burton on, 62, 64–65, 68

Arapesh, 205–7, 211, 307

armchair anthropology, 14, 16, 92, 97, 102. *See also* Frazer, E. Franklin; Hartland, Edwin Sidney; Thomas, Northcote W.

Arnhem Land, 238–42, 331; abuse of women in, 240; adultery in, 239; conception beliefs of, 239, 343n5; homosexuality in, 240; and image of oversexed savages, 239, 240; marriage in, 239, 241; marriage by capture in, 239–40; moral code in, 239, 241; premarital promiscuity in, 239, 241; and regional sexual differences, 241, 343n6; sexual discourse in, 241; sexual license in, 241; women's rights in, 241. *See also* Australian Aborigines

Arnold, Matthew, 16

artificial insemination, 322

Arundell (Burton), Isabel. *See* Burton, Isabel

Arunta, 90–93, 96; Lang on, 108; Thomas on, 108–9

Asama Island, 136

atavism, 104

Atkinson, J. J.: and Andrew Lang, 106; patriarchal theory of, 106–8; theory of primal horde, 107

Augustine, 6

Aunger, Robert V., 313

Australia, 226, 229; as living kindergarten, 83–99

Australian Aborigines, 38, 73, 74, 83–94; and adultery, 86; Burton on, 61; and conception by spirits, 91; elopement among, 86; and exogamy, 85; Fison and Howitt on, 83–90; Freud on, 107; and genital operations, 83, 90, 92; and group marriage, 85–91, 99, 109; and incest, 85–86; and infanticide, 92; kinship terms, 84–85; Lang on monotheism of, 108; and marriage, 77, 83–91, 108–9, 149, 164; and marriage by capture, 77, 83, 87, 89, 91; and matrilineal descent, 85; on modesty, 118; morality of, 45, 90, 109, 118; and nescience of maternity, 182; and nescience of paternity, 108–9, 178, 181–83; polygyny of, 83, 85, 86; and primitive promiscuity, 86, 111; and racial ranking, 30–31, 45; and sexual communism of Lubbock, 77; and sexual license, 83, 89–90, 91; stereotypes

Australian Aborigines (*cont.*)
of, 238; Thomas on, 108–9; and totemism, 86, 87, 91, 92–94, 337n10; as zero point of cultural evolution, 131. *See also* Arnhem Land; images; Spencer, Baldwin
Aveling, Edward, 123
Azande. *See* Evans-Pritchard, E. E.; Zande

Bachman, John, 36
Bachofen, Johann Jakob, 55, 73–74, 76, 198; admired by Morgan, 80, 336n2; on the family, 82; and feminism, 80; on homosexuality, 81; Howitt on, 89; oblivious to class, 81–82; on matriarchy, 80–82; on matriliny, 82; on race, 81–82
Baden-Powell, Robert, 120
Baiga people, 181, 233–34; love among, 233
Bailey, Robert C., 313
Baker, Frank. *See* Burton, Sir Richard F.
Baker, Samuel White, 136, 137–38, 146
Baldwin, James, 187
baloma spirits, 178–79
Bancroft, Hubert Howe, 128
Banks, Joseph, 20
Barker, Pat, 97
Barnes, R. H., 319
Barrow, John, 44
"Bartmann, Sarah," 33. *See also* Saat-Jee
Barton, Roy Franklin, 181
Basden, G. T., 154
Basongye people, 272
Bateson, Mary Catherine, 209–10, 214
Beach, Frank A., 213, 263, 268. *See also* Ford, Clellan S., and Frank A Beach; Kinsey Report
beard, 33; African, 134; Native American, 8, 27, 46. *See also* hair
Beauvoir, Simone de, 214–15
Bedborough, George, 13, 120, 167
Beddoe, John, 122
Behar, Ruth, 293
behaviorism, 168
Behn, Aphra, 42
Benedict, Ruth, 11, 188, 205, 228, 276; on American sexual culture, 250; on berdache, 250, 251–52; and configurationism, 251, 253–

54; on creativity, 253; on Dakota, 252; on Dobuan as "paranoid," 252; and Gorer, 231; on homosexuality, 250–54, 298; on infantile sexuality, 253; on Japan, 250; Kardiner and, 262, 343n9; and Kinsey Report, 266; on Kwakiutl as "paranoid," 252; language of pathology in, 252; lesbianism of, 251; on life cycle, 253; on love, 250; and Mead, 199; relativism of, 252, 254, 298; and "safety-valve" theory, 251, 298; on sexual object choice, 253; on trance, 251; on Zuni as "Apollonians," 250, 252
Benga, Féral, 229
Benin, 145
berdache, 8, 18, 274, 292–93, 297–99, 310, 317–18; among Basongye, 272; among Dakota, 252; and homoeroticism, 289; and Kroeber, 247; Mohave, 247–49; as not synonymous with homosexuality, 26, 272; as pathological, 298; "safety-valve" theory of, 249; sexual techniques of, 299; and sodomy, 298; suppression of, 298–99; Whitehead on, 289; among Zuni, 250. *See also* cross-dressing; gender crossing; "two spirit"
Bernadin de Saint-Pierre, Jacques Henri, 32
Berndt, Ronald M., and Catherine H. Berndt, 228–29, 238–42, 331, 343n4; and colonialism, 242; functionalism of, 239–40; and image of oversexed savages, 239, 240; and missionaries, 239, 241
Besant, Annie, 52, 54, 119, 123
Besnier, Niko, 321–22
bestiality, 70, 238, 240, 269, 284
Bettelheim, Bruno, 227
Bible, 34, 35, 58, 76
Bimin-Kuskusmin people, 289–90
Bingham, Hiram, 79
biology, 41
birth control. *See* contraception
Birth Control Review, 164, 170
bisexuality, 209–10
blacks: and biological difference, 15; fiction of sex between "orangs" and, 38–40; intelligence of, 41. *See also* Africans, Negroes
Blainville, Henri de, 33

capitalism, 186, 219

Caribs, 41

Carlyle, Thomas, 61

Carpenter, Edward, 122–23; on Christianity and Judaism, 128–29; friendship with Ellis, 122, 128; homosexuality of, 122; on homosexuality, 128–29, 253–54; on military pederasty, 129; and Symonds, 129; on Westermarck, 128–29

Casas, Bartolomé de Las, 25–26

case histories: Dora, 100; Devereux's, 247; Elwin's, 233; in Kinsey Report, 263, 266; Malinowski's work as psychiatric, 159

castration, 310

categories, 14, 277–78, 279, 280–81, 297–98, 303; arbitrariness of "male" and "female," 301; desire and social, 300; of disease, 283

Catholic Church: and confession, 157–58; and Malinowski, 176; and New Guinean initiation, 347–48n1

Catlin, George, 44

Caucasian: term (Blumenbach), 27

Cayapa people, 272

celibacy: Elwin and, 232, 233; Russell on, 162. See also chastity

Central States Anthropological Association, 271

Cesara, Manda (Karla Poewe), 327

chastity, 6, 150, 198; among Africans, 313; among Busama, 227; Crawley on, 116, 123; Ellis on, 166; feminists and male, 121; Hemyng on, 50; Kgatlan, 224; Malinowski on, 166, 180; among Manus, 197; among Muria, 235; among Native Americans, 46; among New Zealanders, 47; among Samoans, 193, 292; among Tikopians, 220. See also celibacy

Cheyenne, 26

Cherry Grove. See Fire Island

Chesser, Eustace, 13

child abuse, 319

childhood: pathologization of, 259; sexuality, 270

"childhood determinism," 272

child marriage, 48, 96, 143–44, 147, 151–52

children: and desire, 239; and fieldwork, 326; Manus as civilized, 196. See also adolescence; pederasty

Christianity, 6–7, 62, 123, 176, 228, 273, 283, 290, 321, 330; Carpenter on, 128–29; and confession, 158; conversion to, 158, 223; Crawley's, 116, 123; Evangelical, 53–54, 56; and the family, 54; and initiation camps, 177; morality of, 20, 22, 179, 242; as phallic religion, 58–59; Protestant, 192; Russell on, 162; Samoan, 292; Tahitian, 283; Wake on, 88; Westermarck on, 123. See also Anglican Church, Catholic Church; Dutch Reformed Church; High Leigh conference; Lambeth Conference, Livingstone House conference; missionaries

Cipriani, Lidio, 184

circumcision, 2; Australian, 83, 89, 337n8; Burton on, 64; Hall on, 58; as index of primitivity, 65; Jewish, 318; 19th century and, 64–65; as phallic rite, 58; among Turu, 272. See also female circumcision; genital mutilation; genital operation

class, 4, 14, 81–82, 161, 198, 280–81, 305; Bachofen oblivious to, 81–82; bourgeoisie, 186, 194; colonial, 139; Foucault and, 13–15; Kinsey on, 264; lesbian working, 301, 303–5, 329; lumpen proletariat, 33–34; Mead oblivious to, 193–94, 200; middle, 54, 75, 105, 118, 130, 171, 194, 217, 264; ruling, 74, 77, 117, 210; and Victorian debates, 43–50; working, 44, 54, 75, 118, 130, 161, 162

clitoridectomy, 2, 318, 324; Boddy on, 319; Burton on, 64–65; in Nigeria, 330; among Turu, 272; in Victorian era, 65. See also female circumcision; genital mutilation; genital operation

cold war, 10, 210, 217

collective representations, 321; and AIDS education, 311; of beliefs, 182; of the colonial class, 139; of homosexuality and "naturalization," 302; of primitive sexuality, 242; and sex, 197, 282; of sexuality and spirituality, 245; trope of oversexed savage in, 280

colonialism, 5, 7, 11, 14, 174–78, 218–19, 229,

Contraception (*cont.*)
advocates persecuted, 119–20; and AIDS, 313; Ellis on, 126–27, 155, 167, 173; and eugenicists, 121, 126–27; and knowledge, 52, 121, 167, 171; and Lindsey, 170–71; Malinowski on, 9, 155, 156, 167, 173, 176, 180, 181, 199; Mead on, 199, 208; and reaction, 184; Russell on, 155, 173; Spencer and Gillen on, 92; Stopes and, 156, 161

Cook, Frederick, 116
Cook, James, 20–21, 32
Cooper, James Fenimore, 41
Coote, William A., 120–21
Coréal, François, 26
Corriere della Sera, 184
cosmology, 10, 245, 282, 283, 296, 307
Côté, James E., 203
countertransference: Devereux on, 249–50; in fieldwork, 331–32; Kinsey Report on, 265–66
Counts, Dorothy Ayers, 194–95; on Kaliai, 296–97
couvade, 164
Coward, Rosalind, 75
cranium: and intelligence, 3, 7; size and regular gradation, 30
craniometry. *See* body measurement; cranium; intelligence
Crawley, Ernest, 9, 17, 101–2, 129–30, 329; Anglicanism of, 116, 123; on celibacy, 116, 123; and Ellis, 113; and Malinowski, 164, 168, 170; on marriage, 113, 329; on marriage by capture, 221; on McLennan, 112; on menstruation, 117; nonrelativism of, 116; on origin of sexual restraint, 115; on periodicity, 114, 115, 116; and primitive sexual excess, 113; and "patriarchal" theory, 106; and representations of primitive sexuality, 101; on savage intelligence, 117; on sexual morality, 116; on taboos, 113, 115; on underdevelopment of sex organs, 116
creation (Genesis), 36, 37
Crewe, Robert Offley Ashburton, 147
"criminal" anthropology, 121
Criminal Law Amendment Act (1885), 53, 120
Criminal Law Amendment White Slavery Bill

(1912), 120
criminology, 104
cross-cultural research, 310
Cross-Cultural Survey (Yale), 262
cross-dressing, 10, 26, 289, 297, 299, 300, 321; in India, 310; Marshall on, 274; among Mohave, 244, 245, 247; in South and Central America, 25; in Tahiti, 284. *See also* berdache
Cueva people, 25
Cultural Anthropology, 306
cultural critique, 334n5; anthropology as, 18–19
culture and personality: and Gorer, 257; and Kardiner, 257; and Linton, 257; and Malinowski, 169, 257; and Mead, 194, 257; movement, 4, 218–19, 243, 257; and sexuality, 242–63; and Whiting, 257, 334n13
Curr, Edward Micklethwaite, 92
Curtin, Philip M., 132
Cuvier, Georges, 33, 35

Dahomey, 57, 61, 62, 63, 133
Dakota, 252
dala, 173, 179
Damascus, 64
dance: Falk on African, 131–32; in *ghotul*, 235; Johnston on African, 141–43; Lehner on Busama, 227; Reade on African, 134–35; Samoan, 292; as trope, 131–32, 134
Dapper, Ofert, 31
Darwin, Charles, 2, 15, 105–6; on primitive promiscuity, 105; and sexual selection, 31, 105. *See also* evolutionary theory; evolutionism
Darwinism, 7; of Ellis, 118, 126; ends debate over species, 41; model of courtship, 118; post-, 7, 35; of Westermarck, 110–13, 118, 124, 125–26. *See also* evolutionary theory; evolutionism
Davenport, John, 57
Davis, Madeline D., 301, 303–5
debate over species, 34–41
degeneration, 4, 20, 36, 129; and Africans, 21, 103–4; and Native Americans, 24, 27
"Demetrian principle" (Bachofen), 80–81

"desexualization" of sexuality, 10, 95, 103, 174–78, 183, 217–18, 280–83

desire, 48, 115, 288–89, 303, 305; alterity and, 198, 323; of Arnhem Land children, 239; female, 119, 196, 198; Freud on incestuous, 107; homoerotic, 300; homosexual, 240, 293; male, 198, 281, 286; of Malinowski during fieldwork, 159, 327; "natural" human, 295; in New Guinean homoerotic initiation, 294; primate, 308; silence on heterosexual female, 309; and social categories, 300; as social construction, 300; and subjectivity, 13, 185, 347–48n1; and theories of race, 38; and transgendered identity, 284; as unhealthy, 199

determinism: biological, 188, 199, 307; and constructionism, 307; cultural, 202–3, 207, 270, 323; and Ortner and Whitehead, 286; racial, 188, 278; relativism and, 286

Devereux, George, 242–50; on alcohol, 244–45, 246, 248–49, 251; on anal fixations, 241, 243–44; on anal sex, 244–45; and berdache, 247–49; on countertransference, 249–50; and diagnosis, 242, 244, 248; and discourse of social engineering, 249; and Freudian interpretations, 250; Freudian stages of development in, 243–44; and Gorer, 231; on heterosexuality, 244, 245, 247; on homosexuality, 242–45, 249; ignores social context, 246, 248–50; on masturbation, 242, 243–44; on Mohave sexuality, 10, 231, 242–50; and morality, 249; pathologizes homosexuality, 245, 249; on pederasty, 245–46; on practical joke, 246; on relativism, 249; reports social problems as normative, 245–46; and "safety-valve" theory, 249, 251; on transvestism, 244, 245, 247

deviance, 11, 301; of women, 43; of working class, 43

de Waal, Frans B. M., 308

diagnosis, 13, 129, 201; and alterity, 304–5, 312, 345n8; of desire as unhealthy, 199; Devereux and, 242, 244, 248; discourses of, 186; Mead and, 188, 190–91, 196, 198–200, 208–9, 210; and silence of discourses on

heterosexuality, 185–86. See also Foucault, Michel; medicalization of sexuality; therapy

Diáz, Bernal del Castillo, 25

Dictionary of National Biography, 122

Diderot, Denis, 20–22, 32, 47

Dieri, 86, 88–90, 96, 109

difference: biological, 15–16; gender, 16; racial, 16, 101; sexual, 101. See also alterity

diffusionism: in British anthropology, 103, 148; of Hartland, 97; Malinowski rejects, 174

Dilke, Charles, 52

discourses, 4–7, 13, 54, 215, 321; AIDS and distancing, 317; and alterity, 160; anthropological, 12, 55–57, 61–64, 103, 278; in Arnhem Land, 241; of "blaming the mother," 257–58; of cannibalism, 136; on companionate marriage, 173; and conscription, 18; and construction of sexuality, 307; of evolution, 3; fin de siècle, 101, 130; of homosexuality, 297, 345n8; inequality and Samoan, 292; of Kinsey, 211; 19th-century sexual, 13–14, 52, 55–56, 103, 167, 198; on phallic worship, 107; polygenist, 38–40; racialized, 7–8; of reform, 119; and silence on heterosexuality, 185–86; of social engineering, 249; and social movements, 119–29; scientific, 156–57; Trobriand sexual, 173, 217; and women's experience, 211

divorce: among Alor, 260, 262; colonial elites on, 149–51; Lindsey on, 171; Mead on, 193, 208; among Muria, 237; Russell on, 162, 172; among Trobrianders, 172

disease: homosexuality as, 274. See also AIDS; diagnosis; medicalization of sexuality; venereal disease

Dobuan people, 252

Dollard, John, 254, 258

dominance: female, 5; male, 5, 278, 286, 308; mother, 272

Draper, Patricia, 313–14

dreams, 170

Duban people, 252

Du Bois, Cora, 10, 257; on Alor, 258–61; on Alorese gender roles, 258–59; collaboration with Kardiner, 254, 258; critiqued, 261; and

Du Bois, Cora (*cont.*)
culture-bound syndromes, 258; and developmental periods, 260; on economics and sexual practices, 259; on marriage, 261; on "modal personality," 258; pathologization of Alor by, 259, 260
Du Chaillu, Paul, 60
Duchet, Michèle, 22
Durkheim, Émile, 16, 84, 93, 100, 217–18; on Atkinson, 106; on gender differentiation, 189; on nescience of paternity, 338n2
Dutch Reformed Church, 223
Dykes, Eva Beatrice, 42
dysphoria, sexual, 199–200, 312
dystopia: and Alor, 18; and Marquesas, 18; and Native America, 24

Eddystone, 181
Edo, 149–50
Edwardian period, 5, 101, 127, 217
Egypt, 58, 82, 87, 137, 145
Elele, 131
Elgin, Suzette Hayden, 210–11
elopement: among Australian Aborigines, 86; Kgatlan, 224; among Muria, 237; Samoan, 192
Ellis, Edith (née Lees), 123, 128, 140
Ellis, Havelock, 2, 9, 13, 71, 100–102, 118–19, 129–30, 240, 263, 278, 339n4; on adultery, 172; on Briffault, 168; and Carpenter, 129; on chastity, 166; on companionate marriage, 124–25, 170–72, 275, 305, 329; on contraception, 126–27, 155, 167, 173; and Crawley, 113; on criminals, 121; Darwinism of, 118, 126; and environmentalism, 166; and eugenics, 121–22, 126–27; and "facts," 168, 278; on the family, 126; and feminism, 121, 126–27; and Freud, 113, 167; friendship with Carpenter, 122, 128; friendship with Sanger, 127; friendship with Marie Stopes, 127; friendship with Symonds, 122, 127–28; on homosexuality, 122, 127–28, 165; on intelligence, 126; and Kinsey Report, 265; and Malinowski, 130, 155, 161, 163–73, 199; on marriage by capture, 119; marriage to Edith Lees, 123, 128, 140, 171; on masturbation, 120, 173; on menstruation, 117, 126; on modesty, 118–19, 165, 170, 198; and the National Council for Public Morals, 126–27; Nazis burn books of, 184; on origin of sexual restraint, 115; on periodicity, 114, 115, 116–17, 263; on primitive promiscuity, 112, 329; on prostitution, 127; and primitive sexuality, 100–102, 165; on rape, 118; and Russell, 163; on secular morality, 155; and sex education, 155, 166, 173; and sexual reform, 155–56; and science, 167–68; socialism of, 122; on taboos, 115; theory of neoteny of, 126; on underdevelopment of sex organs, 115–16; and Westermarck, 128, 164; Wieringa on, 302; on women's status, 126, 329
Elliston, Deborah A., 345n2; critique of Herdt on "ritualized homosexuality," 296–97
Elwin, Verrier, 10, 228, 231–38; on Baiga, 181, 233–34; on conception, 233; and conscription, 238; critique of, 234–35; on homosexuality, 237–38, 240; on marriage, 235–37; on Muria, 234–38; primitivism of, 233; on racism, 238; sexual ignorance of, 233
empiricism, 156–57
endogamy, 77, 82, 97
Engels, Friedrich, 78, 198
Enlightenment, 6, 15–17, 20, 40, 43, 47, 334n5
environmental deprivation, 50
environmentalism, 43; in American anthropology, 218; in Baker, 138; in Buffon, 24; in Burton, 63, 70–71; in Ellis, 166; in Malinowski, 166; and monogenism, 35, 37; in Stanley, 137. *See also* "sotadic zone"
equality: gender, 5, 16, 31, 78, 235–36, 329; racial, 16, 40, 138; sexual, 162; social, 162
Erikson, Erik, 205, 208, 211–12
Eskimo. *See* Inuit
essentialism, 11, 278, 302–3, 309–10, 321, 323, 345–46n10; and debates with constructionism, 11, 309–10, 321, 323; in Levy, 285
ethics: Elwin's alleged breach of, 234; and fieldwork, 2
Ethiopia, 154
ethnoanthropologies, 23

"ethnocartography" of sexuality (Weston), 222, 298–99, 304

ethnography, 8; colonial foundation for, 133; of heterosexuality, 306–7; of homosexuality, 127; of "systems" of sexuality and gender, 291

ethnohistory, 301, 304–5

Ethnological Society, 55, 56, 73

ethnology: romantic, 4; and sexual reform, 4

ethnopsychiatry, 241, 243

Eton, 120

eugenicism, 121; of Stopes, 161

eugenics movement, 100, 121–22; and the family, 123, 126–27; Russell on, 162

Evangelical Christianity, 53–54, 56

Evans-Pritchard, E. E., 217; on Mead, 187; support for Rentoul, 180; on Zande sexuality, 10, 220

evolution, 278; and atavism, 104, 140; Darwinian theory of, 35; discourse of, 3; gender differentiation and, 189; of sexuality in psychoanalysis, 106; social, 16, 98, 102, 103, 107, 111

evolutionary anthropology, 74, 148–49, 174, 218, 221

evolutionary theory, 35, 74–75, 84, 102, 108, 280, 287, 307–9, 345n16; and anthropology's roots, 55. See also Darwin, Charles; Darwinism; Rushton, J. Phillippe

evolutionism: of Briffault, 238; and gender and class, 198; and group marriage, 98, 337n7; of Hall, 189–90; Lang on, 95, 108; and morality, 74; of Morgan, 78, 198; 19th-century, 3, 8, 44, 101, 218; and polygenism, 75; reification in, 75; of Rivers, 97; of Russell, 162; and totemism, 93; 20th-century, 99; of Tylor, 95; of Wake, 58; of Westermarck, 113. See also Darwin, Charles; Darwinism

excision, 318, 334n4. See also female circumcision; genital mutilation; genital operation

existentialism, 215

exogamy, 77, 85, 97, 235; Burton on, 60; Fison on, 84; Lang on, 106, 108; McLennan on, 76, 82, 86; as problem in Freud, 107

Eyre, Edward, 44, 56

fa'afafine, 195

"facts," 5, 9, 19, 168, 183–84, 202, 241; Ellis on, 168, 278; and AIDS, 311; narratives presented as, 250; scientific, 182, 282

Falk, E. M., 131–33, 149, 150–53, 331; and Igbo Women's Rebellion, 132, 152–54; report on African dance ceremony, 131–32

Falk, Mrs. E. M., 152–53

family, 10, 217; in Atkinson, 106; Bachofen on, 82; Burton on, 54; and capitalism, 219; Christian, 54; eugenicists on, 123; Ellis on, 126; in evolutionary theory, 74–75, 78–79; feminists on, 123; Freeman on, 203; in Freud, 106–7; Kardiner on, 262; Malinowski on, 168, 175; in matriarchal theory, 74, 78–79, 82; nuclear, 208; in patriarchal theory, 106–8; Russell on, 162–63; social purity movements on, 123; Victorian, 54, 163

Farmer, Paul, 312, 315, 317

Fawcett, Millicent, 121

female circumcision, 313, 317–18; in diaspora, 318–19; emic perspective on, 319–20; and sex education, 320; and sexual response, 319; Sudanese, 319; term as political choice, 317–18. See also clitoridectomy

female dominance, 5

feminism, 4, 7, 15, 80, 204, 210, 215, 277, 285–86; and advocacy around genital mutilation, 318–20; and "claiming a voice," 293, 345n8; Ellis and, 121, 126–27; on the family, 123; First Wave, 271; gay, 286; Kardiner on, 261; lesbian, 304; Malinowski on, 155; and mother right, 80, 155; and nescience of paternity debate, 182; of Ortner and Whitehead, 286; and prostitution, 129; Second Wave, 275, 286; and social purity movements, 121, 123; Victorian, 52, 53–54; Westermarck's, 125–26, 140

feminist anthropology, 4, 278, 287

feminist historians, 104

Ferguson, Adam, 1

Fernández-Alemany, Manuel, 300

Fernando Póo, 133, 146

Ferrero, Guglielmo, 103

fertility: and Australian myth, 239, 241; Bachofen on, 80; breast size as index of, 3;
Frazer on, 93, 95; Montagu on delayed, 181;
Sellon and, 58
fiction. *See* Victorian literature
"fictions," 12, 19, 23, 101, 103; around anal
penetration, 291; and countertransference,
331; of sex between blacks and "orangs,"
38–40
fieldwork, 8, 140, 152, 159, 168, 182, 189, 192,
225; and conscription, 327; countertransference during, 331–32; and ethics, 2, 326–27,
331; and funding, 327; rape during, 327; sex
during, 311–12, 326–28. *See also* participant
observation
Fiji, 83
fin de siècle, 5; anthropology, 103; and companionate marriage, 124–25; discourses, 101;
images, 101, 103–4
Fire Island, 305–6, 329; and communitas, 305;
Lévi-Strauss on, 305–6
First International Congress on Sexual Questions (Berlin), 167
Firth, Sir Raymond, 10, 217, 220–22, 276; and
conscription, 222; on marriage by capture,
220–21, 222; relativism of, 222
Fison, Lorimer, 83–87, 93; on Australian
kinship terms, 84–85; on evolution of the
family, 74, 109; morality in, 86; on primitive
promiscuity, 74; on totemism, 87
Florentine Museum, 184
"Flynt, Josiah," 127
foil: primitives as, 101; sexuality as, 15, 50;
Tahitians as, 22
folklore, 95–96, 102, 180, 220, 238; of AIDS,
151, 314–15; of anthropology, 189; love and
Manu'a, 201; Zuni, 250
Folklore Society, 95
Ford, Clellan S., and Frank A. Beach, 213,
263, 268–70, 271; on childhood sexuality,
270; comparative zoology, 269–70; on
homosexuality, 269; on masturbation, 269,
270; on premarital sex, 269–70; relativism
of, 268; on universals in sexual behavior,
269. *See also* Kinsey Report

Forde, Daryll, 217
Forster, Georg, 20–21, 41
Fortes, Meyer, 165, 183, 217, 220
Fortune, Reo F., 205, 265, 342n7
Foucault, Michel, 4, 8–9, 12–15, 54, 100–101,
124, 156–57, 173, 185–86, 191, 197, 198, 279,
303, 305, 325, 331, 345n8, 345n9; challenged
by Murray on homosexuality, 300; on
confessional mode, 123; on discourses of
reform, 119; on Ellis, 157; on homoeroticism as definitive of homosexuality, 300;
Malthusian couple of, 13, 101, 127, 173, 185–
86; 19th-century public discourse, 13–14,
52; omissions in theory, 13–15; and race, 14;
on reification, 185–86; on *scientia sexualis*,
100, 127, 156–57; on surveillance, 193. *See
also* confessional mode; panopticon; power;
sexology
Frazer, E. Franklin, 280
Frazer, James G., 84, 148; as armchair anthropologist, 92, 97; on Arunta, 93; corn god in,
107; evolutionism of, 94; on fertility, 93, 95;
on nescience of paternity, 93–95, 180 ; on
totemism, 93–95, 337n10
free love, 9, 155, 156, 168
Freeman, Derek, 2, 47, 188, 203, 292; on
Marshall, 273. *See also* Mead-Freeman
controversy
Freeman, Henry Stanhope, 62
freethinkers, 122, 123
French Army Surgeon (Jacobus X): in Ellis,
112; in Rushton, 3, 112
Freud, Sigmund, 2, 101, 102, 115, 129, 227, 231,
281; and American anthropology, 218; and
Devereux, 243–44; and Ellis, 113, 167, 197;
and gender identity, 295; and Malinowski,
167, 169; and the Oedipus complex, 106–7,
169, 218; theory of totemism of, 106–7, 280–
81; recapitulation hypothesis in, 107, 196
Friedan, Betty, 207–8, 209
Friedl, Ernestine, 2
Frye, Marilyn, 210
functionalism, 132, 174–78, 183–84, 239–40;
and African representations, 138; in British
anthropology, 103, 154, 218–19; in Devereux,

249; of Evans-Pritchard, 296; of Firth, 221–22, 223; of Malinowski, 17, 175–78, 179, 183–84, 218; of Radcliffe-Brown, 183; of Schapera, 224
"functional substitution," 177
Fundamentalists, 171

Gabon, 133, 139
Gallagher, Catherine, 42
Galton, Francis, 105, 121–22
Gambia, 133
Gandhi, Mahatma, 232, 233
Ganowanian kinship terminology, 82–83, 85, 99
Gason, Samuel, 83, 86
Gauguin, Paul, 23
gay: activists, 298; history, 300; liberation, 275, 329; men and AIDS, 315; man murdered, 325; natives and berdache tradition, 299; promiscuity, 305; rights, 296, 315; sex in field, 311
gay anthropology, 129, 251, 293, 300, 306, 325; and gay political issues, 293–94
gay ethnohistory, 301, 304–5
Gays and Lesbians of Zimbabwe (GALZ), 315
Gebhard, Paul H., 263, 265, 271
Geertz, Clifford, 187
Gell, Simeran M. S., 237
gender, 4, 14, 154, 198, 277–78, 280–81, 305; ambiguity among Bimin-Kuskusmin, 289–90; categories, 297–98; classification as non-dualistic, 301; as cultural construction, 301; cultural variability in, 205–9; differentiation and evolution, 189–90; hierarchies, 5, 16, 287; ideologies, 292; identity, 295; and Igbo Women's rebellion, 132; multiple, 297, 300–302; "naturalness" of, 16; "patterns" of, 205, 209; as performance, 302, 320–22; redefined in non-sexual terms, 10; among Sambians, 295; as sense of "sex," 285, 309; as social construction, 300; "system," 286, 304; and transgendered identity, 284; Victorian ranking of, 119; Victorian system of, 75, 101, 104–5. See also "third gender"
gender balance: in colonies, 145, 147; and gender crossing, 289

gender crossing: Native American, 289; Samoan, 195. See also berdache
gender equality, 5, 16, 78, 329; and bachelor huts, 235; among Hottentot and San, 31; among Muria, 235–36
gender hierarchies, 5. See also matriarchy; mother right; patriarchy
gender identity, 11
gender roles, 329; anxiety concerning, 10; Benedict on, 252–53; Burton on, 67; and conscription, 257; Du Bois on, 258–59; female, 326; Levy on, 285; Mead on, 205–9; Native American and alternative, 298; as performance, 302, 320–22; in Tahiti, 285
gender studies, 320
General Medical Council, 120
genital cutting, 318. See also female circumcision
genitalia: and constrictor vaginae, 180; in debate over species, 36; exaggerated, 7; gradation in female, 30; and hair, 282; as index of degeneration among Africans, 20, 28; as index of primitivity, 66, 225; Hottentot and San women's, 31–34, 66, 225; large, 347n16; underdevelopment of, 115–16. See also breasts; circumcision; clitoridectomy; genital mutilation; genital operation; penis size; steatopygia
genital mutilation: bans of, 318; Burton on, 64–66; female, 318; feminism and advocacy around, 318–20; and racial hierarchies, 64; and relativism, 2, 318, 320, 335n4. See also circumcision; clitoridectomy; female circumcision; genital operation
genital operation, 92, 278, 319; and beauty, 32, 225; female, 2, 31–32, 64, 83, 90, 92, 225, 273, 313, 317–18; male, 64, 83, 220, 226, 274; and Malinowski, 278; and relativism, 318, 320, 335n4; and stigmatization, 318. See also circumcision; clitoridectomy; genital mutilation
Ghana, 133, 229
ghotul, 234–37; wife, 237
Gillen, F. J. See Spencer, Baldwin
Gilman, Sander L., 33, 43, 103–4, 311

Ginsburg, Faye, 322
Gisu people, 314
Gobineau, Arthur, comte de, 15–16, 333n2
Goldenweiser, Alexander, 253–54
Goldfrank, Esther Schiff, 254
Gordon, Deborah A., 293
Gorer, Geoffrey, 11, 228–31, 254, 257, 267, 270, 343n3; on African dances, 229–30; as neo-Freudian, 231
gorillas. *See* primates
Gosse, Edmund, 51
Gosselin, Claudie, 320
Goulaine de Laudonnière, René, 26
government anthropology, 102, 132, 154, 232; and Igbo Women's Rebellion, 132, 154; and Elwin, 232; and Thomas, 102
gradualism, 144
Grant, Nicole J., 212–13
Great Chain of Being, 23, 29, 40, 225; Negroes and orangutans as equivalent in, 38
Great Depression, 9–10, 217; and functional anthropology, 183–84
Greece: ancient, 13, 26, 44, 70, 80–82, 87, 122, 148; and military pederasty, 129, 294, 302
Green, Margaret M., 154
Greenberg, David F., 129, 265
Gregor, Thomas, 306, 309
Griffiths, Alison, 92
group marriage, 78–79, 82–91, 97–99, 105, 109, 239; Briffault on, 340n6; and incest taboos, 280; in India, 82; Morgan on, 82–83, 149; Thomas on, 88–90, 108–9; Westermarck on, 112. *See also* jus primae noctis; marriage
Grosskurth, Phyllis, 164
Gruenbaum, Ellen, 319

Haddon, A. C., 187
Haggard, H. Rider, 129, 134
hair, 282–83, 291–92. *See also* beard
Haiti, 312, 315, 317
Hall, G. Stanley: on adolescence, 188–90, 194; on circumcision, 58; evolutionism of, 189–90; and Mead, 188–90, 194; on motherhood, 190; and recapitulation, 190
Haller, John and Robin, 104, 208
Hallpike, Christopher, 283

Hamitic hypothesis, 141
Hammond, Dorothy, 132
Hankey, Fred, 61
Haraway, Donna J., 219, 222, 249, 280–81
Harris, Frank, 61
Harris, Helen, 202, 204, 274
Hartland, Edwin Sidney, 84, 95–97, 102; as armchair anthropologist, 97; and pederasty, 96; and primitive nescience of paternity, 95–96, 181
Hawaii, 79
Heald, Suzette, 314
health: sexual, 8–9, 188, 190–91, 196, 198–200, 208–9, 210; women's, 318–20. *See also* AIDS; sex education; venereal disease
Heape, Walter, 117
hegemony: and heterosexuality, 214; Western sexual, 299
High Leigh conference (Hoddesdon, UK), 174–77, 218–19, 278
hemaneh, 26
Hemyng, Bracebridge, 44–50, 51
Henry, Jules, 257
Herdt, Gilbert, 4, 251, 253, 294–97, 301, 329; and AIDS, 311; on colonialism, 219; "cultural hygiene" rebuttal to critics by, 296; neo-Freudianism of, 295; and Turnerian models, 321. *See also* Sambians
hereditarian theory, 329
hermaphrodites, 26, 297
Herodotus, 6, 15, 23
Hesiod, 23
"hetaerism," 74, 80, 105
heterosexuality: Burton on, 66–70; "compulsory," 15, 286; denial of homosexuality as freedom for, 293; Evans-Prichard on, 10, 296; Foucault on, 101, 185–86; and hegemony, 214; and homosexuality, 307; Mead on, 191–92; and primitive sexuality, 5; as problem for study, 306, 309, 324; silence on, 185–86, 276; among Zande, 10, 296. *See also* homoeroticism, homosexuality
hierarchies: gender, 5, 16, 287; evolutionary, 44, 77; in Mayhew and Hemyng, 44; monogenism and racial, 36; moral, 118; and

19th-century discourse, 52; polygenism and racial, 36, 40; racial, 7, 8, 16, 30–31, 36, 40, 42, 61–62, 64, 141–42, 198, 328; of sexual practices, 326; social, 18, 43

hijras, 310, 329

Hinduism, 232

Hinton, James, 123, 165

Hirschfeld, Magnus, 128

history of anthropology, 17, 101, 140, 187, 202

HIV. *See* AIDS

Hobhouse, Leonard, 164

Hogbin, H. Ian, 174, 181, 220, 225–28; on morality, 228

Holmberg, Allan R., 262–63; and food drive, 262

Holmes, Lowell D., 201

"hominterns" (Marshall and Suggs), 275

homoeroticism (behavior, practice), 195; among ancient Greeks, 129; among Andalusians, 290–91; and berdache, 289; "ethnocartographic" phase of study of, 298–99; and Keraki initiation, 253; and Melanesian initiation, 18; Native American, 303; as often defining factor for "homosexuality," 300; as resistance, 303; and Sambian initiation, 295, 329; as transgressive performance, 302, 321

homophobia, 238, 252, 271, 276, 286, 290, 305, 330, 345–46n10; and AIDS, 312

homosexuality, 6, 7, 13, 122, 286, 324; among Africans, 149; and alterity, 308; anthropology of, 11, 287, 291; in Arabia, 71; among Arapesh, 206; in Arnhem Land, 240; Bachofen, 81; Benedict, 250–54; Burton on, 70–72, 128; among Busama, 227; among Capaya, 272; Carpenter on innovators and, 128–29, 253–54; configurationism and, 251, 253–54; conscription of, 129, 297; and constructionism, 302, 309; and Contagious Diseases Act, 53, 120; and creativity, 253–54; criminalized, 120; cross-cultural studies of, 293–94; among Cueva, 25; denials of, 274, 293; Devereux on, 242–45; as disease, 274; as disturbance in gender identity, 295; Ellis on, 122, 127–28; Elwin on, 237–38, 240; ethnographic literature on, 292–93; Ford

and Beach on, 269, 270; Goldenweiser on, 253–54; and heterosexuality, 307; Hogbin on, 226–27; and homoeroticism, 300; and homophobia, 238, 252; Human Relations Area Files on, 270; and identity, 295, 297; in India, 310; in "Inis Beag," 272–73; and initiation, 18, 227, 247, 294–96; institutionalized, 8, 221, 227, 253; and Japanese, 250; Kardiner on, 261; and Kinsey Report, 266, 267, 280; latent, 271–72; among Lepcha, 231; Lévi-Strauss on, 289; Malinowski on, 156, 159, 176, 199, 240, 302; among mammals, 270; among Mangaians, 274; Marquesan, 256; Marshall on, 274; Mead on, 191, 192, 194–96, 199, 200–201, 206, 207, 210, 254; and the military, 127, 129, 275, 296, 345n5; among Mohave, 242, 243, 244–45, 249; among Muria, 237–38; among Native Americans, 18, 23, 26, 71, 128, 288–89; "naturalization" of, 302; in New Guinea, 227, 294–96; no such thing as, 299; among Omaha, 196; among Ontong, 225–26; Ortner on, 289; pathologization of, 245, 249, 254, 293, 295–96; among primates, 308; reification of, 303; "safety-valve" theory of, 249, 251, 293, 298; among Sambians, 294–96, 297, 329, 345n5; among Samoans, 191, 192, 194–96, 212; Schapera on, 224; silence around, 224, 276; social roots of, 253; and the "Sotadic zone," 70–72; Symonds on, 127–28; in Tahiti, 285; as threat, 104; among Tikopians, 221–22; among Trobrianders, 165, 176, 251; tropes of tolerance toward, 274; in Victorian society, 127; Voltaire on, 26; Westermarck on, 127, 128–29; Whitehead on, 288–89; among Wogeo, 227; Zande, 10, 296. *See also* berdache, lesbianism

Hopkins, Ellice, 121, 123

Hoppius (Christian Emanuel Hoppe), 35

Horney, Karen, 254

Hotten, John Camden, 57

Hottentot (Khoi), 30–34; egalitarianism of, 31; images of, 20, 103; monochordism, 31, 334n4; steatopygia among, 31, 33, 225; women, 31–34

Institute for Sex Research (Kinsey Institute), 11, 263, 270, 271

intelligence, 3, 278, 280; African, 7, 28, 34, 41, 132, 134, 136, 141, 148, 153; and African brain development, 3, 138, 139; Australian Aborigines and, 181; breast size and, 3; Burton on, 68; Crawley on savage, 117; in debate over species, 36, 40–41; Ellis on women's and men's, 126; Indian, 142; Jefferson on black, 40; Johnston on Negro, 141; Native American, 24; penis size and, 3, 28–30; primitive, 7, 9, 94, 280, 282; Rushton on, 3; of women, 28, 105, 122, 126, 190. *See also* neoteny

"intermediate sex" (Carpenter), 129

"intermediate types" (Westermarck), 128–29

International African Association, 154

International African Institute, 174

International Association of the Congo, 137

International Encyclopedia of the Social Sciences, 271

Inuit, 20, 27, 116, 345n14

"invention" of kinship, 102

inversion. *See* homosexuality

Iroquoian kinship terminology. *See* Ganowanian kinship terminology

Iroquois, 20, 41, 78, 83; pairing marriage, 86

Islam, 48, 62, 64, 65, 67, 146, 290, 330

Ismail, khedive of Egypt, 137

Jacobs, Sue-Ellen, 300

Jaenen, Cornélius, 23

Jaga, 135

Jahoda, Gustav, 40, 132, 136

jankhas, 310

Jankowiak, William, 204; on love as universal, 201–2, 346n14

Jefferson, Thomas, 40

Jews, 64–65, 318; and reproduction, 322; as "threat," 104. *See also* anti-Semitism;, Judaism

Johnston, Harry Hamilton, 140–45, 148; on African dances, 141–43; and colonial officials, 141; gradualism of, 144; Hamitic hypothesis in, 141–42

Jong, Erica, 185, 187

Jordan, Winthrop D., 25, 28, 42

Journal of the American Medical Association, 315

Judaism (Mosaic), 128–29

jus primae noctis, 89, 109, 112, 337n7n9, 333n1. *See also* group marriage

Kahn, Susan, 322

Kaliai people, 296

Kamilaroi, 84–85, 90; totemism among, 87

Kant, Immanuel, 37

Karachi, 60

Kardiner, Abram, 10, 259; on Alorese, 260–62; anti-relativism of, 262; on "basic personality structure," 255–57; on Benedict, 262; and "blaming the mother," 261–62; conscription by, 261; collaboration with Du Bois, 254, 258; on cultural patterns, 262; ecology of, 255–57; on the family, 262; on feminism, 261; on homosexuality, 261; on Marquesans, 255–57; and pathologization of Alorese, 260; and projective systems, 255, 256; psychoanalytic theory of, 254–55; on race, 262; seminar group of, 254, 258, 343n9; and working mothers, 261–62

Kennedy, Elizabeth Lapovsky, 301, 303–5

Kent, Susan Kingsley, 104

Kenya, 145, 147, 318

Keraki people, 253

Kgatla: Schapera on, 10, 223–25; Suggs on, 343n2

Khoi. *See* Hottentot

Killick, Andrew P., 327

Kingsley, Maria Henrietta, 138–40

Kinsey Institute (Institute of Sex Research), 11, 263, 270, 271

Kinsey, Alfred C., 11, 263–64; on marriage, 264; on morality, 264; and sex education, 223, 264. *See also* Kinsey Report

Kinsey Report, 11, 213, 233, 263–68, 270, 271–72, 275–76, 268, 271, 275; on anxiety, 266; attack on, 267–68; and Benedict, 266; case histories in, 263, 266; and critique of anthropological studies, 265; ethical issues of, 265; and Ellis, 265; and Gorer, 267; on homosexuality, 266, 267, 270; impact of, 267;

Kinsey Report (*cont.*)
on infant sexuality, 266; and Linton, 265;
and Malinowski, 264, 265; on mammalian
sexual behavior, 266; on masturbation, 266,
267; and McCarthyism, 267–68; and Mead,
211, 265, 266, 267; on morality, 265, 266–67;
on premarital sex, 264–65; on prostitution,
266–67; and psychoanalysis, 265–66, 267; rejects countertransference, 265–66; relativism
of, 263, 264; and Schapera, 224, 265; and
sexual liberation, 267; and statistics, 263,
267; and variation in nature, 263. *See also*
Kinsey, Alfred C.
kinship terminologies and theory, 133, 280–
81, 336n3; and desexualization, 280; in fin
de siècle anthropology, 103; and Firth,
222; and Fison and Howitt, 84–87, 89–90;
"invention of," 102; and McLennan, 82–83;
and Morgan, 78–79; and Rivers, 98–99
Kirghiz, 119
kiteshas, 272
Knauft, Bruce M., 347–48n1
knowledge: and power, 101, 177
Knowlton, Charles, 52, 119
Knox, Robert, 16
Krafft-Ebing, Richard von, 100, 128
Kroeber, Alfred, 17, 243; and berdache, 247;
and kin terms, 98
Kuklick, Henrika, 217
kula, 173
Kulick, Don, 300
Kunandaburi, 89
Kuper, Adam, 102
Kurnai, 83, 86–87, 90
Kwakiutl, 268; Benedict on, 252

labial elongation, 64, 66. *See also* genital
mutilation; genital operation; Hottentot
apron
Ladies Association of Nigeria, 153
Lafitau, Père Joseph, 128
Lambeth Conference (Church of England),
161
Lancaster, Roger N., 321
Landes, Ruth, 265
Lang, Andrew, 84, 101, 102, 149; and Atkinson,

106; on Australian nescience of paternity, 108–9; evolutionism of, 95, 108; on
exogamy, 106, 108; patriarchy in, 108; on
totemism, 108
language: of anthropology, 305; of educated
classes, 161; of Elwin, 235, 238; Ford and
Beach on, 268; Hottentot and Khoisan,
31, 39; kinship and, 78, 98; of love, 202;
of Malinowski, 235, 238; Mead and, 195,
197, 211–12, 213, 235, 238; of mental illness
and psychoanalysis, 257; of passion, 205;
of pathology in Benedict, 252; primate, 39;
and race, 55; Tahitian, 284; Trobriand, 158;
women and, 210–12, 213–15
Lapps, 20, 27
Lapsley, Hilary, 250
Laqueur, Thomas, 117
lata, 258
Lawrence, D. H., 13, 233
Leach, Edmund, 74, 281–83; and nescience
of paternity, 178, 182, 282; on primitive
promiscuity, 74, 282; on psychosexual
universals, 282
Lees, Edith. *See* Edith Ellis
Lehner, Stephen, 227–28
Leith-Ross, Sylvia, 154
Legba, 57
Le Moyne, Jacques, 26
Lentswe, king of the Kgatla, 223
Leonardo, Micaela di, 209
Leopold II, king of the Belgians, 53, 137
Lepcha people, 230–31, 270; absence of love
among, 230; aggression among, 230–31
Leprosy Relief Commission, 153
Lepowsky, Maria, 235
lesbian communities, 287, 322, 347n18
lesbianism, 121, 210, 286–87, 296; of Benedict,
199, 214, 251; and feminism, 304; of Mead,
199, 214; among Native Americans, 23; and
rights, 315; working-class, 301, 303–5, 329.
See also butch-femme
LeVine, Robert A., 295, 318, 344n13
LeVine, Sarah, 318
levirate, 230; as survival of group marriage,
86

Lévi-Strauss, Claude, 7, 10, 280–81; on homosexuality, 280, 306; on incest, 86, 280; on male couples on Fire Island, 305–6; and racism, 280; on totemism, 280; and trope of the oversexed savage, 280; women's loss of agency in, 281

Levy, Anita, 43–44, 75, 104–5

Levy, Robert I., 283–85, 324; on masturbation, 284; psychoanalytic approach of, 283, 285; on transgendered *māhū*, 283, 284–85

liberalization: in fin de siècle, 119

liberation, 13; black, 15; gay, 275, 329; sexual, 2, 11, 54, 81; women's, 15, 121

Liberia, 145

libertarians, 122; sexual, 54

liminality, 253, 320–22, 342n3; in 16th-century representation, 23; in rituals of reversal, 115

Lindenbaum, Shirley, 311

Lindsey, Ben: on companionate marriage, 125, 170–71, 275; on contraception, 170–71; on divorce, 171; persecution of, 170; on sex education, 170–71; on sexual reform, 156

Linnaeus, 32, 35, 37, 333n3

Linton, Ralph, 10, 254–65; and culture and personality, 257; errors of fact in, 256–57; on Marquesans, 255–56; theory of "race suicide" in, 255

Littleton, Edward, 120

Livingstone, David, 43, 137, 146

Livingstone House conference ("The Contact of Modern Civilizations with Ancient Cultures and Tribal Customs"), 175–76

lock hospitals, 52, 145, 179, 335n1

Lombroso, Cesare, 103, 121

London Anthropological Society, 56–57

Long, Edward, 36, 38–39

Lopez, V. F., 70

love, 113, 161, 200–204, 309, 346n13; absence of romantic, 138, 140, 196, 197, 200–203, 215, 226, 230, 273, 274; among Africans, 138–40; among Baiga, 233; Benedict on, 250; "feminization" of, 204; free, 9, 155, 156, 168, 205; among Gisu, 314; Hogbin on, 226; among Lepcha, 231; Malinowski on, 200–201, 230; among Mangaians, 202–3, 274; in

Manus, 197; Mead on, 18, 190, 196, 197, 200–201, 202–5, 208, 215; in Samoa, 18, 196, 197, 200–202, 208; in Tahiti, 284; among Turu, 272; as universal, 201–2, 204; as "work," 204

Lubbock, John, 55, 73–74, 75, 76–78, 105, 198; on hetaerism, 105; on marriage by capture, 76–78; on sexual communism, 77; Westermarck on, 111–12

Lugard, Lord Frederick, 141, 148, 149, 154, 174; and Malinowski, 175

lumpen proletariat: equated with degraded primitives, 33–34

lupanars, 70

Lutkehaus, Nancy C., 187, 209

Lyell, Charles, 35

Lyons, Andrew P., 249, 324–25, 330

Lyons, Harriet D., 55–56, 238, 249, 330, 341n1, 346–47n15; on genital mutilations, 318, 324–25

machismo, 321

Macmillan (publisher), 125

"madwoman in the attic," 52

Mageo, Jeannette, 291–92, 321–22

māhū, 283, 284–85, 345n2

Mailu, 159

Maine, Sir Henry, 73–74; on patriarchy, 74, 82, 89, 196

Malayan kinship terminology, 86, 99

male dominance, 5

Mali, 320

Malinowski, Bronislaw, 2, 4, 8–10, 13, 93, 102, 155–84, 188, 198, 217, 223, 225, 262, 306, 322, 329, 339n4; on abortion, 181; on adolescence, 18, 155, 169–70, 171–72, 181, 192; on adultery, 172, 176, 180; and Anglicanism, 176; and applied anthropology, 218–19, 226, 278; and Briffault, 168, 340n6; and Catholicism, 176; on chastity, 166, 180; and colonial administration, 174–78, 208, 219; on companionate marriage, 9, 125, 155, 170–71, 177, 275, 305; confessional mode in, 157–59; and contraception, 9, 155, 156, 161, 167, 173, 176, 180, 181, 199; and conscription of sex, 18–19, 160; and Crawley, 164, 168, 170; and "desexualization" of sex, 174–78, 183; diary

Malinowski, Bronislaw (*cont.*)

of, 159–60, 327; dispute with Rentoul, 180; on divorce, 172; and Ellis, 130, 155, 161, 163–73, 199; on environmentalism, 166; on the family, 168, 175; on feminism, 155; and fieldwork, 152; and Firth, 220, 221; and Freud, 167, 169, 184; functionalism of, 17, 175–78, 179, 183–84, 218; and genital operations, 278; on group marriage, 164, 178; and the High Leigh conference, 174–77, 218–19, 278; on homosexuality, 156, 165, 176; in Kinsey report, 264, 265; on Lang, 164; liberalism of, 219; Leach on, 282; and the Livingstone House conference, 175–76; on love, 18, 200–201, 230; on marriage, 18, 155–56, 164, 168–69, 172, 175–76, 178, 199, 339–40n5; on masturbation, 173; on matriarchy, 163, 178; on matriliny, 178–79, 282; and Mead, 205; and missionaries, 175–78; as modernist, 88, 336n6; on modesty, 165, 170; on monogamy, 168; on nescience of paternity, 159, 163, 178–82, 183, 282; notebook on Ellis of, 165–66, 170; on the Oedipus complex, 169, 179, 182; and participant observation, 157; on periodicity, 130, 170; and persecution, 333n1; on polyandry, 176; on polygamy, 176; on premarital sex, 18, 169, 176; on primitive promiscuity, 155, 168, 178; on primitive sexuality, 155–56, 165, 257; questionnaire of, 176–77; on racism, 175; rejection of primitives as models of human nature by, 155; and relativism, 176; and Russell, 155, 161, 163, 199; and science, 167; seminars of, 219–20; on sex education, 166, 173; on sexual communism, 163; sexual desires during fieldwork of, 159, 327; on sexual license, 168–69, 176; and sexual morality, 156, 176; as sexologist, 13, 155–84; and sexual reform, 155–56, 161, 167–73, 179, 199, 200; and Society for Constructive Birth Control and Racial Progress, 161; on Spencer and Gillen, 178; on "stratified morality," 156; and Stopes, 161, 167, 170, 173, 340n8; therapeutic intent of work of, 159, 174, 208–9; on Watson, 168; and

Westermarck, 164; as womanizer, 199. *See also* Trobrianders

Malinowski Papers (Yale University), 163–64

Malthusian couple, 13, 101, 127, 173, 185–86

'*ma:mam* relationship, 239

mammalian sexuality, 74, 266, 270

Man, 165, 180, 182, 261

Man, E. H., 111

mana, 292

Mandela, Nelson, 315

Mandela, Winnie, 315

Manderson, Lenore, 346–47n15

Mandeville, John, 23, 335–36n1

Manet, Édouard, 103

Mangaians, 270, 273–77; love among, 202–3; sexual segregation of, 273; sleep crawling among, 273

Manu'a (American Samoa). *See* Mead, Margaret; Samoans

Manus: Mead on, 9, 196–98, 200, 212, 226, 228, 261; as civilized children, 196; and conversion to Christianity, 158; love among, 197; and "tumescence," 197, 198–99; as undersexed savages, 197

Maori, 47

Marcus, George E., 18

Marcus, Steven, 56, 57, 73, 292

Marett, Robert R., 148

marriage, 10, 89, 119, 120, 201, 208, 217; African, 44, 63, 96, 135, 139–40, 143–44, 147, 149, 150–52, 313–14; among Alor, 260, 261–62; in Americas, 44; in Arnhem Land, 239, 241; in ancient Greece and Rome, 44, 80–82; Australian aboriginal, 44, 83–91, 108–9, 149; Bachofen on, 80–82; Burton on, 66–70; among Busama, 226; child, 48, 96, 143–44, 147, 151–52; Christian, 6; "communal," 105; companionate, 9, 13; Crawley on origin of, 113, 329; Darwin on, 105; and Diderot, 22; Du Bois on, 261; Elwin on, 235–37; European, 22; as exchange for Howitt, 89; Falk on, 149, 150–51; in fin de siècle anthropology, 103; Foucault on, 185–86; Japanese, 250; Jewish, 322; Johnston on, 143–44; Kgatlan, 223–24; Kinsey on, 264;

among Lepcha, 230–31; Malinowski on, 18, 155–56, 164, 168–69, 172, 175–76, 178, 199, 339–40n5; among Mangaians, 273; McLennan on, 82; Mead on, 18, 190, 192–94, 199, 204, 213; among Mohave, 245; among Muria, 235–37; Morgan on, 78–80; in New Guinea, 294; origin of, 7; Polynesian, 44, 291; primitive, 201; and prostitution, 129; Russell on, 162; among Sambians, 294; Samoan, 18, 190, 192–93, 199, 213, 292; Schapera on, 223–24; silence around, 186; among Sindh, 64; Tahitian, 22, 283; Thomas on, 109; Tikopian, 220; Toda, 97–98; and totemism, 87; Trobriander, 18, 130, 155, 169, 199; among Turu, 272; as universal, 156; Victorian, 54, 56, 111, 139, 140; Westermarck on, 109–12, 125, 164, 168, 329; among Wogeo, 226; in work of Mayhew and Hemyng, 44. *See also* companionate marriage; group marriage; jus primae noctis; marriage by capture; miscegenation; monogamy; polyandry; polygamy; polygyny

marriage by capture, 3, 181, 220, 220–22; and anthropology's roots, 55; in Arnhem Land, 239–40; Australian, 83, 87, 89, 91; Ellis on, 119; as fantasy, 73–99, 101; Firth on, 220–21, 222; Fortune on, 342n7; Howitt on, 89; Lubbock on, 76-77; McLennan on, 76, 105; Morgan on, 82; as stage, 74; Tikopian, 220–21, 222; Wake on, 87, 105

marriage manuals, 56, 120

Marquesans, 18, 255–57, 258, 262, 262; and ecology, 256–57; gender relations of, 255–56; Kardiner on, 255–57, 262; Linton on, 255–56; and negative conscription, 18, 257; pathologization of, 257; sexual freedom of, 255; Suggs on, 256–57, 272

Marshall, Donald: on homosexuality, 274; on Mangaians, 202, 273–74; on transvestism, 274; work as male-centered, 274. *See also* Marshall, Donald, and Robert Suggs

Marshall, Donald, and Robert Suggs, 217, 270–76; homophobia in work of, 271; on homosexuality, 274; masculine bias in, 271; sensationalize Ra'ivavae sexuality, 272–73

Martin, Clyde E., 263

Martyr, Peter, 25

Marx, Eleanor, 54, 123

Marx, Karl, 54

masculinity: crisis in fin de siècle, 129–30

Mason, Michael, 51

Mason, Peter, 23

Masson, Elsie, 160

Masters, William, and Virginia Johnson, 270

masturbation, 6, 101, 104, 120–21, 173, 191, 192, 212, 218, 225, 226, 258–59; as dangerous, 120, 141; and clitoridectomy, 65; Ellis on, 120, 173; Ford and Beach on, 269, 270; Human Relations Area Files on, 270; Kinsey Report on, 266, 267; Levy on, 284; Malinowski on, 173; among mammals, 270; Mead on, 192; 19th-century discourses and, 13, 52, 208; Rovers and, 120; White Cross Society and, 120

materialism, 287

Mathew, John, 88, 111

Mathews, Hugh, 148, 150

matriarchal communalism (Briffault), 168

matriarchal theorists, 76, 78, 82–83, 88, 105, 107; Lang's rejection of, 108; and nescience of paternity, 182

matriarchy, 73–99, 163, 178; and anthropology's roots, 55; Bachofen on, 80–82; Briffault on, 340n6; Howitt on, 89; Leach on, 282; Morgan on, 78; rival schools of, 82. *See also* matriliny

matrilineal theorists, 76, 78

matriliny, 74, 85, 87, 168; and anthropology's roots, 55; Bachofen on, 82; Malinowski on, 178–79, 212; Morgan on, 78, 82, 86; Wake on, 87; Westermarck on, 112. *See also* matriarchy

Maugham, Somerset, 23

Mauss, Marcel, 243, 341n1

Mayhew, Henry, 43–50, 51

McCarthyism, 11, 267–68

McIlwaine, Rev. Joshua, 73

McLennan, John F., 55, 73–74, 76–77, 82–83, 84, 98, 198; Crawley's attack on, 113; on exogamy, 77, 82, 86; Howitt on, 89; on

McLennan, John F. (*cont.*)
infanticide, 76; on kinship terminologies,
82–83, 112; on marriage, 82; on marriage
by capture, 76; and Morgan, 82; on mother
right, 76, 155; on nescience of paternity, 180,
335–36n11; on polyandry, 76; on totemism,
87; Westermarck on, 111–12
McLynn, Frank, 61
Mead, Margaret, 2, 4, 9–11, 23, 58, 186–215,
225, 226, 228, 270, 295, 306–7, 326, 329, 341–
42n1; on adolescence, 18, 188–90, 194, 213;
on adultery, 192–93, 196–97; and alterity,
187, 198, 210; on American culture, 194,
197, 200, 203–5; on Arapesh, 205–7, 211,
342n7; and Baldwin, 187; and Benedict,
199; and bisexuality, 209–10; and Boas,
188, 202–3, 342n2; on chastity, 193, 198; and
configurationism, 254; and conscription,
18–19, 203, 215; and contraception, 199,
208; and culture and personality, 194, 257;
and cultural variability in gender roles,
205–9; on determinism, 190, 203, 207; and
diagnosis of sexual health, 188, 190–91, 196,
198–200, 208–9, 210; on divorce, 193, 208;
on dysphoria, 199–200; and emotions, 194,
197; and Erikson, 205, 208, 211–12; Evans-
Pritchard on, 187; and female sexuality, 198–
99, 202, 215; Friedan on, 207–8, 209; on
gender roles, 205–9; and Gorer, 231; and
Hall, 188–90, 194; on hierarchical rank,
188, 192–94; hoaxing of, 202–3, 328; on
homosexuality, 191, 192, 194–96, 199, 200–
201, 206, 207, 210, 254; on incest, 192, 271;
and infant care, 187, 206–8, 213, 215; and
Kardiner, 343n9; and Kinsey Report, 211,
265, 266, 267; and language, 195, 197, 211–
12, 213–15; and lesbianism, 199, 210, 214;
on love, 18, 190, 196, 197, 200–201, 202–
5, 208, 215, 230; and Malinowski, 205; on
marriage, 18, 190, 192–94, 199, 204, 213;
on Manus, 9, 196–98, 200, 212, 226, 228,
261; on masturbation, 192; on morality,
188, 200; on motherhood, 190, 207, 214–
15; on Mundugumor, 205, 207; oblivious
to class, 193–94, 200; on "patterns" of

gender, 205, 209; and periodicity, 213; and
perversion, 195, 196, 199; politics of, 187–
88; and popular advice genres, 208, 211,
215; on premarital sex, 18, 190–94, 206;
and primitive sexuality, 188, 198, 257; on
prostitution, 194, 210; and psychoanalytic
theory, 254; and race, 187, 210; on rape, 192;
and relativism, 188, 211, 254; and Samoan
sex terms, 212; and sex education, 190, 208,
329; and sexual reform, 199–200, 211; on
sexual technique, 197, 190, 194, 212–13; and
stigmatization, 209; and surveillance, 208;
on "tumescence," 197, 198–99; on virginity,
192–93, 212–13; and Western discourse about
sex, 198; and women's experience, 192,
210–11, 214–15, 293. *See also* determinism;
Manus; Omaha; Samoans
Mead-Freeman controversy, 2, 47, 186, 188,
202–3, 291, 329
medical anthropology, 278–79, 315
medicalization of sexuality: and AIDS, 311–
12. *See also* diagnosis; Foucault, Michel;
therapy
Meek, Charles Kingsley, 154
Mehinka people, 309
Melanesia, 226; as communist for Rivers, 155;
homoerotic initiation in, 18
Melville, Herman, 44
men: monorchidism among Khoi, 31; primitive, 104–5; promiscuous working-class, 130;
middle class, 104–5, 130
Mendel, Gregor, 15, 35
Menninger, Karl, 243
menstruation, 27–30, 117, 121, 126, 181, 211, 215,
220, 226, 231, 233, 239, 245, 289, 317; and
male initiation, 226
Merriam, Alan P., 271; on Basongye berdache,
272
Merrill, George, 122–23
Messenger, John C.: on "Inis Beag," 271–72
Mill, John Stuart, 161
Milnes, Monckton, 63
miscegenation, 25; and debate over species,
20, 34, 37–38; by East Indians and Whites,
145–46, 335n7; by Europeans, Blacks, and

Indians, 321; and images of primitive sexuality, 41–42, 65; white-Amerindian, 25; white-black, 25, 34, 42, 144–47, 321; in West Indies, 147. *See also* marriage

misogyny: of Burton, 59, 71; of Mehinaku, 309

missionaries, 14, 43, 58, 69, 76, 79, 98, 111, 112, 132, 136, 139, 141, 143, 147, 150, 195, 208, 212, 213, 222, 223, 229–30, 239, 338n1, 347–48n1; Berndts on sexual attractions of, 241; and Elwin, 234; and the High Leigh conference, 174–77, 219; and Hogbin, 227–28; and Malinowski, 175–78, 179–80, 219

Mitchell, Philip, 174, 219, 226

Mithraism, 58–59

"modal personality" studies, 11, 218, 258

modernism, 88, 99, 103, 204, 217, 336n6; anti-, 219

modesty, 118–19, 165, 170, 258

moetotolo (sleep crawling), 192

Moffat, Robert, 43

Mohave, 10, 231, 242–50; and alcohol, 244–45, 246, 248–49; anal sex among, 244–45; and berdache, 247–49; connections between sexuality and spirituality, 245; heterosexuality among, 244, 245, 247; homosexuality among, 242, 243, 244–45, 249; marriage among, 245; masturbation among, 242, 243; narratives, 244, 246–47, 248, 250; and rape, 246, 248, 250; and sex as play, 245; taboos, 245; transvestism among, 244, 245, 247; venereal disease among, 246, 247; and virginity, 245; and witchcraft, 245, 248

Moll, Albert, 128

"momism" (Wylie), 261

monogamy, 171, 218, 305, 330; Burton on, 68–70; European, 22; Foucault on, 185–86; Wake on, 59; Westermarck on, 110, 124, 125

monogenism, 34, 35–41; and degeneration, 35; environmentalism and, 35, 37

monorchids: Khoi men as, 31

monotheism: of Australian Aborigine religion, 108

Montagu, M. F. Ashley, 164–65, 333n1; on adolescent sterility, 181, 237; on concep-

tion and Australian Aborigines, 181–82; and Malinowski, 181–82; and nescience of maternity, 182; and nescience of paternity, 179, 182; on racism, 280

morality: African, 45, 135–36, 139, 142, 148, 149, 230, 331; in Arnhem Land, 239, 241; Australian Aboriginal, 45, 90, 109, 118; and conscription, 330; Christian, 20, 22, 179, 242; in debate over species, 40; of Devereux, 249; Ellis on, 155; evolution of, 74; and fin de siècle society, 103; hierarchies of, 118; and high status, 48; Hogbin on, 226; ideas of decline in, 24, 48–50, 124; Indian, 48; Kgatlan, 224; Kinsey on, 264; Kinsey Report on, 265, 266–67; new secular, 155; Polynesian, 291; primitive, 9, 79–80, 109, 111; and primitive sexuality, 5; and relativity, 22; Russell on, 155; savage, 136; sexual, 4, 19, 103, 116, 136, 176, 200, 242, 276, 277; Stanley on, 136; Stopes on, 161; Tasmanian, 118; Tikopian, 220; Toda, 98; Victorian, 69–70; Westermarck and, 113, 118, 124

Moreno, Eva, 327

Morgan, Lewis Henry, 16, 55, 72, 73–74, 78–80, 84, 98, 102, 198; and Bachofen, 80, 336n2; and the "consanguine family," 78–79, 86, 99; on evolution of family, 78–79, 82, 108; on gender equality, 78; on incest, 78; on kinship terminologies, 78–79, 98–99, 112; on group marriage, 82–83, 149; on marriage, 78–80; on marriage by capture, 78, 82; as matriarchal theorist, 76, 78, 82–83; on matriarchy, 78; on matriliny, 78, 82, 86; and McLennan, 82; on primitive morality, 79–80; on primitive promiscuity, 78, 82, 86; Westermarck on, 111–12

Mormons, 67–69, 328

Morocco, 128

Morrow, William, 212

motherhood, 190, 207, 214–15

mother right, 3, 87; Bachofen on, 80; Hartland on, 95. *See also* matriarchy; matriliny; primitive promiscuity

motoro, 273

M'pongwe, 139

Mugabe, Robert, 315
mulattoes, 38, 42
Muller-Lyer, Franz, 238
Mundugumor, 205, 207
Murdock, George Peter, 262, 265
murdus, 86
Muria, 234–38; gender equality among, 235; and sexual utopia, 234; conscription of, 238
The Muria (BBC film), 237
Murray, John (publisher), 234
Murray, Stephen O., 129, 188, 265, 299–300, 327–28; challenges Foucault, 300; on types of homosexualities, 299–300; on new anthropology of sex, 303
myth, 268, 281; Alorese, 260; of the Fall, 58; Mohave, 244, 246–47, 248, 254; as projective system (Kardiner), 255; and vagina dentata, 272; Zuni, 250

Nadel, S. F., 229–30
Nanda, Serena, 310
Napier, Charles, 64, 70
national character studies. *See* "modal personality" studies
National Council for Public Morals, 126
National Council of Women, 154
nationalism, 318, 331
National Vigilance Association, 53, 120–21
Native Americans, 6; Burton on, 61–62, 68; alternative gender roles among, 298; chastity among, 46; as degenerate, 27; as effeminate, 24; 18th-century representations of, 23–24; gay, 300; gender categories of, 298; homosexuality among, 18, 23, 26, 71, 128, 288–89; as ignoble savages, 24, 41; as innocent, 24; and matriliny, 87; menstruation among, 28; as noble savages, 41, 334n5; pathologizing of, 289; and rape, 25; sexual honor code of, 24–25; and slavery, 42; and status of women, 45–46; as undersexed, 8, 20, 24, 45; Voltaire on, 26
"native ethnographer," 306
naturalization: of Africans, 138; of cultural expectations, 211; of heterosexuality, 101; of homosexuality, 71; of gender relations, 75; of monogamy, 124; of Muria sexuality, 234

Nature, 102
nature-culture, 14, 17, 162, 322–23; and AIDS, 306–12
Nazis, 184, 333n2
Negroes: American, 144, 153; on adjacent rung to orangutans on Long's Great Chain of Being, 38; Burton on, 62; Ellis on, 126; image of, 20; Johnston on, 141–42; language of, 38–39; "matriarch," 258; and mothers, 258; Reade on, 135–36; and theory of neoteny, 126. *See also* Africans; blacks
neo-Freudian school, 4, 215, 231, 276, 295; and "childhood determinism," 272; and Kinsey Report, 265; and language of mental illness, 257
neoteny, 114, 126. *See also* intelligence
nescience of paternity. *See under* conception
New Guinea, 225–26, 229, 294–97, 309, 321, 345n6, 347–48n1. *See also* Busama people; Manus; Sambians; Wogeo
Newton, Esther, 287–88, 305–6, 329, 345–46n10
New York Psychoanalytic Institute, 254
New York Society for the Suppression of Vice, 121
Nicaragua, 321
Niebuhr, Reinhold, 267
Nigeria, 131, 141, 145, 148, 149–52, 324–25, 330–31
"niggers," 159, 160
noa marriage, 88–89
noble savage, 41–42
Northeast Frontier Agency, 232
Nott, Josiah Clark, 16, 333n2; polygenism of, 36
Núñez de Balboa, Vasco, 25
Nunga, 150
"nymphae" (White), 30

objectivity, 155, 156, 167
Oceania, 220, 226
O'Donnell, J. M., 89
Oedipus complex, 106–7, 169, 179, 182, 218
Ogilby, John, 28
Ojibwa, 253
Old Testament, 35

polygamy: among Africans, 64, 69, 135, 138, 328; among Arabs, 64, 67; Baker on, 138; Burton on, 60, 64, 67–70, 328; Malinowski on, 176; among Mormons, 67–69, 328; Reade on, 135; in Sindh, 67; Westermarck on, 110

polygenism, 34, 36–41; and evolutionism, 75; fantasies underpinning, 38–40, 63; use of Old Testament, 36; plantation folk-, 137; and reproductive isolation, 38; scientific, 40

polygyny: African, 138, 139–40, 313–14; in Arnhem Land, 239; Australian, 83, 85, 86; Burton on, 68, 71, 140; Kgatlan, 223; Morgan on, 79; Nigerian, 330; Westermarck on, 124

Polynesia, 270, 273, 275; alterity of, 203; homosexuality in, 128, 121; permissiveness in, 291; portrayed by Mayhew and Hemyng, 46–47; as sexual paradise, 20–23, 25, 41, 45, 202, 220, 292; transsexuality in, 322

Pomeroy, Wardell B., 163

Poole, Fitz-John Porter: on Bimin-Kuskusmin gender ambiguity, 289–90

popular advice genres: and "blaming the mother," 257; and Mead, 208, 211, 215

pornography: and anthropology, 3, 17, 56–57, 180; Victorian, 55, 56

Porter, Roy, 20

positivism, 329

postmodernism, 8, 279, 327

poverty: and AIDS, 312, 317; Westermarck on homosexuality and, 124

Powdermaker, Hortense, 261

power: colonial, 174; in confessional mode, 158; excessive female, 271; and functionalism, 222; and the Kinsey Report, 265; and knowledge, 101, 177, 278–79, 347–48n1; male genitals as site of, 290; Mehinaku envy of female, 309; and pleasure, 303; and sexuality, 4, 12–15, 191, 193, 300, 325; and sexual norms, 119; surveillance and, 193

Pratt, George, 212

Pratt, Mary Louise, 132

prejudice. See misogyny; racism

premarital sex: among Africans, 313; among Busama, 226; in Carnaval, 321; as "de-

grading" to women, 177; Polynesian, 291; Samoan, 9, 18, 190–94, 213; in Tahiti, 283; Tikopian, 220; Trobriander, 9, 18, 169, 228; Westermarck on, 111, 124. See also adolescent promiscuity

Prichard, James Cowles, 40

primal horde: Atkinson on, 107; Freud on, 106–7

primates, 29–30, 45, 74, 105, 106, 110, 124, 181, 234, 308, 345n13; and Africans, 313; and alterity, 308; conscription of, 308, 329; and Kinsey Report, 268; Negroes on same rung as in Long's Great Chain of Being, 38; in species debate, 35, 36, 38–40; fiction of sex between blacks and, 38–40, 63

primitive communism: Briffault on, 340n6; Morgan on, 78; in Tahiti, 21–22

primitive confession, 158

primitive intelligence, 3, 7, 9, 40, 94, 117, 138, 139, 141, 280, 282

primitive morality, 9, 155; Hartland on, 95–96; Morgan on, 79–80; Westermarck on decline in, 111

primitive promiscuity, 4, 7, 55, 109–14, 116–17, 118, 140, 155, 169, 182, 186; and anthropology's roots, 55; and Atkinson, 107; Bachofen on, 80–81, 82; Crawley against, 113; criticisms of, 105, 329; Darwin on, 105; demise of, as fantasy, 74, 87–89, 101; in Dieri myth, 86; Ellis on, 112, 329; Fison and Howitt on, 74, 86, 89; and free love, 155; and Freud, 107; Leach on, 74, 282; Maine on, 105; Malinowski on, 155, 168, 178; Morgan on, 78, 82, 86; and Spencer and Gillen, 178; as stage, 75; and Tylor, 105; and Victorian women, 65, 104–5; Wake on, 105; Westermarck on, 88, 105, 109–14, 115–16, 124, 329

primitive sexuality, 5, 96, 130; and anthropological belief, 282; Burton on, 68; Carpenter on, 254; Ellis on, 100–102, 165; images of, 66, 75, 104, 140; Leach on, 282; Malinowski on, 155–56, 166; Mead on, 188; and modern relativity, 113; representations of, 101

primitivism, 5, 8, 155, 328, 334n5; of Elwin, 233; of the elite and AIDS, 317 privacy, 158

professionalization: of anthropology, 4–5

progress, 75, 111, 162, 328

promiscuity: adolescent, 4; of Victorian women, 65. *See also* primitive promiscuity

prostitution, 6, 104, 129; African, 150; Athenian, 78; in Bangkok, 310; and Burton, 60–61, 67, 68; among Busama, 227; as community threat, 104; and Contagious Diseases Act, 53–54; and Criminal Law Amendment Act, 120; Ellis on, 127; environmental deprivation and, 50; equated with primitive peoples, 34, 44–45, 74–75, 103, 124; and feminism, 129; during fieldwork, 327; Indian, 65, 70, 145; in Kinsey Report, 266–67; male, 310; in Mayhew and Hemyng, 49–50, 51; Mead on, 194, 210; in Oman, 310; among Ontong, 225; among Samoans, 47–48; among Sind, 64; South Asian, 346–47n15; temple, 25, 48, 77–78, 128; and venereal disease, 52, 53, 145; Westermarck on poverty and, 124

Protestantism, 158

psychoanalysis, 100, 106–7, 184, 210, 247, 262, 268, 277, 309; and "blaming the mother," 257–58; and conscription, 276; and countertransference, 249–50; of Kardiner, 254–55; Leach on, 282–83; of Levy, 283, 285; and the Oedipus complex, 106–7, 169, 179, 182; as processual, 295; revisionist (Horney), 254; and symbols, 10. *See also* Bettelheim, Bruno; Erikson, Erik; Freud, Sigmund; neo-Freudian school; Spiro, Melford

psychoanalytic anthropology, 231, 243, 281. *See also* Devereux, George; Herdt, Gilbert; Levy, Robert I.; Spiro, Melford

psychoanalytic movement, 161, 210; and relativism, 249

psychology, 14, 155, 264; and "blaming the mother," 257

Public Morality Council, 121

punaluan marriage, 79

pursütpumi ceremony, 97

queer theory, 15, 278, 301–2; on heterosexuality as problem for study, 306

Rabinow, Paul, 327

race, 4, 14, 15–16, 36, 55, 81–82, 132–33, 210, 252, 277–78, 280–81, 303, 305; and Anthropological Society of London, 56; Bachofen oblivious to, 81–82; Buffon on, 36; Ellis's theory of neoteny and, 126; and fin de siècle alterity, 101; Foucault and, 14; Johnston on, 141; Kardiner on, 262; and Lévi-Strauss, 280; and Montagu, 280; Rushton on, 3; and sexualized discourses, 8; "suicide" (Linton), 255; ranking of, 119

racial determinism, 278; Boas's critique of, 188

racial equality, 16, 40, 138

racial hierarchies, 7, 8, 30–31, 141–42, 198; in Burton, 61–62; and monogenism, 36; and polygenism, 36, 40. *See also* anti-Semitism; color bar; racial inequality; racism

racial inequality, 11, 54. *See also* anti-Semitism; color bar; racial hierarchies; racism

racialism. *See* racism

racial prejudice. *See* racism

raciology, 14, 15–16, 41

racism, 7–8, 41–42, 34, 96, 218, 258; advocacy against, 318; and AIDS, 312, 314–17; and berdache, 298; and Boas, 198, 218; of Burton, 56, 59, 61–64, 71; in colonial service, 149; Elwin on, 238; Malinowski on, 175; Montagu on, 182; and negative conscription, 18; scientific, 3, 15–16; in Stanley, 137. *See also* anti-Semitism; color bar; racial hierarchies; racial inequality

Radcliffe-Brown, A. R., 180, 217–18, 225; structuralism of, 17

Ra'ivavae, 270

Raleigh, Walter, 23

rape, 66; and Africans, 151, 230; and Alorese, 261; Ellis on, 118; during fieldwork, 327; LeVine on, 344n13; in Marquesan myth, 256; among Mohave, 246, 248, 250; and Native Americans, 25; and Samoans, 192; and Tikopians, 220–22; and white women, 147

Rapp, Rayna, 322

Ray, John, 35

Raymonde, Natalie, 251

Raynal, Guillaume Thomas François, 24

Reade, W. Winwood, 133–36, 146, 326; on African dance, 134–35; on African penis, 134; on African sexuality, 134–35; on Amazons, 135; and Burton, 133; representations of Africans, 134–35

recapitulation hypothesis, 107, 190

Redbook, 208–9, 211

rediscovery of sex, 11, 277, 285, 294

Reece Committee, 268

"regular gradation," 30

Rehebother Bastaards, 34

Reich, Wilhelm, 161

Reichard, Gladys, 265

reification, 211, 222; of conventional morality, 265–66; in evolutionist works, 75; of "homosexual," 303; of ideologies, 287; of sexual categories, 185; of the sexual subject, 185

relationship terminologies. *See* kinship terminologies and theory

relativism, 322; and activism, 318; and anthropology, 8, 15, 103, 219, 277–79, 287; of Benedict, 252, 254, 298; and conscription, 330; and determinism, 286; Devereux on, 249; and gender, 138; and genital mutilation, 2, 318, 320, 335n4; and Kardiner, 262; of Kinsey Report, 263, 264; of Malinowski, 176; of Mead, 188, 211, 254; and morals, 22, 113, 116, 222; and nescience of paternity, 182, 282; and Ortner and Whitehead, 286; and psychoanalysis, 249; and racial stereotypes, 132–33

religion, 15; African, 314; ancient Greek, 80–81; Aryan, 59; Australian monotheistic, 108; and berdache, 248, 298; conflict with science, 35, 264; in debate over species, 35–37; genital operations and, 318, 320, 335n4; and homosexuality, 128; Leach on, 282; Montagu on, 182; prejudice toward, 36; primitive, 9; psychoanalysis and, 106–7, 258; Tahitian, 283; theories of, 102; Westermarck on, 128. *See also* animism; phallic worship; totemism

representations: accuracy of, 329; of Africans, 134, 137–38, 139, 338n1; and alterity, 330; of colonialism and sex, 311; of primitives, 130; of primitives as undersexed, 103; of primitive sexuality, 101. *See also* collective representations; images; stereotypes; tropes

reproductive isolation, 37, 38

Renan, Ernest, 16

Rentoul, Alex, 180, 182

repression: and civilization, 20; Samoa as free from sexual, 2, 200

repressive hypothesis (Foucault), 13

Rhodes, Cecil, 140–41

Rhodes House library files (Bodleian, Oxford), 148

Rhyne, Wilhelm ten, 31

Rich, Adrienne, 210, 286

Richards, Audrey, 154, 183

ritual, 10, 264, 289–90; bleeding, 294, 343n5; among Ndembu, 295; puberty, 189; AIDS and voodoo, 315. *See also* initiation ritual

Rivers, W. H. R., 9, 96, 97–99, 148, 155, 181; and "depopulation of Melanesia," 179; and group marriage, 97; on Northcote Thomas, 99; on Toda, 97–98

Rivet, Paul, 243

roles: gender, 10, 67, 205–9, 252–53, 257, 258–59, 285, 298, 302, 320–22, 326, 329; lesbian, 304

romanticism, 4, 42, 276, 303

Rome, ancient, 13, 44, 70, 80–82, 148

Roosevelt, Theodore, 144

Roscoe, Will, 247, 248

Rosenberg, Rosalind, 186

Rowbotham, Sheila, 122

Roth, W. E., 83, 93

Rovers, 120

Royal Anthropological Institute, 165

Rubens, Peter Paul, 119

Rubin, Gayle, 281

Rushton, J. Phillippe, 3, 112; on racial difference and AIDS, 314–16; trope of oversexed savage in, 280, 315–16, 347n16

Russell, Bertrand: on adolescence, 171; on adultery, 162, 172; on Briffault, 163; on celibacy, 162; on Christianity, 162; on companionate marriage, 125, 162, 170–72, 275; on contraception, 155, 173; on divorce, 162, 172; on Ellis, 163; on eugenics, 162; evolutionism of, 162; on the family, 162–63; and Malinowski, 155, 161, 163; on marriage, 162; and masturbation, 173; and science, 167; on secular morality, 155; on sex education, 155, 162, 173; on sexual reform, 155–56, 167–68, 199, 200; and the Society for Constructive Birth Control and Racial Progress, 161; and Trobrianders, 163

Russell, Dora, 156

Saat-Jee ("Hottentot Venus"), 33, 66, 103
Sabine women, 119
"safety-valve" theory of homosexuality, 249, 251, 293, 298
sahelis, 310
Sambians, 294–97; and anal intercourse, 294; and gender categories, 302; ritualized homoeroticism among, 294–96, 297, 329, 345n5
same-sex eroticism, 299, 300. *See also* homoeroticism
Samoans, 130, 212, 291–92; adolescence of, 4, 18, 188–89, 192, 193, 213, 328; adultery among, 192–93; chastity among, 193, 292; and Christianity, 292; compared to 19th-century England, 292; confession among, 194; conscription of, 18–19, 203; discourse and inequality among, 292; divorce among, 193; elopement among, 192; and *fa'afafine*, 195; as free of sexual repression, 2, 200; Freeman on, 2; and gender crossing, 195; hair symbolism of, 291–92; hierarchical rank and, 188, 192–94; homosexuality among, 191, 192, 194–96, 212; and the image of Tahiti, 23; and incest, 192; and love, 18, 196, 197, 200–202, 204, 230; and marriage, 18, 190, 192–93, 199, 213, 292; masturbation among, 191, 192, 212; Mayhew and Hemyng on, 47–48; Mead on, 188; Mead's conscription of, 18–19; and premarital sex, 18, 190–94, 213; and prostitution, 47–48; and Protestantism, 192; rape among, 192; sex terms, 212; and sexual technique, 190, 194,

212–13; and *taupou*, 192, 194, 292; virginity among, 192–94, 212–13, 291–92; women and *mana*, 292. *See also* Mead, Margaret; Mead-Freeman controversy
Samoyeds, 26
San (Bushman), 30–31, 33, 225; as noble savages, 334n6; women, 31–32
Sandwich Islands, 79
Sanger, Margaret, 127, 161
Sapir, Edward, 254
Sappho, 81
Schapera, Isaac, 220, 265, 334n4; on Kgatla, 10, 223–25; on Hottentot apron, 225
Schmidt, Wilhelm, 155
Schneider, Harold K.: on Turu, 272
Schoepf, Brooke G., 312, 315, 317
Schreiner, Olive, 121
science, 3, 7, 167–68, 182, 221, 222, 233, 336n6; anthropology as, 155, 157, 278, 339n4; and conflict with religion, 35; of kinship, 218; and Mead, 187; of sexuality, 56, 168. *See also* discourse; Foucault, Michel; *scientia sexualis*; sexology
scientia sexualis, 100, 127, 156–57; Malinowski and, 164–65. *See also* discourse; Foucault, Michel; sexology
secrets, 328
segregation. *See* color bar; gender balance; racism; sexual segregation
Seligman, Brenda Z., 261
Seligman, Charles, 141, 164
Sellon, Edward, 55, 58–59, 76
Seneca, 78
Sepik River, 206, 226
sex, 4, 277–78, 28–81; collective representations and, 197; double sense of, 285; and fin de siècle alterity, 101; in fin de siècle anthropology, 103; and food, 260, 262–63, 281; and gender, 309–10; and gender ideologies, 292; as ludic, 197, 238, 245, 321–22, 342n3; and power, 4, 12–15, 191, 193, 300, 325; premarital, 9, 18, 111, 124, 177, 169, 190–94, 213, 220, 226, 228, 283, 291, 313, 321; Ra'ivavae ritual, 272; rediscovery of, 11, 277, 285, 294; as social construction, 300;

and Benedict, 276; as conscription, 330; of discourse on heterosexuality, 185–86, 276; Firth on, 217, 276; on heterosexual female desire, 309; on homosexuality, 224, 276; on marriage, 186

Simmel, Georg, 328

Sindh, 64

Sinus pudoris (Linnaeus). *See* Hottentot apron

Sioux, 61–62

Siriono, 262–63

skull. *See* body measurement

slavery, 7, 14, 34, 39–40, 55, 74, 111, 132, 133, 137, 139, 141, 149, 150; and the Criminal Law Amendment White Slavery Bill, 120; and debate over species, 36, 40; literature, 42; and miscegenation, 42, 321; white, 52–53, 120

Slessor, Mary, 146

Slobodin, Richard, 97

Smellie, William, 37

Smith, Elliot, 141, 148, 155

Smith, Samuel Stanhope, 36, 40

Smith, Southwood, 43

Smith, William, 25

Smith, William Robertson, 73–74, 84, 87

Smithers, Leonard, 57, 70

"social communism" (Howitt), 90

socialism, 121–22, 155

social hygiene. *See* social purity movements

social movements, 119–29

social purity movements, 6–7, 54, 101, 120–21, 145; on the family, 123, 126; and prostitution, 129

social structure, 10, 154, 182, 201, 282, 283

Society for Constructive Birth Control and Racial Progress, 161, 340n8

Society for Psychical Research, 149

Society of Lesbian and Gay Anthropologists, 294, 298

sociobiology, 277, 329

Soemmering, Samuel Thomas von, 40

Solinus, 23

Solomon Islands, 225–26

"Sotadic Zone," 70–72; definition of, 71

Spanton, Canon E., 175, 177

Sparrman, Anders, 32

species, 35; biological concept of, 20; debate over, 34–41. *See also* monogenism, polygenism

Speke, John Hanning, 59

Spencer, Baldwin, 83–84, 90–93, 96–97; on Arunta, 90–93, 178; on evolution of the family, 108; on group marriage, 90–91, 149, 178, 337n9; and nescience of paternity, 178, 180; on phallic worship, 337n9; on totemism, 91, 93, 337n10

Sperling, Susan, 308

Spiro, Melford, 283; and nescience of paternity, 182

Stanley, Henry Morton, 136–37

status of women, 286, 329; among Africans, 138, 149–50; and Australian Aborigines, 45; Baker on, 138; Bimin-Kuskusmin and, 289–90; divorce and, 171; Ellis on, 126, 329; and evolutionists, 74; and morality, 48; Native America and, 45–46; in Polynesia, 291–92; in Samoa, 291–92; Westermarck on, 111, 125–26

Stead, W. T., 53, 54

steatopygia, 31, 33, 63

Stern, Pamela R., 346n14

stereotypes: of abuse of women, 118, 240; African colonial, 132, 134–35; and AIDS, 313; of Asian sexuality, 310; of Australian Aborigines, 238; combating, 182, 240; and female circumcision, 313. *See also* collective representations; images; representations; tropes

Stevenson, Robert Louis, 129

St. Hilaire, Geoffroy, 33

stigmatization, 231, 345n3; and AIDS, 2–3, 311, 312, 317; and African males, 134; and alterity, 131; and bestiality, 240; of genital operations, 318; and Mead, 209

Stimson, J. Frank, 273

Stirling, Edward Charles, 92

Stirling, Nina, 160

Stocking, George W., Jr., 17, 94, 159, 212

Stolyhwo, Kazimierz, 184

"stone butch," 304

Stopes, Marie, 127, 156, 161, 167, 170, 340n8

Street, Brian, 132

Strehlow, T. G. H., 83

Strachey, Lytton, 51

"stratified morality" (Malinowski), 156

structural anthropology, 279–83, 295, 320

structural functionalism, 223

structuralism: of Levy, 285; of Ortner and Whitehead, 285; political agenda of, 280; post-, 279, 301; of Radcliffe-Brown, 17; symbols, psychoanalysis, and, 10

Sturt, Charles, 92

subculture: homosexuality as, 274–75; and same-sex eroticism, 300; Western sexual, 278

subincision: Australian, 83, 92; Burton on, 64; Spencer and Gillen on, 92, 337n8

subject: desire and the, 13, 185, 347–48n1; reification of sexual, 185

Sudan, 141, 147

suffragists, 126

Suggs, David N., 255; on Linton's and Kardiner's Marquesan facts, 256

Suggs, Robert. See Marshall, Donald, and Robert Suggs

supercision, 274. See also genital mutilation; genital operation

Supúlveda, Juan Ginés de, 25–26

surveillance, 193, 208

suttee, 48

symbolic anthropology, 285, 287–88, 295

symbolism, 320; sexual, 10, 279, 281–83, 287, 289–90; of hair, 282–83, 291–92; of milk and semen, 290. See also beards

Symonds, John Addington, 54, 71, 100; and Carpenter, 128; friendship with Ellis, 122, 127–28; homosexuality of, 122–23; on homosexuality, 127–28

Symons, Donald, 308, 346n13

syndyasmian marriage, 86

taboos, 9, 47, 206, 231, 233, 264, 314; Crawley on, 113, 115; Ellis on, 115; Elwin on, 233; in fin de siècle debates, 103; incest, 3, 9, 22, 106, 230; Kardiner on, 255; Kinsey on, 264;

Lang on, 108; Westermarck on, 110, 115. *See also* incest taboos

Tahiti: adultery in, 283, 284; Christianity in, 283; cross-dressing in, 285; as hell, 23; institutionalized transgendered identity in, 283–85; love in, 284; marriage in, 21, 283; masturbation in, 284; premarital sex in, 283; prostitution in, 21; as sexual paradise, 20–23, 25, 41, 47, 276, 282. *See also under* images

Tanala people, 255

tapu, 47

Tarnowsky, Pauline, 103

Tartars, 27

Tasmanians, 118

taupou (Samoan ceremonial virgin), 192, 194, 292

taure'are'a, 283–84

Tavris, Carol, 204

Tchambuli, 205

Tembandumba, Queen of the Jaga, 135

Temple, Richard C., 148

teratology, 23, 33

Thackeray, William Makepeace, 61

theory: racial, 7; Victorian, 7

therapy: anthropology as, 159, 174, 208–9, 247, 257; Malinowski's auto-, 159

"third gender," 278, 300–301; in India, 310; in South and Central America, 25

Thomas, Northcote W., 84, 99, 100, 108–9, 148, 149, 151–52; African fieldwork of, 152; on African marriage, 149, 151–52; as armchair anthropologist, 102; on Australian kinship, 108–9; on Australian marriage, 108–9; and government anthropology, 102, 133, 148, 151–52; and Malinowski, 164; on nescience of paternity, 109; on rules, 151–52; transcends color bar, 152; on Westermarck, 109

Thomas, Wesley, 300

Thurnwald, Richard, 184, 265

Tikopians: Firth on, 10, 220–22; and marriage, 220; and marriage by capture, 220–21, 222; and premarital sex, 220; sexual techniques of, 220

Tilapoi, 180

Timacuan people, 26

Todas: Hartland on, 96

Torgovnick, Marianna, 132, 327

totemism: in Australia, 85, 87, 91, 92–94, 337n10; "conceptional," 93–95; Fison on, 87; Frazer on, 93–95, 337n10; Freud's theory of, 106–7; Gason on, 85; Lévi-Strauss on, 280–81; McLennan on, 87; Robertson Smith on, 87; Spencer and Gillen on, 91, 93, 337n10; Victorian theories of, 87

transgendered: in Native America, 288–89, 297–98, 303; phenomena, 300; stigmatization of, 345; in Tahiti, 283, 284–85

transsexuality, 209, 322; as transgressive performance, 302, 346n11

transvestism. See cross-dressing

Treichler, Paula A., 312

trial marriage. See companionate marriage

trickster tales, 246

Trilling, Lionel, 267

Trobrianders, 130, 165, 168, 174, 200, 322; absence of romantic love among, 200, 230; adolescence of, 18, 155, 169–70, 171–72, 181, 192; adultery among, 172, 180, 181; baloma spirits of, 178–79; bukumatula, 235; and companionate marriage, 170–73; and confessional mode, 157–59; conscripted by Malinowski, 18–19; and contraception, 181; and divorce, 172; and homosexuality, 165, 176, 251; and image of Tahiti, 23; and marriage, 9, 18, 169, 171–73, 339n1; as matrilineal, 168, 173; and nescience of paternity, 159, 173, 178–83, 321; Oedipus complex and, 169, 182; and premarital sex, 9, 18, 169, 228; and rank, 192–93; Russell and, 163; sexual discourse of, 173; sexual knowledge of, 181; and venereal disease, 179–80. See also Malinowski, Bronislaw

tropes, 105, 135, 283, 346–47n15; of absence of love, 201; of African inferiority, 140; of African ritual dance, 131–32, 134; of African sexuality and intelligence, 132; of African women, 134; of colonial encounter, 141; of motherhood, 215; in period of silence,

276; of sexual freedom, 234; of sexually unimaginative savage, 247; of tolerance for homosexuality, 274. See also images; stereotypes; representations

truth, 278, 293, 311, 328, 329, 332; partial, 312, 332

Tswana people, 270

Tully river blacks: and paternity, 93

Tunis, 141

Turanian kinship terminologies, 83, 85, 99

Turner, Edith, 321

Turner, Victor, 279, 295, 320–21

"tumescence" (Mead), 197, 198–99

Tupi-Guarani, 262

Turu people, 272

Tuzin, Donald, 2, 307, 309

"two-spirit," 18, 247, 310; berdache as, 298; critique of term, 303, 317–18

Tylor, Edward, 72, 73, 102, 108; evolutionism of, 95

Tyson, Edward, 40

Uhombo people, 137

Ulrichs, Karl Heinrich, 122

unawa, 108

"undivided commune" (Fison and Howitt), 74, 86, 88

undersexed savage. See under images; representations

universals: psychosexual, 282; in sexual behavior, 269

Universities' Mission to Central Africa, 177

Urning, 122

USAID, 317

utopia, 23, 45, 68, 155, 156; anti-, 24, 25; Muria and sexual, 234

vagina dentata, 272

vaginal introcision, 83

Vaillant, François Le, 32

Valentine, Ruth: and Benedict, 251

Vance, Carole, 11, 285, 299, 345n8–9

venereal disease, 278; Falk on, 151; and feminists, 121; and Fire Island, 305; and images of oversexed other, 313–14; among Mohave, 246, 247; and prostitution, 53, 145; and rape,

15; blamed for pathologized personality characteristics, 257; blamed for raised color bar, 147; Burton on, 68–69; Christianity's degradation of, 123; Darwin on, 105; and deviant sexuality, 43; experience of, 192, 210–11, 214–15, 286, 293; health of, 318–20; image of seductive, 130; Indian, 145–47; intelligence of, 28, 105, 122, 126, 190; issues of, 132, 152–54; Khoi, 31–34; and language, 210–12; and marriage, 129; middle-class, 54, 75; and morality, 48; as objects of desire, 281; as oversexualized in Victorian era, 104; as passive, 40, 118, 126; promiscuity of Victorian, 65; and rape, 25, 26, 66, 118, 147; and resistance to colonial rule, 152–54; San, 31–32; slaves, 40; South American, 45–46; and suffrage, 141; and theory of neoteny, 126; Trobriand, 180; Westermarck on, 123–24; working-class, 54, 75, 161. *See also* Igbo Women's Rebellion; status of women

women's liberation, 15–21

women's magazines: and Mead, 208, 211, 215

women's rights: in Arnhem Land, 241

Women's Social and Political Union, 121

women's studies, 286

work ethic, 48–49

World War I, 16, 100–101, 121, 129

World War II, 10, 183, 208, 217, 226, 261

Worsley, Peter, 187

Wright, Thomas, 57

Wylie, Philip, 261

xaniths, 310, 329

Yahgans, 115

Yerkes, R. M., 269

Yoruba, 62

Young, Brigham, 68

Young, Robert J. C., 16, 37–38

Zande, 220; boy wives, 296; gender categories, 302; heterosexuality among, 10, 296; homosexuality among, 10, 296

"zero" point: of cultural evolution, 131; of evolutionist theory, 75–76; of stories of social evolution (Atkinson and Freud), 107

Zola, Émile, 53, 54

Zuni: as "Apollonians," 250, 252; berdache among, 250